Dash Diet Cookbook for Beginners

2 in 1: Improve Your Health By Lowering Your Blood Pressure And Cholesterol With 1200+ of The Best, Low-Sodium DASH Diet Recipes | BONUS 100-Days Meal Plan Included for Diabetics

Dash Diet Cookbook

A Complete Guide with 600 Easy & Delicious Low- Sodium, Low Sugar, Heart- Healthy Recipes for Hypertension. BONUS 28-Days Natural Meal Plan Included

Diabetic Cookbook

The Guide for the Newly Diagnosed to Manage Type 2 Diabetes Effortlessly, Detox Cleanse With 600 Healthy Low-Carb Recipes. Includes 100 Days of Natural Meal Plan

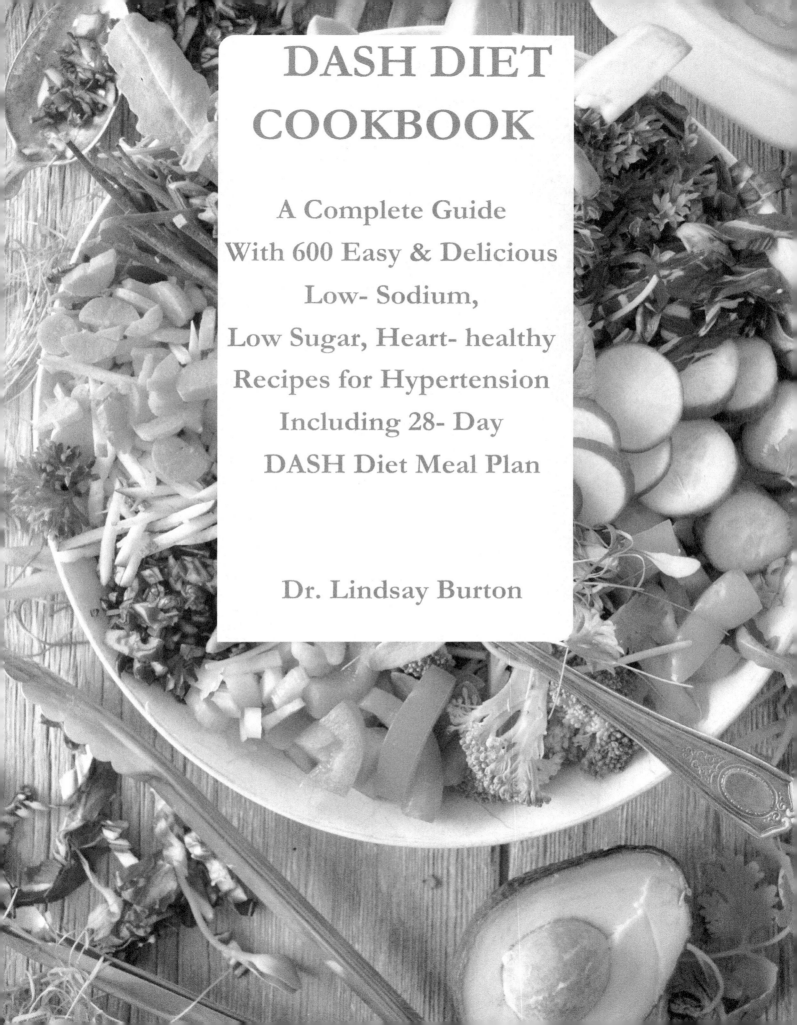

DASH DIET COOKBOOK

A Complete Guide
With 600 Easy & Delicious
Low- Sodium,
Low Sugar, Heart- healthy
Recipes for Hypertension
Including 28- Day
DASH Diet Meal Plan

Dr. Lindsay Burton

Table of Content

Introduction

Dietary Approaches to Control high blood pressure is DASH Diet. The DASH diet is a nutritious eating plan that will help one manage or avoid hypertension. Foods high in calcium, magnesium & potassium are included in this DASH diet. These nutrients aid with blood pressure regulation. The diet restricts sodium-rich, saturated-fat-rich, and sugar-rich foods

The DASH diet has been proven in studies to reduce blood pressure in as little as 14 days. Low- density lipoprotein (bad/LDL) cholesterol levels in the body may also be reduced by eating the DASH Diet. Two significant risk factors for cardiovascular disease and stroke are hypertension and high bad cholesterol levels. Many diet regimens have disappeared, but DASH is here to stay because it works. The DASH diet has been around for years since it is backed up by scientific evidence.

High blood pressure affects one out of every three people in the United States and is a significant risk factor for cardiovascular disease. Potassium, a healthy mineral for your heart, is consumed in greater quantities when one follows the DASH diet. One also eats less salt, which will aid in the reduction of blood pressure and the improvement of heart health.

The advantages of the DASH Diet are well-known. According to users, individuals who had to follow DASH decreased their blood pressure in few weeks. However, it isn't only about lowering blood pressure. The DASH diet may help one lose weight and lower the chances of developing certain health issues.

According to research, the following DASH may reduce the risk of:
Breast cancer
Colorectal cancer is a kind of cancer that affects the colon.
Metabolic syndrome is a collection of symptoms that increase the risk of stroke, Type 2 diabetes & heart disease.
The DASH diet's greatest feature? It's adaptable. It doesn't need specific meals, and one does
not have to go hungry or sacrifice sweets. DASH advises integrating heart-healthy meals into one's routine instead.

Promotes vegetables, whole grains, fruits in the DASH eating pattern
Dairy products that are low-fat or fat-free, fish, beans, nuts, poultry, and vegetable oils are all included.
Saturated fat-rich foods are avoided. Fatty meats, tropical oils including coconut oil, palm oils and palm kernel. Sugar-sweetened drinks and desserts are restricted.

Other lifestyle modifications, in addition to DASH, may help one reduce their blood pressure. They include maintaining a healthy weight, exercising regularly, and refraining from smoking and drinking.

Causes of hypertension

Hypertension is caused by a variety of variables that are likely to function together.

If one has a family history of hypertension, they are more prone to developing it. Therefore, genetics is likely to play a part.

Some individuals, especially the elderly, African Americans, overweight individuals, and those with chronic kidney illness, have high salt consumption or salt sensitivity, contributing to high blood pressure.

Vascular dysfunction causes some people's blood vessels to stiffen and lose flexibility. Arteriolar tightness causes greater resistance to blood flow and elevated blood pressure when it affects the small arteries (arterioles). Obesity, high salt consumption, and being older are all factors that contribute to this.

The DASH Diet

The DASH diet is a customizable and well-balanced eating plan that promotes a lifetime of heart- healthy eating habits that control or reduces hypertension. It's simple to make using groceries from the local supermarket. Vegetables, whole grains and fruits are abundant in the DASH diet. Dairy items that are low-fat or fat-free, fish, poultry, nuts, beans, and are all included. Foods rich in saturated fat, like full-fat dairy products and fatty meats, are restricted.

It's essential to eat high calcium, fiber, protein, magnesium and potassium while following the DASH diet. Choose foods that are:

Saturated fat-free

Sodium-free

A billion people and more around the world suffer from high blood pressure, and the number is growing. In reality, the number of individuals with hypertension has doubled in the past 40 years, posing a significant public health threat since hypertension is related to an increased risk of heart disease, renal failure, and stroke. Because food is believed to have a significant part in the development of hypertension, scientists and dietitians have devised specialized dietary recommendations to assist people in lowering their blood pressure. The DASH diet has less salt than the average American diet, including up to 2,300 mg of sodium per day or even less

It complies with the Dietary Guidelines' that Americans should consume less than 2,300 mg of salt per day. That's about how much sodium is in one teaspoon of regular salt.

A salt-reduced variant of DASH limits sodium intake to 1,500 mg per day. One may choose the diet that best suits their health requirements. Consult the doctor if one is not sure what sodium level is best for them.

The DASH diet plan does not need any specific meals and sets nutritional objectives for each day and week. This strategy suggests:

Fruits, whole grains, lean meats and vegetables are all part of the DASH diet. The diet was developed when researchers discovered that individuals who ate a vegetarian or vegan diet had lower blood pressure.

As a result, the DASH diet prioritizes vegetables, fruits while also include lean protein sources such as fish, legumes and chicken. Salt, added sugars, fat and Red meat, are all restricted on the DASH diet.

Scientists think that one of the major reasons this diet may help individuals with hypertension is because it lowers salt consumption.

The DASH diet recommends no more than a teaspoon of salt (2,300 mg) each day, consistent with most national recommendations.

The low-sodium version suggests consuming no more than 1,500 mg (3/4 teaspoon) of sodium each day.

Potassium, a heart-healthy mineral, is consumed in greater quantities when one follows the DASH diet. One also eats less salt, which will help in the reduction of blood pressure and the improvement of heart health. The advantages of DASH are well-known.

Starting with The Dash Diet

Adding DASH to your diet does not imply making dramatic adjustments overnight. Instead, start with the smallest adjustments that seem most doable to you. Consider the following scenario:

Include one serving of vegetables or fruits in each meal.

Each week, consider 2 or more meatless meals.

Use spices and herbs instead of salt to make meals more flavorful.

Rather than a bag of chips, munch on almonds or nuts.

When feasible, replace white flour with whole-wheat flour.

After lunch or supper, go for a 15-minute stroll (or both).

Phases of the DASH Diet

The primary research study's DASH diet recommendations included two degrees of salt reduction.

In phase one of the DASH diet, salt is restricted to 2300mg each day or approximately 1 teaspoon.

In phase 2 of the DASH diet, salt is decreased to 1500mg.

To achieve phase 2's objective, the individual should eliminate all table salt and add no salt to their food. When one eats packaged or processed meals or dine out, they consume more salt than is advised. Salt is the most common source of sodium in the diet, and the two terms are often used interchangeably unless we're talking about particular biochemical processes.

The DASH Diet is best followed in two phases. Phase 1 is a low-carb diet that does not include fruit and whole grains and will last for 2 weeks. Phase 1 of the Dash Diet is intended to increase the natural calorie-burning mechanisms and reset the metabolism. One will lose weight quickly and visibly throughout this low-carb, protein-rich, and sugar-free diet. Stage 1 of the Dash Diet is intended to reboot the body to establish good eating habits for the rest of life. It will reset the body, and one will learn how to satiate their appetite and feel fuller for longer. It will help one control their blood sugar levels and reduce hunger. You stay away from all fruits and entire grains, which include a lot of natural sugar and alcohol (that includes sugars as well). Low-fat dairy may be consumed in two to three portions each day. 1 cup of skim milk or low-fat yogurt is an example of this. Cheese, whether normal or fat-free, is rich in salt and should be avoided.

Dash Diet Tips

Include a veggie serving for lunch and supper.

Include a fruit dish in regular meals or as a snack. It's simple to eat canned or dried fruits, but make sure they don't contain any added sugar.

Use half the amount of margarine or salad dressing or butter you normally would, and it should be fat-free or low-fat

Replace full-fat cream/dairy with low-fat or skim dairy products wherever possible.

Limit yourself to 6 oz. of meat each day. Make some vegetarian dishes.

Increase the intake of veggies and dry beans.

Snack on unsalted pretzels or almonds, nuts, fat-free or low-fat yogurt, frozen yogurt, plain popcorn without butter, and raw veggies rather than chips or sweets.

Read the food labels to choose items with reduced sodium levels.

Changes may be made gradually. Begin by restricting the salt intake to 2,300 mg each day (~1 teaspoon). After the body has acclimated to the diet, reduce daily salt intake to 1,500. These figures include total sodium consumed, including sodium from food items and sodium from other ingredients used in cooking or added at the table.

When combined with physical exercise, the DASH diet becomes even more successful in lowering blood pressure

This is hardly unexpected, given the many health advantages of exercise.

It is suggested that one engages in 30 minutes of moderate exercise on most days, and one must pick an activity that they like so they can stick to it.

The following are some examples of moderate activity:

Walking at a fast pace (15 minutes/mile or 9 minutes/km)
running (ten minutes/mile or 6 minutes/km)
Cycling is a popular sport (6 minutes/mile or 4 minutes/km)
Lap swimming (20 minutes)
Household chores (60 minutes)

Health Benefits of DASH Diet

The DASH diet was created to lower blood pressure without the use of medication. The NIH (National Institutes of Health) in the United States funded the diet study. The diet did decrease blood pressure as well as first-line hypertension medicine, according to preliminary studies. Consequently, it is regarded as a natural method of lowering blood pressure without the need for medications. The DASH Diet has been shown to decrease various illnesses such as diabetes and cancer in later studies, that is why it has been ranked as the no. 1 diet by US News and World Report for 6 years in a row, beginning in 2011.

Fruits and vegetables, as well as low-fat or nonfat dairy, are abundant in the diet. Whole grains, fish, poultry, lean meats, as well as nuts and legumes, are all included, which helps in:

lowering Blood pressure- blood pressure typically lowers a few points after only 2 weeks of adopting the DASH diet, and if maintained, the systolic blood pressure may drop by 8- 14 points.

The enhanced calcium intake from low-fat dairy products and green leafy vegetables in the DASH diet also helps to enhance bone strength and reduce the risk of osteoporosis.

A high consumption of fruits and vegetables is linked to a reduced long-term risk of cancer.

The DASH diet's controlled food intake reduces metabolic diseases, including heart disease and diabetes and cerebrovascular illness, by lowering fat consumption and increasing the replacement of complex carbs for simple sugars. This results in lower total and LDL cholesterol levels in the blood, with lower blood pressure.

Another advantage of the DASH diet is that it lowers the risk of gout by lowering uric acid levels in hyperuricemia patients.

Surprisingly, the DASH diet has been shown to decrease blood pressure in both healthy and hypertensive individuals. Individuals on the DASH diet had reduced blood pressure in trials even if they didn't lose weight or limit salt consumption. On the other hand, the DASH diet reduced blood pressure significantly more when salt consumption was limited. In fact, the individuals who ate the least salt had the largest decreases in blood pressure. These reduced-salt DASH diet outcomes were particularly remarkable in individuals with hypertension, lowering systolic & diastolic blood pressure by a mean of 12 & 5 mmHg, respectively.

It decreased systolic blood pressure by four mmHg and diastolic blood pressure by two mmHg in individuals who had normal blood pressure.

This is consistent with previous studies that show that limiting salt consumption may lower blood pressure, particularly in those with hypertension.

Bear in mind that a lower blood pressure level does not necessarily imply a lower risk of Dash diet can help you lose weight. This is because the more weight you have, the higher the blood pressure is going to be. Losing weight has also been proven to decrease blood pressure.

People may discover that by eliminating many high-fat, sugary items from their diet, they naturally decrease their calorie intake and lose weight. Others may need to deliberately limit their consumption. In any case, if one wants to lose weight on the DASH diet, they will need to eat fewer calories.

Lowers cancer risk: According to a recent study, individuals who followed the DASH diet had a reduced risk of some malignancies, such as colorectal and breast cancer

According to some studies, the DASH diet may lower the risk of metabolic syndrome by up to 81 percent

Reduces the risk of diabetes: A low-carbohydrate diet has been related to a reduced risk of type 2 diabetes in certain trials. It helps with insulin resistance.

Lowers the risk of heart disease and stroke: A DASH-like diet was linked to a 20 percent reduced risk of heart disease and a 29 percent lower risk of stroke in a recent study of women.

The Dash technique may help avoid diseases like osteoporosis and diabetes by allowing you to eat meals high in iron and capable of repairing your bones.

However, the advantages of this regimen do not stop there. In reality, the foods included in this diet plan (particularly fruits and vegetables) are high in substances that may combat free radicals, which are the primary cause of cellular aging.

DASH Diet's Servings & Food list

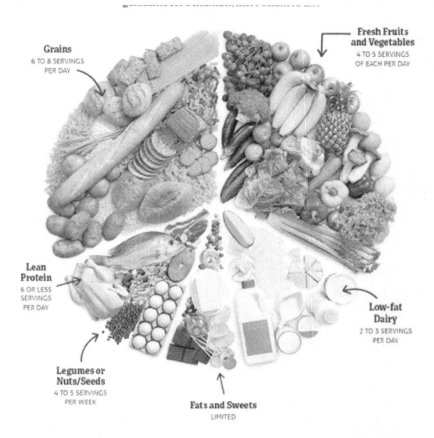

DASH Diet is quite customizable, and you do not need to follow a strict diet. Instead, you can create your meal plan for yourself with various fruits, vegetables, healthy fats, oils, grains, seeds, nuts, legumes, and low-fat dairy and natural sugars.

What to eat on DASH Diet?

People often inquire about the foods allowed on the DASH diet. The excellent thing is that it offers a broad range of foods as well as many choices. The DASH diet is straightforward. Eat more fruit, particularly vegetables, and less high-salt meals (sodium). For instance, instead of a cheeseburger with fries for lunch, go for a salad with protein, low-fat dairy products like Greek yogurt rather than fruity, sugary yogurt.

Vegetables, fruit, bean spreads such as black bean dip or hummus, and unsalted almonds are also good options for snacking. Whole grains like quinoa or brown rice and lean meats like chicken, fish, and lean pork are recommended.

DASH is an adaptable and well-balanced diet plan that promotes a lifetime of heart-healthy eating habits. The DASH diet plan does not need any specific meals, but it recommends servings. This strategy suggests: Consumption of whole grains, fruits, vegetables.

low-fat dairy or Fat-free products such as fish, poultry, legumes, nuts, vegetable oils are all good options.

Saturated fat-rich foods, like full-fat dairy products, fatty meats, tropical oils including coconut, and palm oils, palm kernel, should be avoided.

Sugar-sweetened drinks and desserts should be limited.

The meals are simple to make using groceries from your local supermarket.

When following the DASH diet, it's critical to eat foods that are:

Potassium, magnesium, calcium, fiber, and protein are all abundant.

Saturated fat content is low

They should be sodium-free

Foods to avoid on DASH Diet

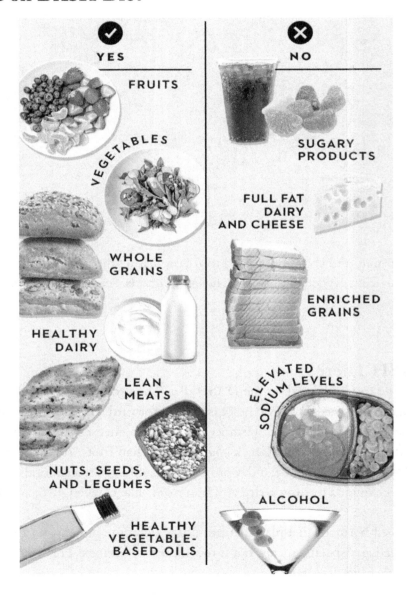

DASH also urges you to eat less high-blood-pressure-raising meals. Fatty foods, such as skin-on chicken and red meat, are among them.

- Dairy products with high-fat content, such as butter, whole milk and cream, should be avoided.
- Coconut and palm oils that are Solid-at-room-temperature should be avoided.
- Sweets, baked products, and desserts with a lot of sugar.
- Sugary beverages, including soda, juice, and sweetened tea or coffee.

These foods are not needed to be completely avoided all of a sudden if you follow the DASH diet. Instead, make daily efforts to make better choices. It will be simpler to keep to the strategy. Consider switching out a meat entrée once a week for a vegetarian alternative.

The majority of Americans consume much more meat than is required at the cost of their vegetable consumption. DASH suggests that you consume no more than 6 oz. of meat each day. Eat more fruits and vegetables that are high in fiber, disease-fighting antioxidants, and other nutrients. Also, eat less

- Meats with a lot of fat,
- Dairy items with high-fat content,
- Drinks with added sugar,
- Sodium (salt)
- The dash diet highlights fruits and vegetables while also including lean protein such as fish, legumes, and chicken. Red meat, added sugars, fat, salt is all limited in the diet.
- Scientists think that one of the major reasons this diet may help individuals with hypertension is because it lowers salt consumption.

Since the initial study, experts have shown that the DASH diet plan may help people lose weight also.

People who follow the Dash diet and increase their physical activity lose weight, improve metabolic markers like insulin sensitivity. Nevertheless, compared to low-carb diets, the DASH diet was less effective as a weight-loss approach. Individuals' blood pressure improved significantly when the DASH diet was combined with exercise and calorie restriction, dropping by 16 to 9 mmHg diastolic and losing weight. People who follow the DASH diet and decrease their blood pressure may find that they don't require as much medication. Discuss any food-related adjustments with your doctor, and if the blood pressure is below target (140/80), you may be able to reduce your medicines and manage the blood pressure only via diet.

Thus, it is necessary to avoid these foods while on DASH Diet, especially foods that are high in sodium:

Cookies

Packaged pasta & rice dishes

- Candy
- Sodas
- Sugary beverages
- Cold cuts & cured meats
- Salted nuts & seeds
- Chips
- Pastries
- Salted Snacks

- Salted Cheese

Using a potassium-based salt replacement not only serves as a replacement in the kitchen but may also help reduce blood pressure. People taking potassium-increasing blood pressure medicines should ask their physicians to assist them in assessing their potassium levels in the blood while making adjustments.

Is there a link between red meat & heart disease?

Grass-fed buffalo and beef, although not explicitly suggested, can be eaten on a dash diet. The composition of grass-fed beef differs significantly from that of grain-fed beef. Grass-fed beef is rich in omega-3s and chemically comparable to salmon. Grain-fed red meat is rich in omega 6 fatty acids and saturated fat, both of which lead to heart disease, obesity, high blood pressure and obesity. It's prohibited to consume red meat that hasn't been raised on grass.

DASH Diet Servings

It's helpful to know how much of a particular food is deemed a "serving" while sticking to a balanced eating plan. One serving consists of:

- Milk: 8 oz.
- 1 slice of bread
- Oil: 1 tsp.
- Uncooked vegetables or fruit: 1 cup
- Rice or pasta: half cup, cooked
- Tofu: 3 oz.
- Vegetables or fruit: half cup, cooked
- Cooked meat: 3 oz.

The DASH diet plan is simple to follow and uses common grocery store items. The DASH diet consists of daily portions from several food categories. Your daily calorie requirements determine the number of servings you should consume.

Considering your age and degree of physical activity when calculating the calorie requirements. If you want to stay at your present weight, consume only as many calories as you expend via physical activity. This is referred to as "energy balance."

If you want to lose weight, consume fewer calories than you can burn or raise the activity level to expend more calories than consuming.

For a 2,000-calorie-per-day DASH diet, these are the required servings out of each food group:

- 6–8 servings of grains per day: One piece of bread, dry cereal (1 oz.), half cup cooked cereal, pasta or rice equals=1 serving.
- 4-5 servings of vegetables each day. Raw leafy green vegetable (1 cup), half cup raw or cooked veggies, or half cup vegetable juice = 1 serving.

- 4-5 servings of fruits each day. One medium fruit, half cup of fresh, frozen, or half cup fruit juice equals= 1 serving

- 2-3 servings of low-fat or fat-free dairy products each day. 1 cup milk or yogurt, or 1 1/2 oz. cheese= 1 serving.

- 6 (1-oz.) meals of lean meats, fish, poultry per day are recommended. 1 egg = 1 serving.

- 4-5 servings of nuts, legumes, seeds each week.   Nuts (1/3 cup), 2 teaspoons of peanut butter, seeds (2 tbsp.), or cooked legumes (half cup) = 1 serving.

- 2-3 servings of fats, oils per day. mayonnaise (1 tbsp.), or salad dressing (2 tbsp.) = 1 serving

- 5 servings or less per week of sweets & added sugars. Sugar, jam (1 tbsp.), sorbet (half cup), or lemonade (1 cup) equals one serve.

DASH Diet Sodium Limits

Many people in the United States consume too much sodium. A high-sodium diet may also raise blood pressure and raise the risk of heart disease. The DASH diet restricts salt consumption to 2,300 mg per day. However, if you want more powerful effects, stick to the DASH diet, where you should consume no more than 1,500 mg of salt each day.

As part of a balanced diet, the NIH'S (National Institutes of Health) Dietary Guidelines for Americans suggest eating less than 2,300 mg of salt per day.

Ways to Cut Sodium

The majority of sodium consumed does not originate from the saltshaker. Salt is frequently high in packaged and processed meals, even if it does not feel salty. Sodium levels in restaurant and takeaway meals may be very high. If you're following the DASH diet, look for salt levels on food labels and keep note of how much one is consuming.

If you're dining out, consider these sodium-reduction tips:

- If available, inquire about the salt content of meals. Request that the meal be made without any additional salt, MSG, or spices that include salt.

- Limit or avoid high-salt sauces and seasonings, or ask for them to be served on the side.

- Look for terms like smoked, pickled, cured, soy sauce, and broth that suggest high salt content.

- Rather than salty snack items like chips or fries, provide vegetables and fruits as a side dish.

- One can decrease sodium in the diet even further by:

- Rather than salt, use sodium-free spices or flavorings.

- When cooking pasta, hot porridge, and rice, don't use salt.

- Selecting unprocessed frozen, canned veggies or fresh.

- Choosing skinless chicken, fish, lean meat cuts

- Read food labels carefully and choose low-sodium or alternatives like no-salt-added.

You may find that your food tastes different when you reduce your intake of processed, high-sodium meals. It may take some time for your taste buds to adapt. However, when it does, you may discover that your preference is the DASH diet.

- Using spices, lemon juice, garlic, herbs as seasonings throughout the cooking process

- If you consume alcohol, restrict to no more than two drinks per day for women and 3 drinks per day for men, with a weekly maximum of 15 drinks. Consult your doctor if you are worried about how drinking is contributing to hypertension.
- Don't smoke. If you have hypertension, it is critical to quit smoking. Smoking raises your chances of getting heart disease and other illnesses. It's also a good idea to keep your house and workplace smoke-free.
- Follow your doctor's instructions for taking your medicine.
- Check your blood pressure regularly.
- Stay away from sugar-sweetened drinks.

Changing your diet involves committing to a healthy lifestyle for the rest of your life. People who make modest adjustments to their diet over time rather than making a drastic shift all at once are more likely to stick to a better diet. If you're thinking about beginning the DASH diet, talk to your doctor about it first.

There are two methods to begin the DASH diet. Gradually alter:

- If you now consume one or two servings of veggies each day, increase to two servings at lunch and supper.
- If you don't eat fruit or drink juice in the morning, try adding a portion of fruit to daily meals or substituting the entire fruit for the juice.
- Eat approximately 6 oz. of meat and substitutes over two meals.
- Make more plant-based protein choices.
- For sweets or snacks, choose fruits, vegetables, whole grains, or protein meals.
- Eat a wide range of healthy foods.

DASH Diet Smoothie & Drinks Recipes

1. Chocolate Berry Smoothie

(Prep time: 10 minutes | Serving: 1)

Ingredients

- Frozen blueberries: ¼ cup
- Honey, to taste
- Cashews: 2 tbsp.
- Unsweetened cocoa powder: 2 tbsp.
- Vanilla extract: half tsp.
- Coldwater: 12 oz.
- Half avocado

Instructions

1. In a blender, add all ingredients.
2. Blend until smooth, pour and serve.

Nutrition: Calories 250 | Fat 17.2 g | Sugar 8 g | Protein 6.4 g | Sodium 55 mg

2. Strawberry DASH Smoothie

(Prep time: 10 minutes | Serving: 1)

Ingredients

- Almond milk: ¾ cup
- Cottage cheese, low fat: half cup, low salt
- Strawberries: 1 cup

Instructions

1. In a blender, add all ingredients.
2. Blend until smooth, pour and serve.

Nutrition: Calories 215 | Protein 22g | Sugar: 21g | Fat 2.8g | Sodium 141mg | Carbs 26g

3. Ultimate Green Smoothie

(Prep time: 5 minutes | Serving: 1)

Ingredients

- Packed baby spinach: 1 cup
- Frozen mango: 3/4 cup
- Fat-free milk: half cup
- 1 banana
- Vanilla: half tsp.
- Whole oats: 1/4 cup
- Nonfat yogurt: ¼ cup

Instructions

1. In a blender, add all ingredients.
2. Blend until smooth, pour and serve.

Nutrition: Calories 98 | Fat: 0 g | Sodium: 20 mg | Sugars: 2 g

4. Banana Breakfast Smoothie

(Prep time: 5 minutes | Serving: 1)

Ingredients

- 1% milk: half cup
- Ice: half cup
- Honey: 1 tbsp.
- 1 frozen banana
- Fat-free vanilla yogurt: 6 oz.

Instructions

1. In a blender, add all ingredients.
2. Blend until smooth, pour and serve.

Nutrition: Calories 109 | Fat 8 g | Sugar 3 g | Protein 6 g | Sodium 30 mg

5. Blackberry Iced Tea

(Prep time: 5 minutes | Cook time: 5 minutes | Serving: 6)

Ingredients

- Honey, to taste
- Blackberry herbal: 12 tea bags
- Cranberry juice: 1 cup, unsweetened
- 8 small cinnamon sticks
- 6 cups of water

- Minced ginger: 1 tbsp.

Instructions

1. In a pan, add water and let it come to a boil.
2. Add ginger, tea bags and cinnamon, turn the heat off. Cover and steep for 15 minutes.
3. Strain and pour in a pitcher; add juice and honey. Mix and serve with ice.

Nutrition: Calories 108| Fat 0 g | Sugar 2 g | Protein 0 g |Sodium 3 mg | Carbs 6 g

6. Carrot Juice Smoothie

(Prep time: 5 minutes | Serving: 2-3)

Ingredients

- 1 banana
- Carrot juice: half cup (carrots blended with water & filtered)
- Grated ginger: half tbsp.
- Turmeric: ¼ tsp.
- Pineapple: 1 cup
- Almond milk: 1 cup, unsweetened
- Cinnamon: half tsp.
- Lime juice: 1 tbsp.

Instructions

1. In a blender, add all ingredients.
2. Blend until smooth, pour and serve.

Nutrition: Calories 144 | Fat 2.3 g | Sugar 17 g | Protein 2.4 g |Sodium 112 mg | Carbs 32 g

7. Oatmeal Smoothie

(Prep time: 5 minutes | Serving: 2)

Ingredients

- Ice: half cup
- Milk: 1 cup
- Mixed berries: 1 cup, frozen
- Low-fat yogurt: half cup
- Rolled oats: half cup
- Honey: 1 tsp.
- 1 banana

Instructions

1. In a blender, add all ingredients.
2. Blend until smooth, pour and serve.

Nutrition: Calories 209 | Fat 16 g | Sugar 9 g | Protein 2

g |Sodium 58 mg | Carbs 2 g

8. Blueberry Lavender Lemonade

(Prep time: 5 minutes | Cook time: 5 time | Serving: 2-4)

Ingredients

- 2 cups of water
- Lemon juice: 1 cup
- Blueberries: 16 oz.
- Granulated sugar substitute: ¼ cup
- Coldwater, as needed
- Lavender flowers dried: 1 tbsp.
- Splenda sweetener: 2 tbsp.

Instructions

1. In a pitcher, add ice (4 cups).
2. In a pan, add water and boil. Add lavender, sugar and berries. Let it boil for five minutes.
3. Strain over ice and add Splenda and lemon juice. Add enough cold water to your taste. Mix and serve.

Nutrition: Calories 33 | Fat 13 g | Sugar 7 g | Protein 0 g |Sodium 7 mg | Carbs 8 g

9. Perfect Green Smoothie

(Prep time: 10 minutes | Serving: 4)

Ingredients

- 2 apples
- Half cucumber
- 1 celery
- 3 carrots
- Spinach: 2 cups
- Chia Seeds: 1 tsp.
- Half bunch of parsley
- 1 bunch of mint
- Lime, Orange, lemon & pineapple: 1/4 part of each

Instructions

1. In a blender, add all ingredients.
2. Blend until smooth, pour and serve.

Nutrition: Calories 251 | Fat 18 g | Sugar 7 g | Protein 3 g |Sodium 58 mg | Carbs 4 g

10. Green Monster Smoothie

(Prep time: 5 minutes | Serving: 2)

Ingredients

- Spinach: 1 to 2 cups
- Chia seeds: 1 tbsp.
- Almond milk: 1 cup
- 1 frozen banana
- Pineapple: half cup

Instructions

1. In a blender, add all ingredients.
2. Blend until smooth, pour and serve.

Nutrition: Calories 198 | Fat 11 g | Sugar 4 g | Protein 4 g |Sodium 45 mg | Carbs 3g

11. Cranberry Spritzer

(Prep time: 5 minutes | Serving: 10)

Ingredients

- Lemon juice: half cup
- Raspberry sherbet: 1 cup
- Sparkling water: 4 cups
- Cranberry juice: 4 cups, low-calorie
- Sugar substitute: ¼ cup
- 10 lemon wedges

Instructions

1. In a pitcher, add all ingredients (chilled), mix well.
2. Serve with lemon wedges.

Nutrition: Calories 100 | Fat 1 g | Sugar 22 g | Protein 0 g |Sodium 9 mg | Carbs 24 g

12. Fruit Smoothie

(Prep time: 5 minutes | Serving: 2)

Ingredients

- 1% milk: ¾ cup
- Orange juice concentrate: 1/4 cup, frozen
- Vanilla frozen yogurt: 1 cup, fat-free

Instructions

1. In a blender, add all ingredients.
2. Blend until smooth, pour and serve.

Nutrition: Calories 189| Fat 9 g | Sugar 4 g | Protein 2 g |Sodium 41 mg | Carbs 3 g

13. Peanut Butter & Banana Smoothie

(Prep time: 5 minutes | Serving: 1)

Ingredients

- Peanut butter: 1 tbsp.

- 1 banana
- Milk: 1 cup

Instructions

1. In a blender, add all ingredients.
2. Blend until smooth, pour and serve.

Nutrition: Calories 355 | Fat 17.2 g | Sugar 15 g | Protein 14 g |Sodium 123 mg | Carbs 41 g

14. Breakfast Strawberry Smoothie

(Prep time: 5 minutes | Serving: 1)

Ingredients

- Coconut powder: 1 tbsp.
- Almond milk: 8 oz.
- Almond butter: 1 tbsp.
- Monk fruit sweetener: 1 tsp.
- Chia seeds: 1 tsp.
- Frozen strawberries: half cup
- Avocado: 2 tbsp.

Instructions

1. In a blender, add all ingredients.
2. Blend until smooth, pour and serve.

Nutrition: Calories 209 | Fat 10 g | Sugar 8 g | Protein 5 g |Sodium 57 mg | Carbs 10 g

15. Watermelon-Cranberry Agua Fresca

(Prep time: 5 minutes | Serving: 8)

Ingredients

- Watermelon: 2 1/2 pounds, diced without seeds
- Cranberry juice: 1 cup
- Lime juice: ¼ cup
- 6 slices of lime

Instructions

1. In a blender, add all ingredients.
2. Blend until smooth, pour and serve.

Nutrition: Calories 84| Fat 0 g | Sugar 8 g | Protein 1 g |Sodium 9 mg | Carbs 20 g

16. Avocado Smoothie

(Prep time: 5 minutes | Serving: 1)

Ingredients

- Half banana

- Half avocado
- Chia seeds: half tsp.
- Cacao powder: 2 tbsp.
- Almond milk: ¼ cup

Instructions
1. In a blender, add all ingredients.
2. Blend until smooth, pour and serve.

Nutrition: Calories 391 | Fat 16 g | Sugar 9 g | Protein 6 g |Sodium 60 mg | Carbs 5 g

17. Blueberry Smoothie

(Prep time: 5 minutes | Serving: 10-12)

Ingredients
- Coconut water: 8 cups
- Pineapple: 4 cups
- 2 apples
- Watermelon: 4 cups
- Spinach & blueberries, to taste

Instructions
1. In a blender, add all ingredients.
2. Blend until smooth, pour and serve.

Nutrition: Calories 250 | Fat 17 g | Sugar 8 g | Protein 6.4 g |Sodium 55 mg | Carbs

18. Strawberry Mockarita

(Prep time: 5 minutes | Serving: 5)

Ingredients
- Lime juice: ¼ cup
- Water: 2 cups
- Sliced strawberries: 4 cups
- Ice: 2 cups
- Honey, to taste

Instructions
1. In a blender, add all ingredients.
2. Blend until smooth, pour and serve.

Nutrition: Calories 64 | Fat 17.2 g | Sugar 13 g | Protein 1 g |Sodium 3 mg | Carbs 16 g

19. Blueberry & Brain-Boosting Smoothie

(Prep time: 5 minutes | Serving: 1)

Ingredients
- Flax meal: 1 tbsp.

- Cinnamon, a pinch
- Low-fat cream: 1 tbsp.
- Frozen blueberries: half cup
- Almond milk: 8 oz.
- Honey: 1 tsp.
- Cayenne pepper, a pinch

Instructions
1. In a blender, add all ingredients.
2. Blend until smooth, pour and serve.

Nutrition: Calories 310 | Fat 14 g | Sugar 8 g | Protein 5 g |Sodium 55 mg | Carbs 10 g

20. Chocolate Smoothie with Avocado & Banana

(Prep time: 5 minutes | Serving: 2)

Ingredients
- Half avocado
- 2 packs of Splenda
- 1 banana, peeled
- Vanilla soy milk: 2 cups
- Cocoa powder: ¼ cup, unsweetened

Instructions
1. In a blender, add all ingredients.
2. Blend until smooth, pour and serve.

Nutrition: Calories 252 | Fat 12 g | Sugar 8 g | Protein 11 g |Sodium 102 mg | Carbs 33 g

21. Chocolate & Cherry Smoothie

(Prep time: 5 minutes | Serving: 2)

Ingredients
- ¼ cucumber, seedless
- Cinnamon, a pinch
- Baby spinach: ¾ cup
- Raw cacao: 1 tbsp., unsweetened
- Frozen cherry: half cup
- Lemon peel: 1 small piece
- Almond milk: 8 oz.
- Lemon juice, to taste

Instructions
1. In a blender, add all ingredients.
2. Blend until smooth, pour and serve.

Nutrition: Calories 310 | Fat 14 g | Sugar 8 g | Protein 5 g |Sodium 58 mg | Carbs 10 g

22. Fresh Fruit Smoothie

(Prep time: 5 minutes | Serving: 4)

Ingredients

- Melon chunks: half cup
- Honey: 1 tbsp.
- Coldwater: 1 cup
- Fresh strawberries: 1 cup
- Pineapple: 1 cup
- 2 oranges' juice

Instructions

1. In a blender, add all ingredients.
2. Blend until smooth, pour and serve.

Nutrition: Calories 72| Fat 1 g | Sugar 13 g | Protein 1 g |Sodium 7 mg | Carbs 17 g

23. Raspberry Green Smoothie

(Prep time: 5 minutes | Serving: 4)

Ingredients

- Chia seeds: 1 tbsp.
- Almond butter: 1 tbsp.
- 1 cup of raspberries
- 1 cup of water
- Lemon juice: 2 tbsp.
- 1 banana
- 1/4 cup of spinach

Instructions

1. In a blender, add all ingredients.
2. Blend until smooth, pour and serve.

Nutrition: Calories 187| Fat 7 g | Sugar 4 g | Protein 4 g |Sodium 34 mg | Carbs 7 g

24. Creamy Kale Smoothie

(Prep time: 5 minutes | Serving: 4)

Ingredients

- Low-fat yogurt: half cup
- Chopped kale: 1 cup
- Honey: 1 tsp.
- Frozen pineapple: 1 ½ cups
- Almond milk: half cup, unsweetened

Instructions

1. In a blender, add all ingredients.

2. Blend until smooth, pour and serve.

Nutrition: Calories 296| Fat 8.5 g | Sugar 36 g | Protein 14 g |Sodium 45 mg | Carbs 45 g

25. Vanilla Fruit Smoothie

(Prep time: 5 minutes | Serving: 2)

Ingredients

- 1 banana
- Wheat germ: 2 tbsp.
- Vanilla yogurt: 1 cup, low-fat
- Protein powder: 2 tbsp., optional
- 1% milk: 1 cup

Instructions

1. In a blender, add all ingredients.
2. Blend until smooth, pour and serve.

Nutrition: Calories 608 | Fat 20 g | Sugar 23 g | Protein 30 g |Sodium 208 mg | Carbs 75 g

26. Peach Blueberry Smoothie

(Prep time: 5 minutes | Serving: 2)

Ingredients

- Almond milk: 1 cup
- Chopped peach: half cup
- Blueberries: ¼ cup
- Cinnamon: ¼ tsp.
- Kale: half cup

Instructions

1. In a blender, add all ingredients.
2. Blend until smooth, pour and serve.

Nutrition: Calories 170 | Fat 4 g | Sugar 17 g | Protein 8.5 g |Sodium 35 mg | Carbs 26 g

27. Mixed Berry Yogurt Smoothie

(Prep time: 5 minutes | Serving: 2-3)

Ingredients

- 2 frozen bananas
- Coldwater: half cup
- Vanilla yogurt: 1 cup, low-fat
- Mixed frozen berries: 2 ½ cups
- Honey, to taste
- Low-fat milk: 1 to 2 cups

Instructions

1. In a blender, add all ingredients.

2. Blend until smooth, pour and serve.

Nutrition: Calories 234 | Fat 10 g | Sugar 9 g | Protein 4 g | Sodium 45 mg | Carbs 12g

28. Ultimate Fruit Smoothie

(Prep time: 5 minutes | Serving: 2)

Ingredients

- 2 strawberries
- Half peach
- Orange juice: half cup
- 2% milk: half cup
- Half mango
- Pineapple chunks: ¼ cup

Instructions

1. In a blender, add all ingredients.

2. Blend until smooth, pour and serve.

Nutrition: Calories 224 | Fat 3.1 g | Sugar 39 g | Protein 6 g | Sodium 57 mg | Carbs 46

29. Banana-Blueberry-Soy Smoothie

(Prep time: 5 minutes | Serving: 2)

Ingredients

- Vanilla extract: 1 tsp.
- Frozen blueberries: half cup
- Half banana, frozen
- Soy milk: 1 ¼ cup or more

Instructions

1. In a blender, add all ingredients.

2. Blend until smooth, pour and serve.

Nutrition: Calories 125 | Fat 5 g | Sugar 11 g | Protein 3 g | Sodium 56 mg | Carbs 25 g

30. Hurricane Punch

(Prep time: 5 minutes | Serving: 2-4)

Ingredients

- Citrus fruit: 2 cups
- Ice: 1 cup
- Lemon juice: 2 tbsp.
- Diced pineapple: 1 1/2 cups
- Cranberry juice: 8 oz.

Instructions

1. In a blender, add all ingredients.

2. Blend until smooth, pour and serve.

Nutrition: Calories 64 | Fat 12 g | Sugar 12 g | Protein 1 g | Sodium 6 mg | Carbs 15 g

31. Peaches & Cream Oatmeal Smoothie

(Prep time: 5 minutes | Serving: 2)

Ingredients

- Almond milk: half cup
- Ice: half cup
- Rolled oats: half cup
- Frozen peaches: 1 cup
- Low-fat yogurt: half cup
- Half banana, frozen

Instructions

1. In a blender, add all ingredients.

2. Blend until smooth, pour and serve.

Nutrition: Calories 217 | Fat 5.5 g | Sugar 8 g | Protein 11 g | Sodium 24 mg | Carbs 33g

32. Blueberry Matcha Smoothie

(Prep time: 5 minutes | Serving: 2)

Ingredients

- Matcha powder: 1 tsp.
- Baby spinach: 1 cup
- Old-fashioned oats: 2 tbsp.
- 1 banana
- Frozen blueberries: 1 cup
- Almond milk: 1 cup, unsweetened

Instructions

1. In a blender, add all ingredients.

2. Blend until smooth, pour and serve.

Nutrition: Calories 131 | Fat 2 g | Sugar 14 g | Protein 3 g | Sodium 89 mg | Carbs 28 g

33. Iced latte

(Prep time: 5 minutes | Serving: 2)

Ingredients

- brown sugar: 2 tbsp.
- whipped topping: 1 cup, fat-free
- 1% milk: 1 ½ cups
- almond syrup: 2 tbsp., sugar-free

- brewed espresso coffee: 2 cups, decaffeinated & cooled
- espresso beans, ground: 1 tsp.
- Ice

Instructions

1. In a blender, add all ingredients except for ground beans & whipped topping.
2. Blend until smooth, pour and serve with ground beans & whipped topping on top.

Nutrition: Calories 84 | Fat 1 g | Sugar 11 g | Protein 3 g |Sodium 82 mg | Carbs 18 g

34. Pineapple Passion Smoothie

(Prep time: 5 minutes | Serving: 2)

Ingredients

- Vanilla yogurt, low fat: 1 cup
- Ice cubes
- Pineapple chunks: 1 cup

Instructions

1. In a blender, add all ingredients.
2. Blend until smooth, pour and serve.

Nutrition: Calories 283 | Fat 3.5 g | Sugar 48 g | Protein 13 g |Sodium 55 mg | Carbs 53 g

35. Blueberry Turmeric Zinger Smoothie

(Prep time: 10 minutes | Serving: 2)

Ingredients

- Frozen mango: 1 cup
- Grated ginger: 1 tsp.
- Frozen blueberries: 1 cup
- Apple cider vinegar: 1 tbsp.
- Fresh turmeric: 1 tbsp., chopped
- Coconut oil: 1 tbsp.
- Black pepper, a pinch
- Orange zest: 2 tsp.
- 1 ½ cups of almond milk

Instructions

1. In a blender, add all ingredients.
2. Blend until smooth, pour and serve.

Nutrition: Calories 189 | Fat 6 g | Sugar 2 g | Protein 4

36. Minty-Lime Iced Tea

(Prep time: 10 minutes | Serving: 1)

Ingredients

- Brewed tea: 1 cup, unsweetened & cooled
- Lime juice: 2 tbsp.
- Mint leaves: 2 tbsp., fresh
- Ice cubes
- Honey, to taste

Instructions

1. In a blender, add all ingredients.
2. Blend until smooth, pour and serve.

Nutrition: Calories 16| Fat 0 g | Sugar 8 g | Protein 0 g |Sodium 9 mg | Carbs 4 g

37. Milk & Honey Smoothie

(Prep time: 10 minutes | Serving: 2)

Ingredients

- Almond milk: 1 ½ cups
- 1 cucumber
- Grape: 1 cup, seedless
- 2 stalks celery, sliced
- Honey, to taste

Instructions

1. In a blender, add all ingredients.
2. Blend until smooth, pour and serve.

Nutrition: Calories 124 | Fat 2 g | Sugar 21 g | Protein 2 g |Sodium 49 mg | Carbs 26 g

38. Cleansing Greens Smoothie

(Prep time: 10 minutes | Serving: 2)

Ingredients

- Cayenne powder: 1/8 tsp.
- Vegan protein powder, vanilla flavor: 2 scoops
- Fresh parsley: ¾ cup
- Half avocado
- Ginger powder: 1/8 tsp.
- ¼ cucumber
- Almond milk: 8 oz.
- Turmeric powder: 1/8 tsp.
- Cinnamon, a pinch

Instructions

1. In a blender, add all ingredients.

Top of right column: g |Sodium 50 mg | Carbs 11 g

2. Blend until smooth, pour and serve.

Nutrition: Calories 260 | Fat 6 g | Sugar 4 g | Protein 40 g | Sodium 171 mg | Carbs 18 g

39. Morning Glory Smoothie

(Prep time: 10 minutes | Serving: 4)

Ingredients
- Apple juice: half cup
- Stevia: half tsp.
- Walnuts: 2 tbsp.
- 1 carrot, small
- Coconut flakes: 2 tbsp., unsweetened
- Vanilla extract: half tsp.
- 1 cup of almond milk
- 2 frozen bananas
- Cinnamon: half tsp.
- Ice cubes: 2 cups

Instructions
1. In a blender, add all ingredients.
2. Blend until smooth, pour and serve.

Nutrition: Calories 276 | Fat 8 g | Sugar 30 g | Protein 6 g | Sodium 72 mg | Carbs 46 g

40. Boosting Blueberry Smoothie

(Prep time: 10 minutes | Serving: 2)

Ingredients
- Oats: 1 to 2 tbsp.
- Almond milk: half cup
- Ice cubes: half cup
- Blueberries: half cup
- Baby spinach: ¼ cup
- 1 banana
- Ground chia seeds: 1 tbsp.

Instructions

In a blender, add all ingredients.

Blend until smooth, pour and serve.

Nutrition: Calories 203 | Fat 5 g | Sugar 8 g | Protein 3 g | Sodium 172 mg | Carbs 40 g

41. Orange Dream Smoothie

(Prep time: 10 minutes | Serving: 4)

Ingredients

- Chilled light soy milk: 1 cup, vanilla-flavored
- Vanilla extract: half tsp.
- Soft tofu: 1/3 cup
- Chilled orange juice: 1 1/2 cups
- Honey: 1 tbsp.
- Orange zest: 1 tsp.
- Ice cubes

Instructions
1. In a blender, add all ingredients.
2. Blend until smooth, pour and serve.

Nutrition: Calories 250 | Fat 12 g | Sugar 4 g | Protein 3 g | Sodium 40 mg | Carbs 20 g

42. Cherry Berry Watermelon Smoothie

(Prep time: 10 minutes | Serving: 3-4)

Ingredients
- Frozen strawberries: half cup
- Cubed watermelon: 1 cup
- Frozen raspberries: half cup
- Almond milk: half cup
- 1 banana, frozen
- Frozen cherries: half cup

Instructions
1. In a blender, add all ingredients.
2. Blend until smooth, pour and serve.

Nutrition: Calories 137 | Fat 1.2 g | Sugar 19 g | Protein 2.3 g | Sodium 56 mg | Carbs 33 g

43. Blueberry, Brazil Nut & Tahini Smoothie

(Prep time: 10 minutes | Serving: 2)

Ingredients
- Frozen blueberries: ¾ cup
- Vanilla extract: half tsp.
- Almond milk: 1 cup
- Tahini: 1 tbsp.
- 1 frozen banana
- Brazil nuts: 2 tbsp., raw

Instructions
1. In a blender, add all ingredients.

2. Blend until smooth, pour and serve.

Nutrition: Calories 201 | Fat 8 g | Sugar 8 g | Protein 3 g |Sodium 56 mg | Carbs 11 g

44. Silky Skin Smoothie

(Prep time: 10 minutes | Serving: 2-3)
Ingredients
- 1 apricot, chopped
- Low-fat yogurt: half cup
- Ice cubes: half cup
- Grated carrot: ¼ cup
- 2 dried apricots
- Honey: 1 tsp.
- Cinnamon: half tsp.

Instructions
1. In a blender, add all ingredients.
2. Blend until smooth, pour and serve.

Nutrition: Calories 130 | Fat 3.5 g | Sugar 17 g | Protein 8 g |Sodium 52 mg | Carbs 21 g

45. Strawberry Banana Milkshake

(Prep time: 10 minutes | Serving: 1)
Ingredients
- 6 frozen strawberries
- 1 banana
- Soy milk: half cup
- Vanilla frozen yogurt: 1 cup, fat-free

Instructions
1. In a blender, add all ingredients.
2. Blend until smooth, pour and serve.

Nutrition: Calories 183 | Fat 1 g | Sugar 17 g | Protein 6 g |Sodium 117 mg | Carbs 40 g

46. Clementine Sunshine Smoothie

(Prep time: 10 minutes | Serving: 4)
Ingredients
- 4 chilled clementine
- Ice: half cup
- Almond milk: ¼ cup

Instructions
In a blender, add all ingredients.

Blend until smooth, pour and serve.

Nutrition: Calories 176 | Fat 2.4 g | Sugar 8 g | Protein 4.6 g |Sodium 32 mg | Carbs 39 g

47. Vegan Berry Protein Smoothie

(Prep time: 10 minutes | Serving: 2-3)
Ingredients
- Frozen strawberries: half cup
- Frozen raspberries: ¼ cup
- 1/4 avocado
- Cauliflower rice: half cup, frozen
- Almond milk: 1 cup, unsweetened
- Frozen blueberries: ¼ cup
- Protein powder: 1 scoop, vanilla & vegan

Instructions
1. In a blender, add all ingredients.
2. Blend until smooth, pour and serve.

Nutrition: Calories 346| Fat 21 g | Sugar 12 g | Protein 18 g |Sodium 215 mg | Carbs 30 g

48. Lean, Mean & Green Smoothie

(Prep time: 10 minutes | Serving: 1)
Ingredients
- 1 banana
- 1 kiwi
- Almond milk: 1 cup
- Spinach: 1 cup
- Coconut water: half cup
- Oats: 2 tbsp.

Instructions
1. In a blender, add all ingredients.
2. Blend until smooth, pour and serve.

Nutrition: Calories 287 | Fat 5 g | Sugar 8 g | Protein 14 g |Sodium 52 mg | Carbs 8 g

49. Almond Butter Banana Oatmeal

(Prep time: 10 minutes | Serving: 1)
Ingredients
- Almond butter: 1 tbsp.

- Oats: 3 tbsp.
- Vanilla almond milk: half cup, unsweetened
- 1 frozen banana

Instructions

1. In a blender, add all ingredients.
2. Blend until smooth, pour and serve.

Nutrition: Calories 278 | Fat 11 g | Sugar 16 g | Protein 7.3g |Sodium 55 mg | Carbs 42 g

50. Blueberry Muffin Smoothie

(Prep time: 10 minutes | Serving: 2-3)

Ingredients

- Low-fat vanilla yogurt: 6 oz.
- Frozen blueberries: half cup
- Oats: ¼ cup
- Lemon zest: ¼ tsp.
- Almond milk: half cup
- Half banana, frozen
- Ice cubes: half cup

Instructions

1. In a blender, add all ingredients.
2. Blend until smooth, pour and serve.

Nutrition: Calories 234 | Fat 12 g | Sugar 9 g | Protein 4 g |Sodium 62 mg | Carbs 12 g

51. Turmeric Milk

(Prep time: 10 minutes | Serving: 2)

Ingredients

- Turmeric powder: half tsp.
- Olive oil: 1 tbsp.
- Vanilla extract: half tsp.
- Almond milk: 2 cups, warm

Instructions

1. In a blender, add all ingredients.
2. Blend until smooth, pour and serve.

Nutrition: Calories 250 | Fat 17.2 g | Sugar 8 g | Protein 6.4 g |Sodium 55 mg | Carbs

52. Raspberry Basil Iced Tea

(Prep time: Overnight & 10 minutes | Serving: 10)

Ingredients

- 6 packs of sweetener (no-calorie)
- Raspberries: 2 cups
- Fresh basil: 8 leaves

- Unsweetened iced tea: 8 cups, decaffeinated

Instructions

1. In a pitcher, add all ingredients, stir well keep in the fridge overnight.
2. Strain and serve.

Nutrition: Calories 2 | Fat 0 g | Sugar 0 g | Protein 0 g |Sodium 0 mg | Carbs 0.4 g

53. Pumpkin Spice Smoothie

(Prep time: 10 minutes | Serving: 2)

Ingredients

- Low-fat yogurt: 1/3 cup
- Pumpkin pie spice: half tsp.
- Honey: 2 tsp.
- Almond milk: 1/3 cup
- Canned pumpkin: half cup
- Rolled oats: 2 tbsp.
- 3 to 4 ice cubes

Instructions

1. In a blender, add all ingredients.
2. Blend until smooth, pour and serve.

Nutrition: Calories 199 | Fat 1.5 g | Sugar 26 g | Protein 11 g |Sodium 106 mg | Carbs 38 g

54. Low Sodium Michelada

(Prep time: 15 minutes | Serving: 1)

Ingredients

- Tabasco: 4 dashes, low-sodium
- 1 Lime's juice
- Ice: 2 cups
- Chili-Lime Sugar: ¼ cup
- No-sodium Chili powder: 1 tsp.
- Tomato Juice: 3 oz., low-sodium
- Worcestershire sauce: 4 dashes, low-sodium
- 1 corona Beer

Instructions

1. With some lime juice, coat the glass's rim well.
2. Roll the wet rim in chili-lime sugar, add ice to the glass.
3. Add the rest of the ingredients except for beer, stir well. Add enough beer to fill the glass. Serve.

Nutrition: Calories 172 | Fat 17.2 g | Sugar 4 g | Protein 2.5 g |Sodium 152 mg | Carbs 20 G

55.   Cilantro Jalapeno Margarita

(Prep time: 10 minutes | Serving: 2)

Ingredients

- Cointreau: 1 oz.
- 1 Jalapeno, cut into lengthwise
- 3 sprigs of Cilantro
- Lime Juice: 1 oz.
- Ice
- White Tequila: 1 1/2 oz.
- Cilantro Jalapeno syrup: half oz.

Instructions

1. In a pan, add water (1 cup) with sugar (1 cup) and boil.

2. When sugar is dissolved, add jalapeno slices and cilantro. Boil for 2 minutes, turn the heat low and cook for 2 minutes.

3. Turn the heat off and let it cool.

4. Moist the edges of the glass with lime juice. Add ice.

5. In a different glass, add the rest of the ingredients with the cooled jalapeno syrup.

6. Mix well, pour in the glass and serve.

Nutrition: Calories 199| Fat 17.2 g | Sugar 8 g | Protein 0.1 g |Sodium 0.6 mg | Carbs 10 g

DASH Diet Breakfast Recipes

56. Peanut Butter Overnight Oats

(Prep time: 6 hours & 10 minutes | Cook time: 0 minutes | Serving: 1)

Ingredients

- Oats
- Chia seeds: ¾ tbsp.
- Rolled oats: half cup
- Almond butter: 2 tbsp.
- Almond milk: half cup, unsweetened
- Maple syrup: 1 tbsp.
- Toppings
- Granola, Fresh sliced fruits & chia seeds

Instructions

1. In a mason jar, add all ingredients except for toppings. Mix well press down with a spoon.
2. Keep in the fridge covered overnight.
3. Serve with desired dressings on top.

Nutrition: Calories 452 | Fat 15.8 g | Sugar 8 g | Protein 14.6 g | Sodium 229 mg | Carbs 52 g

57. Healthy Egg Bake

(Prep time: 5 minutes | Cook time: 30 minutes | Serving: 6)

Ingredients

- 12 eggs, whisked
- Black pepper: ¼ tsp.
- ¼ cup of low-fat milk
- Chopped spinach: 10 oz., frozen
- Dijon mustard: 1 tsp.
- Low-fat cheddar cheese: half cup, shredded
- Dried thyme: 1 tsp.
- Salt: ¼ tsp.
- Ground nutmeg: ¼ tsp.

Instructions

1. Preheat the oven to 350 F. oil spray a nine" pan.
2. Add squeezed spinach to the pan.
3. Whisk eggs with milk. Add nutmeg, mustard, salt, pepper and thyme, and mix well.
4. Pour in the pan over spinach. Spread cheese on top.
5. Bake in the oven for half an hour, cool for 5-10 minutes.
6. Slice and serve.

Nutrition: Calories 190 | Fat 9 g | Sugar 1g | Protein 7.8 g | Sodium 289 mg | Carbs 14.8 g

58. Blueberry Multigrain Pancakes

(Prep time: 5 minutes | Cook time: 20 minutes | Serving: 6)

Ingredients

- Whole-wheat flour: ¾ cup
- All-purpose flour: 1 cup
- Rolled oats: 1/3 cup
- Stevia: 2 tbsp.
- Baking powder: 2 tsp.
- Buttermilk: 1 & ¾ cup
- Yellow cornmeal: 1/3 cup
- Unsalted plant butter: ¼ cup
- Baking soda: half tsp.
- Fresh blueberries: 1 cup
- Nutmeg: half tsp.
- Honey: 1/3 cup
- 3 eggs

Instructions

1. In a bowl, add all the dry ingredients, and mix.

2. Add the wet ingredients and mix, add blueberries and fold.

3. Oil spray a skillet and place on medium flame.

4. Add batter (1/4 cup) and cook undisturbed until bubble forms.

5. Flip and cook until browned. Serve.

Nutrition: Calories 250 | Fat 17.2 g | Sugar 8 g | Protein 6.4 g |Sodium 55 mg | Carbs 76 g

59. Very Berry Muesli

(Prep time: 6 hours & 5 minutes | Cook time: 0 minutes | Serving: 4)

Ingredients
- 1% milk: half cup
- Rolled oats: 1 cup
- Chopped apple: half cup
- Frozen blueberries: half cup
- Dried fruits: half cup, mixed
- Fruit yogurt: 1 cup, low-fat
- Toasted chopped walnuts: ¼ cup

Instructions
1. In a bowl, add milk, oats, and yogurt. Mix and keep in the fridge for 6 to 12 hours, covered.

2. Before serving, add the rest of the ingredients. Serve.

Nutrition: Calories 257| Fat 17 g | Sugar 4 g | Protein 6 g |Sodium 77 mg | Carbs 21 g

60. Zucchini Bread

(Prep time: 35 minutes | Cook time: 30 minutes | Serving: 18)

Ingredients
- Canola oil: ¼ cup
- Sugar substitute: half cup
- 6 egg whites
- Vanilla extract: 2 tsp.
- All-purpose flour: 1 ¼ cups
- Baking powder: 1 tsp.
- Baking soda: 1 tsp.
- Cinnamon: 3 tsp.
- Crushed pineapple: 1 ½ cups, unsweetened

- Whole-wheat flour: 1 ¼ cups
- Shredded zucchini: 2 cups
- Applesauce: half cup, unsweetened
- Chopped walnuts: half cup

Instructions
1. Let the oven preheat to 350 F. Oil spray two loaf pans (9 by 5 inches).

2. In a bowl, add vanilla, egg whites, applesauce, canola oil, and sugar. Mix with an electric mixer and whisk until foamy and thick.

3. In a bowl, add all flour, take the half cup out and set it aside.

4. Add cinnamon, baking soda and powder to the flour.

5. Add dry to wet ingredients and whisk with an electric mixer. Mix until well-mixed.

6. Add pineapples, walnuts and zucchini. Mix and add the half cup of flour as required, do not add all at once. It should not be runny.

7. Add half of the batter to one pan, bake for 50 minutes.

8. Cool in the pan for ten minutes. Slice and serve.

Nutrition per slice: Calories 141 | Fat 5 g | Sugar 5 g | Protein 4 g |Sodium 103 mg | Carbs 22 g

61. Ulli's Granola

(Prep time: 10 minutes | Cook time: 40 minutes | Serving: 26)

Ingredients
- Cashews, almonds, pumpkin seeds, dried cranberries, raisins, sunflower seeds & walnuts: 2 cups each
- Coconut flakes: 3 cups, unsweetened
- Maple syrup: half cup
- Rolled oats: 4 cups
- Canola oil: ¼ cup
- Orange oil: 1/3 cup

Instructions
1. Let the oven preheat to 300 F.

2. In a bowl, add oats, coconut flakes, nuts and seeds.

Mix well.

3. In a bowl, add the rest of the ingredients (except for cranberries and raisins) and whisk well. Pour over the dry mixture and mix.

4. Oil spray generously on a baking sheet and spread the mixture on it.

5. Bake for 35 to 40 minutes rotates the sheet halfway through.

6. Let it cool and mix with cranberries and raisins.

7. Serve and store in the fridge.

Nutrition: Calories 190| Fat 9 g | Sugar 1g | Protein 21 g |Sodium 119 mg | Carbs 14.8 g

62. Whole-Wheat Pretzels

(Prep time: 80 minutes | Cook time: 30 minutes | Serving: 14)

Ingredients

- Brown sugar: 2 tsp.
- Kosher salt: half tsp.
- Active dry yeast: 1 pack
- Whole-wheat flour: 3 cups
- Baking soda: ¼ cup
- 1 1/2 cups of warm water
- Olive oil: 1 tbsp.
- Wheat gluten: half cup
- Sesame seeds: 1 tbsp.
- 1 egg white
- Bread flour: 1 cup

Instructions

1. In a food processor, add warm water, yeast, salt, and sugar. Mix and let it rest for 5 minutes.

2. Add gluten, oil and flour. Mix with a hook attachment for 5 to 10 minutes, or until the dough starts pulling away from the bowl.

3. Oil spray the dough and the bowl, cover and keep in a warm place for 60 minutes.

4. Cut into 14 parts. Make each part into a long rope and shape it into a pretzel.

5. In a large pot, add water (8 to 10 cups) with 3 tbsp. of baking soda. Let it come to a boil

6. Boil pretzel one at a time and cook for half a minute. Take out on a baking sheet lined with parchment paper.

7. With egg white brush the boiled pretzels, sprinkle sesame seeds.

8. Bake for 10 to 15 minutes at 450 F.

Nutrition per pretzel: Calories 148 | Fat 2 g | Sugar 8 g | Protein 8 g |Sodium 76 mg | Carbs 27 g

63. Muesli Scones

(Prep time: 20 minutes | Cook time: 30 minutes | Serving: 16)

Ingredients

- Celtic sea salt: half tsp.
- Dried apricots: ¼ cup, chopped
- Baking soda: half tsp.
- Almond flour: 2 cups, blanched
- Honey: 2 tbsp.
- Dried cranberries: ¼ cup
- 1 egg
- Sesame seeds, sunflower seeds & pistachios (chopped): ¼ cup each

Instructions

1. In a bowl, mix soda, flour and salt. Add nuts, dried fruits and seeds.

2. In a bowl, whisk honey with egg. Add wet to dry ingredients.

3. Mix with hands and make into a dough.

4. Shape into dough into ¾" thick. Cut into 16 parts, make each part into a square.

5. Bake for 10 to 12 minutes at 350 F on a parchment-lined baking sheet.

6. Serve.

Nutrition: Calories 121 | Fat 7.3 g | Sugar 5 g | Protein 8.2 g |Sodium 112 mg | Carbs 18.1 g

64. Tofu Turmeric Scramble

(Prep time: 10 minutes | Cook time: 20 minutes | Serving: 2)

Ingredients

- Extra-firm tofu: 8 oz.
- Olive oil: 1 tbsp.
- ¼ red onion, chopped
- 1 red & 1 green bell pepper, chopped
- Fresh spinach: 2 cups, chopped
- Button mushrooms: half cup, sliced
- Salt & pepper: ¼ tsp. Each
- Garlic powder: 1 tsp.
- Nutritional yeast: ¼ cup
- Turmeric: half tbsp.

Instructions

1. Squeeze tofu gently to get rid of excess water and crumble in a bowl.
2. In a skillet, add oil on medium flame. Sauté bell peppers and onion with salt and pepper for 5 minutes.
3. Add mushrooms and cook for 2 minutes. Add tofu and cook for 3 minutes.
4. Add the rest of the ingredients (except for spinach) and mix. Cook for 5-8 minutes.
5. Add spinach, let it cook for 2 minutes, covered. Serve.

Nutrition: Calories 253 | Fat 17.2 g | Sugar 2 g | Protein 6.4 g |Sodium 85 mg | Carbs 11 g

65. Turkey Sausage & Mushroom Strata

(Prep time: 8 hours & 10 minutes | Cook time: 60 minutes | Serving: 4)

Ingredients

- Turkey sausage: 12 oz.
- Fat-free milk: 2 cups
- Egg substitute: 12 oz.
- Cheddar cheese: 4 oz., low-fat, shredded
- Paprika: half tsp.
- Sliced mushrooms: 1 cup
- Whole-grain ciabatta bread: 8 oz., sliced into one "cubes
- 3 eggs
- Black pepper, to taste
- Green onion: half cup, chopped

Instructions

1. Let the oven preheat to 400 F.
2. Bake the bread cubes on a baking tray for 8 minutes.
3. In a skillet, add oil on medium heat. Cook sausage and cook for 7 minutes.
4. In a bowl, add the rest of the ingredients, whisk well.
5. Add bread cubes and toss to coat. Spread on a baking dish (13 by 9"). 4
6. Keep in the fridge, covered for 8 hours. Bake for 50 minutes at 350 F.
7. Slice and serve.

Nutrition: Calories 276 | Fat 14 g | Sugar 2.7 g | Protein 7.1 g |Sodium 178 mg | Carbs 12g

66. Apple and Peanut Butter Oatmeal

(Prep time: 10 minutes | Cook time: 20 minutes | Serving: 4)

Ingredients

- Cinnamon, a pinch
- Peanut butter: 1 tbsp.
- 3 granny smith apples, chopped
- Water: 4 cups
- Steel-cut oats: 1 cup

Instructions

1. Cook oats to your desired consistency.
2. Add apples and peanut butter, mix. Add cinnamon and enjoy.

Nutrition: Calories 245 | Fat 11.3 g | Sugar 7 g | Protein 12 g |Sodium 108 mg | Carbs 14 g

67. Asparagus Frittata

(Prep time: 10 minutes | Cook time: 10 minutes | Serving: 4)

Ingredients

- Low-fat mozzarella cheese: 1 cup, shredded
- No-fat cream: ¼ cup
- 10 large asparagus, chopped
- Canola oil: 1 to 2 tsp.
- 6 eggs
- 3 mushrooms, sliced
- Black pepper: 1 tsp.

Instructions

1. Sauté mushrooms in oil for 4 to 5 minutes.
2. Add asparagus and cook for 2 to 3 minutes.
3. In a bowl, whisk eggs with cream and pepper.
4. Pour over the asparagus mixture. Cook until almost runny but mostly set.
5. Spread cheese on top and broil in oven for 4 to 5 minutes. Do not burn.
6. Serve.

Nutrition: Calories 254 | Fat 14 g | Sugar 2.7 g | Protein 12 g | Sodium 128 mg | Carbs 12g

68. Smoked Salmon Avocado Toast

(Prep time: 10 minutes | Cook time: 0 minutes | Serving: 1)

Ingredients

- Half avocado
- Garlic & herb seasoning, salt-free: 1 pinch
- Whole grain bread: 2 slices
- Smoked Salmon: 3 oz. (no sodium)

Instructions

1. Toast the bread slices and spread avocado on top.
2. Sprinkle seasoning and top with salmon. Serve.

Nutrition: Calories 307 | Fat 21 g | Sugar 2 g | Protein 24 g | Sodium 450 mg | Carbs 7 g

69. Healthy Breakfast Cookies

(Prep time: 10 minutes | Cook time: 14 minutes | Serving: 6)

Ingredients

- Honey: ¼ cup
- Chopped nuts: 2/3 cup
- Vanilla extract: 1 tsp.
- Cinnamon: 1 tsp.
- 2 bananas, mashed

- Peanut butter: 1 cup
- Dried cranberries: half cup
- Salt: half tsp.
- Quick oats: 2 1/4 cups

Instructions

1. Let the oven preheat to 325 F.
2. In a stand mixer, add all wet ingredients, mix with a paddle attachment.
3. Add the rest of the ingredients and mix until combined.
4. With a scooper, scoop cookie dough on a parchment-lined baking tray. Flatten every cookie dough scoop.
5. Bake for 14-16 minutes, cool and serve.

Nutrition: Calories 276 | Fat 15 g | Sugar 14 g | Protein 9 g | Sodium 197 mg | Carbs 31 g

70. Whole-Grain Pancakes

(Prep time: 10 minutes | Cook time: 12 minutes | Serving: 9)

Ingredients

- Millet flour: 1/4 cup
- Honey: 3 tbsp.
- Flaxseed flour: 2 tbsp.
- Soy milk: 2 1/4 cups
- Whole-wheat flour: 1 cup
- Rolled oats: 1/4 cup
- Baking powder: 1 1/2 tbsp.
- Barley flour: half cup
- Oil: 1 tbsp.
- 3 egg whites, whisked

Instructions

1. In a bowl, add all dry ingredients.
2. In a different bowl, add the wet ingredients and whisk.
3. Add wet to dry ingredients. Mix until combined.
4. Let it rest for half an hour in the fridge.
5. In a pan, add oil on medium flame.
6. Add batter (1/4 cup) and cook on both sides until dry and browned.
7. Serve.

Nutrition (2 pancakes): Calories 180 | Fat 4 g | Sugar 168 g | Protein 6 g | Sodium 55 mg | Carbs 30 g

71. Mushroom & Sausage Quiche

(Prep time: 10 minutes | Cook time: 35 minutes | Serving: 9)

Ingredients

- Olive oil: 1 tsp.
- 3 egg whites
- Mushrooms: 6 oz.
- Turkey sausage: 8 oz., no casing
- Black pepper: half tsp.
- 1% milk: 1 cup
- Sliced scallions: ¼ cup
- Swiss Cheese (grated): ¼ cup, low-fat
- 5 eggs

Instructions

1. In a bowl, whisk milk with eggs and whites.
2. In a pan, add oil on medium flame. Cook sausage for 6-8 minutes, take it out in a bowl.
3. In the same pan, add oil. Sauté mushrooms and cook for 5-7 minutes. Take them out in a bowl.
4. Cook for 5 minutes, add the rest of the ingredients. Mix well.
5. Pour into oil sprayed muffin cups. Add cooked sausage on top.
6. Bake at preheated 325 F for 25 minutes. Cool for 5 minutes, serve.

Nutrition: Calories 132 | Fat 4 g | Sugar 3 g | Protein 5 g | Sodium 192 mg | Carbs 10 g

72. Red Pepper, Kale & Cheddar Frittata

(Prep time: 10 minutes | Cook time: 45 minutes | Serving: 6-8)

Ingredients

- Shredded cheddar cheese: 1 cup, low fat
- Olive oil: 1 tsp
- Sliced scallions: 1/3 cup
- 12 eggs
- Baby kale & spinach: 5 oz.
- Salt, a pinch
- 3/4 cup of 1% milk
- 1 diced red pepper
- Black pepper: 1/4 tsp.

Instructions

1. Let the oven preheat to 375 F. Oil spray a 12" baking dish.
2. In a pan, add oil and sauté red peppers until soft. Add spinach, kale and cook for three minutes.
3. In the prepared dish, spread the vegetables and add scallions on top.
4. In a bowl, whisk milk, eggs, salt and pepper. Pour over the vegetable pan and spread cheese on top.
5. Bake for 35 to 40 minutes, until set. Broil for 1 to 3 minutes. Cool slightly and serve.

Nutrition: Calories 192 | Fat 14 g | Sugar 8 g | Protein 5 g | Sodium 149 mg | Carbs 10 g

73. Breakfast Fruit Pizza

(Prep time: 10 minutes | Cook time: 0 minutes | Serving: 2-3)

Ingredients

- 2 pita bread, whole wheat
- Low-fat cream cheese: 7 oz.
- Manuka honey: 1 to 2 tsp.
- Vanilla extract: half tsp.
- 3 kiwis, sliced
- Sliced strawberries: half cup
- Blackberries: half cup
- Blueberries: ¼ cup
- 2 raspberries

Instructions

Toast the pita bread and spread cream cheese, arrange fruits in the desired manner.

Slice and serve.

Nutrition: Calories 234 | Fat 17.2 g | Sugar 11.6 g | Protein 6.2 g | Sodium 217 mg | Carbs 20 g

74. Poached Eggs with Avocado & Balsamic Tomatoes

(Prep time: 10 minutes | Cook time: 10 minutes | Serving: 2-3)

Ingredients

- 8-10 tomatoes, chopped
- Balsamic vinegar: 2 tbsp.
- 2 to 3 eggs (for each person)
- Italian mixed herbs: 1 tbsp.
- Olive oil: 2 tbsp.
- 2 avocados, sliced

Instructions

1. In a pot, add water, and boil. Add cracked eggs in the water and cook on low for two minutes.
2. Take the eggs out of water. Sprinkle herbs and pepper.
3. Serve with avocados and tomatoes.

Nutrition: Calories 211 | Fat 5.2 g | Sugar 23 g | Protein 2.8 g | Sodium 30.8 mg | Carbs 39 g

75. Whole Grain Cottage Cheese Pancakes

(Prep time: 10 minutes | Cook time: 20 minutes | Serving: 4)

Ingredients

- Sorghum flour: half cup
- Tapioca starch: 1 tbsp. + 1/3 cup
- Oat flour: 1 cup
- Baking powder: 1 tbsp.
- Salt: half tsp.
- Sugar substitute: 3 1/2 tsp.
- Low-fat cottage cheese: 1/3 cup
- Water: 3 tbsp.
- Flax meal: half tsp.
- Teff flour: 2 tbsp.
- Buttermilk: 3/4 cup
- Maple syrup: half cup
- 3 eggs
- Vanilla extract: half tsp.
- Lemon juice: 1 tsp.
- Canola oil: 4 tsp.

- Salt, a pinch
- Blueberries: 4 cups

Instructions

1. In a pot, add maple syrup, salt, blueberries, water and lemon juice. Mix well on low flame.
2. In a bowl, add the rest of the dry ingredients. Mix well.
3. In a different bowl, add the wet ingredients and mix.
4. Add the wet to dry ingredients, gradually and whisk until combined.
5. Let it rest for 12-15 minutes.
6. In an oil-sprayed preheated pan, add the batter.
7. Add the batter and cook on both sides. Serve with blueberries compote.

Nutrition: Calories 211 | Fat 15.2 g | Sugar 23 g | Protein 2.8 g | Sodium 130.8 mg | Carbs 39 g

76. Sweet Millet Congee

(Prep time: 10 minutes | Cook time: 60 minutes | Serving: 8)

Ingredients

- Hulled millet: 1 cup
- Cinnamon: 1 tsp.
- 5 cups of water
- Bacon strips: 8
- Peeled sweet potato: 1 cup, diced
- Ginger minced: 2 tsp.
- Honey: ¼ cup
- Brown sugar: 2 tbsp.
- 1 apple, diced

Instructions

1. In a skillet, cook bacon until crispy. Take them out on a paper towel.
2. In a pot, add millet, brown sugar, ginger, water, cinnamon and sweet potato.
3. Let it come to a boil, turn the heat low and let it cook for 60 minutes.
4. Turn the heat off, add bacon crumbles, apple and honey. Serve.

Nutrition: Calories 215 | Fat 3 g | Sugar 10.2 g | Protein 12 g | Sodium 98.3 mg | Carbs 21g

77. Breakfast Open Sandwich

(Prep time: 5 minutes | Cook time: 0 minutes | Serving: 1)

Ingredients

- 1 or half banana, sliced
- Almond butter: 1 tbsp.
- Chia seeds
- Whole grain bread: 1 slice

Instructions

1. Toast the bread and spread almond butter.
2. Lay banana slices and top with chia seeds.
3. Serve.

Nutrition: Calories 184 | Fat 12 g | Sugar 17 g | Protein 4 g | Sodium 127 mg | Carbs 31 g

78. Pumpkin Overnight Oats

(Prep time: 8 hours & 5 minutes | Cook time: 0 minutes | Serving: 1)

Ingredients

- Unsweetened almond milk: ¾ cup
- Pumpkin puree: ¼ cup
- Pumpkin spice: ¼ tsp.
- Salt, a pinch
- Cinnamon: half tsp.
- Rolled oats: half cup
- Maple syrup: half tsp.

Instructions

1. In a mason jar, add all ingredients and mix.
2. Keep in the fridge overnight and serve.

Nutrition: Calories 188 | Fat 3.3 g | Sugar 17 g | Protein 6.4 g | Sodium 187 mg | Carbs 35 g

79. Apple Cinnamon Steel-Cut Oatmeal

(Prep time: 8 hours & 5 minutes | Cook time: 0 minutes | Serving: 7)

Ingredients

- 1 % milk: 1 ½ cups
- Cinnamon: half tsp.
- Water: 1 ½ cups
- Peeled apples: 2-3 cups chopped
- Steel-cut oats: 1 cup
- Ground flaxseed: 1 tbsp.
- Brown sugar: 2 tbsp.
- Salt, a pinch

Instructions

1. In a slow cooker (3 ½ qt.), add all ingredients after oil spraying it.
2. Stir and cook for 7 hours on low.
3. Serve with fresh fruits.

Nutrition: Calories 149 | Fat 3.6 g | Sugar 8 g | Protein 6.4 g | Sodium 65 mg | Carbs 27.3 g

80. Raspberry Chocolate Scones

(Prep time: 10 minutes | Cook time: 12 minutes | Serving: 12)

Ingredients

- Baking powder: 1 tbsp.
- Pastry flour: 1 cup, whole-wheat
- All-purpose flour: 1 cup
- Baking soda: ¼ tsp.
- Buttery spread: 1/3 cup, fat-free
- Cinnamon: ¼ tsp.
- Raspberries: half cup
- Fat-free yogurt: 1 cup + 2 tbsp.
- Honey: 2 tbsp.
- Chocolate chips: ¼ cup
- Sugar: half tsp.

Instructions

1. In a bowl, mix baking soda, flours, and baking powder. Add buttery spread mix until it crumbles.
2. Add chocolate chips and berries. Mix well.
3. Add honey and yogurt in a bowl and mix, then add to the flour mixture.
4. Mix until combined, and make into a dough. Knead 1-2 times.
5. Make it into a circle and cut it into 12 parts (triangle).
6. Place on an oil sprayed baking sheet. Sprinkle sugar-cinnamon mixture on top.

7. Bake for ten to twelve minutes at 400 F.

Nutrition per scone: Calories 149 | Fat 5 g | Sugar 3 g | Protein 4 g |Sodium 143 mg | Carbs 22 g

81.   Dash Diet French Toast

(Prep time: 10 minutes | Cook time: 12 minutes | Serving: 6)
Ingredients
- Sugar: 2 tbsp.
- Milk: half cup
- Whole wheat bread: 6 slices
- Cinnamon: 1 tsp.
- 2 eggs
- Applesauce: ¼ cup, unsweetened

Instructions
1. In a bowl, add all ingredients except for bread. Mix well and add bread slices until soaked lightly.
2. Place on an oil-sprayed pan and cook until browned on both sides.
3. Serve with fresh fruits.

Nutrition: Calories 150 | Fat 3 g | Sugar 8 g | Protein 8 g |Sodium 220 mg | Carbs 8 g

82.   Guacamole Deviled Eggs

(Prep time: 15 minutes | Cook time: 0 minutes | Serving: 12)
Ingredients
- Green onion: 1 tbsp.
- Half jalapeno pepper
- Cilantro: 1 tbsp.
- 6 eggs, hard-boiled
- Lime: 1 tbsp.
- 2 avocados
- Low-fat sour cream: 1 tbsp.

Instructions
1. Cut the egg in half, take the yolk out and mash with the rest of the ingredients.
2. Stuff the mixture in the egg whites and serve.

Nutrition: Calories 210 | Fat 2.8 g | Sugar 8 g | Protein 6.4 g |Sodium 141 mg | Carbs 12 g

83.   Berry & Quinoa Breakfast Cereal

(Prep time: 25 minutes | Cook time: 0 minutes | Serving: 4)
Ingredients
- 3/4 cup of water
- 1 cup of strawberries
- 4 strawberries
- Blueberries: ¼ cup
- 1/4 cup of hemp seeds
- Honey: 1 tbsp.
- Cooked quinoa: 2 cooked
- Walnuts: 2 tbsp.

Instructions
1. In a blender, add all ingredients except for quinoa, nuts and fruits. Pulse until smooth.
2. Pour over quinoa and serve with toppings.

Nutrition: Calories 493| Fat 20 g | Sugar 8 g | Protein 20 g |Sodium 22 mg | Carbs 60 g

84.   Avocado Egg Cups

(Prep time: 10 minutes | Cook time: 30 minutes | Serving: 4)
Ingredients
- Coarse salt, a pinch
- 4 eggs
- Black pepper, to taste
- 2 avocados
- Herbs & chopped vegetables for toppings
- Olive oil: half tsp.
- Grated low-fat cheese: 1 tbsp.

Instructions
1. Let the oven preheat to 375 F.
2. Cut the avocados in half and remove enough flesh to make space for the egg.
3. Sprinkle salt and pepper and place on a foil-lined baking sheet. Add one egg in each half and top with cheese. With foil, cover the avocado egg loosely.
4. Bake for 20-25 minutes. Add toppings and serve.

Nutrition: Calories 166 | Fat 6 g | Sugar 15 g | Protein 4 g |Sodium 132 mg | Carbs 21 g

85. Summer Breakfast Quinoa Bowls

(Prep time: 10 minutes | Cook time: 25 minutes | Serving: 2)

Ingredients

- Rinsed quinoa: 1/3 cup
- Vanilla extract: half tsp.
- Honey: 2 tsp.
- 1 peach, sliced
- Brown sugar: 2 tsp.
- 12 raspberries
- Low-fat milk: 2/3 cup plus 3/4 cup
- 14 blueberries

Instructions

1. In a pan, add brown sugar, quinoa, vanilla and milk (2/3 cup) on medium flame.
2. Boil for 5 minutes, turn the heat low and cook covered for 15-20 minutes.
3. On a preheated grill, grill the peaches for 2-3 minutes. In a pan, add the rest of the milk and warm.
4. In 2 serving bowls, add quinoa and add warm milk.
5. Serve with fresh and grilled fruits with a drizzle of honey.

Nutrition: Calories 250 | Fat 12 g | Sugar 8 g | Protein 11 g | Sodium 71 mg | Carbs 67 g

86. Egg Muffin with Cheese & Spinach

(Prep time: 25 minutes | Cook time: 10 minutes | Serving: 2)

Ingredients

- Low-fat Swiss cheese: half cup, shredded
- Olive oil: 1 tsp.
- 2 English muffins, whole-grain, halved
- 8 egg whites, beaten
- Hot sauce, a dash
- 4 to 6 Spinach leaves, chopped
- Grape tomatoes: half cup, quartered
- Black Pepper

Ingredients

1. Toast the muffins.

2. In a pan, sauté spinach for 2-3 minutes, add eggs and seasonings.
3. Keep stirring and cook until set. Place on toast with cheese and tomatoes.

Nutrition: Calories 144 | Fat 10 g | Sugar 5.4 g | Protein 17.8 g | Sodium 128 mg | Carbs 11 g

87. Portobello Mushroom & Avocado Sandwich

(Prep time: 10 minutes | Cook time: 25 minutes | Serving: 2)

Ingredients

- Baby Spinach leaves: half cup
- 1 Avocado, thinly sliced
- Any DASH dressing
- 1 tomato, sliced into 4 slices
- 2 Portobello Mushrooms
- Low-fat Cheese: 2 oz., shredded
- 2 poached eggs
- Italian herbs, as needed

Instructions

1. In a pan, add some oil and place on medium flame.
2. Season the mushrooms with pepper and cook for two minutes in the pan, on each side.
3. Season the tomatoes with herbs and pepper.
4. Poach eggs in boiling water to your desired consistency.
5. Place cheese on mushrooms, spinach, tomato and eggs on top.
6. Serve with a sprinkle of dried herbs on top.

Nutrition: Calories 124 | Fat 3.2 g | Sugar 5.3 g | Protein 9 g | Sodium 118 mg | Carbs 10 g

88. Vegetarian Breakfast Salad

(Prep time: Overnight & 12 minutes | Cook time: 5 minutes | Serving: 1)

Ingredients

- Olive oil: 1 1/2 tsp.

- Baby arugula: 1 1/2 cups
- Avocado: half cup
- Sea salt, a pinch
- Lemon Juice: 1 tbsp.
- Grape Tomatoes: 3/4 cup
- Black Pepper: 1/8 tsp.
- Red Onion: 1/4 cup
- 2 Eggs

Instructions

1. In a bowl, whisk oil and lemon juice. Add the vegetables, do not toss.
2. Keep in the fridge overnight, covered.
3. Before serving, toss and add salt and pepper.
4. Top with fried eggs, and serve.

Nutrition: Calories 114 | Fat 3.2 g | Sugar 8 g | Protein 19 g | Sodium 118 mg | Carbs 30 g

89. Blueberry Banana Spelt Muffins

(Prep time: 12 minutes | Cook time: 30 minutes | Serving: 12)

Ingredients

- Almond milk: 2 tbsp. + ¾ cup
- Apple cider vinegar: 1 tsp.
- Mashed banana: ¾ cup
- Cane sugar (natural): 4-6 tbsp.
- Maple syrup: ¼ cup
- Baking soda: half tsp.
- White spelt flour: 2 cups
- Vanilla extract: 1 tsp.
- Canola oil: ¼ cup
- Sea salt: 1/8 tsp.
- Baking powder: 2 tsp.
- Cinnamon: 1 ½ tsp.
- Blueberries: 1 1/4 cups

Instructions

1. Let the oven preheat to 350 F and oil spray a muffin tin.
2. In a bowl, add mashed bananas with vanilla, milk, maple syrup and vinegar. Do not stir.

3. In a bowl, add dry ingredients. Add oil in the wet ingredients, mix and pour over dry ingredients. Do not overmix.
4. Add blueberries and fold lightly.
5. In each muffin cup, add the batter (3/4 full). Bake for 23-27 minutes at 350 F. Do not burn.
6. Cool for 5-8 minutes in the pan and serve.

Nutrition per muffin: Calories 180 | Fat 5 g | Sugar 12 g | Protein 4 g | Sodium 160 mg | Carbs 31 g

90. Almond & Apricot Biscotti

(Prep time: 12 minutes | Cook time: 30 minutes | Serving: 12)

Ingredients

- All-purpose flour: ¾ cup
- Almond extract: half tsp.
- Baking powder: 1 tsp.
- 2 eggs, whisked
- Whole-wheat flour: ¾ cup
- 1 % low-fat milk: 2 tbsp.
- Chopped almonds: ¼ cup
- Brown sugar: ¼ cup, packed
- Dried apricots: 2/3 cup, chopped
- Canola oil: 2 tbsp.
- Honey: 2 tbsp.

Instructions

1. Let the oven preheat to 350 F.
2. In a bowl, add baking powder, sugar and flours; mix.
3. Add wet ingredients with eggs. Mix with a wooden spoon until dough forms.
4. Add almonds and apricots. Mix until combined.
5. Shape the dough into high (1"), wide (3") and long (12") after wrapping in plastic wrap.
6. Take the plastic wrap off and bake for 25-30 minutes.
7. Take out and place on another baking sheet to cool for ten minutes.
8. Cut with a knife and into 24 slices (half-inch wide).

Place slices cut side down on the baking sheet.

9. Bake for 15-20 minutes until crisp. Serve.

Nutrition per cookie: Calories 75 | Fat 2 g | Sugar 6 g | Protein 2 g |Sodium 17 mg | Carbs 12g

91. Spinach Scramble Eggs

(Prep time: 5 minutes | Cook time: 10 minutes | Serving: 2)

Ingredients

- 2 eggs
- Milk & water, a splash of each
- Olive oil, as needed
- Spinach: 2 cups
- Black pepper, to taste

Instructions

1. Whisk eggs with water and milk.
2. Cook eggs in hot oil with spinach.
3. Keep stirring and make into a scramble.
4. Serve with black pepper on top.

Nutrition: Calories 216 | Fat 8 g | Sugar 2 g | Protein 3.9 g |Sodium 141 mg | Carbs 12 g

92. Tofu & Mushroom Scramble

(Prep time: 5 minutes | Cook time: 10 minutes | Serving: 2)

Ingredients

- 2 garlic cloves
- 4 white mushrooms, sliced
- Half red bell pepper, diced
- Half avocado
- Grated carrot: ¼ cup
- Red onion: 1/4 cup, diced
- Extra-firm tofu: 1 pack, crumbled
- Garlic powder, cumin, turmeric, chia seeds, chili powder: half tsp. Each mixed with water (3 tsp.)
- Spring onions: 2, chopped
- Lemon juice, a drizzle

Instructions

1. In a pan, sauté all vegetables (except for spring onion and avocado) with garlic for 6-7 minutes in a non-stick pan. Add a splash of water if necessary.

2. Add tofu and spice mixture.

3. Mix well and serve with avocado and spring onion on top, with a drizzle of lemon juice.

Nutrition: Calories 210 | Fat 2.8 g | Sugar 8 g | Protein 6.4 g |Sodium 141 mg | Carbs 12 g

93. Breakfast Egg Muffin Sandwiches

(Prep time: 5 minutes | Cook time: 14-16 minutes | Serving: 12)

Ingredients

- 12 eggs
- Low-fat Swiss cheese: 3 slices (1 oz. each) sliced into fours
- 12 English muffins, halved

Instructions

1. Let the oven preheat to 375 F. Oil spray 12 ramekins of 10 oz. Place onto 2 baking sheets.
2. In each ramekin, add 1 egg and whisk it. Add black pepper.
3. Bake for 14-16 minutes, and let them cool.
4. In each muffin, place one egg and cheese. Serve right away with desired sliced vegetables, or freeze after wrapping in plastic wrap.

Nutrition: Calories 229 | Fat 10 g | Sugar 8 g | Protein 13 g |Sodium 92 mg | Carbs 21 g

Spinach Sunshine Smoothie Bowl

(Prep time: 5 minutes | Cook time: 0 minutes | Serving: 1)

Ingredients

- Fresh mixed fruits, for topping
- 1 banana
- Orange juice: 1 cup
- Ice cubes: half cup
- Baby spinach: 1 cup, packed
- Half avocado

Instructions

1. In a blender, add all ingredients and pulse until smooth.
2. Pour in the bowl and serve with mixed fruits.

Nutrition: Calories 119 | Fat 3.5 g | Sugar 4 g | Protein 4 g |Sodium 114 mg | Carbs 25 g

94. Strawberry Breakfast Sandwich

(Prep time: 10 minutes | Cook time: 0 minutes | Serving: 8)

Ingredients

Honey: 1 tbsp.

Sliced strawberries: 2 cups

Lemon zest: 1 tsp.

Low-fat cream cheese: 8 oz.

4 English muffins, halved & toasted

Instructions

In a food processor, add zest, honey and cheese. Process until well combined.

On each muffin, half spread the cheese mixture and serve with sliced strawberries on top.

Nutrition: Calories 139 | Fat 3.5 g | Sugar 4 g | Protein 4 g |Sodium 114 mg | Carbs 25 g

95. Strawberry Pancakes

(Prep time: 5 minutes | Cook time: 30 minutes | Serving: 4)

Ingredients

- Sugar: 2 tbsp. + 1/3 cup
- Whole wheat flour: 3/4 cup
- Low-fat unsalted plant butter: 2 tbsp.
- Fresh strawberries: 3 cups, sliced
- Vanilla yogurt: 1 cup, fat-free
- Almond milk: 1 ½ cups
- 3 eggs
- Vanilla extract: half tsp.

Instructions

1. Toss the strawberries with sugar (2 tbsp.).
2. Let the oven preheat to 375 F, melt butter in a pan (9").
3. In a bowl, whisk milk and egg. Add vanilla, sugar and flour; mix well.
4. Add batter to the pan and place in the oven (middle rack).
5. Bake for 25 to 30 minutes, cut in wedges. Serve with strawberries and yogurt.

Nutrition: Calories 86 | Fat 5 g | Sugar 7 g | Protein 2 g |Sodium 115 mg | Carbs 10 g

96. Avocado Egg Sandwich

(Prep time: 15 minutes | Cook time: 0 minutes | Serving: 8)

Ingredients

- Hard-boiled eggs: 6, diced
- Fresh herbs: 1 to 2 tbsp., chopped
- Yogurt: half cup, low-fat
- Dijon mustard: half tsp.
- 1 avocado
- Light mayo: half cup
- Black pepper, paprika and chia seeds, as needed

Instructions

1. In a bowl, whisk all ingredients except for eggs and avocado.
2. Dice the hard-boiled eggs and add to the other ingredients.
3. Before serving, add diced avocado.
4. Serve on top of whole-grain bread.

Nutrition: Calories 100 | Fat 1.5 g | Sugar 9 g | Protein 4 g |Sodium 55 mg | Carbs 18 g

97. Instant Pot Steel Cut Oats

(Prep time: 5 minutes | Cook time: 6 minutes | Serving: 6)

Ingredients

Steel-cut oats: 2 1/2 cups

Cinnamon sticks: 2

7 cups of water

Instructions

1. In an instant pot, add all ingredients and stir.
2. Secure the lid and cook for 6 minutes. Release the pressure naturally.
3. Take the lid off and take the cinnamon sticks out and stir well.
4. Serve with fresh fruits on top.

Nutrition: Calories 201| Fat 5.5 g | Sugar 7 g | Protein 11 g |Sodium 109 mg | Carbs 12 g

98. Mocha Overnight Oats

(Prep time: 15 minutes & overnight | Cook time: 0 minutes | Serving: 1)

Ingredients

- Brewed coffee: 1/3 cup, cooled
- Low-fat yogurt: 1/3 cup
- Cocoa powder: 1 tsp.
- Rolled oats: 1/3 cup
- Vanilla protein powder: 1 scoop
- Chia seeds: 1 tsp.
- Cocoa powder: 1 tsp.
- Mixed fresh berries for toppings

Instructions

1. In a mason jar, add all ingredients, mix and keep in the fridge overnight.
2. Serve with mixed berries on top.

Nutrition: Calories 133 | Fat 5 g | Sugar 2.27 g | Protein 8 g | Sodium 86 mg | Carbs 16.5 g

99. Apple Cinnamon Muffins

(Prep time: 15 minutes | Cook time: 22 minutes | Serving: 16)

Ingredients

- 2 eggs
- Canola oil: 2 tbsp.
- Vanilla extract: 2 tsp.
- Low-fat yogurt: 1 cup
- All-purpose flour: 1 cup
- Baking powder: 1 ½ tsp.
- Cinnamon: 2 ¼ tsp.
- 2 granny smith apples, peeled & chopped
- Milled oats: 3/4 cup
- Flaxseed meal: ¼ cup
- Sugar: 2 tbsp. + 1 cup
- Salt: half tsp.

Instructions

1. Let the oven preheat to 400 F. oil spray 2 muffin tins.
2. In a bowl, whisk vanilla, oil, yogurt and eggs.
3. In a cup, mix cinnamon with sugar (2 tbsp.).
4. In a bowl, add the rest of the dry ingredients and mix.

5. Add wet ingredients mix until just combined. It will be lumpy.
6. Fold in the apples.
7. Pour into muffin cups and sprinkle with cinnamon mixture.
8. Bake for 22 minutes, serve.

Nutrition per muffin: Calories 152 | Fat 17 g | Sugar 8 g | Protein 4 g | Sodium 122 mg | Carbs 29 g

100. Breakfast Tacos

(Prep time: 15 minutes | Cook time: 0 minutes | Serving: 4)

Ingredients

- 4 Corn tortillas
- Scrambled eggs: 1 cup
- Salsa, avocado & shredded low-fat cheese, as needed

Instructions

1. In each corn tortillas, add scrambled eggs with the rest of the ingredients.
2. Roll and serve.

Nutrition: Calories 189 | Fat 9 g | Sugar 3 g | Protein 26 g | Sodium 186 mg | Carbs 21 g

101. Basic Egg Muffin

Ingredients

(Prep time: 15 minutes | Cook time: 15 minutes | Serving: 12-14)

Ingredients

- Black pepper: half tsp.
- 10 eggs
- Salt: ¼ tsp.
- Sun-dried tomatoes: half cup, chopped & soaked
- Chopped spinach: ¾ cup
- Fresh basil: ¼ cup, chopped
- Low-fat parmesan cheese: 1 cup, grated

Instructions

In a bowl, whisk eggs with salt and pepper.

Pour into oil–sprayed muffin cups. Top with the rest of the ingredients.

Bake for 12 to 15 minutes at preheated 400 F.

Serve right away.

Nutrition: Calories 123 | Fat 5.4 g | Sugar 2.17 g | Protein 11.2 g |Sodium 106 mg | Carbs 13 g

102. Breakfast in a Jar

(Prep time: 15 minutes & overnight | Cook time: 0 minutes | Serving: 1)

Ingredients

- Oatmeal: ¼ cup
- Chia seeds: 1 tbsp.
- Coconut flakes: 1 tbsp., unsweetened
- Kefir: ¾ cup
- Raisins: 2 tbsp.

Instructions

1. In a mason jar, layer all the ingredients, dry at the bottom.
2. Keep in the fridge covered overnight.
3. Before serving, mix and serve.

Nutrition: Calories 155 | Fat 12 g | Sugar 7.9 g | Protein 12 g |Sodium 123 mg | Carbs 18.9 g

103. Steel Cut Oat Blueberry Pancakes

(Prep time: 15 minutes | Cook time: 15 minutes | Serving: 2-3)

Ingredients

- 1-1/2 cups of water
- Sea salt: 1/8 tsp.
- Baking soda: half tsp.
- Agave nectar: 2 tbsp. + half cup
- Whole wheat flour: 1 cup
- Steel-cut oats: half cup
- Baking powder: half tsp.
- Low–fat yogurt: half cup, vanilla flavor
- 1 egg
- 1 cup of almond milk
- Frozen blueberries: 1 cup

Instructions

1. In a pot, add water and boil. Add oats with salt.
2. Turn the heat low and cook for ten minutes. Turn

off the heat.

3. In a bowl, add yogurt, flour, milk, baking soda, powder, and egg. Mix.
4. Fold in cooked oats and blueberries.
5. Oil spray a pan and place on medium flame.
6. Add ¼ cup of batter, cook for 2 to 3 minutes on each side.
7. Serve with agave nectar.

Nutrition: Calories 298 | Fat 11 g | Sugar 7 g | Protein 10 g |Sodium 123 mg | Carbs 18.9 g

104. Dash Diet Cinnamon Waffles

(Prep time: 15 minutes | Cook time: 10 minutes | Serving: 2-3)

Ingredients

- Almond flour: 3/4 cup
- Cornstarch: 1/3 cup
- Baking powder: 2 tsp.
- Sweet white rice flour: 1 cup
- Ground chia seeds: 1/3 cup
- Protein powder: 1/3 cup
- Vanilla extract: 2 tsp.
- Cinnamon: 1 tsp.
- Buttermilk: 1 1/2 cups
- Sugar: 2 tbsp.
- 4 eggs
- Melted unsalted plant butter: 4 tbsp.

Instructions

1. In a bowl, add all dry ingredients and mix.
2. In a different bowl, add yolks, vanilla and buttermilk, mix. Add to the dry ingredients and mix until combined; if it is too thick adding more buttermilk.
3. In a stand mixer, whisk 2 egg whites for 30-60 seconds. Gradually add sugar and whisk on medium-hi speed until stiff peaks form.
4. Add ¼th of the stiff egg whites into the batter

and fold the rest in. While mixing, add butter.

5. Oil spray the waffle iron and pour the batter and cook. Serve with fresh fruits.

Nutrition: Calories 288 | Fat 16.3 g | Sugar 1 g | Protein 30.5 g | Sodium 104 mg | Carbs 4.3 g

105.   Simple Banana Muffins

(Prep time: 10 minutes | Cook time: 22 minutes | Serving: 6)
Ingredients

- Granulated sugar: ¼ cup
- 1 egg
- All-purpose flour: half cup
- 2 overripe bananas
- Avocado oil: ¼ cup
- Baking powder: 1 tsp.
- Cinnamon: half tsp.
- Vanilla extract: half tsp.
- Whole wheat flour: half cup
- Salt: ¼ tsp.

Instructions

1. Let the oven preheat to 350 F, oil spray muffin tin with 6 cups.
2. In a bowl, mash the bananas, add sugar and mix.
3. Add eggs and mix until combined.
4. Add vanilla, oil and mix.
5. In a bowl, add flour(s), cinnamon, baking powder and salt. Mix and add wet ingredients. Stir well.
6. Pour into muffin tin and bake for 20 to 22 minutes.

Nutrition: Calories 149 | Fat 3 g | Sugar 0 g | Protein 30 g | Sodium 143 mg | Carbs 12 g

106.   Banana Oatmeal Pancakes

(Prep time: 10 minutes | Cook time: 15 minutes | Serving: 4)
Ingredients

- Boiling water: 1 cup
- All-purpose flour: half cup
- Canola oil: 2 tbsp.
- Rolled oats: half cup
- Whole-wheat flour: half cup
- Brown sugar: 2 tbsp.
- Baking powder: 1 ½ tsp.
- Baking soda: ¼ tsp.
- Skim milk: half cup
- Salt: ¼ tsp.
- Cinnamon: ¼ tsp.
- 1 banana, mashed
- Yogurt: ¼ cup, low-fat
- 1 egg

Instructions

1. In a bowl, add boiling water and oats. Let it rest for 1-2 minutes.
2. Add sugar and oil and mix; let it cool.
3. In a bowl, add flour and all the dry ingredients. Mix.
4. Add the wet to dry ingredients with oats mixture. Mix until just combined.
5. On a heated pan, add some batter and cook for 2-3 minutes on each side.
6. Serve warm.

Nutrition for 3 pancakes: Calories 288 | Fat 9 g | Sugar 12 g | Protein 9 g | Sodium 455 mg | Carbs 45

107.   Healthy Porridge Bowl

(Prep time: 10 minutes | Cook time: 20 minutes | Serving: 2)
Ingredients

- 1 orange, half sliced & half juiced
- Almond butter: 2 tbsp.
- Porridge oats: 5.2 oz.
- Goji berries: 1 tbsp.
- Frozen raspberries: 7 oz.
- Milk: ¼ cup
- Half banana, sliced
- Chia seeds: 1 tbsp.

Instructions

1. In a pan, add orange juice and half of the raspberries. Simmer for 5 minutes.
2. In a pan, add milk, oats and water (~2 cups) on low flame. Cook until creamy.

3. Serve with raspberry compote and the rest of the ingredients on top.

Nutrition: Calories 533 | Fat 19 g | Sugar 14 g | Protein 17 g | Sodium 271 mg | Carbs 66 g

108. Healthy Banana Bread

(Prep time: 20 minutes | Cook time: 1 hour & 15 minutes | Serving: 8-10)

Ingredients

- Whole meal flour: 5 oz.
- 3 eggs, whisked
- Baking soda: 1 tsp.
- Low-fat yogurt: ¾ cup
- Baking powder: 1 tsp.
- Mashed overripe bananas: 10 oz.
- Self-rising flour: 3.5 oz.
- Agave syrup: 4 tbsp.

Instructions

1. Let the oven preheat to 320 F.
2. Oil spray a 2 lb. baking pan and line with parchment paper, let it hang over the pan.
3. In a bowl, add all dry ingredients and mix.
4. In a different bowl, mix the wet ingredients. Add the wet to dry ingredients.
5. Pour in the prepared pan, bake for 70-75 minutes.
6. Cool in the pan, slice and serve.

Nutrition: Calories 145 | Fat 2 g | Sugar 9 g | Protein 6 g | Sodium 76 mg | Carbs 24 g

109. Banana & Walnut Pancakes

(Prep time: 20 minutes | Cook time: 1 hour & 15 minutes | Serving: 8-10)

Ingredients

- Baking powder: 2 tsp.
- Salt: ¼ tsp.
- Chopped walnuts: 2 tbsp.
- Whole wheat flour: 1 cup
- Cinnamon: ¼ tsp.
- Vanilla: 1 tsp.
- 3 egg whites

- 1 mashed banana
- 1% milk: 1 cup
- Oil: 2 tsp.

Instructions

1. In a bowl, add all dry ingredients and mix.
2. In a bowl, add all wet ingredients and mix; add the wet to dry ingredients. Mix, but do not over mix.
3. Place a skillet on medium flame. Oil spray the pan and pour the batter (1/4 cup). Cook on both sides for 2 to 3 minutes.
4. Serve.

Nutrition: Calories 146 | Fat 4 g | Sugar 8 g | Protein 6.4 g | Sodium 67 mg | Carbs 22g

110. Spinach & Eggs on Potato Toast

(Prep time: 10 minutes | Cook time: 15 minutes | Serving: 1)

Ingredients

- 1 egg, fried
- Sweet potato: 1 large slice, ¼" thick
- Hot sauce: half tsp.
- Cooked spinach: 1/3 cup
- Fresh chives: half tsp., sliced

Instructions

1. In a toaster, toast the potato slice for 12-15 minutes.
2. Add hot sauce, spinach, egg and chives on top.

Nutrition: Calories 243 | Fat 10 g | Sugar 7.9 g | Protein 11.9 g | Sodium 104 mg | Carbs 12 g

111. Spinach, Mushroom & Feta Cheese Scramble

(Prep time: 10 minutes | Cook time: 10 minutes | Serving: 1)

Ingredients

- 1 egg + 2 egg whites
- Sliced fresh mushrooms: half cup
- Black pepper
- Fresh spinach: 1 cup, chopped
- Feta cheese: 2 tbsp.

Instructions

1. Place a pan (8 ") on medium flame, and oil spray the pan.
2. Sauté spinach and mushrooms for 2 to 3 minutes, till the spinach wilts.
3. In a bowl, whisk egg and whites with pepper and feta.
4. Pour in the pan and cook, stirring for 3 to 4 minutes.
5. Serve with whole-grain toast.

Nutrition: Calories 219 | Fat 6 g | Sugar 3 g | Protein 12 g | Sodium 143 mg | Carbs 4 g

112. Honey Whole-Wheat Bread

(Prep time: 4 hours & 10 minutes | Cook time: 25 minutes | Serving: 17)

Ingredients
- Rolled oats: 1 cup
- Soy flour: 3/4 cup
- Flaxseed meal: 3/4 cup
- Sea salt: half tsp.
- Flaxseed: 3 tbsp.
- Sesame seeds: 3 tbsp.
- Poppy seeds: 3 tbsp.
- Water: 3 cups
- Whole-wheat flour: 3 cups
- Honey: half cup
- Yeast: 4 ½ tbsp.
- White flour: 5 cups
- Applesauce: 1 cup, unsweetened
- Olive oil: ¼ cup

Instructions
1. In a bowl, add oats and water, microwave until soft.
2. In a stand mixer, add all dry ingredients (except for white flour), mix.
3. Add oil, honey and applesauce. Mix and add oats mixture, mix with hands.
4. Then, mix with hook attachment for three minutes.

5. Gradually add white flour, and until a dough forms, it should be elastic and smooth.
6. Keep the dough in a warm place, covered for 1-2 hours.
7. Roll the dough and cut it into 4 pieces, make each piece in a loaf.
8. Oil spray the loaf pans. Place the loaf in the pans and keep it in a warm place, covered for 1-2 hours.
9. Bake for 25 minutes at 350 F. Serve in half" thick slices.

Nutrition per slice: Calories 90 | Fat 2 g | Sugar 2 g | Protein 6.4 g | Sodium 88 mg | Carbs 15 g

113. Crunchy Oat Clusters

(Prep time: 20 minutes | Cook time: 15 minutes | Serving: 6)

Ingredients
- Rapeseed oil: half tbsp.
- Vanilla extract: 1 tbsp.
- Low-fat yogurt: 12 oz.
- 3 egg whites
- 7 dried apricots
- Porridge oats: 5 oz.
- Flaked almonds: 0.8 oz.
- Cinnamon: 1 tbsp.
- Pumpkin seeds: 0.8 oz.
- Desiccated coconut: 0.8 oz.

Instructions
1. Let the oven preheat to 356 F, line a baking tray with parchment paper.
2. In a blender, add egg whites, oil and apricots. Blend until smooth.
3. Add vanilla, cinnamon and oats, mix with a spatula and fold in pumpkin seeds, almonds, and desiccated coconut.
4. Make the mixture into clusters by pinching with hands, and spread onto the baking tray.
5. Bake for 15 minutes, flip and bake for ten minutes.
6. Cool and serve with peach slices.

Nutrition: Calories 298 | Fat 12 g | Sugar 10 g | Protein 14 g | Sodium 65 mg | Carbs 30 g

114. Pumpkin Macadamia Nut Pancakes

(Prep time: 20 minutes | Cook time: 15 minutes | Serving: 3-4)

Ingredients

- Puréed pumpkin with spices: 1 cup
- Pancake mix: 1 cup, gluten-free
- Macadamia nuts: 1 cup, chopped
- Milk: half cup, low-fat
- 1 egg
- Olive oil: 2 tbsp.

Instructions

1. In a bowl, add all ingredients and mix.
2. Heat a pan on medium flame, add little oil.
3. Pour batter and cook for 2-3 minutes on both sides.
4. Serve with yogurt and berries.

Nutrition: Calories 159 | Fat 3 g | Sugar 5 g | Protein 12 g | Sodium 214 mg | Carbs 3g

115. Tuna & Avocado Toast

(Prep time: 20 minutes | Cook time: 15 minutes | Serving: 3-4)

Ingredients

- 1/4 avocado, mashed
- Julienned carrot: 1 tbsp.
- Half lemon's juice
- Oil-packed tuna: 1 tbsp., flaked
- Sliced seaweed
- Sweet potato: 1 large slice, ¼" thick
- Pickled ginger: 1 tsp., chopped
- Sesame seeds: 1/8 tsp.

Instructions

In a toaster, toast the sweet potato for 12-15 minutes.

Add the rest of the ingredients on top in your desired order.

Serve.

Nutrition: Calories 149 | Fat 3 g | Sugar 3 g | Protein 30 g | Sodium 142 mg | Carbs 3g

116. Overnight Oatmeal

(Prep time: Overnight & 10 minutes | Cook time: 0 minutes | Serving: 2)

Ingredients

- 1% milk: half cup
- Old fashion oatmeal: 1 cup
- Chia seeds: 1 tbsp.
- Low-fat vanilla yogurt: 1 cup
- Frozen blueberries: 1 cup

Instructions

1. In a bowl, add all ingredients mix well.
2. Divide into two containers, keep in the fridge covered, overnight.
3. Serve cold.

Nutrition: Calories 159 | Fat 3 g | Sugar 0 g | Protein 30 g | Sodium 134 mg | Carbs 3g

117. Buckwheat Pancakes

(Prep time: 10 minutes | Cook time: 15 minutes | Serving: 3-4)

Ingredients

- Canola oil: 1 tbsp.
- Non-fat milk: half cup
- Baking powder: 1 tbsp.
- Sugar: 1 tbsp.
- All-purpose flour: half cup
- 2 egg whites
- Buckwheat flour: half cup
- Fresh strawberries: 3 cups, sliced
- Sparkling water: half cup

Instructions

1. In a bowl, add milk, egg whites and oil; whisk well.
2. In a different bowl, mix the sugar, flours and baking powder. Add the wet to dry ingredients with sparkling water, do not over mix.
3. Heat a non-stick pan and pour batter (half cup). Cook for 2 minutes on each side.

4. Serve with fresh strawberries.

Nutrition: Calories 143| Fat 3 g | Sugar 5 g | Protein 5 g |Sodium 150 mg | Carbs 24 g

118. Chilled Oatmeal

(Prep time: Overnight & 10 minutes | Cook time: 0 minutes | Serving: 1)

Ingredients

- Fat-free milk: 3 tbsp.
- Mixed fresh fruit: half cup
- Low-fat yogurt: 3 tbsp.
- Chopped walnuts: 2 tbsp., toasted
- Old-fashioned oats: 1/3 cup
- Honey: 1 tbsp.

Instructions

1. In a mason jar, add all ingredients except for nuts and fruits. Mix and add fruits and nuts on top.
2. Keep in the fridge overnight. Serve.

Nutrition: Calories 345 | Fat 13 g | Sugar 8 g | Protein 10 g |Sodium 53 mg | Carbs 53

Cool Summertime Oatmeal

(Prep time: Overnight & 10 minutes | Cook time: 0 minutes | Serving: 4)

Ingredients

Low-fat plain yogurt: ¾ cup

Chopped walnuts: half cup, toasted

1/4 cup of honey

Fat-free milk: ¾ cup

Old-fashioned oats: 1-1/3 cups

Dark sweet cherries: 1 cup, pitted

Blueberries: 1 cup

Instructions

In a bowl, add honey, oats, yogurt and milk. Mix and keep in the fridge overnight, covered.

Add walnuts, cherries and blueberries on top, and serve.

Nutrition: Calories 350 | Fat 12 g | Sugar 31 g | Protein 10 g |Sodium 53 mg | Carbs 55

119. Apple Cinnamon Oats

(Prep time: Overnight & 10 minutes | Cook time: 0 minutes | Serving: 1)

Ingredients

- Half apple, chopped
- Raisins: 1 tbsp.
- Old-fashioned oats: half cup
- Low-fat milk: 1 cup
- Toasted chopped nuts
- Cinnamon: ¼ tsp.

Instructions

1. In a mason jar, add all ingredients, mix and keep in the fridge overnight.
2. Keep in the fridge overnight, sealed. Serve.

Nutrition: Calories 349 | Fat 8 g | Sugar 28 g | Protein 14 g |Sodium 263 mg | Carbs 59

120. Apple Pie Steel-Cut Oatmeal

(Prep time: 10 minutes | Cook time: 8 hours | Serving: 4)

Ingredients

- Steel-cut oats: 1 1/2 cups
- Applesauce: 1 1/2 cups, unsweetened
- Cinnamon: 1 ½ tsp.
- 6 cups of water
- Maple syrup: 1/4 cup
- 1 large apple, chopped
- Ground nutmeg: half tsp.

Instructions

1. In a slow cooker (4 qt.), add all ingredients except for apples.
2. Cook for 6 to 8 hours on low. Add apples, stir and serve.

Nutrition: Calories 171 | Fat 2 g | Sugar 13 g | Protein 4 g |Sodium 39 mg | Carbs 36 g

121. Overnight Maple Oatmeal

(Prep time: Overnight & 10 minutes | Cook time: 0 minutes | Serving: 2)

Ingredients

- Mixed fresh fruit
- 1% milk: 1 cup
- Old-fashioned oats: 2 cups
- Low-fat vanilla yogurt: 1 cup
- Toasted walnuts: half cup, chopped

- Maple syrup: ¼ cup
- Vanilla extract: 2 tsp.

Instructions
1. In a bowl, add all ingredients except for yogurt, toast and fruits. Mix and keep in the fridge covered overnight.
2. Before serving, add yogurt, fruits and walnuts, serve.

Nutrition: Calories 249 | Fat 9 g | Sugar 8 g | Protein 9 g | Sodium 46 mg | Carbs 36 g

122. Overnight Peach Oatmeal

(Prep time: 10 minutes | Cook time: 8 hours | Serving: 6)

Ingredients
- Steel-cut oats: 1 cup
- Almond extract: ¼ tsp.
- Almond milk: 1 cup
- 2 peaches, sliced
- 4 cups of water
- Brown sugar: 3 tbsp.

Instructions
1. In a slow cooker (3 qt.), add all the ingredients except for peaches.
2. Cook on low for 7 to 8 hours.
3. Before serving, add peaches.

Nutrition: Calories 163 | Fat 2 g | Sugar 13 g | Protein 5 g | Sodium 116 mg | Carbs 31 g

123. Avocado & Black Bean Eggs

(Prep time: 5 minutes | Cook time: 10 minutes | Serving: 2)

Ingredients
- 1 red chili, sliced without seeds
- Cumin seeds: ¼ tsp.
- Cherry tomatoes: 7 oz.
- Rapeseed oil: 2 tsp.
- 2 eggs
- Canned black beans: 14 oz.
- 1 avocado, sliced
- 1 sliced garlic clove
- Fresh coriander: ¾ cup, chopped

Instructions
1. In a pan, add oil on medium flame. Sauté garlic and chili till it softens.
2. Add eggs, and as they set, add the beans, tomatoes and cumin seeds.
3. Turn the heat off and add coriander and avocado. Add some lime juice if needed.
4. Serve.

Nutrition: Calories 356 | Fat 20 g | Sugar 18 g | Protein 11 g | Sodium 67 mg | Carbs 4 g

124. Socca Pancake

(Prep time: 10 minutes | Cook time: 10 minutes | Serving: 2)

Ingredients
- Water: 1 cup + 2 tbsp.
- Sea salt: ¾ tsp.
- Olive oil: 2 tbsp.
- Chickpea flour: 1 cup
- Ground cumin: 1/8 tsp.

Instructions
1. In a bowl, add all ingredients except for oil. Mix well.
2. In a pan, add oil and heat it. Add the batter and cook on both sides until cooked through.
3. Serve with onion, tomato and basil on top.

Nutrition: Calories 61 | Fat 8 g | Sugar 0 g | Protein 5.3 g | Sodium 163 mg | Carbs 3.2 g

125. Almond Butter & Banana toast

(Prep time: 10 minutes | Cook time: 15 minutes | Serving: 1)

Ingredients
- Almond butter: 2 tbsp.
- Cinnamon, to taste
- 1 banana, sliced
- 1 large sweet potato slice

Instructions
1. Toast the sweet potato slice for 12 to 15 minutes.
2. Spread peanut butter on toasted sweet potato.

3. Add banana slices on top, serve with cinnamon on top.

Nutrition: Calories 216| Fat 8 g | Sugar 2 g | Protein 34 g |Sodium 173 mg | Carbs 5 g

126. Perfect Granola

(Prep time: 10 minutes | Cook time: 15 minutes | Serving: 4)
Ingredients
- Honey: 4 tbsp.
- Vanilla: 1 ½ tsp.
- Almonds: 1 cup, slivered
- Canola oil: ¼ cup
- Bran flakes: 2 cups
- Old-fashioned rolled oats: 6 cups
- 1 cup of raisins
- Shredded coconut: half cup, sweetened
- Walnuts: 3/4 cup, chopped

Instructions
1. Let the oven preheat to 325 F.
2. In a pan, add vanilla, oil and honey. Cook on low flame for 5 minutes.
3. In a bowl, add the rest of the ingredients, except for raisins. Mix well.
4. Gradually add the honey mixture. Mix well.
5. Oil spray a baking tray and spread the mixture on the prepared tray.
6. Bake for 25 minutes. Let it cool and add raisins, stir and serve.

Nutrition: Calories 250 | Fat 17.2 g | Sugar 8 g | Protein 6.4 g |Sodium 55 mg | Carbs 56 g

127. Cranberry Orange Muffins

(Prep time: 15 minutes | Cook time: 25 minutes | Serving: 16)
Ingredients
- 2 eggs
- Canola oil: ¼ cup
- Granulated sugar: half cup
- Vanilla: 2 tsp.
- 1 3/4 cup of all-purpose flour
- Brown sugar: ¼ cup
- Greek yogurt: 8 oz.
- Baking powder: 1 tsp.
- Unsweetened orange juice: 2 tbsp., concentrate
- 1 1/2 cups of cranberries
- Orange zest: 2 tbsp.
- 1/4 cup of flaxseed meal
- Cinnamon: half tsp.
- Baking soda: 1 tsp.
- Salt, a pinch

Instructions
1. Let the oven preheat to 350 F. oil spray a muffin tin.
2. In a bowl, add wet ingredients and mix.
3. In a different bowl, add the dry ingredients except for cranberries and mix.
4. Gradually add dry to wet ingredients, mix for 1 to 2 minutes.
5. Add cranberries and fold.
6. Pour the batter into the prepared pan and bake for 22 minutes.
7. Serve.

Nutrition per muffin: Calories 155 | Fat 5 g | Sugar 10 g | Protein 4 g |Sodium 148 mg | Carbs 24 g

128. Baked Oatmeal

(Prep time: Overnight & 10 minutes | Cook time: 45 minutes | Serving: 8)
Ingredients
- 2 eggs, whisked
- Packed brown sugar: ¾ cup
- 1 % milk: 3 cups
- Dried blueberries: ¼ cup
- Cinnamon: 1 1 /2 tsp.
- Canola oil: ¼ cup
- Salt: 1/4 tsp.
- Sliced almonds: ¼ cup
- Old-fashioned oats: 2 cups
- Dried cherries: ¼ cup

Instructions
1. In a bowl, add all ingredients except for cherries, oats, almonds and blueberries. Mix and add the

rest of the ingredients (except for almonds).

2. Oil spray an 8" baking dish, spread the oats mixture in this dish.

3. Cover and keep in the fridge for 8 hours.

4. Let the oven preheat to 350 F.

5. Take the overnight oats out and stir; add almonds on top.

6. Bake for 40 to 50 minutes. Serve.

Nutrition for the half cup: Calories 331 | Fat 13 g | Sugar 30 g | Protein 8 g | Sodium 264 mg | Carbs 46 g

129. Maple Apple Baked Oatmeal

(Prep time: 20 minutes | Cook time: 25 minutes | Serving: 8)

Ingredients

- Baking powder: 2 tsp.
- Salt, a pinch
- 3 cups of old-fashioned oats
- Cinnamon: 1 ¼ tsp.
- Ground nutmeg: ¼ tsp.
- 2 eggs
- Low-fat milk: 2 cups
- Maple syrup: half cup
- Sunflower kernels: 1/4 cup
- Canola oil: 1/4 cup
- 1 apple, chopped
- Vanilla extract: 1 tsp.

Instructions

1. Let the oven preheat to 350 F.

2. In a bowl, whisk vanilla, eggs, oil, milk and syrup.

3. Add the rest of the ingredients, except for apples and sunflower kernels, to another bowl and mix.

4. Add the wet to dry ingredients, mix and let it rest for 5 minutes. Add apples and mix.

5. Pour in an 11 by 7" baking dish, add sunflower kernels on top. Bake for 25 to 30 minutes.

6. Serve

Nutrition: Calories 305 | Fat 13 g | Sugar 20 g | Protein 8 g | Sodium 225 mg | Carbs 41

130. Peanut Butter & Cinnamon Toast

(Prep time: 10 minutes | Cook time: 3 minutes | Serving: 1)

Ingredients

- Cinnamon, to taste
- Peanut butter: 1 tbsp.
- Half banana
- Whole-wheat bread: 1 slice, toasted

Instructions

1. Toast the bread slice and spread peanut butter, with banana slices on top.

2. Sprinkle cinnamon and serve.

Nutrition: Calories 266 | Fat 11 g | Sugar 8 g | Protein 6.4 g | Sodium 53 mg | Carbs 21 g

131. Peanut Butter & Jelly Yogurt

(Prep time: 10 minutes | Cook time: 0 minutes | Serving: 1)

Ingredients

- Grape jelly: 4 tsp., low-sugar
- Red seedless grapes: 2 tbsp., halved
- Unsalted peanuts: 1 tsp.
- Low-fat Greek yogurt: 6 oz.
- Peanut butter: 1 tbsp., low-fat

Instructions

1. In a bowl, add yogurt, add peanut butter and jelly on top.

2. Mix and top with grapes and peanuts.

3. Serve.

Nutrition: Calories 143 | Fat 11 g | Sugar 2.9 g | Protein 23.6 g | Sodium 56 mg | Carbs 17 g

132. Muesli Breakfast Bars

(Prep time: 25 minutes | Cook time: 25 minutes | Serving: 24)

Ingredients

- Soy flour: half cup
- Salt: ¼ tsp.
- Dry milk: half cup, fat-free
- Old-fashioned rolled oats: 2 ½ cups

- Wheat germ: half cup, toasted
- Vanilla extract: 2 tsp.
- Dried apples: half cup, chopped
- Peanut butter: half cup
- Raisins: half cup
- Olive oil: 1 tbsp.
- Chopped pecans: half cup, toasted
- Honey: 1 cup

Instructions

1. Let the oven preheat to 325 F.
2. Oil spray a 9 by 13 baking dish.
3. In a bowl, add oats, almonds, dry milk, raisins, salt, flour, apples and wheat germ. Mix well.
4. In a pan, add olive oil, honey and peanut butter on low until combined. Do not boil; add vanilla.
5. Add honey mixture to dry ingredients. it will be sticky, not wet.
6. Pour in the oil sprayed pan, and press down.
7. Bake for 25 minutes, cool for ten minutes.
8. Slice in 24 bars and serve.

Nutrition per bar: Calories 169| Fat 5 g | Sugar 8 g | Protein 5 g |Sodium 76 mg | Carbs 26 g

133. Mushroom Shallot Frittata

(Prep time: 10 minutes | Cook time: 25 minutes | Serving: 4)

Ingredients

- Unsalted plant butter: 1 tbsp.
- Fresh parsley: 2 tsp., chopped
- 4 shallots, diced
- 5 egg whites
- Dried thyme: 1 tsp.
- Low-fat parmesan cheese: ¼ cup, grated
- Mushrooms: half-pound, chopped
- Black pepper, to taste
- 3 eggs
- Milk: 1 tbsp.

Instructions

1. Let the oven preheat to 350 F.
2. In a skillet, add butter and sauté shallots for 5 minutes.
3. Add thyme, mushrooms, black pepper and parsley.
4. In a bowl, add milk, cheese, eggs and whites; whisk well. Pour in the shallot pan.
5. As it sets, place it in the oven and bake for 15 minutes.
6. Slice and serve.

Nutrition: Calories 276 | Fat 8.1 g | Sugar 3.4 g | Protein 33.2 g |Sodium 213 mg | Carbs 13 g

134. Avocado & White Bean Toast

(Prep time: 10 minutes | Cook time: 0 minutes | Serving: 4)

Ingredients

- Half lime's juice
- Whole-wheat bread: 1 slice, toasted
- Fresh basil leaves: 2 to 3 leaves
- Half avocado, mashed
- Black pepper
- Canned white beans: ¼ cup, mashed

Instructions

1. On the slice, spread avocado, white beans and fresh basil.
2. Serve with a drizzle of lime juice.

Nutrition: Calories 121 | Fat 3 g | Sugar 3 g | Protein 21 g |Sodium 112 mg | Carbs 6 g

135. Asparagus Omelet Tortilla Wrap

(Prep time: 10 minutes | Cook time: 15 minutes | Serving: 1)

Ingredients

2 egg whites

Fat-free milk: 1 tbsp.

1 egg

Plant butter: 1 tsp.

Low-fat parmesan cheese: 2 tsp.

1 green onion, diced

Black pepper

1 (8") whole wheat tortilla

4 asparagus spears

Instructions

1. In a skillet, sauté asparagus for 3 to 4 minutes. Take them out on a plate.

2. In a bowl, add the rest of the ingredients, except for butter and cheese. Whisk well.

3. In the pan, add butter on medium flame.

4. Add in the egg mixture and as it sets, add asparagus on 1 side.

5. Fold the other half on top. Place in a tortilla and serve.

Nutrition: Calories 319 | Fat 13 g | Sugar 4 g | Protein 21 g |Sodium 397 mg | Carbs 28 g

136. White Cheddar & Black Bean Frittata

(Prep time: 20 minutes | Cook time: 15 minutes | Serving: 6)
Ingredients
- 3 egg whites
- 1/4 cup of salsa
- 6 eggs
- Canned black beans: 1 cup, rinsed
- Olive oil: 1 tbsp.
- Fresh parsley: 1 tbsp., minced
- Red pepper: 1/3 cup, chopped
- 2 minced garlic cloves
- Salt & black pepper: 1/8 tsp.
- Green pepper: 1/3 cup, diced
- White cheddar cheese: half cup, shredded
- 3 green onions, diced

Instructions

1. Let the broiler preheat.

2. In a skillet, add oil and sauté peppers for 3 to 4 minutes. Add garlic and sauté for 1 minute.

3. Add beans and turn the heat low.

4. In a bowl, add the rest of the ingredients (except for cheese), and whisk. Pour in the pan.

5. Cook for 4 to 6 minutes, add cheese on top.

6. Broil for 3 to 4 minutes, slice and serve.

Nutrition: Calories 183| Fat 10 g | Sugar 2 g | Protein 13 g |Sodium 287 mg | Carbs 9

137. Grapefruit, Lime & Mint Yogurt Parfait

(Prep time: 15 minutes | Cook time: 0 minutes | Serving: 6)
Ingredients
- 4 red grapefruit
- Lime juice: 2 tbsp.
- Low-fat plain yogurt: 4 cups
- Fresh mint leaves, torn
- Lime zest: 2 tsp.
- Honey: 3 tbsp.

Instructions

1. Cut grapefruit in segments without skin.

2. In a bowl, mix juice, yogurt and lime zest.

3. Add the grapefruits on the bottom and top with yogurt mixture in six parfait glasses and repeat the layers.

4. Before serving, drizzle with honey and top with mint leaves.

Nutrition: Calories 207 | Fat 3 g | Sugar 26 g | Protein 10 g |Sodium 115 mg | Carbs 39 g

138. Peach Parfait

(Prep time: 15 minutes | Cook time: 0 minutes | Serving: 2)
Ingredients
- Fresh raspberries: 1 cup
- Low-fat milk: 1 ½ cups
- Fresh peaches: 1 cup, sliced
- Almond extract: 1/8 tsp.

Instructions

1. In a blender, add all ingredients except for raspberries. Blend until creamy.

2. In a bowl, mash fresh raspberries.

3. In 2 parfait glasses, layer the raspberries and peaches mixture. Serve.

Nutrition: Calories 194 | Fat 3 g | Sugar 1 g | Protein 17 g |Sodium 105 mg | Carbs 27 g

139. Scrambled Eggs with Spinach

(Prep time: 10 minutes | Cook time: 20 minutes | Serving: 4)

Ingredients

- 2 eggs
- Swiss cheese: ¼ cup
- Fresh cilantro: half tsp.
- 1 tomato, chopped
- Cayenne pepper: half tsp.
- Chopped Spinach: 1 cup

Instructions

1. In a bowl, whisk eggs with cayenne pepper and cilantro. Whisk until frothy.

2. Place a skillet on medium flame. Pour the eggs and keep whisking and when some liquid remains. Add tomato and spinach.

3. Cook for 30-60 seconds, serve with cheese on top.

Nutrition: Calories 135 | Fat 3.1 g | Sugar 2 g | Protein 5.2 g |Sodium 389 mg | Carbs 19.8 g

DASH Diet Appetizers, Sides & Snacks Recipes

140. Pumpkin Pie Bites

(Prep time: 30 minutes | Cook time: 0 minutes | Serving: 8)

Ingredients

- Boiling water
- Pumpkin pie spice: 1 ½ tsp.
- Pumpkin puree: ¼ cup
- Medjool dates: ¼ cup, pitted
- Maple syrup: 2 tsp.
- Mini chocolate chips: half cup
- Salt: 1/8 tsp.
- Coconut flour: 2 tbsp.
- Almond butter: ¼ cup
- Oats: 1 1/2 cup

Instructions

1. In some boiling water, add dates and soak for ten minutes.
2. In a food processor, add all ingredients except for chocolate chips.
3. Pulse until smooth. Fold in chips and keep in the fridge for 20 minutes.
4. Make the mixture into small balls and serve chilled.

Nutrition: Calories 191 | Fat 3 g | Sugar 8 g | Protein 15.1 g | Sodium 92 mg | Carbs 12 g

141. Chili-Lime Grilled Pineapple

(Prep time: 15 minutes | Cook time: 7 minutes | Serving: 6)

Ingredients

- Lime juice: 1 tbsp.
- 1 fresh pineapple, trimmed & sliced
- Honey: 1 tbsp.
- Brown sugar: 3 tbsp.
- Salt, a pinch
- Olive oil: 1 tbsp.
- Chili powder: 1 ½ tsp.

Instructions

1. In a bowl, add all ingredients except for pineapple.
2. Brush the pineapple with half of the mixture. Grill for 2 to 4 minutes on 1 side.
3. Keep basting with half of the mixture.
4. Serve.

Nutrition: Calories 97 | Fat 2 g | Sugar 8 g | Protein 1 g | Sodium 35 mg | Carbs 20 g

142. Citrusy Fruit Kabobs

(Prep time: 15 minutes | Cook time: 7 minutes | Serving: 8)

Ingredients

- Lemon juice: 2 tbsp.
- Honey: 4 ½ tsp.
- Lemon zest: 1 ½ tsp.
- Orange juice: 1/3 cup
- Fresh mint: 2 tsp., chopped
- Fresh strawberries: 24
- Cornstarch: 2 tsp.
- 2 bananas, sliced
- Ground allspice: ¼ tsp.
- Fresh pineapple: 16 cubes

Instructions

1. In a pan, add all ingredients except for fruits. Place on medium flame.
2. Let it come to a boil, cook for 2 minutes, turn the heat off.
3. Onto 8 skewers, thread the fruits. Brush with glaze, grill for 5 to 7 minutes, flipping occasionally.
4. Keep basting with the glaze, serve.

Nutrition: Calories 83 | Fat 0 g | Sugar 8 g | Protein 1

g |Sodium 2 mg | Carbs 21 g

143. Zucchini Pizza Boats

(Prep time: 15 minutes | Cook time: 30 minutes | Serving: 6)
Ingredients
- Tomato pasta sauce: half cup, low-sodium
- No salt Italian seasoning blend
- Shredded mozzarella cheese: half cup, low-fat
- 3 zucchinis, small
- Parmesan cheese: 2 tbsp.

Instructions
1. Let the oven preheat to 350 F.
2. Cut the zucchinis in half and take the middle part out.
3. Place the zucchinis onto a baking sheet. Add pasta sauce, all cheeses and Italian seasoning in zucchinis.
4. Bake for 25-30 minutes. Serve.

Nutrition: Calories 181 | Fat 9 g | Sugar 3 g | Protein 13 g |Sodium 89 mg | Carbs 11g

144. Soy Nut & Apricot Trail Mix

(Prep time: 15 minutes | Cook time: 0 minutes | Serving: 8)
Ingredients
- Shelled pistachios: 1 cup, roasted
- Raisins: 1 cup
- Pumpkin seeds: 1 cup
- Roasted soy nuts: 1 cup
- Dried apricots: 1 cup, chopped

Instructions

In a bowl, add all ingredients. Toss to combine. Serve.

Nutrition per ¼ cup: Calories 198 | Fat 11 g | Sugar 8 g | Protein 11 g |Sodium 4 mg | Carbs 18 g

145. Spicy Roasted Broccoli

(Prep time: 15 minutes | Cook time: 30 minutes | Serving: 8)
Ingredients
- Seasoning blend: half tsp., no-salt-added
- Chopped broccoli: 8 cups
- 4 minced garlic cloves

- Olive oil: 4 tbsp.
- Black pepper: ¼ tsp.
- Red pepper flakes, to taste

Instructions
1. Let the oven preheat to 450 F.
2. In a bowl, toss oil (2 tbsp.) and broccoli. Add pepper and seasoning.
3. Spread on a baking sheet, bake for 15 minutes.
4. In a bowl, add the rest of the ingredients.
5. Drizzle the garlic oil over the roasted broccoli and bake for 8-10 minutes.
6. Serve

Nutrition: Calories 86| Fat 7 g | Sugar 1 g | Protein 2 g |Sodium 24 mg | Carbs 5 g

146. Tomato Basil Bruschetta

(Prep time: 15 minutes | Cook time: 0 minutes | Serving: 6)
Ingredients
- Chopped basil: 2 tbsp.
- 2 minced garlic cloves
- Diced fennel: half cup
- Half baguette, whole-grain, sliced
- Olive oil: 1 tsp.
- Chopped parsley: 1 tbsp.
- Black pepper: 1 tsp.
- 3 tomatoes, chopped
- Balsamic vinegar: 2 tsp.

Instructions
1. Toast the bread.
2. In a bowl, add the rest of the ingredients mix well.
3. Spread over toasted bread. Serve.

Nutrition: Calories 142 | Fat 2 g | Sugar 0 g | Protein 5 g |Sodium 123 mg | Carbs 26 g

147. Cheesy Turkey Meatball

(Prep time: 15 minutes | Cook time: 10 minutes | Serving: 6-8)
Ingredients
- Chicken sausage: 12 oz., without casing
- Pecorino Romano: 2 tbsp., grated
- Whole-wheat panko: half cup

- Kosher salt: ¼ tsp.
- Lean ground turkey: 1 pound
- 2 grated garlic cloves
- Fresh parsley: ¼ cup, chopped
- Italian seasoning: 1 tsp.

Instructions

1. In a bowl, add all ingredients and mix.
2. Make into small meat balls.
3. In a skillet, add some oil and cook meatballs in batches, until browned on all sides.
4. Serve right away.

Nutrition: Calories 341 | Fat 18 g | Sugar 0 g | Protein 30 g | Sodium 620 mg | Carbs 13 g

148. Garlic Mashed Potatoes

(Prep time: 15 minutes | Cook time: 30 minutes | Serving: 8)

Ingredients

- Olive oil: ¼ cup
- Red potatoes: 2 pounds, sliced into large chunks
- Black pepper: half tsp.
- 6 garlic cloves
- Seasoning blend: 1 tsp., no-salt-added

Instructions:

In a pan, add potato and garlic cloves (peeled).

Add enough water to cover, let it boil.

Cook on a medium flame for 25 minutes. Turn the heat off.

Drain all but ¾ cup of potatoes water.

Add the rest of the ingredients, mash and serve.

Nutrition: Calories 145 | Fat 7 g | Sugar 1 g | Protein 2 g | Sodium 7 mg | Carbs 19 g

149. Avocado & Shrimp Spring Roll

(Prep time: 15 minutes | Cook time: 7 minutes | Serving: 6)

Ingredients

- Dried rice noodles: 1 oz.
- Cooked & peeled shrimp: 3 oz., halved
- 1 avocado, 12 slices

- Fresh mint: ¼ cup packed, chopped
- Peanut sauce: 1 tbsp.
- 1 mango, sliced into 12 slices
- Red leaf lettuce: 1 cup
- Vietnamese salad roll wrappers: 4 (12")
- Fresh Thai basil: ¼ cup packed, chopped
- Radish sprouts: 1 oz.

Instructions

1. In a pot, boil water and add rice noodles. Turn the heat off and let them rest for 4 minutes.
2. Drain, and take out in a bowl. Add peanut sauce and mix.
3. In a dish, add warm water, soak the roll wrapper and 30 seconds. Place on a plate,
4. Add the rest of the ingredients in, roll tightly and fold the ends.
5. Place seam side down, cut and serve.

Nutrition: Calories 170 | Fat 6.4 g | Sugar 8 g | Protein 7 g | Sodium 46 mg | Carbs 23 g

150. Sweet & Spicy Edamame

(Prep time: 15 minutes | Cook time: 10 minutes | Serving: 4)

Ingredients

- Stevia sweetener: half tsp.
- Liquid stevia: 10 drops
- Soy sauce: 1 tbsp., low-sodium
- 2 cups of water
- Frozen, shelled edamame: 2 cups
- Grated gingerroot: 1 tsp.
- Black pepper: 1/8 tsp.
- Sriracha hot sauce: 2 tsp.
- Rice vinegar: 1 tbsp.
- Toasted sesame oil: 1 tsp.
- Sesame seeds: 1 tsp. + 1 tbsp.
- 1 minced garlic clove

Instructions

1. In a pan, add water and all stevia. Mix and let it come to a boil.
2. Add edamame cook for 3-5 minutes. Drain and set aside.

3. In a pan, add the rest of the ingredients. Cook on low for 1-2 minutes.

4. Add edamame and toss. Serve with sesame seeds on top.

Nutrition: Calories 136| Fat 6.5 g | Sugar 4 g | Protein 11 g |Sodium 154 mg | Carbs 9 g

151. Grilled Stuffed Jalapeños

(Prep time: 15 minutes | Cook time: 10 minutes | Serving: 14)

Ingredients

- Cream cheese: 1 cup, softened
- Center-cut bacon: 2 slices
- Green onions: ¼ cup, chopped
- Lime juice: 1 tsp.
- 14 jalapeño peppers, cut in half without seeds
- Cheddar cheese: 1 oz., shredded
- Kosher salt: ¼ tsp.
- 1 minced garlic clove

Instructions

1. Let the grill preheat to medium heat.
2. Cook bacon until crispy. Take the bacon out on a plate and crumble it.
3. In a bowl, add cheese, bacon and the rest of the ingredients, except for peppers.
4. Stuff the peppers with the cheese mixture.
5. Grill for 8 minutes, cheese side up. Serve.

Nutrition: Calories 56 | Fat 4.1 g | Sugar 8 g | Protein 2.9 g |Sodium 157 mg | Carbs 2.1

152. Spicy Almonds

(Prep time: 10 minutes | Cook time: 30 minutes | Serving: 14)

Ingredients

- Sugar: 1 tbsp.
- Paprika: 1 tsp.
- Cayenne pepper: ¼ tsp.
- Ground coriander: half tsp.
- Cinnamon: half tsp.
- Kosher salt: ¼ tsp.
- Ground cumin: half tsp.

- Almonds: 2 ½ cups
- 1 egg white

Instructions

1. Let the oven preheat to 325 F.
2. In a bowl, add egg whites whisk until foamy. Add almonds and toss.
3. In a bowl, add the rest of the ingredients. Mix and sprinkle over almonds.
4. Spread on an oil-sprayed baking tray bake for half an hour.

Nutrition: Calories 230 | Fat 20 g | Sugar 3 g | Protein 8 g |Sodium 201 mg | Carbs 9 g

153. Sweet & Spicy Snack Mix

(Prep time: 10 minutes | Cook time: 30 minutes | Serving: 12)

Ingredients

- Wheat squares cereal: 2 cups
- Worcestershire sauce: 2 tbsp., low-sodium
- Dried pineapple chunks: 1 cup
- Raisins: 1 cup
- Chili powder: half tsp.
- 2 cans of (15 oz.) Garbanzos, drained
- Honey: 2 tbsp.
- Garlic powder: 1 tsp.

Instructions

1. Let the oven preheat to 350 F.
2. Oil spray a baking sheet and a skillet.
3. Add chickpeas in the skillet, cook for ten minutes.
4. Spread on the baking sheet. Bake for 20 minutes.
5. In a pan, add raisins, pineapples and cereal. Add roasted chickpeas and mix.
6. In a cup, add the rest of the ingredients, mix and pour over the chickpea mixture.
7. Toss to coat, oil spray the mixture. Bake for 10-15 minutes, do not burn, occasionally stir.
8. Cool and serve.

Nutrition: Calories 194 | Fat 2 g | Sugar 3 g | Protein 5 g |Sodium 218 mg | Carbs 39 g

154. Quinoa-Stuffed Tomatoes

(Prep time: 10 minutes | Cook time: 40 minutes | Serving: 4)
Ingredients
- Olive oil: 1 tbsp.
- Quinoa: 1 cup
- Chopped red onions: 2 tbsp.
- 4 medium tomatoes
- Cooked mixed vegetables: 1 cup
- Fresh parsley: 1 tbsp., chopped
- Black pepper: ¼ tsp.
- Chicken broth: 1 cup, low-sodium
- Half avocado, diced

Instructions
1. Let the oven preheat to 350 F.
2. Trim the tomatoes by cutting the top off, taking the seeds and membrane out, and making it hollow inside.
3. In a pan, add oil on medium flame. Sauté onion for 1 to 2 minutes.
4. Add cooked vegetables and cook for 1 to 2 minutes.
5. Add quinoa cook for 2 minutes.
6. Add broth, stir and let it come to a boil. Turn the heat off and let it rest for 7 to 10 minutes, covered.
7. Fluff with a fork and add the rest of the ingredients, except for tomatoes.
8. Mix and stuff the quinoa mixture into hollowed tomatoes.
9. Bake for 15 to 20 minutes.

Nutrition: Calories 299 | Fat 10 g | Sugar 8 g | Protein 10 g | Sodium 64 mg | Carbs 46 g

155. Southwestern Potato Skins

(Prep time: 10 minutes | Cook time: 15 minutes | Serving: 12)
Ingredients
- Olive oil: 1 tsp.
- Chili powder: 1 tsp.
- Cooked turkey bacon: 6 slices, chopped
- 6 baking potatoes, large
- Cheddar cheese: half cup, shredded
- Green onions: 2 tbsp., sliced
- Hot pepper sauce: 1/8 tsp.
- 1 tomato, chopped

Instructions
1. Let the oven preheat to 450 F.
2. Pierce the potatoes all over with a fork. Microwave for ten minutes and let them cool.
3. Slice the potatoes half lengthwise, take the flesh out and leave the shell (1/4").
4. Mix hot sauce, olive oil and chili powder, brush the potatoes' inside with chili oil. Slice the potato shells in halves.
5. In a bowl, add the rest of the ingredients, stuff the shells and bake for ten minutes.
6. Serve.

Nutrition: Calories 194 | Fat 6 g | Sugar 8 g | Protein 8 g | Sodium 164 mg | Carbs 27 g

156. Spanakopita

(Prep time: 10 minutes | Cook time: 40 minutes | Serving: 4)
Ingredients
- Corn oil: 1 tsp.
- 1 minced garlic clove
- Crumbled feta: ¼ cup fat-free
- Non-fat ricotta cheese: half cup
- 1 onion, chopped
- 2 eggs
- 5 sheets phyllo: 9 by 14", thawed in the fridge
- Fresh dill weed: 2 tbsp.
- Black pepper: 1/8 tsp.
- Fresh baby spinach: 2 pounds

Instructions
1. Let the oven preheat to 350 F. oil spray a baking dish (8 or 9" square).
2. In a skillet, add oil on medium flame. Sauté onion

for 3 minutes.

3. Add garlic and cook for 1 minute. Turn the heat low and add spinach cook for 1 minute.

4. Turn the heat off when spinach wilts. Drain well.

5. In a bowl, add the rest of the ingredients except for phyllo. Mix and add spinach mixture.

6. Mix and transfer in the prepared dish. Cut the 5 sheets in half.

7. On one sheet of phyllo, add spinach mixture brush with some oil, add the next sheet, brush with oil. Keep repeating the phyllo and oil.

8. Bake for half an hour. Turn the temperature to 375 F, bake for ten minutes.

9. Slice and serve.

Nutrition: Calories 142 | Fat 18 g | Sugar 4 g | Protein 6.4 g | Sodium 234 mg | Carbs 28 g

157. Smoked Salmon Bites

(Prep time: 20 minutes | Cook time: 0 minutes | Serving: 8)
Ingredients
- Cream cheese: 4 oz., softened & low-fat
- Smoked salmon: 4 oz., sliced into 16 strips
- Chopped shallot: 1 tbsp.
- 2 small peeled beets
- Lemon juice: 1 tbsp.
- Lemon zest: 2 tsp.

Instructions

1. Slice the beets with a mandolin into 16 pieces. Make them into squares by trimming.

2. In a bowl, add cheese, zest, juice and shallot.

3. On each salmon strip, spread the cheese mixture on both sides.

4. On 1 beet square, add 1 salmon strip. Serve.

Nutrition: Calories 62 | Fat 4.1 g | Sugar 8 g | Protein 4 g | Sodium 186 mg | Carbs 2 g

158. Potato Nachos

(Prep time: 10 minutes | Cook time: 40 minutes | Serving: 5)
Ingredients

- Small potatoes: 1 pound with skins on
- 1 peeled cucumber, diced
- Diced tomato: ¾ cup
- Chili powder: half tsp.
- Cheddar cheese: half cup, shredded
- ¾ cup of salsa
- Ground turkey: 8 oz., lean
- Lettuce: 1 cup, shredded
- Chopped cilantro: 1 tbsp.

Instructions
1. Slice the potatoes into ¼" thick. Oil spray the potatoes generously and place them on a baking sheet evenly.

2. Bake for 25 to 30 minutes at 450 F.

3. In a skillet, add turkey and chili powder. Cook for 8 to 10 minutes on medium flame.

4. Take the potatoes out and transfer them to a baking dish; add turkey mixture on top.

5. Sprinkle cheese on top. Bake for 3-5 minutes, or broil.

6. Serve with the rest of the ingredients on top.

Nutrition: Calories 267 | Fat 9 g | Sugar 4 g | Protein 11 g | Sodium 81 mg | Carbs 13.9 g

159. Smoked Trout Spread

(Prep time: 10 minutes | Cook time: 40 minutes | Serving: 12)

Ingredients
- Low-fat cottage cheese: half cup
- Hot pepper sauce: 1 tsp.
- Red onion: ¼ cup, chopped
- Broken smoked trout fillet: ¼ pound, without skin
- 1 celery stalk, chopped
- Lemon juice: 2 tsp.
- Worcestershire sauce: half tsp.

Instructions
1. In a food processor, add all ingredients except for celery. Pulse until smooth.

2. Add diced celery and fold.

3. Serve.

Nutrition per 1 tbsp.: Calories 29 | Fat 1 g | Sugar 8 g | Protein 4 g |Sodium 87 mg | Carbs 1 g

160. Cauliflower "Caviar"

(Prep time: 10 minutes | Cook time: 40 minutes | Serving: 12)

Ingredients

- Olive oil: 5 tsp.
- Minced garlic: 1 tbsp.
- Black pepper: ¾ tsp.
- Cauliflower florets: 4 cups, chopped
- Kosher salt: ¼ tsp.
- 24 endive leaves
- Sherry vinegar: 1 tbsp.
- Fresh parsley: ¼ cup, chopped
- Prosciutto: 4 oz., chopped

Instructions

1. Let the oven preheat to 400 F.
2. Spread florets on a baking sheet. Toss with oil (1 tbsp.), salt and pepper.
3. Bake for 40 minutes.
4. In the skillet, add the rest of the oil, sauté prosciutto for ten minutes.
5. Add garlic and cook for 1 minute. Drain.
6. In a bowl, add prosciutto, cauliflowers, vinegar mash with a fork.
7. Serve on top of the endive leaf.

Nutrition: Calories 59 | Fat 3 g | Sugar 8 g | Protein 3.8 g |Sodium 205 mg | Carbs 4.8 g

161. Pickled Asparagus

(Prep time: 10 minutes | Cook time: 0 minutes | Serving: 6)

Ingredients

- Pearl onions: ¼ cup
- Cider vinegar: ¼ cup
- Fresh asparagus: 3 cups
- Fresh dill: 1 sprig
- White wine vinegar: ¼ cup
- 8 black peppercorns

- 1 cup of water
- Whole coriander: 6 seeds
- 3 garlic cloves
- Red pepper flakes: ¼ tsp.
- 2 cloves

Instructions

1. Wash the asparagus well, cut in length that will fit in your jar.
2. Trim the onions, and place all ingredients in an air-tight jar.
3. Mix and keep in the fridge for 4 weeks.

Nutrition for the half cup: Calories 24 | Fat 1 g | Sugar 2 g | Protein 2 g |Sodium 5 mg | Carbs 4 g

162. Serrano Watermelon Bites

(Prep time: 10 minutes | Cook time: 0 minutes | Serving: 8)

Ingredients

- 1 serrano chili, sliced into 16 slices
- Seedless watermelon: 1 pound, sliced into 16 cubes
- Fresh mint: 2 tsp., sliced
- Serrano ham: 2 oz., sliced into 16 strips
- Pomegranate molasses: 1 tbsp.

Instructions

1. On each watermelon cube, wrap the ham slice.
2. Add chili slice on top.
3. Before serving, drizzle with molasses and top with mint.
4. Serve

Nutrition: Calories 38| Fat 1 g | Sugar 5 g | Protein 2 g |Sodium 191 mg | Carbs 6 g

163. Roman-Style Artichokes

(Prep time: 15 minutes | Cook time: 10 minutes | Serving: 4)

Ingredients

- 2 minced garlic cloves
- Chicken broth: half cup, low-sodium
- Water: half cup
- Olive oil: 1 tbsp.
- Dried oregano: half tsp.
- 2 artichokes
- Fresh Italian parsley: 2 tbsp., chopped

- Salt: ¼ tsp.

Instructions

1. Cut the artichoke one" from the top. Peel the outer leaves.

2. Cut in half and scrape the choke protein.

3. In a pressure cooker, add water and broth, place a steaming rack in the cooker.

4. Place the halved artichoke on the rack, round side down.

5. In a bowl, add the rest of the ingredients and mix.

6. Sprinkle on the artichokes. Seal the lid and cook for ten minutes on high pressure.

7. Release the pressure. Serve with a drizzle of oil.

Nutrition: Calories 64 | Fat 0.5 g | Sugar 1 g | Protein 2 g | Sodium 55 mg | Carbs 8 g

164. Maple-Sesame Cauliflower Bites

(Prep time: 15 minutes | Cook time: 40 minutes | Serving: 6)

Ingredients

- 3/4 cup of chickpea flour
- Cauliflower florets: 6 cups
- Sesame oil: 2 tsp., toasted
- Black pepper: half tsp.
- 2% milk: half cup
- Sliced scallions: 1 tbsp.
- Maple syrup: 2 tbsp.
- Kosher salt: ¼ tsp.
- Garlic powder: 1 tsp.
- Sesame seeds: 1 tsp., toasted
- Tamari: 1 tbsp., low-sodium
- Rice vinegar: 2 tsp., unseasoned
- Grated ginger: half tsp.

Instructions

1. Let the oven preheat to 450 F.

2. In a bowl, add ginger, maple syrup, vinegar, tamari and oil. Whisk well.

3. In a bowl, add the rest of the ingredients, except for cauliflower mix and add cauliflower.

4. Toss well.

5. Spread on an oil sprayed baking sheet. Bake for 20 minutes, stirring halfway through.

6. Take the florets out and pour maple mixture on top, toss to coat. Bake for 5 more minutes.

7. Sprinkle sesame seeds and serve.

Nutrition: Calories 120 | Fat 3 g | Sugar 8 g | Protein 6 g | Sodium 227 mg | Carbs 18 g

165. Fruit Skewers & Yogurt Dip

(Prep time: 15 minutes | Cook time: 0 minutes | Serving: 10)

Ingredients

- Yogurt Dip
- Honey: ¼ cup
- Low-fat Greek yogurt: 1 ½ cups
- Non-fat cream cheese: 8 oz.
- Fruit Skewers (all cut in squares)
- 3 fresh kiwis, cubed
- 20 fresh blueberries
- 1 fresh pineapple, cubed
- 10 fresh strawberries

Instructions

1. Thread the fruits cubes onto skewers, alternatively.

2. In a bowl, add all ingredients of dips, mix and serve with fruit kabobs.

Nutrition: Calories 124 | Fat 2 g | Sugar 8 g | Protein 6 g | Sodium 38 mg | Carbs 3 g

166. Polenta-Sausage Triangles

(Prep time: 55 minutes | Cook time: 30 minutes | Serving: 8)

Ingredients

- Chopped yellow onion: ¾ cup
- 3 minced garlic cloves
- Instant polenta: 1 cup
- Non-fat milk: 1 ¼ cups
- Chopped celery: ¾ cup
- Water: 1 ½ cups
- Olive oil: 2 tbsp.
- Low-fat pork sausage: 8 oz.

- Kosher salt: ¼ tsp.

Instructions

1. Add some oil and sausage to a pan, cook for 2 minutes, add garlic and other vegetables, and cook for 8 minutes.

2. Add milk, water, mix and let it come to a boil.

3. Add polenta slowly; keep whisking. Add salt and cook for three minutes.

4. Oil spray a baking dish (11 by 7") and transfer the polenta mixture into the dish.

5. Let it cool to room temperature and keep in the fridge covered for 4 hours.

6. Slice into 8 pieces in a triangle shape.

7. In a skillet, add oil on medium flame. Add polenta triangles and cook for two minutes on 1 side.

8. Serve hot.

Nutrition: Calories 190| Fat 9 g | Sugar 1g | Protein 7.8 g |Sodium 289 mg | Carbs 14.8 g

167. Roasted Potatoes with Garlic & Herbs

(Prep time: 15 minutes | Cook time: 40 minutes | Serving: 4)

Ingredients

- 4 garlic cloves
- Black pepper: ¼ tsp.
- Fresh parsley: 2 tbsp., chopped
- Olive oil: 2 tsp.
- Fresh rosemary: 2 tsp., chopped
- Small potatoes: ¾ pound
- Salt: 1/8 tsp.
- Butter: 2 tsp.

Instructions

1. Let the oven preheat to 400 F and oil spray a baking dish.

2. In a bowl, add all ingredients except for butter and parsley, toss to coat well.

3. Spread on the prepared baking dish and cover with foil and bake for 25 minutes.

4. Take the foil off and bake for 25 minutes.

5. Toss with parsley and butter. Serve.

Nutrition: Calories 104 | Fat 4 g | Sugar 1 g | Protein 2 g |Sodium 103 mg | Carbs 15 g

168. Turnip Rounds with Cranberry Chutney

(Prep time: 15 minutes | Cook time: 15 minutes | Serving: 4)

Ingredients

- Peeled turnips: 2 pounds, sliced into ¾" rounds
- Frozen cranberries: 8 oz.
- Black pepper
- Olive oil: 3 tbsp.
- 1 shallot, diced
- Cayenne pepper, a pinch
- Honey: 3 tbsp.
- Fresh sage: 1 tsp., chopped
- Lemon zest: 1 tsp.

Instructions

1. In a skillet, add oil (half) on medium flame.

2. Add turnips (half) and cook for 4 minutes. Take it out on a plate, sprinkle with black pepper and a pinch of salt.

3. Repeat with the rest of the turnips.

4. Turn the flame to low, add oil and sage, cook for few minutes and take them out on a plate.

5. Add shallots and sauté on medium flame. Cook for three minutes.

6. Add the rest of the ingredients, cook for three minutes.

7. Serve turnips with chutney and sage leaves on top.

Nutrition: Calories 267 | Fat 5 g | Sugar 3 g | Protein 15.1 g |Sodium 81 mg | Carbs 11 g

169. Caramelized Onion & Gruyere Spread

(Prep time: 15 minutes | Cook time: 40 minutes | Serving: 8)

Ingredients

- Low-fat Gruyere cheese: 2 oz., shredded

- Sour cream: ⅓ cup, low-fat
- Fresh chives: 2 tbsp., chopped
- Chopped onion: 3 ½ cups
- 3 cooked bacon slices, crumbled
- Canola mayonnaise: ⅓ cup
- Salt & pepper: ¼ tsp. Each

Instructions
1. Let the oven preheat to 425 F.
2. In a skillet, add some oil on medium heat. Sauté onion for 5 minutes, turn the heat to low.
3. Cook for 20 minutes, let it cool slightly.
4. In a bowl, add cheese (except for 2 tbsp.), onions and the rest of the ingredients.
5. Mix and transfer to an oil-sprayed baking dish, sprinkle the rest of the cheese on top.
6. Bake for 20 minutes. Serve.

Nutrition: Calories 101 | Fat 6.8 g | Sugar 1 g | Protein 4.2 g | Sodium 236 mg | Carbs 5.3 g

170. Crispy Garbanzo Beans

(Prep time: 15 minutes | Cook time: 40 minutes | Serving: 8)
Ingredients
- Pepper: half tsp.
- Salt: ¼ tsp.
- Dried dill: 2 tsp.
- 2 cans of (15 oz.) Garbanzo beans
- 4 garlic cloves
- Onion powder: 1 tsp.
- Parsley flakes: 1 tsp.

Instructions
1. Let the oven preheat to 400 F
2. Drain and dry the beans well. In a bowl, add the rest of the ingredients.
3. Oil spray a baking sheet, spread the beans, and sprinkle with spices.
4. Roast in the oven for 30 to 40 minutes; halfway through, stir the chickpeas.
5. Roast until crispy and golden.

Nutrition: Calories 245 | Fat 7 g | Sugar 4 g | Protein 21 g | Sodium 87 mg | Carbs 13 g

171. Roasted Butternut Squash Fries

(Prep time: 15 minutes | Cook time: 20 minutes | Serving: 6)
Ingredients
- Olive oil: 1 tbsp.
- 1 butternut squash
- Fresh thyme: 1 tbsp., chopped
- Salt: ¼ tsp.
- Fresh rosemary: 1 tbsp., chopped

Instructions
1. Let the oven preheat to 425 F. Oil spray a baking sheet.
2. Peel the squash and slice into sticks (3" long).
3. In a bowl, add squash fries and the rest of the ingredients. Toss to coat evenly.
4. Spread on the prepared baking sheet, bake for ten minutes.
5. Take out and stir the fries and bake for 5-10 minutes more.

Nutrition for the half cup: Calories 62 | Fat 2 g | Sugar 2 g | Protein 1 g | Sodium 168 mg | Carbs 11 g

172. Avocado Salsa

(Prep time: 15 minutes | Cook time: 10 minutes | Serving: 16)
Ingredients
- Salt: 1/8 tsp.
- 1 green bell pepper, chopped
- Black beans: half can
- 16 corn tortillas (6"), sliced into 6 triangles
- 1 seeded cucumber, chopped
- Red pepper flakes: 1/8 tsp.
- 1 celery stalk, chopped
- Lime juice: 2 tbsp.
- Fresh cilantro: 2 to 3 tbsp., chopped
- 2 avocados, chopped

Instructions
1. Let the oven preheat to 350 F.
2. On a baking sheet, place tortilla triangles in one

even layer.

3. Bake for ten minutes, take them out on a plate. Keep repeating until all are baked.

4. In a bowl, add the rest of the ingredients, except for avocados.

5. Mix and fold in avocado, serve with tortilla chips.

Nutrition: Calories 180| Fat 4.5 g | Sugar 1 g | Protein 3 g |Sodium 76 mg | Carbs 16 g

173. Pear Chutney Bruschetta

(Prep time: 15 minutes | Cook time: 25 minutes | Serving: 8)
Ingredients
- Olive oil: 2 tsp.
- Chopped bosc pear: 1 ½ cups
- Baguette: 16 thin slices, toasted
- Pear nectar: half cup
- Chopped shallots: ¼ cup
- Sugar: 2 tbsp.
- Cider vinegar: 1 ½ tbsp.
- Crumbled blue cheese: 7 tsp.
- Dried apricots: ¼ cup, chopped
- 1 cinnamon stick, 3"
- Fresh thyme: 1 tsp., chopped
- Chopped pecans: 8 tsp., toasted
- Fresh chives: 1 tsp., chopped

Instructions
1. In a skillet, add oil on medium heat.
2. Sauté shallots for 2 minutes. Add pears and the rest of the ingredients except for bread, herbs; let it come to a boil.
3. Turn the heat low, simmer for 20 minutes.
4. Spread over bread and serve with fresh herbs on top.

Nutrition: Calories 124| Fat 3.6 g | Sugar 3 g | Protein 2.4 g |Sodium 155 mg | Carbs 21.9

174. Grilled Pineapple

(Prep time: 20 minutes | Cook time: 10 minutes | Serving: 8)
Ingredients
- Olive oil: 1 tbsp.
- Lime juice: 1 tbsp.
- Lime zest: 1 tbsp.
- Dark honey: 2 tbsp.
- Cinnamon: 1 tsp.
- Ground cloves: ¼ tsp.
- 1 pineapple, cut into strips

Instructions
1. Let the grill heat. Oil spray the grates away from the heat source.
2. In a bowl, add all the ingredients, except for pineapples.
3. Onto skewers, thread the pineapple. Brush with marinade and grill for 5 minutes on 1 side.
4. Serve warm.

Nutrition: Calories 145 | Fat 16 g | Sugar 0 g | Protein 1 g |Sodium 8 mg | Carbs 13 g

175. Peanut Butter Energy Balls

(Prep time: 20 minutes | Cook time: 0 minutes | Serving: 17)
Ingredients
- Peanut butter: 1 cup
- Shredded coconut: ¼ cup, unsweetened
- Rolled oats: 2 cups
- Honey: half cup
- Mini chocolate chips: ¼ tsp.

Instructions
In a bowl, add all ingredients and mix well.

Make the mixture into 1 tbsp. of balls. Serve.

Nutrition for 2 balls: Calories 174 | Fat 9.2 g | Sugar 9 g | Protein 6.4 g |Sodium 47.7 mg | Carbs 18.2 g

176. Buffalo Cauliflower Bites

(Prep time: 20 minutes | Cook time: 30-40 minutes | Serving: 4)
Ingredients
- Hot sauce: 2 tbsp.
- Cauliflower florets: 4 cups
- Ketchup: 3 tbsp., no-salt-added
- Red wine vinegar: 1 tsp.
- 1 egg white
- Blue cheese: 1 tbsp.

- Panko: ¾ cup
- Black pepper: ¼ tsp.
- Sour cream: ¼ cup, low-fat
- 1 minced garlic clove

Instructions

1. In a bowl, whisk egg white, ketchup and hot sauce.
2. In a bowl, add panko. Toss florets with hot sauce mixture and then toss in panko.
3. Work in batches. Oil spray the breaded cauliflower spread on an oil-sprayed baking sheet.
4. Bake for 30-40 minutes at 320 F. stir halfway through or more than once. Do not burn.
5. In a bowl, add the rest of the ingredients, whisk and serve with buffalo cauliflower.

Nutrition: Calories 125 | Fat 4 g | Sugar 1 g | Protein 5 g | Sodium 255 mg | Carbs 17 g

177. Fiesta Rolls

(Prep time: 6 hours & 20 minutes | Cook time: 30 minutes | Serving: 8-10)

Ingredients

- 2 red bell peppers
- Lime juice: 2 tsp.
- Non-fat cream cheese: half cup
- Fresh poblano peppers: 2 large
- 2 minced garlic cloves
- Fresh cilantro: 1 tbsp., chopped
- Red pepper: 1/8 tsp.
- 4 tortillas (7-8")

Instructions

1. Cut the poblano and bell peppers in half and take the seeds out.
2. Bake on a foil-lined baking sheet, round side down, for 20-25 minutes at 425 F.
3. Wrap in foil and rest for 15-20 minutes. Peel the skin off and slice in strips.
4. In a bowl, add the rest of the ingredients except

for tortillas. Spread over tortillas, add pepper slices. Roll and warp in plastic wrap.
5. Keep in the fridge for 6 hours. Slice and serve.

Nutrition: Calories 224 | Fat 7 g | Sugar 3 g | Protein 16 g | Sodium 98 mg | Carbs 13 g

178. California Quinoa

(Prep time: 20 minutes | Cook time: 30 minutes | Serving: 4)

Ingredients

- Olive oil: 1 tbsp.
- Crumbled feta cheese: half cup
- Greek olives: ¼ cup, chopped
- 2 cups of water
- 1 tomato, diced
- Quinoa: 1 cup
- Fresh basil: 2 tbsp., chopped
- 1 zucchini, chopped
- Canned chickpeas: 3/4 cup
- 2 minced garlic cloves
- Black pepper: ¼ tsp.

Instructions

1. In a pan, add oil on medium heat.
2. Add garlic and quinoa, cook for 2 to 3 minutes. Add water and zucchini and let it come to a boil; turn the heat low and simmer for 12 to 15 minutes.
3. Add the rest of the ingredients. Cook for few minutes.
4. Serve.

Nutrition: Calories 310 | Fat 11 g | Sugar 3 g | Protein 11 g | Sodium 350 mg | Carbs 42 g

179. Sweet & Spicy Pumpkinseeds

(Prep time: 20 minutes | Cook time: 5 minutes | Serving: 8)

Ingredients

- Canola oil: 1 tbsp.
- Red pepper, a pinch
- Chipotle Chile powder: half tsp.
- Sugar: 1 tsp.
- Kosher salt: ¼ tsp.
- Pumpkinseed kernels: 1 cup, unsalted

- Ground cumin: half tsp.
- Cinnamon: ¼ tsp.

Instructions

1. In a skillet, add pumpkin seeds on medium heat. Cook for 4 minutes.
2. In a bowl, add the rest of the ingredients, add seeds. Toss to coat.
3. Cool the seeds after spreading on a baking tray.

Nutrition: Calories 158 | Fat 13 g | Sugar 8 g | Protein 8.8 g |Sodium 67 mg | Carbs 4.3 g

180. Quick Pickled Dilly Green Beans

(Prep time: 2 hours & 10 minutes | Cook time: 5 minutes | Serving: 12)

Ingredients

- Fresh dill: ¼ cup, chopped
- Sugar: 2 tsp.
- Green beans: half-pound, trimmed
- 1 peeled garlic clove
- 1 cup of water
- Salt: 1 tsp.
- White wine vinegar: 1 cup
- Pickling spice: 2 tsp.

Instructions

1. In a bowl, add green beans and dill.
2. In a pan, add all the ingredients. Let it come to a boil, and cook for 1 minute.
3. Pour over the bean mixture and rest for 2 hours.
4. Drain and serve.

Nutrition: Calories 6 | Fat 17.2 g | Sugar 4 g | Protein 0.4 g |Sodium 41 mg | Carbs 1.4 g

181. Wonton Chips

(Prep time: 10 minutes | Cook time: 8 minutes | Serving: 12)

Ingredients

- Wonton wrappers: 18
- Olive oil, as needed
- Garlic powder, red pepper & cheese: as needed

Instructions

With olive oil, brush the wonton. Cut into 8 triangles.

Spread on a baking sheet and sprinkle the rest of the ingredients on top.

Bake for 8 minutes at 350 F. Serve.

Nutrition: Calories 145 | Fat 8 g | Sugar 2.3 g | Protein 1 g |Sodium 12 mg | Carbs 9 g

182. Savory Bites

(Prep time: 10 minutes | Cook time: 15 minutes | Serving: 12)

Ingredients

- Olive oil: 4 tsp.
- Dried basil: half tsp., crushed
- Worcestershire sauce: 2 tsp.
- Toast rounds: 5 ¼ oz.
- Cayenne pepper, a dash
- Water: 2 tsp.
- Garlic powder: ¼ tsp.

Instructions

1. In a bowl, add toast rounds.
2. In a bowl, add the rest of the ingredients and mix. Pour over the toast rounds and toss.
3. In a baking pan, add the toast rounds in 1 layer.
4. Bake for 15 minutes at 300 F. Serve.

Nutrition: Calories 217 | Fat 7 g | Sugar 3 g | Protein 16 g |Sodium 65 mg | Carbs 16 g

183. Garlic-Parsley Shrim

(Prep time: 10 minutes | Cook time: 10 minutes | Serving: 4)

Ingredients

- Kosher salt: ¼ tsp.
- Dry white wine: ¼ cup
- 2 minced garlic clove
- Raw large shrimp: ¾ pound, peeled & deveined
- 1 jalapeño, chopped without seeds
- Plant butter: 2 tbsp., unsalted
- Fresh ginger: 1 tsp., minced
- Olive oil: 2 tsp.
- Fresh parsley: ¼ cup, chopped

Instructions

1. Cut the shrimps in half lengthwise, then crosswise. Toss with salt and place in a colander. Let it rest for 5 minutes.
2. Rinse well.
3. In a bowl, add shrimp and toss with jalapenos, ginger and garlic.
4. In a skillet, add oil on medium-high heat.
5. Add shrimps and cook for three minutes.
6. Add wine and cook for 2 minutes.
7. Add butter and parsley, cook, until it melts. Serve.

Nutrition: Calories 254 | Fat 10 g | Sugar 1 g | Protein 17 g |Sodium 304 mg | Carbs 21 g

184. Roasted Pepper Roll-Ups

(Prep time: 20 minutes | Cook time: 0 minutes | Serving: 16)

Ingredients

- Soft goat cheese: 4 oz.
- Low-fat milk: 1 tbsp.
- Roasted red sweet peppers: half cup, without liquid, chopped
- Low-fat cream cheese: 4 oz. Softened
- Black pepper: ¼ tsp.
- Fresh spinach: 2 cups, packed
- 1 minced garlic clove
- Fresh basil: ¼ cup, chopped
- 8-inch whole wheat tortillas: 8 tortillas

Instructions

1. In a bowl, add cream cheese and whisk with an electric mixer for 30 seconds on high.
2. Add garlic, goat cheese, garlic, black pepper and milk. Mix until smooth.
3. Add basil and red pepper, mix.
4. In each tortilla, add some filling and spinach leaves. Roll tightly.
5. Serve chilled.

Nutrition: Calories 231 | Fat 4 g | Sugar 2.8 g | Protein 14 g |Sodium 66 mg | Carbs 8.1 g

185. Crab & Celery Root Rémoulade

(Prep time: 20 minutes | Cook time: 0 minutes | Serving: 12)

Ingredients

- Red onion: half cup, chopped
- Dijon mustard: 1 tbsp.
- Lump crabmeat: 8 oz., drained
- Shredded celery root: 2 cups
- Mayonnaise: 3 tbsp.
- Kosher salt: ¼ tsp.
- Lemon juice: 1 tbsp.
- Chopped tarragon: 1 tsp.
- Boston lettuce: 24 baby leaves
- Black pepper: half tsp.
- Red pepper: 1/8 tsp.
- Olive oil: 2 tbsp.

Instructions

1. In a bowl, add crabmeat, red and celery root. Mix.
2. In a bowl, add mayo, mustard, salt, lemon juice, pepper and tarragon. Mix and slowly add oil while whisking.
3. Pour the mixture over the crab mixture and mix.
4. Serve in a lettuce leaf.

Nutrition: Calories 70 | Fat 4 g | Sugar 8 g | Protein 4.5 g |Sodium 155 mg | Carbs 4.4 g

186. Mini Corn Bread Crab Cakes

(Prep time: 1 hour & 25 minutes | Cook time: 12 minutes | Serving: 12)

Ingredients

- Green onions: half cup, sliced
- Mayonnaise: ¼ cup, low-fat
- Red bell pepper: 1/3 cup, chopped
- 1 minced garlic clove
- Olive oil: 2 tsp.
- Green bell pepper: 1/3 cup, chopped
- Fresh parsley: 2 tbsp., chopped
- Lemon juice: 1 tbsp.
- Lump crabmeat: 1 pound
- Fresh chives: 2 tbsp., chopped

- Hot pepper sauce: 1 tbsp.
- Buttermilk corn bread: 2 cups, crumbled
- Old bay seasoning: 1 tsp., low-sodium
- Lemon zest: half tsp.
- 1 egg, whisked

Instructions

1. Let the oven preheat to 400 F.
2. In a pan, sauté onion, garlic and bell pepper for three minutes. Turn the heat off and cool.
3. In a bowl, add mayo (1/4 cup), bell pepper mixture and the rest of the ingredients except for crabmeat and corn bread.
4. Mix and then add corn bread and crabmeat. Make into 16 portions and place onto baking sheets, oil spray the portions.
5. Keep in the fridge covered for 1 hour.
6. Bake for 12 minutes at 400 F. Serve with desired sauce.

Nutrition: Calories 83| Fat 3.2 g | Sugar 8 g | Protein 7.4 g |Sodium 317 mg | Carbs 6.4 g

187. Oat & Nut Crunch Mix

(Prep time: 15 minutes | Cook time: 22 minutes | Serving: 20)

Ingredients

- Apple pie spice: half tsp.
- Sliced almonds: half cup
- Plant butter: 2 tbsp., melted
- Oat square cereal: 4 cups
- Dried cherries: 1 cup

Instructions

1. In a baking pan (15 by 10 by 1"), add almonds and cereal.
2. In a bowl, add the rest of the ingredients (except for cherries) and mix, drizzle over almonds and cereal.
3. Toss well, bake for 20 minutes at 300 F.
4. Cool for 20 minutes in the pan, add cherries, mix

and serve.

Nutrition: Calories 234 | Fat 4.1 g | Sugar 3 g | Protein 17 g |Sodium 23 mg | Carbs 13 g

188. Sun-Dried Tomato Palmiers

(Prep time: 1 hour & 25 minutes | Cook time: 12 minutes | Serving: 10)

Ingredients

- 1 sheet of puff pastry dough, frozen & thawed
- Sun-dried tomatoes: 4 oil-packed, drained
- Olive oil: 1 tbsp.
- Kalamata olives: half cup, pitted
- Fresh thyme leaves: 1 tsp.
- 1 minced garlic clove

Instructions

1. In a food processor, add all ingredients instead of phyllo. Pulse until chopped.
2. Roll the dough into 10 by 9" rectangle.
3. Spread the mixture over the dough; leave half" space from the border.
4. Roll from both sides and meet in the center; keep in the fridge for 20 minutes.
5. Let the oven preheat to 400 F.
6. Slice the dough into 20 pieces, and arrange on parchment paper on a baking sheet.
7. Bake for 15 minutes.

Nutrition: Calories 168 | Fat 12.5 g | Sugar 8 g | Protein 2 g |Sodium 158 mg | Carbs 12.1 g

189. Brown Rice Pilaf

(Prep time: 15 minutes | Cook time: 45 minutes | Serving: 8)

Ingredients

- 2 cups of water
- Orange juice: 3 tbsp.
- Turmeric: ¼ tsp.
- Dried apricots: ¼ cup, chopped
- Orange zest: half tsp.
- Dark brown rice: 1 1/8 cups, rinsed
- Canola oil: 1 ½ tbsp.

- Pistachio nuts: ¼ cup, chopped

Instructions

1. In a pan, add water, turmeric and rice on high flame.
2. Let it come to a boil, turn the heat low and simmer for 45 minutes.
3. In a bowl, add the rest of the ingredients. Pour over freshly cooked rice and toss to coat.
4. Serve.

Nutrition for a half cup: Calories 153 | Fat 5 g | Sugar 8 g | Protein 3 g | Sodium 157 mg | Carbs 24 g

190. Stuffed Sweet Potato

(Prep time: 15 minutes | Cook time: 15 minutes | Serving: 1)

Ingredients

- Canned black beans: 1 cup, rinsed
- 1 sweet potato, large
- Water: 2 tbsp.
- Chopped kale: ¾ cup
- Hummus: ¼ cup

Instructions

1. With a fork, pierce the potato all over. Microwave for 7-10 minutes, on high.
2. Wash kale and place in a pan, cook on medium flame, covered. Stir occasionally until it wilts.
3. Add beans and some water. Keep stirring for 1-2 minutes.
4. Cut the potato in half and add kale-bean mixture on top.
5. In a bowl, whisk hummus with water (2 tbsp.) pour over sweet potato and serve.

Nutrition: Calories 472 | Fat 7 g | Sugar 19.9 g | Protein 21.1 g | Sodium 489 mg | Carbs 85.3 g

191. Oysters with Peppercorn Mignonette

(Prep time: 15 minutes | Cook time: 0 minutes | Serving: 8)

Ingredients

- Pink peppercorns: 2 tsp., crushed
- 32 oysters on the half shell
- Champagne vinegar: half cup
- Shallots: 2 tbsp., chopped
- Fresh tarragon: 1 ½ tsp., chopped

Instructions

1. In a bowl, add all ingredients except for oysters, mix and pour over oysters
2. Serve.

Nutrition: Calories 47 | Fat 1.4 g | Sugar 0 g | Protein 4.1 g | Sodium 120 mg | Carbs 4.4 g

192. Wild Rice Pilaf

(Prep time: 15 minutes | Cook time: 60 minutes | Serving: 8)

Ingredients

- 3 cups of water
- Olive oil: 2 tbsp.
- Wild rice: 1 1/2 cups, rinsed well
- Slivered almonds: ¼ cup
- 2 cored apples (granny smith), diced
- Dried cranberries: half cup, unsweetened
- Sugar substitute: 1 tbsp.
- Red wine vinegar: 1 tbsp.

Instructions

1. Let the oven preheat to 325 F. oil spray a baking sheet.
2. Roast almonds on the baking sheet for ten minutes. Let them cool.
3. In a pan, add water (3 cups) and rice.
4. Let it come to a boil, turn the heat low and simmer for 45-60 minutes. Keep adding the water if it gets dry.
5. Drain and add cranberries. Mix and let it rest, covered.
6. In a bowl, add sugar, oil and vinegar. Pour over rice with apples. Toss to coat, serve with sliced almonds on top.

Nutrition for 1 cup: Calories 213 | Fat 5 g | Sugar 4 g | Protein 5 g | Sodium 6 mg | Carbs 37 g

193. Lemon Chicken Kabobs

(Prep time: 15 minutes | Cook time: 15 minutes | Serving: 6)

Ingredients

- Lemon juice: 1/4 cup
- Red pepper flakes: 1 ½ tsp.
- 2 lemons, halved
- Olive oil: 4 tbsp.
- Chicken breasts: 1 1/2 pounds, boneless & skinless, cubed (1")
- White wine: 3 tbsp.
- Fresh rosemary: 1 tsp., chopped

Instructions

1. In a dish, add all ingredients except for lemons; coat well.
2. Keep in the fridge for 3 hours.
3. Thread the chicken onto six skewers, grill for 10-12 minutes, flipping once.
4. Squeeze lemon and serve.

Nutrition for 1 skewer: Calories 182 | Fat 8 g | Sugar 1 g | Protein 23 g | Sodium 55 mg | Carbs 2 g

194. Romano Baked Tomatoes

(Prep time: 15 minutes | Cook time: 15 minutes | Serving: 4)

Ingredients

- Low-fat Romano cheese: 2 Tbsp., grated
- Garlic powder: 1/4 tsp.
- Fresh oregano: 1 tbsp., chopped
- Olive oil: 1 tbsp.
- 2 tomatoes, halved
- Pepper: 1/4 tsp.

Instructions

1. Let the oven preheat to 400 F.
2. On a baking sheet place, the tomatoes, Add the rest of the ingredients on top.
3. Bake for 20 minutes. Serve.

Nutrition: Calories 57 | Fat 4.5 g | Sugar 2 g | Protein 1 g | Sodium 60 mg | Carbs 4 g

195. Garlic Rosemary Mushrooms

(Prep time: 15 minutes | Cook time: 10 minutes | Serving: 4)

Ingredients

- Sliced mushrooms: 2 cups
- Black pepper
- Dry white wine: ¼ cup
- 2 minced garlic cloves
- Bacon: 1 to 2 slices, chopped
- Fresh rosemary:2 tsp., chopped

Instructions

1. Cook bacon in a pan for 4 minutes, add the rest of the ingredients except for wine, cook on medium for 8 minutes.
2. Add wine and cook until evaporated.
3. Serve.

Nutrition: Calories 154 | Fat 3 g | Sugar 3 g | Protein 11 g | Sodium 61 mg | Carbs 3 g

196. Acorn Squash with Apples

(Prep time: 15 minutes | Cook time: 15 minutes | Serving: 2)

Ingredients

Low-fat margarine: 2 tsp.

Brown sugar: 2 tbsp.

1 acorn squash, ~ 6" in diameter

1 peeled Granny Smith apple, cored & sliced

Instructions

1. In a bowl, toss apples with sugar.
2. With a knife, pierce the squash all over, microwave for 5 minutes, flipping halfway through.
3. Cut in half and take the seeds out, stuff with apples.
4. Microwave for 2 minutes. Serve with margarine on top.

Nutrition for 1/4: Calories 204 | Fat 4 g | Sugar 6 g | Protein2 g | Sodium 46 mg | Carbs 40 g

197. Brussels Sprouts with Shallots & Lemon

(Prep time: 15 minutes | Cook time: 15 minutes | Serving: 4)

Ingredients

- 3 shallots, sliced thin

- Black pepper: ¼ tsp.
- Salt: 1/8 tsp.
- No-salt-added broth: half cup
- Lemon zest: ¼ tsp.
- Olive oil: 3 tsp.
- Brussels sprouts: 1 pound, quartered
- Lemon juice: 1 tbsp.

Instructions

In a pan, add oil (2 tsp.) on medium flame. Sauté shallots for 6 minutes and take them out in a bowl.

Add more oil to the pan and sauté Brussels sprouts for 3-4 minutes.

Add broth and let it simmer for 5-6 minutes.

Add shallots back in the pan, add the rest of the ingredients. Stir and serve.

Nutrition: Calories 104 | Fat 4 g | Sugar 3 g | Protein 5 g | Sodium 191 mg | Carbs 12 g

198. Broccoli with Onions & Pine Nuts

(Prep time: 15 minutes | Cook time: 25 minutes | Serving: 4)

Ingredients

- Pine nuts: 3 tbsp.
- Broccoli florets: 4 cups
- Oil: 2 tsp.
- Black pepper
- Onion: 1 cup, chopped
- Balsamic vinegar: 2 tsp.

Instructions

1. In a skillet, add pine nuts and toast for 2-3 minutes.
2. In a pan, add oil and sauté onion for 15-20 minutes on medium flame.
3. Steam the florets for 4-6 minutes, take them out in a bowl.
4. Add the rest of the ingredients. Toss to coat, serve.

Nutrition: Calories 232 | Fat 6 g | Sugar 5 g | Protein 6.9

g | Sodium 81 mg | Carbs 7.1 g

199. Baked Black Beans with Chorizo

(Prep time: 15 minutes | Cook time: 55 minutes | Serving: 6)

Ingredients

- Spanish chorizo: half cup, diced
- Chicken broth: ¾ cup, low-sodium
- 1 jalapeño pepper, thinly sliced
- Seeded tomato: 1 cup, chopped
- Ground cumin: half tsp.
- Red pepper: ¼ tsp.
- Olive oil: 1 tbsp.
- Chopped onion: 1 ½ cups
- Monterey jack cheese: half cup, shredded
- 5 minced garlic cloves
- Green onions: ¼ cup, sliced
- Black beans: 2 cans (15 oz.), rinsed

Instructions

1. Let the oven preheat to 425 F.
2. In a skillet, add oil and sauté chorizo for 2 minutes. Take it out in a bowl.
3. Add all spices and garlic to the pan, cook for 1 minute.
4. Add beans, broth. Let it come to a boil and simmer for 5 minutes.
5. Mash it roughly, transfer it to an oil-sprayed baking dish (8"-square).
6. Add tomato, chorizo and cheese on top.
7. Bake for half an hour. Serve with scallions on top.

Nutrition: Calories 189 | Fat 8.4 g | Sugar 2 g | Protein 10.2 g | Sodium 298 mg | Carbs 19.4 g

200. Cheesy Baked Zucchini

(Prep time: 15 minutes | Cook time: 35 minutes | Serving: 2)

Ingredients

- Garlic powder: 1/8 tsp.
- 1 zucchini, ~6 inches
- Low-fat parmesan cheese: 2 tbsp., grated
- Olive oil: 1 tsp.

- Onion powder: 1/8 tsp.

Instructions

1. Let the oven preheat to 375 F.
2. Cut the ends off zucchini. Cut the zucchini in half-inch, but do not cut all the way through.
3. Place it on a foil-lined baking sheet. Pour olive oil and sprinkle with onion and garlic powder. Wrap in foil and bake for 30-35 minutes.
4. Unwarp, Sprinkle cheese on top. Bake for 1-2 minutes.
5. Serve.

Nutrition for half: Calories 64 | Fat 11 g | Sugar 2 g | Protein 3 g | Sodium 85 mg | Carbs 4 g

201. Eggplant Crostini

(Prep time: 15 minutes | Cook time: 35 minutes | Serving: 8)

Ingredients

- Olive oil: ¼ cup
- 1 minced garlic clove
- Arugula: 1 cup
- Multigrain baguette: 16 slices
- Low-fat Greek yogurt: ¼ cup
- Red, yellow, green & orange cherry tomatoes: 1 cup, quartered
- 1 eggplant: 1 pound
- Lemon juice: 2 ½ tbsp.
- Low-fat Parmigiano-Reggiano cheese: 1 oz., shaved
- Black pepper: half tsp.
- Fresh mint: 2 tbsp., chopped

Instructions

1. Let the grill preheat to medium-high.
2. Cut eggplant in one" thick slice, and brush with olive oil on both sides.
3. Oil spray the grates and grill eggplant on both sides until tender.
4. Toast the bread also for 1 minute on 1 side.
5. In a bowl, add mint, arugula, tomato, oil (1 tbsp.), juice (1 ½ tbsp.) toss to coat
6. In a food processor, add eggplant, juice (1 tbsp.), a pinch of salt, the rest of the ingredients except for

cheese. Pulse until smooth.

7. Spread the mixture on each bread slice and top with salad, cheese. Serve.

Nutrition: Calories 175 | Fat 5.3 g | Sugar 1 g | Protein 6.2 g | Sodium 298 mg | Carbs 17.7 g

202. Baked Apples with Cherries & Almonds

(Prep time: 15 minutes | Cook time: 60 minutes | Serving: 6)

Ingredients

- Dried cherries: 1/3 cup, chopped
- 6 golden apples, ~ 1 3/4 pounds
- Chopped almonds: 3 tbsp.
- Apple juice: half cup
- Brown sugar: 1 tbsp., packed
- Cinnamon: half tsp.
- Wheat germ: 1 tbsp.
- Ground nutmeg: 1/8 tsp.
- Canola oil: 2 tsp.
- 1/4 cup of water
- Dark honey: 2 tbsp.

Instructions

1. Let the oven preheat to 350 F.
2. In a bowl, add all ingredients except for apples, honey, oil and apple juice; mix well.
3. Core each apple and stop ¾" inch from the bottom.
4. Stuff the apples with the mixture and place them on a baking dish.
5. Pour the rest of the ingredients on top, bake for 50-60 minutes, covered with foil.
6. Serve with juice.

Nutrition for 1 apple: Calories 200 | Fat 4 g | Sugar 31 g | Protein 2 g | Sodium 55 mg | Carbs 39 g

203. Grape Leaves Stuffed

(Prep time: 15 minutes | Cook time: 60 minutes | Serving: 8)

Ingredients

- Long-grain rice: half cup
- Green onions: half cup, chopped

- Flat-leaf parsley: 2 tbsp., chopped
- Pine nuts: 2 tbsp.
- Onion: 1 cup, chopped
- 24 large grape leaves
- Non-fat yogurt: half cup
- 1 cup of water
- Dried currants: 2 tbsp.
- Black pepper & salt: ¼ tsp., each
- Fresh mint: 1 ½ tbsp., chopped
- Fresh dill: 1 ½ tbsp., chopped
- Cinnamon: 1/8 tsp.

Instructions

1. Wash the grape leaves and pat dry.
2. In a skillet, oil spray and place on medium flame.
3. Sauté onion for 7 minutes. Add nuts, rice, scallions and cook for 4 minutes.
4. Add water and rest of the ingredients, simmer for 15 minutes, covered.
5. Serve the rice in grape leaves. Fold and serve.

Nutrition: Calories 88 | Fat 17.2 g | Sugar 8 g | Protein 2.7 g |Sodium 475 mg | Carbs 16.5 g

204. Asparagus with Hazelnut Gremolata

(Prep time: 15 minutes | Cook time: 5 minutes | Serving: 4)
Ingredients

- Lemon zest: ¼ tsp.
- 1 minced garlic clove
- Fresh flat-leaf parsley: 1 tbsp., chopped
- Asparagus: 1 pound, trimmed
- Lemon juice: 2 tsp.
- Olive oil: 1 tsp.
- Toasted hazelnuts: 1 tbsp., chopped
- Salt, a pinch

Instructions

1. Steam the asparagus for 4 minutes.
2. In a bowl, add the rest of the ingredients, add asparagus. Toss to coat.
3. Serve.

Nutrition: Calories 50 | Fat 2 g | Sugar 8 g | Protein 3 g |Sodium 148 mg | Carbs 5 g

205. Picnic Cole Slaw

(Prep time: 15 minutes | Cook time: 0 minutes | Serving: 8)
Ingredients

- Carrot strips: 1 cup
- 1 bell pepper, chopped
- Sugar: 3 tbsp.
- Apple cider vinegar: ¼ cup
- Chopped onion: half cup
- Packaged coleslaw: 8 oz.
- Pepper: ¼ tsp.
- 6 radishes, halved & sliced
- Salt, a pinch

Instructions

1. In a bowl, add all ingredients. Toss and keep in the fridge covered for 15 minutes.

Nutrition: Calories 34 | Fat 0 g | Sugar 6 g | Protein 1 g |Sodium 121 mg | Carbs 8 g

206. Avocado Jicama Appetizer

(Prep time: 15 minutes | Cook time: 0 minutes | Serving: 8)
Ingredients

- Top of Form
- 1 avocado, grated
- Pumpkin seeds: 1 tbsp., unsalted
- Mango: 1/3 cup, diced
- 1 to 2 lime's zest
- 12 jicamas, sliced thin
- Green onions: 1 tbsp., chopped
- Chili Verde: 1 tbsp., low-sodium

Instructions

2. Cut a 2" round in every slice of jicama with a cookie cutter.
3. In a bowl, add the rest of the ingredients, add on top of jicama slices.
4. Serve.

Nutrition: Calories 224 | Fat 7 g | Sugar 3 g | Protein 16 g |Sodium 88 mg | Carbs 13 g

207. Corn Pudding

(Prep time: 15 minutes | Cook time: 30 minutes | Serving: 8)

Ingredients

- Ginger, clove & nutmeg: 1/8 tsp. Each
- 3 cups of skim milk
- Cinnamon: ¼ tsp.
- 2 cups of coarse cornmeal
- 3 cups of water
- 1/4 cup of maple syrup
- Raisins: half cup

Instructions

1. In a pan, add milk and water and boil.
2. Add cornmeal, keep stirring. Let it come to a boil, turn the heat low and cook for 10-15 minutes, stirring occasionally.
3. Turn the heat off, add the rest of the ingredients, mix and let it rest for 10-15 minutes.
4. Serve.

Nutrition for 1 cup: Calories 213| Fat 1 g | Sugar 7 g | Protein 6 g |Sodium 44 mg | Carbs 45 g

208. Lentil Ragout

(Prep time: 15 minutes | Cook time: 20 minutes | Serving: 6)

Ingredients

- Olive oil: 1 tsp.
- Chopped onions: 1 cup
- Black pepper: ¼ tsp.
- Fresh thyme: 1 tbsp., chopped
- 6 tomatoes, diced
- Red lentils: 1 cup
- 4 minced garlic cloves
- 5 cups of water
- Kosher salt: ¼ tsp.

Instructions

1. In a pan, add oil and sauté onions for three minutes on medium flame.
2. Add tomatoes and cook for 3 minutes.

3. Add lentils, water and cook for 20 minutes. Add the rest of the ingredients.
4. It will be thick, not dry. Serve.

Nutrition for the half cup: Calories 512 | Fat 1 g | Sugar 5 g | Protein 10 g |Sodium 145 mg | Carbs 27 g

209. Artichokes with Roasted Garlic Dip

(Prep time: 15 minutes | Cook time: 2 hours & 10 minutes| Serving: 4)

Ingredients

- 4 artichokes: ~ 3 1/2 pounds
- Unsalted plant butter: 1 tbsp.
- Dry white wine: half cup
- 2 garlic heads, whole
- Vegetable broth: 1 cup
- Kosher salt, a pinch

Instructions

1. Let the oven preheat to 400 F.
2. Trim the garlic head but do not separate or peel.
3. Wrap every garlic head in foil, bake for 45 minutes, let it cool for ten minutes.
4. Squeeze the garlic out and peel.
5. Take the stems off artichokes and cut half" from the top.
6. In a Dutch oven, add the artichokes and water (2/3). Let it come to a boil.
7. Turn the heat low and simmer for 45 minutes.
8. In a pan, add wine, garlic pulp (half) and let it come to a boil for 2 minutes.
9. Add broth and cook for 8 minutes.
10. Turn the heat off, add salt and butter. Pulse with a stick blender.
11. Serve with artichokes.

Nutrition: Calories 135 | Fat 3.1 g | Sugar 2 g | Protein 5.2 g |Sodium 389 mg | Carbs 19.8 g

210. Creamed Swiss Chard

(Prep time: 15 minutes | Cook time: 15 minutes | Serving: 8)

Ingredients

- All-purpose flour: 1 ½ tbsp.
- 3 minced garlic cloves
- Black pepper: half tsp.
- Olive oil: 2 tbsp.
- Low-fat soy milk: 1 ¼ cups
- Swiss chard: 2 pounds, sliced into half' strips with stems
- Parmesan cheese: 1 tbsp., grated

Instructions

1. In a pan, add oil on medium flame. Add flour while keep whisking and make a paste.
2. Add garlic, cook for 30 seconds.
3. Slowly add milk; while whisking, cook until it thickens.
4. Add chard and coat well. Cook, covered for 2 minutes.
5. Add pepper and cheese, serve.

Nutrition: Calories 80 | Fat 4 g | Sugar 2 g | Protein 3 g | Sodium 265 mg | Carbs 8 g

211. Twice-Baked Potatoes

(Prep time: 15 minutes | Cook time: 55 minutes | Serving: 12)

Ingredients

- Olive oil: 1 tsp.
- Black pepper: half tsp.
- Fat-free milk: 2 tbsp.
- Red potatoes: 2 pounds
- Smoked salmon: 2 tbsp., chopped
- Unsalted plant butter: 1 tbsp.
- White cheddar cheese: 2 oz., grated

Instructions

1. Let the oven preheat to 400 F.
2. Toss potatoes with oil and a pinch of salt.
3. Spread on an oil sprayed baking sheet, bake for 35 minutes. Cool for ten minutes.
4. Slice the potatoes in half, and slice a little bit from the bottom so they will stand.
5. Take some of the pulp out, leave a shell.

6. In a bowl, add the pulp and the rest of the ingredients except for salmon, mix and spoon onto potato shells.
7. Add salmon on top. Bake for 15 minutes at 400 F.

Nutrition: Calories 96 | Fat 2.9 g | Sugar 2 g | Protein 3.5 g | Sodium 159 mg | Carbs 13.6 g

212. Chinese-Style Asparagus

(Prep time: 15 minutes | Cook time: 10 minutes | Serving: 6)

Ingredients

- Fresh asparagus: 1 1/2 pounds
- Soy sauce: 1 tsp., low-sodium
- Water: half cup
- Sugar: half tsp.

Instructions

1. In a pan, add all ingredients except for asparagus. Boil and add asparagus.
2. Simmer for 3-4 minutes.
3. Serve.

Nutrition: Calories 24 | Fat 1 g | Sugar 0 g | Protein 2 g | Sodium 26 mg | Carbs 4 g

213. Deviled Eggs with Smoked Salmon

(Prep time: 10 minutes | Cook time: 15 minutes | Serving: 19)

Ingredients

- Fresh dill: 2 tsp., chopped
- Sour cream: ¼ cup, non-fat
- Dijon mustard: 1 tbsp.
- Fresh chives: 1 tbsp., chopped
- 8 eggs
- Smoked salmon: 2 oz.
- Mayonnaise: 2 tbsp., low-fat
- Fresh tarragon: 2 tsp., chopped
- Black pepper: ¼ tsp.

Instructions

1. Boil eggs for 15 minutes, drain and rinse.
2. Slice in half, and take yolks out in a bowl.

3. Add the rest of the ingredients with yolks. Mix and spoon in the egg white.

4. Serve.

Nutrition: Calories 95 | Fat 5.8 g | Sugar 0 g | Protein 8.1 g |Sodium 295 mg | Carbs 2.6 g

214. Minted Sugar Snap Peas

(Prep time: 10 minutes | Cook time: 10 minutes | Serving: 6)

Ingredients
- 1 carrot, cut into strips
- Garlic powder: ¼ tsp.
- Sugar snap peas: 8 oz.
- Pepper: 1/8 tsp.
- Olive oil: 1 tsp.
- Chopped fresh mint: 1 tbsp.
- Salt, a pinch

Instructions
1. In a skillet, add oil on medium heat.

2. Sauté carrots for 1-2 minutes. Add snap peas and sauté for 30 seconds.

3. Add the rest of the ingredients and cook for 10-15 seconds.

4. Serve.

Nutrition: Calories 40| Fat 1.5 g | Sugar 3 g | Protein 2 g |Sodium 157 mg | Carbs 6 g

215. Coconut Shrimp

(Prep time: 15 minutes | Cook time: 15 minutes | Serving: 6)

Ingredients
- Sweetened coconut: ¼ cup
- 12 large shrimp, peeled & deveined
- Kosher salt: ¼ tsp.
- Coconut milk: half cup
- Panko breadcrumbs: ¼ cup

Instructions
1. Let the oven preheat to 375 F. Oil spray a baking sheet.

2. In a food processor, add panko, salt and coconut and pulse until even. Take it out in a bowl.

3. In a different bowl, add coconut milk. Coat shrimps in milk then in panko mix.

4. Place on a baking tray. Oil spray the shrimps. Bake for 10-15 minutes.

Nutrition for 2 shrimps: Calories 75 | Fat 4 g | Sugar 2 g | Protein 5 g |Sodium 278 mg | Carbs 4 g

216. Spicy Root Vegetable Wedges

(Prep time: 10 minutes | Cook time: 50 minutes | Serving: 6)

Ingredients
- 2 carrots
- Olive oil: 2 tbsp.
- Cinnamon: half tsp.
- 1 lime's juice
- 2 parsnips
- Black pepper
- Coriander seeds: 2 tbsp., crushed
- Peeled sweet potatoes: 1 ½ pound

Instructions
1. Let the oven preheat to 400 F.

2. Slice the carrots in half, and cut each half in quarters. Cut the parsnips in quarters also

3. In a pan, add parsnips, carrots and enough water to cover.

4. Let it come to a boil, turn the heat low and simmer for few minutes.

5. In a roasting tray, add pepper, lime juice, cinnamon and olive oil.

6. Slice the potatoes in quarters, roll in spice mixture and place on one side on the tray.

7. Add the drained vegetables and toss to coat. Place on a roasting tray.

8. Bake for 40 minutes. Cool and serve.

Nutrition: Calories 287 | Fat 12 g | Sugar 3 g | Protein 18 g |Sodium 143 mg | Carbs 13 g

217. Herb Scallops with Balsamic Cream

(Prep time: 4 hours & 10 minutes | Cook time: 10 minutes | Serving: 6)

Ingredients

- Olive oil: ¼ cup
- Fresh mint: 2 tbsp., chopped
- Balsamic vinegar cream: 1 tbsp., low-fat
- Fresh flat-leaf parsley: 2 tbsp., chopped
- 1 minced garlic clove
- 8 sea scallops: ~ 1 lb.
- Lemon zest: 1 tsp.
- Balsamic cream: half cup, low-fat
- Parmesan cheese: 1 tbsp., low-fat
- Baby arugula: 2 cups

Instructions

1. Pat dry the scallops, place them in a plastic bag.
2. In a bowl, add the rest of the ingredients except for arugula, whisk and pour over oysters.
3. Toss to coat, keep in the fridge for 2-4 hours. Flipping bag once or twice.
4. Drain and thread onto skewers.
5. Grill over medium-high flame for 6-8 minutes. Serve with arugula.

Nutrition: Calories 258 | Fat 12 g | Sugar 2 g | Protein 16.4 g | Sodium 143 mg | Carbs 11 g

218. Chickpea Polenta with Olives

(Prep time: 1 hour & 20 minutes | Cook time: 15 minutes | Serving: 8)

Ingredients

- Polenta
- Soy milk: 2 cups
- Chopped fresh thyme: 1 tbsp.
- Olive oil: half tbsp.
- Chickpea flour: 1 ¾ cups
- 3 chopped garlic cloves
- Dry mustard: 1 tsp.
- Chicken stock: 1 cup, low-sodium

- 3 egg whites
- Black pepper: ¼ tsp.
- Topping
- Chopped olives, onion, sun-dried tomatoes & fresh herbs.

Instructions

1. In a food processor, add milk, pepper, broth, thyme, mustard, garlic, oil and flour.
2. Pulse until smooth. Transfer to a bowl and let it rest for 1 hour in the fridge.
3. Let the oven preheat to 425 F. oil spray a baking pan (9 by 13")
4. In a bowl, beat the egg whites to stiff peaks, and fold in the batter.
5. Pour in the pan, bake for 15 minutes, cool for 15 minutes.
6. In a pan, add some oil and sauté the toppings. Pour over polenta and broil until light brown. Slice in wedges and serve.

Nutrition for 2 wedges: Calories 157 | Fat 5 g | Sugar 4 g | Protein 8 g | Sodium 160 mg | Carbs 20 g

219. Broccoli-Cheddar Quinoa Bites

(Prep time: 15 minutes | Cook time: 35 minutes | Serving: 8)

Ingredients

- Quinoa: half cup
- Baking powder: half tsp.
- Chopped broccoli: ¾ cup
- Ground pepper: 1/4 tsp.
- Cheddar cheese: ¾ cup, shredded, low-fat
- Garlic powder: half tsp.
- Salt: 1/8 tsp.
- Onion powder: ¼ tsp.
- 1 egg, whisked

Instructions

1. Let the oven preheat to 350 F.
2. Place mini muffin cups (16) in the muffin tin.

3. As per the pack's instructions, cook quinoa with salt.

4. Add the rest of the ingredients in quinoa and stir.

5. Pour in the muffin cups and press down. Oil spray the muffin tops.

6. Bake for 22-25 minutes. Cool for 20 minutes, serve.

Nutrition for 2 muffins: Calories 87 | Fat 4.2 g | Sugar 0.4 g | Protein 4.6 g | Sodium 198 mg | Carbs 7.8 g

220. Grilled Fruit Kebabs with Balsamic Drizzle

(Prep time: 15 minutes | Cook time: 15 minutes | Serving: 8)

Ingredients

- 2 bananas, into large chunks
- Strawberries: 1 pound without stems
- Watermelon chunks: 2 cups
- Canola oil: 1 tbsp.
- Pineapple chunks: 2 cups
- Balsamic vinegar: 2 tbsp.
- Honey: 2 tsp.

Instructions

1. Let the grill preheat to medium-high heat.

2. Onto 8 skewers, thread the fruits alternatively.

3. In a bowl, whisk the rest of the ingredients. Brush over fruit skewers with only half the mixture.

4. Grill for 8-0 minutes, flipping often. Keep basting with the rest of the mixture.

5. Serve.

Nutrition: Calories 199 | Fat 4.1 g | Sugar 29.9 g | Protein 2.4 g | Sodium 5.2 mg | Carbs 43.1 g

221. Indian-Spiced Roasted Nuts

(Prep time: 15 minutes | Cook time: 20 minutes | Serving: 8)

Ingredients

- Honey: 1 ½ tsp.
- Salt: 1/8 tsp.
- Canola oil: 1 tsp.
- Brown sugar: 1 ½ tsp.

- Ground cloves: 1/8 tsp.
- Blanched almonds: ¼ cup
- Cinnamon: 3/4 tsp.
- Ground cardamom: 1/8 tsp.
- Hazelnuts: ¼ cup
- Black pepper, a pinch
- Cashews: ¼ cup

Instructions

1. Let the oven preheat to 350 F.

2. In a bowl, add all ingredients except for nuts. Mix and microwave for 30 seconds.

3. Mix well.

4. Add nuts, toss to coat. Line a baking sheet with parchment paper.

5. Spread on the baking sheet and bake for 15 minutes.

6. Cool and serve.

Nutrition: Calories 60 | Fat 5 g | Sugar 8 g | Protein 1.5 g | Sodium 44 mg | Carbs 3.4 g

222. Fresh Shrimp Spring Rolls

(Prep time: 35 minutes | Cook time: 0 minutes | Serving: 12)

Ingredients

- 12 lettuce leaves
- Shredded carrots: 1 cup
- Half cucumber, sliced thin
- 12 basil leaves
- Rice paper: 12 sheets
- Cooked shrimp: 1 ¼ pounds, de-veined & peeled
- Fresh cilantro: ¾ cup

Instructions

1. Rinse rice paper in warm water till just wet and place on a plate.

2. In each rice paper, add 1 of each basil & lettuce leaf. Add the rest of the vegetables and shrimp.

3. Roll tightly and serve.

Nutrition: Calories 250 | Fat 17.2 g | Sugar 8 g | Protein 6.4 g | Sodium 165 mg | Carbs 19 g

223. Seared Endive

(Prep time: 15 minutes | Cook time: 10 minutes | Serving: 4)

Ingredients

Black pepper, a pinch

Washed Belgian endive: 8 heads, halved

Water: 1 tbsp.

1 lemon's juice

Salt: 1/8 tsp.

Instructions

1. In a pan, add water on medium flame.

2. Add trimmed endive cook until the outer leaves turn translucent.

3. Turn the heat off and add lemon juice and the rest of the ingredients. Serve.

Nutrition for 2 heads: Calories 24 | Fat 0 g | Sugar 1 g | Protein 6.4 g | Sodium 143 mg | Carbs 5 g

4. Broil again till cheese melts.

5. Serve.

Nutrition: Calories 213 | Fat 9 g | Sugar 9 g | Protein 12 g | Sodium 89 mg | Carbs 11 g

224. Zucchini Pizza Bites

(Prep time: 10 minutes | Cook time: 10 Minutes | Serving: 1)

Ingredients

- Shredded mozzarella cheese: 2 tbsp., low-fat
- large zucchini: 4 slices of ¼" thick
- Black pepper, to taste
- Pizza sauce: 4 tbsp., low-sodium

Instructions

1. Preheat the broiler to high.

2. Oil spray the zucchini on all sides and season with black pepper.

3. Broil for 4 minutes' total, then add pizza sauce and cheese on top.

DASH Diet Vegan & Meatless Recipes

225. Vegetarian Black Bean Pasta

(Prep time: 15 minutes | Cook time: 20 minutes | Serving: 6)

Ingredients

- Portobello baby mushrooms: 1 3/4 cups, sliced
- Olive oil: 1 tbsp.
- 1 can of (15 oz.) Diced tomatoes with juices
- 1 minced garlic clove
- Whole wheat fettuccine: 9 oz.
- Baby spinach: 2 cups
- Dried rosemary: 1 tsp.
- 1 can of (15 oz.) Black beans, rinsed
- Dried oregano: half tsp.

Instructions

1. Cook pasta as per the pack's instructions.
2. Heat oil in a skillet on medium flame, sauté mushrooms, cook for 4 to 6 minutes.
3. Add garlic and cook for 1 minute.
4. Add the rest of the ingredients, toss well and serve.

Nutrition for 1 ¼ cups: Calories 255 | Fat 3 g | Sugar 4 g | Protein 12 g | Sodium 230 mg | Carbs 45 g

226. Roasted Root Vegetables with Cheese Polenta

(Prep time: 15 minutes | Cook time: 40 minutes | Serving: 4)

Ingredients

- **Polenta**
- Black pepper: ¼ tsp.
- Polenta: half cup
- Chicken broth: 2 cups, low-sodium
- Goat cheese: ¼ cup
- Olive oil: 1 tbsp.
- **Vegetables**
- 1 minced garlic clove
- Pesto: 2 tsp.
- Roasted root vegetables: 2 cups
- Olive oil: 1 tbsp.
- Fresh sage: 1 tbsp.

Instructions

1. Let the oven preheat to 425 F with racks in the upper and lower third.
2. To roast the vegetables, toss with herbs, oil, salt and pepper. Spread on the baking sheets, lined with parchment paper.
3. Roast for 30-40 minutes.
4. In a pan, add broth and boil. Turn the heat to low, add slowly, add polenta, whisk well.
5. Cook, covered for ten minutes. Cook, stirring for ten minutes.
6. Add oil, cheese and pepper. In a skillet, add oil, sauté garlic for 1 minute.
7. Add roasted vegetables, cook for 2-4 minutes. Add sage and cook for 1 minute.
8. Serve the polenta with vegetables, with pesto on top.

Nutrition: Calories 442 | Fat 7.2 g | Sugar 7.7 g | Protein 9.1 g | Sodium 432 mg | Carbs

227. Eggplant Parmesan

(Prep time: 15 minutes | Cook time: 1 hour & 40 minutes | Serving: 6)

Ingredients

- 2 eggs
- Water: 2 tbsp.
- 1 cup of whole-wheat panko breadcrumbs
- Fresh basil: ¼ cup, torn
- Parmesan cheese: ¼ cup
- 2 eggplants: 2 pounds total, sliced into ¼" thick slices
- Mozzarella cheese: 1cup, low-fat
- 2 minced garlic cloves
- Black pepper: half tsp.
- 1 jar of (24 oz.) Tomato sauce, unsalted
- Italian seasoning: 1 tsp.
- Red pepper flakes: half tsp.

Instructions

1. Let the oven preheat to 400 F.
2. Oil spray a 9 by 13 baking dish.
3. In a bowl, whisk water and egg.
4. In a dish, add parmesan, Italian seasoning and bread crumbs.
5. Coat eggplant in whisked egg, then in bread crumbs, press to adhere.
6. Place the breaded eggplant on the baking sheet. Oil spray the eggplant on both sides.
7. Bake for half an hour, switch racks after flipping the eggplant in the upper and third rack.
8. Sprinkle pepper.
9. In a bowl, add tomato sauce, red pepper, garlic and basil. Mix.
10. In the baking dish, add half a cup of the sauce, place the eggplant slices, add one cup of sauce on top, sprinkle parmesan on top.
11. Bake for 20-30 minutes, cool for 5 minutes. Serve.

Nutrition: Calories 241 | Fat 9 g | Sugar 9 g | Protein 14 g | Sodium 487 mg | Carbs 28 g

228. Spinach Soufflés

(Prep time: 15 minutes | Cook time: 1 hour & 20 minutes | Serving: 4)

Ingredients

- 4 egg whites
- Dried parsley: 1 tsp.
- Cream of tartar: ¼ tsp.
- Whole-wheat bread crumbs: 1 tbsp. + 1 ½ tsp.
- Minced garlic: 1 tsp.
- Milk: 2/3 cup, non-fat
- Parmesan cheese: 2 oz.
- Baby spinach: 6 oz.
- All-purpose flour: 2 tbsp.
- Black pepper: 1/8 tsp.
- 2 egg yolks

Instructions

1. Let the oven preheat to 425 F.
2. Oil spray 4 ramekins of six oz. and sprinkle with crumbs on all sides.
3. In a bowl, add egg and tartar, whisk well.
4. Oil spray a pan and sauté garlic and spinach for 3-4 minutes. Turn the heat off and add parsley.
5. In a pan, add flour, milk and black pepper, whisk well and let it come to a boil, simmer for 4-5 minutes, keep whisking. Turn the heat off and let it cool.
6. Whisk the egg white to medium peaks.
7. In the milk mixture, add spinach mixture, add yolks, parmesan and mix.
8. Fold in egg whites in batches. Pour in the prepared ramekins, tap to get the excess air out and place on a baking tray.
9. Bake for 5 minutes, change the temperature to 350 F, Bake for 20 minutes. Serve.

Nutrition: Calories 144 | Fat 6.0 g | Sugar 3 g | Protein 14 g | Sodium 354 mg | Carbs 9 g

229. Lentil Medley

(Prep time: 20 minutes | Cook time: 25 minutes | Serving: 8)

Ingredients

- 2 cups of water
- 1 red onion, diced

- 2 cups of mushrooms, sliced
- Lentils: 1 cup
- 1 zucchini, cubed
- Soft sun-dried tomato: half cup (not in oil)
- Fresh mint: ¼ cup
- Olive oil: 3 tbsp.
- 1 cucumber, cubed
- Dried oregano: 1 tsp.
- Honey: 2 tsp.
- Rice vinegar: half cup
- Baby spinach: 4 cups, chopped
- Dried basil: 1 tsp.
- Feta cheese: 1 cup

Instructions
1. Cook lentils in water after rinsing for 20 to 25 minutes, drain and rinse with cold water.
2. Transfer to a bowl, add the rest of the ingredients, toss and serve.

Nutrition for 1 ¼ cup: Calories 225 | Fat 8 g | Sugar 11 g | Protein 6.4 g | Sodium 400 mg | Carbs 29 g

230. Huevos Rancheros

(Prep time: 15 minutes | Cook time: 25 minutes | Serving: 4)
Ingredients
- Diced onion: half cup
- Canned crushed tomatoes: 15 oz., fire-roasted
- Water: 2 tbsp.
- Diced poblano pepper: half cup, without seeds
- Canola oil: 1 tsp.
- 1 jalapeño pepper, fresh
- Minced garlic: 1 ½ tsp.

For Huevos
1 avocado, cut in fours

canola oil: 1 tsp.

4 corn tortillas (6")

4 eggs

1 can of (15 oz.) black beans, rinsed

Mexican blend cheese: ¼ cup, shredded & low-fat

Instructions
1. In a pan, add oil on medium flame, sauté onion for 2 minutes.

2. Add peppers and cook for 2 minutes. Add garlic and cook for 1 minute.
3. Add water, salt and tomatoes, let it come to a boil, turn the heat low and simmer for 5 minutes. Turn the heat off, and keep warm.
4. In a skillet, add oil and cook egg for 3-4 minutes.
5. In each tortilla, add eggs and beans, tomato salsa, and the rest of the ingredients.
6. Roll and serve.

Nutrition: Calories 334 | Fat 13.5 g | Sugar 9 g | Protein 17 g | Sodium 265 mg | Carbs 37 g

231. Zucchini Black Bean Tacos

(Prep time: 20 minutes | Cook time: 0 minutes | Serving: 4)
Ingredients
- Salsa, as needed
- For tacos
- Chili powder: half tsp.
- 8 corn tortillas
- Chipotle powder: half tsp.
- 1 can of (15 oz.) Black beans, rinsed
- Paprika: ¼ tsp.
- Garlic powder: ¼ tsp.
- 1 zucchini, grated

Avocado Crema (blend all ingredients)
Greek yogurt: half cup, low-fat

1 avocado

1 lime's juice

Instructions
1. In a bowl, add all ingredients of tacos, except for tortillas.
2. Warm the tortillas in the oven.
3. Add the taco mix, salsa and avocado crema on top.
4. Serve.

Nutrition: Calories 245 | Fat 10 g | Sugar 5 g | Protein 6.4 g | Sodium 321 mg | Carbs 35 g

232. Zucchini with Corn

(Prep time: 20 minutes | Cook time: 20 minutes | Serving: 6)
Ingredients
- Olive oil: 1 tbsp.

- Diced onion: 1/4 cup
- 3 zucchinis, cut into ¼" thick slices
- Fresh corn kernels: 4 cups
- Black pepper: ¼ tsp.
- 1 minced garlic clove
- 1 fresh jalapeño, chopped without seeds
- Crumbled cotija cheese: 1/4 cup
- Salt: 1/8 tsp.

Instructions

Boil the corn in water, cook on low for ten minutes, cover, then drain.

Sauté garlic and onion in hot oil for 5 minutes, add zucchini.

Cook for 5 minutes. Add jalapenos, pepper, corn and pepper, cook for ten minutes.

Turn the heat off, serve with cheese on top.

Nutrition: Calories 202 | Fat 5 g | Sugar 8 g | Protein 7 g |Sodium 164 mg | Carbs 40 g

233. Zucchini Pad Thai

(Prep time: 20 minutes | Cook time: 20 minutes | Serving: 6)

Ingredients

- Sauce
- Chicken stock: ¼ cup, low-sodium
- Sriracha: half tbsp.
- Coconut sugar: 1 ½ tbsp.
- Tamari: 1 ½ tbsp., low-sodium
- Tamarind paste: ¼ cup
- Half lime's juice
- **Noodles**
- 2 large peeled carrots, spiralized
- 4 zucchinis, spiralized
- **Pad Thai**
- 2 eggs, whisked
- Chopped peanuts: ¼ cup
- Mushrooms: 2 cups, sliced
- 3 cups of bean sprouts
- Pepper
- Sliced scallions: 2 tbsp.
- Olive oil: 2 tsp.

Instructions

1. In a bowl, add all ingredients of the sauce, mix and

set it aside.

2. In a skillet, add oil (half) and cooks with a sprinkle of pepper. Take them out in a bowl.

3. Add the rest of the oil to the pan, cook mushrooms until wilted, take them out in a bowl.

4. In the pan, add sauce, cook for few minutes, add carrots, zucchini cook for 5 minutes,

5. Add mushrooms, eggs and sprouts; toss to coat.

6. Serve with peanuts and scallions on top.

Nutrition: Calories 320 | Fat 11 g | Sugar 17 g | Protein 34 g |Sodium 401 mg | Carbs 31g

234. Couscous with Beans & Vegetables

(Prep time: 20 minutes | Cook time: 20 minutes | Serving: 6)

Ingredients

- 1 diced onion
- 1 red bell pepper, cut into thin strips
- 1 carrot, sliced
- Olive oil: 2 tsp.
- Vegetable broth: 1 cup, low-fat
- 1 zucchini, cut into half-moons
- 1 celery rib, sliced
- 1 tomato, diced
- Minced garlic: 1 tsp.
- 2 cans of (16 oz.) Red kidney beans, rinsed
- 1 sweet potato, small, cubed
- Dried thyme: 1 tsp.
- Salt: 1/8 tsp.
- Ground cumin: 1 tsp.
- Minced parsley: ¼ cup
- Paprika: half tsp.
- Cayenne: 1/8 tsp.
- Whole-wheat couscous: 1 cup

Instructions

1. In a skillet, add oil on medium heat. Sauté all vegetables for 5 minutes, add garlic and cook for 30 seconds.

2. Add the rest of the ingredients, except for couscous, let it come to a boil on high heat,

turn the heat low and simmer for 12-15 minutes.

3. Cook couscous as per pack's instruction.

4. Serve the vegetables with fluffed couscous.

Nutrition: Calories 330 | Fat 2.5 g | Sugar 8 g | Protein 16 g |Sodium 241 mg | Carbs 65 g

235. Roasted Kabocha with Wild Rice

(Prep time: 20 minutes | Cook time: 2 hours | Serving: 4)

Ingredients

Olive oil: ¼ cup

Chili powder: 1 tsp.

Black pepper

Wild rice: half cup

Kabocha squash: 3 pounds

Pumpkin seeds: half cup

Pomegranate seeds: half cup

Fresh parsley: ¼ cup, chopped

Lime juice: 1 tbsp.

Honey: 1 tsp.

Lime zest: 1 tsp.

Instructions

1. Let the oven preheat to 375 F.

2. With a fork, pierce the squash all over and place it on a baking sheet lined with foil.

3. Roast for 80 minutes.

4. Cut the squash into 5-6 pieces lengthwise. Take the middle part out.

5. Season the squash with oil (1 tbsp.) and sprinkle with pepper; place on a baking sheet flesh side up.

6. Broil the squash for 5-7 minutes.

7. In a skillet, add pumpkin seeds and oil (1 tbsp.). Cook for 3 minutes. Add chili powder and honey, cook for 30 seconds. Take them out on a plate and cool.

8. In a pan, add water (1 ½ cups), and let it boil. Add rice and let it come to a boil, turn the heat low, cover and simmer for 20-25 minutes, drain.

9. Add rice, pumpkin seeds, zest, juice, parsley, oil (2 tbsp.), and toss well in a bowl.

10. Serve with broiled squash on top.

Nutrition: Calories 250 | Fat 17.2 g | Sugar 8 g | Protein 6.4 g |Sodium 155 mg | Carbs

236. Chickpea Quinoa Bowl

(Prep time: 20 minutes | Cook time: 0 minutes | Serving: 4)

Ingredients

- ¼ Cup of slivered almonds

- Olive oil: 4 tbsp.

- 2 cups of cooked quinoa

- 1 minced garlic clove

- 1 jar of (7 oz.) Roasted red peppers, washed

- Paprika: 1 tsp.

- Fresh parsley: 2 tbsp., chopped

- Ground cumin: half tsp.

- Kalamata olives: ¼ cup, chopped

- Chopped cucumber: 1 cup

- Chopped red onion: ¼ cup

- 1 can of (15 oz.) Chickpeas, rinsed

- Feta cheese: ¼ cup, crumbled

Instructions

1. In a food processor, add garlic, cumin, almonds, oil (2 tbsp.), peppers and paprika. Pulse until smooth.

2. In a bowl, toss quinoa with oil (2 tbsp.), onion, and olives.

3. In serving bowls, add quinoa with cucumber, chickpeas and pepper sauce.

4. Serve with parsley and feta on top.

Nutrition for 1 ½ cups: Calories 479 | Fat 24 g | Sugar 8 g | Protein 12.4 g |Sodium 476 mg | Carbs 48 g

237. Acorn Squash & Coconut Creamed Greens Casserole

(Prep time: 20 minutes | Cook time: 2 hours | Serving: 4)

Ingredients

- 1 can of (15 oz.) coconut milk
- Half jalapeno, minced without seeds
- Grapeseed oil: 2 tbsp.
- Cornstarch: 1 tbsp.
- Chopped ginger: 2 tbsp.
- 4 minced garlic cloves
- Black pepper
- Lime juice: 1 tbsp.
- 2 plum tomatoes, diced
- 1 sweet onion, chopped
- Light agave syrup: 1 tsp.
- Tuscan kale: 10 cups, packed, chopped
- Ground cumin: 2 tsp.
- Acorn squash: 1 1/4 pounds, sliced into 1/8" of thickness
- Swiss chard: 7 packed cups, chopped

Instructions

1. Let the oven preheat to 425 F. mix coconut milk with the cornstarch.
2. In a skillet, add oil on medium heat. Sauté onion for 4 minutes.
3. Add garlic, ginger, jalapenos and cook for 2 minutes; add black pepper.
4. To the onion mixture, add tomato and cook for 2 minutes, add cumin and cook for 1 minute.
5. Add kale and chard, cook until wilted and liquid evaporates.
6. Add agave syrup and coconut milk. Let it simmer and cook for 3 minutes.
7. Add lime juice.
8. Into a baking dish (8 by 10"), add the creamed greens, add squash on top.
9. Bake for 25-30 minutes. Serve.

Nutrition: Calories 248 | Fat 17.2 g | Sugar 8 g | Protein 11 g |Sodium 164 mg | Carbs 33 g

238. Gnocchi Pomodoro

(Prep time: 20 minutes | Cook time: 35 minutes | Serving: 4)

Ingredients

- 1 onion, chopped
- Butter: 1 tbsp.
- 2 minced garlic cloves
- Olive oil: 3 tbsp.
- 1 pack of frozen cauliflower gnocchi: 12 oz.
- Canned whole tomatoes: 1 ½ cups, chopped
- Chopped fresh basil: ¼ cup
- Red pepper flakes: ¼ tsp.

Instructions

1. In a skillet, add oil (2 tbsp.) on medium heat. Sauté onion and cook for 5 minutes.
2. Add pepper flakes, garlic and sauté for 1 minute.
3. Add tomatoes and let it simmer for 20 minutes, turn the heat off, add basil and butter.
4. In a skillet, add oil (1 tbsp.) on medium flame. Add gnocchi and cook for 5-7 minutes, transfer to the tomato sauce and toss to coat. Serve.

Nutrition for ¾ cup: Calories 448 | Fat 14.2 g | Sugar 8 g | Protein 10 g |Sodium 306 mg | Carbs 65 g

239. Portobello Mushrooms Florentine

(Prep time: 20 minutes | Cook time: 12 minutes | Serving: 4)

Ingredients

- Garlic salt & pepper: 1/8 tsp., each
- 2 eggs
- Olive oil: half tsp.
- 2 Portobello mushrooms, without stems
- 1 onion, chopped
- Goat cheese: 1/4 cup crumbled
- Baby spinach: 1 cup

Instructions

1. Let the oven preheat to 425 F.
2. Oil spray the mushrooms and place in a 15 by 10 by 1" pan, round side down.
3. Add pepper and garlic salt, bake for ten minutes.

4. In a skillet, add oil on medium heat. Sauté onion till tender; add spinach until it wilts.

5. Add whisked eggs, cook until all liquid is gone.

6. Stuff the mushrooms, add cheese on top. Serve

Nutrition for 1 mushroom: Calories 126 | Fat 5 g | Sugar 4 g | Protein 11 g | Sodium 401 mg | Carbs 10 g

240. Brown Rice Bowl

(Prep time: 20 minutes | Cook time: 20 minutes | Serving: 4)

Ingredients
- Pico de Gallo, as needed
- **Rice**
- 1 shallot, diced
- Fresh cilantro: 2 cups, chopped
- Olive oil: half cup
- Brown rice: 2 cups
- 1 clove garlic
- Red wine vinegar: 2 tbsp.
- Red pepper flakes: half tsp.

Instructions
1. In a blender, add all ingredients except for rice and pulse until smooth.

2. As per the pack's instructions, cook the brown rice, omitting salt.

3. Serve the rice with cilantro vinaigrette, beans, mixed fresh vegetables on top.

Nutrition: Calories 148 | Fat 3 g | Sugar 3 g | Protein 16 g | Sodium 115 mg | Carbs 15 g

241. Warm Spiced Cabbage Bake

(Prep time: 20 minutes | Cook time: 60 minutes | Serving: 4)

Ingredients
- Raisins: 2 tbsp., chopped
- Black pepper
- Fresh dill: half cup, chopped
- Toasted pine nuts: 1/3 cup, chopped
- Olive oil: 5 tbsp.
- Savoy cabbage: 1 1/2 pounds, 6 wedges
- 1 sweet onion, chopped
- 4 sliced garlic cloves

- 1 can of (~15 oz.) Whole tomatoes, peeled & crushed
- Allspice, a pinch
- Sweet paprika: 1 tsp.
- Sour cream: half cup, low-fat
- Ground cinnamon: ¼ tsp.
- Red pepper flakes: ¼ tsp.

Instructions
1. Let the oven preheat to 400 F.

2. In a bowl, mix dill, nuts and raisins.

3. In a skillet, add 2 tbsp. of oil on medium-high flame. Cook cabbage wedges for 5-6 minutes on both sides, take it out on a plate and sprinkle black pepper.

4. Add the rest of the oil in the pan, sauté garlic and onion on low flame for 4 minutes.

5. Add spices, cook for 1 minute.

6. Add water (1 cup) and tomatoes, add the nut mixture (half). Let it simmer with a pinch of salt.

7. Add the cabbage wedges to the skillet and transfer the skillet to the oven.

8. Bake for half an hour.

9. Serve with the rest of the nut mixture and sour cream on top.

Nutrition: Calories 131 | Fat 3 g | Sugar 3 g | Protein 21 g | Sodium 145 mg | Carbs 6 g

242. Polenta Squares with Cheese & Pine Nuts

(Prep time: 20 minutes + Cooling | Cook time: 40 minutes | Serving: 30)

Ingredients
- Quick-cooking polenta: 1 cup
- Crumbled gorgonzola cheese: 1/3 cup, low-fat
- Unsalted butter: 1 tbsp.
- ¼ cup of boiling water

- 4 cups of water
- ⅔ cup of balsamic vinegar
- Toasted pine nuts: 3 tbsp.
- Flat-leaf fresh parsley: 2 tbsp., chopped
- Grated zest: 1 tsp.
- Currants: 3 tbsp.

Instructions

1. In a pan, add water (4 cups) and boil; slowly add polenta while whisking.
2. Whisk on low flame for 4 minutes till it thickens.
3. Add butter and pour in an oil sprayed baking pan (square-9").
4. Cover with plastic wrap on top; it should touch the polenta surface, keep in the fridge for 60 minutes. Slice in 30 squares.
5. In a bowl, add currants and boiling water (1/4 cup). Let it rest for ten minutes, then drain.
6. In a bowl, add currants, zest, pine nuts, and cheese.
7. In a pan, add vinegar, cook on medium heat for ten minutes, until reduced by 2 tbsp. Let it cool.
8. In a skillet, add oil on medium heat. Add polenta squares and cook for 6 minutes on one side.
9. Serve with cheese mixture and drizzle of vinegar.

Nutrition: Calories 130 | Fat 1.1 g | Sugar 8 g | Protein 3.1 g | Sodium 201 mg | Carbs 18 g

243. Curried Cauliflower with Chickpeas

(Prep time: 20 minutes | Cook time: 75 minutes | Serving: 4)
Ingredients

- Dried chickpeas: 3/4 cup, rinsed
- Minced ginger: 2 tbsp.
- Canola oil: 2 tsp.
- 1 onion, chopped
- 3 cups of water

- 1 cauliflower, medium head, broken into florets
- 1 diced red bell pepper
- 3 minced garlic cloves
- Curry powder: 2 tbsp.
- Salt: 1/8 tsp.
- Vegetable broth: 1 1/2 cups, low-sodium

Instructions

1. Cook chickpeas in a pressure cooker with water for 45 minutes on high pressure.
2. Let the pressure release naturally for 15 minutes, drain.
3. Sauté onion for 3 minutes in hot oil, add bell pepper, cook for 3 minutes.
4. Add garlic and ginger, cook for 30 seconds.
5. In the pressure cooker, add cauliflower, salt, broth and curry powder. Add chickpeas with sautéed vegetables, cook for 3 minutes on high pressure. Release the pressure. Serve.

Nutrition: Calories 224 | Fat 5.5 g | Sugar 10 g | Protein 11 g | Sodium 201 mg | Carbs 37 g

244. Turkish Red Lentil Soup

(Prep time: 20 minutes | Cook time: 1 hour & 45 minutes | Serving: 4)
Ingredients

- 3 Garlic cloves
- 5 medium Carrots
- 1 Onion, large
- 2 Celery sticks
- Dried Oregano: 1 tbsp.
- Tomato paste: 5 tbsp.
- Red Lentils: 17 oz.
- Olive Oil & Black Pepper, as needed
- Chicken stock, as needed, low-sodium

- Dried Mint: 1 tbsp.

Instructions

1. In a food processor, add vegetables, process until crumbly.
2. Transfer to a pan with some olive oil. sauté for few minutes until tender.
3. Add tomato paste, black pepper. Cook for few minutes.
4. In a large pan, add lentils and enough stock to cover the vegetables, add herbs.
5. Simmer for 90 minutes. Serve with the vegetable mixture on top.

Nutrition: Calories 251 | Fat 9 g | Sugar 10 g | Protein 19 g | Sodium 55 mg | Carbs 28 g

245. Lentil Fritters with Red Cabbage Slaw

(Prep time: 20 minutes | Cook time: 10 minutes | Serving: 4)

Ingredients

- Fresh cilantro leaves: half cup
- 1 minced garlic clove
- Lemon juice: 2 tbsp.
- 2 cans of (15 oz.) Lentils, rinsed
- Ground cumin: half tsp.
- Bread crumbs: half cup
- Fresh parsley leaves: half cup
- Greek yogurt: half cup, low-fat
- Black pepper
- Red pepper flakes: ¼ tsp.
- 4 pitas, pocket less
- Red cabbage, shredded: 1½ cups
- Olive oil: 3 tbsp.

Instructions

1. Add garlic, cilantro, lentils (1 can), parsley, cumin in a food processor, pulse until smooth. Take it

out in a bowl, add breadcrumbs, black pepper, a pinch of salt, rest of the lentils; mix and make it into half' thick patties.

2. In a bowl, toss the cabbage with oil (1 tbsp.), lemon juice, black pepper.
3. In a bowl, add yogurt, water (1/4 cup), red pepper flakes. Whisk well.
4. In a skillet, add oil on medium flame. Cook patties for 3-4 minutes on 1 side.
5. Serve the patties with yogurt sauce, cabbage mixture.

Nutrition: Calories 181 | Fat 11.5 g | Sugar 3 g | Protein 12 g | Sodium 109 mg | Carbs 11 g

246. Baked Feta with Olive Tapenade & Romesco

(Prep time: 20 minutes | Cook time: 35 minutes | Serving: 12)

Ingredients
Romesco

- Peeled plum tomato: 2 cups, chopped
- Chopped hazelnuts: 2 tbsp., toasted
- 1 slice of white bread, chopped
- 5 minced garlic cloves
- 1 red bell pepper
- Black pepper: ¼ tsp.
- Chicken broth: half cup, low-sodium
- Tapenade
- Fruity olives: half cup, pitted
- Sherry vinegar: 2 tbsp.
- Black pepper: ¼ tsp.
- Flat-leaf parsley: ¼ cup, chopped
- Kalamata olives: half cup, pitted
- Olive oil: 1 tbsp.

Instructions

1. Let the broiler preheat to high.

2. Slice the bell peppers in half and take the seeds out. Place on the foil-lined baking sheet, cut side down.

3. Broil for 7-8 minutes until charred. Transfer to a plastic bag, close and let it rest for ten minutes, peel and slice.

4. Let the oven preheat to 425 F.

5. In a skillet, add oil on medium flame. Add garlic and tomato, cook for 4 minutes.

6. Add broth and bell pepper, cook for ten minutes, covered. Add bread, nuts and cook for 60 seconds.

7. Puree with a stick blender, season with black pepper.

8. In a food processor, add olives and the rest of the ingredients, pulse until chopped.

9. Oil spray a baking dish (1 ½ qt.) spread the romesco sauce with cheese (3/4 cup).

10. Add tapender on top, layer them again. Bake for 20 minutes, serve.

Nutrition: Calories 88| Fat 6.1 g | Sugar 2 g | Protein 3.6 g |Sodium 208 mg | Carbs 4.9 g

247. White Bean & Quinoa Burgers

(Prep time: 20 minutes | Cook time: 35 minutes| Serving: 5)
Ingredients
- Chili powder: 1 tsp.
- 1 can of cannellini beans, rinsed
- Garlic powder: 1 tsp.
- 1 avocado
- 1 egg
- Smoked paprika: 1 tsp.
- Ground cumin: half tsp.
- Mayonnaise: ¼ cup, low-fat
- Black pepper: 1/8 tsp.

- 10 lettuce leaves
- Cooked quinoa: 1 cup
- Sriracha sauce: 1 ½ tsp.

Instructions
1. Let the oven preheat to 375 F.
2. In a bowl, add beans and mash well; add half of the avocado and mash.
3. Add spices and mix well.
4. Add quinoa, chopped avocado to the bean mixture.
5. Make into 5 patties, bake for half an hour.
6. Serve in whole-wheat buns with fresh sliced vegetables, sriracha and mayo

Nutrition: Calories 343| Fat 11.5 g | Sugar 9 g | Protein 12 g |Sodium 378 mg | Carbs 52 g

248. Roasted Root Vegetables

(Prep time: 20 minutes | Cook time: 45 minutes| Serving: 4)
Ingredients
- 1 parsnip: 1/4 pound
- 2 red onions: half pound
- Mixed new potatoes: 1 pound
- Olive oil: 1 tbsp.
- Ground cumin: half tsp.
- 1 turnip: 1/4 pound
- Fresh thyme: 2 tsp., chopped
- Smoked paprika: ¼ tsp.
- Ground coriander: half tsp.

Instructions
1. Let the oven preheat to 400 F.
2. Slice the potatoes, turnips and parsnips into ¾ to 1" pieces.
3. Cut the onion into half" segments. Transfer all the vegetables to a bowl. Toss with oil, paprika, cumin, thyme and coriander.

4. Spread on a baking sheet, roast for 40 minutes. Serve.

Nutrition: Calories 163 | Fat 4 g | Sugar 2 g | Protein 3 g |Sodium 444 mg | Carbs 30 g

Veggie-Stuffed Quesadillas

(Prep time: 20 minutes | Cook time: 10 minutes| Serving: 10)

Ingredients

- 1 red onion, cut into strips
- Chili powder: half tsp.
- Olive oil: 2 tsp.
- 2 sweet peppers, sliced into thin strips
- 5 flour tortillas (6-7")
- Cream cheese: 1/3 cup, low-fat
- Ground cumin: half tsp.
- Fresh parsley: 2 tbsp., chopped

Instructions

In a pan, sauté onion and sweet peppers in hot oil for 3-5 minutes.

Add chili powder and cumin. Cook for 1 minute. Add parsley.

On each tortilla, spread the cream cheese, add pepper mixture.

Fold and serve.

Nutrition: Calories 226| Fat 17.2 g | Sugar 6 g | Protein 28 g |Sodium 235 mg | Carbs 15 g

249. Veggie Burger

(Prep time: 20 minutes | Cook time: 35 minutes| Serving: 6-8)

Ingredients

- Portobello mushrooms: 2 cups, chopped
- Chopped carrots: half cup
- White miso: 1 tsp.
- Chopped peeled zucchini: half cup,
- Fresh basil: 2 tbsp., chopped
- Chopped red onions: half cup
- Fresh parsley: 2 tbsp., chopped
- 2 minced garlic cloves
- Cooked brown rice: 1 cup
- Whole wheat bread crumbs: 1 cup
- Sunflower seeds: half cup, ground

Instructions

1. Let the oven preheat to 300 F.
2. In a pan, add water (1/8 cup), sauté all vegetables for ten minutes.
3. Add miso and stir. In a food processor, add all the ingredients with sautéed vegetables. Pulse until smooth.
4. Make the mixture into patties and bake for ten minutes on each side. Serve.

Nutrition: Calories 215 | Fat 12 g | Sugar 7.8 g | Protein 21 g |Sodium 152 mg | Carbs 17 g

250. Vegan Coconut Chickpea Curry

(Prep time: 20 minutes | Cook time: 15 minutes| Serving: 4)

Ingredients

- Chopped onion: 1 cup
- 1 can of (15 oz.) Chickpeas, rinsed
- Diced bell pepper: 1 cup
- Canola oil: 2 tsp.
- 1 zucchini, half-moons
- Baby spinach: 4 cups
- Coconut curry sauce: 1 ½ cups, no-salt-added
- Brown rice: 2 cups, cooked
- Vegetable broth: half cup

Instructions

1. In a skillet, heat oil on medium flame.
2. Sauté vegetables for 5-6 minutes. Add sauce, broth, chickpeas, simmer on low flame, cook for 4-6 minutes.

3. Add spinach, cook, until it wilts. Serve.

Nutrition: Calories 471| Fat 17.2 g | Sugar 12 g | Protein 10.4 g |Sodium 405 mg | Carbs 65 g

251. Spicy Pumpkin Burritos

(Prep time: 20 minutes | Cook time: 10 minutes| Serving: 4)
Ingredients
- Frozen corn kernels: half cup
- Cooked brown rice: 1 cup
- Canned black beans: ~15 oz. Rinsed
- 1 tsp. Of olive oil
- Canned packed pumpkin: 15 oz.
- 1 tsp. Of ground cumin
- Cayenne pepper: ¼ tsp.
- 1 tsp. Of chili powder
- 1/4 cup of water
- Sour cream: half cup, non-fat
- 8 whole-grain tortillas: 8-inches
- Chopped tomato: half cup
- Sliced green onions: half cup
- Shredded lettuce: half cup
- Dried oregano: half tsp.

Instructions
1. In a pan, add oil on medium flame.
2. Sauté corn for 4-5 minutes.
3. Add the rest of the ingredients, except for tortillas. Simmer for 4-5 minutes.
4. In each tortilla, add filling, roll and serve.

Nutrition: Calories 259 | Fat 3 g | Sugar 9 g | Protein 10 g |Sodium 366 mg | Carbs 49 g

252. Carbonara with Spinach & Mushrooms

(Prep time: 20 minutes | Cook time: 30 minutes| Serving: 5)
Ingredients
- 3 eggs, whisked
- Olive oil: 1 tbsp.
- Parmesan cheese: 1 cup
- Peeled sweet potatoes: 2 pounds
- Baby spinach: 5 oz.
- Black pepper: ¼ tsp.
- 2 minced garlic cloves
- Center-cut bacon: 3 strips, chopped
- Sliced mushrooms: 8 oz.

Instructions
1. In a pot, boil water.
2. Spiralizerd sweet potatoes, add to the boiling water and cook for 2-3 minutes.
3. Drain all but ¼ cup of water.
4. In the water, add eggs, parmesan and pepper with noodles, toss to coat.
5. In a skillet, add oil on medium heat. Cook mushrooms, bacon for 6-8 minutes.
6. Add garlic, sauté for 1 minute, add spinach, cook for 1-2 minutes until wilted.
7. Transfer to the noodle pan, toss and serve.

Nutrition: Calories 312 | Fat 17.2 g | Sugar 8 g | Protein 14 g |Sodium 387 mg | Carbs 37 g

253. Chickpea Curry

(Prep time: 20 minutes | Cook time: 10 minutes| Serving: 6)
Ingredients
- 4 garlic cloves
- Fresh ginger: two", chopped
- Ground coriander: 2 tsp.
- 1 sweet onion, chopped
- Ground turmeric: half tsp.
- Canned diced tomatoes: 2 ¼ cups, undrained
- 1 serrano pepper, sliced lengthwise
- Canola oil: 6 tbsp.
- 2 cans of (15 oz.) Chickpeas, rinsed

- Ground cumin: 2 tsp.

- Garam masala: 2 tsp.

Instructions

1. In a food processor, add garlic, serrano and ginger, pulse until smooth, and onion and pulse until chopped.

2. In a pan, heat oil on medium flame. sauté onion mixture and cook for 3-5 minutes, add spices and cook for 2 minutes.

3. In a food processor, add tomatoes until chopped. Transfer to the pan, simmer for 4 minutes.

4. Add chickpeas and simmer for 5 minutes, serve with fresh herbs on top.

Nutrition for 1 cup: Calories 278 | Fat 15 g | Sugar 3.1 g | Protein 5.8 g | Sodium 325 mg | Carbs 30 g

254. Whole Wheat Veggie Pizza

(Prep time: 60 minutes | Cook time: 25 minutes | Serving: 4)

Ingredients

- 2 packs of (1/4 oz.) yeast, quick-rise

- Garlic powder: 1 tsp.

- Olive oil: 2 tbsp.

- Whole wheat flour: half cup

- All-purpose flour: 2 ½ cups

- 1 cup of water

- **Sauce**
- Pizza sauce, low sodium & no-sugar-added: as needed

- **Toppings**
- Fresh sliced vegetables & shredded skim mozzarella

Instructions

1. In a bowl, add all ingredients of dough except for oil, all purpose (1 ½ cups) and water.

2. Add water and oil to a pan and heat up to 120 to 130 F.

3. Add the dry to wet ingredients and beat for three minutes on medium speed.

4. Add the rest of the flour as needed to make a soft dough.

5. Knead the dough for five minutes. oil spray a bowl, place the dough inside, lightly oil spray the top of the dough. Let it rest for half an hour, in a warm place, covered.

6. Let the oven preheat to 400 F.

7. Cut the dough in half and roll, place in oil sprayed pizza pans (12") and pierce with a fork all over, bake for 8-10 minutes.

8. Take the crust out, add sauce and toppings, bake for 12 to 15 minutes till the cheese melts.

9. Serve.

Nutrition: Calories 190 | Fat 6 g | Sugar 3 g | Protein 7 g | Sodium 201 mg | Carbs 28 g

255. Spaghetti-Squash Spaghetti

(Prep time: 15 minutes | Cook time: 1 hour & 25 minutes | Serving: 4)

Ingredients

- Olive oil: 1 tsp.

- Spaghetti squash: 3 pounds

- Half onion, diced

- Tomatoes: 1 cup, diced

- Red pepper flakes: 1/8 tsp.

- Canned tomato sauce: 16 oz., salt-free

- Minced garlic: 1 tsp.

- Black pepper: 1/4 tsp.

- Salt-free mixed dried herbs: 1/4 tsp.

- Dried basil: 1 tsp.

- Small mozzarella balls: half cup, sliced

Instructions

1. Let the oven preheat to 350 F.

2. Slice the squash in half and place on an oil sprayed baking sheet.

3. Bake for 60 minutes.

4. In a skillet, add oil on medium heat.

5. Sauté onion, garlic for 5 to 7 minutes. add rest of the ingredients except for tomato sauce and cheese, cook for 2 to 3 minutes.

6. Add sauce, stir and cook on low for 10 minutes.

7. With a fork, scrape the tender squash into noodles, serve with sauce and cheese.

Nutrition for 6 rolls: Calories 265 | Fat 12 g | Sugar 6.5 g | Protein 21.1 g | Sodium 445 mg | Carbs 16 g

256. Sweet Corn & White Bean Succotash

(Prep time: 15 minutes | Cook time: 10 minutes | Serving: 4)

Ingredients

- Diced onion: ¼ cup
- Olive oil: 2 tbsp.
- Black pepper: ¼ tsp.
- 1 cup of corn
- Sugar snap peas: half cup
- Halved cherry tomatoes: half cup
- Canned white beans: ¾ cup
- Nondairy butter: 1 tsp.

Instructions

1. In a skillet, add oil on medium heat. Sauté onion and corn for 5 minutes.

2. Add rest of the ingredients, except for butter and tomatoes, cook on high flame for 1 minute.

3. Add butter and tomatoes, toss well. Serve with fresh herbs on top.

Nutrition: Calories 315 | Fat 17.2 g | Sugar 7.9 g | Protein 21 g | Sodium 145 mg | Carbs 16 g

257. Orecchiette with Broccoli Rabe

(Prep time: 15 minutes | Cook time: 25 minutes | Serving: 6)

Ingredients

- Red pepper flakes: half tsp.
- Broccoli rabe: 2 pounds
- Whole wheat orecchiette pasta: 3 1/2 cups
- Olive oil: ¼ cup
- Cherry tomatoes: 2 cups, halved
- 3 chopped garlic cloves
- Mushrooms chopped: 1 ½ cups

Instructions

1. As per the pack's instructions, cook the pasta. Drain all but half cup of water.

2. Wash and Slice the rabe into 2" pieces.

3. In a skillet, add oil on medium heat. Sauté mushrooms, garlic and red pepper till they are browned.

4. Add rabe and cook for 6-10 minutes. add tomatoes and cook for two minutes.

5. Add pasta and coat well, with some of the pasta water. Serve.

Nutrition for 1 ½ cups: Calories 359 | Fat 12 g | Sugar 2.6 g | Protein 15 g | Sodium 212 mg | Carbs 48 g

258. Cabbage Roll Skillet

(Prep time: 15 minutes | Cook time: 25 minutes | Serving: 6)

Ingredients

- Lean ground beef: 1 pound
- Pepper: half tsp.
- 1 large onion, diced
- Canned whole plum tomatoes: 28 oz., with juices
- Cooked brown rice: 4 cups
- Canned tomato sauce: 8 oz., salt-free
- Sliced cabbage: 6 cups
- Brown sugar: 1 tbsp.

- Dried oregano: 1 tsp.
- Cider vinegar: 2 tbsp.
- Dried thyme: 1 tsp.
- 1 green pepper, thin strips

Instructions
1. Chop the tomatoes.
2. In a skillet, cook onion and beef for 6 to 8 minutes, on medium flame, until it is cooked.
3. Add rest of the ingredients, except for cabbage and rice. Mix well.
4. Add cabbage and cook for 6 minutes, covered. Stir, cook uncovered for 6 to 8 minutes.
5. Serve with rice.

Nutrition: Calories 332 | Fat 5 g | Sugar 12 g | Protein 22 g |Sodium 431 mg | Carbs 50 g

259. General Tso Cauliflower

(Prep time: 15 minutes | Cook time: 35 minutes| Serving: 6)
Ingredients
- All-purpose flour: 1 cup
- Milk: 1 cup
- Vegetable oil: 1 tbsp.
- Sweet chili sauce: ¾ cup
- Panko bread crumbs: 1 cup
- 1 cauliflower: large head, broken into florets
- 2 minced garlic cloves
- Ground ginger: 1 tsp.
- 1 lime's juice
- Black pepper
- Low-sodium soy sauce: 1/3 cup

Instructions
1. Let the oven preheat to 400 F. Coat the cauliflower in flour, then in milk and lastly in crumbs.
2. Place on a baking sheet lined with parchment paper, sprinkle with a pinch of salt and pepper.
3. Bake for 20-30 minutes.

4. In a pan, add oil on medium heat. Sauté garlic, ginger, cook for 2 minutes
5. Add the rest of the ingredients, cook for 5 minutes. add baked cauliflower, toss and serve.

Nutrition: Calories 315 | Fat 17.2 g | Sugar 7.8 g | Protein 22.2 g |Sodium 245 mg | Carbs 16 g

260. Spaghetti Pesto Sauce & Zucchini

(Prep time: 15 minutes | Cook time: 25 minutes| Serving: 6)
Ingredients
- Whole-wheat spaghetti: 12 oz.
- Almonds: 2 tbsp.
- Fresh basil: 2 cups, tightly packed
- Olive oil: 1 ½ tbsp.
- Zucchini chopped: 8 cups
- 1 minced garlic clove
- Salt & pepper: 1/8 tsp., each
- Chicken broth: 2 tbsp., low-sodium
- Shredded parmesan cheese: 1 ½ tbsp.

Instructions
1. Oil spray a pan and cook zucchini for 10-12 minutes on medium flame.
2. Cook the pasta as per pack's instructions, drain all but ¼ cup of water.
3. Add the rest of the ingredients with only 2 cups of zucchini, pulse until smooth.
4. In a bowl, add pasta, some pasta water, pesto. Toss and serve with rest of the zucchini.

Nutrition: Calories 211 | Fat 7.1 g | Sugar 3 g | Protein 14 g |Sodium 106 mg | Carbs 15 g

261. Yellow Lentils with Spinach & Ginger

(Prep time: 15 minutes | Cook time: 25 minutes| Serving: 6)
Ingredients
- Shallot chopped: 2 tbsp.

- Chicken stock: 1 ½ cups, low-sodium
- Olive oil: 1 tbsp.
- Curry powder: half tsp.
- Ground turmeric: half tsp.
- Baby spinach leaves: 2 cups, chopped
- Ground ginger: 1 tsp.
- Yellow lentils: 1 cup, rinsed
- Light coconut milk: half cup

Instructions

1. In a pan, add oil on medium heat. Sauté ginger, turmeric, shallot, and curry powder, cook for 1 minute.
2. Add stock, milk and lentils. Let it come to a boil, turn the heat low and simmer for 12 minutes. If it is too dry, add some water.
3. Add spinach and stir, cook for 3 minutes. serve with cilantro and toasted sesame seeds on top.

Nutrition for ¾ cup: Calories 263 | Fat 7 g | Sugar 4 g | Protein 14 g | Sodium 301 mg | Carbs 36 g

262. Black Bean Cakes

(Prep time: 75 minutes | Cook time: 1 hour & 15 minutes | Serving: 8)

Ingredients

- Olive oil: 2 tbsp.
- 4 cups of water
- Salt: 1/8 tsp.
- 8 minced garlic cloves
- Dried black beans: 2 cups, soaked overnight
- Fresh cilantro: half cup, chopped

Instructions

1. In a pan, add water and beans, let it boil.
2. Turn the heat low and simmer for 60-70 minutes, partially covered. Drain.
3. In a bowl, add garlic and beans, mash them. Add

salt and cilantro, mix and make into 8 cakes. Keep in the fridge for 1 hour.

4. Cook the cakes hot oil for 5 minutes, until crispy on both sides.

Nutrition for 1 cake: Calories 196 | Fat 4 g | Sugar 0 g | Protein 10 g | Sodium 113 mg | Carbs 30 g

263. Cauliflower Fried Rice

(Prep time: 15 minutes | Cook time: 20 minutes | Serving: 6)

Ingredients

- Vegetable oil: 2 tbsp.
- Soy sauce: 2 tbsp., low-sodium
- 1 orange pepper, sliced thin strips
- Half head of cauliflower
- Two-inch piece of ginger, thin strips
- Chili garlic paste: 2 tsp.
- Sugar substitute: 2 tsp.
- Edamame: 1 cup
- 1 scallion, sliced
- 4 eggs
- Peas: 1 cup

Instructions

1. Break the cauliflower into florets, and pulse in a food processor for 15 seconds, to get a rice consistency. Do it in batches.
2. In a skillet, add oil on medium heat. Sauté ginger, scallion (white part only), pepper for 2 minutes. Add cauliflower rice and cook for 5 minutes.
3. In a bowl, add chili garlic paste, sugar and soy sauce.
4. In a different bowl, whisk the eggs.
5. Make room for eggs in the same skillet, by pushing them to a side. Add oil and eggs, cook for 2 minutes.
6. Turn the heat off, add the rest of the ingredients,

toss everything and serve.

Nutrition: Calories 109 | Fat 1.5 g | Sugar 3 g | Protein 2 g | Sodium 126 mg | Carbs 12 g

264. Grilled Eggplant & Tomato Pasta

(Prep time: 15 minutes | Cook time: 25 minutes | Serving: 4)
Ingredients

- Eggplant: 1 ½ pounds, half'' thick slices
- Olive oil: 4 tbsp.
- Fresh oregano: 2 tsp., chopped
- Salt: 1/8 tsp.
- 1 clove garlic, grated
- Fresh basil: half cup, chopped
- Plum tomatoes: 1 pound, chopped
- Black pepper: half tsp.
- Red pepper flakes: ¼ tsp.
- Whole-wheat penne: 8 oz.
- Crumbled feta cheese: ¼ cup

Instructions

1. Let the grill preheat to medium-high.
2. In a bowl, add tomatoes, red pepper, salt, pepper, garlic, oil (3 tbsp.), and oregano. Toss well.
3. Oil brush the eggplant slices and grill for four minutes on each side. Cool for ten minutes then chop and toss with tomatoes.
4. Cook pasta as per pack's instructions. Toss with tomato mixture and serve with cheese on top.

Nutrition for 2 cups: Calories 449 | Fat 19 g | Sugar 10 g | Protein 13 g | Sodium 221 mg | Carbs 62 g

265. Chipotle-Lime Cauliflower Taco Bowls

(Prep time: 15 minutes | Cook time: 20 minutes | Serving: 4)
Ingredients

- Chipotles chopped: 1 to 2 tbsp., in adobo sauce
- 1 cauliflower: small-head, broken into small florets
- Honey: 1 tbsp.
- Lime juice: ¼ cup
- 2 garlic cloves
- 1 avocado
- Cooked quinoa: 2 cups
- Shredded red cabbage: 1 cup
- Canned black beans: 1 cup, rinsed
- 1 red onion, sliced thin
- Queso fresco: half cup, crumbled

Instructions

1. Let the oven preheat to 450 F.
2. In a blender, add honey, lime juice, garlic and chipotles. Pulse until smooth.
3. Toss the cauliflower with chipotles sauce. Spread on a foil-lined baking sheet.
4. Add onion on top, roast for 18-20 minutes. flipping halfway through.
5. In each serving bowl, add quinoa, top with cauliflower, cheese, cabbage, avocado and beans. Serve.

Nutrition: Calories 345 | Fat 13 g | Sugar 8 g | Protein 13 g | Sodium 350 mg | Carbs 46 g

266. Ginger Veggie Pasta

(Prep time: 15 minutes | Cook time: 20 minutes | Serving: 8)
Ingredients

- Olive oil: 1 tbsp.
- Whole-wheat elbow pasta: 2 cups
- Garlic paste: 2 tsp.
- Brussels sprouts: 1 ½ cups, chopped
- Sliced red cabbage: half cup
- Ginger paste: 2 tsp.
- Half red onion, sliced
- Shredded carrots: half cup

- Mushrooms: 2 cups, sliced
- Sweet red pepper: half, chopped
- Ancho chili pepper: ¼ tsp.
- 2 scallions, chopped
- Black pepper: ¼ tsp.

Instructions

1. Cook pasta as per the pack's instructions.
2. In a skillet, add oil on medium heat. Sauté red onion, garlic, ginger for 2 minutes.
3. Add all vegetables cook for 4 to 6 minutes.
4. Drain all but 1 cup of water, add vegetable mixture, add little water.
5. Toss and serve.

Nutrition for 1 cup: Calories 270 | Fat 7 g | Sugar 2 g | Protein 21 g | Sodium 217 mg | Carbs 29 g

267. Crispy Tofu with Black Pepper Sauce

(Prep time: 15 minutes | Cook time: 12 minutes | Serving: 4)
Ingredients

- Chili garlic sauce: 2 tbsp.
- Brown sugar: 1 tbsp.
- Extra-firm tofu: 8 oz., drained
- Soy sauce: 2 tbsp., low-sodium
- Sugar snap peas: 2 cups, sliced
- Rice vinegar: 1 tbsp.
- 4 scallions, sliced & color-separated
- Cornstarch: 3 tbsp.
- Canola oil: 6 tbsp.
- Grated ginger: 2 tsp.
- Black pepper: 1 tsp.
- 3 minced garlic cloves

Instructions

1. Slice tofu in half" cubes and dry with paper towels, and toss with cornstarch.

2. In a skillet, add oil (4 tbsp.) on medium heat. Cook tofu for 5-7 minutes. Take it out on paper towels.
3. In a pan, add oil (1 tbsp.), sauté peas for 2-3 minutes, take it out on a plate.
4. Add the rest of the oil to the same pan, add pepper. Sauté for half a minute.
5. Add ginger, scallions, garlic, cook for 30 to 45 seconds.
6. Add the rest of the ingredients, cook until it thickens. Turn the heat off, add peas and tofu, toss and serve.

Nutrition for 1 cup: Calories 250 | Fat 24 g | Sugar 8 g | Protein 7 g | Sodium 381 mg | Carbs 20 g

268. Stuffed Eggplant

(Prep time: 15 minutes | Cook time: 30 minutes | Serving: 2)
Ingredients

- 1 cup of water
- Olive oil: 1 tbsp.
- Chopped mixed bell peppers: half cup
- Chopped celery: ¼ cup
- 1 eggplant, medium
- Canned tomatoes: 1 cup, with ¼ cup of juices
- Whole-wheat bread crumbs: ¾ cup
- Sliced mushrooms: 2 cup
- 1/4 cup of diced onion

Instructions

1. Let the oven preheat to 350 F.
2. Cut the eggplant in half lengthwise. Take the pulp out.
3. Place the eggplant shells on an oil sprayed baking tray, round side down.
4. Chop the pulp and set it aside.
5. In a skillet, add oil on medium heat. Add all vegetables and sauté for 8-10 minutes.

6. Add bread crumbs, season with black pepper.

7. Stuff the eggplant with this mixture.

8. Bake, covered with foil for 15 minutes. Serve.

Nutrition: Calories 334 | Fat 10 g | Sugar 16 g | Protein 26 g | Sodium 55 mg | Carbs 35 g

269. Pea & Spinach Carbonara

(Prep time: 15 minutes | Cook time: 12 minutes | Serving: 4)
Ingredients

- Whole-wheat panko breadcrumbs: half cup

- Fresh parsley: 3 tbsp., chopped

- Parmesan cheese: 8 tbsp., grated

- Olive oil: 1 ½ tbsp.

- 3 egg yolks

- 1 minced garlic clove

- 1 egg

- Salt & pepper: 1/8 tsp. Each

- 1 cup of peas

- Whole wheat linguine: 9 oz.

- 8 cups of baby spinach

Instructions

1. Cook pasta without salt and add peas, spinach in the last 2 minutes, drain all but ¼ cup of water.

2. In a skillet, add oil on medium heat. Sauté garlic, bread crumbs for 2 minutes. Take it out in a bowl and toss with parsley (2 tbsp.) and parmesan.

3. In a bowl, whisk egg, parmesan, salt, egg yolk and pepper.

4. Gradually add the pasta water to the egg mixture, add the egg mixture to pasta, toss and serve toasted breadcrumbs.

Nutrition for 1 cup: Calories 430 | Fat 14.5 g | Sugar 2.5 g | Protein 20 g | Sodium 387 mg | Carbs 54 g

270. Lemon-Pepper Linguine with Squash

(Prep time: 15 minutes | Cook time: 12 minutes | Serving: 8)
Ingredients

- Olive oil: 3 tbsp.

- Zucchinis: 1 pound, sliced lengthwise

- Unsalted butter: 2 tbsp.

- Manchego cheese: half cup, grated, low-fat

- Whole-wheat spaghetti: 1 pound

- Fresh herbs: 1 cup, chopped

- Lemon juice: 3 tbsp.

- Black peppercorns: 1 1/2 tbsp., roughly ground

- Yellow squash: 8 oz., sliced lengthwise

- Lemon zest: 2 tbsp.

Instructions

1. Cook pasta as per the pack's instructions. Drain all but ¾ cup of water.

2. In a skillet, add oil and butter on medium heat. Sauté pepper for 30 seconds.

3. Add squash, zucchinis, cook for 3-4 minutes. Transfer to the pasta bowl, add the rest of the ingredients with as much pasta water as needed. Toss and serve.

Nutrition for 1 1/3 cup: Calories 316 | Fat 11.9 g | Sugar 3.6 g | Protein 11.1 g | Sodium 201 mg | Carbs 46 g

271. Sweet Potato-Black Bean Burgers

(Prep time: 45 minutes | Cook time: 7 minutes | Serving: 4)
Ingredients

- Rolled oats: half cup

- Tomato paste: 1 tbsp., salt-free

- Canned black beans: 1 cup, rinsed

- Salt: 1/8 tsp.

- Grated sweet potato: 2 cups

- Vegan mayonnaise: ¼ cup
- Chopped scallions: half cup
- Lemon juice: 2 tbsp.
- Curry powder: 1 tsp., salt-free
- Low-fat yogurt: half cup
- Sliced cucumber: 1 cup
- Fresh dill: 2 tbsp., chopped
- Olive oil: 2 tbsp.

Instructions

1. In a bowl, whisk yogurt, lemon juice and dill.
2. In a food processor, add oats and pulse until ground.
3. With paper towels, squeeze the sweet potato and transfer it to a bowl. Add ground oats.
4. Add the rest of the ingredients, except for cucumbers. Mix and make into half" thick cakes. Keep in the fridge for half an hour.
5. In a skillet, add oil on medium heat. Cook patties for 3 minutes on each side.
6. Serve in buns with cucumber and yogurt sauce.

Nutrition for 1 burger: Calories 454 | Fat 22.2 g | Sugar 8.8 g | Protein 11 g |Sodium 387 mg | Carbs 54 g

272. Sweet Roasted Beet & Arugula Pizza

(Prep time: 15 minutes | Cook time: 10 minutes| Serving: 2)

Ingredients

- 1 whole-wheat crust (8"), low-sodium
- Toppings
- 1 cup of arugula
- Goat cheese: half cup, crumbled
- 2 small beets, roasted
- Honey: 2 tbsp.
- Balsamic vinegar: 2 tbsp.
- 1 cup of blackberries

- Instructions
- Roll the crust and top with toppings except for arugula.
- Bake at 350 F for 8-10 minutes.
- Top with arugula and serve.

Nutrition: Calories 284 | Fat 11 g | Sugar 3 g | Protein 12 g |Sodium 187 mg | Carbs 32 g

273. Chickpea & Potato Curry

(Prep time: 15 minutes | Cook time: 20 minutes| Serving: 4)

Ingredients

- Canola oil: 3 tbsp.
- Curry powder: 2 tsp.
- 1 onion, chopped
- Peeled gold potatoes: 1 pound, 1-inch pieces
- 3 minced garlic cloves
- Garam masala: half tsp.
- Cayenne pepper: ¼ tsp.
- ¾ cup of water
- Salt: 1/8 tsp.
- 1 can of (15 oz.) chickpeas, rinsed
- 1 can of (14 oz.) diced tomatoes, salt-free
- 1 cup of frozen peas

Instructions

Steam the potatoes for 6-8 minutes.

In a pot, add oil on medium heat. Sauté onion and cook for 3-5 minutes.

Add garlic and spices, except for garam masala and cook for 1 minute.

Add tomatoes and juice, cook for 2 minutes. Puree with a stick blender with a half cup of water.

Add the rest of the water in sauce, add peas, potatoes, chickpeas and garam masala. Cook for 15 minutes.

Nutrition for 1 ¼ cups: Calories 321 | Fat 11.6 g | Sugar 6.6 g | Protein 8.9 g |Sodium 343 mg | Carbs 46 g

274. Summer Skillet Vegetable & Egg Scramble

(Prep time: 15 minutes | Cook time: 20 minutes | Serving: 4)

Ingredients

Baby potatoes: 12 oz., sliced

Chopped fresh herbs: 1 tsp.

Sliced mixed vegetables: 4 cups

Leafy greens: 2 cups

Olive oil: 2 tbsp.

3 scallions, sliced & color-separated

6 eggs, whisked

Instructions

In a skillet, add oil on medium heat.

Sauté potatoes for 8 minutes. Add scallions (whites), vegetables, cook for 8-10 minutes. Add herbs and push the vegetables to one side of the pan.

Turn the heat to low, add green scallions and eggs and cook for 2 minutes.

Add leafy greens, mix everything and serve.

Nutrition for 1 ½ cups: Calories 254 | Fat 17.2 g | Sugar 4.5 g | Protein 12 g | Sodium 302 mg | Carbs 19 g

275. Southwestern Vegan Bowl

(Prep time: 15 minutes | Cook time: 20 minutes | Serving: 6)

Ingredients

Chopped red onion: 1 cup

- 1 chili pepper, minced
- Canola oil: 2 tsp.
- Sweet potato: 1 cup, chopped
- Tomato: 1 cup, chopped
- Ground cumin: ¾ tsp.
- 2 minced garlic cloves
- Green bell pepper: 2 cups, chopped
- Green & red lentils: half cup, each
- Black pepper: ¾ tsp.

- Canned black beans: 1 cup, rinsed
- 2 cups of vegetable stock, low-sodium
- Red wine vinegar: 1 tbsp.
- 1 cup of brown rice
- 4 wedges of lime
- 2 cups of water
- Chopped kale: 4 cups
- Fresh cilantro: 2 tbsp., chopped

Instructions

1. In a pan, heat oil on medium flame.
2. Sauté garlic, tomato, potato, onion and peppers for 10-15 minutes.
3. Add water, spices, rice, stock and lentil. Let it come to a boil, turn the heat low and simmer for 45 minutes.
4. Toss with cilantro, beans and kale, serve with lime.

Nutrition for 2 cups: Calories 376 | Fat 4 g | Sugar 0 g | Protein 18 g | Sodium 67 mg | Carbs 68 g

276. Curried Quinoa & Chickpeas

(Prep time: 15 minutes | Cook time: 20 minutes | Serving: 4)

Ingredients

- Orange juice: half cup
- 1 red bell pepper, julienned
- 1 can of (15 oz.) Chickpeas, rinsed
- 1 1/2 cups of water
- 1 red onion, chopped
- 2 tomatoes, chopped without seeds
- Fresh cilantro: half cup, chopped
- 1 cup of quinoa
- Raisins: half cup
- Curry powder: 1 tsp.

Instructions

1. In a pan, add liquids, let it come to a boil.
2. Add tomatoes, curry, and the rest of the ingredients. Let it come to a boil, turn the heat low and simmer for 15 to 20 minutes.
3. Turn the heat off and fluff. Serve.

Nutrition for 1 ½ cups: Calories 355 | Fat 5 g | Sugar 20 g | Protein 12 g |Sodium 155 mg | Carbs 70 g

277. Stuffed Potatoes with Salsa & Beans

(Prep time: 15 minutes | Cook time: 20 minutes| Serving: 4)
Ingredients
- 4 russet potatoes, medium
- Pickled jalapeños: 4 tsp., chopped
- Salsa: half cup
- 1 sliced avocado
- 1 can of (15 oz.) pinto beans, rinsed & roughly mashed

Instructions
1. With a fork, pierce the potatoes all over.
2. Microwave for 20 minutes, turning twice. Take it out and let it cool.
3. Cut the potato in half, do not cut all the way through.
4. Add the rest of the ingredients on top, serve.

Nutrition: Calories 324| Fat 8 g | Sugar 5 g | Protein 9.2 g |Sodium 387 mg | Carbs 56 g

278. Soba Noodles with Ginger-Sesame Dressing

(Prep time: 15 minutes | Cook time: 20 minutes| Serving: 4)
Ingredients
- Brown sugar substitute: ¼ cup
- Minced gingerroot: 1 tbsp.
- Rice vinegar: 2 tbsp.
- Orange juice: 2 tbsp.
- 1 minced garlic clove

- Canola oil: 2 tbsp.
- Soy sauce: ¼ cup, low-sodium
- Hot pepper sauce: half tsp.
- Sesame oil: 1 tsp.
- Water, as needed
- **Salad**
- Sesame seeds: 3 tbsp.
- Coleslaw mix: 14 oz.
- Shelled edamame: 2 cups
- Japanese soba noodles: half pound
- Shredded carrots: 1 cup
- Scallions sliced: 1 cup

Instructions
1. In a bowl, add all ingredients, except for the salad. Mix well.
2. As per the pack's instructions, cook soba and edamame, drain and wash with cold water.
3. In a bowl, add noodles, edamame, rest of the ingredients and pour the dressing.
4. Toss and serve.

Nutrition for 1 1/3 cup: Calories 349 | Fat 11 g | Sugar 8 g | Protein 14 g |Sodium 444 mg | Carbs 54g

279. Vegan Mushroom Bolognese

(Prep time: 15 minutes | Cook time: 55 minutes| Serving: 4)
Ingredients
- Chopped celery: ⅔ cup
- Olive oil: 2 tbsp.
- Chopped onion: half cup
- White button mushrooms: 1 pound
- Canned crushed tomatoes: 1 cup
- Chopped carrots: ⅔ cup
- A pinch of salt
- Dry white wine: half cup

- Whole-wheat pasta: 8 oz.

- Oat milk: half cup, unsweetened

- Nutmeg: ¼ tsp.

Instructions

1. In a food processor, add mushrooms (half), process until chopped. Dice largely the rest of the mushrooms.

2. In a skillet, add oil on medium heat. Sauté onion until translucent.

3. Add celery and carrots, cook for 3-4 minutes.

4. Add all mushrooms, cook until they wilt. Add milk and cook until it evaporates.

5. Add nutmeg, wine, cook until it evaporates, add tomatoes and let it come to a boil.

6. Turn the heat low, simmer for 45 minutes. If It gets too dry, add some water.

7. Cook pasta as per the pack's instructions. Toss pasta with sauce and serve.

Nutrition for 1 ½ cups: Calories 393 | Fat 10.2 g | Sugar 8.2 g | Protein 14 g |Sodium 190 mg | Carbs 63 g

280.   Slow-Cooked Ratatouille

(Prep time: 15 minutes | Cook time: 6 hours| Serving: 10)
Ingredients

- 2 onions, sliced thin

- Olive oil: 3 tbsp.

- 4 tomatoes, diced

- 1 peeled eggplant, 1" cubes

- 3 zucchinis, sliced into ¾" slices

- Fresh basil: 1/3 cup, chopped

- 2 celery ribs, diced

- Dried basil: 2 tsp.

- 1 can of (~3 oz.) Sliced ripe olives, without juices

- 1 can of (6 oz.) Tomato paste

- 4 minced garlic cloves

- Black pepper: ¼ tsp.

Instructions

1. Pat dry the eggplant well with paper towels.

2. In a slow cooker (5-6 qt.), add all ingredients except olives, basil and tomato paste.

3. Cook on low for 5-6 hours.

4. Before serving, add basil, olives and tomato paste. Serve.

Nutrition for ¾ cup: Calories 102| Fat 5 g | Sugar 8 g | Protein 3 g |Sodium 276 mg | Carbs 13 g

281.   Mushroom Pizzas with Arugula Salad

(Prep time: 15 minutes | Cook time: 30 minutes| Serving: 4)
Ingredients

- Olive oil: 2 tbsp. + 1 tsp.

- Shredded mozzarella cheese: half cup, low-fat

- Black pepper: half tsp.

- Sun-dried tomatoes: half cup, chopped

- Tomato sauce: half cup, salt-free

- 8 Portobello mushroom large caps without gills

- Dried Italian seasoning: half tsp.

- Baby spinach: 2 cups, chopped

- 1 can of (14 oz.) Artichoke hearts, chopped & rinsed

- Fresh basil leaves: ¼ cup, sliced

- Lemon juice: 1 tbsp.

- Feta cheese: ¼ cup, crumbled

- Baby arugula: 2 cups

Instructions

1. Let the oven preheat to 400 F.

2. With one tbsp. of oil brush the mushroom caps, place them on a wire rack on a baking sheet, round side down.

3. Roast for ten minutes, roast on the other side for 5 minutes.

4. In a bowl, add oil (1 tsp. + 1tbsp.), pepper (half), lemon juice and arugula. Toss.

5. Season with half of the pepper and add 1 tbsp. of sauce on every mushroom cap.

6. Add the rest of the ingredients in each cap equally and bake for 10-15 minutes.

7. Serve with arugula salad.

Nutrition: Calories 264 | Fat 17.2 g | Sugar 8 g | Protein 14 g |Sodium 345 mg | Carbs 25 g

282. Mushroom-Bean Bourguignon

(Prep time: 15 minutes | Cook time: 60 minutes| Serving: 10)

Ingredients

- 5 carrots, 1" pieces
- 2 minced garlic cloves
- Dried thyme: half tsp.
- 8 large Portobello mushrooms, 1" pieces
- Tomato paste: 1 tbsp., salt-free
- 2 onions, sliced
- Dry red wine: 25 oz.
- Olive oil: 4 tbsp.
- All-purpose flour: 3 tbsp.
- Vegetable broth: 2 cups, low-sodium
- Pepper: half tsp.
- Pack of frozen pearl onions: ~15 oz.
- 2 cans of (~15 oz.) navy beans, rinsed

Instructions

1. Heat oil (2 tbsp.) in a Dutch oven, sauté onions, carrots and cook for 8 to 10 minutes.

2. Add garlic and cook for 1 minute; take it out of the pan.

3. In a pan, add oil (1 tbsp. + 1tsp.) on medium flame, sauté mushrooms until lightly browned.

4. Add tomato paste and cook for 1 minute. Add onion mixture, wine, pepper, thyme, broth (1 ½ cups), let it come to a boil, turn the heat low, cover and simmer for 25 minutes.

5. Add onions, beans and cook for half an hour.

6. In a bowl, add flour and rest of the broth, mix and pour in the pan. Cook for 2 minutes, until it thickens.

Nutrition for 1 cup: Calories 234 | Fat 6 g | Sugar 6 g | Protein 9 g |Sodium 402 mg | Carbs 33g

283. Southwestern Vegetable Chowder

(Prep time: 15 minutes | Cook time: 20 minutes| Serving: 6)

Ingredients

- Chili powder: 1 tbsp.
- 1 cup of chopped celery
- All-purpose flour: half cup
- 1 cup of chopped onion
- Diced sweet potato: 2 cups
- Ground cumin: 1 ½ tsp.
- Dried oregano: 1 tsp.
- Vegetable broth: 4 cups, low-sodium
- Olive oil: 3 tbsp.
- 2 cans of (15 oz.) Black beans, rinsed
- 1 cup of 1% milk
- 2 poblanos peppers, diced

Instructions

1. In a pan, heat oil on medium flame.

2. Sauté celery and onion for 3-6 minutes. Add spices and flour, cook for 1 minute.

3. Add milk, broth and let it come to a boil.

4. Add peppers, sweet potato, stir and simmer for 12-15 minutes, uncovered.

5. Add black beans, cook for 2-4 minutes.

6. Serve with fresh herbs on top.

Nutrition: Calories 307 | Fat 10 g | Sugar 7 g | Protein 11.2 g |Sodium 276 mg | Carbs 44 g

284. Asparagus Tofu Stir-Fry

(Prep time: 15 minutes | Cook time: 20 minutes| Serving: 4)
Ingredients
- Canola oil: 3 tsp.
- Sugar substitute: half tsp.
- Soy sauce: 4 tsp., low-sodium
- Minced ginger: 2 tsp.
- Cornstarch: 1 tbsp.
- Vegetable broth: 1 ¼ cups, low-sodium
- 1" pieces of asparagus: 1 pound
- 2 scallions, sliced
- Sliced almonds: 2 tbsp.
- Extra-firm tofu: 14 oz., cut into half" cubes
- 1 yellow squash, cut into half-moons
- Salt & pepper: 1/8 tsp. each

Instructions
1. In a bowl, mix sugar, soy sauce, cornstarch and broth. Mix well.
2. In a pan, heat oil (1 tsp.) and sauté half of the ginger. Add asparagus and cook for 2 minutes.
3. Add squash, cook for 2 minutes. Add onions, cook for 1 minute, take them out on a plate.
4. Cook tofu with ginger, salt and pepper in the rest of the oil for 7 to 9 minutes, take it out on a plate.
5. Add soy sauce mixture, cook for 2 minutes, add vegetables and tofu, cook and serve with rice.

Nutrition for 1 cup: Calories 278 | Fat 11 g | Sugar 4 g | Protein 14 g |Sodium 55 mg | Carbs 34 g

285. Vegan Moroccan Lettuce Wraps

(Prep time: 20 minutes | Cook time: 0 minutes| Serving: 6)
Ingredients
- Bean & Chickpea Mix: 2 cups
- Bibb lettuce: 2 heads, leaves separated
- Salad greens: 2 cups, chopped
- Cooked quinoa: 1 1/2 cups

Instructions
1. In 3 lettuce leaves, add quinoa, bean mix and salad greens. Roll and serve.

Nutrition: Calories 425 | Fat 19 g | Sugar 2.9 g | Protein 13.7 g |Sodium 341 mg | Carbs 50 g

286. Black Bean & Corn Quinoa

(Prep time: 15 minutes | Cook time: 20 minutes| Serving: 4)
Ingredients
- 1 onion, chopped
- Pepper: ¼ tsp.
- 1 red bell pepper, chopped
- Salt: ¼ tsp.
- 1 celery rib, chopped
- Canola oil: 2 tbsp.
- Chili powder: 2 tsp.
- 1 can of (15 oz.) Black beans, rinsed
- 2 cups of low-sodium vegetable stock
- 1 cup of quinoa
- Fresh cilantro: 2 tbsp. + 1/3 cup
- 1 cup of frozen corn

Instructions
2. In a skillet, add oil on medium heat.
3. Sauté celery, red pepper, seasoning and onion, cook for 5 to 7 minutes.
4. Add corn, stock, let it come to a boil. Add quinoa, turn the heat low, simmer for 12 to 15 minutes.
5. Add beans and cilantro, mix and serve.

Nutrition for 1 ¼ cup: Calories 375 | Fat 10 g | Sugar 8 g | Protein 13 g | Sodium 55 mg | Carbs 60 g

287. Spinach & Mushroom Quiche

(Prep time: 20 minutes | Cook time: 40 minutes | Serving: 6)

Ingredients

- Fresh mushrooms: 8 oz., sliced
- Sweet onion: 1 ½ cups, sliced
- Sliced garlic: 1 tbsp.
- Olive oil: 2 tbsp.
- Dijon mustard: 1 tbsp.
- Shredded gruyere cheese: 1 ½ cups
- Salt & pepper: ¼ tsp. Each
- Baby fresh spinach: 8 cups, chopped
- 6 eggs
- Low-fat cream: ¼ cup
- Fresh thyme: 1 tbsp.

Instructions

1. Let the oven preheat to 375 F.
2. Oil spray a pie pan (9").
3. In a skillet, add oil on medium heat. Sauté mushrooms for 8 minutes.
4. Add garlic, onion and cook for 5 minutes. Add spinach and cook for 1-2 minutes. Turn the heat off.
5. In a bowl, add the rest of the ingredients, whisk.
6. Add the mushroom mixture and pour in the pie pan; bake for half an hour.
7. Slice and serve.

Nutrition per slice: Calories 277 | Fat 20 g | Sugar 3.2 g | Protein 17.1 g | Sodium 387 mg | Carbs 6.8 g

288. Black Bean & Sweet Potato Rice Bowls

(Prep time: 15 minutes | Cook time: 30 minutes | Serving: 4)

Ingredients

- Sweet chili sauce: 2 tbsp.
- Water: 1 1/2 cups
- Garlic salt: 1/8 tsp.
- Long grain rice: ¾ cup
- Chopped fresh kale: 4 cups, without stems
- 1 large peeled sweet potato, diced
- 1 red onion, diced
- Olive oil: 3 tbsp.
- 1 can of (15 oz.) Black beans, rinsed

Instructions

1. In a saucepan, add water, garlic salt and rice, let it come to a boil, turn the heat low and simmer for 15 to 20 minutes; turn the heat off. Let it rest for 5 minutes.
2. In a skillet, add oil on medium heat. Sauté potato for 8 minutes, add onion and cook for 4 to 6 minutes.
3. Add kale and cook for 3 to 5 minutes. Add beans and cook for few minutes.
4. Add chili sauce, rice to the potato mixture, toss and serve.

Nutrition for 2 cups: Calories 435 | Fat 11 g | Sugar 15 g | Protein 10 g | Sodium 400 mg | Carbs 74 g

289. Vegetarian Bolognese

(Prep time: 15 minutes | Cook time: 4-8 hours | Serving: 8)

Ingredients

- Dry white wine: half cup
- Water: half cup
- Chopped carrot: half cup
- 1 cup of diced onion
- 1 can of (28 oz.) Diced tomatoes, salt-free
- Whole-wheat spaghetti: 1 pound
- Chopped celery: half cup
- Olive oil: 3 tbsp.

- Minced garlic: 2 tbsp.
- 2 cans of (15 oz.) Cannellini beans, rinsed
- Italian seasoning: 1 tsp.
- Low-fat cream: ¼ cup
- Parmesan cheese: half cup, grated
- Ground pepper: ¼ tsp.
- Fresh basil: ¼ cup, chopped

Instructions

1. In a slow cooker (5-6 qt.), add all ingredients except pasta, cream and beans. Stir and cook for 4 hours on high, for 8 hours on low.
2. Add cream, beans and cook for few minutes.
3. Cook pasta as per the pack's instructions. Serve with sauce.

Nutrition: Calories 434 | Fat 12.6 g | Sugar 6.2 g | Protein 15 g |Sodium 356 mg | Carbs 65 g

290. Black Bean-Sweet Potato Skillet

(Prep time: 15 minutes | Cook time: 35 minutes| Serving: 5)
Ingredients

- Olive oil: 1 tbsp.
- 1 can of (~15 oz.) Vegetable broth, low-sodium
- 2 cans of (~15 oz.) Black beans, rinsed
- 1 onion, chopped
- 2 peeled sweet potatoes, chopped
- Dry couscous: 1 ¼ cups, cooked
- Pepper: ¼ tsp.
- Cinnamon: ¼ tsp.
- Chipotle pepper: 1 tsp., chopped, in adobo sauce

Instructions

1. Sauté onion in hot oil, add the rest of the ingredients except for couscous, stir and let it come to a boil, turn the heat low and, cover, simmer for 25 minutes.

2. Take the lid off and simmer for 5 to 10 minutes. Serve with couscous.

Nutrition: Calories 294 | Fat 3 g | Sugar 9 g | Protein 12 g |Sodium 453 mg | Carbs 54 g

291. Linguine with Beans & Summer Squash

(Prep time: 15 minutes | Cook time: 10 minutes| Serving: 4)
Ingredients

- 1 tsp. Of olive oil
- 1 yellow summer squash, half-moons
- Half red onion: sliced
- Dry whole-grain linguine: 8 oz., cooked
- 1 zucchini, half-moons
- 2 tbsp. Of water
- Canned cannellini beans: 15.5 oz., rinsed
- Balsamic vinegar: 2 tbsp.
- 1 large tomato, diced
- 1/4 tsp. Of black pepper
- Chopped, fresh basil: 2 tbsp.
- Grated parmesan cheese: ¼ cup

Instructions

1. Sauté onion in hot oil for 3-4 minutes.
2. Add water, pepper and squash; cook for 6-8 minutes.
3. Add the rest of the ingredients, cook for 3 minutes.
4. Serve with pasta.

Nutrition: Calories 346 | Fat 5.0 g | Sugar 8 g | Protein 15 g |Sodium 218 mg | Carbs 62 g

292. Herbed Veggie Skillet

(Prep time: 15 minutes | Cook time: 10 minutes| Serving: 5)
Ingredients

- 8 oz. Of sliced zucchini
- 1/8 tsp. Of dried marjoram
- Sliced onion: 1/4 cup

- Chopped green bell pepper: 1/4 cup

- 1/8 tsp. Of dried basil

- Kernel corn: ¾ cup

- 1/3 cup of diced tomato

- 1/8 tsp. Of dried oregano

- 2 tsp. Of canola oil

- 2 tbsp. Of water

- Black pepper, to taste

Instructions

1. Sauté onion, zucchini and bell pepper in hot oil for 3 minutes.

2. Add the rest of the ingredients, cook for 5 minutes, covered.

3. Add water if needed, stir and cook. Serve.

Nutrition: Calories 69 | Fat 2.5 g | Sugar 3 g | Protein 2 g |Sodium 9 mg | Carbs 11g

293. Vegetable Quinoa Bowl

(Prep time: 15 minutes | Cook time: 35 minutes| Serving: 4)
Ingredients

- Cremini mushrooms: 3 cups, cut into fours

- Black pepper: ¼ tsp.

- 2 shallots, sliced

- Half cup of water

- 4 cups of broccoli florets

- Olive oil: 2 tbsp.

- 2 cups of cooked quinoa

- ¾ cup of raw cashews

- Fresh parsley leaves: ¼ cup

- Shredded red cabbage: 1 cup

- Cider vinegar: 1 tbsp.

- Tamari: half tsp., low-sodium

Instructions

1. Let the oven preheat to 425 F.

2. In a bowl, add vegetables toss with pepper and oil

(1 tbsp.), spread on a baking sheet.

3. Roast for 20 minutes. In a blender, add water, tamari, oil (1 tbsp.), parsley, cashews, and vinegar. Puree until smooth.

4. In serving bowls, add quinoa, vegetables and sauce. Serve.

Nutrition: Calories 340| Fat 18 g | Sugar 5 g | Protein 12 g |Sodium 310 mg | Carbs 35 g

294. Zucchini & Mushroom Sauté

(Prep time: 10 minutes | Cook time: 7 minutes| Serving: 4)
Ingredients

- 2 zucchinis, julienned

- Black pepper, to taste

- Sliced mushrooms: 1 ½ cups

- Olive oil: 2 tsp.

- Fresh basil: 2 tsp., chopped

Instructions

1. In a skillet, add oil on high heat.

2. Sauté zucchini and cook for 2 minutes. Add mushrooms, basil cook for 1 minute.

3. Serve with black pepper on top.

Nutrition: Calories 37 | Fat 17.2 g | Sugar 1.8 g | Protein 1.5 g |Sodium 55 mg | Carbs 2.8 g

295. Whole-Wheat Veggie Wrap

(Prep time: 15 minutes | Cook time: 0 minutes| Serving: 2)
Ingredients

- Cheddar cheese: 2 tbsp.

- Hummus: 2 tbsp.

- 1 whole-wheat tortilla of 8-inches

- ¼ avocado, mashed

- Mixed fresh vegetables: 1 cup, sliced

Instructions

1. Spread avocado and hummus on the tortilla. Add vegetables and cheese.

2. Roll tightly, slice and serve.

Nutrition: Calories 354| Fat 17.2 g | Sugar 5.1 g | Protein 11.4 g |Sodium 201 mg | Carbs 38 g

296. Lemony Asparagus Pasta

(Prep time: 15 minutes | Cook time: 15 minutes| Serving: 4)
Ingredients

- Asparagus: half bunch, 1" long pieces
- Whole-wheat pasta: 4 oz.
- Whole-grain mustard: 2 tsp.
- Fresh tarragon: 1 tsp.
- Flour: 2 tsp.
- Minced garlic: 2 tbsp.
- Salt, a pinch
- Black pepper: ¼ tsp.
- ¾ cup of 1% milk
- Low-fat parmesan cheese: half cup, grated
- Olive oil: 1 tsp.
- Lemon zest: 1/3 tsp.

Instructions

1. Cook pasta as per pack's instruction, omitting slat.
2. In the last 2 minutes, add asparagus, cook and drain.
3. In a bowl, mix flour, mustard, milk and pepper.
4. Sauté garlic in hot oil until golden. Add mustard mixture and simmer until thickens, stirring as needed.
5. Add lemon juice, zest and tarragon. Mix and serve with pasta.

Nutrition: Calories 264 | Fat 11 g | Sugar 3 g | Protein 2 g |Sodium 196 mg | Carbs 12 g

297. Vermicelli with Vegetables

(Prep time: 15 minutes | Cook time: 15 minutes| Serving: 2)
Ingredients

- 6 spears of asparagus
- Minced garlic: 1 tbsp.

- Whole-grain vermicelli: 4 oz.
- Olive oil: 2 tsp.
- 1 tomato, diced
- Black pepper, or to taste
- Fresh basil: 2 tbsp., chopped
- Grated Parmesan: 4 tbsp.

Instructions

1. Sauté asparagus in hot oil (half) until tender-crisp. Take it out and cut it into bite-size pieces.
2. Cook pasta as per pack's instructions, drain.
3. Add the rest of the ingredients with asparagus to the pasta. Toss and serve.

Nutrition for 1 cup: Calories 325 | Fat 9 g | Sugar 3 g | Protein 13 g |Sodium 123 mg | Carbs 48 g

298. Black-Eyed Peas 'n' Pasta

(Prep time: 15 minutes | Cook time: 35 minutes| Serving: 6)
Ingredients

- Diced green pepper: 1 cup
- 1 can of (28 oz.) Crushed tomatoes
- Chopped onion: half cup
- Fresh cilantro: 1-3 tbsp.
- Olive oil: 1 tbsp.
- 1 can of (15 oz.) Black-eyed peas, rinsed
- 1 jalapeno pepper, chopped without seeds
- 3 minced garlic cloves
- Dry bow tie pasta: 8 oz., cooked
- Pepper: 1/8 tsp.
- Cider vinegar: 1 tsp.
- Sugar: half to ¼ tsp.

Instructions

1. In a skillet, add oil on medium heat.
2. Sauté garlic, onion, jalapenos, green peppers, until tender.
3. Add tomatoes, stir and let it come to a boil; turn

the heat low and simmer for ten minutes.

4. Add the rest of the ingredients, cook for ten minutes more.

5. Add cooked pasta, toss and serve.

Nutrition for 1 cup: Calories 266 | Fat 4 g | Sugar 10 g | Protein 11 g |Sodium 432 mg | Carbs 50 g

299. Southwest Style Rice Bowl

(Prep time: 15 minutes | Cook time: 10 minutes| Serving: 6)
Ingredients
- Chopped mixed vegetables: 1 cup
- Shredded cheese: 2 tbsp., low-fat
- Mushrooms: 1 cup, chopped
- Vegetable oil: 1 tsp.
- Sour cream: 2 tbsp., low-fat
- Cooked brown rice: 1 cup
- Salsa: 4 tbsp.

Instructions
1. Sauté vegetables in hot oil for 3-5 minutes.
2. Add rice and beans cook for few minutes.
3. Serve with cheese, salsa and sour cream on top.

Nutrition: Calories 175 | Fat 2 g | Sugar 2 g | Protein 10 g |Sodium 286 mg | Carbs 30 g

300. Fettuccine with Shiitake Mushrooms

(Prep time: 15 minutes | Cook time: 10 minutes| Serving: 6)
Ingredients
- 3 minced garlic cloves
- Black pepper to taste
- Shitake mushrooms: 1 1/2 cups, sliced
- Lemon zest: 2 tsp.
- Basil, fresh: half cup
- Olive oil: 2 tbsp.
- Grated parmesan: half cup
- Lemon juice: 2 tbsp.
- Dry whole-wheat fettuccine: 8 oz., cooked

Instructions
1. Sauté garlic in hot oil for 1 minute. Add mushrooms and cook for 4-5 minutes.
2. Add pepper, lemon juice, zest. Stir and turn the heat off.
3. In a skillet, add basil, parmesan, some of the pasta water, pasta and mushrooms. Toss and serve.

Nutrition: Calories 378| Fat 8 g | Sugar 17 g | Protein 32 g |Sodium 209 mg | Carbs 36 g

301. Vegan Lasagna

(Prep time: 15 minutes | Cook time: 55 minutes| Serving: 6)
Ingredients
- Olive oil: 3 tbsp.
- 3 cloves garlic, minced
- 1 onion, chopped
- Whole-wheat lasagna noodles: 8 oz.
- Dry red wine: ¼ cup
- Mushrooms: 12 oz., sliced
- Nutritional yeast: 2 tsp.
- Dried oregano: 1 tsp.
- Chopped broccoli: 2 cups
- Silken tofu: 16 oz., crumbled & dry
- 1 can of (16 oz.) Crushed tomatoes
- Dried basil: 1 tsp.
- Black pepper: ¼ tsp.

Instructions
1. Let the oven preheat to 400 F.
2. Oil spray a 9 by 13" baking dish.
3. Cook the pasta noodles as per the pack's instructions and drain.
4. Sauté onion, garlic, mushroom and broccoli in hot oil for 7-9 minutes.
5. Add the rest of the ingredients, except for yeast and tofu. Simmer for ten minutes.

6. Add yeast and tofu to a bowl, and mix

7. In the baking dish, spread the tomato sauce on the bottom.

8. Layer the noodles, tofu mixture and tomato sauce in 3 layers.

9. Bake, covered, for 30-40 minutes. Slice and serve.

Nutrition: Calories 325 | Fat 10.2 g | Sugar 7.7 g | Protein 14 g |Sodium 323 mg | Carbs 42 g

302. Polenta with Fresh Vegetables

(Prep time: 15 minutes | Cook time: 1 hour & 10 minutes| Serving: 4)

Ingredients

- 4 cups of water
- Broccoli florets: 1 cup
- Polenta: 1 cup
- Garlic chopped: 1 tsp.
- Fresh mushrooms: 1 cup, sliced
- Parmesan cheese: 2 tbsp.
- Sliced onions: 1 cup
- Sliced zucchini: 1 cup

Instructions

1. Let the oven preheat to 350 F. oil spray a (3 qt.) baking dish

2. Add polenta, garlic and water to the dish. Bake for 40 minutes, uncovered.

3. In a pan, sauté onion and mushrooms, cook for 5 minutes.

4. Steam the broccoli and zucchini for 2-3 minutes.

5. Serve the polenta with vegetables, herbs and cheese.

Nutrition: Calories 178 | Fat 1 g | Sugar 3 g | Protein 6 g |Sodium 55 mg | Carbs 35 g

303. Zucchini Lasagna Rolls

(Prep time: 15 minutes | Cook time: 1 hour & 10 minutes| Serving: 4)

Ingredients

- Olive oil: 2 tsp.
- Black pepper: ¼ tsp.
- Smoked skim mozzarella: 8 oz., shredded
- Fresh basil: 2 tbsp., chopped
- Frozen spinach: 10 oz., thawed & squeezed
- Marinara sauce: ¾ cup, low-sodium
- 2 zucchinis, large
- 1 egg, whisked
- Parmesan cheese: 3 tbsp., grated
- 1 minced garlic clove

Instructions

1. Let the oven preheat to 425 F. oil spray 2 baking sheets.

2. Cut the zucchini lengthwise into 24 strips. Toss with oil and half of the black pepper.

3. Place the zucchini onto baking sheets in 1 even layer. Bake for ten minutes.

4. In a bowl, add parmesan (1 tbsp.) and mozzarella (2 tbsp.), mix.

5. In a bowl, add egg, garlic, all cheese, pepper and spinach, mix.

6. In a baking dish (8" square), add marinara sauce (1/4 cup).

7. Add the egg mixture on each strip of zucchini, roll and place in the baking pan.

8. Add half a cup of marinara on top. Top with cheese mixture.

9. Bake for 20 minutes, rest for 5 minutes. Serve.

Nutrition for 6 rolls: Calories 315 | Fat 17.2 g | Sugar 7.8 g | Protein 22.2 g |Sodium 445 mg | Carbs 16 g

304. Charred Vegetable & Bean Tostadas

(Prep time: 15 minutes | Cook time: 35 minutes | Serving: 6)

Ingredients

- **Lime Crema**
- Lime juice: 2 tsp.
- Sour cream: 5 tbsp.
- Kosher salt, a pinch
- Lime zest: 1/8 tsp.
- **Tostadas**
- Canola oil: 2 tsp. + 2tbps.
- Water: ¼ cup, or more
- 4 sliced garlic cloves
- 2 cans of (15 oz.) Black beans, rinsed
- 6 corn tortillas
- Ground cumin: 1 ½ tsp.
- Chipotle chili powder: 1/8 tsp.
- Sliced cabbage: 1 cup
- 2 red sweet peppers, sliced
- 1 red onion, half-moons
- Black pepper: ¼ tsp.
- 2 zucchinis, half-moons
- Cotija cheese: 6 tbsp., crumbled
- Corn kernels: 1 cup
- Fresh cilantro: ¼ cup, chopped

Instructions

1. In a bowl, add all ingredients of crema, mix and set it aside.
2. Let the oven preheat to 400 F with a rack in the upper third of the oven.

3. Oil spray or brush the tortillas with oil (1 tbsp.) and bake on a baking tray for ten minutes, flipping halfway through. Let them cool.
4. In a skillet, heat 2 tsp. of oil, sauté garlic (1 clove) for 30 seconds.
5. Add spices and cook for 30 seconds, add beans and cook for half an hour.
6. Puree with a stick blender with water (1 tbsp. at a time) and pulse until smooth.
7. Let the broiler preheat.
8. Add all vegetables and garlic to a bowl, toss with oil (1 tbsp.), and broil on a baking sheet for 8-12 minutes.
9. Serve tostadas with bean mixture, vegetables, rest of the ingredients and crema on top.

Nutrition: Calories 327 | Fat 12 g | Sugar 6 g | Protein 13 g | Sodium 378 mg | Carbs 43 g

DASH Diet Poultry & Meat Recipes

305. Pork Chops with Tomato Curry

(Prep time: 15 minutes | Cook time: 25 minutes | Serving: 6)

Ingredients

- 6 pork loin chops, boneless
- 1 onion, diced
- Sugar: 4 tsp.

- Unsalted butter: 4 tsp.

- Apples sliced: 5 cups

- 1 can of (28 oz.) Whole tomatoes, undrained

- Chili powder: half tsp.

- Curry powder: 2 tsp.

- Salt: ¼ tsp.

Instructions

1. In a pot (6 qt.), add butter (2 tsp.) on medium flame. Sear pork chops and take them out.

2. Add the rest of the butter, sauté onion for 2-3 minutes, add the rest of the ingredients, let it come to a boil, keep breaking the tomatoes.

3. Add the chops back in the pot. Turn the heat low and simmer for 5 minutes.

4. Flip the chops and cook for 3-5 minutes until the internal temperature of the meat reaches 145 F.

5. Serve.

Nutrition: Calories 478| Fat 14 g | Sugar 15 g | Protein 38 g |Sodium 387 mg | Carbs 50 g

306. Chicken with Crushed Harissa Chickpeas

(Prep time: 15 minutes | Cook time: 15 minutes | Serving: 4)
Ingredients

- Rapeseed oil: 2 tbsp.

- Za'atar: 1 tbsp.

- 1 red & 1 yellow pepper, sliced

- Red harissa paste: 1 ½ tbsp.

- 4 chicken breasts

- 1 onion, diced

- Half bunch parsley, chopped

- Canned chickpeas: 14 oz.

- Baby spinach: 5 oz.

Instructions

1. In a pan, add oil (half) on medium flame. Sauté

peppers and onion for 7 minutes.

2. Pound the chicken into 0.7" of thickness.

3. In a bowl, add za'atar and oil, mix and rub all over the chicken.

4. Grill, the chicken for 3-4 minutes on 1 side.

5. Add chickpeas on medium flame in a pan, add harissa paste, water (2 tbsp.), and mash with a masher.

6. In a different pan, sauté spinach with some water. Add the onion-pepper mixture, transfer to the chickpeas with parsley.

7. Serve with grilled chicken.

Nutrition: Calories 366 | Fat 12 g | Sugar 6 g | Protein 44 g |Sodium 285 mg | Carbs 16 g

307. Thai Chicken Pasta Skillet

(Prep time: 15 minutes | Cook time: 10 minutes | Serving: 6)
Ingredients

- Canola oil: 2 tsp.

- Sugar snap peas: 10 oz., cut into strips

- Thai peanut sauce: 1 cup, low-sodium

- 1 cucumber, halved & sliced diagonally, without seeds

- Whole wheat spaghetti: 6 oz.

- Julienned carrots: 2 cups

- Cooked chicken: 2 cups, shredded

Instructions

1. Cook pasta as per the pack's instructions.

2. In a skillet, add oil on medium flame. Add carrots and peas, cook for 6 to 8 minutes.

3. Add pasta, peanut sauce and chicken. Toss well.

4. Serve with cucumber and fresh herbs on top.

Nutrition: Calories 403 | Fat 15 g | Sugar 15 g | Protein 6.4 g |Sodium 432 mg | Carbs 25 g

308. Steaks with Goulash Sauce

(Prep time: 15 minutes | Cook time: 20 minutes | Serving: 6)

Ingredients

- Peeled sweet potatoes: 8 oz., cut into thin chips
- 1 green pepper, diced
- Fresh thyme: 1 tbsp.
- Rapeseed oil: 4 tsp.
- Baby spinach: 7 oz., wilted
- 2 small onions, sliced into half-moons
- Cherry tomatoes: 3 oz., halved
- 2 sliced garlic cloves
- Smoked paprika: 1 tsp.
- Vegetable bouillon: 1 tsp.
- Tomato purée: 1 tbsp.
- 2 fillet steaks, brushed with oil

Instructions

1. Let the oven preheat to 460 F.
2. Toss the thyme and potatoes with oil (2 tsp.) and spread on a wire rack on top of a baking sheet.
3. In a pan, add oil and sauté onion for 5 minutes, cook, covered.
4. Add the garlic, pepper, stir and cook, covered for 5 minutes more.
5. Bake the chips for 15 minutes.
6. Add ¾ cup of water to the onion mixture and add bouillon, tomatoes and puree. Stir and simmer for ten minutes.
7. In a pan, add the oil-brushed steaks and sear for 2-3 minutes on one side.
8. Rest for few minutes, serve with sauce, spinach and sauce.

Nutrition: Calories 374| Fat 14 g | Sugar 3.8 g | Protein 28 g |Sodium 204 mg | Carbs 21 g

309. Italian Sausage-Stuffed Zucchini

(Prep time: 25 minutes | Cook time: 25 minutes | Serving: 6)

Ingredients

- Italian turkey sausage: 1 pound, without casing
- Parmesan cheese: 1/3 cup, grated
- Fresh oregano: 2 tbsp., chopped
- 2 tomatoes, chopped without seeds
- Black pepper: ¼ tsp.
- 6 zucchinis, medium
- Panko bread crumbs: 1 cup
- Fresh parsley: 1/3 cup, chopped
- Fresh basil: 2 tbsp., chopped
- Shredded skim mozzarella cheese: 3/4 cup

Instructions

1. Let the oven preheat to 350 F.
2. Slice every zucchini in half, lengthwise. Take the pulp out, and dice the pulp.
3. In a dish, add the zucchini boats, microwave for 2 to 3 minutes on high, and cover plastic wrap.
4. Add zucchini pulp with sausage in a skillet, cook for 6-8 minutes, then drain.
5. Add pepper, tomatoes, cheese (half), herbs and crumbs. Mix and stuff the zucchini boats.
6. Place in a baking dish and bake for 15 to 20 minutes, covered.
7. Add cheese on top and bake for 5 to 8 minutes, uncovered.

Nutrition: Calories 206| Fat 9 g | Sugar 5 g | Protein 17 g |Sodium 456 mg | Carbs 16 g

310. Chicken Quinoa Bowl

(Prep time: 25 minutes | Cook time: 20 minutes | Serving: 4)

Ingredients

- Salt & pepper: ¼ tsp. Each
- Olive oil: 4 tbsp.
- Chicken breasts: 1 pound, boneless & skinless
- Red onion: ¼ cup, chopped

- Slivered almonds: ¼ cup

- Ground cumin: half tsp.

- 1 minced garlic clove

- Chopped cucumber: 1 cup

- Paprika: 1 tsp.

- 1 jar of (7 oz.) Roasted red peppers, washed

- Cooked quinoa: 2 cups

- Kalamata olives: half cup, chopped

- Fresh parsley: 2 tbsp., chopped

Instructions

1. Let the broiler preheat, place a rack in the upper third of the oven.

2. Season chicken with salt and pepper. Place on a foil-lined baking sheet and broil for 14-18 minutes until the internal temperature of the meat reaches 165 F.

3. Shred the cooked chicken.

4. In a food processor, add paprika, almonds, peppers, cumin, oil (2 tbsp.) and garlic. Pulse until smooth.

5. In a bowl, toss quinoa, oil (2 tbsp.), onion and olives.

6. In serving bowls, add quinoa, add chicken, sauce and cucumber.

7. Serve with parsley on top.

Nutrition: Calories 498 | Fat 27 g | Sugar 2.5 g | Protein 27 g |Sodium 545 mg | Carbs 31 g

311. Roasted Brussels Sprouts, Chicken & Potatoes

(Prep time: 25 minutes | Cook time: 35 minutes | Serving: 4)
Ingredients
- Dijon mustard: 2 tsp.

- Red potatoes: 3 cups, diced small

- Fresh oregano: 1 ½ tsp.

- Onions: 1 cup, diced

- Chicken breasts: 1 lb. Boneless & skinless, cut into 4 pieces

- Vinaigrette dressing: 1/3 cup

- 1 lemon's juice

- Black pepper

- Kalamata olives: ¼ cup, quartered

- Quartered Brussels sprouts: 4 cups

- Garlic salt: 1/8 tsp.

Instructions

1. Let the oven preheat to 400 F.

2. In a sheet pan, place the chicken. Arrange Brussels sprouts on one side and potatoes and onion on different sides.

3. In a bowl, add the rest of the ingredients. Pour over the sheet pan, and coat the vegetables.

4. Bake for 20 minutes for chicken, take the chicken out, cook the vegetables for 15 minutes more. Serve.

Nutrition: Calories 361 | Fat 10 g | Sugar 8 g | Protein 32 g |Sodium 589 mg | Carbs 37 g

312. Mexican Bake

(Prep time: 15 minutes | Cook time: 45 minutes | Serving: 6)
Ingredients
- Chicken breasts: 1 lb. Boneless & skinless, bite-size pieces

- 2 cans of (15 oz.) Tomatoes, diced, unsalted

- Corn kernels: 1 cup

- Brown cooked rice: 1 ½ cups

- 1 can of (15 oz.) Black beans, rinsed

- Poblano pepper: 1 cup, chopped

- Monterey jack cheese: 1 cup, shredded (low-fat)

- Chili powder: 1 tbsp.
- Red bell pepper: 1 cup, chopped
- Cumin: 1 tbsp.
- 4 minced garlic cloves

Instructions
1. Let the oven preheat to 400 F.
2. In a casserole dish (3 qt.), add rice and spread, add chicken on top.
3. Add the rest of the ingredients except for cheese, mix, and pour over chicken in a bowl.
4. Spread cheese on top, bake for 45 minutes. Serve.

Nutrition: Calories 325 | Fat 7.2 g | Sugar 8 g | Protein 28.4 g |Sodium 355 mg | Carbs 36.9 g

313. Chicken & Vegetable Penne with Walnut Pesto

(Prep time: 15 minutes | Cook time: 35 minutes | Serving: 4)
Ingredients
- Parsley leaves: 1 cup
- 2 crushed garlic cloves
- Parmesan cheese: 1/3 cup
- Salt & pepper: 1/8 tsp., each
- Cauliflower florets: 2 cups
- Chopped walnuts: ¾ cup
- Green beans: 8 oz., halved
- Whole-wheat penne: 6 oz.
- Olive oil: 2 tbsp.
- Shredded chicken breast: 1 ½ cups

Instructions
1. Toast the walnuts in the microwave for 2 to 3 minutes, let them cool.
2. In a food processor, add half a cup of walnuts, pepper, salt, garlic and parsley, pulse until combined.
3. Slowly add oil while the machine is pulsing. Add parmesan and pulse until mixed.

4. Transfer the pesto to a bowl, add chicken.
5. Cook pasta as per the package's instructions. In the last 7 minutes, add cauliflower and beans, cook and drain all but ¾ cup of water.
6. Add the pasta water to the pesto bowl and add the pasta and vegetables.
7. Toss to coat. Serve with walnuts on top.

Nutrition: Calories 514 | Fat 26 g | Sugar 4.8 g | Protein 31.4 g |Sodium 536 mg | Carbs 43 g

314. Beef Kabobs with Sauce

(Prep time: 15 minutes | Cook time: 15 minutes | Serving: 4)
Ingredients
- Garlic powder: ¼ tsp.
- Dried rosemary: half tsp.
- Onion powder: half tsp.
- Dried oregano: half tsp.
- Pepper: 1/8 tsp.
- Lean ground beef: 1 pound
- Ground cumin: half tsp.
- Salt: ¼ tsp.

Instructions
1. In a bowl, add all ingredients and mix until combined.
2. Make it into 12 portions. Make each portion into a long patty with the help of a skewer (6-inch). Place on a plate.
3. Oil spray a pan and cook the skewer kabobs for 5-7 minutes until browned on all sides. Serve with tzatziki sauce

Nutrition: Calories 226 | Fat 9.5 g | Sugar 8 g | Protein 30 g |Sodium 325 mg | Carbs 6 g

315. Greek Chicken with Roasted Vegetables

(Prep time: 20 minutes | Cook time: 20 minutes | Serving: 4)
Ingredients
- Lemon Vinaigrette

- Feta cheese: 1 tbsp., crumbled
- 1 lemon's zest & juice
- Honey: half tsp.
- Olive oil: 1 tbsp.
- **Chicken & Vegetables**
- Light mayonnaise: ¼ cup
- Grape tomatoes: 1 ½ cups, cut in half
- 6 minced garlic cloves
- 2 chicken breast halves: skinless, boneless, halved lengthwise
- Panko bread crumbs: half cup
- Cremini mushrooms: 1 ½ cups, sliced
- Kosher salt: ¼ tsp.
- Parmesan cheese: 3 tbsp., grated
- Black pepper: half tsp.
- 1" pieces of asparagus: 2 cups
- Olive oil: 1 tbsp.

Instructions

1. In a bowl, add 1 tbsp. of lemon juice, zest (half tsp.), and the rest of the dressings ingredients.
2. With a baking pan (15 by 10") in the oven, let the oven preheat to 475 F.
3. Pound the chicken with a mallet into half" thickness. Transfer to a bowl, add mayo, garlic cloves (2) and mix well.
4. In a dish, add cheese, breadcrumbs, half of the salt and pepper, mix.
5. Coat chicken in cheese mixture, oil spray the breaded chicken.
6. In a bowl, add the rest of the garlic, salt and pepper, oil, and vegetables.
7. In the baking pan, add chicken on one side and vegetables on the other.

8. Roast for 18-20 minutes. Serve the chicken, vegetables with vinaigrette.

Nutrition: Calories 306 | Fat 15.1 g | Sugar 3.6 g | Protein 29.5 g | Sodium 378 mg | Carbs 12.1 g

316. Huli Huli Chicken

(Prep time: 20 minutes | Cook time: 10 minutes | Serving: 4)
Ingredients
- Fresh pineapple: 1 Cup, diced
- Chicken breast, boneless & skinless: 12 oz., cubed
- **Sauce**
- Lite soy sauce: 2 Tbsp.
- Honey: 2 tbsp.
- Minced ginger: 1 tsp.
- Orange juice: 2 tsp.
- Ketchup: 2 Tbsp.
- Minced garlic: 1 tsp.

Instructions

1. Let the broiler preheat, onto 8 skewers, thread chicken and pineapple pieces alternatively.
2. In a bowl, add all sauce's ingredients, mix and set it aside.
3. Broil/grill the chicken for 3 to 5 minutes; keep brushing with sauce after each minute. Discard the rest of the sauce
4. Serve until the internal temperature of the meat reaches 165. Serve.

Nutrition: Calories 156 | Fat 17.2 g | Sugar 8 g | Protein 18 g | Sodium 320 mg | Carbs 16 g

317. Beef & Blue Cheese Pesto Penne

(Prep time: 20 minutes | Cook time: 15 minutes | Serving: 4)
Ingredients
- 2 (6 oz.) beef tenderloin steaks
- Baby spinach: 6 cups, chopped

- Salt & pepper: ¼ tsp. Each
- Grape tomatoes: 2 cups, halved
- Gorgonzola cheese: ¼ cup, crumbled
- Whole wheat penne pasta: 2 cups
- Pesto:1/3 cup
- Chopped walnuts: ¼ cup

Instructions

1. Cook pasta as per the pack's instructions.
2. Season the steaks with salt and pepper, grill or broil them for 5 to 7 minutes until the internal temperature of the meat reaches 135 F.
3. In a bowl, add cooked pasta and the rest of the ingredients, except for cheese.
4. Toss and serve with sliced steak with cheese on top.

Nutrition: Calories 532| Fat 22 g | Sugar 3 g | Protein 35 g |Sodium 434 mg | Carbs 49 g

318. Sheet Pan Chicken Fajitas

(Prep time: 15 minutes | Cook time: 20 minutes | Serving: 8)

Ingredients

- Chicken breast tenderloin: 2 lbs., halved lengthwise
- Fajita seasoning mix: 1 ½ tbsp., low-salt
- 1 green & 1 red pepper sliced
- Olive oil: 1 tbsp.
- 1 onion, sliced

Instructions

1. Let the oven preheat to 350 F.
2. Oil spray a sheet pan and arrange onion and pepper slices.
3. Add chicken on top of vegetables and add seasoning and oil on vegetables and chicken.
4. Toss well and bake for 20 minutes until the internal temperature of the meat reaches 165 F
5. Serve in whole-wheat tortillas.

Nutrition: Calories 168| Fat 4 g | Sugar 4 g | Protein 24

g |Sodium 140 mg | Carbs 5 g

319. Citrus-Herb Pork Roast

(Prep time: 15 minutes | Cook time: 5 hours & 10 minutes | Serving: 8)

Ingredients

- Dried oregano: 1 tsp.
- 2 onions, sliced into thin wedges
- Ground ginger: half tsp.
- 1 (3-4 pounds) pork sirloin roast, boneless
- Sugar: 1 tbsp.
- Black pepper: half tsp.
- White grapefruit juice: 1 tbsp.
- Orange zest: 1 tsp.
- Salt: ¼ tsp.
- Steak sauce: 1 tbsp.
- Orange juice: 3 tbsp. + 1 cup
- Cornstarch: 3 tbsp.
- Soy sauce: 1 tbsp., low-sodium

Instructions

1. Slice pork in half.
2. Add pepper, oregano and ginger, in a bowl, mix and rub all over the roast.
3. Add oil in a skillet, sear the pork on all sides, and put in a slow cooker (4 qt.)
4. Add onion to the roast.
5. In a bowl, add the rest of the ingredients (except for salt, cornstarch, orange juice (3 tbsp.) and zest), mix and pour over roast.
6. Cook, covered for 4 to 5 hours on low. Take onions and meat out on a tray.
7. Transfer the (without fat) to a pan, add salt and zest. Let it boil., add juice and cornstarch. Mix until smooth, cook for 2 minutes.
8. Serve the roast with the sauce.

Nutrition for 5 oz.: Calories 289| Fat 10 g | Sugar 8 g |

Protein 35 g |Sodium 326 mg | Carbs 13 g
Nutrition Facts

320. Fall Curry Chicken

(Prep time: 15 minutes | Cook time: 20 minutes | Serving: 4)

Ingredients

- Salt: ¼ tsp.
- Canola oil: 1 ½ tsp.
- Golden raisins: ¼ cup
- Lite coconut milk: 1 cup
- Curry powder: 2 tsp.
- Chicken breasts: 1 pound, boneless & skinless, sliced into 1/4" strips
- Cayenne pepper: ¼ tsp.
- 2 pods of cardamom
- 1 onion, diced
- Pumpkin seeds: ¼ cup, roasted
- Tomato paste: 1 tbsp.
- Butternut squash: ~ 1 pound, peeled & cubed
- 1 granny smith apple, chopped

Instructions

1. Season chicken with half of the salt and oil (half tsp.) and sear the chicken for 2 minutes in hot oil on each side. Do it in batches.
2. In a pan, add the rest of the oil, sauté onion on a medium flame for 2 minutes.
3. Add tomato paste, curry powder, cardamom, and cayenne pepper mix.
4. Add milk and deglaze the pan, and mix. Add squash, stir and cover.
5. Simmer for 15 minutes, add the chicken back to the pan with juices.
6. Cook for 2 minutes, add raisins and apples. Serve with seeds on top.

Nutrition: Calories 354| Fat 13 g | Sugar 5 g | Protein 29 g |Sodium 444 mg | Carbs 32 g

321. Turkey Meat Loaf

(Prep time: 15 minutes | Cook time: 70 minutes | Serving: 10)

Ingredients

- 1 onion, diced
- Fat-free milk: half cup
- Quick-cooking oats: 1 cup
- Garlic powder: 1 tsp.
- Egg substitute: ¼ cup
- Ketchup: 2 tbsp.
- Lean ground turkey: 2 pounds
- Shredded carrot: half cup
- Pepper: ¼ tsp.
- **Toppings**
- quick-cooking oats: ¼ cup
- ketchup: ¼ cup

Instructions

1. Let the oven preheat to 350 F.
2. In a bowl, add all ingredients except for toppings. Mix until combined, do not over mix.
3. In a bowl, mix the toppings.
4. Oil spray a 9 by 5" loaf pan. Add the turkey mixture and add toppings on top.
5. Bake for 60 to 65 minutes until the internal temperature of the meat reaches 165 F.
6. Rest it for ten minutes, slice and serve.

Nutrition: Calories 195 | Fat 8 g | Sugar 4 g | Protein 20 g |Sodium 188 mg | Carbs 12 g

322. One-Pan Lemon & Chicken Bake

(Prep time: 20 minutes | Cook time: 70 minutes| Serving: 10)

Ingredients

- 1/3" piece of ginger, grated
- Lemon juice: 1/3 cup
- Chili powder: half tsp.
- Fresh thyme leaves: 2 tsp.
- 2 minced garlic cloves
- 1 lemon, sliced

- Fresh oregano: 1 tbsp., chopped
- Chicken stock: 1/3 cup, salt-free
- Orange juice: 1/3 cup
- Sweet paprika: 1 tsp.
- Baby potatoes: 17 oz.
- Olive oil: 1 tbsp.
- 1 sweet onion, chopped
- 8 chicken thigh cutlets, skinless
- 1 orange, sliced
- Green beans: 3.5 oz., cut into thirds

Instructions

1. Let the oven preheat to 390 F.
2. In a bowl, add herbs, garlic, ginger, lemon juice, orange juice, stock, and chili powder.
3. Slice the potatoes paper-thin slices of every potato, do not cut all the way through.
4. On a roasting pan, spread the onion, add chicken on top.
5. Add potatoes around the chicken, and pour the liquid mixture on top.
6. Add paprika, oil and place lemon and orange slices. Sprinkle salt and pepper.
7. Bake for 50 minutes, keep basting with pan juices.
8. Add beans and make sure they are covered in pan juices.
9. Cook for ten minutes more. Serve.

Nutrition: Calories 630 | Fat 41.7 g | Sugar 8 g | Protein 36.1 g | Sodium 265 mg | Carbs 24 g

323. Chicken Parmesan

(Prep time: 20 minutes | Cook time: 15 minutes | Serving: 10)

Ingredients

- 8 chicken breast halves, boneless & skinless
- 1 onion, chopped
- All-purpose flour: half cup

- Butter: 2 tbsp.
- Sugar: 2 tbsp.
- Parmesan cheese: 1 ½ cups
- 4 minced garlic cloves
- 3 cans (~15 oz.) Crushed tomatoes
- Wine: ¾ cup
- Fresh parsley: ¼ cup, chopped
- Salt & pepper: ¼ tsp. each

Instructions

1. On a plate, add flour, half of the salt and pepper.
2. Season the chicken with the rest of the salt and pepper, and coat in the flour mixture.
3. In a pan, add butter and a bit of canola oil. Cook the chicken on both sides for three minutes.
4. Take the chicken out, add garlic and onion, cook for 2 minutes.
5. Add wine and deglaze the pan, cook for three minutes, until reduced by half.
6. Add tomatoes and sugar, cook for half an hour, add parmesan and parsley.
7. Serve chicken with sauce.

Nutrition: Calories 342 | Fat 18 g | Sugar 3 g | Protein 24 g | Sodium 124 mg | Carbs 21 g

324. Chicken Burritos

(Prep time: 20 minutes | Cook time: 70 minutes | Serving: 4)

Ingredients

- 1 jalapeno pepper, chopped without seeds
- Fresh oregano: 2 tbsp.
- 4 (10") whole-wheat tortillas
- 1 yellow onion, diced
- Oil: 1 tsp.
- Cooked chicken breast: 8 oz.
- Cumin seed: 2 tbsp.
- 1 red bell pepper, diced

- 2 ribs celery, diced
- Grape tomatoes: 2 cups
- Canned black beans: half cup, rinsed
- 2 chopped garlic cloves
- Green cabbage: 2 cups, shredded

Instructions

1. In a skillet, add oil on medium heat. Sauté vegetables and cumin for 10 to 15 minutes.
2. Add garlic, oregano and tomatoes. Cook for 5 to 10 minutes, transfer to a blender. Puree until smooth.
3. In each tortilla, add chicken and top with beans, sauce and cabbage. Roll tightly and Serve.

Nutrition for each burrito: Calories 286 | Fat 6 g | Sugar 8 g | Protein 20 g |Sodium 382 mg | Carbs 38 g

325. Creamy Chicken & Mushrooms

(Prep time: 15 minutes | Cook time: 15 minutes | Serving: 4)

Ingredients

- Dry white wine: half cup
- 4 chicken cutlets (4-5-oz.)
- Fresh parsley: 2 tbsp., chopped
- Mixed mushrooms: 4 cups, sliced
- Heavy cream: half cup
- Salt & pepper: ¼ tsp. each

Instructions

1. Season the chicken with salt and pepper.
2. In a pan, add oil (1 tbsp.) and cook chicken on medium for 7-10 minutes, until browned all over. Take them out.
3. In the pan, add oil (1 tbsp.) sauté mushrooms for 4 minutes. Turn the heat to high, and add dry wine and cook for 4 minutes. Turn the heat low and add cream and chicken juices.
4. Add the chicken back in the pan, stir well and

serve.

Nutrition: Calories 325 | Fat 19.6 g | Sugar 2.5 g | Protein 29.1 g |Sodium 229 mg | Carbs 4.2 g

326. Italian Pot Roast

(Prep time: 15 minutes | Cook time: 7 hours & 10 minutes | Serving: 8)

Ingredients

- 6 peppercorns
- 3 allspice berries
- 2 carrots, sliced
- Olive oil: 2 tsp.
- 1 (3") cinnamon stick
- 4 minced garlic cloves
- Beef chuck roast, boneless (2 pounds)
- 2 celery ribs, sliced
- 1 can of (28 oz.) Crushed tomatoes
- 1 onion, diced
- 4 cloves
- Beef broth: 1 cup, low-sodium
- Salt: ¼ tsp.

Instructions

1. In double cheesecloth, add all spices and secure tightly.
2. In a skillet, add oil on medium heat. Sear roast on all sides and place in a slow cooker (4 qt.).
3. Add spices and vegetables except for garlic and onion.
4. In the pan, add onion and sauté until soft, add garlic and cook for 1 minute.
5. Add broth and cook, let it come to a boil, turn the heat low and simmer until it is reduced by 2/3 cup. Add salt and tomatoes, mix and pour in the slow cooker.
6. Cook on low for 6 to 7 hours, then take the meat and spice bag out.

7. Remove fat and serve.

Nutrition for 3 oz.: Calories 251 | Fat 12 g | Sugar 2 g | Protein 6.4 g |Sodium 271 mg | Carbs 11g

327. Maple-Glazed Pork Tenderloin

(Prep time: 20 minutes | Cook time: 30 minutes | Serving: 4)

Ingredients

- Fresh rosemary: 1 tbsp.
- Cauliflower florets: 1 pound
- Ground coriander: half tsp.
- Dried apricots: ¼ cup, chopped
- Whole-grain mustard: 1 tbsp.
- Salt: ¼ tsp.
- 1 pork tenderloin, 1-pound
- Olive oil: 2 tsp.
- Ground cumin: half tsp.
- Maple syrup: 1 tbsp.

Instructions

1. Let the oven preheat to 425 F.
2. In a bowl, mix rosemary and mustard.
3. In a bowl, add the rest of the ingredients with half of the salt and except for pork. Toss well.
4. Let a sauté pan (10") preheat on medium flame.
5. Season the pork with maple syrup and salt. Sear the pork in the hot pan for 1 minute on each side. Take the pork out.
6. Add water (1 tbsp.) to the pan, and deglaze the pan. Add cauliflower mixture and cook for 5 minutes.
7. On a baking sheet, add pork and top with cauliflower, brush with rosemary-mustard mixture.
8. Roast for 20 minutes until the internal temperature of the meat reaches 145 F
9. Rest it for 5 minutes, slice and serve with cauliflower and juices.

Nutrition: Calories 214| Fat 5 g | Sugar 5 g | Protein 26 g |Sodium 543 mg | Carbs 15 g

328. Slow-Cooker Chicken & Orzo

(Prep time: 20 minutes | Cook time: 2-4 hours & 30 minutes | Serving: 4)

Ingredients

- Chicken broth: 1 cup, low-sodium
- Herbes de Provence: 1 tsp.
- 2 tomatoes, chopped
- Salt & pepper: ¼ tsp. Each
- 1 onion, cut in half-moon
- Chicken breasts: 1 pound, boneless & skinless
- 1 lemon's juice & zest
- Fresh parsley: 2 tbsp., chopped
- Whole-wheat orzo: ¾ cup
- Green olives: 1/3 cup, cut in fours

Instructions

1. Slice every chicken breast into 4 pieces.
2. In a slow cooker (6 qt.), add all the ingredients except for olives & orzo; cook for 4 hours on low or 2 hours on High.
3. Add olives and orzo, cook for half an hour. Serve.

Nutrition: Calories 278 | Fat 4.7 g | Sugar 3.1 g | Protein 29 g |Sodium 387 mg | Carbs 29.5 g

329. Philly Cheesesteak Stuffed Peppers

(Prep time: 20 minutes | Cook time: 40 minutes | Serving: 4)

Ingredients

- Olive oil: 1 tbsp.
- Top round steak: 12 oz., sliced thin
- 1 onion, cut into half-moons
- 2 bell peppers, halved & seeded

- Black pepper: half tsp.
- Mushroom: 8 oz., sliced
- Salt: ¼ tsp.
- Italian seasoning: 1 tbsp.
- Low-fat provolone cheese: 4 slices
- Worcestershire sauce: 1 tbsp.

Instructions

1. Let the oven preheat to 375 F.
2. On a baking sheet, place the halved peppers, bake for half an hour.
3. In a pan, add oil on medium flame. Sauté onion for 4-5 minutes.
4. Add mushrooms, sauté for 5 minutes.
5. Add steak, spices and seasonings. Cook for 3 to 5 minutes, turn the heat off and add Worcestershire.
6. Let the broiler preheat to high, stuff the pepper halves with filling and place 1 cheese slice on top.
7. Broil for 2-3 minutes, 5" away from heat source.

Nutrition for halved pepper: Calories 308 | Fat 16.9 g | Sugar 5.8 g | Protein 29 g | Sodium 454 mg | Carbs 11.9 g

330. Pork & Mushroom Casserole

(Prep time: 20 minutes | Cook time: 2 hours | Serving: 4)
Ingredients

- Brown mushrooms: 17 oz., sliced
- **Pork** shoulder: 35 oz., boneless & cut into 1" pieces
- 2 celery stalks, diced
- Olive oil: 2 tbsp.
- Plain flour: 2 tbsp.
- 1 onion, sliced
- 2 garlic cloves, sliced
- Fresh rosemary: 2 tbsp., chopped
- Fresh thyme: 1 tbsp., chopped

- Lemon zest: 2 tsp.
- Chicken stock: 1 1/2 cups, low-sodium
- Pearl barley: ¾ cup
- Fresh sage: 1 tbsp., chopped
- Fresh flat-leaf parsley: 2 tbsp., chopped

Instructions

1. In a ziplock bag, add flour and pepper. Mix and add pork; shake well.
2. In a skillet, add half the oil, and place on high flame.
3. Sear pork for 5 minutes until browned. Take it out on a plate.
4. Add the rest of the onion and add vegetables and herbs. Cook for 8-10 minutes.
5. Add water (1 ½ cups) and stock. Let it come to a boil, add the pork back and transfer to the oven; bake for 1 hour & 20 minutes, covered.
6. Cook barley as per the pack's instructions.
7. Take the cover off the skillet, bake for 25 minutes.
8. Serve the pork with zest on top and barley.

Nutrition: Calories 381 | Fat 15.5 g | Sugar 2 g | Protein 7.1 g | Sodium 32 mg | Carbs

331. Chicken Cutlets with Tomato Cream Sauce

(Prep time: 20 minutes | Cook time: 15 minutes | Serving: 4)
Ingredients

- Salt & pepper: ¼ tsp. Each
- Sun-dried tomatoes in oil: half cup, sliced with only 1 tbsp. Of oil
- Chicken cutlets: 1 pound
- Low-fat cream: half cup
- Chopped shallots: half cup, chopped
- Dry white wine: half cup
- Fresh parsley: 2 tbsp., chopped

Instructions

1. Season chicken with half of the salt and pepper.

2. In a pan, add oil from tomatoes on medium flame. Add chicken and cook for 6 minutes until the internal temperature of the meat reaches 165 F.

3. Add shallots and sun-dried tomatoes. Cook for 1 minute.

4. Turn the flame high and add wine, deglaze the pan, cook for 2 minutes.

5. Turn the heat to medium and add cream and chicken juices with the rest of the salt and pepper; cook for 2 minutes.

6. Add chicken back to the pan, serve.

Nutrition for 3 oz.: Calories 324 | Fat 18.9 g | Sugar 1.8 g | Protein 25 g |Sodium 249 mg | Carbs

332. Grilled Basil Chicken & Tomatoes

(Prep time: 60 minutes | Cook time: 10 minutes | Serving: 4)
Ingredients
- Fresh basil: 1/4 cup, packed
- 4 chicken breast halves, boneless & skinless (4 oz., each)
- Olive oil: 2 tbsp.
- 8 tomatoes, plum
- 1 minced garlic clove
- Balsamic vinegar: 3/4 cup
- Salt: ¼ tsp.

Instructions
1. In a blender, add all ingredients except for chicken and tomatoes.

2. Add only 4 tomatoes to the blender. Pulse until smooth.

3. In a bowl, add tomato mixture (2/3 cup) and chicken. Mix and keep in the fridge for 60 minutes.

4. Take the chicken out and discard the liquids.

5. Grill the chicken for 4-6 minutes on 1 side until the

internal temperature of the meat reaches 165 F.

6. Cut the rest of the tomatoes in half and grill for 2 to 4 minutes on each side.

7. Serve tomatoes and chicken with the rest of the tomato sauce.

Nutrition: Calories 177 | Fat 5 g | Sugar 7 g | Protein 24 g |Sodium 171 mg | Carbs 8

333. Spicy Mediterranean Lamb Kebabs

(Prep time: 30 minutes | Cook time: 10 minutes | Serving: 4)
Ingredients
- 2 yellow onions, chopped
- Black pepper: half tsp.
- Grind bulgur: 2 cups
- Chopped pine nuts: ¼ cup
- Ground cinnamon: half tsp.
- 2 minced garlic cloves
- Very lean lamb: 1 1/2 pounds
- Salt: 1/4 tsp.
- Ground cumin: 1 tsp.
- Lemon juice: 2 tbsp.
- Ground cardamom: half tsp.

Instructions
1. In a food processor, add onions and puree them.

2. Strain it and discard the pulp. Add lemon juice to this liquid and water to make it 1 1/2cups.

3. In a bowl, add the liquids and bulgur, let it soak for ten minutes.

4. Add the rest of the ingredients to the bulgur. Mix well.

5. Make the mixture into 16 long kebabs, and thread onto skewers.

6. Use little water if it is too dry. Keep in the fridge for half an hour.

7. Let the broiler preheat. Oil spray a broiling pan and

place 4-6 inches away from the heat source.

8. Broil the kebabs for 8 minutes, turning and serve with yogurt.

Nutrition: Calories 317 | Fat 19 g | Sugar 1.8 g | Protein 24.7 g | Sodium 301 mg | Carbs 17.2 g

334. Dijon-Honey Pork Chops

(Prep time: 10 minutes | Cook time: 10 minutes | Serving: 4)

Ingredients

- Lemon-pepper seasoning: 1 tsp., salt-free
- Canola oil: 2 tsp.
- 4 pork loin boneless chops
- Dijon mustard: 1 tbsp.
- Orange juice: half cup
- Honey: 1 tbsp.

Instructions

1. Season the chops with lemon pepper.

2. In a skillet, add oil on medium, sear the chops on both sides.

3. In a bowl, add the rest of the ingredients and pour in the pan.

4. Let it come to a boil, turn the heat low and simmer for 5 to 8 minutes until the internal temperature of the meat reaches 145 F.

5. Take the chops out and let the sauce boil, and let it reduce by ¼ cup.

6. Serve the sauce with chops.

Nutrition for 1 chop: Calories 244 | Fat 11 g | Sugar 7 g | Protein 28 g | Sodium 134 mg | Carbs 9 g

335. Cherry-Chicken Lettuce Wraps

(Prep time: 15 minutes | Cook time: 10 minutes | Serving: 4)

Ingredients

- Ground ginger: 1 tsp.
- Shredded carrots: 1 ½ cups
- Salt & pepper: ¼ tsp. Each
- Chicken breasts: 3/4 pound, boneless & skinless, cubed
- Olive oil: 2 tsp.
- Fresh sweet fresh cherries: 1 1/4 cups, pitted & chopped
- Almonds: 1/3 cup, chopped
- Rice vinegar: 2 tbsp.
- 4 scallions, chopped
- 8 lettuce Boston leaves
- Teriyaki sauce: 2 tbsp., low-sodium
- Honey: 1 tbsp.

Instructions

1. Season the chicken with salt, pepper and ginger.

2. In a skillet, add oil on medium heat. Add chicken and cook for 3 to 5 minutes.

3. Turn the heat off and add almonds, cherries, carrots and scallions.

4. In a cup, mix the rest of the ingredients, mix and pour over chicken, toss and serve in lettuce leaves.

Nutrition for 2 lettuce rolls: Calories 257 | Fat 10 g | Sugar 15 g | Protein 21 g | Sodium 381 mg | Carbs 22 g

336. Heart Healthy Lasagna Rolls

(Prep time: 15 minutes | Cook time: 20 minutes | Serving: 4)

Ingredients

- Ground turkey breast: 6 oz.
- Ricotta cheese: 1 cup, low-fat
- Chopped spinach: 10 oz., frozen & thawed, drained
- Mozzarella cheese: ¾ cup, low-fat
- Long whole-grain: 12 lasagna noodles
- Red pepper flakes: ¼ tsp.
- 2 cups of marinara sauce

Instructions

1. Cook lasagna noodles as per the pack's instructions.

2. Cut every cooked noodle in half crosswise.

3. In a pan, add turkey meat and cook until browned.

Drain and add red pepper flakes and spinach, cook until spinach is warmed.

4. Turn the heat off and let it cool.

5. Add ricotta cheese and mix well.

6. Let the oven preheat to 400 F.

7. In a baking dish (13 by 9"), add half a cup of marinara and spread; onto every lasagna noodle, add the filling mixture (1 tbsp.) and roll tightly.

8. Place in the baking dish. Add the rest of the marinara sauce on top, add cheese on top. Bake for 15 minutes, covered. Serve.

Nutrition: Calories 377 | Fat 13 g | Sugar 7 g | Protein 24.7 g | Sodium 227 mg | Carbs 21 g

337. Chicken & Asparagus Bake

(Prep time: 15 minutes | Cook time: 20 minutes | Serving: 4)
Ingredients

- Carrots: 8 oz., cut into 1" pieces
- Olive oil: 3 tbsp.
- Baby potatoes: 12 oz., halved
- Salt: ¼ tsp.
- Black pepper: half tsp.
- Ground coriander: 2 tsp.
- Asparagus: 1 pound, trimmed
- 2 chicken breasts, boneless & skinless, halved crosswise
- Lemon juice: 2 tbsp.
- Shallot: 2 tbsp., chopped
- Fresh flat-leaf parsley: 2 tbsp., chopped
- Whole-grain mustard: 1 tbsp.
- Honey: 2 tsp.
- Fresh dill: 1 tbsp.

Instructions

1. Let the oven preheat to 375 F.

2. Pound a chicken with a mallet into half' thickness.

Place on the baking sheet on 1 side, and place carrots and potatoes on the other half.

3. Add oil (1 tbsp.), half of salt & pepper, and coriander (1 tsp.) on the tray. Toss but keep the vegetables, chicken separate, and bake for 15 minutes.

4. In a bowl, add the rest of the ingredients.

5. Take the tray out from the oven and place asparagus on the vegetable side.

6. Add the rest of the ingredients on top, and broil until the internal temperature of the meat reaches 165 F. Serve.

Nutrition: Calories 325 | Fat 13.8 g | Sugar 8 g | Protein 27 g | Sodium 465 mg | Carbs 30 g

338. Balsamic-Seasoned Steak

(Prep time: 15 minutes | Cook time: 13 minutes | Serving: 4)
Ingredients

- Coarsely black pepper: ¼ tsp.
- Beef sirloin steak: 1 pound
- Steak sauce: 2 tsp., salt-free
- Balsamic vinegar: 2 tbsp.
- Low-fat Swiss cheese: 2 oz., thin strips

Instructions

1. Let the broiler preheat.

2. Season the steak with pepper and broil for 7 minutes, 4-inches from heat.

3. In a bowl, mix steak sauce with vinegar.

4. Flip the steak and drizzle with sauce mixture (1 tbsp.)

5. Broil for 4 to 6 minutes until the internal temperature of the meat reaches 140 F.

6. Take the steak out and let it rest for 5 minutes, slice the steak and add the rest of the vinegar mixture on top.

7. Add cheese and broil, serve.

Nutrition for 3 oz.: Calories 188 | Fat 1 g | Sugar 8 g | Protein 26 g |Sodium 116 mg | Carbs 2g

339. Chicken Pesto Pasta with Asparagus

(Prep time: 15 minutes | Cook time: 10 minutes | Serving: 6)

Ingredients

- Whole-wheat penne: 8 oz.
- Low-fat parmesan cheese: ¼ cup, grated
- Chicken breast: 3 cups, cooked & shredded
- Fresh asparagus: 1 pound, 2" pieces
- Basil pesto: 7 oz.
- Salt & pepper: ¼ tsp. each

Instructions

1. According to the package's instructions, cook the pasta.
2. In the last 2 minutes, add asparagus and drain all but half a cup of water.
3. Add the rest of the ingredients to the same pot. Mix and serve.

Nutrition for 1 cup: Calories 309 | Fat 18.4 g | Sugar 3.5 g | Protein 31 g |Sodium 345 mg | Carbs 32 g

340. Chicken Fried Rice

(Prep time: 15 minutes | Cook time: 10 minutes | Serving: 6)

Ingredients

- 4 eggs, whisked
- Tiny green beans: 1 pound
- Diced onion: 3/4 cup
- Vegetable oil: 3 tbsp.
- Red bell pepper: 3/4 cup, diced
- Asian chili-garlic sauce: 2-3 tsp.
- Soy sauce: 1/3 cup, low sodium
- Cooked chicken: 2 cups, chopped
- Cooked basmati rice: 4 cups

Instructions

1. In a skillet, add some oil on medium heat.
2. Add eggs, cook for 1-2 minutes, stir, take them out

on a plate, and chop.

3. Add some oil (2 tbsp.) on medium heat, sauté all vegetables for 3-4 minutes.
4. Add chicken and cook for 2 minutes.
5. Add the rest of the ingredients, stir for 3-4 minutes.
6. Add eggs, toss and serve.
7. Stir in scrambled eggs; sprinkle with desired toppings.

Nutrition: Calories 371 | Fat 19 g | Sugar 2 g | Protein 27 g |Sodium 314 mg | Carbs 25 g

341. Chicken & Spinach Skillet Pasta

(Prep time: 15 minutes | Cook time: 20 minutes | Serving: 4)

Ingredients

- Fresh spinach: 10 cups, chopped
- Olive oil: 2 tbsp.
- 4 minced garlic cloves
- Chicken breasts: 1 pound, boneless & skinless, cubed
- Dry white wine: half cup
- Whole-wheat penne pasta: 8 oz.
- Salt & pepper: ¼ tsp. Each
- 1 lemon's juice & zest
- Grated parmesan cheese: 4 tbsp.

Instructions

1. As per package instructions, cook pasta.
2. In a skillet, add oil on medium heat. Cook chicken with salt and pepper for 5-7 minutes.
3. Add garlic and cook for 1 minute. Add zest, lemon juice and wine. Let it simmer and turn the heat off.
4. Add spinach and pasta, stir and let it rest, covered, until spinach wilts.
5. Serve with cheese on top.

Nutrition: Calories 335 | Fat 12.3 g | Sugar 1.1 g | Protein 28 g |Sodium 378 mg | Carbs 25 g

342. Carolina-Style Vinegar BBQ Chicken

(Prep time: 15 minutes | Cook time: 5 hours | Serving: 6)
Ingredients

- 1 cup of white vinegar
- Red pepper flakes: 1 tsp.
- Salt: ¼ tsp.
- 1/4 cup of sugar substitute
- 2 cups of water
- Chicken base: 1 tbsp., low-sodium
- Chicken breasts: 1 1/2 pounds, boneless & skinless

Instructions

1. In a slow cooker (6 qt.), add all ingredients stir and cook for 4 to 5 hours on low.
2. Take the chicken out, drain all but 1 cup of juice.
3. Shred the chicken and add the chicken back to the cooker with reserved juice.
4. Heat it well and serve in whole wheat buns.

Nutrition for the half cup: Calories 134| Fat 3 g | Sugar 3 g | Protein 23 g |Sodium 228 mg | Carbs 3 g

343. Grilled Peanut Chicken

(Prep time: 15 minutes | Cook time: 15 minutes | Serving: 6)
Ingredients

- Lime juice: 1 tbsp.
- Peanut butter: 2 tbsp., low-fat
- Cayenne pepper: a pinch
- 1 minced garlic clove
- Curry powder: 1/3 tsp.
- 4 chicken breast halves, skinless & boneless
- Soy sauce: 2 tsp.

Instructions

1. Let the grill preheat to high.
2. In a bowl, add all ingredients except for chicken, mix well.
3. Oil spray the grill grates, place chicken and brush with half of the sauce; cook for 6-8 minutes.
4. Flip and brush with the rest of the sauce. Cook for 6-8 minutes. Serve.

Nutrition: Calories 340 | Fat 17 g | Sugar 8 g | Protein 32 g |Sodium 302 mg | Carbs 13 g

344. Skillet Lemon Chicken & Potatoes

(Prep time: 15 minutes | Cook time: 20 minutes | Serving: 4)
Ingredients

- Chicken thighs: 1 pound, boneless & skinless
- Baby gold potatoes: 1 pound, halved lengthwise
- Baby kale: 6 cups
- Chicken broth: half cup, low sodium
- Olive oil: 3 tbsp.
- 1 lemon, sliced without seeds
- Salt & pepper: 1/4 tsp. Each
- 4 minced garlic cloves
- Fresh tarragon: 1 tbsp., chopped

Instructions

1. Let the oven preheat to 400 F.
2. In a pan, add oil (1 tbsp.) and season chicken with half of the salt and pepper.
3. Cook for 5 minutes, and take it out on a plate.
4. Add the rest of the oil and season potatoes with salt and pepper.
5. Cook potatoes for 3 minutes cut side down. Add the rest of the ingredients (except for kale) and place the chicken back in the pan.
6. Place the pan in the oven and bake for 15 minutes, add kale and cook for 3-4 minutes more. Serve.

Nutrition: Calories 374| Fat 19.3 g | Sugar 1.8 g | Protein 24.7 g |Sodium 334 mg | Carbs 25 g

345. Carne Guisada

(Prep time: 15 minutes | Cook time: 7-9 hours | Serving: 12)

Ingredients

- 1/4 cup of all-purpose flour
- 1 bay leaf
- Beer: 12 oz.
- 1 jalapeno pepper, chopped without seeds
- Worcestershire sauce: 4 tsp.
- Chili powder: 2 tsp.
- Salt: ¼ tsp.
- Ground cumin: 1 ½ tsp.
- Paprika: half tsp.
- Tomato paste: 2 tbsp.
- Red pepper flakes: 2-3 tsp.
- Pork shoulder roast: 3 pounds, boneless & cut into 2" pieces
- 2 minced garlic cloves
- 1 onion, chopped
- Red wine vinegar: half tsp.
- 2 red potatoes, unpeeled & chopped

Instructions

1. In a slow cooker (4-5 qt.), add all ingredients, stir well and cook for 7 to 9 hours on low.
2. Take the meat out and shred it, discard the bay leaf and take the fat off.
3. Serve shredded meat with sauce.

Nutrition for 2/3 cup: Calories 261 | Fat 12 g | Sugar 3 g | Protein 21 g |Sodium 200 mg | Carbs 16 g

346. Delmonico Steak with Mushroom Sauce

(Prep time: 15 minutes | Cook time: 22 minutes | Serving: 2)

Ingredients

- Margarine: 1 tsp., trans-free
- Button mushrooms: 2 oz.
- 3 minced garlic cloves
- Rosemary: ¼ tsp.
- 2 (4 oz.) New York strip steaks
- Shiitake mushrooms: 2 oz., sliced
- Thyme: ¼ tsp.
- Broth, low-sodium: ¼ cup

Instructions

1. Let the grill preheat.
2. Place the grates 4-6" away from the heat source. Oil spray the grates.
3. Grill the steak for ten minutes on 1 side until the internal temperature of the meat reaches 145-160 F. Take it out on a plate.
4. In a pan, add margarine on medium flame.
5. Sauté garlic and herbs, for 1-2 minutes. Add broth and deglaze the pan, cook, until it thickens and reduces, serves with steak.

Nutrition: Calories 351 | Fat 21 g | Sugar 5.5 g | Protein 29 g |Sodium 265 mg | Carbs 13 g

347. Chicken Tortilla Casserole

(Prep time: 15 minutes | Cook time: 30 minutes | Serving: 6)

Ingredients

- Olive oil: 2 tbsp.
- 1 leek, sliced, color-separated
- Cornstarch: 1 tbsp.
- Sliced mushrooms: 8 oz.
- Chicken breasts: 1 pound, boneless & skinless
- 3 sliced garlic cloves
- Mexican cheese blend: 1/3 cup, shredded
- 1% milk: 2 cups
- Baby spinach: 4 cups
- Green salsa: 1/3 cup
- Pickled jalapeños: ¼ cup, chopped
- Goat cheese: 4 oz.
- Salt & pepper: half tsp. Each
- 12 corn tortillas, cut in half

Instructions

1. Let the oven preheat to 400 F. Oil spray a 9 by 13" baking dish.

2. In a pan, add chicken and water to cover it.

3. Let it come to a boil, covered, turn the heat low and simmer for 1-12 minutes.

4. Take the chicken out and chop.

5. Add oil on medium flame, sauté garlic, mushroom and leek, and cook for 4 minutes in a skillet.

6. Add cornstarch and milk add to the skillet, cook for 3 minutes until it thickens.

7. Add the rest of the ingredients, except for tortillas, cheese and salsa, cook for 2 minutes. Turn the heat off and add the chicken; stir well.

8. In the baking dish, add tortillas and cover the dish, add filling (1 ½ cups).

9. Layer the tortilla and filling, and spread salsa and cheese on top.

10. Bake for 20-25 minutes, let it rest for ten minutes. Serve.

Nutrition: Calories 351 | Fat 21 g | Sugar 8 g | Protein 29 g |Sodium 303 mg | Carbs 13 g

348. Chicken & Wild Rice Casserole

(Prep time: 15 minutes | Cook time: 27 minutes | Serving: 4)
Ingredients

- 3 cups, cooked wild brown rice
- Chicken thighs: 1 1/4 pounds, boneless & skinless, bite-size pieces
- 1 sweet onion, diced
- Olive oil: 4 tbsp.
- Parmesan cheese: half cup, grated
- Salt & pepper: ¼ tsp. Each
- Fresh thyme: 1 tbsp., chopped
- Peeled butternut squash: 5 cups cubes

- Cranberries: ¾ cup, dried

Instructions

1. Let the oven preheat to 350 F. oil spray a baking dish (9 by 13").

2. In a skillet, add oil (2 tsp.) on medium heat. Cook the chicken for 6 minutes, take it out on a plate.

3. Add the rest of the oil to a pan, and sauté all vegetables with salt for 2 minutes.

4. Cook, covered for 6 to 8 minutes. Add rice, parmesan (1/4 cup), chicken, cranberries and thyme. Cook for a few minutes and transfer in the baking dish.

5. Bake for 20 minutes, take the dish out and sprinkle with the rest of the cheese on top.

6. Bake for 5 minutes. Serve with fresh herbs on top.

Nutrition: Calories 323 | Fat 15.1 g | Sugar 8 g | Protein 29 g |Sodium 301 mg | Carbs 11.1 g

349. Chicken Tenders with Salad

(Prep time: 15 minutes | Cook time: 10 minutes | Serving: 4)
Ingredients

- 1 egg
- Whole wheat breadcrumbs: half cup
- 1 pound of chicken tenders
- Black pepper: 1/8 tsp.
- Canola oil: ¼ cup
- All-purpose flour: 2 tbsp.
- White-wine vinegar: 1 tbsp.
- Olive oil: 2 tbsp.
- Everything bagel seasoning: 1 tbsp.
- Mixed baby greens: 5 oz.
- Honey: 1 tsp.
- Dijon mustard: 1 tsp.

Instructions

1. In a bowl, whisk egg; in a different dish, add flour.

2. In a separate bowl, add everything seasoning and breadcrumbs. Mix.

3. Coat chicken in flour, then in egg and lastly in crumbs.

4. In a skillet, add oil on medium heat. Add chicken and cook for 7 minutes; the internal temperature of the meat reaches 165 F.

5. In a bowl, add the rest of the ingredients, toss and serve with chicken.

Nutrition: Calories 394| Fat 25 g | Sugar 2.1 g | Protein 26 g |Sodium 402 mg | Carbs 13.8 g

350. Roasted Chicken Thighs

(Prep time: 15 minutes | Cook time: 10 minutes | Serving: 8)
Ingredients

- 2 red & 2 green peppers
- Fresh rosemary: 3 tsp., chopped
- Olive oil: 2 tbsp.
- Red potatoes: 2 pounds
- Fresh thyme: 4 tsp., chopped
- Salt & pepper: ¼ tsp. each
- 2 onions
- 8 chicken thighs, boneless & skinless

Instructions

1. Let the oven preheat to 450 F.

2. Cut the onions, potatoes and peppers into one" piece, place on a roasting sheet.

3. Add oil (1 tbsp.) and herbs (2 tsp. each), toss to coat.

4. Arrange chicken on top of vegetables, brush with oil and add herbs, salt & pepper on top.

5. Roast for 35 to 40 minutes until the internal temperature of the meat reaches 175 F.

Nutrition: Calories 308| Fat 12 g | Sugar 5 g | Protein 24 g |Sodium 221 mg | Carbs 25 g

351. Chicken Rice with Onion & Tarragon

(Prep time: 45 minutes | Cook time: 70-80 minutes | Serving: 6)
Ingredients

- 1 1/2 cups of chopped celery
- Long-grain white rice: ¾ cup, uncooked
- Chicken broth: 2 cups, low-sodium
- 1 1/2 cups of pearl onions
- Chicken breast: 1 pound, boneless & skinless, halves
- 1 1/2 cups of dry white wine
- Fresh tarragon: 1 tsp.
- Wild rice: ¾ cup, uncooked

Instructions

1. Let the oven preheat to 300 F.

2. Slice the chicken into one" piece.

3. In a pan, add chicken, broth (1 cup), onion, tarragon and celery. Cook for ten minutes on medium flame and let it cool.

4. Add rice, broth (1 cup), wine to a baking dish and soak for half an hour.

5. Add vegetables and chicken to the dish, bake for 1 hour, covered.

6. Add more broth; if it gets dry in-between, serve.

Nutrition for 1 ½ cups: Calories 313 | Fat 17 g | Sugar 2 g | Protein 6.4 g |Sodium 104 mg | Carbs 38 g

352. Golden Apricot-Glazed Turkey Breast

(Prep time: 15 minutes | Cook time: 2 hours | Serving: 15)
Ingredients

- 1 turkey breast, 5 pounds, bone-in
- Balsamic vinegar: 1/4 cup
- Apricot preserves: half cup
- Pepper: ¼ tsp.

- Salt, a pinch

Instructions

1. Let the oven preheat to 325 F.
2. In a bowl, add all ingredients except for the turkey. Mix.
3. In a roasting pan, place turkey. Bake for 1 to 2 hours until the internal temperature of the meat reaches 175 F.
4. Keep basting with the apricot mixture every half an hour.
5. Let it rest for 15 minutes and serve.

Nutrition for 4 oz.: Calories 236| Fat 8 g | Sugar 5 g | Protein 32 g |Sodium 84 mg | Carbs 8 g

353. Roast Pork with Apples & Onions

(Prep time: 15 minutes | Cook time: 60 minutes | Serving: 8)

Ingredients

- Pork loin roast, boneless, 2 pounds
- 3 golden apples, large, sliced into one" wedges
- Salt & pepper: ¼ tsp. Each
- Fresh rosemary: 1 tbsp., chopped
- Olive oil: 1 tbsp.
- 2 onions, cut into ¾" wedges
- 5 garlic cloves

Instructions

1. Let the oven preheat to 350 F.
2. Season the roast with pepper and salt.
3. In a skillet, add oil on medium heat. Sear the roast on all sides and take it out on a plate.
4. Add the rest of the ingredients in the pan, and place the roast back in.
5. Roast for 45 to 55 minutes until the internal temperature of the meat reaches 145 F.
6. Flipping garlic, onion and apples once. Rest it for ten minutes, slice and serve.

Nutrition: Calories 210 | Fat 7 g | Sugar 9 g | Protein 23 g |Sodium 109 mg | Carbs 14 g

354. Turkey & Black Bean Chili

(Prep time: 15 minutes | Cook time: 6-8 hours | Serving: 8)

Ingredients

- 1 can of diced tomato, with liquids
- Turkey breast: 2 pounds, skinless
- 2 cans of tomato sauce
- Dried oregano: 2 tsp.
- 2 cans of black beans, rinsed
- Corn kernels: 1 cup
- Cumin: 1 tbsp.
- Red pepper flakes: half tsp.
- 4 minced garlic cloves
- Chili powder: 1 tbsp.
- Coriander: 2 tsp.

Instructions

1. In a bowl, add all ingredients and divide into 2 portions.
2. Cook or freeze, both or one portion, add to the slow cooker.
3. Cook for 6-8 hours on low. Serve.

Nutrition: Calories 406| Fat 2.4 g | Sugar 16 g | Protein 49 g |Sodium 123 mg | Carbs 47 g

355. Mixed Spice-Burgers

(Prep time: 15 minutes | Cook time: 10 minutes | Serving: 6)

Ingredients

- Fresh parsley: 3 tbsp., chopped
- 1 onion, chopped
- 1 minced garlic clove
- Cinnamon: half tsp.
- Ground allspice: ¾ tsp.
- Lean ground beef: 1 1/2 pounds
- Black pepper: ¾ tsp.
- Fresh mint: 2 tbsp., chopped

- Salt: ¼ tsp.
- Ground nutmeg: ¼ tsp.

Instructions
1. In a bowl, add all ingredients except for beef, mix well add beef.
2. Mix well, but do not over mix. Make it into 6 long patties.
3. Grill or broil for 4 to 6 minutes, 4 inches from heat (if broiling), cook until the internal temperature of the meat reaches 160 F. Sever.

Nutrition: Calories 192 | Fat 9 g | Sugar 2 g | Protein 6.4 g | Sodium 245 mg | Carbs 3 g

356. Chicken Chili Verde
(Prep time: 15 minutes | Cook time: 20 minutes | Serving: 6)
Ingredients
- Canola oil: 1 tbsp.
- Chicken stock: 4 cups, salt-free
- Chicken thighs: 1 ½ pound, boneless & skinless, bite-size pieces
- Yellow onion: 2 cups, chopped
- Spinach: 2 cups, chopped
- 2 cans of (15 oz.) Pinto beans, rinsed
- Poblano peppers: 2 cups, chopped
- Corn kernels: 2 cups
- 5 chopped garlic cloves
- Salsa Verde: 1 ½ cups
- Fresh cilantro: 1 ½ cups, chopped
- Salt: ¼ tsp.
- Sour cream: 6 tbsp.

Instructions
1. In a bowl, add beans (1 cup) and mash them
2. In a pot, add oil on high heat. Add chicken and cook for 4-5 minutes.
3. Add garlic, onion and poblano and cook for 4 to 5 minutes.

4. Add all the beans, salt, salsa and stock, let it come to a boil, turn the heat low and simmer for three minutes.
5. Add the rest of the ingredients, cook for 1 minute. Serve.

Nutrition: Calories 408 | Fat 13 g | Sugar 8.6 g | Protein 31.6 g | Sodium 509 mg | Carbs 40 g

357. Charred Lemon Chicken Piccata
(Prep time: 15 minutes | Cook time: 18 minutes | Serving: 6)
Ingredients
- 2 lemons, sliced
- 4 chicken breast halves, skinless, boneless, ¾" thickness
- Sugar: 1 1/2 tsp.
- 4 cloves of garlic
- Unsalted butter: 2 tbsp.
- Kosher salt: ¼ tsp.
- Olive oil: 1 tbsp.
- Grated shallot: 1 tsp.
- Chicken stock: 1 cup, unsalted
- Fresh flat-leaf parsley: 2 tbsp., chopped
- Grated garlic: half tsp.
- 1 oregano & 1 thyme sprig
- Black pepper: half tsp.
- Capers: 1 tbsp., rinsed
- Dry white wine: half cup
- All-purpose flour: 1 tsp.

Instructions
1. In a bowl, add garlic, sugar and lemon slices.
2. Season the chicken with half of the salt and pepper.
3. In a skillet, add oil (2 tsp.) on medium heat. Cook chicken for 4 minutes on 1 side, take it out on a

plate.

4. Add lemon slices in the pan, cook for 1 minute, flipping as needed. Take them out in the bowl.

5. In the pan, add butter and sauté garlic and shallots, herbs, cook for 1 minute.

6. Add wine and deglaze the pan, let it come to a boil, cook for 3 minutes.

7. Add flour, salt and stock; keep whisking. Let it come to a boil, turn the heat low, and simmer for 3 minutes until it is reduced by 2/3 cup. Turn the heat off and take the sprigs out.

8. Add capers and chicken, stir and serve with lemon mixture.

Nutrition: Calories 351 | Fat 21 g | Sugar 8 g | Protein 29 g |Sodium 401 mg | Carbs 13 g

358. Greek Meatball Mezze Bowls

(Prep time: 15 minutes | Cook time: 15 minutes | Serving: 4)

Ingredients

- Lean ground turkey: 1 pound
- Dried oregano: half tsp.
- Feta cheese: half cup, crumbled
- Chopped spinach: 1 cup, frozen & thawed
- Garlic powder: half tsp.
- Sliced cucumber: 2 cups
- Salt & pepper: ¼ tsp.
- Cooked quinoa: 2 cups, cooled
- Chopped parsley: half cup
- ¼ cup of tzatziki
- Lemon juice: 2 tbsp.
- Olive oil: 1 tbsp.
- Chopped mint: 3 tbsp.
- Cherry tomatoes: 2 cups

Instructions

1. Squeeze the spinach to get rid of extra water,

transfer to a bowl.

2. Add half of the salt, pepper, turkey, garlic powder, feta, and oregano. Mix until combined.

3. Make into 12 balls, and coat the pan with oil spray.

4. Add meatballs and cook for 10-12 minutes, until browned all over.

5. In a bowl, mint, quinoa, oil, salt, pepper, lemon juice, mix.

6. In each serving bowl, add the quinoa mixture, meatballs, tomatoes and cucumbers, served with tzatziki.

Nutrition: Calories 392 | Fat 17.2 g | Sugar 5.3 g | Protein 32 g |Sodium 327 mg | Carbs 14 g

359. Firehouse Enchiladas

(Prep time: 15 minutes | Cook time: 30 minutes | Serving: 6)

Ingredients

- Olive oil: 1 tbsp.
- Ground cumin: 1 tsp.
- Salt: ¼ tsp.
- Chopped onion: half cup
- 2 cans of (8 oz.) Tomato sauce, salt-free
- Chili powder: 2 tsp.
- ¾ cup of water
- Scallions: ¼ cup, sliced
- All-purpose flour: 1 tbsp.
- Lean ground beef: 1 ½ pound
- Monterey jack cheese: 3 oz., low-fat shredded
- 12 corn tortillas of 6"
- 1 can of (4 oz.) Green chili peppers, diced & undrained

Instructions

1. Let the oven preheat to 375 F.

2. In a pot, add oil on medium flame. Add cumin, flour, chili powder and salt in hot oil.

3. Cook for 1 minute, add water and tomato sauce.

4. Cook until it comes to a boil, turn the heat low and simmer for 5 minutes, covered.

5. Turn the heat off.

6. In a pan, add beef and brown it, drain and add half cup of sauce, chili peppers, and cheese (1/4 cup).

7. In a baking dish (3 qt., rectangle), add half a cup of sauce at the bottom.

8. Warm tortillas in the microwave.

9. Add meat mixture (1/4 cup) in each tortilla, roll and place in the tray.

10. Add the rest of the meat mixture in sauce, and spoon all over the rolled tortillas.

11. Add sprinkled cheese on top. Bake for 20 minutes, serve.

Nutrition for 2 tortillas: Calories 363 | Fat 11.7 g | Sugar 5.5 g | Protein 32 g |Sodium 387 mg | Carbs 32 g

360. Chicken Gyros

(Prep time: 6 hours & 15 minutes | Cook time: 10 minutes | Serving: 6)

Ingredients

- Fresh mint: 3 tbsp., chopped
- Lemon-pepper marinade: half cup, salt-free
- Chicken breasts: 1-1/2 pounds, boneless & skinless, cubed
- **Sauce**
- Garlic powder: half tsp.
- Lemon juice: 2 tbsp.
- Dill weed: 1 tsp.
- Greek yogurt: half cup, low-fat
- **Assembly**
- Chopped cucumber, tomato, onion & feta cheese

Instructions

1. In a dish, add marinade, mint and chicken, toss well.

2. Cover and keep in the fridge for 6 hours.

3. Before cooking, drain the marinade.

4. In a skillet, add little oil on medium heat. Add

chicken and cook for 4 to 6 minutes.

5. In a bowl, mix all the sauce's ingredients.

6. Serve in pita pockets, with chicken, sauce, and desired toppings.

Nutrition for 1 gyro: Calories 248 | Fat 4 g | Sugar 8 g | Protein 30 g |Sodium 251 mg | Carbs 22g

361. Chicken Souvlaki

(Prep time: 45 minutes | Cook time: 10 minutes | Serving: 6)

Ingredients

1. 2 pita pockets

2. Spinach leaves: 1 cup

3. Low-fat Greek yogurt: 2 tbsp.

4. 1 tomato, thinly sliced

5. 1 chicken breast, large

6. Smoked paprika, chili powder, thyme & oregano: 1/8 tsp.

7. Half cucumber, sliced

8. Olive oil: 1 tbsp.

9. Salt and pepper: 1/8 tsp. Each

10. Feta: 0.7 oz.

11. Lemon juice: 3 tbsp.

12. 2 cloves of garlic

13. Sprinkle a little chili powder – optional

Instructions

- In a bowl, mix cucumber, lettuce, feta and tomato.
- Cut the chicken into chunks, and transfer to a ziplock bag.
- Add the rest of the ingredients, except for pita, shake well and keep in the fridge for half an hour.
- Preheat a griddle pan, thread the chicken onto skewers and grill for few minutes, turning, until cooked.
- Serve in a pita with vegetable mix on top.

Nutrition: Calories 352 | Fat 21 g | Sugar 8 g | Protein 29 g |Sodium 301 mg | Carbs 13 g

362. Chipotle Chicken Quinoa Bowl

(Prep time: 45 minutes | Cook time: 15 minutes | Serving: 4)

Ingredients

- Olive oil: 1 tbsp.
- Garlic powder: half tsp.
- Shredded cheddar: ¼ cup
- Chipotle peppers in sauce (adobo): 1 tbsp., chopped
- Cooked quinoa: 2 cups
- Pico de Gallo: ¼ cup
- Ground cumin: half cup
- Chicken breast: 1 pound boneless & skinless
- 1 avocado, diced
- Salt: ¼ tsp.
- Romaine lettuce: 2 cups, shredded
- Canned pinto beans: 1 cup, rinsed

Instructions

1. Let the grill preheat to medium heat.
2. In a bowl, add garlic powder, chipotles and oil.
3. Oil spray the grill grates sprinkle chicken with salt.
4. Grill for 5 minutes. Flip and brush with oil mixture and cook until the internal temperature of the meat reaches 165 F, for 3-5 minutes.
5. Take off the grill and chop.
6. In each serving bowl, add quinoa, chicken, and the rest of the ingredients, equally. Serve.

Nutrition for 1 bowl: Calories 452 | Fat 18.7 g | Sugar 2.6 g | Protein 35 g |Sodium 460 mg | Carbs 36 g

363. Basil Turkey Burgers

(Prep time: 15 minutes | Cook time: 10 minutes | Serving: 4)

Ingredients

- Smoked barbecue sauce: 3 tbsp.
- Lean ground turkey: 1 pound
- Oat bran: 2 tbsp.
- Chopped fresh basil: 1/4 cup
- 4 buns, whole wheat, split
- Garlic salt: 1/8 tsp.
- 1 minced garlic clove
- Pepper: 1/8 tsp.

Instructions

1. In a bowl, add all ingredients, mix and make into half' thick patties.
2. Oil spray a griddle pan and add burgers, cook for 5 to 7 minutes until the internal temperature of the meat reaches 165 F.
3. Serve in toasted buns.

Nutrition for 1 burger: Calories 315 | Fat 11 g | Sugar 8 g | Protein 27 g |Sodium 378 mg | Carbs 29 g

364. Grilled Lemon Rosemary Chicken

(Prep time: 2 hours & 15 minutes | Cook time: 12 minutes | Serving: 6)

Ingredients

Honey: 3 tbsp.

Salt & pepper: 1/8 tsp., each

Canola oil: 2 tsp.

Lemon juice: ¼ cup

6 chicken breast halves, boneless & skinless

Dried rosemary: 1 tsp.

Instructions

Add all ingredients in a zip lock bag, shake well, and keep in the fridge for 2 hours.

Take the chicken out and drain the marinade.

Preheat a griddle pan and oil spray it; grill chicken for 6 to 8 minutes until the internal temperature of the meat reaches 170 F.

Nutrition for 1 half of breast: Calories 187| Fat 4 g | Sugar 8 g | Protein 34 g |Sodium 102 mg | Carbs 1 g

365. Turkey Medallions with Tomato Salad

(Prep time: 30 minutes | Cook time: 12 minutes | Serving: 6)

Ingredients

- Red wine vinegar: 1 tbsp.
- 1 green pepper, chopped
- Red onion: ¼ cup, chopped
- Olive oil: 2 tbsp.
- Sugar: half tsp.
- Dried oregano & salt: ¼ tsp. Each
- 3 tomatoes
- 1 celery rib, chopped
- Fresh basil: 1 tbsp., chopped
- **Turkey**
- Lemon juice: 2 tbsp.
- Turkey breast tenderloins: 20 oz.
- Panko whole-wheat bread crumbs: 1 cup
- Salt & pepper: ¼ tsp. Each
- Lemon-pepper seasoning: 1 tsp., salt-free
- Parmesan cheese: half cup
- 1 egg
- Chopped walnuts: half cup
- Olive oil: 3 tbsp.

Instructions

1. Slice tomatoes in wedges, add the rest of the salad ingredients, toss and keep in the fridge.
2. In a bowl, whisk lemon juice and egg.
3. In a different bowl, add lemon pepper, crumbs, walnuts and cheese.
4. Slice turkey into one" slices, and pound into half" thickness. Season with salt and pepper.
5. Coat the turkey tenderloin in egg, then in crumb mixture.
6. In a skillet, add oil and cook the tenderloin for 2 to 3 minutes on each side.
7. Serve with tomato salad.

Nutrition: Calories 351 | Fat 21 g | Sugar 8 g | Protein 29 g | Sodium 401 mg | Carbs 13 g

366. White Chicken Chili

(Prep time: 15 minutes | Cook time: 20 minutes | Serving: 8)

Ingredients

- 2 cans of (15 oz.) white beans, low-sodium, without liquid
- 1 onion, chopped
- 1 can of (~15 oz.) diced tomatoes, low-sodium
- 1 can of (10 oz.) white chunk chicken
- Chicken broth: 4 cups, salt-free
- Chili powder: 2 tsp.
- Cayenne pepper: 1/8 tsp.
- Half green pepper, chopped
- 1 red pepper, chopped
- Monterey jack cheese: 8 tbsp., low-fat
- 2 minced garlic cloves
- Dried oregano: 1 tsp.
- Fresh cilantro: 3 tbsp., chopped
- Ground cumin: 1 tsp.

Instructions

1. In a pot, add tomatoes, broth, beans and chicken. Simmer on medium flame, covered.
2. In a pan, add some oil and sauté garlic and other vegetables for 3-5 minutes.
3. Add the vegetable mixture to the pot, add the rest of the ingredients.
4. Cook for ten minutes, serve.

Nutrition for 1 ½ cups: Calories 212 | Fat 4 g | Sugar 4 g | Protein 19 g | Sodium 241 mg | Carbs 25 g

367. Grilled Chicken with Cauliflower Rice

(Prep time: 20 minutes | Cook time: 15 minutes | Serving: 4)
Ingredients

- Ground cumin: 2 ½ tsp.
- Cayenne pepper: ¼ tsp.
- Dried marjoram: 1 ½ tsp.
- Olive oil: 5 tbsp.
- Riced cauliflower: 2 cups
- Salt: 1/8 tsp.
- Ground allspice: ¼ tsp.
- Cherry tomatoes: 1 cup, halved
- Chicken breast: 1 pound, boneless & skinless
- Lemon juice: ¼ cup
- Diced cucumber: 1 cup
- Sliced scallions: ¼ cup
- Flat-leaf parsley leaves: 2 cups

Instructions

1. Let the grill preheat to medium heat.
2. In a bowl, add oil (2 tbsp.), cayenne, allspice, salt, cumin (2 tsp.) and marjoram. Mix and brush all over the chicken.
3. Grill chicken for 10-12 minutes until the internal temperature of the meat reaches 165 F.
4. In a bowl, add the rest of the oil, cumin, parsley, scallions, cauliflower, tomatoes and cucumbers, toss to coat.
5. Slice the grilled chicken and serve with cauliflower rice mixture.

Nutrition: Calories 341| Fat 21.1 g | Sugar 3.2 g | Protein 28 g |Sodium 411 mg | Carbs 8.5 g

368. Spinach & Mushroom Smothered Chicken

(Prep time: 15 minutes | Cook time: 10 minutes | Serving: 4)
Ingredients

- Sliced mushrooms: 1 3/4 cups
- 3 green onions, sliced
- 4 chicken breast halves, boneless & skinless
- Baby spinach: 3 cups
- Olive oil: 1 ½ tsp.
- Provolone cheese: 2 slices, halved, low-fat
- Chopped pecans: 2 tbsp.
- Rotisserie chicken seasoning: half tsp., low-sodium

Instructions

1. Let the broiler preheat.
2. In a skillet, add oil on medium heat. Sauté green onion and mushroom until soft.
3. Add pecans, spinach, cook until wilted. Turn the heat off.
4. Season chicken with seasoning, broil four inches from heat, for 4-5 minutes on 1 side, until the internal temperature of the meat reaches 165 F
5. Add cheese on top, broil until melted. Serve with mushroom mixture.

Nutrition: Calories 203 | Fat 9 g | Sugar 8 g | Protein 27 g |Sodium 210 mg | Carbs 3 g

369. Grilled Pork Fajitas

(Prep time: 15 minutes | Cook time: 10 minutes | Serving: 8)
Ingredients

- Oregano: half tsp.
- Paprika: half tsp.
- 1 small onion, thinly sliced
- Ground coriander: ¼ tsp.
- Diced tomatoes: 3 cups
- Garlic powder: ¼ tsp.
- Pork tenderloin: 1 pound, cut into strips
- 8 whole-wheat tortillas, (8")
- Ground cumin: 1 tsp.
- Cheddar cheese: half cup, shredded
- 4 cups of shredded lettuce
- 1 cup of salsa

Instructions

1. Preheat a grill to medium-high.
2. In a bowl, add herbs and spices, coat the pork in this spice mix.
3. Grill the onion and pork for 5 minutes, until browned on all sides, flipping as needed.
4. In each tortilla, add pork, onions, the rest of the ingredients on top.
5. Roll and serve.

Nutrition for 1 fajita: Calories 180 | Fat 3g | Sugar 4 g | Protein 17 g | Sodium 380 mg | Carbs 29 g

370. Coconut-Curry Chicken Cutlets

(Prep time: 15 minutes | Cook time: 15 minutes | Serving: 4)

Ingredients

- 1 pound of chicken cutlets
- 1 can of (14 oz.) light coconut milk
- Lime juice: 1 tbsp.
- Brown sugar: 1 tbsp.
- 2 cups of cooked quinoa
- Grapeseed oil: 2 tbsp.
- Thai curry red paste: 1 tbsp.

Instructions

1. In a skillet, add oil to medium flame.
2. Cook chicken for 1-3 minutes on 1 side, take it out on a plate.
3. Turn the heat off.
4. In a pan, add oil and the rest of the ingredients. Cook on high flame for 5-10 minutes, until reduced by half.
5. Serve chicken with sauce and quinoa.

Nutrition: Calories 387 | Fat 16 g | Sugar 4.5 g | Protein 31 g | Sodium 194 mg | Carbs 27 g

371. Asparagus Turkey Stir-Fry

(Prep time: 15 minutes | Cook time: 15 minutes | Serving: 4)

Ingredients

- Soy sauce: 1 tsp.
- 1/4 cup of chicken broth
- Cornstarch: 2 tsp.
- Lemon juice: 1 tbsp.
- Canola oil: 2 tbsp.
- Turkey breast tenderloins: 1 pound, cut into half" strips
- 1 jar of (2 oz.) Sliced pimientos, without liquid
- 1 minced garlic clove
- Fresh asparagus: 1 pound, 1 1/2" pieces

Instructions

1. In a bowl, add lemon juice, cornstarch, soy sauce, broth, mix well.
2. In a skillet, add oil on medium, cook meat until all cooked through.
3. In the pan, sauté asparagus, cook for few minutes, add pimientos, add soy sauce mixture, cook for 1 minute.
4. Add turkey back in the pan, toss and serve.

Nutrition: Calories 205 | Fat 9 g | Sugar 1 g | Protein 28 g | Sodium 204 mg | Carbs 5 g

372. Mango-Chutney Chicken

(Prep time: 15 minutes | Cook time: up to 7 hours | Serving: 4)

Ingredients

- Chicken breasts: 3 pounds
- Mango chutney: ¼ cup
- 1 onion, sliced into wedges
- Barbecue sauce: 1/3 cup, low-calorie
- Curry powder: half tsp.
- Black pepper: 1/8 tsp.
- 2 scallions, chopped
- Cooked brown rice: 1 ⅓ cups
- 1 mango, chopped

Instructions

1. Add chicken, curry powder, pepper, chutney, and BBQ sauce in a slow cooker (3-4 qt.). Stir and cook for 6-7 hours on low. Or 3 to 3 ½ hours on high.

2. Take the chicken out, add onion and sauce to the cooker.

3. In a bowl, toss mango with rice and scallions.

4. Serve the rice with onion and chicken.

Nutrition: Calories 433| Fat 8.2 g | Sugar 25.7 g | Protein 41.7 g |Sodium 419 mg | Carbs 47 g

373. Harissa Chicken & Vegetables

(Prep time: 15 minutes | Cook time: 30 minutes| Serving: 4)
Ingredients

- Sliced mixed bell peppers: 4 cups

- Kosher salt: ¼ tsp.

- Cauliflower florets: 4 cups

- Harissa paste: 2 tsp. + half tsp.

- Black pepper: 1/8 tsp.

- Brown sugar: 1 tsp.

- Fresh parsley: 1 tsp., chopped

- 1 minced garlic clove

- Olive oil: 3 tbsp.

- Lemon juice: 2 tbsp.

- 2 chicken breasts, boneless & skinless

- Greek yogurt: half cup, low-fat

- Lemon zest: 1 tsp.

- Fresh mint: 1 tsp., chopped

Instructions

1. Let the oven preheat to 400 F.

2. Toss florets with half of the salt, oil (2 tbsp.) and peppers.

3. Spread on a baking sheet, roast for 15 minutes.

4. In a bowl, add the rest of the oil, salt, garlic, harissa paste (2 tsp.), garlic and sugar. Mix and rub all over

the chicken, add vegetables and spread on the baking sheet.

5. Bake for 20 minutes.

6. Add the rest of the ingredients in a bowl, mix and pour over chicken and vegetables, and serve.

Nutrition: Calories 341 | Fat 13 g | Sugar 9 g | Protein 31.8 g |Sodium 431 mg | Carbs 15 g

374. Chicken Breasts with Balsamic Strawberries

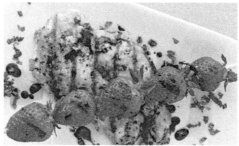

(Prep time: 15 minutes | Cook time: 30 minutes| Serving: 4)
Ingredients

- 1 lemon's juice

- Balsamic strawberries: half cup

- Fresh tarragon: 1 ½ tbsp., chopped

- Olive oil: 2 tsp.

- 4 chicken breasts, boneless & skinless, pounded thin

- 2 minced garlic cloves

- Kosher salt & pepper: 1/8 tsp. each

Instructions

1. In a bowl, add chicken and the rest of the ingredients, except for berries. Mix and keep in the fridge for half an hour.

2. Grill chicken for 4-5 minutes on each side, serve with strawberries tossed with balsamic.

Nutrition: Calories 268 | Fat 8 g | Sugar 5 g | Protein 32 g |Sodium 316 mg | Carbs 14 g

DASH Diet Fish & Seafood Recipes

375. Easy Roasted Salmon

(Prep time: 10 minutes | Cook time: 25 minutes | Serving: 4)

Ingredients

- One lemon, quartered
- 4 minced garlic cloves
- Black pepper
- 4 wild salmon fillets of (6 oz.)
- Fresh dill: ¼ cup, chopped

Instructions

1. Let the oven preheat to 400 F. Oil spray a glass baking dish and place fish in it.
2. Drizzle lemon juice on each fillet. One wedge for 1 fillet.
3. Add the rest of the ingredients on top.
4. Bake for 20-22 minutes. serve

Nutrition (for 6 oz.): Calories 251 | Fat 2 g | Sugar 0.9 g | Protein 34 g | Sodium 78 mg | Carbs 2 g

376. Walnut-Rosemary Crusted Salmon

(Prep time: 10 minutes | Cook time: 25 minutes | Serving: 4)

Ingredients

- 1 minced garlic clove
- Lemon juice: 1 tsp.
- Fresh rosemary: 1 tsp.
- Honey: half tsp.
- Lemon zest: ¼ tsp.
- Crushed red pepper: ¼ tsp.
- Panko breadcrumbs: 3 tbsp.
- Dijon mustard: 2 tsp.
- Kosher salt: ¼ tsp.
- Skinless salmon fillet: 1 pound
- Walnuts: 3 tbsp., chopped
- Olive oil: 1 tsp.

Instructions

1. Let the oven preheat to 425 F.
2. In a bowl, add oil, panko and walnuts and mix.
3. In another bowl, add the rest of the ingredients except for fish, and mix.
4. Place fish on a parchment-lined baking sheet.
5. Pour the mustard mixture and spread all over the fish, add walnut mixture and press to adhere. Oil spray the breaded salmon.
6. Bake for 8-12 minutes.
7. Serve with lemon juice on top.

Nutrition for 3 oz.: Calories 222 | Fat 17.2 g | Sugar 0 g | Protein 24 g | Sodium 223 mg | Carbs 4g

377. Spiced Salmon

(Prep time: 10 minutes | Cook time: 15 minutes | Serving: 8)

Ingredients

- Soy sauce: 1 tbsp.
- Paprika: half tsp.
- Pepper: half tsp.
- Olive oil: 1 tbsp.
- Plant butter: 1 tbsp., melted
- Packed brown sugar: 2 tbsp.
- Garlic powder: half tsp.
- Cayenne pepper, salt & tarragon, a pinch
- Ground mustard: half tsp.
- Dill weed: ¼ tsp.
- 1 salmon fillet: 2 pounds

Instructions

1. In a bowl, add all ingredients except for fish, mix and brush all over salmon.

2. Oil spray the grill grates and grill for 10 to 15 minutes. Or broil four inches away from the heat source till it flakes.

Nutrition for 3 oz.: Calories 256 | Fat 17 g | Sugar 5 g | Protein 20 g | Sodium 330 mg | Carbs 5 g

378. Dijon Salmon with Green Bean Pilaf

(Prep time: 10 minutes | Cook time: 25 minutes | Serving: 4)

Ingredients

- Olive oil: 3 tbsp.

- Salt: ¼ tsp.

- Wild salmon: 1 ¼ pound, cut into 4 portions without skin 2 tablespoons mayonnaise: 2 tbsp.

- Whole-grain mustard: 2 tsp.

- Thin green beans: 12 oz., cut into bite-size

- Minced garlic: 1 tbsp.

- 1 lemon's zest & quartered

- Water: 2 tbsp.

- Pine nuts: 2 tbsp.

- Ground pepper: half tsp.

- Cooked brown rice: 8 oz.

Instructions

1. Let the oven preheat to 425 F.

2. Coat salmon in oil (1 tbsp.) and place on a parchment-lined baking sheet.

3. With a fork, mash salt and garlic. Add 1 tsp. of garlic mixture in a bowl, add black pepper (1/4 tsp.), mustard and mayo. Spread all over the fish.

4. Bake for 6-8 minutes for each inch of thickness.

5. In a skillet, add oil and sauté the garlic mixture with beans, nuts, black pepper and zest for 2-4 minutes.

6. Add water and rice, stir and cook for 2-3 minutes.

7. Serve the pilaf with salmon and lemon wedges.

Nutrition: Calories 442 | Fat 24.8 g | Sugar 0 g | Protein 33 g | Sodium 504 mg | Carbs 21.6 g

379. Teriyaki Salmon with Cauliflower Rice

(Prep time: 1 hour & 20 minutes | Cook time: 25 minutes | Serving: 4)

Ingredients

- Water: 1 tbsp.

- Balsamic vinegar: 1 tbsp.

- 4 skinless salmon fillets of (6-oz.)

- White vinegar: 1 tsp.

- No-calorie sweetener: half tsp.

- Minced ginger: 1 tsp.

- Soy sauce: 2 tbsp., low-sodium

- Canola oil: 1 tsp.

- Minced garlic: 1 tsp.

- Sesame oil: 1 tbsp.

- Chopped, fresh cilantro: 1 cup

- Cauliflower: 1 head, chopped

- Half sweet onion, chopped

- 2 scallions, diced

- Sesame seeds: 1 tsp.

Instructions

1. In a baking pan (8"), add sweetener, ginger, garlic, soy sauce, sesame oil, water, vinegar and sherry. Whisk well and add fish, coat the fish in marinade and keep in the fridge for 1-24 hours.

2. Let the oven preheat to 450 F.

3. In a food processor, add onion and cauliflower and pulse until crumbly. Do it in batches.

4. Bake the fish in the baking pan for 10-12 minutes. Broil for 2-4 minutes, till it flakes easily.

5. In a pan, add canola oil and sauté cauliflower rice

for 5-6 minutes. Turn the heat off, add cilantro, and mix.

6. Serve fish with juices and cauliflower rice topped with sesame and scallions.

Nutrition: Calories 178 | Fat 5.4 g | Sugar 2.17 g | Protein 26 g |Sodium 176 mg | Carbs 11 g

380. Roasted Oysters with Pancetta & Breadcrumbs

(Prep time: 10 minutes | Cook time: 10 minutes | Serving: 6)

Ingredients

- Pine nuts: 2 tbsp., toasted
- Fresh flat-leaf parsley: 2 tbsp., chopped
- Whole-wheat bread: 2 slices
- 18 oysters on the half shell
- Chopped pancetta: 1 oz.
- Black pepper: ¼ tsp.

Instructions

1. Let the oven preheat to 450 F.
2. In a food processor, pulse nuts and bread until ground.
3. In a pan, add pancetta and cook for 2 minutes. Turn the heat off add bread mixture, pepper and parsley.
4. Place oysters in 1 even layer and add 1 tbsp. of nut mixture on oysters.
5. Bake for 5 minutes, serve with lemon wedges.

Nutrition: Calories 92 | Fat 4.9 g | Sugar 0 g | Protein 4.7 g |Sodium 212 mg | Carbs 7.7 g

381. Creamy Lemon Pasta with Shrimp

(Prep time: 15 minutes | Cook time: 25 minutes | Serving: 4)

Ingredients

- Olive oil: 1 tbsp.
- Unsalted butter: 2 tbsp.
- Whole-wheat fettuccine: 8 oz.

- Chopped garlic: 1 tbsp.
- Arugula: 4 cups
- Lemon zest: 1 tsp.
- Shrimps: 12 oz., peeled and deveined
- Red pepper flakes: ¼ tsp.
- Low-fat parmesan cheese: 1/3 cup, grated
- Yogurt: ¼ cup, low-fat
- Salt: ¼ tsp.
- Fresh basil: ¼ cup, sliced
- Lemon juice: 2 tbsp.

Instructions

1. Cook pasta as per the pack's instructions. Drain all but half a cup of water.
2. In a skillet, add oil on medium flame. Cook shrimps for 2-3 minutes. Take it out in a bowl.
3. In the pan, add butter, cook garlic and pepper flakes for 1 minute.
4. Add arugula and cook for 1 minute. Turn the heat low.
5. Add pasta with water, zest, yogurt, toss well. Add lemon juice, shrimps, salt toss well and serve with grated cheese and basil on top.

Nutrition for 1 ½ cups: Calories 403 | Fat 13.9 g | Sugar 3 g | Protein 28.3 g |Sodium 396.3mg| Carbs 45.5 g

382. Peppered Sole

(Prep time: 15 minutes | Cook time: 10 minutes | Serving: 4)

Ingredients

- 2 green onions, sliced
- 2 minced garlic cloves
- Cayenne pepper: 1/8 tsp.
- 4 sole fillets of (4 oz.)
- Mushrooms: 2 cups, sliced
- Unsalted butter: 2 tbsp.

- Paprika: ¼ tsp.
- Lemon-pepper seasoning: ¼ tsp.
- 1 tomato, chopped

Instructions

1. In a skillet, add butter on medium heat. Sauté mushroom until tender.
2. Add garlic, sauté for 1 minute. Add fish fillet over mushrooms and add cayenne pepper, paprika and lemon pepper on top.
3. Cook for 5-10 minutes, covered on medium flame.
4. Serve with scallions and tomatoes.

Nutrition: Calories 174 | Fat 7 g | Sugar 2 g | Protein 23 g |Sodium 166 mg | Carbs 4 g

383. Shrimp Ceviche

(Prep time: 3 hours & 15 minutes | Cook time: 0 minutes | Serving: 8)

Ingredients

- 2 lemons' zest & juice
- Olive oil: 2 tbsp.
- Cumin: 2 tsp.
- Minced garlic: 2 tbsp.
- Shrimp: half-pound, sliced in ¼" pieces
- Red onion: half cup, chopped
- Serrano chili pepper: ¼ cup, chopped without seeds
- 2 limes' zest & juice
- Diced tomato: 1 cup
- Chopped cilantro: ¼ cup
- Canned black beans: 1 cup
- Peeled diced cucumber: 1 cup, without seeds

Instructions

1. In a pan, add shrimp and lemon, lime juice. Keep in the fridge for 3 hours.
2. In a different bowl, add the rest of the ingredients.
3. Serve shrimps with juices and the rest of the ingredients.

Nutrition: Calories 98 | Fat 4 g | Sugar 8 g | Protein 7 g |Sodium 167 mg | Carbs 10 g

384. Roasted Salmon with Smoky Chickpeas

(Prep time: 15 minutes | Cook time: 45 minutes | Serving: 4)

Ingredients

- Smoked paprika: 1 tbsp.
- Salt: ¼ tsp.
- 1 can of (15 oz.) Chickpeas, rinsed
- Chopped kale: 10 cups
- Buttermilk: 1/3 cup
- Olive oil: 2 tbsp.
- Garlic powder: ¼ tsp.
- Mayonnaise: ¼ cup
- Fresh chives: ¼ cup, chopped
- Wild salmon: 1 ¼ pounds, cut into 4 pieces
- Pepper: half tsp.
- Water: ¼ cup

Instructions

1. Let the oven preheat to 425 F, with racks in the middle and the upper third racks.
2. In a bowl, add half salt, oil (1 tbsp.) and paprika. Mix and add dried chickpeas, toss well.
3. Spread on a baking sheet and bake for half an hour in the upper rack; move the chickpeas twice.
4. In a blender, add mayo, pepper (1/4 tsp.), garlic powder, herbs and buttermilk. Pulse until smooth.
5. In a pan, add oil and sauté kale for 2 minutes. Add water and cook for 5 minutes. Turn the heat off.
6. Season the salmon with salt and pepper and place on 1 side of the chickpeas tray.
7. Bake for 5-8 minutes in the middle rack.
8. Serve with a drizzle of dressing, chickpeas and kale.

Nutrition: Calories 447 | Fat 21.8 g | Sugar 2.2 g | Protein 37 g |Sodium 512 mg | Carbs

385.   Shrimp Orzo with Feta

(Prep time: 15 minutes | Cook time: 25 minutes | Serving: 4)
Ingredients

- Olive oil: 2 tbsp.

- Lemon juice: 2 tbsp.

- 2 minced garlic cloves

- Feta cheese: half cup, crumbled

- Uncooked shrimp: 1 1/4 pounds, peeled & deveined

- Whole wheat orzo pasta: 1-1/4 cups

- Pepper: ¼ tsp.

- 2 tomatoes, diced

- Fresh cilantro: 2 tbsp., chopped

Instructions

1. As per the pack's instructions, cook the pasta.

2. In a skillet, add oil to sauté garlic on a medium flame for 1 minute.

3. Add lemon juice and tomatoes, let it come to a boil, add shrimps.

4. Turn the heat low and simmer for 4 to 5 minutes.

5. Add cooked pasta and the rest of the ingredients, toss and serve.

Nutrition for 1 cup: Calories 406 | Fat 12 g | Sugar 2 g | Protein 33 g |Sodium 307 mg | Carbs 40 g

386.   Snapper Over Tomatoes & Sautéed Spinach

(Prep time: 15 minutes | Cook time: 12 minutes | Serving: 4)
Ingredients

- Tomatoes: 1 cup, chopped

- Italian dressing: 3 tbsp., low-fat

- Fresh spinach: 10 cups

- 4 red snapper fillets

- 4 lemon wedges

- Dijon mustard: 3 tbsp.

- Chopped onion: half cup

Instructions

1. Let the broiler preheat.

2. In a bowl, whisk dressing and mustard.

3. On a baking sheet lined with foil, place fish, skin side down and brush with half of the marinade.

4. Broil for 8 minutes.

5. In a skillet, add the rest of the marinade and onion on medium flame.

6. Cook for 2 minutes, covered. Add spinach (half) and cook for 1 minute, covered.

7. Add the rest of the spinach and tomatoes, cook for 1 minute covered. Mix well.

8. Serve with fish and lemon wedges.

Nutrition: Calories 276 | Fat 8.1 g | Sugar 3.4 g | Protein 33.2 g |Sodium 223 mg | Carbs 13 g

387.   Oven-Baked Fish & Chips

(Prep time: 25 minutes | Cook time: 35 minutes | Serving: 4)
Ingredients

- **Canola oil: 4 tsp.**
- 2 egg whites, whisked

- 2 cups of cornflakes

- Russet potatoes: 1 1/2 pound, cut into wedges (1/4")

- All-purpose flour: ¼ cup

- Salt: ¼ tsp.

- Cajun seasoning: 1 ½ tsp., no-salt-added

- Cod: 1 pound, cut into 4 pieces

Instructions

1. Let the oven preheat to 425 F, with racks in the lower third upper racks.

2. Wash the potatoes and pat dry, toss with oil and Cajun (3/4 tsp.), toss well and spread on an oil-

lined baking sheet. Bake for 30-35 minutes, flipping every ten minutes on the lower rack.

3. In a food processor, add cornflakes and grind and transfer to a dish.

4. In a dish, add egg white; in a different dish, add salt, Cajun and flour.

5. Coat fish in flour mixture then in egg and lastly coat in cornflakes.

6. Place on an oil-sprayed wire rack on a baking tray, generously oil spray the breaded fish.

7. Bake on the upper rack and bake for 20 minutes, serve with chips.

Nutrition: Calories 256 | Fat 5.1 g | Sugar 2.16 g | Protein 28.9 g |Sodium 112 mg | Carbs 14 g

388. Grilled Tilapia with Pineapple Salsa

(Prep time: 15 minutes | Cook time: 8 minutes | Serving: 8)
Ingredients
- 2 green onions, chopped
- Pepper: 1/8 tsp.
- Green pepper: ¼ cup, chopped
- Salt: ¼ tsp.
- Fresh cilantro: ¼ cup, chopped
- 8 tilapia fillets
- Fresh pineapple: 2 cups, cubed
- Lime juice: 2 tbsp. + 4 tsp.
- Cayenne pepper, a pinch
- Canola oil: 1 tbsp.

Instructions
1. In a bowl, add pineapple, cayenne, salt (half), lime juice (4 tbsp.), green pepper, scallions and cilantro, toss and keep in the fridge.

2. In a bowl, mix lime juice and oil. Pour over fish, season with salt and pepper.

3. Broil from 4 inches for 2 to 3 minutes on 1 side. Serve with salsa.

Nutrition: Calories 131 | Fat 3 g | Sugar 3 g | Protein 21 g |Sodium 145 mg | Carbs 6 g

389. Tuna Pita Pockets

(Prep time: 15 minutes | Cook time: 0 minutes | Serving: 6)
Ingredients
- Chopped tomatoes: ¾ cup
- Green bell peppers: half cup, diced
- Shredded carrots: half cup
- 3 pita pockets, whole-wheat, halved
- Chopped broccoli: half cup
- 2 cans of (6 oz.) Tuna packed in water, without water
- Shredded romaine lettuce: 1 1/2 cups
- Chopped onion: ¼ cup
- Ranch dressing: half cup, low-fat

Instructions
1. In a bowl, add all vegetables and toss.
2. In a bowl, add dressing and tuna, mix and add to the vegetable mixture; mix.
3. In each half pocket, add the tuna mixture and serve.

Nutrition for 1 half: Calories 209 | Fat 5 g | Sugar 3 g | Protein 18 g |Sodium 378 mg | Carbs 23 g

390. Salmon with Lemon-Garlic Butter Sauce

(Prep time: 15 minutes | Cook time: 20 minutes | Serving: 4)
Ingredients
- Asparagus: 1 pound, trimmed
- Lemon zest: 1 tsp.
- Salt & pepper: ¼ tsp. Each
- Grated garlic: half tbsp.
- Lemon juice: 1 tbsp.

- Salmon fillet: 1 pound, cut into 4 pieces
- Unsalted butter: 3 tbsp.
- Olive oil: 1 tbsp.

Instructions
1. Let the oven preheat to 375 F.
2. On an oil sprayed baking sheet, place salmon and asparagus, sprinkle salt and pepper.
3. In a skillet, add the rest of the ingredients on a medium flame.
4. Mix well and pour over salmon and asparagus.
5. Bake for 12-15 minutes.

Nutrition: Calories 270 | Fat 17.2 g | Sugar 2.2 g | Protein 25.4 g | Sodium 298 mg | Carbs 5.6 g

391. Grilled Black Sea Bass

(Prep time: 15 minutes | Cook time: 20 minutes | Serving: 4)
Ingredients
Dressing
- Minced ginger: half tsp.
- 1 shallot, chopped
- Soy sauce: 1 tsp., low-sodium
- Canola oil: 1 ½ tbsp.
- Lemon juice: 1 tbsp.
- Rice wine vinegar: 1 tbsp.
- Orange juice: 2 tbsp.
- 1 minced garlic clove
- Sesame oil: ¼ tsp.
- Sugar substitute: ¼ tsp.

Others
- Asparagus: half pound
- Washed mixed greens: 6 oz., dried
- Corn kernels: 2 cups
- 4 skinless black sea bass fillets, bones removed

Instructions
1. Let the broiler preheat.

2. In a blender, add all ingredients of dressing with water (1 tbsp.) pulse until smooth.
3. In a pot, add water and boil. Add corn, cook for 2 minutes, take out, wash with water, and transfer to a bowl.
4. Add asparagus in the boiling water, cook for 2 minutes. Take out, wash with water.
5. Broil the fish for 6 minutes on 1 side, until tender.
6. In the corn bowl, add greens, add dressing and toss well.
7. On each serving plate, add the corn salad. Top with fish and asparagus.
8. Serve.

Nutrition: Calories 178 | Fat 5.4 g | Sugar 2.17 g | Protein 26 g | Sodium 212 mg | Carbs 11 g

392. Lemon-Pepper Tilapia with Mushrooms

(Prep time: 15 minutes | Cook time: 15 minutes | Serving: 4)
Ingredients
- Fresh mushrooms: half-pound, sliced
- 4 tilapia fillets
- Lemon-pepper seasoning: ¾ tsp.
- 3 scallions, sliced
- Unsalted butter: 2 tbsp.
- 3 minced garlic cloves
- 1 tomato, chopped
- Paprika: ¼ tsp.
- Cayenne pepper: 1/8 tsp.

Instructions
1. In a skillet, add butter on medium heat.
2. Sauté mushrooms with lemon pepper (1/4 tsp.) for 3 to 5 minutes.
3. Add garlic, cook for half a minute.
4. Add fish on top of mushrooms, add the rest of the

ingredients on top.

5. Cook for 5 to 7 minutes, covered. Serve.

Nutrition: Calories 216 | Fat 8 g | Sugar 2 g | Protein 34 g | Sodium 173 mg | Carbs 5 g

393. Garlicky Shrimp & Spinach

(Prep time: 15 minutes | Cook time: 15 minutes | Serving: 4)
Ingredients

- 6 sliced cloves garlic
- Lemon zest: 1 ½ tsp.
- Spinach: 1 pound
- Shrimps: 1 pound, peeled & deveined
- Olive oil: 3 tbsp.
- Fresh parsley: 1 tbsp., chopped
- Salt: ¼ tsp.
- Lemon juice: 1 tbsp.
- Red pepper flakes: ¼ tsp.

Instructions

1. In a pan, add oil on medium flame.
2. Add garlic and cook for 1-2 minutes. Add half salt and spinach and cook for 3-5 minutes.
3. Turn the heat off and add lemon juice; take it out in a bowl.
4. Add the rest of the oil in a pan on medium-high flame.
5. Sauté garlic for 1-2 minutes, add shrimps and the rest of the ingredients. Cook for 3-5 minutes. Serve with sautéed spinach.

Nutrition: Calories 226 | Fat 11.6 g | Sugar 0.7 g | Protein 26 g | Sodium 359 mg | Carbs 6.1 g

394. Peppered Tuna Kabobs

(Prep time: 15 minutes | Cook time: 15 minutes | Serving: 4)
Ingredients

- 1 mango, cubed
- 1 jalapeno pepper, diced without seeds

- Tuna steaks: 1 pound, cubed
- 2 sweet red peppers, cut into pieces (2 by 1")
- Corn: half cup
- 4 scallions, chopped
- Fresh parsley: 2 tbsp., chopped
- Lime juice: 2 tbsp.
- Coarsely black pepper: 1 tsp.

Instructions

1. Season the tuna with pepper, and thread onto skewers with mango, red pepper alternatively.
2. Add the rest of the ingredients to a bowl, mix and keep in the fridge.
3. Grill the skewers for 10-12 minutes on medium flame. Flipping occasionally.
4. Serve with salsa.

Nutrition: Calories 205 | Fat 2 g | Sugar 12 g | Protein 29 g | Sodium 50 mg | Carbs 20 g

395. Louisiana Jambalaya

(Prep time: 15 minutes | Cook time: 40 minutes | Serving: 4)
Ingredients

- 3 onions, chopped
- 2 minced garlic cloves
- Shrimp: half pound
- Water: half cup
- Olive oil: 2 tbsp.
- Dry white wine: half cup
- One can of (28 oz.) Diced tomatoes
- Basil: half tsp.
- Paprika: ¼ tsp.
- Uncooked rice: 1 cup
- Beef bouillon: 1 tsp., low-sodium
- Green pepper: 1 cup, chopped
- Thyme: half tsp.
- Tabasco sauce: ¼ tsp.

- Kielbasa: half-pound, low-fat & sliced

Instructions
1. Sauté garlic and onion on a medium flame for 5 minutes.
2. Add the rest of the ingredients, except for green peppers. Stir well. Simmer for half an hour, covered.
3. Add chopped peppers, and simmer for ten minutes. Serve.

Nutrition: Calories 301 | Fat 5.8 g | Sugar 2.11 g | Protein 29 g | Sodium 181 mg | Carbs 12 g

396. Salmon Cakes
(Prep time: 20 minutes | Cook time: 15 minutes | Serving: 4)
Ingredients
- 1 onion, small, chopped
- Cooked salmon: 1 1/2 cups
- Dijon mustard: 1 ½ tsp.
- 1 stalk of celery, chopped
- Olive oil: 3 tsp.
- Whole-wheat breadcrumbs: 1 ¾ cups
- Fresh parsley: 2 tbsp., chopped
- 1 egg, whisked
- Black pepper: half tsp.

Instructions
1. Let the oven preheat to 450 F.
2. In a pan, add oil (half) and sauté onion and celery for 3 minutes. Add parsley, turn the heat off.
3. In a bowl, add salmon and flake, remove skin and bones.
4. Add mustard, egg, mix and add the crumbs, pepper and onion mixture. Mix and make into 8 patties.
5. In a pan, add the rest of the ingredients. Add patties and cook for 2-3 minutes on 1 side. Serve.

Nutrition: Calories 310 | Fat 12.2 g | Sugar 5.7 g | Protein 32 g | Sodium 461 mg | Carbs 25.8 g

397. Firecracker Salmon
(Prep time: 15 minutes | Cook time: 20 minutes | Serving: 4)
Ingredients
- Salt & pepper: ¼ tsp. Each
- Hot sauce: ¼ cup
- Parsley: 2 tbsp., chopped
- Apple cider vinegar: 1 tbsp.
- Salmon: 1 1/4 lb.
- Red pepper flakes: ¼ tsp.
- Onion powder: half tsp.
- Brown sugar: half cup
- Minced garlic: 2 tsp.

Instructions
1. Let the oven preheat to 375 F, with a rack in the oven.
2. In a pan, add all ingredients except for fish, let it come to a boil, turn the heat low and simmer for 8 to 10 minutes.
3. Turn the heat and cool for 3 to 5 minutes.
4. Make a foil packet, and place the salmon, pack it.
5. Bake in the oven on a baking tray for 8-10 minutes.

Nutrition: Calories 178 | Fat 5.4 g | Sugar 2.17 g | Protein 26 g | Sodium 286 mg | Carbs 11 g

398. Garlic Shrimp Pasta
(Prep time: 15 minutes | Cook time: 18 minutes | Serving: 4)
Ingredients
- Baby spinach leaves: 4 cups
- Onion chopped: half cup
- Cherry tomatoes: 1 ½ cups, halved
- Multigrain spaghetti: 8 oz.
- Olive oil: 3 tsp.
- Red pepper flakes: ¼ tsp.

- Medium shrimp: 1 1/2 lb., peeled & deveined
- 3 cloves garlic, finely chopped
- Dry white wine: half cup
- Low-sodium chicken broth: 8oz.
- Salt & pepper: 1/8 tsp., each
- Fresh parsley: 3 tbsp., chopped
- Unsalted butter: 2 tbsp.

Instructions
1. Cook pasta as per the pack's instructions. Drain and add to a pan, add oil (2 tsp.), tomato and spinach. Stir and keep warm.
2. In a skillet, add oil and sauté onion for 1 minute. Add garlic, pepper flakes and shrimp for 2 minutes.
3. Add the rest of the ingredients, except for butter and parsley. Cook for 2 minutes, turn the heat off.
4. Add butter and parsley, transfer to the pasta pan, toss and serve.

Nutrition: Calories 287 | Fat 8 g | Sugar 2 g | Protein 29 g |Sodium 132 mg | Carbs 21 g

399. Scallops with Snow Peas & Orange

(Prep time: 15 minutes | Cook time: 12 minutes | Serving: 4)
Ingredients
- Olive oil: 1 tbsp. + 2 tsp.
- 1 orange
- 16 sea scallops
- 1 cup of couscous
- Black pepper
- Snow peas: 3/4 pound, halved in length

Instructions
1. Cook couscous as per pack's instructions.
2. In a skillet, add oil (half) and season the scallops with a pinch of salt and pepper.

3. Cook for 2-3 minutes on 1 side. Take them out on a plate.
4. Thinly slice 1/8th part of an orange peel.
5. Clean the pan, add oil and sauté snow peas and orange peel with a pinch of salt and pepper.
6. Serve with couscous and scallops.

Nutrition: Calories 298 | Fat 11 g | Sugar 7.9 g | Protein 30 g |Sodium 123 mg | Carbs 18.9 g

Blackened Shrimp Tacos

(Prep time: 15 minutes | Cook time: 5 minutes | Serving: 4)
Ingredients
Lime juice: 1 tbsp.

1 minced garlic clove

Cilantro leaves: half cup

Cajun spice: 2 tbsp., salt-free

1 avocado

Iceberg lettuce: 2 cups, chopped

Salt: 1/8 tsp.

Large shrimp: 1 pound, peeled & deveined

Pico de Gallo: half cup

8 corn tortillas

Instructions
Let the grill preheat to medium heat.

In a bowl, add avocado and mash, add salt, garlic and lime juice. Mix.

Toss the pat dried shrimps with Cajun seasoning.

Thread onto skewers. Grill for 2 minutes on each side.

Serve in tacos with the rest of the ingredients.

Nutrition for 2 tacos: Calories 286 | Fat 17.2 g | Sugar 3.5 g | Protein 24 g |Sodium 409 mg | Carbs 30.4 g

400. Clams Casino with Pancetta

(Prep time: 15 minutes | Cook time: 12 minutes | Serving: 12)
Ingredients

- Diced pancetta: ¾ cup
- Minced shallots: 3 tbsp.
- Black pepper: ¼ tsp.
- 1 minced garlic clove
- Parmigiano-Reggiano cheese: 1 ½ tbsp.
- White bread: 1 slice (day old)
- Dry white wine: 2 tbsp.
- Red bell pepper: 1/3 cup, chopped
- Fresh parsley: 2 tbsp., chopped
- 36 cleaned clams

Instructions
1. In a skillet, add oil on medium heat.
2. Cook pancetta for 6 minutes. Add wine and deglaze the pan, add garlic, shallots and pepper, cook for 4 minutes. Take it out in a bowl.
3. In a food processor, add bread and pulse until crumbly. Add to the pancetta mixture with cheese, pepper and parsley. Mix well.
4. Let the broiler preheat. Do not use the open/broken shells of clams.
5. Discard the top shell, add pancetta mixture to each clam, broil for 4 minutes, and rotate the pan and broil for three minutes. Serve.

Nutrition: Calories 61 | Fat 8 g | Sugar 0 g | Protein 5.3 g | Sodium 163 mg | Carbs 3.2 g

401. Chilean Sea Bass with Dill Relish

(Prep time: 15 minutes | Cook time: 12 minutes | Serving: 4)
Ingredients
- Baby capers: 1 tsp., drained
- Dijon mustard: 1 tsp.
- Fresh dill: 1 ½ tsp., chopped
- 4 white sea bass fillets
- Chopped onion: 1 ½ tbsp.

- Lemon juice: 1 tsp.
- 4 lemon wedges

Instructions
1. Let the oven preheat to 375 F.
2. In a bowl, add all ingredients except for fish and mix well.
3. On a foil sheet, place the fish and squeeze 1 lemon wedge, add ¼ of the mixture and spread.
4. Wrap the fish in foil and bake for 10-12 minutes. Serve.

Nutrition: Calories 245 | Fat 5.1 g | Sugar 8 g | Protein 29.3 g | Sodium 175 mg | Carbs 12 g

402. Coriander & Lemon Crusted Salmon

(Prep time: 15 minutes | Cook time: 15 minutes | Serving: 4)
Ingredients
- Lemon zest: 1 tsp.
- Wild salmon: 1 pound, cut into 4 portions
- Red pepper flakes: half tsp.
- White vinegar: 1 tbsp.
- Asparagus: 1 pound, trimmed
- Water: 8 cups
- Olive oil: 2 tbsp.
- Lemon juice: 1 tbsp.
- Coriander seeds: 1 tbsp.
- Fresh mint: 1 tbsp., chopped
- 4 eggs
- Sea salt: ¼ tsp.
- Fresh tarragon: 1 tbsp., chopped
- Black pepper: ¼ tsp.

Instructions
1. Let the broiler preheat.
2. In a skillet, toast coriander for 3 minutes. Transfer

to a grinder, add salt and zest, grind well.

3. Season the salmon with coriander mixture, and place on an oil-sprayed baking sheet.

4. Toss the trimmed asparagus with the rest of the ingredients, except for eggs, water and vinegar. Broil salmon for 3-6 minutes.

5. In a pan, boil water with vinegar. Turn the heat low and simmer; swirl water with a spoon.

6. Add eggs, one by one in the water, cook for 3-4 minutes.

7. Serve the salmon with asparagus salad and poached eggs.

Nutrition: Calories 288| Fat 16.3 g | Sugar 1 g | Protein 30.5 g |Sodium 304 mg | Carbs 4.3 g

403. Baked Cod with Lemon & Capers

(Prep time: 15 minutes | Cook time: 25 minutes | Serving: 4)

Ingredients

- 1 lemon, halved
- Unsalted butter: 1 tbsp.
- 4 cod fillets
- Chicken bouillon: 1 tsp., low-sodium
- Capers: 4 tsp., rinsed
- Hot water: 1 cup
- All-purpose flour: 1 tbsp.

Instructions

1. Oil spray 4 sheets of foil and preheat the oven to 350 F.

2. In each foil sheet, place 1 piece of salmon, add the lemon juice from the half lemon on 4 fillets.

3. Slice the other half in slices and place lemon slices in each packet.

4. Seal the packets.

5. Bake for 20 minutes.

6. In a bowl, add bouillon with hot water. Mix well.

7. In a bowl, mix flour and butter, transfer to a pan. Mix on medium flame, add the bouillon while whisking.

8. Add capers, turn the heat off. Serve with baked fish.

Nutrition: Calories 159 | Fat 3 g | Sugar 0 g | Protein 30 g |Sodium 294 mg | Carbs 3g

404. Cilantro Lime Shrimp

(Prep time: 30 minutes | Cook time: 10 minutes | Serving: 4)

Ingredients

- Lime zest: 1 ½ tsp.
- Olive oil: 2 tbsp.
- 1/3 cup of lime juice
- Fresh cilantro: 1/3 cup, chopped
- Salt: ¼ tsp.
- 1 jalapeno pepper, chopped without seeds
- Ground cumin: ¼ tsp.
- Shrimp: 1 pound, peeled & deveined
- 3 minced garlic cloves
- Pepper: ¼ tsp.
- Lime slices, as needed

Instructions

1. In a bowl, add all ingredients except for shrimps. Mix and add shrimps, toss and let it rest for 15 minutes.

2. Thread lime slices and shrimp onto skewers. Grill for 2 to 4 minutes on 1 side and serve.

Nutrition: Calories 167| Fat 8 g | Sugar 1 g | Protein 19 g |Sodium 284 mg | Carbs 4 g

(Prep time: 30 minutes | Cook time: 10 minutes | Serving: 4)

Ingredients

- 4 tilapia fillets
- Fresh parsley: 1/4 cup, chopped

- Salt: ¼ tsp.
- 1 shallot, chopped
- Olive oil: 2 tbsp.
- Lemon juice: 1 ½ tbsp.
- Lemon zest: 2 tsp.
- Black pepper: ¼ tsp.
- Hazelnuts: 1/3 cup, chopped

Instructions
1. Let the oven preheat to 450 F.
2. In a bowl, add shallot, oil (1 tsp.), salt (half), hazelnuts, zest, pepper (half) and parsley.
3. Place fish in oil sprayed baking tray and brush with oil (2 tsp.) and lemon juice.
4. Season with salt and pepper. Add hazelnut mixture on top, press to adhere.
5. Roast for 7-10 minutes. Serve.

Nutrition: Calories 262| Fat 15 g | Sugar 0.8 g | Protein 30 g |Sodium 250 mg | Carbs 3.3 g

405. Curried Cod

(Prep time: 10 minutes | Cook time: 25 minutes | Serving: 4)
Ingredients
- 1 onion, diced
- Canned chopped tomatoes: 28 oz.
- Medium curry powder: 2 tbsp.
- 1" piece of ginger, peeled & grated
- 4 lemon wedges
- 3 minced garlic cloves
- Coriander, chopped
- Oil: 1 tbsp.
- Canned chickpeas: 14 oz.
- 4 cod fillets

Instructions
1. Sauté onion in hot oil for few minutes, add ginger,

garlic and curry powder, cook for 1 to 2 minutes.
2. Add chickpeas, salt, pepper, and tomatoes. Cook for 8 to 10 minutes.
3. Add cod and cook, covered for 5 to 10 minutes.
4. Serve with lemon zest and coriander on top, on the side of lemon wedges.

Nutrition: Calories 296| Fat 6 g | Sugar 10 g | Protein 34 g |Sodium 209 mg | Carbs 22 g

406. Blackened Salmon

(Prep time: 10 minutes | Cook time: 15 minutes | Serving: 4)
Ingredients
- Rice vinegar: 1 tbsp. + 1/4 cup
- Black pepper
- Salmon fillet: 1 1/4 lb., skinless, cut into 4 fillets
- Grated ginger: 1 tbsp.
- Honey: 2 tsp.
- Blackening seasoning: 1 tbsp., salt-free
- 1/4 white onion, sliced
- Snap peas: 8 oz., cut into pieces
- 2 cucumbers, sliced
- 6 radishes, sliced into half-moons
- Fresh mint: ¼ cup, chopped

Instructions
1. Let the oven preheat to 425 F.
2. Brush the salmon with vinegar (1 tbsp.), place salmon on an oil-sprayed baking sheet.
3. Sprinkle with blackening seasoning and a pinch of salt. Bake for 10-12 minutes.
4. In a bowl, add the rest of the ingredients, toss and serve with salmon.

Nutrition: Calories 222 | Fat 8 g | Sugar 2.11 g | Protein 24 g |Sodium 130 mg | Carbs 12.7 g

407. Shrimp & Grits Stuffed Peppers

(Prep time: 10 minutes | Cook time: 30 minutes | Serving: 4)

Ingredients

- Chicken broth: 1 cup, salt-free
- Quick grits: ¾ cup., (do not use instant)
- Large shrimp: 1 pound, peeled & deveined, chopped
- Tabasco: half tsp.
- Water: 1 ½ cups
- Salt: ¼ tsp.
- Black pepper: half tsp.
- Sharp cheddar cheese: ¾ cup, shredded
- 4 bell peppers
- Garlic powder: half tsp.
- 1 bunch of scallions, sliced
- Olive oil: 1 tbsp.

Instructions

1. Let the oven preheat to 350 F
2. In a pan, boil water and broth on medium flame.
3. Add grits and whisk, add half black pepper, turn the heat low and cook for 5 to 7 minutes, stirring occasionally. Turn the heat off and add cheese, hot sauce and mix.
4. Cut the top off the bell peppers and take the middle part out, place on baking sheets. Bake for five minutes.
5. In a bowl, toss the rest of the ingredients and spread them on a baking sheet. Bake for ten minutes rotates the tray once or twice.
6. Mix the shrimps with grits and stuff in the peppers.
7. Bake for ten minutes and serve.

Nutrition: Calories 406| Fat 12.7 g | Sugar 7.5 g | Protein 33 g |Sodium 444 mg | Carbs 40 g

408. Fish Tacos

(Prep time: 15 minutes | Cook time: 10 minutes | Serving: 4)

Ingredients

- Salsa, as needed
- **Fish**
- Beer: 1/3 cup
- Cumin, cayenne pepper & salt: 1/8 tsp. Each
- All-purpose flour: 3 tbsp.
- Tilapia fillet: 8 oz., cut into strips (1-inch wide)
- 4 corn tortillas
- Canola oil: 2 tsp.

Instructions

1. In a bowl, add all seasonings with flour. Add beer and mix.
2. Add fish pieces and coat well.
3. In a pan, add oil on medium flame. Add fish and cook on one side for 2-4 minutes.
4. Serve in a tortilla with salsa on top.

Nutrition: Calories 234| Fat 11.1 g | Sugar 12 g | Protein 27 g |Sodium 217 mg | Carbs 19 g

409. Roast Salmon with Chimichurri Sauce

(Prep time: 15 minutes | Cook time: 15 minutes | Serving: 4)

Ingredients

Chimichurri Sauce

- Lemon juice: 3 tbsp.
- Flat-leaf parsley: 2 cups
- Red pepper flakes: half tsp.
- Salt & pepper: ¼ tsp. Each
- 5 cloves of garlic
- Olive oil: half cup
- Fresh oregano: 1 tbsp.

Salmon

- Salt & pepper: ¼ tsp. Each

- Olive oil: 2 tsp.
- 4 salmon fillets

Instructions
1. Let the oven preheat to 425 F.
2. In a food processor, add all ingredients of the sauce, except for oil. Pulse and gradually add oil until smooth.
3. Season the salmon with salt, pepper and brush with oil before. Place on an oil-sprayed baking sheet.
4. Bake for 8-10 minutes for each inch of thickness.
5. Serve with chimichurri sauce.

Nutrition: Calories 378 | Fat 24.7 g | Sugar 0.3 g | Protein 34.6 g | Sodium 378 mg | Carbs 2.5 g

410. Coconut Curry with Cod

(Prep time: 15 minutes | Cook time: 20 minutes | Serving: 4-6)
Ingredients
- Chopped red onion: half cup
- Red chili flakes: half tsp.
- 2 minced garlic cloves
- Matchstick carrots: half cup
- Garam masala: 2 tsp.
- 1/4 cup of canola oil
- 1 red pepper, sliced into 1" pieces
- Coconut milk: 2 cups
- Greens: 2 cups, chopped
- Turmeric: half tsp.
- Sea salt: ¼ tsp.
- 1 lime's juice
- Cod: 1 pound, sliced into 2" pieces

Instructions
1. Sauté onion and garlic in hot oil for 5 minutes.
2. Add spices and cook for 30 seconds. Add milk,

lime juice, carrots and pepper.
3. Add fish and stir, simmer for 18-20 minutes. Do not stir too much.
4. Add greens and turn the heat off. Serve.

Nutrition: Calories 278 | Fat 11 g | Sugar 7.9 g | Protein 30.1 g | Sodium 203 mg | Carbs 12 g

411. Halibut with Mango-Avocado Salsa

(Prep time: 15 minutes | Cook time: 12 minutes | Serving: 4)
Ingredients
- 1 avocado, cubed
- Red cabbage: half cup, chopped
- Diced mango: 1 ½ cups
- Fresh cilantro: ¼ cup, chopped
- Ground cumin, a pinch
- 1 scallion, chopped
- Lime juice: 1 tbsp.
- Fresh jalapeno: 2 tsp., chopped
- Olive oil: 1 tbsp.

For halibut
- 4 skinless halibut fillets of 7 oz.
- Olive oil: 3 tbsp.

Instructions
1. Let the oven preheat to 450 F.
2. In a bowl, add all ingredients of salsa, toss and add black pepper.
3. In a skillet, add oil on medium heat.
4. When oil gets hot, add fish fillet, cook for 3 minutes, check if the sear is to your desired color.
5. Put it in the oven for 4-5 minutes, flip and take it out of the oven. Let it rest in hot oil.
6. Serve with salsa with a pinch of salt and pepper on top.

Nutrition: Calories 208 | Fat 5.5 g | Sugar 2.11 g | Protein 32 g | Sodium 127 mg | Carbs 9.2 g

412.   Cod en Papillote

(Prep time: 15 minutes | Cook time: 15 minutes | Serving: 4-6)

Ingredients

- 4-6 oz. cod fillet: boneless & skinless
- Crème fraiche: 1 tbsp., low-fat
- Unsalted plant butter: 1 tsp.
- Mixed dried herbs
- Salt and pepper: 1/8 tsp. Each
- Dry white wine: 1 tbsp.
- Lemon zest: half tsp.

Instructions

1. Let the oven preheat to 400 F.
2. In a large foil sheet, add butter.
3. Season fish with salt and pepper, place on the foil sheet.
4. Add the rest of the ingredients on top. Close the packet.
5. Bake for 15 minutes. Serve.

Nutrition: Calories 208 | Fat 7 g | Sugar 2.21 g | Protein 30 g | Sodium 206 mg | Carbs 9 g

413.   Halibut Lemon Piccata

(Prep time: 15 minutes | Cook time: 20 minutes | Serving: 2)

Ingredients

- Canola oil: 2 tbsp.
- Almond flour: 4 to 5 tbsp.
- Avocado oil: 2 tbsp.
- 2 halibut fillets of 8 oz. Bone & skin removed
- **Sauce**
- Lemon juice: 3 to 4 tbsp.
- Capers: 1 ½ tbsp. Drained
- Fresh flat parsley: 2 tbsp. Chopped

- Chicken stock: ¾ cup, low-sodium

Instructions

1. In a skillet, add oil on medium heat.
2. Season the fish with a pinch of salt, coat in almond flour on both sides.
3. Add fish to the skillet, cook for 2 to 3 minutes on 1 side. Keep basting with juices and oil.
4. Take the fish out and add the sauce's ingredients to the pan, simmer until it is reduced by half. Add a pinch of salt and serve with fish.

Nutrition: Calories 401 | Fat 31 g | Sugar 1 g | Protein 26 g | Sodium 225 mg | Carbs 6 g

414.   Mustard & Coriander Crusted Salmon

(Prep time: 15 minutes | Cook time: 10 minutes | Serving: 4)

Ingredients

- Mustard seeds: 1 tsp.
- Crushed red pepper, a pinch
- Flat-leaf parsley: 1 cup, packed
- Dijon mustard: half tsp. + 1 tbsp.
- Lemon juice: 1 tbsp.
- Coriander seeds: 1 tbsp.
- Skinless salmon: 1 1/4 pounds
- Olive oil: 1 tbsp. + 1 tsp.
- Watercress: 6 oz., without thick stems

Instructions

1. Let the oven preheat to 425 F.
2. In a grinder, add all seeds with red pepper and coarsely grind.
3. Season the salmon with a pinch of salt and pepper, and spread the mustard (1 tbsp.) all over.
4. Add the ground spices and press to adhere to the fish.
5. In a skillet, add oil (1 tsp.) on medium heat. Place fish and cook for 2-3 minutes on 1 side.

6. Take it out on a plate.

7. In a bowl, whisk the rest of the ingredients except for parsley and watercress.

8. Add the watercress and parsley, toss to coat. Serve with salmon.

Nutrition: Calories 218 | Fat 5.4 g | Sugar 2.17 g | Protein 26 g |Sodium 136 mg | Carbs 13 g

415. Pepper & Spice Crusted Salmon

(Prep time: 15 minutes | Cook time: 10 minutes | Serving: 2)
Ingredients
- Coriander seeds: 1 tsp., crushed
- Dry white wine: 1/4 cup
- Green peppercorns: 1 tsp., crushed
- White peppercorns: 1 tsp., crushed
- 1 egg, beaten
- Salmon fillet: 12 oz., with skin
- Pink peppercorns: 1 tsp., crushed

Instructions
1. In a bowl, add all peppercorns and seeds mix.

2. In a bowl, add the egg. Coat the fish in egg, then in the spice mix, patting to adhere.

3. In a pan, add some oil and place fish skin side down, cook for five minutes.

4. Flip and cook for 2-3 minutes.

5. Add the wine and some more oil, whisk and deglaze the pan.

6. Pour over salmon and serve.

Nutrition: Calories 238 | Fat 4.1 g | Sugar 2.15 g | Protein 27 g |Sodium 316 mg | Carbs 12 g

416. Walnut-Sage Crusted Salmon

(Prep time: 15 minutes | Cook time: 10 minutes | Serving: 4)
Ingredients

- 1 minced garlic clove
- Dijon mustard: 2 tsp.
- Olive oil: 1 tsp.
- Lemon juice: 1 tsp.
- Honey: half tsp.
- Lemon zest: ¼ tsp.
- Skinless salmon fillet: 1 pound
- Fresh sage: 1 tbsp.
- Crushed red pepper: ¼ tsp.
- Panko breadcrumbs: 3 tbsp.
- Kosher salt: ¼ tsp.
- Walnuts: 3 tbsp., chopped

Instructions
1. Let the oven preheat to 425 F.

2. In a bowl, add oil, panko and walnuts and mix.

3. In another bowl, add the rest of the ingredients except for fish, and mix.

4. Place fish on a parchment-lined baking sheet.

5. Pour the mustard mixture and spread all over the fish, add walnut mixture and press to adhere. Oil spray the breaded salmon.

6. Bake for 8-12 minutes.

7. Serve with lemon juice on top.

Nutrition for 3 oz.: Calories 217| Fat 17.2 g | Sugar 0 g | Protein 22 g |Sodium 223 mg | Carbs 4g

417. Garlic Lemon Shrimp

(Prep time: 15 minutes | Cook time: 8 minutes | Serving: 4)
Ingredients
- Shrimp: 1 pound, peeled & deveined
- Ground cumin: 1 tsp.
- 3 sliced garlic cloves
- Fresh parsley: 2 tbsp., chopped
- Olive oil: 2 tbsp.

- Lemon juice: 1 tbsp.
- Salt: ¼ tsp.

Instructions
1. Sauté shrimps in hot oil for 3 minutes, add the rest of the ingredients, cook for 2 to 3 minutes more.
2. Serve.

Nutrition: Calories 163| Fat 8 g | Sugar 0 g | Protein 19 g |Sodium 284 mg | Carbs 2g

418.   Charred Shrimp, Pesto & Quinoa Bowls

(Prep time: 15 minutes | Cook time: 10 minutes | Serving: 4)
Ingredients
- Balsamic vinegar: 2 tbsp.
- Arugula: 4 cups
- Olive oil: 1 tbsp.
- Pesto: 1/3 cup
- Salt & pepper: ¼ tsp. Each
- Large shrimp: 1 pound, peeled and deveined
- Cooked quinoa: 2 cups
- Cherry tomatoes: 1 cup, halved
- 1 avocado, diced

Instructions
1. In a bowl, add salt, pesto, pepper, oil and vinegar. Take out 4 tbsp. and reserve.
2. In a skillet, add oil on medium heat. Cook shrimps for 4-5 minutes, take them out on a plate.
3. In the pesto mixture, add quinoa and arugula, toss well.
4. In serving bowls, add the quinoa mixture, add shrimps, tomato and avocado on top.
5. Drizzle with reserved pesto mixture on top, serve.

Nutrition: Calories 429 | Fat 22 g | Sugar 5 g | Protein 30 g |Sodium 571 mg | Carbs 28 g

419.   Swordfish with Roasted Lemons

(Prep time: 15 minutes | Cook time: 70 minutes | Serving: 4)
Ingredients
- Sugar: 1 tbsp.
- Chopped garlic: half tsp.
- Sea salt: ¼ tsp.
- 2 lemons, cut into fours without seeds
- 4 chopped parsley: 1/4 cup
- Swordfish fillets
- Canola oil: half tsp.

Instructions
1. Let the oven preheat to 375 F.
2. In a bowl, toss lemon wedges with sugar and salt.
3. Roast in a dish covered with foil for 60 minutes.
4. Oil spray a baking pan. Brush the fish with oil and add garlic on top.
5. Broil for 5 minutes on 1 side.
6. Serve with roasted lemons and parsley on top.

Nutrition: Calories 280 | Fat 12 g | Sugar 4 g | Protein 34 g |Sodium 287 mg | Carbs 9 g

420.   Ahi Tuna with Soy Ginger Avocado

(Prep time: 15 minutes | Cook time: 5 minutes | Serving: 4)
Ingredients
- Grated ginger: 4 tsp.
- 4 minced garlic cloves
- Olive oil: 2 tbsp. + ¼ cup
- 2 sliced jalapeno pepper
- 4 lime's juice
- Fresh cilantro: 1 bunch, chopped
- Soy sauce: half cup, low-sodium
- 2 avocado: sliced
- No calorie sweetener: 1/8 tsp

- Tuna steak: 6 oz.

Instructions

1. In a bowl, add all ingredients with oil (1/4 cup), except for fish and avocado. whisk well
2. In a pan, add oil on medium flame.
3. Season the tuna with black pepper.
4. Sear the tuna in oil for 60 seconds on 1 side.
5. Add half of the sugar mixture in the pan, coat fish.
6. Serve with avocado and the rest of the mixture.

Nutrition: Calories 265 | Fat 5 g | Sugar 5 g | Protein 28 g | Sodium 186 mg | Carbs 13 g

421. Scallops with Charred Lemon & Bean Ragu

(Prep time: 15 minutes | Cook time: 20 minutes | Serving: 4)

Ingredients

- Spinach: 1 pound, sliced
- 2 minced garlic cloves
- 1 can of (15 oz.) Cannellini beans, rinsed
- Olive oil: 3 tsp.
- Capers: 1 tbsp., rinsed
- Butter: 1 tbsp.
- Black pepper: half tsp.
- Fresh parsley: 2 tbsp.
- Dry white wine: 1/3 cup
- Dry sea scallops: 1 pound, trimmed
- Chicken broth: 1 cup, low-sodium
- 1 lemon, halved

Instructions

1. In a pan, add oil on medium flame. Cook greens for 4 minutes, add pepper (half), garlic and capers, cook for 30 seconds.
2. Add wine, beans and broth. Let it come to a boil, turn the heat low and simmer for 5 minutes,

covered.
3. Turn the heat off and add butter.
4. Season scallops with pepper in a pan, add oil and cook scallops on both sides for 4 minutes' total.
5. Take it out on a plate, add lemons to the pan, round side up, cook for 2 minutes.
6. Serve the scallops with bean mixture and charred lemons.

Nutrition: Calories 255 | Fat 17.2 g | Sugar 1.4 g | Protein 21.4 g | Sodium 587 mg | Carbs 21 g

422. Oat Crusted Salmon with Vegetable Skewers

(Prep time: 15 minutes | Cook time: 30 minutes | Serving: 4)

Ingredients

- Rolled oats: 1 tbsp.
- Lemon juice: 1 tsp.
- Almonds: 1 tbsp.
- 2 salmon fillets
- Fresh dill: 1 tbsp.
- 1 zucchini, sliced into chunks
- Lemon zest: 2 tsp.
- 1 red capsicum, sliced into chunks
- Half onion, sliced into chunks
- Black pepper: half tsp.
- 6 cherry tomatoes
- Olive oil: 1 tbsp.
- 2 minced garlic cloves

Instructions

1. Let the oven preheat to 366 F.
2. In a food processor, add lemon juice, zest, oats, olive oil, dill and almonds. Pulse until smooth.
3. In an oil sprayed baking dish, add the salmon and spread the oat mixture on top.

4. Bake for 10 to 15 minutes.

5. In a bowl, add all vegetables and toss. Thread onto skewers.

6. Bake for 10-15 minutes, serve with crusted salmon.

Nutrition: Calories 175 | Fat 4.2 g | Sugar 3.4 g | Protein 25 g |Sodium 216 mg | Carbs 17 g

423. Grilled Salmon in Grape Leaves

(Prep time: 15 minutes | Cook time: 10 minutes | Serving: 4)
Ingredients
- Salt & pepper: ¼ tsp., each
- 4 salmon fillets
- Olive oil
- 12 large grape leaves rinsed, dried

Instructions
1. Season the fish with salt and pepper.
2. On a plate, place 2-3 grape leaves, add salmon in the middle, fold and seal the edges with oil.
3. Preheat the grill to medium, grill the grape leaves packet for 5-6 minutes, on 1 side.
4. Serve with Tomato-Raisin Relish. (Recipe 29 in sauce's chapter).

Nutrition: Calories 178 | Fat 5.4 g | Sugar 2.17 g | Protein 26 g |Sodium 386 mg | Carbs 11 g

424. Roasted Garlic Salmon & Brussels Sprouts

(Prep time: 15 minutes | Cook time: 25 minutes | Serving: 6)
Ingredients
- Fresh oregano: 2 tbsp., chopped
- Brussels sprouts: 6 cups, sliced
- Olive oil: ¼ cup
- 14 garlic cloves
- Salt: ¼ tsp.

- Salmon fillet: 2 pounds, without skin, cut into six portions
- Black pepper: ¾ tsp.
- White wine: ¾ cup

Instructions
1. Let the oven preheat to 450 F.
2. In a bowl, add garlic cloves (2) oregano (half), salt & pepper (half) and oil. Mince them.
3. Cut the rest of the cloves in half and toss with Brussels sprouts and oil (3 tbsp.). Spread on a baking tray and roast for 15 minutes.
4. In the minced garlic mixture, add wine.
5. Add salmon on top of roasted Brussels sprouts. Pour the wine mixture on top of the fish.
6. Add the salt, pepper, oregano on top.
7. Bake for 5-10 minutes. Serve.

Nutrition: Calories 334 | Fat 15.4 g | Sugar 2 g | Protein 33 g |Sodium 385 mg | Carbs 11 g

425. Grilled Shrimp Skewers

(Prep time: 15 minutes | Cook time: 5 minutes | Serving: 6)
Ingredients
- Lemon juice: ⅓ cup
- Fresh chives: 2 tbsp., chopped
- Olive oil: 3 tbsp.
- Lemon zest: 1 tsp.
- Fresh sage: 2 tbsp., chopped
- Black pepper: 1 tsp.
- Fresh oregano: 2 tbsp., chopped
- 2 cans of (15 oz.) Cannellini beans, rinsed
- 24 raw shrimps, peeled & deveined
- Salt: ¼ tsp.
- 12 cherry tomatoes, cut into fours
- Diced celery: 1 cup

Instructions

1. In a bowl, add herbs, zest, salt, pepper, juice, zest, and oil whisk well and reserve 2 tbsp. of the mixture.
2. In the rest of the mixture, add celery, beans, and tomatoes, toss to combine.
3. Let the grill preheat to medium. Onto 6 skewers, thread the shrimps.
4. Oil spray the grill pan or grill rack, grill for 4 minutes, serve with white bean salad with reserved dressing on top.

Nutrition: Calories 212 | Fat 17.2 g | Sugar 1.5 g | Protein 16.9 g | Sodium 467 mg | Carbs 23 g

426. Snap Pea & Shrimp Curry

(Prep time: 15 minutes | Cook time: 7 minutes | Serving: 6)
Ingredients

- Curry powder: 2 tbsp.
- Lite coconut milk: 1 cup
- Raw shrimps: 1 1/2 pounds, peeled & deveined
- Canola oil: 2 tbsp.
- Sugar snap peas: 1 pound, trimmed
- Lemon juice: ¼ cup

Instructions

1. In a skillet, add oil on medium heat.
2. Sauté curry powder for 1-2 minutes, add shrimps, snap peas and cook for 4 minutes.
3. Add the rest of the ingredients with a pinch of salt. Let it come to a boil, cook for 2 minutes. Serve.

Nutrition: Calories 289 | Fat 13.4 g | Sugar 1 g | Protein 27 g | Sodium 389 mg | Carbs 1 g

427. Roasted Salmon & Tomatoes

(Prep time: 15 minutes | Cook time: 12-15 minutes | Serving: 4)
Ingredients

- Kalamata olives: ¼ cup, quartered
- Salmon fillet: 1 ¼ pound, cut into 4 fillets
- Olive oil: 2 tbsp.,
- Cherry tomatoes: 2 cups, halved
- Fresh thyme: 1 tbsp., chopped
- Minced garlic: 4 tsp.
- Salt & pepper: ¼ tsp. each

Instructions

1. Let the oven preheat to 400 F.
2. In a bowl, add half of the salt, pepper, oil (1 tbsp.), thyme and garlic. Mix and spread it on a baking sheet (half sheet).
3. Brush the salmon with oil (1 tbsp.) and sprinkle with salt and pepper.
4. Place on the empty half side of the baking sheet. Add tomatoes on the mixture side and bake for 12-15 minutes.
5. Serve.

Nutrition: Calories 276 | Fat 15 g | Sugar 2 g | Protein 29 g | Sodium 476 mg | Carbs 4.9 g

428. Honey Mustard Salmon with Mango Quinoa

(Prep time: 15 minutes | Cook time: 12 minutes | Serving: 2)
Ingredients

- Honey: 2 tsp.
- Cooked quinoa: ⅔ cup
- Spicy brown mustard: 2 tsp.
- Salmon fillet: 8 oz., skinless
- Jalapeño: 1-2 tbsp., chopped without seeds
- Fresh cilantro: 2 tbsp., chopped
- 1 minced garlic clove
- Mango: half cup, chopped
- Salt & pepper: 1/8 tsp. Each
- Sliced almonds: 1 tbsp., toasted (see tip)
- Olive oil: 1 tsp.

Instructions

1. In a bowl, add garlic, honey and mustard. Mix and brush all over Salmon on all sides.
2. Preheat the grill on medium heat. Grill the fish for 4-6 minutes for each inch of thickness.
3. In a bowl, add the rest of the ingredients. Toss and serve with salmon.

Nutrition: Calories 326| Fat 17.2 g | Sugar 12 g | Protein 26.4 g |Sodium 281 mg | Carbs 26.6 g

429. Salmon & Escarole Packets

(Prep time: 15 minutes | Cook time: 12-15 minutes | Serving: 4)

Ingredients

- Chopped escarole: 6 cups
- 2 lemons, 1 juiced & 1 sliced
- Canola oil: 2 tbsp.
- Fresh tarragon: 2 tbsp., chopped
- Salmon fillet: 1-1 1/4 pounds, cut into 4 fillets
- 2 minced garlic cloves
- Scallions: 1 bunch, sliced

Instructions

1. Let the oven preheat to 400 F.
2. Take 20-24" long pieces of foil or parchment, and make them into a packet.
3. In a pan, add oil and one lemon juice. Mix on low flame, turn the heat off and add garlic and tarragon in hot oil. Mix and take out 2 tbsp.
4. Add the rest to a bowl, add escarole, scallions, a pinch of salt and pepper. Toss well.
5. In each packet, add some greens and place fish fillet, sprinkle a pinch of salt and pepper.
6. Add the 2 tbsp. of sauce on top. Drizzle some lemon juice and place lemon slices on top. Seal the packet and bake for 15 minutes. Serve.

Nutrition: Calories 213 | Fat 17.2 g | Sugar 1.4 g | Protein 24 g |Sodium 376 mg | Carbs 6.4 g

430. Salmon Chowder

(Prep time: 15 minutes | Cook time: 20 minutes | Serving: 4)

Ingredients

- Water: 1 ½ cups
- Sweet pepper: ¾ cup, chopped
- Skinless salmon fillets: 1 ½ pound
- Green onions: ¼ cup, sliced (color separated)
- All-purpose flour: 3 tbsp.
- Salt & pepper: half tsp. Each
- Low-sodium vegetable stock: 3 ½ cups
- Olive oil: 2 tbsp.
- Lime zest: 1 tsp.
- Red-skinned potatoes: 3 cups, (half' pieces)
- Low-fat milk: 2 ½ cups
- Ground ancho chili: ¼ tsp.
- Kernel corn: 2 cups

Instructions

1. In a pan, add water and boil.
2. Add washed & dried fish and let it come to a boil; turn the heat low and simmer for 6-8 minutes, covered.
3. Take fish out and drain, flake the salmon.
4. In a Dutch oven (6 qt.), add oil on medium flame.
5. Sauté bell pepper and scallion (white part) for 3 minutes. Add flour and cook for 1 minute.
6. Add broth, slowly. Add milk, salt, chili powder, pepper, and potatoes. Let it come to a boil, turn the heat low and simmer for 15 minutes.
7. Add corn and cook for 2 minutes; add the salmon and zest. Cook for few minutes.
8. Serve with green onion on top.

Nutrition: Calories 280 | Fat 10 g | Sugar 7.9 g | Protein 22 g |Sodium 287.4 mg | Carbs 24.9

431. Grilled Snapper Curry

(Prep time: 15 minutes | Cook time: 18 minutes | Serving: 4)

Ingredients

- Skim milk: 1 cup
- Cornstarch: 1 tsp.
- Canola oil: 1 tsp.
- Fennel seed: half tsp.
- Ground cumin: 1 tsp.
- Ground cumin: 1 tsp.
- Turmeric: 1 tbsp.
- Coconut extract: half tsp.
- 2 minced garlic cloves
- Black pepper, to taste
- Ground coriander: 1 tsp.
- Paprika: 1 tsp.
- Minced ginger: 2 tbsp.
- Onion: 1 cup, sliced
- Bok choy: 2 cups, sliced
- Red bell pepper: 1 cup, sliced
- Sliced celery: 2 cups
- 1 poblano pepper, chopped
- 4 red snapper fillets

Instructions

1. In a bowl, add all spices, milk, cornstarch and extract. Mix.
2. In a skillet, add oil on medium heat.
3. Sauté all vegetables with garlic and ginger for few minutes.
4. Add milk mixture, cook on low, do not boil. Turn the heat off.
5. Broil or grill the fish until the internal temperature reaches 145 F. It will take ten minutes.
6. Serve snapper with vegetable curry.

Nutrition: Calories 240 | Fat 12 g | Sugar 8 g | Protein 34 g | Sodium 160 mg | Carbs 17 g

432. Ginger-Steamed Fish

(Prep time: 15 minutes | Cook time: 12-15 minutes | Serving: 6)

Ingredients

Fish

- 6 slices peeled ginger (1/4")
- 6 portions of halibut

Sauce

- Soy sauce: ¼ cup, low-sodium
- Chopped garlic: ¼ cup
- Sesame oil: 2 tbsp., toasted
- Sesame seeds: ¼ cup
- Minced ginger: ¼ cup
- Canola oil: 2 tbsp.

Instructions

1. In a pot, boil 1-2" of water, place a steamer basket. Place fish with ginger on top. And steam for 7 minutes for every inch of thickness.
2. In a bowl, add all ingredients of sauce except for soy sauce and oils, mix.
3. In a skillet, add oil on medium flame, add the mixture cook for 1 minute.
4. Add sesame oil, cook for 30 seconds and add soy sauce; cook for 1 minute.
5. Serve with fish, do not serve ginger slices.

Nutrition: Calories 270 | Fat 13.2 g | Sugar 0.2 g | Protein 28.7 g | Sodium 455 mg | Carbs 6.8 g

433. Salmon & Spring Vegetables

(Prep time: 15 minutes | Cook time: 10-12 minutes | Serving: 2)

Ingredients

- Fresh dill: 1 tsp., chopped

- Asparagus: 10 oz., trimmed
- Canola oil: 1 tsp.
- Small potatoes: 6 oz., cut into one" pieces
- 2 salmon fillets, skinless
- Balsamic vinegar: 2 tbsp.
- Salt & pepper: 1/8 tsp. each

Instructions

1. In a baking dish (2 qt. square), add salmon and place potatoes and asparagus around the salmon.
2. In a bowl, add the rest of the ingredients, mix and pour over vegetables and salmon.
3. Cover with plastic wrap and microwave for 10-12 minutes on High. Serve.

Nutrition: Calories 329 | Fat 17.2 g | Sugar 5.2 g | Protein 27.5 g |Sodium 289 mg | Carbs 23g

434. Barbecue-Glazed Shrimp

(Prep time: 15 minutes | Cook time: 12-15 minutes | Serving: 4)

Ingredients

- Paprika: 1 tsp.
- Garlic powder: half tsp.
- Cayenne pepper: 1/8 tsp.
- Chopped zucchini: 2 cups
- Dried oregano: half tsp.
- Jumbo shrimp: 1 pound, peeled & deveined
- Salt & pepper: ¼ tsp., each
- Sliced celery: half cup
- Whole-grain orzo: 1 cup
- Cherry tomatoes: 1 cup, halved
- Olive oil: 2 tbsp.
- Chopped bell pepper: 1 cup
- 3 scallions
- Barbecue sauce: 2 tbsp., low-sodium

Instructions

1. In a bowl, add spices and herbs, mix and sprinkle

over shrimp. Toss.
2. Cook pasta as per the pack's instructions.
3. In a pan, add oil (1 tbsp.) sauté all vegetables with the only white part of the scallion for 5 minutes.
4. Add the sautéed vegetables to the cooked pasta, add salt and combined.
5. In the pan, add oil and cook shrimp for 4-6 minutes. Add BBQ sauce, cook for 1 minute.
6. Serve with pasta.

Nutrition: Calories 360| Fat 7.2 g | Sugar 3 g | Protein 30 g |Sodium 491 mg | Carbs 40.6 g

435. Salmon with Horseradish Pistachio Crust

(Prep time: 15 minutes | Cook time: 12-15 minutes | Serving: 6)

Ingredients

- Sour cream: 1/3 cup
- Chopped shallots: half cup
- Bread crumbs: 2/3 cup
- 6 salmon fillets
- Orange zest: half tsp.
- Horseradish: 1-2 tbsp.
- Chopped pistachios: 2/3 cup
- Olive oil: 2 tbsp.
- Red pepper flakes: ¼ tsp.
- Fresh dill: 1 tbsp., chopped
- 1 minced garlic clove

Instructions

1. Let the oven preheat to 350 F.
2. Take a baking pan and place salmon in it; spread sour cream on salmon.
3. Add the rest of the ingredients in a bowl, press onto salmon, pat to adhere.
4. Bake for 12-15 minutes. Serve.

Nutrition: Calories 376 | Fat 25 g | Sugar 8 g | Protein 24

g |Sodium 219 mg | Carbs 15 g

436. Salmon Burgers with Green Sauce

(Prep time: 2 hours & 20 minutes | Cook time: 5 minutes | Serving: 4)

Ingredients

- Red onion: 2 tbsp., chopped
- Fresh cilantro: 2 tbsp., chopped
- 1 anchovy fillet, chopped
- Mayonnaise: 3 tbsp., low fat
- Peeled ginger: half tsp., chopped
- Fresh parsley: 1 tsp., chopped
- Salmon fillet: 1 pound, skinless
- Capers: 1 tsp., rinsed
- Sea salt: ¼ tsp.
- Black pepper: 1/8 tsp.
- Sour cream: 1 tbsp., low fat
- Lemon juice: half tsp.
- Fresh chives: 2 tsp., chopped
- Lemon zest: half tsp.
- Olive oil: 1 tbsp.

Instructions

1. Cut salmon into ¼" pieces and mix with ginger, onion, cilantro, half of salt and pepper. Mix and make into 4 patties. Keep in the fridge for 2 hours.
2. In a bowl, add the rest of the ingredients, except for oil. Mix well.
3. In a skillet, add oil and cook salmon burgers for 2-3 minutes on each side.
4. Serve with sauce.

Nutrition: Calories 197 | Fat 9.8 g | Sugar 0.6 g | Protein 23.1 g |Sodium 235 mg | Carbs 2.9 g

437. Korean Grilled Mackerel

(Prep time: 15 minutes | Cook time: 12-15 minutes | Serving: 4)

Ingredients

- Canola oil: 1 tbsp.
- 2 whole mackerel
- Soy sauce: 1 tbsp., low-sodium
- Korean chili paste: 2 tbsp.
- Rice vinegar: 2 tsp.
- Grated ginger: 1 tsp.

Instructions

1. In a bowl, add all ingredients except for fish, mix and take 2 tbsp. of the marinade out and set it aside.
2. Place the fish on a baking sheet opening like a paperback. Pour the rest of the marinade on top and keep it in the fridge for half an hour.
3. Let the grill preheat to medium and oil spray the grates. Grill fish, skin side up for three minutes, flip and brush with the reserved marinade, cook for 3-4 minutes more.
4. Serve.

Nutrition: Calories 221 | Fat 6.8 g | Sugar 0.3 g | Protein 33.9 g |Sodium 589 mg | Carbs 3.9 g

438. Salmon & Edamame Cakes

(Prep time: 35 minutes | Cook time: 8 minutes | Serving: 4)

Ingredients

- Whole-wheat panko: ¼ cup
- Fresh cilantro: 1 tbsp., chopped
- 2 egg whites
- Cooked salmon: 2 cups, flaked

- 1 scallion, chopped

- 1 minced garlic clove

- Fresh ginger: 1 tbsp., minced

- Edamame: half cup

Instructions

1. In a bowl, add all ingredients. Mix and make into 4 patties.

2. Keep in the fridge for 15-30 minutes.

3. Oil spray a pan and place on a medium flame.

4. Add the patties and cook for 3-4 minutes on 1 side. Serve.

Nutrition: Calories 267| Fat 1 g | Sugar 1 g | Protein 21 g |Sodium 166 mg | Carbs 5 g

DASH Diet Soups, Sandwiches & Salad Recipes

439. Shrimp & Nectarine Salad

(Prep time: 15 minutes | Cook time: 6 minutes | Serving: 4)

Ingredients

Dressing

- Cider vinegar: 3 tbsp.

- Fresh tarragon: 1 tbsp., chopped

- Dijon mustard: 1 1/2 tsp.

- 1/3 cup of orange juice

- Honey: 1 1/2 tsp.

Salad

- Corn: 1 cup

- Shrimps: 1 pound, peeled & deveined

- 2 nectarines, sliced into one" pieces

- Chopped red onion: half cup

- Lemon-pepper seasoning: half tsp., salt-free

- Salt: 1/8 tsp.

- Canola oil: 4 tsp.

- Mixed salad greens: 8 cups

- Grape tomatoes: 1 cup, halved

Ingredients

1. In a bowl, add all ingredients of dressing, whisk well.

2. In a skillet, add (half) oil on medium. Sauté corn for 1 to 2 minutes, take it out on a plate.

3. Season shrimps with salt and lemon pepper.

4. Add the rest of the oil to the skillet, cook shrimps for 3 to 4 minutes. Add corn back to the pan.

5. Add the rest of the ingredients in a bowl, add dressing (1/3 cup), and toss to coat.

6. Serve with shrimps, with a drizzle of dressing.

Nutrition: Calories 252 | Fat 7 g | Sugar 14 g | Protein 23 g | Sodium 432 mg | Carbs 27 g

440. Mexican-Style Bean Soup

(Prep time: 15 minutes | Cook time: 20 minutes | Serving: 2)

Ingredients

- 1 onion, diced
- 2 minced garlic cloves
- Rapeseed oil: 2 tsp.
- Canned black beans: 14 oz.
- Chili powder: 2 tsp., mild
- Ground coriander: 1 tsp.
- Half red chili, chopped without seeds
- Ground cumin: 1 tsp.
- 1 red pepper, sliced into chunks
- Canned chopped tomatoes: 14 oz.
- Vegetable bouillon powder: 1 tsp., salt-free
- Chopped coriander: 1 cup
- Chicken breast (skinless): 4 oz., shredded
- 1 lime's juice

Instructions

1. In a pan, add oil to medium flame.

2. Sauté pepper and onion for ten minutes. Add spices, garlic, beans (with juices), tomatoes, water (half can), bouillon. Stir well and simmer for 15 minutes, covered.

3. In a bowl, add the rest of the ingredients, toss and serve with soup.

Nutrition: Calories 378| Fat 8 g | Sugar 17 g | Protein 32 g | Sodium 209 mg | Carbs 36 g

441. Feta & Kale Loaded Sweet Potato

(Prep time: 15 minutes | Cook time: 50 minutes | Serving: 4)

Ingredients

- 1 can of (14 oz.) chickpeas, drained
- Olive oil: 1tbsp.
- 1 red onion, sliced thin
- Red wine vinegar: 2 tbsp.
- Kale: 3.5 oz.
- 2 sweet potatoes
- Feta: 1 oz.
- Caster sugar: 1 tsp.
- Mixed greens
- Chili flakes, to taste
- Toasted pumpkin seeds: 1tbsp.

Instructions

1. Let the oven preheat to 390 F.

2. Pierce the sweet potatoes all over with a fork, and roast for 40 minutes, turning as needed.

3. Roast the chickpeas on a tray for ten minutes.

4. In a bowl, add vinegar, onion, a pinch of salt and sugar.

5. In a bowl, mix feta with chili flakes and oil.

6. In a pan, add some water and cook kale for three minutes, till wilted. Add some black pepper.

7. Cut the potatoes in half and top with the rest of the mixtures and ingredients on top. Serve.

Nutrition: Calories 422 | Fat 15 g | Sugar 19 g | Protein 15 g | Sodium 287 mg | Carbs 51 g

442. Broccoli Pasta Salad

(Prep time: 15 minutes | Cook time: 20 minutes | Serving: 2)

Ingredients

- Whole-wheat penne: 2.6 oz.
- Grated ginger: 1 tsp.
- Broccoli florets: 6.7 oz.
- 2 eggs
- Beans: 6.7 oz., halved
- Sunflower seeds: 2 tbsp.
- White miso paste: 1 tbsp.
- Rapeseed oil: 1 tbsp.

Instructions

1. Boil the eggs for 8 minutes, then peel and cut in half.
2. Cook pasta per pack's instructions; in the last 5 minutes, add beans and broccoli and cook until tender.
3. Drain all but 4 tbsp. of water.
4. Add vegetables and pasta to a bowl.
5. In the pasta water, add oil, miso and ginger, whisk well and pour over the pasta.
6. Toss well and serve with eggs.

Nutrition: Calories 436 | Fat 22 g | Sugar 5 g | Protein 24 g | Sodium 209 mg | Carbs 31 g

443. Mediterranean Chicken & Chickpea Soup

(Prep time: 15 minutes | Cook time: 4-8 hours | Serving: 6)
Ingredients

- 1 sweet onion, chopped
- 1 can of (15 oz.) diced roasted tomatoes, salt-free
- 4 cups of water
- Dried chickpeas: 1 ½ cups, soaked for 8-10 hours
- Tomato paste: 2 tbsp.
- 4 chopped garlic cloves
- Chicken thighs: 2 pounds, bone-in & without skin
- 1 bay leaf

- Ground cumin: 4 tsp.
- Paprika: 4 tsp.
- Olives: ¼ cup, halved & oil-cured
- Cayenne pepper: ¼ tsp.
- Pepper: ¼ tsp.
- Salt: ¼ tsp.
- 1 can of (14 oz.) Artichoke hearts, quartered
- Chopped fresh parsley: ¼ cup

Instructions

1. In a slow cooker (6 qt.), add all ingredients except olives, artichoke, stir and cover.
2. Cook for 4 hours on high or 8 hours on low.
3. Take the bay leaf out and discard; take the chicken out and shred the chicken.
4. Add olives, artichokes to the cooker, stir.
5. In serving bowls, add shredded chicken, soup and serve.

Nutrition: Calories 447 | Fat 15.3 g | Sugar 8.5 g | Protein 33.4 g | Sodium 555 mg | Carbs 43 g

444. Tuna Salad & Spinach Sandwiches

(Prep time: 15 minutes | Cook time: 0 minutes | Serving: 4)
Ingredients

- Half peeled cucumber, diced without seeds
- Dill weed: half tsp.
- Red onion, diced: 1/4 cup
- 1 pouch (6 oz.) Tuna, in water
- Black pepper: ¼ tsp.
- 2 ribs celery, chopped
- Olive oil: 2 tbsp.
- Baby spinach: 1 cup
- Whole wheat bread: 8 slices
- One lemon's juice

- Seasoning blend: half tsp., no-salt-added

Instructions

1. In a bowl, mix onion, dill, cucumber, celery and tuna. Add lemon juice and oil, mix.
2. Add the rest of the ingredients and mix.
3. Serve in toasted bread.

Nutrition: Calories 194 | Fat 3 g | Sugar 1 g | Protein 17 g |Sodium 455 mg | Carbs 27 g

445. Zesty Tomato Soup

(Prep time: 15 minutes | Cook time: 15 minutes| Serving: 2)
Ingredients
- Milk: 10.5 oz., non-fat
- Low-fat parmesan cheese: 1 tbsp.
- 1 tomato, chopped
- 1 can of (~12 oz.) Condensed tomato soup, low-sodium & low-fat
- Fresh cilantro: 1 tbsp., chopped
- Croutons: 2 tbsp.

Instructions
1. In a pan, add milk and soup.
2. Whisk until smooth, place on medium flame.
3. Cook for 7 to 10 minutes. Add herbs and tomatoes. Cook for 5 minutes.
4. Serve with cheese and croutons.

Nutrition for 1 ½ cups: Calories 178 | Fat 1 g | Sugar 22 g | Protein 9 g |Sodium 220 mg | Carbs 31g

446. Kale, White Bean & Tomato Sorghum Soup

(Prep time: 15 minutes | Cook time: 25 minutes| Serving: 10)
Ingredients
- Chicken broth: 7 cups, low-sodium
- Kosher salt & pepper: ¼ tsp. Each
- Olive oil: 1 tbsp.
- Whole grain sorghum: half cup, uncooked

- 2 chopped garlic cloves
- Hot sauce: 1 tsp.
- 1 onion, chopped
- 1 can of (15 oz.) Diced tomatoes, undrained
- Kale: 12 oz., chopped without stems
- 2 cans of (15 oz.) white beans, rinsed

Instructions
1. In a pan, add broth (3 cups) let it boil.
2. Add sorghum and simmer for 20 to 25 minutes. If there is liquid, it is okay.
3. In a skillet, add oil to medium. Sauté garlic, pepper, salt and onion for 6 to 8 minutes.
4. Add sriracha and kale, cook for 4 minutes.
5. In a food processor, add half a cup of beans and process until mashed.
6. Add mashed beans and the rest of the ingredients to the soup.
7. Stir well, let it come to a boil, turn the heat low and simmer for 20 minutes. Serve.

Nutrition: Calories 175 | Fat 2 g | Sugar 2 g | Protein 10 g |Sodium 286 mg | Carbs 30 g

447. Grilled Chicken Salad with Fig Vinaigrette

(Prep time: 15 minutes | Cook time: 0 minutes| Serving: 1)
Ingredients
Dressing
- Fresh basil: 2 tbsp., chopped
- ¼ cup of dried figs
- Balsamic vinegar: half cup
- Pepper, to taste
- ¼ cup of olive oil
- Lemon zest: 1 tsp.

Salad
- Grilled chicken breast: 4 oz., diced

- Half pear, sliced
- Pea shoots: ¼ cup
- 1 radish, thinly sliced

Instructions

1. In a blender, add all ingredients of the dressing. Pulse until combined.
2. In a bowl, add all ingredients of salad, except for chicken. Toss and add chicken on top.
3. Serve with dressing.

Nutrition: Calories 224 | Fat 15 g | Sugar 11 g | Protein 9 g |Sodium 172 mg | Carbs 14 g

448. Open-Faced Garden Tuna Sandwich

(Prep time: 15 minutes | Cook time: 0 minutes| Serving: 2)
Ingredients

- Olive oil: 2 tbsp.
- Black pepper
- Lemon juice: 2 tbsp.
- 1 can of (5 oz.) Tuna in water, drained
- Fresh parsley: 2 tbsp., chopped
- Cherry tomatoes: 1/3 cup, sliced
- 2 green onions, chopped
- 2 slices hearty multigrain bread: 2 slices
- Cream cheese: ¼ cup, low-fat
- Leafy greens: 1/3 cup

Instructions

1. In a bowl, whisk all ingredients except for tuna, tomatoes, arugula and cream cheese; whisk well.
2. In a bowl, add tuna and parsley mixture (2/3 cup), mix.
3. Brush the bread with some of the parsley mixture and toast in a skillet.
4. On toasted bread, spread cream cheese and top with arugula, tomatoes and tuna mixture. Serve.

Nutrition: Calories 361 | Fat 22 g | Sugar 5 g | Protein 24 g |Sodium 273 mg | Carbs 18 g

449. Chicken Caesar Pasta Salad

(Prep time: 15 minutes | Cook time: 15 minutes| Serving: 6)
Ingredients

- Parmesan cheese: ¾ cup
- Greek yogurt: ¼ cup, low-fat
- Olive oil: 3 tbsp.
- Dijon mustard: 2 tsp.
- Lemon juice: 2 tbsp.
- Buttermilk: half cup, low-fat
- Black pepper: half tsp.
- Anchovy paste: 1 ½ tsp.
- 1 garlic clove
- Romaine lettuce: 5 cups, chopped
- Whole-wheat penne: 8 oz.
- Cooked chicken breast: 3 cups, shredded
- Salt: ¼ tsp.
- Cherry tomatoes: 2 cups, halved

Instructions

1. Add lemon juice, yogurt, half of salt & pepper, garlic, oil, parmesan (half cup), anchovy paste, buttermilk, and mustard in a blender. Pulse until smooth.
2. As per package instructions, cook the pasta. Drain all but 1 cup of water.
3. In the pasta and water, add tomatoes, chicken, salt and pepper. Toss well, add buttermilk dressing.
4. Cook for a few minutes until thickens.
5. Serve hot or chilled, with parmesan on top.

Nutrition: Calories 383| Fat 13.6 g | Sugar 4 g | Protein 32 g |Sodium 408 mg | Carbs 33 g

450. Tomato Green Bean Soup

(Prep time: 15 minutes | Cook time: 20 minutes| Serving: 9)
Ingredients

- 1 cup of chopped carrots

- Fresh basil: ¼ cup, chopped
- Oil: 2 tsp.
- Tomatoes: 3 cups, diced
- 1 minced garlic clove
- Vegetable broth: 6 cups, no-salt-added
- 1 cup of chopped onion
- Pepper: ¼ tsp.
- Green beans: 1 pound, 1-inch pieces

Instructions
1. In a pan, sauté onion, carrots in hot oil for 5 minutes.
2. Add garlic, beans cook for 1 minute, add broth.
3. Let it come to a boil, turn the heat low and simmer for 20 minutes.
4. Add basil, tomatoes, pepper.
5. Simmer for 5 minutes, covered. Serve.

Nutrition: Calories 58 | Fat 1 g | Sugar 5 g | Protein 4 g | Sodium 302 mg | Carbs 10 g

451. Roasted Vegetable Farro Salad

(Prep time: 15 minutes | Cook time: 60 minutes | Serving: 15)
Ingredients
- Cauliflower florets: ~ 3 cups
- Sea salt & pepper: ¼ tsp. Each
- Broccoli florets: ~ 3 cups
- 3 cups of dry farro
- 2 lemons' juice & zest
- 2 onions, sliced in wedges
- Olive oil: 2 tbsp.
- Fresh parsley: 3 tbsp., chopped
- Chopped hazelnuts: 1 cup
- Dried cranberries: 1 cup

- ¼ cup of apple cider vinegar
- Olive oil: half cup

Instructions
1. In a pan, add the farro and add enough water to cover by two inches of water.
2. Let it come to a boil, turn the heat low and simmer for 50 minutes. Drain and let it cool.
3. Let the oven preheat to 450 F.
4. Toss florets, onion with oil, salt and pepper. Roast for 20 to 25 minutes, take it out of the oven and cool.
5. In a bowl, whisk lemon juice, zest. Pour in a cup and add enough cider vinegar to make it half cup. Slowly add olive oil while whisking.
6. In the farro, add the rest of the ingredients, drizzle with vinaigrette.
7. Toss and serve.

Nutrition: Calories 322 | Fat 16 g | Sugar 7 g | Protein 9 g | Sodium 137 mg | Carbs 40 g

452. Chicken & Vegetable Tortellini Salad

(Prep time: 15 minutes | Cook time: 18 minutes | Serving: 6)
Ingredients
- 2 bay leaves
- Salad creamy dressing: ¼ cup, (choose from dressing chapter)
- 6 cups of water
- 1 pack of (20 oz.) Cheese tortellini, low-sodium
- Chicken breast: 1 pound, boneless & skinless
- Marinated artichokes: half cup, diced
- Peas: half cup
- Fresh herbs: 5 tbsp., chopped
- Sunflower seeds: 2 tbsp.
- Radishes: half cup, sliced thin

- Red-wine vinegar: 2 tbsp.
- Baby arugula: 1 cup

Instructions
1. In a pan, add chicken, water and bay leaves.
2. Let it come to a boil, turn the heat low and simmer for 10-12 minutes until the internal temperature of the meat reaches 165 F.
3. Take the chicken and bay leaf out. In the water, add tortellini, cook for three minutes.
4. Add peas, cook for 1 minute. Drain, then rinse.
5. In a bowl, add dressing, herbs (3 tbsp.), artichoke marinade, vinegar. Mix and add shredded chicken, the rest of the ingredients except for seeds, toss and combined.
6. Serve with fresh herbs, sunflower seeds on top.

Nutrition for 1 ½ cups: Calories 357 | Fat 12.7 g | Sugar 2.9 g | Protein 23.6 g |Sodium 367 mg | Carbs 47 g

453. Romaine Lettuce with Dressing

(Prep time: 15 minutes | Cook time: 8 minutes| Serving: 4)
Ingredients
- Whole wheat-bread: 1 slice
- Creamy dressing: 4 tsp. (low-sodium)
- Romaine lettuce: 2 heads, halved
- 16 cherry tomatoes, halved
- Olive oil: 4 tsp.
- Parmesan cheese: 4 tbsp., shredded

Instructions
1. Let the grill preheat to high heat.
2. Cut the bread into cubes, and toast in the oven until medium brown. Let it cool.
3. With olive oil (1 tsp.), brush the romaine lettuce and place it on the grill.
4. Cook for 2 to 5 minutes. Take it out on a serving plate.
5. Add bread cubes, dressing and the rest of the ingredients on top. Serve.

Nutrition: Calories 162 | Fat 8 g | Sugar 8 g | Protein 6.4 g |Sodium 241 mg | Carbs 17 g

454. Wedge Salad Skewers

(Prep time: 15 minutes | Cook time: 0 minutes| Serving: 8)
Ingredients
- 4 Roma tomatoes, halved
- 1 red onion, sliced into one" pieces
- Cream dressing, as needed
- Blue cheese crumbled: 5 oz.
- 1 cucumber, sliced
- Iceberg lettuce: 1 head, sliced into wedges
- 2 avocados, sliced into one" pieces
- Cooked bacon: 5 pieces
- 2 scallions, diced

Instructions
1. Thread all the ingredients onto skewers except for cheese, dressing and scallions.
2. Serve with cheese, dressing and scallions on top.

Nutrition: Calories 238 | Fat 19 g | Sugar 3 g | Protein 8 g |Sodium 307 mg | Carbs 10 g

455. Minestrone Soup

(Prep time: 15 minutes | Cook time: 55 minutes| Serving: 16)
Ingredients
- 1 minced garlic clove
- 1 can of (6 oz.) tomato paste
- Chopped onion: 1⅓ Cup
- Olive oil: ¼ Cup
- Chopped celery: 1 ½ cups
- Fresh parsley: 1 tbsp., chopped
- Whole-wheat Spaghetti: 2 cups, broken
- 1 can of (1 lb.) Tomatoes, diced

- Sliced carrots: 1 cup

- 1 can of (~16 oz.) Red kidney beans, rinsed

- Dash of hot sauce

- Peas: 1½ Cups

- Shredded cabbage: 4¾ Cup

- Fresh green beans: 1½ Cups

- Water: 11 Cups

Instructions

1. In a pan, heat oil. Add celery, garlic, and onion for 5 minutes.

2. Add the rest of the ingredients, except for the pasta and stir well

3. let it come to a boil, turn the heat low, cover and simmer for45 minutes.

5. Add pasta and simmer for 2 to 3 minutes, serve.

Nutrition: Calories 153 | Fat 4 g | Sugar 2 g | Protein 11 g |Sodium 191 mg | Carbs 21 g

456. Butternut Squash Soup

(Prep time: 15 minutes | Cook time: 25 minutes| Serving: 6)
Ingredients

- 2 shallots, diced

- Peeled butternut squash, cubed: 3 cups

- Minced gingerroot: 2 tsp.

- Corn oil: 2 tsp.

- Low-fat cream: 1/3 cup

- Vegetable broth: 3 cups, low-sodium

- Salt: 1/8 tsp.

- Black pepper: ¼ tsp.

- Ground nutmeg: ¼ tsp.

Instructions

1. Select sauté on a pressure cooker, sauté onions for 3 minutes.

2. Cancel the sauté function. Add gingerroot, squash, broth, salt and pepper.

3. Stir and Cook for 20 minutes, on high. Release the pressure for ten minutes, naturally. Take the lid off.

4. Puree the soup with a stick blender.

5. Add cream and cook for 2-3 minutes. Serve.

Nutrition: Calories 64 | Fat 1.5 g | Sugar 3 g | Protein 2 g |Sodium 126 mg | Carbs 12 g

457. Pasta e Faggioli Soup

(Prep time: 5 days & 15 minutes | Cook time: 8 hours| Serving: 6)
Ingredients

- 2 cups of diced onions

- Dried Italian seasoning: 4 tsp.

- 1 cup of diced celery

- Cooked chicken thighs: 1 pound, diced

- 1 cup of diced carrots

- Whole-wheat rotini pasta: 4 cups, cooked

- 4 cups of baby spinach

- Parmigiano-Reggiano cheese: half cup, grated

- Chicken broth: 6 cups, low-sodium

- Salt: ¼ tsp.

- Fresh basil: 4 tbsp., chopped

- 1 can of (15 oz.) White beans, rinsed

- Olive oil: 2 tbsp.

Instructions

1. In a zip lock bag, add celery, onion and carrots.

2. In a different bag, add pasta and chicken. Keep both zip lock bags in the freezer for 5 days.

3. A night before cooking, keep them in the fridge.

4. In a bowl cooker, add the vegetable bag, seasonings and broth.

5. Cook, covered for 7 ¼ hours on low.

6. Add basil, spinach, beans and the pasta bag. Cook for 45 minutes.

7. Serve with cheese on top.

Nutrition for 2 cups: Calories 457 | Fat 18 g | Sugar 4.4 g | Protein 33 g | Sodium 403 mg | Carbs 42 g

458. Honey Lemon Fruit Salad

(Prep time: 30 minutes | Cook time: 5 minutes | Serving: 6)

Ingredients

Dressing

- Water: 3 tbsp.
- Lemon juice: ¼ cup
- 2 lemons' zest
- Honey: 2 tbsp.

Salad

- 6 oz. of blueberries
- Grapes: 1 cup, halved
- 6 oz. of raspberries
- 6 oz. of blackberries
- Strawberries: 1 lb., sliced

Instructions

1. In a pan, add all ingredients of dressing, let it come to a boil.
2. Turn the heat low and simmer for 3 to 5 minutes. Cool for 25 minutes.
3. In a bowl, add all ingredients of salad, toss and pour the dressing. Toss and serve.

Nutrition for 1 cup: Calories 92 | Fat 17.2 g | Sugar 16 g | Protein 1 g | Sodium 2 mg | Carbs 23 g

459. Strawberry Jicama Cucumber Salad

(Prep time: 30 minutes | Cook time: 0 minutes | Serving: 4)

Ingredients

- 1 peeled jicama, chopped
- 1 peeled cucumber, chopped
- Lime juice: 2 tbsp.
- Fresh cilantro: 1 tbsp., chopped
- 2 cups of strawberries, chopped
- 1 jalapeño, chopped without seeds
- Poppy seeds: 1 tsp.
- Olive oil: 1 tbsp.
- No-calorie sweetener: 1 tbsp.

Instructions

1. In a bowl, whisk oil, sweetener and lime juice until dissolved.
2. Add the rest of the ingredients in a bowl, toss and add dressing, toss and serve.

Nutrition: Calories 130 | Fat 4 g | Sugar 8 g | Protein 3 g | Sodium 10 mg | Carbs 24 g

460. Salmon Couscous Salad

(Prep time: 30 minutes | Cook time: 7 minutes | Serving: 4)

Ingredients

- ¼ cup of diced eggplant
- Whole-wheat Israeli couscous: ¼ cup, cooked
- 3 cups of baby spinach
- Goat cheese: 2 tbsp., crumbled
- Sliced mushrooms: ¼ cup
- White-wine vinaigrette: 2 tbsp.
- Cooked salmon: 4 oz.
- Dried apricots: ¼ cup, sliced

Instructions

1. In a skillet, add oil on medium flame.
2. Sauté eggplant and mushroom for 3-5 minutes. Turn the heat off.
3. In a bowl, toss spinach with vinaigrette (half) and transfer to a plate.
4. Toss couscous with the rest of the vinaigrette and add on top of spinach.
5. Serve with the rest of the ingredients on top.

Nutrition: Calories 464 | Fat 22 g | Sugar 18 g | Protein 34 g | Sodium 350 mg | Carbs 34.7 g

461. Vegetable Turkey Soup

(Prep time: 15 minutes | Cook time: 8 hours | Serving: 6)

Ingredients

- 3 carrots, sliced
- 3 zucchinis, sliced
- Chicken broth: 4 cups, low-sodium
- 1 can of (~16 oz.) Cannellini beans, rinsed
- Salt & pepper: ¼ tsp. Each
- 1 onion, diced
- Ground turkey breast: 1 lb., skinless
- 1 can of (28 oz.) Tomato sauce, no-salt-added
- 2 minced garlic cloves
- Dried Italian seasoning: 1 tbsp.

Instructions

1. In a slow cooker, add all ingredients, stir and cook for 8 hours on low.
2. Serve.

Nutrition: Calories 224 | Fat 1.9 g | Sugar 11 g | Protein 26 g | Sodium 275 mg | Carbs 27 g

462. Quinoa Power Salad

(Prep time: 15 minutes | Cook time: 30 minutes | Serving: 2)

Ingredients

- Half red onion, sliced into 1/4" thick wedges
- Chicken tenders: 8 oz.
- Olive oil: 2 tbsp.
- 1 peeled sweet potato, sliced into half" thick wedges
- Garlic powder: half tsp.
- Salt: ¼ tsp.
- Baby greens: 4 cups
- Whole-grain mustard: 2 tbsp.
- Cider vinegar: 1 tbsp.
- Sunflower seeds: 1 tbsp., toasted
- Chopped shallot: 1 tbsp.
- Maple syrup: 1 tbsp.
- Cooked red quinoa: half cup

Instructions

1. Let the oven preheat to 425 F.
2. Toss sweet potato with garlic powder, oil (1 tbsp.), and half of the salt.
3. Toss and spread on a baking sheet, roast for 15 minutes.
4. In a bowl, add mustard (1tbsp.) and chicken toss well.
5. Take the vegetable tray out after 15 minutes, add chicken to the sheet.
6. Bake for ten minutes.
7. Add the rest of the ingredients in a bowl, except for baby greens and quinoa, whisk well.
8. Shred the chicken and toss with dressing. Add vegetables, quinoa and greens.
9. Toss and serve.

Nutrition: Calories 466 | Fat 11.6 g | Sugar 6 g | Protein 28 g | Sodium 515 mg | Carbs

463. Zucchini Salad

(Prep time: 15 minutes | Cook time: 0 minutes | Serving: 6)

Ingredients

- Olive oil: 2 tsp.
- 1 minced garlic clove
- Feta cheese: ¼ cup, nonfat
- Pepper: ¼ tsp.
- Dried dill: 2 tsp.
- 4 zucchinis, spiralized
- 1 lemon's juice
- Dried parsley: 1 tsp.
- Chopped red onion: 2 tbsp.

Instructions

1. In a bowl, whisk pepper, oil, garlic and lemon juice
2. In a bowl, add the rest of the ingredients, toss and pour dressing.
3. Toss and serve chilled

Nutrition: Calories 65 | Fat 3 g | Sugar 0 g | Protein 4

g |Sodium 101 mg | Carbs 8 g

464. Buffalo Chicken Salad Wrap

(Prep time: 20 minutes | Cook time: 10 minutes| Serving: 4)

Ingredients

- 2 chipotle peppers
- 1/4 cup of white wine vinegar
- Jicama: half cup, sliced thin
- 3 chicken breasts
- Celery diced: half cup
- 2 carrots: half cup, into matchsticks
- 1/4 cup of mayonnaise, low-fat
- 2 (12") whole-grain tortillas
- Onion diced: half cup
- Spinach chopped: 4 cups

Instructions

1. Let the oven preheat to 375 F.
2. Grill chicken for ten minutes until the internal temperature of the meat reaches 165 F.
3. Cut the cooked chicken into cubes.
4. Ad mayo, peppers and vinegar in a blender, pulse until smooth.
5. In a bowl, add all ingredients, except for tortilla and spinach. Mix well.
6. In each tortilla, add chicken mixture, top with spinach. Roll and serve.

Nutrition for half wrap: Calories 247 | Fat 8 g | Sugar 3 g | Protein 25 g |Sodium 374 mg | Carbs 21g

465. Asian Vegetable Salad

(Prep time: 25 minutes | Cook time: 0 minutes| Serving: 4)

Ingredients

- Julienned red sweet pepper: half cup
- Yellow onion: half cup, julienned
- Red cabbage: 1 cup, sliced
- Julienned carrot: 1 1/2 cup
- Sliced spinach: 1 1/2 cups
- Fresh cilantro: 1tbsp., chopped
- Soy sauce: 2 tsp., low-sodium
- Julienned bok choy: 1 1/2 cup
- Snow peas: 1 1/2 cups
- Minced garlic: 1 tbsp.
- Chopped cashews: 1 1/2 tbsp.
- Sesame oil: 2 tsp, toasted

Instructions

1. In a bowl, add all ingredients, toss well and serve.

Nutrition: Calories 113 | Fat 4 g | Sugar 6 g | Protein 3 g |Sodium 55 mg | Carbs 14 g

466. Chicken Sliders

(Prep time: 15 minutes | Cook time: 10 minutes| Serving: 4)

Ingredients

- Black pepper: 1 tbsp.
- Diced onion: half cup
- Minced garlic: 1 tbsp.
- Ground chicken breast: 10 oz.
- Fennel seed: 1 tbsp., crushed
- Balsamic vinegar: 1 tbsp.
- 1 chili pepper, fresh & chopped

Instructions

2. In a bowl, add all ingredients, mix and make into 4 patties.
3. Grill until the internal temperature of the meat reaches 165 F
4. Serve in buns with fresh vegetables.

Nutrition: Calories 224 | Fat 4 g | Sugar 6 g | Protein 22 g |Sodium 183 mg | Carbs 25 g

467. White Bean Hummus Wraps

(Prep time: 20 minutes | Cook time: 0 minutes | Serving: 4)

Ingredients

- Lemon juice: 1 tbsp.
- Black pepper: 1/4 tsp.
- Water: 3 tbsp.
- 1 can of (~16 oz.), white beans, drained, low-sodium
- Sweet paprika: 1/4 tsp.

For Wraps

- 1 avocado, sliced
- 1 cucumber, sliced
- 4 whole-grain wraps (10")
- 1 tomato, sliced
- 1 bell pepper, sliced without seeds
- Lettuce: 4 cups

Instructions

1. In a food processor, add beans and the rest of the ingredients. Pulse until smooth.
2. On each wrap, spread the white bean spread. Add sliced vegetables.
3. Roll and serve.

Nutrition: Calories 345 | Fat 12.1 g | Sugar 5 g | Protein 13 g | Sodium 88 mg | Carbs 49 g

468. French Onion Soup

(Prep time: 15 minutes | Cook time: 2 hours & 45 minutes | Serving: 4)

Ingredients

- Sliced sweet onion: 4 cups
- Fresh thyme: ¼ tsp., chopped
- Sliced red onion: 4 cups
- Beef broth: 8 cups, low-sodium
- Dry white wine: ¼ cup
- Sugar: half tsp.
- Olive oil: 2 tsp.
- Black pepper: half tsp.
- Swiss cheese: 8 slices, low-fat & low-sodium
- Salt: ¼ tsp.
- French bread: 8 slices, cubed

Instructions

1. In a Dutch oven, add olive oil on medium heat.
2. Sauté onions for 5 minutes, add salt, pepper and sugar.
3. Turn the heat low and cook for 20 minutes. Turn the heat to medium, cook for 5 minutes.
4. Add wine, cook for 60 seconds.
5. Add thyme, broth and let it boil. Simmer on low flame for 2 hours, covered.
6. Let the broiler Preheat.
7. Broil bread cubes on a baking sheet for 3 minutes, turning as needed.
8. Serve the soup with croutons and cheese slices. Broil and serve.

Nutrition: Calories 103 | Fat 15 g | Sugar 12 g | Protein 5 g | Sodium 294 mg | Carbs 8 g

469. Vegetable Weight-Loss Soup

(Prep time: 15 minutes | Cook time: 35 minutes | Serving: 8)

Ingredients

- 1 onion, chopped
- 2 minced garlic cloves
- 2 carrots, chopped
- 2 stalks celery, diced
- Green beans: 12 oz., half" pieces
- 4 cups of chopped kale
- Salt: ¼ tsp.
- Vegetable broth: 8 cups, low-sodium
- Olive oil: 2 tbsp.
- 2 cans of (15 oz.) Cannellini, rinsed & low-sodium

- Red-wine vinegar: 2 tsp.

- 2 zucchinis, diced

- Pesto: 8 tsp.

- 4 Roma tomatoes, chopped without seeds

- Pepper: half tsp.

Instructions

1. In a pot, add oil on medium flame.

2. Sauté all vegetables with garlic, cook for ten minutes.

3. Add broth and let it come to a boil; turn the heat low and simmer for ten minutes.

4. Add the rest of the ingredients, except for pesto, turn the heat to high. Simmer for ten minutes.

5. Serve with pesto on top.

Nutrition for 1 ¾ cup: Calories 225 | Fat 8.4 g | Sugar 5.3 g | Protein 12.7 g |Sodium 305 mg | Carbs

470. Veggie & Hummus Sandwich

(Prep time: 15 minutes | Cook time: 0 minutes| Serving: 1)
Ingredients

- Mixed salad greens: half cup

- Hummus: 3 tbsp.

- ¼ cup of shredded carrot

- ¼ avocado, mashed

- ¼ red sweet pepper, sliced

- Whole-grain bread: 2 slices

- ¼ cup of sliced cucumber

Instructions

1. On one slice of bread, spread hummus.

2. On the other slice of bread, spread avocado.

3. Add the rest of the ingredients in between 2 slices. Serve.

Nutrition: Calories 25| Fat 14.3 g | Sugar 6.8 g | Protein 12 g |Sodium 407 mg | Carbs 39 g

471. Couscous Salad

(Prep time: 15 minutes | Cook time: 35 minutes| Serving: 8)

Ingredients

- ¼" Zucchini piece: 1 cup

- Lemon juice: 1 tbsp.

- Black pepper: half tsp.

- 1 red sweet pepper, sliced into ¼" pieces

- Olive oil: 2 tbsp.

- Red onion: half cup, chopped

- Whole-wheat couscous: 1 cup

- Ground cumin: ¾ tsp.

Instructions

1. As per package instructions, cook couscous.

2. Add the rest of the ingredients in the couscous, toss well and serve chilled.

Nutrition for 2/3 cup: Calories 136 | Fat 4 g | Sugar 8 g | Protein 4 g |Sodium 3 mg | Carbs 21g

472. Shrimp Cobb Salad with Dijon Dressing

(Prep time: 20 minutes | Cook time: 0 minutes| Serving: 4)
Ingredients

- White-wine vinegar: 3 tbsp.

- Chopped shallot: 2 tbsp.

- Olive oil: 3 tbsp.

- Cucumber chunks: 1 cup

- Dijon mustard: 1 tbsp.

- 10 cups of mixed greens

- Salt: ¼ tsp.

- 12 peeled extra-large shrimp, cooked & halved

- 1 avocado, chopped

- Cherry tomatoes: 1 cup, halved

- Black pepper: half tsp.

- Crumbled blue cheese: ¼ cup

- 2 hard-boiled eggs, halved

- Cooked bacon: 2 slices, crumbled

Instructions

1. In a bowl, whisk salt, pepper, vinegar, shallots, oil and mustard.
2. In a bowl, add the salad. Drizzle with dressing, toss and serve.

Nutrition for 2 ½ cups: Calories 378 | Fat 25 g | Sugar 3.2 g | Protein 6.4 g | Sodium 416 mg | Carbs 12.7 g

473.   Tuscan Bean Soup

(Prep time: 20 minutes | Cook time: 30 minutes | Serving: 6)
Ingredients

- Half red onion, diced
- 1 can of (~16 oz.) Northern beans, rinsed
- 1 celery, chopped
- Olive oil: 1 tsp.
- Chicken broth: 2 cups, low-sodium
- 2 cups of spinach
- 1 can of (~15 oz.) Diced tomatoes with liquid
- 1 minced garlic clove
- Dried oregano: 1 tsp.
- Red pepper flakes: ¼ tsp.
- Dried thyme: half tsp.
- Grated Parmesan cheese: 1/3 cup

Instructions

1. In a Dutch oven, add oil on medium flame.
2. Sauté celery, onion and garlic for 4-5 minutes.
3. Add the rest of the ingredients except for spinach. Turn the heat to high, simmer.
4. Turn the heat low and simmer, covered for 20 minutes,
5. Add spinach and cook for 2-3 minutes, serve.

Nutrition: Calories 100 | Fat 2 g | Sugar 5 g | Protein 7 g | Sodium 207 mg | Carbs 14 g

474.   Fig & Goat Cheese Salad

(Prep time: 20 minutes | Cook time: 0 minutes | Serving: 6)
Ingredients

- 4 dried figs, sliced
- Olive oil: 2 tsp.
- Goat cheese: 1 oz., crumbled
- Mixed salad greens: 2 cups
- Slivered almonds: 1 ½ tbsp., toasted
- Honey: half tsp.
- Balsamic vinegar: 2 tsp.

Instructions

1. In a bowl, whisk honey, vinegar, oil with a pinch of salt and pepper.
2. Add the rest of the ingredients to a bowl. Toss and add the dressing on top.
3. Toss and serve.

Nutrition: Calories 340 | Fat 21 g | Sugar 3 g | Protein 10 g | Sodium 300 mg | Carbs 31 g

475.   Apple Lettuce Salad

(Prep time: 20 minutes | Cook time: 0 minutes | Serving: 4)
Ingredients

- Lemon juice: 2 tbsp.
- Apple pie spice: ¼ tsp.
- Canola oil: 1 tbsp.
- Apple juice: 1/4 cup, no-sugar-added
- Mixed salad greens: 8 cups
- Dijon mustard: half tsp.
- Brown sugar: 2 ¼ tsp.
- 1 red apple, diced

Instructions

1. Add lemon juice, pie spice, oil, apple juice, mustard, and brown sugar in a bowl. Mix and add apples, toss.
2. Add salad greens, toss and serve.

Nutrition: Calories 124 | Fat 4 g | Sugar 7 g | Protein 2 g | Sodium 44 mg | Carbs 20 g

476. Mediterranean Breakfast Sandwiches

(Prep time: 20 minutes | Cook time: 0 minutes| Serving: 4)

Ingredients

- 8 slices of tomato
- Olive oil: 4 tsp.
- Dried rosemary: half tsp.
- Multigrain bread: 8 slices
- 4 eggs
- Baby spinach: 2 cups
- Feta cheese: 4 tbsp., low-fat

Instructions

1. Let the oven preheat to 375 F.
2. Toast the bread slices.
3. In a skillet, add oil on medium flame. Add rosemary and eggs, one at a time.
4. Cook for 60 seconds. Flip and cook on the other side, turn the heat off.
5. On 4 toasted bread, add the vegetables, egg and feta. Add the other toast on top. Serve.

Nutrition: Calories 242 | Fat 17.2 g | Sugar 3.2 g | Protein 13 g |Sodium 435 mg | Carbs 25 g

477. Tomato Basil Soup

(Prep time: 20 minutes | Cook time: 15 minutes| Serving: 6)

Ingredients

- Non-fat milk: 2 cups
- Salt, a pinch
- Garlic powder: half tsp.
- 3 cans of (~14 oz.) Diced tomatoes, salt-free
- Pepper: half tsp.
- Fresh basil: 1 ½ cups

Instructions

1. In a pan, add all ingredients, except for basil.
2. Let it come to a boil, turn the heat low and simmer for 15 minutes.
3. Add basil leaves. Cook for 5 minutes.
4. Puree with an immersion blender, serve.

Nutrition: Calories 79 | Fat 0 g | Sugar 10 g | Protein 5 g |Sodium 176 mg | Carbs 14 g

478. Baby Beet & Orange Salad

(Prep time: 20 minutes | Cook time: 50 minutes| Serving: 4)

Ingredients

- Chopped celery: half cup
- 1 orange's zest & juice
- Chopped Napa cabbage: 1 1/2 cups
- 1 orange, cut into segments after peeling
- Baby beets: 4 cups with 1 cup of greens
- Black pepper, to taste
- Onion chopped: half cup
- Olive oil: half tbsp.

Instructions

1. Let the oven preheat to 400 F.
2. Slice the green from beets and wash well.
3. Rinse the beets and toss with olive oil, and wrap in aluminum foil.
4. Bake for 45 minutes, let them cool, then peel and slice.
5. In a bowl, add chopped beets' greens with other vegetables.
6. In a bowl, whisk orange juice with half tbsp. of olive oil. Add pepper.
7. Pour over salad with beets, toss and serve.

Nutrition for 2 cups: Calories 250 | Fat 2 g | Sugar 15 g | Protein 3 g |Sodium 135 mg | Carbs 22 g

479. Black Bean Salad

(Prep time: 20 minutes | Cook time: 0 minutes| Serving: 4)

Ingredients

- 1 ripe avocado, chopped
- Cilantro leaves: ¼ cup
- Red onion: half cup, sliced
- Olive oil: 2 tbsp.

- Lime juice: ¼ cup

- 1 can of (15 oz.) Black beans, rinsed

- Corn kernels: 2 cups

- 1 minced garlic clove

- Salt: 1/8 tsp.

- Grape tomatoes: 2 cups, halved

- 8 cups of mixed salad greens

Instructions

1. In a bowl, add onion and enough water to cover them.

2. In a food processor, add oil, avocado, garlic, salt, cilantro and lime juice, pulse until smooth.

3. In a bowl, add the rest of the ingredients, drained onions, with avocado dressing.

4. Toss and serve.

Nutrition for 2 cups: Calories 322 | Fat 16 g | Sugar 12 g | Protein 10 g |Sodium 305 mg | Carbs 40 g

480. Three Sisters Soup

(Prep time: 20 minutes | Cook time: 30 minutes| Serving: 4)
Ingredients
- Yellow corn: 16 oz.

- Canned kidney beans: 16 oz., rinsed

- Canned cooked pumpkin: 15 oz.

- 1 onion, diced

- Curry powder: half tsp.

- Vegetable stock: 6 cups, low-sodium

- 1 rib celery, diced

- Dried sage: half tsp.

Instructions

1. In a pan, add stock and boil.

2. Add celery, corn, onion and beans, cook for ten minutes.

3. Add the rest of the ingredients, simmer for 20

minutes.

4. Serve.

Nutrition: Calories 145 | Fat 1.0 g | Sugar 6 g | Protein 9 g |Sodium 55 mg | Carbs 28 g

481. Calypso Bean Salad with Pesto

(Prep time: 20 minutes | Cook time: 70 minutes| Serving: 4)
Ingredients
- Dried calypso beans: 2 cups, soaked 8-10 hours

- 1 carrot, chopped

- Basil pesto: half cup

- Water: 8 cups

- 1 celery stalk, chopped

- Olive oil: 2 tbsp.

- Half onion, chopped

Instructions

1. In a pan, add all ingredients, except for pesto. Stir and let it come to a boil, turn the heat low and simmer for 60 minutes.

2. Take the beans out, strain and throw the vegetables away.

3. In a pan, sauté beans in hot oil. Toss in pesto and serve.

Nutrition: Calories 103 | Fat 1.5 g | Sugar 2 g | Protein 5 g |Sodium 294 mg | Carbs 8 g

482. Beef Stew

(Prep time: 20 minutes | Cook time: 2 hours| Serving: 6)
Ingredients
- Boneless lean beef meat: 1 pound, 1 ½" cubes

- Canola oil: 2 tbsp.

- Black pepper: ¾ tsp.

- Half fennel bulb, sliced thin

- All-purpose flour: 3 tbsp.

- Vegetable stock: 3 cups, salt-free

- Flat-leaf parsley: 1/3 cup, chopped

- Shallots chopped: 3 tbsp.
- 4 peeled potatoes, chunks
- 2 thyme sprigs, fresh
- 4 carrots, chunks
- Boiling onions: 10 oz., halved
- 1 bay leaf
- 3 Portobello mushrooms, chunks

Instructions

1. On a plate, add flour, and coat the beef cubes in flour.
2. In a pan, add oil on medium flame.
3. Cook beef for 5 minutes, on all sides, take it out on a plate.
4. Sauté shallots, fennel for 7 to 8 minutes.
5. Add bay leaf, thyme and half of the pepper. Cook for 1 minute.
6. Add beef back in the pan, with wine and stock.
7. Let it come to a boil, turn the heat low and simmer for 45 minutes.
8. Add vegetables and cook for half an hour.
9. Take the bay leaf and sprig out, sprinkle pepper and serve.

Nutrition for 1 cup: Calories 244| Fat 8 g | Sugar 8 g | Protein 21 g |Sodium 185 mg | Carbs 22g

483. Turkey & Vegetable Barley Soup

(Prep time: 20 minutes | Cook time: 20 minutes | Serving: 6)
Ingredients

- 5 carrots, chopped
- Baby spinach: 2 cups
- 1 onion, chopped
- Cooked turkey breast: 2 cups, cubed
- Pepper: half tsp.
- Canola oil: 1 tbsp.

- Quick-cooking barley: 2/3 cup
- Chicken broth: 6 cups, low-sodium

Instructions

1. Sauté onion, carrots in hot oil for 4 to 5 minutes.
2. Add the rest of the ingredients. Let it come to a boil, turn the heat low and simmer for 10 to 15 minutes.

Nutrition for 1 1/3 cup: Calories 208 | Fat 4 g | Sugar 8 g | Protein 21 g |Sodium 402mg | Carbs 23 g

484. Spinach Bean Soup

(Prep time: 10 minutes | Cook time: 22 minutes | Serving: 6)
Ingredients

- Minced garlic: 2 tbsp.
- Cumin: 1 tsp.
- Canned tomatoes, diced: 15 oz., with liquid
- Pepper: 1/4 tsp.
- Canned vegetable broth: 14.5 oz., low-sodium
- 1 small onion (chopped)
- Canned chickpeas: 16 oz., with liquid
- Fresh spinach: 4 cups, packed

Instructions

1. In a pot, add some oil on medium heat.
2. Sauté garlic and onion for 5 minutes.
3. Add the rest of the ingredients, except for spinach, stir and let it boil.
4. Turn the heat low and add spinach and cook for 10 to 15 minutes; serve.

Nutrition: Calories 95 | Fat 17.2 g | Sugar 5 g | Protein 6 g |Sodium 45 mg | Carbs 17 g

485. Creamy Asparagus Soup

(Prep time: 10 minutes | Cook time: 22 minutes | Serving: 6)
Ingredients

- Fresh asparagus: half-pound, ¼" pieces
- Canola oil: 2 tbsp.
- Chopped onion: half cup
- 2 stalks celery, diced

- Peeled potatoes: 2 cups, diced
- 4 cups of water
- 1 1/2 cups of milk, non-fat
- Whole-wheat flour: half cup

Instructions

1. Add water, potatoes, onion, asparagus, celery, and onion on high heat in a pot.
2. Let it come to a boil, turn the heat low and simmer for 15 minutes.
3. In a bowl, add oil, whisk the milk and flour. Gradually add the mixture to the soup.
4. Cook on medium-high heat, cook for 5 minutes, until soup thickness.
5. Serve with black pepper on top.

Nutrition for 1 ½ cups: Calories 140 | Fat 4 g | Sugar 2 g | Protein 6 g |Sodium 76 mg | Carbs 22g

486. Cranberry Bean Salad

(Prep time: 10 minutes | Cook time: 40 minutes | Serving: 4)

Ingredients

- Cranberry beans: 2 cups
- Half onion, diced
- 1 carrot, diced
- Fresh parsley: half cup, chopped
- 1 lemon, cut into fours
- Water: 8 cups
- 1 celery stalk, diced
- Olive oil: 1 tbsp.
- Grapeseed oil: ¼ cup
- Olives: half cup, pitted

Instructions

1. Add water, cranberry beans, and other ingredients in a pan except for lemon, olives, and oil stir.
2. Let it come to a boil, turn the heat low and simmer for 25 minutes.

3. Take the beans out.
4. In a pot, add oil and lemon, cook for 20 minutes on low.
5. Take the lemons out and dice, transfer to the bean bowl. Add olives and fresh herbs.
6. Toss and serve.

Nutrition: Calories 113 | Fat 8.9 g | Sugar 2 g | Protein 12 g |Sodium 114 mg | Carbs 8 g

487. Southwestern Steak Salad

(Prep time: 10 minutes | Cook time: 20 minutes | Serving: 4)

Ingredients

- Salt: 1/8 tsp.
- Multigrain bow tie pasta: 2 cups
- Ground cumin: ¼ tsp.
- Olive oil: 1 tbsp.
- 2 sweet corn ears, without husks
- Pepper: ¼ tsp.
- 2 tomatoes
- 1 beef top sirloin steak: ¾ pound
- 3 poblano peppers, cut in half without seeds
- 1 sweet onion, cut into half' rings

Dressing

- Fresh cilantro: 1/3 cup, chopped
- Olive oil: 1 tbsp.
- Lime juice: ¼ cup
- Ground cumin: ¼ tsp.
- Pepper: ¼ tsp.

Instructions

1. Season steak with spices.
2. With oil, brush onion, peppers and corn.
3. Grill the steak for 6 to 8 minutes on one side and cook until the meat's internal temperature reaches 140 F.
4. Grill the vegetables for 8 to 10 minutes.
5. As per package instructions, cook the pasta.

6. Chop the grilled vegetables and take them out in a bowl.

7. Add dressing ingredients, pasta, toss and serve with sliced steak.

Nutrition: Calories 456 | Fat 13 g | Sugar 15 g | Protein 30 g | Sodium 370 mg | Carbs 58 g

488. Carrot Soup

(Prep time: 10 minutes | Cook time: 40 minutes | Serving: 6)

Ingredients

10 carrots, sliced

All-purpose flour: 3 tbsp.

Black pepper: ¼ tsp.

Sugar: 1 ½ tbsp.

Fresh parsley: 2 tbsp., chopped

2 cups of water

Ground nutmeg: ¼ tsp.

Non-fat milk: 4 cups

Instructions

In a pan, add water, sugar and carrots.

Cook, covered for 20 minutes. Save some carrot water, drain the rest.

In a saucepan, add flour on medium flame. Whisk nutmeg, pepper, and milk. Cook until it thickens.

In a blender, add white sauce and carrots, pulse until smooth.

Add some reserved water if needed to get the desired consistency.

Serve with fresh herbs on top.

Nutrition for 1 ½ cups: Calories 124 | Fat 17.2 g | Sugar 16 g | Protein 7 g | Sodium 140 mg | Carbs 24 g

489. Turkey Wrap

(Prep time: 15 minutes | Cook time: 0 minutes | Serving: 4)

Ingredients

- 1/4 cup of salsa
- Sliced tomatoes: half cup
- 2 (12") whole-wheat tortillas
- Sliced cooked turkey: 12 oz.
- 1/4 cup of avocado
- Green cabbage: 1 cup, shredded
- Thinly sliced carrots: half cup

Instructions

1. Mix salsa with avocado, and spread over tortillas.

2. Add vegetables and turkey slices in the middle, wrap tightly, cut in half and serve.

Nutrition for half wrap: Calories 226 | Fat 6 g | Sugar 0 g | Protein 28 g | Sodium 253 mg | Carbs 15 g

490. Hungarian Mushroom Soup

(Prep time: 10 minutes | Cook time: 40 minutes | Serving: 4)

Ingredients

- Hungarian paprika: 1 tbsp.
- Mixed mushrooms, sliced: 1 pound
- Unsalted butter: 3 tbsp.
- Chopped onions: 2 cups
- Dried dill weed: 2 tsp.
- Almond milk: 1 cup
- Soy sauce: 1 tbsp., low-sodium
- Greek yogurt: half cup, low-fat
- Veggie broth: 2 cups, low-sodium
- Black pepper, to taste
- Lemon juice: 2 tsp.
- All-purpose flour: 3 tbsp.
- Fresh parsley: 2 tbsp.

Instructions

1. In a pot, add butter on medium flame.

2. Sauté onion for 5 minutes, add mushrooms and cook for 5 minutes.

3. Add broth, dill, soy sauce and paprika, simmer on

low flame, covered for 15 minutes.

4. In a bowl, mix flour and milk, add to the soup and mix well. Simmer for 15 minutes more, covered. Stir as needed.

5. Add rest of the ingredients, mix well and heat on low for 5 minutes. Serve.

Nutrition: Calories 113 | Fat 1.5 g | Sugar 2 g | Protein 5 g |Sodium 114 mg | Carbs 8 g

491. White-Bean, Tomato, Cucumber Salad with Basil Vinaigrette

(Prep time: 15 minutes | Cook time: 0 minutes | Serving: 4)
Ingredients

- Olive oil: ¼ cup
- Red-wine vinegar: 3 tbsp.
- Black pepper: ¼ tsp.
- Honey: 1 tsp.
- Chopped shallot: 1 tbsp.
- Fresh basil leaves: half cup
- 1 can of (15 oz.) Cannellini beans, rinsed
- Dijon mustard: 2 tsp.
- Salt: 1/8 tsp.
- Half cucumber, sliced
- Mixed salad greens: 10 cups
- Cherry tomatoes: 1 cup, halved

Instructions

1. In a food processor, add all ingredients except for cucumber, tomatoes, greens and beans.

2. Pulse until smooth; take it out in a bowl. Add the rest of the vegetables, toss and serve.

Nutrition: Calories 246 | Fat 15.3 g | Sugar 1 g | Protein 7.5 g |Sodium 245 mg | Carbs

492. Warm Rice & Pintos Salad

(Prep time: 10 minutes | Cook time: 25 minutes | Serving: 4)
Ingredients

- Frozen corn: 1 cup
- Ground cumin: 1 ½ tsp.
- 1 small onion, diced
- 2 minced garlic cloves
- Chili powder: 1 ½ tsp.
- 1 can of (15 oz.) Pinto beans, rinsed
- Cheddar cheese: ¼ cup, shredded
- Salsa: half cup
- Cooked brown rice: 8.8 oz.
- Olive oil: 1 tbsp.
- 1 can of (4 oz.) Chopped green chilies
- Fresh cilantro: 1/4 cup, chopped
- 1 bunch of romaine, cut in fours

Instructions

1. In a skillet, add oil on medium heat.

2. Sauté onion and corn for 4-5 minutes. Add spices and garlic cook for 1 minute.

3. Add rice, salsa, beans, cilantro, chilies, and mix well. Cook for 2-3 minutes.

4. Serve in romaine wedges, with cheese on top.

Nutrition: Calories 331 | Fat 8 g | Sugar 5 g | Protein 12 g |Sodium 432 mg | Carbs 50 g

493. Roasted Beet with Wild Arugula Salad

(Prep time: 10 minutes | Cook time: 30 minutes | Serving: 8)
Ingredients

- Wild arugula: 6 cups
- Olive oil: 7 tbsp.
- Pignoli nuts: half cup
- 4 lb. Of beets
- Kosher salt: 1/4 tsp.
- Goat cheese: 6 oz.
- Reduced balsamic vinegar: 6 tbsp.

Instructions

1. In a pan, add nuts and toast until golden brown.

2. Toss the beets with olive oil (2 tsp.) and bake at 350 F, until soft.

3. Take them out, peel and slice thinly.

4. In a bowl, add salt, balsamic and arugula; toss well.

5. Serve salad with arugula, beet slices, goat cheese and toasted nuts on top.

Nutrition: Calories 246 | Fat 15.3 g | Sugar 1 g | Protein 7.5 g |Sodium 205 mg | Carbs

494. Asian Chicken Wraps

(Prep time: 15 minutes | Cook time: 10 minutes | Serving: 4)
Ingredients

- Cooked skinless white meat chicken: 1 cup, shredded
- 5 scallions, sliced
- Coleslaw mix: 1-pound pack
- Sesame oil: 1 tsp.
- Hoisin sauce: 3 tbsp.
- Minced ginger: 1 tbsp.
- Garlic chili sauce: 1 tsp.
- 1 minced garlic clove
- Whole wheat tortillas: 4 tortillas (8")
- Shiitake mushrooms: 3 oz., sliced without stems

Instructions

In a skillet, add oil on medium-high heat.

Add coleslaw, ginger, chicken, garlic, scallions and mushrooms. Cook for 3 minutes.

Add chili sauce and hoisin, cook for 1 minute.

Warm the tortillas. In each tortilla, add the filling, roll and serve.

Nutrition: Calories 275 | Fat 13 g | Sugar 8 g | Protein 12 g |Sodium 135 mg | Carbs 12g

495. Mixed Vegetable Salad with Lime Dressing

(Prep time: 15 minutes | Cook time: 0 minutes | Serving: 6)
Ingredients

- ¼ Cup of olive oil
- 6 leaves of lettuce
- Fresh cilantro: 1 ½ tbsp., chopped
- ¼ cup of canola oil
- Salt & pepper: 1/8 tsp. Each
- 1 sliced hard-boiled egg
- 2 cups of mixed vegetables
- Lime juice: 3 tbsp.
- 1 watercress, small bunch without stems
- 1 red onion, thickly sliced into rounds & separated

Instructions

1. In a bowl, whisk salt, oils, cilantro, lime juice, and pepper.

2. Add vegetables and toss.

3. On the serving plate, place the lettuce, top with vegetables, cheese, onion and egg. Serve.

Nutrition for 1 ½ cups: Calories 214 | Fat 17.2 g | Sugar 1.8 g | Protein 2.6 g |Sodium 198 mg | Carbs 7.7 g

496. Cream of Turkey & Wild Rice Soup

(Prep time: 15 minutes | Cook time: 20 minutes | Serving: 4)
Ingredients

- Sliced mushrooms: 2 cups
- ¾ cup of diced celery
- Olive oil: 1 tbsp.
- ¾ cup of diced carrots
- Salt & pepper: ¼ tsp. Each
- Shredded cooked turkey: 3 cups
- ¼ cup of all-purpose flour
- Chicken broth: 4 cups, low-sodium
- ¼ cup of diced shallots
- Fresh parsley: 2 tbsp., chopped
- Instant wild rice: 1 cup

- Sour cream: half cup, low-fat

Instructions
1. In a pan, add oil on medium heat.
2. Sauté vegetables for 5 minutes, add salt, pepper and flour and cook for 2 minutes.
3. Add broth, stir, let it come to a boil.
4. Add rice and lower the heat, cook for 5 to 7 minutes, covered.
5. Add turkey, parsley and sour cream. Cook for 2 minutes. Serve.

Nutrition: Calories 378 | Fat 10.6 g | Sugar 2.8 g | Protein 36 g |Sodium 287 mg | Carbs 28 g

497. Garden Vegetable Beef Soup

(Prep time: 15 minutes | Cook time: 1 hour & 10 minutes | Serving: 8)
Ingredients
- 1 onion, diced
- 1/4 cup of tomato paste
- 2 minced garlic cloves
- Lean ground beef: 1 1/2 pounds
- 2 celery ribs, diced
- 1 can of (~15 oz.) Diced tomatoes with liquid
- Julienned carrots: 10 oz.
- Pepper: ¼ tsp.
- Shredded cabbage: 1 1/2 cups
- Cut green beans: half cup
- 1 zucchini, chopped
- Dried basil: 1 tsp.
- 4 cans of (~15 oz.) Beef broth, low-sodium
- Red potato: 5 oz., chopped
- Dried oregano: half tsp.

Instructions
1. In a pot (6 qt.), add garlic, beef, onion and cook

for 6 to 8 minutes. Drain.
2. Add celery and carrots, cook for 6 to 8 minutes. Add tomato paste and cook for 1 minute.
3. Add the rest of the ingredients, let it come to a boil, turn the heat low and simmer for 35 to 45 minutes, covered. Serve.

Nutrition for 1 ¾ cup: Calories 207 | Fat 7 g | Sugar 7 g | Protein 21 g |Sodium 359 mg | Carbs 14 g

498. Potato-Fennel Soup

(Prep time: 15 minutes | Cook time: 20 minutes | Serving: 8)
Ingredients
- Olive oil: 1 tsp.
- Chopped red onion: 1 cup
- Lemon juice: 2 tsp.
- 2 peeled russet potatoes, sliced
- Fennel bulb: 2 pounds, chopped
- Chicken broth: 3 cups, low-sodium
- Fennel seeds: 2 tsp., toasted
- Milk: 1 cup, non-fat

Instructions
1. In a pot, sauté onion and fennel in hot oil for 5 minutes.
2. Add lemon juice, potatoes, milk and broth. Cook on low flame for 15 minutes.
3. With a stick blender, puree the soup.
4. Serve with fennel seeds on top.

Nutrition for ¾ cup: Calories 149 | Fat 1.5 g | Sugar 8 g | Protein 6 g |Sodium 104 mg | Carbs 28 g

499. Pesto Chicken & Cannellini Bean Soup

(Prep time: 15 minutes | Cook time: 45 minutes | Serving: 8)
Ingredients
- Chopped onion: 1 cup
- 8 cups of chicken broth, low-sodium
- Dried oregano: 1 tsp.

- Olive oil: 2 tbsp.

- Dried marjoram: 1 tsp.

- Chicken breasts: 2 pounds, skin removed & bone-in

- 1 can of (15 oz.) Cannellini beans, rinsed

- 3 cups of sliced fennel

- Black pepper: half tsp.

- 2 minced garlic cloves

- Broccoli: 3 cups

- Chopped tomatoes: 2 cups

- Salt: 1/8 tsp.

- Pesto: ¼ cup

Instructions
1. sauté garlic and onion for 2-3 minutes in hot oil.

2. Add dried herbs, cook for 1 minute. Add chicken and broth, cook on high flame.

3. Cook until the internal temperature of the meat reaches 165 F, for 20-22 minutes.

4. Take the chicken out and shred.

5. Add tomatoes, fennel, tomatoes and broccolini to the pot. Simmer for 4-10 minutes.

6. Add beans, chicken, pepper, and salt. Cook for 3 minutes.

7. Turn the heat off, add pesto. Stir and serve.

Nutrition for 1 ¾ cup: Calories 271 | Fat 10 g | Sugar 8 g | Protein 26 g | Sodium 289 mg | Carbs 17 g

500. . Grilled Veggie Sandwich

(Prep time: 15 minutes | Cook time: 10 minutes | Serving: 2)
Ingredients
- 3 minced garlic cloves

- Olive oil: 1/8 cup

- Light mayonnaise: 3 tbsp.

- 1 cup of sliced red bell peppers

- 1 squash, small, sliced

- 1 zucchini, sliced

- Lemon juice: 1 tbsp.

- Crumbled feta cheese: half cup, low-fat

- 1 red onion, sliced

- 2 slices of focaccia bread

Instructions
1. In a bowl, mix lemon juice, mayo and garlic.

2. With olive oil, brush the vegetables on both sides and grill on oiled grates.

3. Grill for 3 minutes on each side.

4. On each slice of bread, spread the mayo mixture and add feta cheese on top.

5. Grill for 2-3 minutes, but do not burn.

6. Serve the bread with grilled vegetables.

Nutrition: Calories 246 | Fat 15.3 g | Sugar 1 g | Protein 7.5 g | Sodium 213 mg | Carbs 12 g

501. Quinoa & Asian Pear Salad

(Prep time: 15 minutes | Cook time: 15 minutes | Serving: 6)
Ingredients
- 4 oz. of trimmed snow peas

- 1 scallion, chopped

- Uncooked quinoa: 1 cup

- Diced red bell pepper: 1/4 cup

- 1/4 cup of roasted pecans, chopped

- Salt & pepper: ¼ tsp.

- Toasted sesame oil: 1 tsp.

- Toasted sesame seeds: 1 tsp.

- Peeled Asian pear, half' pieces

- Lemon juice: 2 tbsp.

- Olive oil: 1 tbsp.

Instructions
1. Cook the quinoa without salt, as per package instructions, fluff with a fork.

2. Cook the snow peas in boiling water for 45

seconds. Drain and wash with cold water.

3. Add the sesame seeds, pear, pecans, bell peppers, snow peas, scallion to the quinoa.

4. Add the rest of the ingredients in a bowl and whisk, pour over quinoa mixture. Toss to coat. Let it rest for 15 minutes and serve.

Nutrition: Calories 198 | Fat 8.5 g | Sugar 6 g | Protein 5 g | Sodium 101 mg | Carbs 26 g

502. Curried Squash & Chicken Soup

(Prep time: 15 minutes | Cook time: 10 minutes | Serving: 2)

Ingredients

- Lite coconut milk: half cup
- Lime juice: 2 tsp.
- Water: half cup
- Pureed winter squash: 10 oz.
- Brown sugar: 2 tsp.
- Chicken breast: 8 oz., boneless & skinless, sliced
- Thai red curry paste: half to 1 tsp.
- Baby spinach: 6 oz.

Instructions

1. In a pan, add milk, water and squash on medium heat.

2. Cook for ten minutes, stirring occasionally.

3. Add chicken and cook for 3 minutes. Add the rest of the ingredients, cook for 3 minutes. Serve.

Nutrition 1 ¾ cup: Calories 284 | Fat 7.2 g | Sugar 8 g | Protein 28 g | Sodium 287 mg | Carbs 29 g

503. Vegetable-Barley Soup

(Prep time: 15 minutes | Cook time: 15 minutes | Serving: 4)

Ingredients

- Half onion, diced
- 1 celery rib
- 1 1/2 cups of mixed vegetables, frozen
- 1 cup of chopped kale
- 1 minced garlic clove
- 1 tsp. Of olive oil
- Canned diced tomatoes: 15 oz., with liquid
- Water: half cup
- 1 1/2 cups of vegetable broth, low-sodium
- Dried basil: half tsp.
- 1/8 tsp. Of pepper
- Dried oregano: half tsp.
- 1/4 cup of barley

Instructions

1. In a Dutch oven, add some oil, sauté celery and onion for 3 minutes on medium flame.

2. Add garlic, cook for ten seconds. Add the rest of the ingredients, let it come to a boil, turn the heat low and simmer for 10-12 minutes. Serve.

Nutrition: Calories 261 | Fat 13.5 g | Sugar 6 g | Protein 4 g | Sodium 145 mg | Carbs 11 g

504. Macaroni Salad with Avocado Dressing

(Prep time: 15 minutes | Cook time: 15 minutes | Serving: 12)

Ingredients

- Red bell pepper: 1 cup, chopped
- Celery: half cup, sliced
- Salt: ¼ tsp.
- 1 avocado
- 2 scallions, diced
- Whole-wheat macaroni: 8 oz.
- Fresh cilantro: 2 tbsp., chopped
- Black pepper: ¼ tsp.
- Rice vinegar: 2 tbsp.
- Dried minced garlic: half tsp.
- ¼ cup of light mayonnaise

Instructions

1. Cook pasta as per package instructions. Drain, take it out in a bowl.

2. Add celery, cilantro, scallions and bell peppers.

3. In a food processor, add avocado (half) and the rest of the ingredients. Pulse until smooth.

4. Pour in the macaroni salad, toss and serve.

Nutrition for the half cup: Calories 130 | Fat 6.2 g | Sugar 0.8 g | Protein 3.4 g | Sodium 181 mg | Carbs 16 g

505. Pickled Onion Salad

(Prep time: 65 minutes | Cook time: 0 minutes | Serving: 4)
Ingredients
- 4 scallions, chopped
- Sugar: 2 tbsp.
- Cider vinegar: half cup
- Sliced red onions: 2 cups
- Lime juice: 1 tbsp.
- Olive oil: 2 tsp.
- 4 lettuce leaves
- Fresh cilantro: half cup, chopped

Instructions
1. In a bowl, whisk sugar, oil, onions and vinegar.
2. Keep in the fridge for 60 minutes, covered.
3. Before serving, add lime juice, cilantro, stir and serve on lettuce leaves.

Nutrition for half cup: Calories 86 | Fat 2 g | Sugar 12 g | Protein 1 g | Sodium 21 mg | Carbs 16 g

506. Curried Carrot & Apple Soup

(Prep time: 15 minutes | Cook time: 35 minutes | Serving: 4)
Ingredients
- 1 onion, chopped
- 1 stick of celery, chopped
- Curry powder: 1 tbsp.
- 1 bay leaf
- Olive oil: 1 tbsp.
- 6 carrots, thinly sliced
- Broth: 4 cups, low-sodium
- 2 large peeled apples, chopped
- A pinch of salt

Instructions
1. Sauté celery and onion for 8 to 12 minutes, on medium heat.
2. Add apples, curry powder, bay leaf, carrots and cook for 2 minutes with a pinch of salt.
3. Let it come to a boil, turn the heat low and simmer for 20-25 minutes, covered.
4. Take the bay leaf out, puree the soup with a stick blender.
5. Add black pepper, and serve.

Nutrition: Calories 276 | Fat 14 g | Sugar 2.7 g | Protein 7.1 g | Sodium 178 mg | Carbs 12g

507. Chicken & Shredded Brussels Sprout Salad

(Prep time: 15 minutes | Cook time: 20 minutes | Serving: 4)
Ingredients
- Olive oil: 2 tbsp.
- Chopped shallot: 1/4 cup
- Pepper: 1/8 tsp.
- Red-wine vinegar: 2 tbsp.
- Center-cut bacon: 4 slices
- Dijon mustard: half tsp.
- Cooked chicken breast: 2 cups, shredded

- Brussels sprouts: 1 pound, shredded
- Honey: 1 tsp.
- 2 Fuji apples, sliced

Instructions

1. In a skillet, cook bacon until crispy and take it out on a plate. Crumble the bacon.
2. Drain the fat, sauté shallots and cook for 1-2 minutes, turn the heat off.
3. Add mustard, vinegar, pepper, mustard, honey, whisk well.
4. Add Brussels and toss well. Cook for 2-3 minutes.
5. Add chicken and apples, toss to coat. Serve with crumbled bacon on top.

Nutrition for 2 cups: Calories 357| Fat 17.2 g | Sugar 15 g | Protein 34 g |Sodium 309 mg | Carbs 28 g

DASH Diet Sauces, Dips & Dressing Recipes

508. Artichoke Dip

(Prep time: 10 minutes | Cook time: 35 minutes | Serving: 8)

Ingredients

- Spinach: 4 cups, chopped
- Fresh thyme: 1 tsp., chopped
- 2 minced garlic cloves
- 1 can of (~16 oz.) Artichoke hearts, drained
- Canned white beans: 1 cup
- Black pepper: 1 tsp.
- Parmesan cheese: 2 tbsp.
- Fresh parsley: 1 tbsp., chopped
- Low-fat sour cream: half cup

Instructions

1. In a bowl, add all ingredients and mix.
2. Pour in a glass baking dish and bake for half an hour at 350 F.

Nutrition for the half cup: Calories 78 | Fat 2 g | Sugar 1.5 g | Protein 5 g |Sodium 130 mg | Carbs 10 g

509. Pesto Yogurt Dip

(Prep time: 10 minutes | Cook time: 0 minutes | Serving: 8)

Ingredients

- Basil leaves: 2 cups
- Kosher salt: ¼ tsp.
- Low-fat Greek yogurt: 1 1/3 cups
- Parmigiano-Reggiano: half cup
- 1 garlic clove
- Low-fat buttermilk: half cup

Instructions

1. In a food processor, add all ingredients, pulse until smooth.
2. Add cheese in the end.
3. Serve.

Nutrition: Calories 68 | Fat 3 g | Sugar 3 g | Protein 7 g |Sodium 188 mg | Carbs 3 g

510. Tzatziki Sauce

(Prep time: 10 minutes | Cook time: 0 minutes | Serving: 8)

Ingredients

- 2 peeled cucumbers, seeded
- Lemon juice: 3 tbsp.
- Salt & pepper: ¼ tsp., each
- Plain yogurt: 3 cups, low-fat
- 1 minced garlic clove
- Fresh dill: 1 tbsp., chopped

Instructions

1. On a bowl, place a strainer lined with cheese cloth.
2. Add yogurt to the cheese cloth and keep it in the fridge for 2 hours.
3. Grate the cucumbers and toss with salt. Squeeze in paper towels to get all the moisture out. Add to the thick yogurt.
4. Add the rest of the ingredients, mix and serve.

Nutrition for 2 tbsp.: Calories 28 | Fat 0 g | Sugar 2 g | Protein 4 g |Sodium 21 mg | Carbs 3g

511.   French Onion Dip

(Prep time: 10 minutes | Cook time: 2 hours & 45 minutes | Serving: 9)

Ingredients

- Olive oil: 5 tsp.
- Yellow onion: 8 oz., sliced
- Peeled sweet potatoes: 1 pound, trimmed
- 2 minced garlic cloves
- Greek yogurt: 1 cup, low-fat
- Chopped shallots: half cup
- Kosher salt: ¼ tsp.
- Fresh chives: 1 tbsp., chopped
- Fresh thyme: 1 tsp., chopped
- Black pepper: half tsp.
- Worcestershire sauce: 1 ½ tsp., low-sodium
- Soft tofu: 10 oz., pat dried
- Lemon juice: 1 tbsp.

Instructions

1. Let the oven preheat to 200 F.
2. Slice the potatoes with a mandolin into 1/8" slices. Transfer to a bowl and toss with oil (2 tsp.).
3. On 2 parchment-lined baking sheets, layers the potatoes in 1 even layer.
4. Sprinkle salt and bake for 90 minutes.
5. Change the temperature to 400 F, and bake for ten minutes more.
6. Let them cool.
7. In a blender, add tofu, juice and yogurt. Pulse until smooth.
8. In a pan, add oil and sauté onion for 8-10 minutes. Turn the heat low and add shallots and the rest of the ingredients except for Worcestershire and garlic. Cook for 40 minutes.
9. Turn the heat to medium, add Worcestershire and garlic cook for 5 minutes.
10. Let it cool for 15 minutes. Add to the tofu mixture, mix and serve with potatoes.

Nutrition: Calories 144| Fat 7 g | Sugar 4 g | Protein 6 g |Sodium 300 mg | Carbs 16 g

512.   Sweet & Spicy Mustard Dip

(Prep time: 10 minutes | Cook time: 0 minutes | Serving: 4)

Ingredients

- Sour cream: half cup, low-fat
- Baby carrots: 2 cups
- Honey: 1 tbsp.
- Red pepper flakes: ¼ tsp.
- Cider vinegar: 1 tbsp.
- Cream cheese: 1/3 cup, low-fat
- Mustard powder: 2 tsp.
- Cherry tomatoes: 2 cups

Instructions

1. In a bowl, add sour and cream cheese.
2. Add flakes, honey, mustard and vinegar; mix well.
3. Serve with cherry tomatoes.

Nutrition: Calories 132 | Fat 1.5 g | Sugar 14 g | Protein 8 g | Sodium 233 mg | Carbs 23 g

513. Roasted Red Pepper Hummus

(Prep time: 10 minutes | Cook time: 0 minutes | Serving: 10)
Ingredients
- Roasted red bell pepper: 1 cup, sliced without seeds
- Olive oil: 1 tbsp.
- White sesame seeds: 2 tbsp.
- 2 cups of chickpeas
- Lemon juice: 1 tbsp.
- Cayenne pepper: ¼ tsp.
- Cumin: 1 ¼ tsp.
- Garlic powder: 1 tsp.
- Kosher salt: ¼ tsp.
- Onion powder: 1 tsp.

Instructions
1. Add all ingredients to a food processor, pulse until smooth.
2. Serve.

Nutrition for 3 tbsp.: Calories 53 | Fat 2 g | Sugar 1 g | Protein 2 g | Sodium 89 mg | Carbs 7 g

514. Peanut Dipping Sauce

(Prep time: 10 minutes | Cook time: 0 minutes | Serving: 6)
Ingredients
- Greek yogurt: ¼ cup, low-fat
- Apple cider vinegar: 1 tbsp.
- 1 minced garlic clove
- Peanut butter: ¼ cup, low-fat
- Red pepper flakes: ¼ tsp.

- Lime juice: 1 tbsp.
- Sesame oil: 1 tsp.
- Lite soy sauce: 1 tbsp.
- Grated ginger: 1 tsp.
- Sugar: 1 tsp.

Instructions
1. In a bowl, add all ingredients, mix and serve.

Nutrition: Calories 103 | Fat 12 g | Sugar 2 g | Protein 5 g | Sodium 24 mg | Carbs 8 g

515. Cannellini Bean Hummus

(Prep time: 15 minutes | Cook time: 0 minutes | Serving: 10)
Ingredients
- 1 can of (15 oz.) cannellini beans, rinsed
- Salt: ¼ tsp.
- Tahini: 1/4 cup
- 2 garlic cloves
- Fresh parsley: 2 tbsp., chopped
- Lemon juice: 3 tbsp.
- Ground cumin: 1 ½ tsp.
- Pita breads, for serving
- Red pepper flakes: ¼ tsp.
- Mixed fresh vegetables, for serving

Instructions
2. In a food processor, add garlic and pulse until minced.
3. Add the rest of the ingredients, pulse until smooth.
4. Serve with vegetables and pita bread.

Nutrition for 2 tbsp.: Calories 78 | Fat 4 g | Sugar 0 g | Protein 3 g | Sodium 114 mg | Carbs 8 g

516. Edamame Hummus

(Prep time: 15 minutes | Cook time: 0 minutes | Serving: 6)
Ingredients
- Tahini: 2 tbsp.
- 1 lemon's juice
- 1 minced garlic clove

- Water: half cup

- Cooked edamame: 1 1/1 cups, without shells

- Pepper & salt: ¼ tsp. Each

- Lemon zest: 1 tsp.

- Olive oil: 2 tsp.

Instructions
1. In a food processor, add all ingredients. Pulse until smooth.
2. Serve.

Nutrition: Calories 103 | Fat 1.5 g | Sugar 2 g | Protein 5 g |Sodium 94 mg | Carbs 8 g

517. Peach Honey Spread

(Prep time: 20 minutes | Cook time: 15 minutes| Serving: 4)
Ingredients
- Honey: 2 tbsp.

- 1 can of (15 oz.) Peach halves, unsweetened, drained

- Cinnamon: half tsp.

Instructions
1. In a bowl, add all ingredients, mash with a fork.
2. Serve chunky.

Nutrition: Calories 58 | Fat 0 g | Sugar 8 g | Protein 0.5 g |Sodium 55 mg | Carb 14 g

518. Whipped Red Beet Dip

(Prep time: 15 minutes | Cook time: 2 hours| Serving: 8)
Ingredients
- Yellow beets: 1 1/2 pounds, trimmed & washed

- Sesame seeds: 1 tbsp.

- Olive oil: 5 tbsp.

- Red beets: 12 oz., trimmed & washed

- White wine vinegar: 2 tbsp. + 2 tsp.

- 2 peeled mandarins, bite-size pieces

- Black pepper

- Fennel seeds: ¾ tsp.

- Toasted almonds: ¼ cup, chopped

- Cumin seeds: 1 tsp.

- Coriander seeds: 1 tsp.

- Low-fat feta: 8 oz., half sliced & half crumbled

Instructions
1. Let the oven preheat to 425 F.
2. Place red beets slices on a foil sheet, place the yellow on the other 2 foils sheets.
3. Drizzle with oil (1 tsp.), vinegar (1 tsp.), a pinch of salt and pepper.
4. Place three packets on a baking sheet, bake for 80 minutes.
5. Take it out from the oven and let it cool.
6. In a skillet, add the spices. Toast for 2-3 minutes.
7. Grind coarsely and mix with almonds.
8. Chop the peeled red beets, and pulse with feta and vinegar (2 tsp.) and oil (2 tbsp.) until smooth.
9. On serving plates, add the red beets puree, add the vinegar and oil on top.
10. Pinch of salt and pepper. Add yellow beets (slices), sliced feta and mandarins.
11. Add dressing, spices on top, serve.

Nutrition: Calories 135 | Fat 13.5 g | Sugar 3 g | Protein 6.4 g |Sodium 98 mg | Carbs 3 g

519. Baked Spinach Artichoke Yogurt Dip

(Prep time: 15 minutes | Cook time: 25 minutes| Serving: 8)
Ingredients
- Skim shredded Mozzarella cheese: 1 cup, low-fat

- Frozen spinach: 10 oz., thawed & drained

- Red pepper: 2 tbsp., chopped

- Low-fat Greek yogurt: 8 oz.

- 1 can of (14-oz.) Artichoke hearts, chopped

- Green onion: ¼ cup, chopped

- 1 minced garlic clove

Instructions

- Let the oven preheat to 350 F.

- In a bowl, add all ingredients except for red pepper, mix well.

- Transfer to a casserole dish (1 qt.). Bake for 20 to 25 minutes at 350 F. serve with red pepper on top.

Nutrition for 2 tbsp.: Calories 54 | Fat 4 g | Sugar 2 g | Protein 4 g |Sodium 7 mg | Carbs

520. Asparagus with Horseradish Dip

(Prep time: 15 minutes | Cook time: 5 minutes | Serving: 8)
Ingredients
- Parmesan cheese: ¼ cup, low-fat

- Fresh asparagus: 2 pounds, trimmed

- Worcestershire sauce: half tsp.

- Mayonnaise: 1 cup, low-fat

- Horseradish: 1 tbsp.

Instructions
- Steam the asparagus for 2 to 4 minutes.

- In a bowl, add the rest of the ingredients, serve with asparagus.

Nutrition: Calories 63 | Fat 5 g | Sugar 8 g | Protein 1 g |Sodium 146 mg | Carbs 3 g

521. Cajun Hot Crab Dip

(Prep time: 15 minutes | Cook time: 40 minutes | Serving: 12)
Ingredients
- Minced garlic: 1 tsp.

- ¼ cup of water

- Chopped shallots: 2 tbsp.

- Low-fat cream cheese: 1/3 cup

- Tabasco: 1 tbsp.

- Cajun seasoning: 2 tsp., no-salt-added

- Lump crabmeat: 1 pound

- Canola mayonnaise: half cup

- Salt & black pepper: ¼ tsp.

- Fresh chives: 3 tbsp., chopped

- Red bell pepper: ¼ cup, chopped

- Lemon juice: 2 tbsp.

- Panko: 3 tbsp.

Instructions
1. Let the oven preheat to 450 F.

2. In a pan, add garlic, shallots, oil spray the vegetables, sauté for 2 minutes.

3. In a food processor, add crab (1 cup), Cajun, water, tabasco. Pulse until smooth.

4. Take it out in a bowl add the crab and the rest of the ingredients (except for panko).

5. Add to a baking dish (1 qt.) and oil spray the top. Spread panko on top.

6. Bake for half an hour at 450 F.

Nutrition: Calories 95 | Fat 5.3 g | Sugar 0 g| Protein 8.4 g |Sodium 253 mg | Carbs 2 g

522. Baba Ghanoush

(Prep time: 15 minutes | Cook time: 23 minutes | Serving: 12)
Ingredients
- Olive oil: 2-3 tbsp.

- Lemon juice: half cup

- 1/3 cup of tahini

- Black pepper

- Eggplants: ~ 3 pounds

- 2 minced garlic cloves

Instructions
1. Let the oven preheat to 450 F.

2. With olive oil, rub the eggplants on the outside.

3. Roast on a baking tray for 15-20 minutes. Let them cool.

4. Peel chop the eggplant and transfer it to a food

processor.

5. Add the rest of the ingredients, add enough water to get your desired consistency.

6. Sprinkle with a pinch of salt. Serve.

Nutrition: Calories 58| Fat 1 g | Sugar 8 g | Protein 0.4 g |Sodium 3 mg | Carbs 14 g

523. Black Bean Hummus

(Prep time: 15 minutes | Cook time: 0 minutes| Serving: 8)
Ingredients
- Tahini: 2 tbsp.
- Fresh cilantro: half cup, chopped
- Lime juice: 2 tbsp.
- Olive oil: 1 tbsp.
- Water: 2 tbsp.
- 1 garlic clove
- Ground cumin: ¾ tsp.
- Salt: ¼ tsp.
- 3 pitas
- Canned black beans: 15 oz., rinsed
- Half jalapeño pepper, without seeds

Instructions
1. In a food processor, add all ingredients except for pitas. Pulse until smooth.
2. Serve with baked pita wedges.

Nutrition: Calories 127 | Fat 4 g | Sugar 1 g | Protein 5.1 g |Sodium 128 mg | Carbs 18.5 g

524. Tangy Asian Salad Dressing

(Prep time: 15 minutes | Cook time: 0 minutes| Serving: 4)
Ingredients
- Vinegar: 2 tbsp.
- Lemon juice: 2 tsp.
- Soy sauce: 1 tbsp., low-sodium

- Honey: 2 tsp.
- Oil: 4 tbsp.
- Grated gingerroot: 1 tsp.

Instructions
1. In a bowl, add all ingredients and whisk until combined.
2. Serve chilled.

Nutrition: Calories 135 | Fat 13.5 g | Sugar 3 g | Protein 6.4 g |Sodium 98 mg | Carbs 3 g

525. Citrus Drizzle Salad Dressing

(Prep time: 15 minutes | Cook time: 0 minutes| Serving: 4)
Ingredients
- Olive oil: 8 tbsp.
- Lime juice: 4 tbsp.

Instructions
1. In a bowl, add all ingredients and whisk until combined.
2. Serve chilled.

Nutrition: Calories 16 | Fat 18 g | Sugar 0 g | Protein 0 g |Sodium 1 mg | Carbs 1 g

526. House Ranch Dressing

(Prep time: 15 minutes | Cook time: 0 minutes| Serving: 2)
Ingredients
- Garlic powder: half tbsp.
- Lemon juice: 2 tbsp.
- Dill weed: 1 tbsp., dried
- Greek yogurt: 2 cups, non-fat
- Mayonnaise: half cup, low-fat
- Kosher salt: ¼ tsp.
- Onion powder: half tbsp.
- Black pepper: ¼ tsp.

Instructions
1. In a bowl, add all ingredients and whisk until combined.

Nutrition: Calories 30 | Fat 1 g | Sugar 1 g | Protein 2 g |Sodium 78 mg | Carbs 2 g

527. Spicy Peanut Salad Dressing

(Prep time: 15 minutes | Cook time: 0 minutes| Serving: 2)
Ingredients

- Cayenne pepper: ¼ tsp.
- Water: 2 tbsp.
- Cumin: half tsp.
- 2 minced garlic cloves
- Peanut butter: 2 tbsp. No-sugar & low fat
- Soy sauce: 1 tbsp., low-sodium

Instructions

2. In a bowl, add all ingredients and whisk until combined.

Nutrition: Calories 103 | Fat 1.5 g | Sugar 2 g | Protein 5 g |Sodium 294 mg | Carbs 8 g

528. Citrus Remoulade

(Prep time: 15 minutes | Cook time: 0 minutes| Serving: 16)
Ingredients

- Salt, a pinch
- Lite mayonnaise: 1 cup
- Orange zest: 1 tsp.
- Orange juice: 1 tbsp.

Instructions

3. In a bowl, add all ingredients and whisk until combined.

Nutrition: Calories 45 | Fat 4 g | Sugar 2 g | Protein 0 g |Sodium 95 mg | Carbs 2 g

529. Layered Hummus Dip

(Prep time: 15 minutes | Cook time: 0 minutes| Serving: 15)
Ingredients

- Red onion: ¼ cup, chopped
- 1 cucumber, chopped
- Greek olives: half cup, chopped
- Hummus: 10 oz.

- 2 tomatoes, chopped without seeds
- Crumbled feta cheese: 1 cup

Instructions

1. In a round dish (10"), add hummus at the bottom and spread.
2. Add the rest of the ingredients on top in layers.
3. Serve with baked pita chips.

Nutrition: Calories 88 | Fat 5 g | Sugar 0 g | Protein 4 g |Sodium 275 mg | Carbs 6 g

530. Vinegar & Oil Salad Dressing

(Prep time: 10 minutes | Cook time: 0 minutes| Serving: 6)
Ingredients

- Vinegar: 4 tbsp.
- Canola oil: 8 tbsp.

Instructions

1. In a bowl, add all ingredients and whisk until combined.

Nutrition: Calories 167 | Fat 18.5 g | Sugar 0 g | Protein 0 g |Sodium 0 mg | Carbs 0 g

531. Zesty Green Goddess Dip

(Prep time: 15 minutes | Cook time: 0 minutes| Serving: 6)
Ingredients

- Fresh basil: half cup
- Green onions: ¼ cup, chopped
- Canola mayonnaise: 1/3 cup
- Watercress: 2 cups, trimmed
- Fresh flat-leaf parsley: ¼ cup
- Anchovy paste: 1 tsp.
- Black pepper: half tsp.
- White wine vinegar: 1 tbsp.
- Greek yogurt: ¼ cup, fat-free
- Olive oil: 2 tbsp.
- Salt & red pepper: ¼ tsp.

Instructions

1. In a food processor, add all ingredients, pulse until combined.
2. Serve chilled.

Nutrition: Calories 92| Fat 8.7 g | Sugar 0 g | Protein 1.5 g |Sodium 223 mg | Carbs 1.2 g

532. Roasted Red Pepper Bagna Cauda

(Prep time: 15 minutes | Cook time: 2 hours| Serving: 12)
Ingredients

- 1 garlic head, whole
- 6 red bell peppers
- Canned anchovy: 8 small fillets, drained
- Kosher salt: ¼ tsp.
- Crushed red pepper: half tsp.
- Lemon juice: 2 tbsp.
- Fresh parsley: 1 ½ tbsp.
- Black pepper: ¼ tsp.
- Olive oil: ¼ cup

Instructions

1. Let the oven preheat to 350 F
2. Roast the garlic head (unpeeled & unseparated) wrapped in foil for 60 minutes, cool for 10 minutes.
3. Squeeze the cloves out; only use 1 tbsp. of garlic.
4. Let the broiler preheat.
5. Slice the bell peppers in half and take the middle part out.
6. Broil, round side up for 15 minutes, transfer to a ziplock bag and rest for 20 minutes. Then peel the skin off.
7. In a food processor, add peppers, garlic and the rest of the ingredients. Pulse until smooth serve.

Nutrition: Calories 66 | Fat 5.3 g | Sugar 0 g | Protein 1.4 g |Sodium 140 mg | Carbs 4.2 g

533. Red Wine Vinaigrette Salad Dressing

(Prep time: 15 minutes | Cook time: 0 minutes| Serving: 6)
Ingredients

- Olive oil: half cup
- Black pepper, to taste
- Dijon mustard: 1 tbsp.
- Red wine vinegar: 1/3 cup
- Salt, a pinch

Instructions

1. In a bowl, add all ingredients and whisk until combined.

Nutrition: Calories 163 | Fat 2.5 g | Sugar 0 g | Protein 0 g |Sodium 100 mg | Carbs 1g

534. Cilantro Lime Dressing

(Prep time: 15 minutes | Cook time: 0 minutes| Serving: 16)
Ingredients

- Cottage cheese: 2 cups, low-fat
- Cilantro: half cup, chopped
- 1 clove garlic
- 1/4 cup of olive oil
- Black pepper: ¼ tsp.
- Salt: 1/8 tsp.
- 2 limes' juice
- Sugar: half tsp.

Instructions

In a bowl, add all ingredients and whisk until combined.

Nutrition: Calories 54 | Fat 4 g | Sugar 0 g | Protein 4 g |Sodium 100 mg | Carbs 2g

535. Italian Salad Dressing

(Prep time: 15 minutes | Cook time: 0 minutes| Serving: 8)
Ingredients

- Red wine vinegar: 2 tbsp.
- 1 minced garlic clove
- Lemon juice: 1 tbsp.

- Red pepper flakes: 1/8 tsp.
- Olive oil: 3 tbsp.
- Dijon mustard: 2 tsp.
- Dried oregano: 1/8 tsp.
- Dried parsley: 1 tsp.
- Dried basil: 1 tsp., crumbled

Instructions

2. In a bowl, add all ingredients and whisk until combined.

Nutrition: Calories 50 | Fat 5 g | Sugar 0 g | Protein 0 g | Sodium 30 mg | Carbs 0 g

536. Tomato-Raisin Relish

(Prep time: 15 minutes | Cook time: 10 minutes | Serving: 8)
Ingredients

- 1/4 cup of golden raisins
- Diced onion: 1 cup
- Hot water: half cup
- 1/4 cup of raisins
- Olive oil: 1 tbsp.
- Minced garlic: 1 tbsp.
- Lemon zest: 2 tsp.
- Capers: 1 tbsp., drained
- Lemon juice: 3 tbsp.
- Chopped tomatoes: 1 cup, without seeds
- Kalamata olives: ¼ cup, chopped
- Pine nuts: ¼ cup, toasted
- Salt: ¼ tsp.
- Fresh flat-leaf parsley: ¼ cup, chopped
- Black pepper: ¼ tsp.

Instructions

1. In half cup of water, soak the raisins for ten minutes.
2. sauté onion in hot oil for 3 minutes, add garlic and cook for 1 minute.

3. Add the juice, tomatoes and zest cook for 4 minutes.
4. Turn the heat off, add the rest of the ingredients. Mix and Serve.

Nutrition: Calories 64 | Fat 6 g | Sugar 8 g | Protein 0.5 g | Sodium 3 mg | Carbs 2g

537. Greek Seven-Layer Dip

(Prep time: 25 minutes | Cook time: 5 minutes | Serving: 8)
Ingredients

- Chopped mint: 1 tbsp.
- Pepper: 1/8 tsp.
- 6 whole-wheat pita pockets, 2 layers separated, cut into wedges
- Baby spinach: 1 cup, sliced
- Half tomato, chopped
- Water: 2 tbsp.
- Lemon juice: 1 tbsp.
- Dried oregano: 1/8 tsp.
- Canned chickpeas: 1 cup, rinsed
- 1/4 peeled cucumber, chopped
- Crumbled feta: 2 tbsp., fat-free

Instructions

1. Let the oven preheat to 400 F.
2. Bake the wedges for 5 minutes after oil spraying and arranging them in 1 layer.
3. In a food processor, add the chickpeas and pulse until chopped.
4. As the machine is still pulsing, add lemon juice, pepper and water, until smooth.
5. On the serving plate, add spinach, layer chickpea mixture.
6. Then oregano, tomato, cucumber and mint. Add cheese in the last.
7. Serve with baked wedges.

Nutrition: Calories 69 | Fat 0.5 g | Sugar 2 g | Protein 4 g |Sodium 100 mg | Carbs 13 g

538. Basil Butter & Sun-Dried Tomato

(Prep time: 10 minutes | Cook time: 15 minutes| Serving: 4)

Ingredients

- Flour: 1 tbsp.
- Tomato (sun-dried) paste: 1 tbsp.
- Chicken broth: 1 cup
- Unsalted plant butter: 1 tbsp.
- Dried basil: 1 tsp.

Instructions

1. In a pan, melt butter on a low flame.
2. Add flour and whisk for 2 minutes; keep mixing.
3. Add broth on medium flame, keep mixing for 5 minutes.
4. Add tomato paste and basil.
5. Simmer on low flame for 2 minutes. Serve.

Nutrition: Calories 43 | Fat 3 g | Sugar 0 g | Protein 1 g |Sodium 111 mg | Carbs 3 g

539. DASH Diet Vinaigrette

(Prep time: 10 minutes| Cook time: 10 minutes | Serving: 16)

Ingredients

1 minced garlic cloves

Dijon mustard: 1 tbsp.

Olive oil: 5 tbsp.

Orange juice: 6 tbsp.

White-wine vinegar: 1/4 cup

Salt: 1/8 tsp.

Instructions

Add all ingredients in a bowl, with only 4 tbsp. of orange juice.

Whisk and adjust the taste by adding more juice. Serve with salad.

Nutrition for 1 tbsp.: Calories 38| Fat 3 g | Sugar 0.4 g | Protein 0.1 g |Sodium 48 mg | Carbs 0.8 g

540. Skinny Quinoa Veggie Dip

(Prep time: 20 minutes | Cook time: 15 minutes| Serving: 32)

Ingredients

- Ground cumin: 1 ½ tsp.
- Paprika: 1 ½ tsp.
- Chopped cucumber: 3/4 cup
- 2 cans of (15 oz.) Black beans, rinsed
- Water: 1-2/3 cups
- Lime juice: 5 tbsp.
- Low-fat sour cream: ¾ cup + 2 tbsp.
- Pepper to taste
- Cayenne pepper: half tsp.
- Chopped zucchini: 3/4 cup
- 2 avocados, chopped
- Fresh cilantro: ¼ cup, chopped
- 2/3 cup of quinoa
- 3 tomatoes, chopped
- Chopped red onion: ¼ cup

Instructions

1. In a food processor, add beans and spices with water (1/3 cup) pulse until smooth.
2. Cook quinoa in water (1 1/3 cups) and drizzle with lime juice (2 tbsp.)
3. In a bowl, add avocados, cilantro, lime juice and sour cream (2 tbsp.); mash well.
4. In a baking dish (2 ½ qt.), add bean mixture and spread, then add quinoa, sour cream mixture, then the rest of the sour cream, add the rest of

the vegetables on top.

5. Serve right away.

Nutrition for ¼ cup: Calories 65 | Fat 3 g | Sugar 1 g | Protein 2 g |Sodium 54 mg | Carbs 8 g

541. Grilled Mango Chutney

(Prep time: 20 minutes | Cook time: 7 minutes| Serving: 6)
Ingredients

-   1/4 cup of sugar

-   Ground ginger: half tsp.

-   Cider vinegar: 2 tbsp.

-   1 peeled mango

-   Green bell pepper: 2 tbsp., chopped

-   Fresh rosemary: ¼ tsp., chopped

-   Grated ginger: 1 tbsp.

-   Ground cloves: 1/8 tsp.

-   1/4 cup of chopped onion

Instructions

1. Broil the mango 4-6" away from heat for 2-3 minutes on 1 side.

2. Cool for few minutes, and chop.

3. Transfer to a bowl, add the rest of the ingredients. Toss to combined.

4. Serve chilled.

Nutrition: Calories 58| Fat 17.2 g | Sugar 2 g | Protein 0 g |Sodium 1 mg | Carbs 15 g

542. Blue Cheese Dressing

(Prep time: 15 minutes | Cook time: 0 minutes| Serving: 4)
Ingredients

-   Minced garlic: 1 tbsp.

-   Cayenne pepper: half tsp.

-   Mayonnaise: 1 cup, non-fat

-   Buttermilk: half cup, low-fat

-   Blue cheese crumbles: half cup

-   Horseradish: 1 tbsp.

-   Worcestershire sauce: 1 tsp.

Instructions

1. In a food processor, add all ingredients pulse until smooth.

2. Serve chilled.

Nutrition for 2 tbsp.: Calories 32 | Fat 2 g | Sugar 1.4 g | Protein 1 g |Sodium 172 mg | Carbs 2.5 g

Chapter 11: DASH Diet Savory Treats & Desserts Recipes

543. Strawberry Frozen Yogurt Squares

(Prep time: 8 hours & 15 minutes | Cook time: 0 minutes | Serving: 9)

Ingredients

- Sweetened condensed milk: 1 cup, non-fat
- Strawberry yogurt: 3 cups, fat-free
- Crunchy barley & wheat cereal: 1 cup
- Unsweetened frozen strawberries: ~ 2 ½ cups

Instructions

1. Spread the cereal on a foil-lined baking tray (8 by 8").
2. In a blender, add the rest of the ingredients and pulse until smooth.
3. On top of the cereal, pour the mixture and cover with foil.
4. Keep in the freeze for 8 hours until solid.
5. Thaw for 5 to 10 minutes, slice, and serve.

Nutrition: Calories 215 | Fat 12 g | Sugar 8.2 g | Protein 4.4 g | Sodium 78 mg | Carbs 12 g

544. Chocolate Banana Cake

(Prep time: 15 minutes | Cook time: 25 minutes | Serving: 18)

Ingredients

- Splenda brown sugar: half cup
- Baking soda: half tsp.
- All-purpose flour: 2 cups
- Mashed banana: half cup
- Vanilla extract: 1 tsp.
- Soy milk: 3/4 cup
- 1 egg white
- Cocoa powder: 1/4 cup, unsweetened
- Canola oil: ¼ cup
- 1 egg
- Dark semisweet chocolate chips: half cup
- Lemon juice: 1 tbsp.

Instructions

1. Let the oven preheat to 350 F. Oil spray an 11 by 7" pan.
2. In a bowl, mix baking soda, flour and brown sugar.
3. In a different bowl, add the wet ingredients and mix.
4. Add the wet to dry ingredients. Add chocolate chips and mix.
5. Pour the batter into the prepared pan. Bake for 25 minutes.
6. Slice and serve.

Nutrition: Calories 150 | Fat 4 g | Sugar 9 g | Protein 3 g | Sodium 52 mg | Carbs 27 g

545. Strawberries with Peppered Balsamic Drizzle

(Prep time: 1 hour & 5 minutes | Cook time: 0 minutes | Serving: 4)

Ingredients

- Balsamic vinegar: 1 tbsp.
- Low-fat vanilla yogurt: 4 oz.
- Brown sugar: 1 tbsp.
- Fresh strawberries: 2 cups, halved
- Black pepper, a pinch

Instructions

1. In a bowl, add all ingredients except for yogurt, toss and let it rest for 60 minutes at room temperature.

2. Serve with yogurt on top.

Nutrition: Calories 65 | Fat 0 g | Sugar 8 g | Protein 3 g | Sodium 15 mg | Carbs 0 g

546.   Whole Wheat Muffins

(Prep time: 20 minutes | Cook time: 30 minutes | Serving: 12)

Ingredients

- 2 cups of whole wheat flour
- Canola oil: 3 tbsp.
- Sugar: half cup
- White vinegar: 1 tbsp.
- 2 egg whites
- Baking powder: 3 ½ tsp.
- 1 1/3 cups of 1% milk

Instructions

1. Let the oven preheat to 350 F. Oil spray a muffin tin.

2. In two bowls, add the wet and dry ingredients.

3. Pour wet to dry ingredients. Do not overmix.

4. Pour the batter into the muffin cups, bake for 25 to 30 minutes at 350 F.

Nutrition: Calories 276 | Fat 12 g | Sugar 9.2 g | Protein 7.3 g | Sodium 92 mg | Carbs 11 g

547.   Cheesecake Sandwiches

(Prep time: 20 minutes | Cook time: 50 minutes | Serving: 4)

Ingredients

- Sugar: 1 tbsp. + 1 ½ tsp.
- Raspberries: half cup
- Lemon rind: half tsp., grated
- 8 chocolate wafers
- Low-fat cream cheese: 2 oz., softened

- 1 teaspoon lemon juice: 1 tsp.

Instructions

1. In a bowl, whisk cream cheese, lemon rind and sugar (1 tbsp.).

2. Add the rest of the ingredients and mash.

3. Spread the mixture onto half of the chocolate wafers, top with the other half and serve.

Nutrition: Calories 114 | Fat 4.9 g | Sugar 10 g | Protein 2 g | Sodium 139 mg | Carbs 16 g

548.   Vanilla Chia Seed Pudding

(Prep time: 1 hour & 5 minutes | Cook time: 0 minutes | Serving: 10)

Ingredients

- Chia seeds: half cup
- Low-fat vanilla yogurt: 1 cup
- Vanilla extract: half tsp.
- 2 % milk: 2 cups
- Maple syrup: 1 ½ tbsp.

Instructions

1. In a bowl, add all ingredients and whisk well.

2. Keep in the fridge covered for 3-4 hours before serving whisk once.

3. Serve.

Nutrition: Calories 92 | Fat 4 g | Sugar 8 g | Protein 5 g | Sodium 49 mg | Carbs 10 g

549.   Zucchini Walnut Muffins

(Prep time: 25 minutes | Cook time: 25 minutes | Serving: 12)

Ingredients

- All-purpose flour: 1 cup
- Baking soda: half tsp.
- Cinnamon: half tsp.
- Ground nutmeg: ¼ tsp.
- Whole wheat pastry flour: 1 cup
- 1 cup of sugar
- Shredded zucchini: 1 cup

- Baking powder: 1 ½ tsp.
- Salt: ¼ tsp.
- 1 egg
- Low-fat milk: ¾ cup
- Canola oil: 2 tbsp.
- Melted plant butter: 2 tbsp.

Instructions

1. Let the oven preheat to 400 F. oil spray a muffin tin.
2. In different bowls, add wet and dry ingredients except for zucchini. Mix and add the wet to dry ingredients.
3. Add zucchini in the batter and fold.
4. Pour in the muffin cups and bake for 20 to 30 minutes.
5. Cool for 5 minutes and serve.

Nutrition: Calories 217 | Fat 12 g | Sugar 12 g | Protein 6 g |Sodium 78 mg | Carbs 18.1 g

550. Morning Muffins

(Prep time: 5 minutes | Cook time: 25 minutes | Serving: 12)
Ingredients

- Milk: 1 cup, low-fat
- Grated carrots: half cup
- 1/3 cup of sugar
- 1 egg
- Vegetable oil: 2 tbsp.
- Raisins: half cup
- Baking powder: 1 tsp.
- Vanilla: 1 tsp.
- 1 1/2 cups of flour
- Cinnamon: 1 tsp.
- Baking soda: half tsp.
- Old-fashioned oatmeal: 1 cup

Instructions

1. Let the oven preheat to 400 F. oil spray a muffin tin.
2. In different bowls, add wet and dry ingredients. Mix and add the wet to dry ingredients. Mix until just combined.
3. Pour in the muffin tin and bake for 15 minutes.
4. Serve.

Nutrition: Calories 240 | Fat 12 g | Sugar 10 g | Protein 6.4 g |Sodium 98 mg | Carbs 14.8 g

551. Pumpkin Bread

(Prep time: 15 minutes | Cook time: 60 minutes | Serving: 8)
Ingredients

- Milk: ¾ cup, low-fat
- Whole wheat pastry flour: 2 cups
- 1 cup of sugar
- Cinnamon: 1 tsp.
- Pumpkin puree: 1 cup
- Ground cloves: ¼ tsp.
- 2 eggs
- Baking soda: 1 tsp.
- Ground allspice: 1 tsp.
- Baking powder: half tsp.
- Ground nutmeg: ¼ tsp.

Instructions

1. Let the oven preheat to 350 F.
2. Oil spray a loaf pan and sprinkle some flour.
3. In a bowl, add all ingredients, mix and pour in the pan and bake for 50-55 minutes.
4. Cool in the pan and serve.

Nutrition: Calories 166 | Fat 8.2 g | Sugar 12 g | Protein 4 g |Sodium 67 mg | Carbs 18.7 g

552. Lemon Blueberry Oatmeal Muffins

(Prep time: 15 minutes | Cook time: 25 minutes | Serving: 6)
Ingredients

- Packed brown sugar: 2 tbsp.

- Baking powder: 1 tbsp.

- All-purpose flour: 1 cup

- 2 egg whites, whisked

- Quick oats: 1 ¾ cups

- Lemon peel: 1 tsp.

- Splenda sugar: half cup

- Vegetable oil: 2 tbsp.

- Vanilla: 1 tsp.

- Non-fat milk: 1 cup

- Blueberries: 1 cup

Instructions

1. Let the oven preheat to 400 F. oil spray a muffin tin.

2. In a bowl, mix brown sugar and oats (1/4 cup). Set it aside.

3. In a bowl, add dry ingredients with the rest of the oats.

4. In a bowl, add the wet ingredients with lemon peel. Mix.

5. Add the dry to wet ingredients, mix until just combined.

6. Fold in berries and pour in the muffin cups. Add oats and brown sugar mixture on top.

7. Bake for 20-24 minutes. Cool and serve.

Nutrition: Calories 265 | Fat 10 g | Sugar 8 g | Protein 6.1 g |Sodium 87 mg | Carbs 17 g

553. Mango Banana Soft Serve

(Prep time: 10 minutes | Cook time: 0 minutes | Serving: 6)
Ingredients

- Mango chunks: 16 oz., frozen

- Canned coconut light milk: 1 ½ tbsp.

- Sugar: 1-2 tbsp. (for sweeter version otherwise, skip)

- 1 ripe frozen

- Banana

- Lime juice: 1 ½ tbsp.

Instructions

1. In a bowl, mix the sugar and mango, mix and let it rest for 5 minutes.

2. In a blender, add all the ingredients, pulse until smooth and thick.

3. Pour into the bowls and serve.

Nutrition: Calories 85 | Fat 1 g | Sugar 3 g | Protein 1 g |Sodium 3 mg | Carbs 21 g

554. Chickpea Brownies

(Prep time: 10 minutes | Cook time: 20 minutes | Serving: 6)
Ingredients

- Nut butter: half cup

- 1 can of (15 oz.) Chickpeas, rinsed

- Cocoa powder: ¼ cup

- Olive oil: 1 tbsp.

- 1 tsp. Of vanilla

- Chocolate chips: half cup

- Baking powder: ¼ tsp.

- Maple syrup: half cup

- Almond flour: ¼ cup

- Baking soda: ¼ tsp.

Instructions

1. Let the oven preheat to 350 F.

2. Blend the olive oil, chickpeas, nut butter, vanilla and maple syrup in a food processor.

3. Add baking powder, almond flour, baking soda and cocoa powder, pulse until smooth.

4. Take it out in a bowl and add chips, mix.

5. Oil spray an 8 by 8 baking pan and pour the mixture in. bake for 21 to 23 minutes.

6. Slice and serve.

Nutrition: Calories 147 | Fat 7.9 g | Sugar 8.5 g | Protein 4.4 g |Sodium 165.2 mg | Carbs 17 g

Classic Honey Flan

(Prep time: 10 minutes | Cook time: 45 minutes | Serving: 4)

Ingredients

- Egg substitute: half cup
- Lemon zest: half tsp.
- Non-fat milk: half cup
- 1 egg
- Cinnamon: half tsp.
- Honey: 3 tbsp. + ¼ cup
- Vanilla: 1 tsp.

Instructions

1. Let the oven preheat to 325 F. Oil spray 4 custard cups.
2. In a bowl, add cinnamon and honey (2 tbsp.)
3. In a bowl, add all the other ingredients, mix well.
4. On a baking dish, place the custard cups and add some of the honey-cinnamon mixtures in each cup.
5. Add the mixture on top. Place boiling water in the baking dish, only 1" of depth.
6. Bake for 45 minutes.
7. Serve cold or warm by flipping onto serving plates.

Nutrition: Calories 199 | Fat 2 g | Sugar 8 g | Protein 8 g |Sodium 114 mg | Carbs 40 g

555. Pineapple Upside-Down Cake

(Prep time: 10 minutes | Cook time: 45 minutes | Serving: 8)

Ingredients

- Brown sugar blend: ¼ cup, low-calorie
- All-purpose flour: 1 cup
- 1 can of (20 oz.) Pineapple slices with juice (low-sugar)
- Baking powder: 1 tsp.
- No-calorie granulated sweetener: 3/4 cup

- 1 ripe banana, chopped
- Water: 1 tbsp.
- 2 eggs
- 1% buttermilk: half cup
- Baking soda: half tsp.
- 1/2 teaspoon cinnamon: half tsp.
- Canola oil: 1 tbsp.
- Vanilla extract: 1 tsp.

Instructions

1. Let the oven preheat to 350 F
2. In a pot, add canned pineapple liquid, low-calorie (1/4 cup) and sugars, mix and let it come to a boil.
3. Boil until it is reduced by 1/4th, turn the heat off.
4. Oil spray a cake pan (9") and pour the sugar mixture.
5. Add pineapple slices on top of the liquid, which will easily fit.
6. In a bowl, add the dry ingredients with no-calorie sweetener.
7. In a bowl, add banana and mash with a fork. Add the wet ingredients.
8. Add the wet to dry ingredients until mixed.
9. Add the rest of the pineapple slices and mix in the batter.
10. Pour over the pineapple slices, bake for 50 minutes. Cool for ten minutes, slice and serve.

Nutrition: Calories 188 | Fat 3.3 g | Sugar 17 g | Protein 6.4 g |Sodium 187 mg | Carbs 35 g

556. Whole-Wheat Cranberry Muffins

(Prep time: 10 minutes | Cook time: 15 minutes | Serving: 12)

Ingredients

- Toasted wheat germ: ¼ cup

- All-purpose flour: half cup
- Pineapple juice: ¾ cup
- Light brown sugar: half cup, packed
- Whole-wheat flour: half cup
- Baking soda: ¼ tsp.
- Dried cranberries: half cup, unsweetened
- Quick-cooking oatmeal: ¾ cup
- Baking powder: 2 tsp.
- 1 egg
- Corn oil: 1 tbsp.
- Sunflower seeds: 2 tbsp.

Instructions

1. Let the oven preheat to 400 F. Oil spray a muffin tin (12 cups).
2. In a bowl, add the dry ingredients and mix.
3. Add the wet ingredients and mix until just combined. Do not over-mix, and it should be lumpy.
4. Pour the batter into the muffin cups. Add sunflower seeds on top.
5. Bake for 11-12 minutes. Cool and serve.

Nutrition: Calories 143 | Fat 2.5 g | Sugar 15 g | Protein 3 g |Sodium 108 mg | Carbs 28 g

557. Apple Oat Bran Muffins

(Prep time: 10 minutes | Cook time: 20 minutes | Serving: 12)
Ingredients
- ¾ cups of whole wheat flour
- Baking powder: 1 tsp.
- ¾ cups of all-purpose flour
- Baking soda: half tsp.
- Vegetable oil: 2 tbsp.
- Oat bran: half cup

- Cinnamon: 1 ½ tsp.
- Brown sugar: ¼ cup, packed
- 1 egg
- Salt: ¼ tsp.
- Buttermilk: 1 cup
- Golden peeled apples: 1 ½ cups, chopped

Instructions

1. Let the oven preheat to 400 F. oil spray a muffin tin.
2. In two different bowls, add wet and dry ingredients. Mix and add wet to dry ingredients. Mix and fold apples in.
3. Pour in the prepared pan and bake for 18-20 minutes.
4. Serve.

Nutrition: Calories 275 | Fat 9 g | Sugar 10.2 g | Protein 7 g |Sodium 98.3 mg | Carbs 21g

558. Strawberry-Chocolate Yogurt Bark

(Prep time: 4 hours & 10 minutes | Cook time: 0 minutes | Serving: 32)
Ingredients
- Vanilla extract: 1 tsp.
- Low-fat Greek yogurt: 3 cups
- Mini chocolate chips: ¼ cup
- Honey: ¼ cup
- Sliced strawberries: 1 ½ cups

Instructions

1. In a bowl, mix yogurt, vanilla and honey. Spread on a parchment-lined baking sheet (10 x15").
2. Add strawberries and chocolate chips on top.
3. Keep in the freezer until firm. Break and serve.

Nutrition: Calories 34 | Fat 1.3 g | Sugar 3.5 g | Protein 2 g |Sodium 7.6 mg | Carbs 4 g

559. Red Wine Poached Pears

(Prep time: 10 minutes | Cook time: 45 minutes | Serving: 4)

Ingredients

- Low fat cream: 1/3 cup
- Red wine: 25 oz.
- Softened goat cheese: 2 oz.
- 1 cinnamon stick
- Honey: 1 tbsp. + 1/3 cup
- 4 bosc pears

Instructions

1. Peel the pears in a manner to leave the stem intact.
2. In a pan, add all ingredients except for pears, cheese and cream. Add honey (1/3 cup)
3. Let it simmer on low, add pears. Simmer for 20 minutes, partially covered.
4. Take the pears out on a plate. Cook the wine mixture for 15-18 minutes, until ¼ is remaining.
5. In a bowl, whisk cheese, honey, with cream till soft peaks appear.
6. Serve poached pears with wine sauce and a dollop of cheese mixture.

Nutrition per pear: Calories 103 | Fat 1 g | Sugar 8 g | Protein 1 g |Sodium 7 mg | Carbs 24 g

560. Peanut Butter & Chocolate Dipped Pretzels

(Prep time: 15 minutes | Cook time: 7 minutes | Serving: 10)

Ingredients

- Whole-wheat honey pretzel: 30
- Semisweet chocolate: 4 oz., chopped
- Peanut butter: ¼ cup

Instructions

1. Melt the chocolate chips on a double broiler.
2. Dip half the pretzels in chocolate and half in peanut butter.
3. Place on a parchment-lined baking tray.
4. Serve when it sets.

Nutrition: Calories 276 | Fat 17.2 g | Sugar 21 g | Protein 6 g |Sodium 165 mg | Carbs 45 g

561. Tropical Fruit Pops

(Prep time: 15 minutes | Cook time: 0 minutes | Serving: 12)

Ingredients

1 banana, sliced

Chopped mango: 2 cups

Ground ginger: ¼ tsp.

1 can of 8 oz. Crushed pineapple

Orange juice concentrate: ¼ cup

Instructions

In a food processor, add all ingredients, pulse until smooth.

Pour in the pop molds. Add sticks and freeze for 3-4 hours. Serve.

Nutrition: Calories 275| Fat 3 g | Sugar 20 g | Protein 6 g |Sodium 89 mg | Carbs 43 g

562. Buckwheat, Blueberry & Butternut Muffins

(Prep time: 15 minutes | Cook time: 20 minutes | Serving: 10)

Ingredients

3/4 cup of buckwheat flour

Sugar: ¼ cup

1 1/3 cups of all-purpose flour

Cinnamon: 1 tsp.

Baking powder: 1 ½ tsp.

Cooking oil: 2 tbsp.

2 eggs, whisked

Baking soda: half tsp.

Salt: ¼ tsp.

Blueberries: ¾ cup

Orange zest: half tsp.

Cooked butternut squash: 1 cup, mashed

Non-fat milk: half cup

Orange juice: ¼ cup

Instructions

Oil spray a muffin tin (12 cups).

In a bowl, add all dry ingredients and mix.

In a bowl, add all wet ingredients and mix.

Add the wet to dry ingredients and mix. Fold the
blueberries in.

Let the oven preheat to 400 F.

Pour in the muffin tin and bake for 18-22 minutes. Serve.

Nutrition: Calories 166 | Fat 6 g | Sugar 15 g | Protein 4
g | Sodium 65 mg | Carbs 21 g

563. Mango Rice Pudding

(Prep time: 5 minutes | Cook time: 50 minutes | Serving: 4)
Ingredients
2 cups of water

1 mango, mashed

Vanilla soy milk: 1 cup

Vanilla extract: 1 tsp.

Splenda sugar: 2 tbsp.

Brown rice: 1 cup, long grain

Cinnamon: half tsp.

Instructions
In a pan, boil water and add rice. Simmer on low flame and
cook for 35 to 40 minutes, covered.

In the mashed mango, add cooked rice, milk, cinnamon
and sugar. Cook for 10-15 minutes, uncovered.

Turn the heat off, add vanilla, and serve with fresh mangos.

Nutrition: Calories 275 | Fat 3 g | Sugar 8 g | Protein 6
g | Sodium 149 mg | Carbs 58 g

564. Thai Cashew Brittle

(Prep time: 2 hours & 35 minutes | Cook time: 20 minutes |
Serving: 24)
Ingredients
Honey: 1 cup

Planted butter: 1 tbsp.

Water: half cup

Baking soda: 1 tsp.

Roasted cashews: 1 cup, chopped

Grated ginger: 1 tsp.

2 cups of sugar

Chile paste: 1 tbsp.

Grated lemongrass: 1 tsp.

Instructions
In a pan, add water (half cup), honey, sugar mix on medium
flame. Let it come to a boil.

Cook until the thermometer reads 335 F. Turn the heat off.

Add the rest of the ingredients and cashews. Mix and
quickly transfer to a parchment-lined oil-sprayed
baking tray.

Let it cool for two hours, break and serve.

Nutrition: Calories 114 | Fat 3.2 g | Sugar 8 g | Protein
0.9 g | Sodium 118 mg | Carbs 30 g

565. Light & Creamy Chocolate Pudding

(Prep time: 1 hour & 10 minutes | Cook time: 15 minutes |
Serving: 4)
Ingredients
Sugar: 2 tbsp.

Vanilla extract: 1 tsp.

Cornstarch: 3 tbsp.

Baking cocoa: 2 tbsp.

Chocolate soy milk: 2 cups

Instructions
In a pan, add cocoa, sugar and cornstarch, mix and add

milk.

Cook until it thickens. Turn the heat low and cook for 2 minutes.

Turn the heat off, add vanilla, cool for 15 minutes.

Pour in the serving dish, serve chilled.

Nutrition per half-cup: Calories 127 | Fat 2 g | Sugar 8 g | Protein 3 g |Sodium 112 mg | Carbs 25 g

566. Pineapple Nice Cream

(Prep time: 10 minutes | Cook time: 0 minutes | Serving: 6)
Ingredients
Frozen mango chunks: 1 cup

Lime juice: 1 tbsp.

Frozen pineapple chunks: 16 oz.

Instructions
In a food processor, add all ingredients and process until smooth. Add some water if necessary.

Serve.

Nutrition: Calories 55 | Fat 17.2 g | Sugar 12 g | Protein 0.6 g |Sodium 1.1 mg | Carbs 14.2 g

567. Pineapple Sundae

(Prep time: 10 minutes | Cook time: 0 minutes | Serving: 1)
Ingredients
Chopped roasted pistachio: 1 tsp.

Low-fat vanilla yogurt: 2 tbsp.

Canned pineapple tidbits: 4 oz., drained

Instructions

In a serving bowl, add pineapple, add yogurt on top.

Serve with chopped nuts on top.

Nutrition: Calories 210 | Fat 2.8 g | Sugar 8 g | Protein 6.4 g |Sodium 141 mg | Carbs 12 g

568. Pumpkin-Hazelnut Tea Cake

(Prep time: 10 minutes | Cook time: 55 minutes | Serving: 12)
Ingredients

Canola oil: 3 tbsp.

Canned pumpkin puree: ¾ cup, unsweetened

2 eggs, whisked

Ground cinnamon: half tsp.

Honey: half cup

Flaxseed: 2 tbsp.

Packed brown sugar: 3 tbsp.

Baking powder: half tsp.

Chopped hazelnuts: 2 tbsp.

Salt: 1/8 tsp.

Whole-wheat flour: 1 cup

Ground allspice: half tsp.

All-purpose flour: half cup

Ground nutmeg: half tsp.

Ground cloves: ¼ tsp.

Instructions

Let the oven preheat to 350 F. oil spray an 8 x 4" loaf pan.

In a bowl, add eggs, browns sugar, canola oil, honey and puree. Whisk with an electric beater at low speed.

In a bowl, add the rest of the ingredients and mix.

Add dry ingredients to wet ingredients until well combined.

Pour in the pan and spread hazelnuts on top, and press down.

Bake for 50-55 minutes. Cool in the pan, slice and serve.

Nutrition per slice: Calories 166 | Fat 6 g | Sugar 15 g | Protein 4 g |Sodium 65 mg | Carbs 28 g

569. Berry Flag Cake

(Prep time: 2 hours & 30 minutes | Cook time: 0 minutes | Serving: 16)
Ingredients
Toasted pecans: half cup

Salt: ¼ tsp.

Lemon juice: 1 tbsp.

Graham crackers: 7 oz.

Canola oil: 1/3 cup

Lemon zest: 1 tsp.

Low-fat cream cheese: 16 oz., softened

Blueberries: 1 ¼ cups

Confectioners' sugar: ⅔ cup

Greek yogurt: 2 cups, non-fat

Raspberries: 1 ½ cups

Instructions

In a food processor, add salt, pecans and crackers until finely processed.

While pulsing, add oil gradually and transfer to a 9x13" baking dish. Press down with hands.

In a clean food processor, add lemon zest, cream cheese, lemon juice, yogurt and confectioners' sugar. Pulse until smooth.

Pour over the crust and spread in an even layer. Keep in the fridge covered for 2 hours or until set.

Place the berries on top of the cake. Slice in 16 pieces and serve.

Nutrition per piece: Calories 234 | Fat 17.2 g | Sugar 11.6 g | Protein 6.2 g |Sodium 223.7 mg | Carbs 20 g

570.   Southern Cornbread

(Prep time: 20 minutes | Cook time: 15 minutes | Serving: 12)
Ingredients

All-purpose flour: half cup

Whole-wheat flour: half cup

Baking powder: half tsp.

Yellow cornmeal: 1 cup

Cream-style corn: 1 cup, undrained (no-salt)

Sugar: 2 tbsp.

Baking soda: half tsp.

Buttermilk: half cup, non-fat

Salt: 1/8 tsp.

Kernel corn: half cup

Canola oil: 2 tbsp.

Milk: ¼ cup, low-fat

1 egg

Instructions

Let the oven preheat to 425 F. Oil spray a baking dish (9" square).

In a bowl, add all dry ingredients and mix.

In a different bowl, add the rest of the ingredients. Mix and pour in the flour mixture.

Mix until just combined. Pour in the prepared pan.

Bake for 20-15 minutes, cool for 5-10 minutes, slice and serve.

Nutrition: Calories 139 | Fat 3.5 g | Sugar 4 g | Protein 4 g |Sodium 114 mg | Carbs 25 g

571.   Peanut Butter Wreaths

(Prep time: 50 minutes | Cook time: 15 minutes | Serving: 4 ½ dozen)
Ingredients

Granulated sugar substitute: 1 ½ cups

Unsalted plant butter: half cup

Kosher salt: ¼ tsp.

Quick-cooking oats: 3 cups

1% milk: half cup

Light brown sugar: ¼ cup, packed

Chocolate pieces

Low-fat peanut butter: 1 cup

Vanilla extract: 2 tsp.

Instructions

Let the oven preheat to 350 F.

On a baking tray, spread the oats and bake for 8-10 minutes, stirring once halfway through. Take them out of the oven.

In a pan, add milk, sugars, milk and butter on medium until mixed well. Let it come to a boil. Turn the heat off.

Add salt, vanilla and peanut butter. Mix and add oats and let them rest for five minutes.

Scoop onto parchment-lined baking trays (use 3) and press in the center, and add chocolate pieces.

Cool for half an hour. Serve.

Nutrition: Calories 298 | Fat 13.1 g | Sugar 5 g | Protein 6 g | Sodium 67.3 mg | Carbs 12 g

572.   Fruit Sundae

(Prep time: 20 minutes | Cook time: 0 minutes | Serving: 6)

Ingredients

Shredded jicama: ¼ cup

Mixed fresh fruits: 3 cups, chopped

Strawberries: ¾ cup, chopped

6 waffle cones

Instructions

In a blender, puree the strawberries. Mix with chopped fruits, toss to coat and serve in cones with jicama on top.

Nutrition: Calories 215 | Fat 11 g | Sugar 8.9 g | Protein 4 g | Sodium 54 mg | Carbs 8 g

573.   Raspberry Peach Puff Pancake

(Prep time: 15 minutes | Cook time: 20 minutes | Serving: 4)

Ingredients

3 eggs, whisked

Sugar: half tsp.

2 peeled peaches, sliced

Fresh raspberries: half cup

All-purpose flour: half cup

Plant butter: 1 tbsp.

Low-fat milk: half cup

Vanilla yogurt: ¼ cup

Salt, two pinches

Instructions

Let the oven preheat to 400 F.

Toss peaches with sugar, add raspberries and gently mix.

In a pie plate (9"), add butter and let it melt in the oven for 2 to 3 minutes.

In a bowl, add eggs, salt and milk, whisk until combined. Add flour gradually and mix.

Take the pie plate out and coat the entire pan and add batter.

Bake for 18 to 22 minutes. Serve with yogurt and fruits.

Nutrition: Calories 199 | Fat 7 g | Sugar 8 g | Protein 9 g | Sodium 173 mg | Carbs 25 g

574.   Guilt-Free Carrot Cake

(Prep time: 15 minutes | Cook time: 30 minutes | Serving: 6-7)

Ingredients

Whole wheat flour: half cup

Light brown sugar: ¼ cup, packed

All-purpose flour: 1 cup

Dry milk: ¼ cup, non-fat

Cinnamon: 1 tsp.

Baking soda: 1 ¼ tsp.

Sugar substitute (granulated): half cup

Ground cloves: ¼ tsp.

Baking powder: 1 ½ tsp.

Ground allspice: half tsp.

Chopped walnuts: 2 tbsp.

Grated carrots: 1 ½ cups

Canned crushed pineapple: 6 oz., unsweetened, drained

Golden raisins: 2 tbsp.

Canola oil: ¼ cup

Ground nutmeg: half tsp.

1 egg

Egg substitute: ¾ cup

Instructions

Let the oven preheat to 350 F.

Oil spray a spring-foam (10") pan.

In a bowl, add both flours, the rest of the dry ingredients.

Mix well.

With an electric mixer, mix the wet ingredients in the dry ingredients.

Add pineapples, carrots, raisins, walnuts and fold.

Pour the batter into the pan, bake for half an hour.

Slice and serve.

Nutrition: Calories 276 | Fat 11 g | Sugar 9 g | Protein 5 g |Sodium 102 mg | Carbs 15 g

575. Peach Cobbler Dump Cake

(Prep time: 15 minutes | Cook time: 30 minutes | Serving: 12)

Ingredients

Light brown sugar: 3 tbsp.

Yellow organic cake mix: 1 box

Salt, a pinch

Low-fat milk: ¾ cup

Sliced peaches: 3 cups

Grapeseed oil: ¼ cup

Lemon juice: 1 tbsp.

Instructions

Let the oven preheat to 350 F. Oil spray a baking dish (13 by 9")

In a pan, add brown sugar, peaches, salt and mix; let it boil on medium flame.

Turn the heat off and add lemon juice. Pour in the prepared dish.

In a bowl, add oil, cake mix and milk, whisk and pour over the peaches, spread evenly.

Bake for 28-30 minutes. Cool and serve.

Nutrition: Calories 211 | Fat 5.2 g | Sugar 23 g | Protein 2.8 g |Sodium 30.8 mg | Carbs 39 g

576. Fruit & Almond Bites

(Prep time: 3 hours & 15 minutes | Cook time: 0 minutes | Serving: 4x12)

Ingredients

Chopped pistachios: 1 cup, toasted

Almond extract: ¼ tsp.

Dried cherries: 1 cup, chopped

Honey: 1/4 cup

Sliced almonds: 3-3/4 cups

Dried apricots: 2 cups, chopped

Instructions

In a food processor, add almonds (1 1/4 cups), process until finely diced. Take them out in a bowl.

Add the rest of the almonds to the food processor, process until chopped.

Add almond extract, and while the machine is still running, add honey gradually.

Take it out in a bowl. Add cherries and apricots.

Separate this mixture into six parts and roll each part into a half" thick roll. Wrap in plastic wrap, keep in the fridge for one hour.

Cut the chilled rolls into 1 1/2 "pieces, coat in chopped almonds. Roll half of the pieces in pistachios.

Serve and wrap the rest in plastic wrap.

Nutrition per piece: Calories 86 | Fat 5 g | Sugar 7 g | Protein 2 g |Sodium 15 mg | Carbs 10 g

577. Carrot & Zucchini Chia Seed Muffins

(Prep time: 15 minutes | Cook time: 25 minutes | Serving: 10)

Ingredients

Baking powder: 1 tsp.

Salt: half tsp.

Whole-wheat pastry flour: 1 ½ cups

Ground chia seeds: ¼ cup

Nutmeg: ¼ tsp.

Cinnamon: 2 tsp.

1% buttermilk: ¾ cup

Baking soda: 1 tsp.

Chopped walnuts: half cup

Cloves: half tsp.

Applesauce: ¼ cup

Ginger: ¼ tsp.

1 egg

Canola oil: ¼ cup

White grape juice: ¼ cup, concentrate

Grated zucchini: 1 cup

Chopped dates: ¼ cup

Grated carrot: 1 cup

Golden raisins: ¼ cup

Instructions

Let the oven preheat to 400 F. line a muffin tin with paper cups (10 cups).

In a bowl, add all wet egg, juice, oil, buttermilk and applesauce. Mix well. Add dates, carrots, zucchini, raisins and walnuts, fold them in.

Add the rest of the ingredients and mix.

Pour in the muffin cups. Bake for 20-25 minutes.

Serve.

Nutrition: Calories 289 | Fat 10.1 g | Sugar 7.9 g | Protein 3.9 g | Sodium 99.2 mg | Carbs 17 g

578. Mango & Banana Frozen Yogurt

(Prep time: 2 hours & 15 minutes | Cook time: 0 minutes | Serving: 4-6)

Ingredients

Chopped mango: ¾ cup

Skimmed milk: 1 ½ cups

Orange juice: 1/3 cup

Sliced bananas: 1 cup

Vanilla yogurt: 1 cup, low-fat

1 lime's juice

Sugar substitute: ¾ cup

Instructions

In a blender, add lime juice, bananas, and orange juice, pulse until smooth.

Pour in a bowl, add yogurt, milk and sugar, whisk until light.

Freeze and serve.

Nutrition: Calories 272 | Fat 11 g | Sugar 6 g | Protein 3 g | Sodium 79 mg | Carbs 9.9 g

579. Oat Avocado-Berry Bars

(Prep time: 15 minutes | Cook time: 40 minutes | Serving: 15)

Ingredients

Sour cream: half cup, low-fat

Low sugar, non-fat granola: 1 ¾ cups

Packed brown sugar: 2 tbsp.

Canola oil: 2 tbsp.

Whole-wheat flour: 1 ½ cups

Cinnamon: 1 tsp.

Salt: ¼ tsp.

Filling

Avocado: half cup

Cornstarch: 1 tsp.

Blueberries: 1 cup, frozen

Chopped dates: half cup

Orange zest: 1 tbsp.

Instructions

Let the oven preheat to 350 F. Oil spray a 13 by 9 by 2 baking pan.

In a food processor, add granola and pulse 3 times; take it out in a bowl.

Add salt, flour, cinnamon and brown sugar. Mix and add oil and sour cream.

Mix with a fork until crumbly.

In a baking pan, add half of the mixture and press down. Bake for 20 minutes, let it cool.

In a food processor, add oats, pulse until smooth.

Add avocado, mix till smooth. Add cornstarch and other ingredients, pulse until combined.

Transfer to the baked crust and spread, add the rest of the granola mixture on top.

Bake for 15 minutes.

Cool and cut in 15 pieces, serve.

Nutrition: Calories 152 | Fat 4 g | Sugar 10 g | Protein 4 g |Sodium 76 mg | Carbs 28 g

580. Frozen Yogurt Pops

(Prep time: 6 hours & 15 minutes | Cook time: 0 minutes | Serving: 4-6)

Ingredients

Plain yogurt: 1 cup, low-fat

Honey: 1 tbsp.

Frozen & thawed peach slices, unsweetened: 16 oz.

Instructions

In a food processor, add all ingredients with only (1 ½ cups) peaches, pulse until smooth.

Chop the rest of the peach slices.

Take it out in a bowl, add the puree and mix.

Pour in the molds with a stick. Freeze and serve.

Nutrition: Calories 66| Fat 17.2 g | Sugar 9 g | Protein 3 g |Sodium 32 mg | Carbs 13 g

581. Strawberry-Mango Nice Cream

(Prep time: 15 minutes | Cook time: 0 minutes | Serving: 4)

Ingredients

Frozen mango chunks: 12 oz.

Lime juice: 1 tbsp.

Sliced strawberries: 8 oz., frozen

Instructions

In a blender, add all ingredients, pulse until smooth.

Add some water if it is too thick. Serve.

Nutrition: Calories 70 | Fat 0.5 g | Sugar 14.2 g | Protein 1.1 g |Sodium 1.5 mg | Carbs 17.4

582. Chilled Key Lime Mousse

(Prep time: 6 hours & 45 minutes | Cook time: 0 minutes |

Serving: 10)

Ingredients

Unflavored gelatin: 2 1/4 tsp.

Lime juice: 2/3 cup

Sugar substitute: 1 ½ cups

¼ cup of water

Egg whites: 7

Lime zest: 4 tsp.

Egg yolks: 6

Salt: ¼ tsp.

Greek yogurt: 1 ½ cups, low-fat

Instructions

In a bowl, add water and gelatin, let it rest for three minutes.

In a skillet, add water (1 inch) heat on a low flame.

Add the gelatin bowl in hot water and stir until it is dissolved.

In a food processor, add lime zest and sugar (1 cup), pulse until smooth. Take it out in a pan, add salt and lime juice.

Heat and whisk until sugar is dissolved. Turn the heat off.

In a bowl, add yolk and whisk, gradually add lime juice mixture while whisking.

Turn the heat on and cook for 2-4 minutes. Pour in the stand mixer, mix on low speed, then turn to medium speed for 3-5 minutes.

Slowly add gelatin mixture whisk machine is still running, cool for 5 minutes.

In a stand mixer, whisk the egg whites until foamy on medium speed.

Turn the speed to medium-high, add sugar (half cup) gradually, whisk until stiff peaks appear.

Add yogurt in the lime custard, fold the egg whites in

batches.

Pour the batter into 10 ramekins (8 oz.), keep in the fridge for 3-12 hours.

Serve.

Nutrition: Calories 191 | Fat 3.4 g | Sugar 30 g | Protein 7.5 g |Sodium 114 mg | Carbs

583. Tahini & Almond Cookies
(Prep time: 20 minutes | Cook time: 14 minutes | Serving: 54)
Ingredients
Whole wheat flour: 2 tbsp. + 1 cup

White flour: 1 cup

Salt, a pinch

Cold unsalted plant butter: 3 tbsp. + half cup, cubed

Vanilla extract: 1 tsp.

Almond meal: 2/3 cup

¾ cup of sugar

Tahini paste: 2 tbsp. + ¾ cup

Water: 2 tbsp.

Instructions
Let the oven preheat to 350 F.

In a food processor, add all flours, vanilla, salt, sugar and butter, pulse until it becomes crumbly.

Add tahini and water, pulse until a dough forms.

Take the dough and knead with your hands few times. Divide into small dough balls and place onto parchment-lined baking sheets, and flatten slightly.

Bake for 12 to 14 minutes. Cool and serve.

Nutrition: Calories 265 | Fat 9 g | Sugar 3 g | Protein 2 g |Sodium 75 mg | Carbs 10.9 g

584. Protein Energy Bites
(Prep time: 2 hours & 15 minutes | Cook time: 0 minutes | Serving: 7)
Ingredients
1/4 cup of raisins

Vanilla extract: 2 tsp.

Chia seeds: 1 tbsp.

Soaked cashews: 1 cup, drained

4 dates (soaked for ten minutes), chopped

Sunflower seeds: 1/4 cup

Cocoa powder, as needed

Sea salt, a pinch

Dried milk powder: 1/3 cup

Canola oil: 1 tbsp.

Instructions
In a food processor, add all ingredients except for cocoa powder, pulse until smooth.

Take it out in a bowl. Keep in the fridge for 1 hour.

Scoop some and make them into small balls, and roll in cocoa powder. Serve chilled.

Nutrition: Calories 250 | Fat 12 g | Sugar 8 g | Protein 6.4 g |Sodium 77 mg | Carbs 11 g

585. Tofu Chocolate Cake
(Prep time: 15 minutes | Cook time: 25 minutes | Serving: 6)
Ingredients
Soft tofu: 10.5 oz.

Water: ¼ cup

Moist chocolate cake mix: 1 box, low sugar

Instructions
In a food processor, add tofu and cake mix, mix.

Add water and process until smooth.

As per cake box instructions, pour in the pan, but do not add anything else.

Bake as per instructions

Slice and serve.

Nutrition: Calories 189 | Fat 4 g | Sugar 8 g | Protein 2.9 g |Sodium 267 mg | Carbs 35 g

586. Strawberry Cobbler with Cream Cheese
(Prep time: 20 minutes | Cook time: 45 minutes | Serving: 8)
Ingredients
1 egg, whisked

1 cup of all-purpose flour

Unsalted plant butter: half cup

1 cup of sugar substitute

Whole strawberries: 4 cups, cut into fours

1 cup of milk

Baking powder: 3 tsp., no-sodium

Cream cheese: 2 oz., cubed

Instructions

Let the oven preheat to 350 F.

Pour the melted butter into a 9 by 13 baking dish.

In a bowl, add all ingredients except for strawberries and cream cheese. Mix and pour in the dish.

Add strawberries and cubed cream cheese on top.

Bake for 45 minutes.

Nutrition: Calories 323 | Fat 15 g | Sugar 30 g | Protein 4.4 g |Sodium 46 mg | Carbs 44 g

587. Peanut Butter Blossom Cookies

(Prep time: 20 minutes | Cook time: 15 minutes | Serving: 20)

Ingredients

canola oil: half cup

Peanut Butter: ¾ cup

2/3 cup of Granulated Sugar substitute

Hershey's Milk Chocolate: 48 Kisses

Brown Sugar: 1/3 cup

Almond Milk: 2 tbsp.

1 Egg

Baking Soda: 1 tsp., low-sodium

Vanilla Extract: 1 tsp.

All-Purpose Flour: 1 ½ cups

Instructions

Let the oven preheat to 375 F.

In a bowl, add peanut butter and oil and blend well.

Add brown sugar and sugar substitute (1/3 cup), beat until fluffy.

Add vanilla, egg and milk and blend well.

Add the dry ingredients and mix until a dough forms.

Add egg, milk and vanilla, then beat until well blended. Add some more oil if it is too dry.

Scoop and make into small balls, roll in the rest of the sugar substitute and place on a baking sheet.

Bake for 8-10 minutes. Take them out from the oven and instantly press one chocolate on top.

Cool and serve.

Nutrition: Calories 76| Fat 5.6 g | Sugar 8 g | Protein 1.3 g |Sodium 16.7 mg | Carbs 6.5 g

588. Classic Caramel Apples

(Prep time: 1 hour & 20 minutes | Cook time: 20 minutes | Serving: 10)

Ingredients

Dark brown sugar: 2 cups

Kosher salt: ¼ tsp.

Honey: 1 cup

10 granny smith apples

Vanilla extract: 1 ½ tsp.

Unsalted plant butter: half cup

Condensed milk: 14 oz.

Instructions

Take the stems off of apples, add one craft stick to each apple.

Keep in the fridge.

In a saucepan, add the rest of the ingredients except for vanilla, place over medium flame.

Cook for 20 minutes until the thermometer shows 245 F.

Turn the heat off and add vanilla. Let it rest for five minutes.

Take the apples out and pat dry. Roll the apples in caramel sauce, drip the excess off.

Place on parchment-lined baking sheet.

Chill and serve.

Nutrition: Calories 257 | Fat 8 g | Sugar 8 g | Protein 3 g | Sodium 87 mg | Carbs 16 g

589. Cranberry Dreamsicle Trifle

(Prep time: 1 hour & 20 minutes | Cook time: 20 minutes | Serving: 10-12)

Ingredients

Sugar: ¾ cup + 2/3 cup

Orange zest: 1 tbsp.

Orange juice: half cup

Cranberries: 3 ½ cups

2 ½ cups of milk

Cornstarch: 1/3 cup

Vanilla extract: 1 tsp.

Orange juice: 3 tbsp.

Pound cake: 16 oz.

3 egg yolks

Whipping cream: 1 ½ cups, whipped to soft peaks

Instructions

In a pan, add sugar (3/4 cup), cranberries and orange juice. Cook for 6 minutes or until reduced by half. Turn the heat off and cool completely.

In a pan, add milk, sugar, extract and zest and cook until sugar dissolves.

In a bowl, add yolks, orange juice and cornstarch, whisk and slowly add half a cup of the milk mixture. Mix until smooth.

Pour it into the milk mixture and whisk well.

Cook on a medium flame for 3-5 minutes, keep whisking. Cook for 3-5 minutes.

Pour in a bowl, cover with plastic wrap and keep in the fridge for half an hour.

Slice the cake into one" cubed.

Take a 5-qt. Trifle dish, add 1/3 of cake cubes. Layer orange cream, whipped cream and cranberry mixture. Repeat the layers. Serve after chilling.

Nutrition: Calories 250 | Fat 17.2 g | Sugar 8 g | Protein 6.4 g | Sodium 55 mg | Carbs 7 g

Lite Shortcake

(Prep time: 20 minutes | Cook time: 0 minutes | Serving: 6)

Ingredients

Sugar: half cup

Lite cool whip, as needed

Strawberries: 4 cups

6 slices of angel food

Instructions

Toss strawberries with sugar, toss to coat. Let it rest for 20 minutes.

Mash the strawberries. Serve with cool whip on top.

Nutrition: Calories 215 | Fat 11 g | Sugar 8 g | Protein 2 g | Sodium 103 mg | Carbs 12 g

590. Chocolate Avocado Mousse

(Prep time: 20 minutes | Cook time: 0 minutes | Serving: 4)

Ingredients

Canola oil: 2 tbsp.

1 avocado

Vanilla extract: 1 tsp.

Almond milk: ¼ cup

Cacao powder: ¼ cup

Instructions

In a food processor, add all ingredients, blend until smooth.

Serve chilled.

Nutrition: Calories 189 | Fat 5 g | Sugar 8 g | Protein 4 g | Sodium 53 mg | Carbs 7 g

591. Nut Butter Bars

(Prep time: 50 minutes | Cook time: 50 minutes | Serving: 8)

Ingredients

Bars

Olive oil: 1 tbsp.

Creamy cashew butter: half cup, unsweetened

Butternut squash: 2 cups, cubed

Unsalted plant butter: half cup

White rice flour: 2 tbsp. + 1 cup

1 egg

Lite brown sugar: 1 cup

Vanilla extract: 1 ½ tsp.

Salt: 1/8 tsp.

Frosting

Cashew butter: 3 tbsp., unsweetened

Softened cream cheese: 3 oz.

Roasted cashews: 1/3 cup, chopped

Unsalted plant butter: 3 tbsp.

Powdered sugar: ¼ cup

Instructions

Let the oven preheat to 450 F.

Toss oil and squash and spread on a foil-lined baking sheet. Roast for 18 minutes, cool for ten minutes.

Add to a food processor, pulse until smooth. Use only half a cup of puree.

Change the oven temperature to 350 F.

Oil spray a baking dish (8" square) and place parchment paper, let it hang from the sides.

In a pan, add butter on medium flame, cook until it turns golden brown. Turn the heat off.

Add brown sugar and whisk till smooth.

Cool for 15 minutes. Add the rest of the ingredients, add flour in the last. Mix until combined.

Spread on the baking dish, bake for 23-25 minutes. Let it cool.

In a bowl, add all ingredients of frosting (except for cashews), whisk with an electric mixer until fluffy and smooth. Spread over bars, add cashews on top.

Slice and serve.

Nutrition: Calories 255 | Fat 12 g | Sugar 8 g | Protein 6.4 g | Sodium 109 mg | Carbs 11g

592. Oatmeal Cookies

(Prep time: 20 minutes | Cook time: 15 minutes | Serving:)

Ingredients

White sugar substitute: half cup

All-purpose flour: 1 cup

Brown sugar: ¾ cup, packed

¼ cup of water

Plant-based butter: ¾ cup

1 egg, whisked

Vanilla: 1 tsp.

Raisins: 1½ cup

Cinnamon: 2 tsp.

Baking soda: half tsp.

Salt: 1/8 tsp.

Quick-cooking oats: 3 cups

Ground cloves: half tsp.

Chopped nuts: 1 cup

Instructions

Let the oven preheat to 400 F. Oil spray a baking sheet.

In a bowl, add all sugars and butter, cream them.

Add egg, vanilla and water. Whisk well.

Add the dry ingredients, and mix until combined.

Add oats, nuts and raisins, mix.

Make the mixture into small balls and place it on the baking sheet.

Bake for 10 to 13 minutes. Cool and serve.

Nutrition for 2 cookies: Calories 181 | Fat 8 g | Sugar 10 g | Protein 4 g | Sodium 60 mg | Carbs 25 g

593. Easy Coffee Cake

(Prep time: 20 minutes | Cook time: 30 minutes | Serving: 18)

Ingredients

Toppings

Cinnamon: 2 tsp.

Walnuts: 1 cup, chopped

Brown sugar: half cup, packed

Batter

Sugar: half cup

Baking mix: 3 cups

Skim milk: 1 1/3 cups

Salt: ¼ tsp.

2 eggs

Instructions

Let the oven preheat to 350 F. Oil spray a tube pan.

In a bowl, mix cinnamon, nuts, and sugar.

In a bowl, whisk salt, baking mix and sugar; mix well.

In a bowl, whisk egg and milk. Add the wet to dry

   ingredients.

Whisk with a fork for 15 to 20 seconds until just combined.

   It should be lumpy.

Add topping (1/3) in the pan, add half of the batter.

Layer toppings and batter and swirl. Bake for 25 to 30

   minutes.

Cool for ten minutes, slice and serve.

Nutrition per slice: Calories 209 | Fat 12 g | Sugar 14 g |
Protein 7 g |Sodium 118 mg | Carbs 23 g

Chapter 12: 28-Days Healthy DASH Diet Meal Plan

Before starting with the meal plan, serving & portions can be followed from 2.3 (chapter 2 of this book). Cookpasta, rice and grains as per the package instructions (if the recipe indicates) but always omit salt.

COOKING CONVERSION CHART

Measurement

CUP	ONCES	MILLILITERS	TABLESPOONS
8 cup	64 oz	1895 ml	128
6 cup	48 oz	1420 ml	96
5 cup	40 oz	1180 ml	80
4 cup	32 oz	960 ml	64
2 cup	16 oz	480 ml	32
1 cup	8 oz	240 ml	16
3/4 cup	6 oz	177 ml	12
2/3 cup	5 oz	158 ml	11
1/2 cup	4 oz	118 ml	8
3/8 cup	3 oz	90 ml	6
1/3 cup	2.5 oz	79 ml	5.5
1/4 cup	2 oz	59 ml	4
1/8 cup	1 oz	30 ml	3
1/16 cup	1/2 oz	15 ml	1

Temperature

FAHRENHEIT	CELSIUS
100 °F	37 °C
150 °F	65 °C
200 °F	93 °C
250 °F	121 °C
300 °F	150 °C
325 °F	160 °C
350 °F	180 °C
375 °F	190 °C
400 °F	200 °C
425 °F	220 °C
450 °F	230 °C
500 °F	260 °C
525 °F	274 °C
550 °F	288 °C

Weight

IMPERIAL	METRIC
1/2 oz	15 g
1 oz	29 g
2 oz	57 g
3 oz	85 g
4 oz	113 g
5 oz	141 g
6 oz	170 g
8 oz	227 g
10 oz	283 g
12 oz	340 g
13 oz	369 g
14 oz	397 g
15 oz	425 g
1 lb	453 g

Week 1

Monday (Day 1)

Breakfast: **Strawberry DASH Smoothie**

Lunch: **Roasted Root Vegetables with Cheese Polenta**

Snack: **Pumpkin Pie Bites**

Dinner: **Dijon Salmon with Green**

Bean PilafTuesday (Day 2)

Breakfast: **Healthy Egg**

Bake Lunch: **Shrimp &**

Nectarine Salad Snack:

Soy Nut & Apricot Trail

MixDinner: **Mexican Bake**

Wednesday (Day 3)

Breakfast: **Muesli Scones**

Lunch: **Lentil Medley**

Dinner: **Greek Chicken with Roasted Vegetables**

Dessert:

Oatmeal

Cookie

Thursday(Day

4)

Breakfast:

Blueberry

Multigrain

Pancakes

Lunch: **Zucchini Pad Thai**

Snack: **Spicy Almonds**

Dinner: **Grilled Salmon in**

Grape LeavesFriday (Day 5)

Breakfast: **Whole-Wheat**

Pretzels Lunch:

Broccoli Pasta Salad

Snack: **Quinoa-Stuffed**

TomatoesDinner: **Fall**

Curry Chicken

Saturday (Day 6)

Breakfast: **Cherry Berry Watermelon**

SmoothieLunch: **Romaine Lettuce**

with **Dressing** Snack: **Potato Nachos**

Dinner: **Turkey**

Meat Loaf

Sunday (Day 7)

Breakfast: **Strawberry Banana Milkshake**

Lunch: **Minestrone Soup**

Snack: **Non-fat yogurt with berries**

Dinner: **Cherry-Chicken Lettuce Wraps**

Week 2

Monday (Day 8)

Breakfast: **Banana Breakfast**

SmoothieLunch: **Tomato**

Green Bean Soup Dinner:

Heart Healthy Lasagna

Rolls Tuesday (Day 9)

Breakfast: **Almond Butter Banana Oatmeal**

Lunch: **Chickpea Quinoa Bowl**

Dinner: **Skillet Lemon Chicken &**

Potatoes Dessert: **Strawberry Cobbler**

with Cream Cheese Wednesday **(Day**

10)

Breakfast: **Peaches & Cream Oatmeal**

SmoothieLunch: **Tuna Salad &**

Spinach Sandwiches Snack: **Graham**

Crackers with Nut-Butter

Dinner: **Salmon with Horseradish**

Pistachio Crust Thursday **(Day 11)**

Breakfast: **Oatmeal Smoothie**

Lunch: **Couscous with Beans &**

Vegetables Dinner: **Curried**

Cauliflower with ChickpeasFriday

(Day 12)

Breakfast: **Green Monster Smoothie**

Lunch: **Polenta Squares with Cheese &**

Pine Nuts Dinner: **Salmon Burgers with**

Green Sauce Saturday (Day 13)

Breakfast: **Avocado Smoothie**

Lunch: **Carbonara with Spinach &**

MushroomsDinner: **Vegan Coconut**

Chickpea Curry Sunday (Day 14)

Breakfast: **Chocolate Berry Smoothie**

Lunch: **Zesty Tomato Soup**

Snack: **Spicy Almonds**

Dinner: **Warm Spiced Cabbage Bake**

Week 3

Monday (Day 15)

Breakfast: **Carrot Juice**

Smoothie Lunch: **Roasted**

Vegetable Farro Salad

Dinner: **Salmon & Escarole**

Packets

Tuesday (Day 16)

Breakfast: **Blueberry Lavender**

LemonadeLunch: **Honey**

Lemon Fruit Salad Dinner:

Chicken Tenders with Salad

Dessert: **Carrot & Zucchini Chia**

Seed Muffins Wednesday (Day 17)

Breakfast: **Peanut Butter & Banana Smoothie**

Lunch: **Zucchini Salad**

Snack: **Dried Fruits**

Dinner: **Golden Apricot-Glazed**

Turkey Breast Thursday (Day 18)

Breakfast: **Perfect Green**

SmoothieLunch: **French**

Onion Soup Dinner:

Chickpea Curry

Friday (Day 19)

Breakfast: **Fruit Smoothie**

Lunch: **Fig & Goat**

Cheese Salad Dinner:

Cabbage Roll Skillet

Saturday (Day 20)

Breakfast: **Tofu Turmeric Scramble**

Lunch: **Three Sisters Soup**

Dinner: **Roasted Garlic Salmon &**

Brussels Sprouts Sunday (Day 21)

Breakfast: **Apple and Peanut Butter**

Oatmeal Lunch: **Mixed Vegetable Salad**

with Lime Dressing Dinner: **Ginger**

Veggie Pasta

Week 4

Monday (Day 22)

Breakfast: **Healthy Breakfast Cookies with de-caffeinated coffee**

Lunch: **Turkey Wrap**

Snack: **Oat & Nut Crunch Mix**

Dinner: **Yellow Lentils with Spinach & GingerTuesday (Day 23)**

Breakfast: **Mushroom & Sausage Quiche**

Lunch: **Carrot Soup**

Dinner: **Halibut Lemon**

PiccataWednesday (Day 24)

Breakfast: **Sweet Millet**

Congee Lunch: **Grilled**

Veggie Sandwich

Snack: **Wonton Chips**

with salsa

Dinner: **Italian Sausage-Stuffed**

ZucchiniDessert: **Oat Avocado-**

Berry Bars Thursday (Day 25)

Breakfast: **Pumpkin Overnight**

Oats Lunch: **Curried Carrot &**

Apple Soup Dinner: **One-Pan**

Lemon & Chicken Bake Friday

(Day 26)

Breakfast: **Dash Diet French Toast**

Lunch: **Pesto Chicken & Cannellini**

Bean Soup Dinner: **Crispy Tofu with**

Black Pepper Sauce Saturday (Day

27)

Breakfast: **Egg Muffin with Cheese & Spinach**

Lunch: **Garden Vegetable**

Beef Soup Dinner: **Grilled**

Peanut Chicken Sunday

(Day 28)

Breakfast: **Vegetarian Breakfast Salad**

Lunch: **White-Bean, Tomato, Cucumber Salad with Basil**

VinaigretteSnack: **Sweet & Spicy Pumpkinseeds**

Dinner: **Roast Salmon with Chimichurri Sauce**

Conclusion

The National Heart, Lung, & Blood Institute promotes the DASH Diet, which means dietary methods to stophigh blood pressure. It highlights foods rich in blood pressure-lowering minerals like potassium,
protein, calcium, and fiber, which you've always been advised to consume. DASH also prohibits sugar-sweetened drinks and sweets, and foods rich in saturated fat, including fatty meats, full-fat dairy meals, and tropical oils. Following DASH also entails a daily sodium limit of 2,300 mg, which will be gradually reduced to about 1,500 mg. The DASH Diet is well-balanced and long-term sustainable, which is one of the reasons it is ranked as Best Overall Diet, along with the Mediterranean Diet. Even without reducing too much salt consumption, the DASH eating plan has decreased blood pressure in only 14 days. People with slight hypertension, even those with prehypertension, had the best response. The DASH diet may assist improve drugresponsiveness and reduce blood pressure in individuals with severe hypertension who would not be able to go without medication. With weight reduction and exercise, the DASH diet may help decrease cholesterol and improve insulin resistance, lowering the risk of diabetes. The DASH diet is rich in vegetables and fruits both lowers blood pressure. The DASH diet had the biggest impact on blood pressure, with readings dropping within two weeks after beginning the plan. Bad cholesterol is also decreased, with blood pressure.

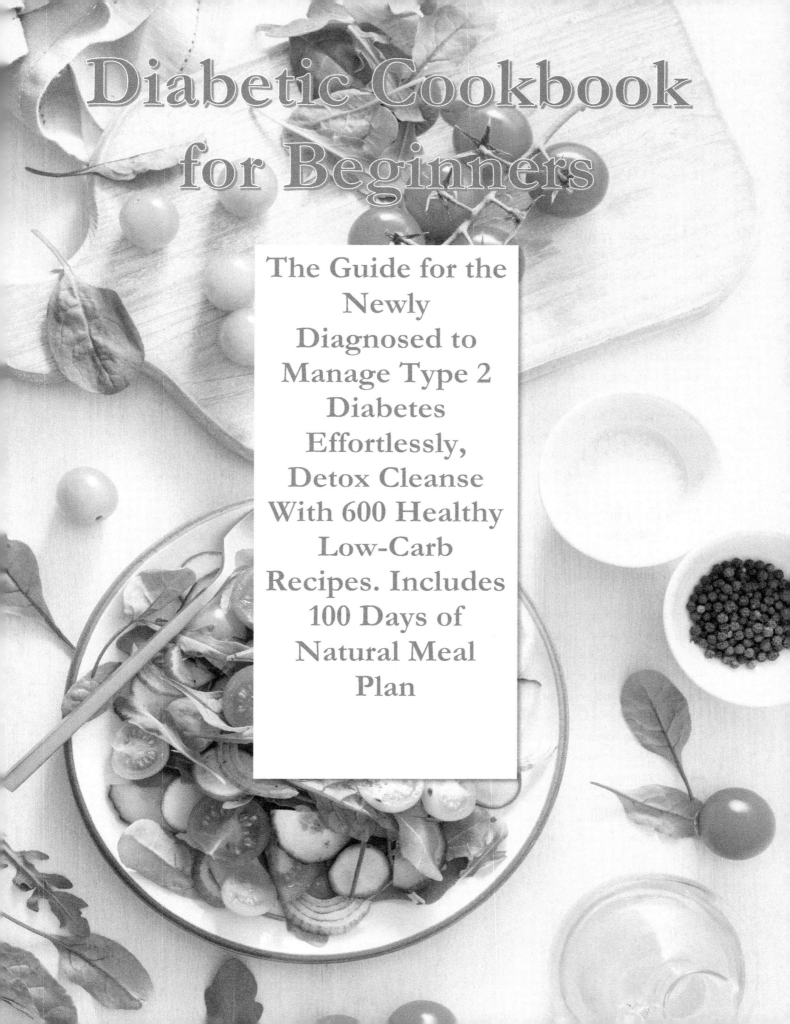

Diabetic Cookbook for Beginners

The Guide for the Newly Diagnosed to Manage Type 2 Diabetes Effortlessly, Detox Cleanse With 600 Healthy Low-Carb Recipes. Includes 100 Days of Natural Meal Plan

Introduction

Diabetes is a disease that caused by high levels of sugar in the blood and it's a serious condition that requires your attention.

If diabetes is not diagnosed and managed in a timely manner, it could lead to complications such as blindness, kidney failure, nerve damage, heart disease and more.

To treat diabetes, you have to control your blood sugar level. You will need to stick to a special diet and exercise regularly along with taking medications.

A healthy diet for diabetics is low in fat, low in cholesterol and sugar and rich in vitamins and fiber. It should also include plenty of protein as this will keep you feeling full longer.

Eating snacks between meals can be beneficial for a diabetic as it helps to keep blood sugar levels under control.

If you are a diabetic, you understand the importance of having healthy recipes to help maintain your condition. As with any diet, it is important to monitor and control carbohydrates which means substituting sugars with other ingredients that have fewer carbs.

There are many recipes which allow you the freedom of creativity while still being able to stick to your dietary needs. The following section will contain some tips for cooking in the kitchen as well specific foods that should be included in a diabetic diet.

Try to choose sugar substitutes that are found naturally such as Stevia and Agave Syrup which have fewer calories than refined sugar. You can find these sweeteners at your local health food store or online.

Avoid foods that are high in fat and cholesterol. This means staying away from fatty meats such as bacon and sausage as well as whole eggs. Fish and chicken can be eaten without the skins if you need less fat in your diet. Chicken and fish are great sources of protein, iron, zinc, Omega-3s and B12 which are all important nutrients for diabetics.

All vegetables contain carbohydrates so it is best to stick with those that are low in sugar such as broccoli, cauliflower, spinach, kale and avocado. You can also use onions, garlic, mushrooms and tomatoes to replace butter for dishes that need more fat.

When making recipes in which you need to add fat such as frying chicken or cooking meat, the healthier ingredients that do not add much of a taste to the dish are olive oil, coconut oil and non-fat yogurt. The same goes for any type of smoothie which includes milk and other dairy products that have carbs. These foods contain calcium which is a vital nutrient for diabetics.

You can also use low-carb fruits such as berries which will make your meal healthier and more filling. You can use the same variety of berries in a smoothie to add some flavor to your food without the glucose content.

The following are some foods you should absolutely avoid or limit because of their high carb content: pasta, bread, potatoes, rice and desserts. Diabetics are told to limit carbohydrates in the diet and decrease the symptoms which are hardest for diabetics to control.

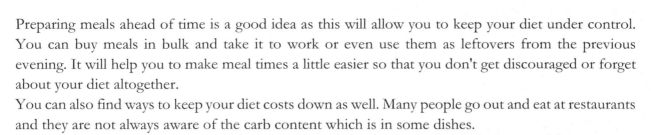

Preparing meals ahead of time is a good idea as this will allow you to keep your diet under control. You can buy meals in bulk and take it to work or even use them as leftovers from the previous evening. It will help you to make meal times a little easier so that you don't get discouraged or forget about your diet altogether.

You can also find ways to keep your diet costs down as well. Many people go out and eat at restaurants and they are not always aware of the carb content which is in some dishes.

Foods are may be high in sugar and fat which you want to avoid if you are trying to keep your blood sugar levels down.

Even restaurant meals that say they are healthy can contain more carbs than necessary or you might add a side dish which was not even part of the original meal. By knowing the carb content in some restaurant meals, you can make your meal healthier at home by substituting one or two items with a healthier version.

You also need to keep track of how much you are drinking to avoid overdoing it. If you are not used to drinking alcohol, just keep it in moderation and try to stick with low-carb liquors and beers so that you can still enjoy a drink without going overboard.

Breakfast Recipes

594. Blueberry Breakfast Cake

Preparation time: 15 minutes
Cooking time: 45 minutes
Servings: 12
Ingredients:
For the topping
- ¼ cup finely chopped walnuts
- 1/2 teaspoon ground cinnamon
- 2 tablespoons butter, chopped into small pieces
- 2 tablespoons sugar

For the cake
- Nonstick cooking spray
- 1 cup whole-wheat pastry flour
- 1 cup oat flour
- ¼ cup sugar
- 2 teaspoons baking powder
- 1 large egg, beaten
- 1/2 cup skim milk
- 2 tablespoons butter, melted
- 1 teaspoon grated lemon peel
- 2 cups fresh or frozen blueberries

Directions:
To make the topping
1.	In a small bowl, stir together the walnuts, cinnamon, butter, and sugar. Set aside.
To make the cake
1.	Preheat the oven to 350f. Spray a 9-inch square pan with cooking spray. Set aside.

2.	In a large bowl, stir together the pastry flour, oat flour, sugar, and baking powder.
3.	Add the egg, milk, butter, and lemon peel, and stir until there are no dry spots.
4.	Stir in the blueberries, and gently mix until incorporated. Press the batter into the prepared pan, using a spoon to flatten it into the dish.
5.	Sprinkle the topping over the cake.
6.	Bake for 40 to 45 minutes, until a toothpick inserted into the cake comes out clean, and serve.
Nutrition: calories: 177; total fat: 7g; saturated fat: 3g; protein: 4g; carbs: 26g; sugar: 9g; fiber: 3g; cholesterol: 26mg; sodium: 39mg

595. Whole-Grain Pancakes

Preparation time: 10 minutes
Cooking time: 15 minutes
Servings: 4 to 6
Ingredients:
- 2 cups whole-wheat pastry flour
- 4 teaspoons baking powder
- 2 teaspoons ground cinnamon
- 1/2 teaspoon salt
- 2 cups skim milk, plus more as needed
- 2 large eggs
- 1 tablespoon honey
- Nonstick cooking spray
- Maple syrup, for serving

- Fresh fruit, for serving

Directions:

1. In a large bowl, stir together the flour, baking powder, cinnamon, and salt.
2. Add the milk, eggs, and honey, and stir well to combine. If needed, add more milk, 1 tablespoon at a time, until there are no dry spots and you have a pourable batter.
3. Heat a large skillet over medium-high heat, and spray it with cooking spray.
4. Using a ¼-cup measuring cup, scoop 2 or 3 pancakes into the skillet at a time. Cook for a couple of minutes, until bubbles form on the surface of the pancakes, flip, and cook for 1 to 2 minutes more, until golden brown and cooked through. Repeat with the remaining batter.
5. Serve topped with maple syrup or fresh fruit.

Nutrition: calories: 392; total fat: 4g; saturated fat: 1g; protein: 15g; carbs: 71g; sugar: 11g; fiber: 9g; cholesterol: 95mg; sodium: 396mg

596. Buckwheat Grouts Breakfast Bowl

Preparation time: 5 minutes, plus overnight to soak
Cooking time: 10 to 12 minutes
Servings: 4
Ingredients:

- 3 cups skim milk
- 1 cup buckwheat grouts
- ¼ cup chia seeds
- 2 teaspoons vanilla extract
- 1/2 teaspoon ground cinnamon
- Pinch salt
- 1 cup water
- 1/2 cup unsalted pistachios

- 2 cups sliced fresh strawberries
- ¼ cup cacao nibs (optional)

Directions:

1. In a large bowl, stir together the milk, groats, chia seeds, vanilla, cinnamon, and salt. Cover and refrigerate overnight.
2. The next morning, transfer the soaked mixture to a medium pot and add the water. Bring to a boil over medium-high heat, reduce the heat to maintain a simmer, and cook for 10 to 12 minutes, until the buckwheat is tender and thickened.
3. Transfer to bowls and serve, topped with the pistachios, strawberries, and cacao nibs (if using).

Nutrition: calories: 340; total fat: 8g; saturated fat: 1g; protein: 15g; carbs: 52g; sugar: 14g; fiber: 10g; cholesterol: 4mg; sodium: 140mg

597. Peach Muesli Bake

Preparation time: 10 minutes
Cooking time: 40 minutes
Servings: 8
Ingredients:

- Nonstick cooking spray
- 2 cups skim milk
- 11/2 cups rolled oats
- 1/2 cup chopped walnuts
- 1 large egg
- 2 tablespoons maple syrup
- 1 teaspoon ground cinnamon
- 1 teaspoon baking powder
- 1/2 teaspoon salt
- 2 to 3 peaches, sliced

Directions:

1. Preheat the oven to 375f. Spray a 9-inch square baking dish with cooking spray. Set aside.

2. In a large bowl, stir together the milk, oats, walnuts, egg, maple syrup, cinnamon, baking powder, and salt. Spread half the mixture in the prepared baking dish.

3. Place half the peaches in a single layer across the oat mixture.

4. Spread the remaining oat mixture over the top. Add the remaining peaches in a thin layer over the oats. Bake for 35 to 40 minutes, uncovered, until thickened and browned.

5. Cut into 8 squares and serve warm.

Nutrition: calories: 138; total fat: 3g; saturated fat: 1g; protein: 6g; carbs: 22g; sugar: 10g; fiber: 3g; cholesterol: 24mg; sodium: 191mg

598. Steel-Cut Oatmeal Bowl With Fruit And Nuts

Preparation time: 5 minutes
Cooking time: 20 minutes
Servings: 4
Ingredients:

- 1 cup steel-cut oats
- 2 cups almond milk
- ¾ cup water
- 1 teaspoon ground cinnamon
- ¼ teaspoon salt
- 2 cups chopped fresh fruit, such as blueberries, strawberries, raspberries, or peaches
- 1/2 cup chopped walnuts
- ¼ cup chia seeds

Directions:

1. In a medium saucepan over medium-high heat, combine the oats, almond milk, water, cinnamon, and salt.

Bring to a boil, reduce the heat to low, and simmer for 15 to 20 minutes, until the oats are softened and thickened.

2. Top each bowl with 1/2 cup of fresh fruit, 2 tablespoons of walnuts, and 1 tablespoon of chia seeds before serving.

Nutrition: calories: 288; total fat: 11g; saturated fat: 1g; protein: 10g; carbs: 38g; sugar: 7g; fiber: 10g; cholesterol: 0mg; sodium: 329mg

599. Whole-Grain Dutch Baby Pancake

Preparation time: 5 minutes
Cooking time: 25 minutes
Servings: 4
Ingredients:

- 2 tablespoons coconut oil
- 1/2 cup whole-wheat flour
- ¼ cup skim milk
- 3 large eggs
- 1 teaspoon vanilla extract
- 1/2 teaspoon baking powder
- ¼ teaspoon salt
- ¼ teaspoon ground cinnamon
- Powdered sugar, for dusting

Directions:

1. Preheat the oven to 400f.

2. Put the coconut oil in a medium oven-safe skillet, and place the skillet in the oven to melt the oil while it preheats.

3. In a blender, combine the flour, milk, eggs, vanilla, baking powder, salt, and cinnamon. Process until smooth.

4. Carefully remove the skillet from the oven and tilt to spread the oil around evenly.

5. Pour the batter into the skillet and return it to the oven for 23 to 25 minutes, until the pancake puffs and lightly browns.

6. Remove, dust lightly with powdered sugar, cut into 4 wedges, and serve.

Nutrition: calories: 195; total fat: 11g; saturated fat: 7g; protein: 8g; carbs: 16g; sugar: 1g; fiber: 2g; cholesterol: 140mg; sodium: 209mg

600. Mushroom, Zucchini, And Onion Frittata

Preparation time: 10 minutes
Cooking time: 20 minutes
Servings: 4
Ingredients:

- 1 tablespoon extra-virgin olive oil
- 1/2 onion, chopped
- 1 medium zucchini, chopped
- 11/2 cups sliced mushrooms
- 6 large eggs, beaten
- 2 tablespoons skim milk
- Salt
- Freshly ground black pepper
- 1 ounce feta cheese, crumbled

Directions:

1. Preheat the oven to 400f.

2. In a medium oven-safe skillet over medium-high heat, heat the olive oil.

3. Add the onion and sauté for 3 to 5 minutes, until translucent.

4. Add the zucchini and mushrooms, and cook for 3 to 5 more minutes, until the vegetables are tender.

5. Meanwhile, in a small bowl, whisk the eggs, milk, salt, and pepper. Pour the mixture into the skillet, stirring to combine, and transfer the skillet to the oven. Cook for 7 to 9 minutes, until set.

6. Sprinkle with the feta cheese, and cook for 1 to 2 minutes more, until heated through.

7. Remove, cut into 4 wedges, and serve.

Nutrition: calories: 178; total fat: 13g; saturated fat: 4g; protein: 12g; carbs: 5g; sugar: 3g; fiber: 1g; cholesterol: 285mg; sodium: 234mg

601. Spinach And Cheese Quiche

Preparation time: 10 minutes, plus 10 minutes to rest
Cooking time: 50 minutes
Servings: 4 to 6
Ingredients:

- Nonstick cooking spray
- 8 ounces yukon gold potatoes, shredded
- 1 tablespoon plus 2 teaspoons extra-virgin olive oil, divided
- 1 teaspoon salt, divided
- Freshly ground black pepper
- 1 onion, finely chopped
- 1 (10-ounce) bag fresh spinach
- 4 large eggs
- 1/2 cup skim milk
- 1 ounce gruyere cheese, shredded

Directions:

1. Preheat the oven to 350f. Spray a 9-inch pie dish with cooking spray. Set aside.

2. In a small bowl, toss the potatoes with 2 teaspoons of olive oil, 1/2 teaspoon of salt, and season with pepper.

Press the potatoes into the bottom and sides of the pie dish to form a thin, even layer. Bake for 20 minutes, until golden brown. Remove from the oven and set aside to cool.

3. In a large skillet over medium-high heat, heat the remaining 1 tablespoon of olive oil.

4. Add the onion and sauté for 3 to 5 minutes, until softened.

5. By handfuls, add the spinach, stirring between each addition, until it just starts to wilt before adding more. Cook for about 1 minute, until it cooks down.

6. In a medium bowl, whisk the eggs and milk. Add the gruyere, and season with the remaining 1/2 teaspoon of salt and some pepper. Fold the eggs into the spinach. Pour the mixture into the pie dish and bake for 25 minutes, until the eggs are set.

7. Let rest for 10 minutes before serving.

Nutrition: calories: 445; total fat: 14g; saturated fat: 4g; protein: 19g; carbs: 68g; sugar: 6g; fiber: 7g; cholesterol: 193mg; sodium: 773mg

602. Spicy Jalapeno Popper Deviled Eggs

Preparation Time: 5 minutes
Cooking Time: 5 minutes
Servings: 4
Ingredients

- 4 large whole eggs, hardboiled
- 2 tablespoons Keto-Friendly mayonnaise
- ¼ cup cheddar cheese, grated
- 2 slices bacon, cooked and crumbled
- 1 jalapeno, sliced

Directions:
1. Cut eggs in half, remove the yolk and put them in bowl
2. Lay egg whites on a platter
3. Mix in remaining ingredients and mash them with the egg yolks
4. Transfer yolk mix back to the egg whites
5. Serve and enjoy!

Nutrition:
Calories: 176
Fat: 14g
Carbohydrates: 0.7g
Protein: 10g

603. Lovely Porridge

Preparation Time: 15 minutes
Cooking Time: Nil
Servings: 2
Ingredients

- 2 tablespoons coconut flour
- 2 tablespoons vanilla protein powder
- 3 tablespoons Golden Flaxseed meal
- 1 and 1/2 cups almond milk, unsweetened
- Powdered erythritol

Directions:
1. Take a bowl and mix in flaxseed meal, protein powder, coconut flour and mix well
2. Add mix to the saucepan (placed over medium heat)
3. Add almond milk and stir, let the mixture thicken
4. Add your desired amount of sweetener and serve
5. Enjoy!

Nutrition:
Calories: 259
Fat: 13g
Carbohydrates: 5g
Protein: 16g

604. Salty Macadamia Chocolate Smoothie

Preparation Time: 5 minutes
Cooking Time: Nil
Servings: 1
Ingredients

- 2 tablespoons macadamia nuts, salted
- 1/3 cup chocolate whey protein powder, low carb
- 1 cup almond milk, unsweetened

Directions:
1. Add the listed ingredients to your blender and blend until you have a smooth mixture
2. Chill and enjoy it!

Nutrition:
Calories: 165
Fat: 2g
Carbohydrates: 1g
Protein: 12g

605. Basil and Tomato Baked Eggs

Preparation Time: 10 minutes
Cooking Time: 15 minutes

Servings: 4

Ingredients

- 1 garlic clove, minced
- 1 cup canned tomatoes
- ¼ cup fresh basil leaves, roughly chopped
- 1/2 teaspoon chili powder
- 1 tablespoon olive oil
- 4 whole eggs
- Salt and pepper to taste

Directions:

1. Preheat your oven to 375 degrees F
2. Take a small baking dish and grease with olive oil
3. Add garlic, basil, tomatoes chili, olive oil into a dish and stir
4. Crackdown eggs into a dish, keeping space between the two
5. Sprinkle the whole dish with salt and pepper
6. Place in oven and cook for 12 minutes until eggs are set and tomatoes are bubbling
7. Serve with basil on top
8. Enjoy!

Nutrition:

Calories: 235

Fat: 16g

Carbohydrates: 7g

Protein: 14g

606. Cinnamon and Coconut Porridge

Preparation Time: 5 minutes

Cooking Time: 5 minutes

Servings: 4

Ingredients

- 2 cups of water
- 1 cup 36% heavy cream
- 1/2 cup unsweetened dried coconut, shredded
- 2 tablespoons flaxseed meal
- 1 tablespoon butter
- 1 and 1/2 teaspoon stevia
- 1 teaspoon cinnamon
- Salt to taste
- Toppings as blueberries

Directions:

1. Add the listed ingredients to a small pot, mix well

2. Transfer pot to stove and place it over medium-low heat
3. Bring to mix to a slow boil
4. Stir well and remove the heat
5. Divide the mix into equal servings and let them sit for 10 minutes
6. Top with your desired toppings and enjoy!

Nutrition:

Calories: 171

Fat: 16g

Carbohydrates: 6g

Protein: 2g

607. An Omelet of Swiss chard

Preparation Time: 5 minutes

Cooking Time: 5 minutes

Servings: 4

Ingredients

- 4 eggs, lightly beaten
- 4 cups Swiss chard, sliced
- 2 tablespoons butter
- 1/2 teaspoon garlic salt
- Fresh pepper

Directions:

1. Take a non-stick frying pan and place it over medium-low heat
2. Once the butter melts, add Swiss chard and stir cook for 2 minutes
3. Pour egg into the pan and gently stir them into Swiss chard
4. Season with garlic salt and pepper
5. Cook for 2 minutes
6. Serve and enjoy!

Nutrition:

Calories: 260

Fat: 21g

Carbohydrates: 4g

Protein: 14g

608. Cheesy Low-Carb Omelet

Preparation Time: 5 minutes

Cooking Time: 5 minutes

Servings: 5

Ingredients

- 2 whole eggs
- 1 tablespoon water

- 1 tablespoon butter
- 3 thin slices salami
- 5 fresh basil leaves
- 5 thin slices, fresh ripe tomatoes
- 2 ounces fresh mozzarella cheese
- Salt and pepper as needed

Directions:

1. Take a small bowl and whisk in eggs and water
2. Take a non-stick Sauté pan and place it over medium heat, add butter and let it melt
3. Pour egg mixture and cook for 30 seconds
4. Spread salami slices on half of egg mix and top with cheese, tomatoes, basil slices
5. Season with salt and pepper according to your taste
6. Cook for 2 minutes and fold the egg with the empty half
7. Cover and cook on LOW for 1 minute
8. Serve and enjoy!

Nutrition:

- Calories: 451
- Fat: 36g
- Carbohydrates: 3g
- Protein:33g

609. Yogurt and Kale Smoothie

Servings: 1

Preparation Time: 10 minutes

Ingredients:

- 1 cup whole milk yogurt
- 1 cup baby kale greens
- 1 pack stevia
- 1 tablespoon MCT oil
- 1 tablespoon sunflower seeds
- 1 cup of water

Directions:

1. Add listed ingredients to the blender
2. Blend until you have a smooth and creamy texture
3. Serve chilled and enjoy!

Nutrition:

Calories: 329

Fat: 26g

Carbohydrates: 15g

Protein: 11g

610. Bacon and Chicken Garlic Wrap

Preparation Time: 15 minutes

Cooking Time: 10 minutes

Servings: 4

Ingredients

- 1 chicken fillet, cut into small cubes
- 8-9 thin slices bacon, cut to fit cubes
- 6 garlic cloves, minced

Directions:

1. Preheat your oven to 400 degrees F
2. Line a baking tray with aluminum foil
3. Add minced garlic to a bowl and rub each chicken piece with it
4. Wrap bacon piece around each garlic chicken bite
5. Secure with toothpick
6. Transfer bites to the baking sheet, keeping a little bit of space between them
7. Bake for about 15-20 minutes until crispy
8. Serve and enjoy!

Nutrition:

- Calories: 260
- Fat: 19g
- Carbohydrates: 5g
- Protein: 22g

611. Grilled Chicken Platter

Preparation Time: 5 minutes

Cooking Time: 10 minutes

Servings: 6

Ingredients

- 3 large chicken breasts, sliced half lengthwise
- 10-ounce spinach, frozen and drained
- 3-ounce mozzarella cheese, part-skim
- 1/2 a cup of roasted red peppers, cut in long strips
- 1 teaspoon of olive oil
- 2 garlic cloves, minced
- Salt and pepper as needed

Directions:

1. Preheat your oven to 400 degrees Fahrenheit
2. Slice 3 chicken breast lengthwise
3. Take a non-stick pan and grease with cooking spray
4. Bake for 2-3 minutes each side

5. Take another skillet and cook spinach and garlic in oil for 3 minutes

6. Place chicken on an oven pan and top with spinach, roasted peppers, and mozzarella

7. Bake until the cheese melted

8. Enjoy!

Nutrition:

Calories: 195

Fat: 7g

Net Carbohydrates: 3g

Protein: 30g

612. Parsley Chicken Breast

Preparation Time: 10 minutes

Cooking Time: 40 minutes

Servings: 4

Ingredients

- 1 tablespoon dry parsley
- 1 tablespoon dry basil
- 4 chicken breast halves, boneless and skinless
- 1/2 teaspoon salt
- 1/2 teaspoon red pepper flakes, crushed
- 2 tomatoes, sliced

Directions:

1. Preheat your oven to 350 degrees F

2. Take a 9x13 inch baking dish and grease it up with cooking spray

3. Sprinkle 1 tablespoon of parsley, 1 teaspoon of basil and spread the mixture over your baking dish

4. Arrange the chicken breast halves over the dish and sprinkle garlic slices on top

5. Take a small bowl and add 1 teaspoon parsley, 1 teaspoon of basil, salt, basil, red pepper and mix well. Pour the mixture over the chicken breast

6. Top with tomato slices and cover, bake for 25 minutes

7. Remove the cover and bake for 15 minutes more

8. Serve and enjoy!

Nutrition:

Calories: 150

Fat: 4g

Carbohydrates: 4g

Protein: 25g

613. Mustard Chicken

Preparation Time: 10 minutes

Cooking Time: 40 minutes

Servings: 4

Ingredients

- 4 chicken breasts
- 1/2 cup chicken broth
- 3-4 tablespoons mustard
- 3 tablespoons olive oil
- 1 teaspoon paprika
- 1 teaspoon chili powder
- 1 teaspoon garlic powder

Directions:

1. Take a small bowl and mix mustard, olive oil, paprika, chicken broth, garlic powder, chicken broth, and chili

2. Add chicken breast and marinate for 30 minutes

3. Take a lined baking sheet and arrange the chicken

4. Bake for 35 minutes at 375 degrees Fahrenheit

5. Serve and enjoy!

Nutrition:

Calories: 531

Fat: 23g

Carbohydrates: 10g

Protein: 64g

614. Balsamic Chicken

Preparation Time: 10 minutes

Cooking Time: 25 minutes

Servings: 6

Ingredients

- 6 chicken breast halves, skinless and boneless
- 1 teaspoon garlic salt
- Ground black pepper
- 2 tablespoons olive oil
- 1 onion, thinly sliced
- 14- and 1/2-ounces tomatoes, diced
- 1/2 cup balsamic vinegar
- 1 teaspoon dried basil
- 1 teaspoon dried oregano
- 1 teaspoon dried rosemary
- 1/2 teaspoon dried thyme

Directions:

1. Season both sides of your chicken breasts thoroughly with pepper and garlic salt

2. Take a skillet and place it over medium heat

3. Add some oil and cook your seasoned chicken for 3-4 minutes per side until the breasts are nicely browned

4. Add some onion and cook for another 3-4 minutes until the onions are browned

5. Pour the diced-up tomatoes and balsamic vinegar over your chicken and season with some rosemary, basil, thyme, and rosemary

6. Simmer the chicken for about 15 minutes until they are no longer pink

7. Take an instant-read thermometer and check if the internal temperature gives a reading of 165 degrees Fahrenheit

8. If yes, then you are good to go!

Nutrition:

Calories: 196

Fat: 7g

Carbohydrates: 7g

Protein: 23g

615. Greek Chicken Breast

Preparation Time: 10 minutes

Cooking Time: 25 minutes

Servings: 4

Ingredients

- 4 chicken breast halves, skinless and boneless
- 1 cup extra virgin olive oil
- 1 lemon, juiced
- 2 teaspoons garlic, crushed
- 1 and 1/2 teaspoons black pepper
- 1/3 teaspoon paprika

Directions:

1. Cut 3 slits in the chicken breast

2. Take a small bowl and whisk in olive oil, salt, lemon juice, garlic, paprika, pepper and whisk for 30 seconds

3. Place chicken in a large bowl and pour marinade

4. Rub the marinade all over using your hand

5. Refrigerate overnight

6. Pre-heat grill to medium heat and oil the grate

7. Cook chicken in the grill until center is no longer pink

8. Serve and enjoy!

Nutrition:

Calories: 644

Fat: 57g

Carbohydrates: 2g

Protein: 27g

616. Chipotle Lettuce Chicken

Preparation Time: 10 minutes

Cooking Time: 25 minutes

Servings: 6

Ingredients

- 1 pound chicken breast, cut into strips
- Splash of olive oil
- 1 red onion, finely sliced
- 14 ounces tomatoes
- 1 teaspoon chipotle, chopped
- 1/2 teaspoon cumin
- Pinch of sugar
- Lettuce as needed
- Fresh coriander leaves
- Jalapeno chilies, sliced
- Fresh tomato slices for garnish
- Lime wedges

Directions:

1. Take a non-stick frying pan and place it over medium heat

2. Add oil and heat it up

3. Add chicken and cook until brown

4. Keep the chicken on the side

5. Add tomatoes, sugar, chipotle, cumin to the same pan and simmer for 25 minutes until you have a nice sauce

6. Add chicken into the sauce and cook for 5 minutes

7. Transfer the mix to another place

8. Use lettuce wraps to take a portion of the mixture and serve with a squeeze of lemon

9. Enjoy!

Nutrition:

Calories: 332

Fat: 15g

Carbohydrates: 13g

Protein: 34g

617. Stylish Chicken-Bacon Wrap

Preparation Time: 5 minutes

Cooking Time: 50 minutes

Servings: 3

Ingredients

- 8 ounces lean chicken breast

- 6 bacon slices
- 3 ounces shredded cheese
- 4 slices ham
-

Directions:
1. Cut chicken breast into bite-sized portions
2. Transfer shredded cheese onto ham slices
3. Roll up chicken breast and ham slices in bacon slices
4. Take a skillet and place it over medium heat
5. Add olive oil and brown bacon for a while
6. Remove rolls and transfer to your oven
7. Bake for 45 minutes at 325 degrees F
8. Serve and enjoy!

Nutrition:
Calories: 275
Fat: 11g
Carbohydrates: 0.5g
Protein: 40g

618. Healthy Cottage Cheese Pancakes

Preparation Time: 10 minutes
Cooking Time: 15
Servings: 1
Ingredients:

- 1/2 cup of Cottage cheese (low-fat)
- 1/3 cup (approx. 2 egg whites) Egg whites
- ¼ cup of Oats
- 1 teaspoon of Vanilla extract
- Olive oil cooking spray
- 1 tablespoon of Stevia (raw)
- Berries or sugar-free jam (optional)

Directions:
1. Begin by taking a food blender and adding in the egg whites and cottage cheese. Also add in the vanilla extract, a pinch of stevia, and oats. Palpitate until the consistency is well smooth.
2. Get a nonstick pan and oil it nicely with the cooking spray. Position the pan on low heat.
3. After it has been heated, scoop out half of the batter and pour it on the pan. Cook for about 2 1/2 minutes on each side.

4. Position the cooked pancakes on a serving plate and cover with sugar-free jam or berries.
Nutrition: Calories: 205 calories per serving Fat – 1.5 g, Protein – 24.5 g, Carbohydrates – 19 g

619. Avocado Lemon Toast

Preparation Time: 10 minutes
Cooking Time: 13 minutes
Servings: 2
Ingredients:

- Whole-grain bread – 2 slices
- Fresh cilantro (chopped) – 2 tablespoons
- Lemon zest – ¼ teaspoon
- Fine sea salt – 1 pinch

Directions:
1. Begin by getting a medium-sized mixing bowl and adding in the avocado. Make use of a fork to crush it properly.
2. Then, add in the cilantro, lemon zest, lemon juice, sea salt, and cayenne pepper. Mix well until combined.
3. Toast the bread slices in a toaster until golden brown. It should take about 3 minutes.
4. Top the toasted bread slices with the avocado mixture and finalize by drizzling with chia seeds.
Nutrition:
Calories: 72 calories per serving
Protein – 3.6 g
Avocado – 1/2
Fresh lemon juice – 1 teaspoon
Cayenne pepper – 1 pinch
Chia seeds – ¼ teaspoon
Fat – 1.2 g
Carbohydrates – 11.6 g

620. Healthy Baked Eggs

Preparation Time: 10 minutes
Cooking Time: 1 hour
Servings: 6
Ingredients:

- Olive oil – 1 tablespoon
- Garlic – 2 cloves
- Eggs – 8 larges
- Sea salt – 1/2 teaspoon
- Shredded mozzarella cheese (medium-fat) – 3 cups
- Olive oil spray
- Onion (chopped) – 1 medium

- Spinach leaves – 8 ounces
- Half-and-half – 1 cup
- Black pepper – 1 teaspoon
- Feta cheese – 1/2 cup

Directions:

1. Begin by heating the oven to 375F.
2. Get a glass baking dish and grease it with olive oil spray. Arrange aside.
3. Now take a nonstick pan and pour in the olive oil. Position the pan on allows heat and allows it heat.
4. Immediately you are done, toss in the garlic, spinach, and onion. Prepare for about 5 minutes. Arrange aside.
5. You can now Get a large mixing bowl and add in the half, eggs, pepper, and salt. Whisk thoroughly to combine.
6. Put in the feta cheese and chopped mozzarella cheese (reserve 1/2 cup of mozzarella cheese for later).
7. Put the egg mixture and prepared spinach to the prepared glass baking dish. Blend well to combine. Drizzle the reserved cheese over the top.
8. Bake the egg mix for about 45 minutes.
9. Extract the baking dish from the oven and allow it to stand for 10 minutes.
10. Dice and serve!

Nutrition:

Calories: 323 calories per serving

Fat – 22.3 g

Protein – 22.6 g

Carbohydrates – 7.9 g

621. Quick Low-Carb Oatmeal

Preparation Time: 10 minutes

Cooking Time: 15 minutes

Servings: 2

Ingredients:

- Almond flour – 1/2 cup
- Flax meal – 2 tablespoons
- Cinnamon (ground) – 1 teaspoon
- Almond milk (unsweetened) – 11/2 cups
- Salt – as per taste
- Chia seeds – 2 tablespoons
- Liquid stevia – 10 – 15 drops
- Vanilla extract – 1 teaspoon

Directions:

1. Begin by taking a large mixing bowl and adding in the coconut flour, almond flour, ground cinnamon, flax seed powder, and chia seeds. Mix properly to combine.
2. Position a stockpot on a low heat and add in the dry ingredients. Also add in the liquid stevia, vanilla extract, and almond milk. Mix well to combine.
3. Prepare the flour and almond milk for about 4 minutes. Add salt if needed.
4. Move the oatmeal to a serving bowl and top with nuts, seeds, and pure and neat berries.

Nutrition:

Calories: calories per serving

Protein – 11.7 g

Fat – 24.3 g

Carbohydrates – 16.7 g

622. Tofu and Vegetable Scramble

Preparation Time: 10 minutes

Cooking Time: 15 minutes

Servings: 2

Ingredients:

- Firm tofu (drained) – 16 ounces
- Sea salt – 1/2 teaspoon
- Garlic powder – 1 teaspoon
- Fresh coriander – for garnishing
- Red onion – 1/2 medium
- Cumin powder – 1 teaspoon
- Lemon juice – for topping
- Green bell pepper – 1 medium
- Garlic powder – 1 teaspoon
- Fresh coriander – for garnishing
- Red onion – 1/2 medium
- Cumin powder – 1 teaspoon
- Lemon juice – for topping

Directions:

1. Begin by preparing the ingredients. For this, you are to extract the seeds of the tomato and green bell pepper. Shred the onion, bell pepper, and tomato into small cubes.
2. Get a small mixing bowl and position the fairly hard tofu inside it. Make use of your hands to break the fairly hard tofu. Arrange aside.
3. Get a nonstick pan and add in the onion, tomato, and bell pepper. Mix and cook for about 3 minutes.

4.   Put the somewhat hard crumbled tofu to the pan and combine well.

5.   Get a small bowl and put in the water, turmeric, garlic powder, cumin powder, and chili powder. Combine well and stream it over the tofu and vegetable mixture.

6.   Allow the tofu and vegetable crumble cook with seasoning for 5 minutes. Continuously stir so that the pan is not holding the ingredients.

7.   Drizzle the tofu scramble with chili flakes and salt. Combine well.

8.   Transfer the prepared scramble to a serving bowl and give it a proper spray of lemon juice.

9.   Finalize by garnishing with pure and neat coriander. Serve while hot!

Nutritional Information:

Calories: 238 calories per serving

Carbohydrates – 16.6 g

Fat – 11 g

623. Breakfast Smoothie Bowl with Fresh Berries

Preparation Time: 10 minutes

Cooking Time: 5 minutes

Servings: 2

Ingredients:

* Almond milk (unsweetened) – 1/2 cup
* Psyllium husk powder – 1/2 teaspoon
* Strawberries (chopped) – 2 ounces
* Coconut oil – 1 tablespoon
* Crushed ice – 3 cups
* Liquid stevia – 5 to 10 drops
* Pea protein powder – 1/3 cup

Directions:

1.   Begin by taking a blender and adding in the mashed ice cubes. Allow them to rest for about 30 seconds.

2.   Then put in the almond milk, shredded strawberries, pea protein powder, psyllium husk powder, coconut oil, and liquid stevia. Blend well until it turns into a smooth and creamy puree.

3.   Vacant the prepared smoothie into 2 glasses.

4.   Cover with coconut flakes and pure and neat strawberries.

Nutrition:

Calories: 166 calories per serving

Fat – 9.2 g

Carbohydrates – 4.1 g

Protein – 17.6 g

624. Chia and Coconut Pudding

Preparation Time: 10 minutes

Cooking Time: 5 minutes

Servings: 2

Ingredients:

* Light coconut milk – 7 ounces
* Liquid stevia – 3 to 4 drops
* Kiwi – 1
* Chia seeds – ¼ cup
* Clementine – 1
* Shredded coconut (unsweetened)

Directions:

1.   Begin by getting a mixing bowl and putting in the light coconut milk. Set in the liquid stevia to sweeten the milk. Combine well.

2.   Put the chia seeds to the milk and whisk until well-combined. Arrange aside.

3.   Scrape the clementine and carefully extract the skin from the wedges. Leave aside.

4.   Also, scrape the kiwi and dice it into small pieces.

5.   Get a glass vessel and gather the pudding. For this, position the fruits at the bottom of the jar; then put a dollop of chia pudding. Then spray the fruits and then put another layer of chia pudding.

6.   Finalize by garnishing with the rest of the fruits and chopped coconut.

Nutrition:

Calories: 201 calories per serving

Protein – 5.4 g

Fat – 10 g

Carbohydrates – 22.8 g

625. Tomato and Zucchini Sauté

Preparation Time: 10 minutes

Cooking Time: 43 minutes

Servings: 6

Ingredients:

* Vegetable oil – 1 tablespoon
* Tomatoes (chopped) – 2
* Green bell pepper (chopped) – 1
* Black pepper (freshly ground) – as per taste
* Onion (sliced) – 1

- Zucchini (peeled) – 2 pounds and cut into 1-inch-thick slices
- Salt – as per taste
- Uncooked white rice – ¼ cup

Directions:

1. Begin by getting a nonstick pan and putting it over low heat. Stream in the oil and allow it to heat through.
2. Put in the onions and sauté for about 3 minutes.
3. Then pour in the zucchini and green peppers. Mix well and spice with black pepper and salt.
4. Reduce the heat and cover the pan with a lid. Allow the veggies cook on low for 5 minutes.
5. While you're done, put in the water and rice. Place the lid back on and cook on low for 20 minutes.

Nutrition:

Calories: 94 calories per serving

Fat – 2.8 g

Protein – 3.2 g

Carbohydrates – 16.1 g

626. Steamed Kale with Mediterranean Dressing

Preparation Time: 10 minutes

Cooking Time: 25 minutes

Servings: 6

Ingredients:

- Kale (chopped) – 12 cups
- Olive oil – 1 tablespoon
- Soy sauce – 1 teaspoon
- Pepper (freshly ground) – as per taste
- Lemon juice – 2 tablespoons
- Garlic (minced) – 1 tablespoon
- Salt – as per taste

Directions:

1. Get a gas steamer or an electric steamer and fill the bottom pan with water. If making use of a gas steamer, position it on high heat. Making use of an electric steamer, place it on the highest setting.
2. Immediately the water comes to a boil, put in the shredded kale and cover with a lid. Boil for about 8 minutes. The kale should be tender by now.
3. During the kale is boiling, take a big mixing bowl and put in the olive oil, lemon juice, soy sauce, garlic, pepper, and salt. Whisk well to mix.

4. Now toss in the steamed kale and carefully enclose into the dressing. Be assured the kale is well-coated.
5. Serve while it's hot!

Nutrition:

Calories: 91 calories per serving

Fat – 3.5 g

Protein – 4.6 g

Carbohydrates – 14.5 g

627. Healthy Carrot Muffins

Preparation Time: 10 minutes

Cooking Time: 40 minutes

Servings: 8

Ingredients:

Dry ingredients

- Tapioca starch – ¼ cup
- Baking soda – 1 teaspoon
- Cinnamon – 1 tablespoon
- Cloves – ¼ teaspoon
- Wet ingredients
- Vanilla extract – 1 teaspoon
- Water – 11/2 cups
- Carrots (shredded) – 11/2 cups
- Almond flour – 1¾ cups
- Granulated sweetener of choice – 1/2 cup
- Baking powder – 1 teaspoon
- Nutmeg – 1 teaspoon
- Salt – 1 teaspoon
- Coconut oil – 1/3 cup
- Flax meal – 4 tablespoons
- Banana (mashed) – 1 medium

Directions:

1. Begin by heating the oven to 350F.
2. Get a muffin tray and position paper cups in all the molds. Arrange aside.
3. Get a small glass bowl and put half a cup of water and flax meal. Allow this rest for about 5 minutes. Your flax egg is prepared.
4. Get a large mixing bowl and put in the almond flour, tapioca starch, granulated sugar, baking soda, baking powder, cinnamon, nutmeg, cloves, and salt. Mix well to combine.
5. Conform a well in the middle of the flour mixture and stream in the coconut oil, vanilla extract, and flax egg. Mix well to conform a mushy dough.

Then put in the chopped carrots and mashed banana. Mix until well-combined.

6.   Make use of a spoon to scoop out an equal amount of mixture into 8 muffin cups.

7.   Position the muffin tray in the oven and allow it to bake for about 40 minutes.

8.   Extract the tray from the microwave and allow the muffins to stand for about 10 minutes.

9.   Extract the muffin cups from the tray and allow them to chill until they reach room degree of hotness and coldness.

10.   Serve and enjoy!

Nutrition:

Calories: 189 calories per serving

Fat – 13.9 g

Protein – 3.8 g

Carbohydrates – 17.3 g

628.   Vegetable Noodles Stir-Fry

Preparation Time: 10 minutes

Cooking Time: 40 minutes

Servings: 4

Ingredients:

- White sweet potato – 1 pound
- Zucchini – 8 ounces
- Garlic cloves (finely chopped) – 2 large
- Vegetable broth – 2 tablespoons
- Salt – as per taste
- Carrots – 8 ounces
- Shallot (finely chopped) – 1
- Red chili (finely chopped) – 1
- Olive oil – 1 tablespoon
- Pepper – as per taste

Directions:

1.   Begin by scrapping the carrots and sweet potato. Make Use a spiralizer to make noodles out of the sweet potato and carrots.

2.   Rinse the zucchini thoroughly and spiralize it as well.

3.   Get a large skillet and position it on a high flame. Stream in the vegetable broth and allow it to come to a boil.

4.   Toss in the spiralized sweet potato and carrots. Then put in the chili, garlic, and shallots. Stir everything using tongs and cook for some minutes.

5.   Transfer the vegetable noodles into a serving platter and generously spice with pepper and salt.

6.   Finalize by sprinkling olive oil over the noodles. Serve while hot!

Nutrition:

Calories: 169 calories per serving

Fat – 3.7 g

Protein – 3.6 g

Carbohydrates – 31.2 g

629.   Cauliflower Mac & Cheese

Preparation Time: 5 Minutes

Cooking Time: 25 Minutes

Effort: Easy

Serving Size: 4

Ingredients:

- 1 Cauliflower Head, torn into florets
- Salt & Black Pepper, as needed
- ¼ cup Almond Milk, unsweetened
- ¼ cup Heavy Cream
- 3 tbsp. Butter, preferably grass-fed
- 1 cup Cheddar Cheese, shredded

Directions:

1.   Preheat the oven to 450 F.

2.   Melt the butter in a small microwave-safe bowl and heat it for 30 seconds.

3.   Pour the melted butter over the cauliflower florets along with salt and pepper. Toss them well.

4.   Place the cauliflower florets in a parchment paper-covered large baking sheet.

5.   Bake them for 15 minutes or until the cauliflower is crisp-tender.

6.   Once baked, mix the heavy cream, cheddar cheese, almond milk, and the remaining butter in a large microwave-safe bowl and heat it on high heat for 2 minutes or until the

cheese mixture is smooth. Repeat the procedure until the cheese has melted.

7.　　Finally, stir in the cauliflower to the sauce mixture and coat well.

Nutrition:

Calories: 294Kcal

Fat: 23g

Carbohydrates: 7g

Proteins: 11g

630.　Easy Egg Salad

Preparation Time: 5 Minutes

Cooking Time: 15 to 20 Minutes

Effort: Easy

Servings: 4

Ingredients:

- 6 Eggs, preferably free-range
- ¼ tsp. Salt
- 2 tbsp. Mayonnaise
- 1 tsp. Lemon juice
- 1 tsp. Dijon mustard
- Pepper, to taste
- Lettuce leaves, to serve

Directions:

1.　　Keep the eggs in a saucepan of water and pour cold water until it covers the egg by another 1 inch.

2.　　Bring to a boil and then remove the eggs from heat.

3.　　Peel the eggs under cold running water.

4.　　Transfer the cooked eggs into a food processor and pulse them until chopped.

5.　　Stir in the mayonnaise, lemon juice, salt, Dijon mustard, and pepper and mix them well.

6.　　Taste for seasoning and add more if required.

7.　　Serve in the lettuce leaves.

Nutrition:

Calories – 166kcal

Fat – 14g

Carbohydrates - 0.85g

Proteins – 10g

Sodium: 132mg

631.　Baked Chicken Legs

Preparation Time: 10 Minutes

Cooking Time: 40 Minutes

Effort: Easy

Servings: 6

Ingredients:

- 6 Chicken Legs
- ¼ tsp. Black Pepper
- ¼ cup Butter
- 1/2 tsp. Sea Salt
- 1/2 tsp. Smoked Paprika
- 1/2 tsp. Garlic Powder

Directions:

1.　　Preheat the oven to 425 F.

2.　　Pat the chicken legs with a paper towel to absorb any excess moisture.

3.　　Marinate the chicken pieces by first applying the butter over them and then with the seasoning. Set it aside for a few minutes.

4.　　Bake them for 25 minutes. Turnover and bake for further 10 minutes or until the internal temperature reaches 165 F.

5.　　Serve them hot.

Nutrition:

Calories – 236kL

Fat – 16g

Carbohydrates – 0g

Protein – 22g

Sodium – 314mg

632. Creamed Spinach

Preparation Time: 5 Minutes
Cooking Time: 10 Minutes
Effort: Easy
Servings: 4
Ingredients:

- 3 tbsp. Butter
- ¼ tsp. Black Pepper
- 4 cloves of Garlic, minced
- ¼ tsp. Sea Salt
- 10 oz. Baby Spinach, chopped
- 1 tsp. Italian Seasoning
- 1/2 cup Heavy Cream
- 3 oz. Cream Cheese

Directions:

1.   Melt butter in a large sauté pan over medium heat.
2.   Once the butter has melted, spoon in the garlic and sauté for 30 seconds or until aromatic.
3.   Spoon in the spinach and cook for 3 to 4 minutes or until wilted.
4.   Add all the remaining ingredients to it and continuously stir until the cream cheese melts and the mixture gets thickened.

5.   Serve hot
Nutrition:
Calories – 274kL
Fat – 27g
Carbohydrates – 4g
Protein – 4g
Sodium – 114mg

633. Stuffed Mushrooms

Preparation Time: 10 Minutes
Cooking Time: 20 Minutes
Servings: 4
Ingredients:

- 4 Portobello Mushrooms, large
- 1/2 cup Mozzarella Cheese, shredded
- 1/2 cup Marinara, low-sugar
- Olive Oil Spray

Directions:

1.   Preheat the oven to 375 F.
2.   Take out the dark gills from the mushrooms with the help of a spoon.
3.   Keep the mushroom stem upside down and spoon it with two tablespoons of marinara sauce and mozzarella cheese.
4.   Bake for 18 minutes or until the cheese is bubbly.
Nutrition:
Calories – 113kL
Fat – 6g
Carbohydrates – 4g
Protein – 7g
Sodium – 14mg

634. Berry-Oat Breakfast Bars

Preparation time: 10 minutes
Cooking time: 25 minutes
Servings: 12
Ingredients:

- 2 cups fresh raspberries or blueberries
- 2 tablespoons sugar
- 2 tablespoons freshly squeezed lemon juice
- 1 tablespoon cornstarch
- 11/2 cups rolled oats
- 1/2 cup whole-wheat flour
- 1/2 cup walnuts
- ¼ cup chia seeds

- ¼ cup extra-virgin olive oil
- ¼ cup honey
- 1 large egg

Directions:

1. Preheat the oven to 350f.
2. In a small saucepan over medium heat, stir together the berries, sugar, lemon juice, and cornstarch. Bring to a simmer. Reduce the heat and simmer for 2 to 3 minutes, until the mixture thickens.
3. In a food processor or high-speed blender, combine the oats, flour, walnuts, and chia seeds. Process until powdered. Add the olive oil, honey, and egg. Pulse a few more times, until well combined. Press half of the mixture into a 9-inch square baking dish.
4. Spread the berry filling over the oat mixture. Add the remaining oat mixture on top of the berries. Bake for 25 minutes, until browned.
5. Let cool completely, cut into 12 pieces, and serve. Store in a covered container for up to 5 days.

Nutrition: calories: 201; total fat: 10g; saturated fat: 1g; protein: 5g; carbs: 26g; sugar: 9g; fiber: 5g; cholesterol: 16mg; sodium: 8mg

30 minutes or less • nut free • vegetarian

635. Whole-Grain Breakfast Cookies

Preparation time: 20 minutes
Cooking time: 10 minutes
Servings: 18 cookies
Ingredients:

- 2 cups rolled oats
- 1/2 cup whole-wheat flour
- ¼ cup ground flaxseed
- 1 teaspoon baking powder
- 1 cup unsweetened applesauce
- 2 large eggs
- 2 tablespoons vegetable oil
- 2 teaspoons vanilla extract
- 1 teaspoon ground cinnamon
- 1/2 cup dried cherries
- ¼ cup unsweetened shredded coconut
- 2 ounces dark chocolate, chopped

Directions:

1. Preheat the oven to 350f.
2. In a large bowl, combine the oats, flour, flaxseed, and baking powder. Stir well to mix.
3. In a medium bowl, whisk the applesauce, eggs, vegetable oil, vanilla, and cinnamon. Pour the wet mixture into the dry mixture, and stir until just combined.
4. Fold in the cherries, coconut, and chocolate. Drop tablespoon-size balls of dough onto a baking sheet. Bake for 10 to 12 minutes, until browned and cooked through.
5. Let cool for about 3 minutes, remove from the baking sheet, and cool completely before serving. Store in an airtight container for up to 1 week.

Nutrition: calories: 136; total fat: 7g; saturated fat: 3g; protein: 4g; carbs: 14g; sugar: 4g; fiber: 3g; cholesterol: 21mg; sodium: 11mg

Appetizer Recipes

636. Cheesy Broccoli Bites

Preparation Time: 10 minutes
Cooking Time: 25 minutes
Serving: 6
Ingredient:

- 2 tablespoons olive oil
- 2 heads broccoli, trimmed
- 1 egg
- 1/3 cup reduced-fat shredded Cheddar cheese
- 1 egg white
- ½ cup onion, chopped
- 1/3 cup bread crumbs
- ¼ teaspoon salt
- ¼ teaspoon black pepper

Direction:
1.   Ready the oven at 400°F (205°C). Coat a large baking sheet with olive oil.
2.   Arrange a colander in a saucepan, then place the broccoli in the colander. Pour the water into the saucepan to cover the bottom. Boil, then reduce the heat to low. Close and simmer for 6 minutes. Allow cooling for 10 minutes.
3.   Blend broccoli and remaining ingredients in a food processor. Let sit for 10 minutes.
4.   Make the bites: Drop 1 tablespoon of the mixture on the baking sheet. Repeat with the remaining mixture.
5.   Bake in the preheated oven for 25 minutes. Flip the bites halfway through the cooking time.
6.   Serve immediately.

Nutrition:
100 calories
13g carbohydrates
3g fiber

637. Easy Caprese Skewers

Preparation Time: 5 minutes
Cooking Time: 0 minute
Serving: 2
Ingredient:

- 12 cherry tomatoes
- 8 (1-inch) pieces Mozzarella cheese
- 12 basil leaves
- ¼ cup Italian Vinaigrette, for serving

Direction

1.   Thread the tomatoes, cheese, and bay leave alternatively through the skewers.
2.   Place the skewers on a huge plate and baste with the Italian Vinaigrette. Serve immediately.

Nutrition:
230 calories
8.5g carbohydrates
1.9g fiber

638. Grilled Tofu with Sesame Seeds

Preparation Time: 45 minutes
Cooking Time: 20 minutes
Serving: 6
Ingredient:

- 1½ tablespoons brown rice vinegar
- 1 scallion
- 1 tablespoon ginger root
- 1 tablespoon no-sugar-added applesauce
- 2 tablespoons naturally brewed soy sauce
- ¼ teaspoon dried red pepper flakes
- 2 teaspoons sesame oil, toasted
- 1 (14-ounce / 397-g) package extra-firm tofu
- 2 tablespoons fresh cilantro
- 1 teaspoon sesame seeds

Direction
1.   Combine the vinegar, scallion, ginger, applesauce, soy sauce, red pepper flakes, and sesame oil in a large bowl. Stir to mix well.
2.   Dunk the tofu pieces in the bowl, then refrigerate to marinate for 30 minutes.
3.   Preheat a grill pan over medium-high heat.
4.   Place the tofu on the grill pan with tongs, reserve the marinade, then grill for 8 minutes or until the tofu is golden brown and have deep grilled marks on both sides. Flip the tofu halfway through the cooking time. You may need to work in batches to avoid overcrowding.
5.   Transfer the tofu to a large plate and sprinkle with cilantro leaves and sesame seeds. Serve with the marinade alongside.

Nutrition:
90 calories
3g carbohydrates

1g fiber

639. Kale Chips

Preparation Time: 5 minutes
Cooking Time: 15 minutes
Serving: 1
Ingredients:

- ¼ teaspoon garlic powder
- Pinch cayenne to taste
- 1 tablespoon extra-virgin olive oil
- ½ teaspoon sea salt, or to taste
- 1 (8-ounce) bunch kale

Direction

1. Prepare oven at 180°C. Line two baking sheets with parchment paper.
2. Toss the garlic powder, cayenne pepper, olive oil, and salt in a large bowl, then dunk the kale in the bowl.
3. Situate kale in a single layer on one of the baking sheets.
4. Arrange the sheet in the preheated oven and bake for 7 minutes. Remove the sheet from the oven and pour the kale into the single layer of the other baking sheet.
5. Move the sheet of kale back to the oven and bake for another 7 minutes.
6. Serve immediately.

Nutrition
136 calories
3g carbohydrates
1.1g fiber

640. Simple Deviled Eggs

Preparation Time: 5 minutes
Cooking Time: 8 minutes
Serving: 12
Ingredients:

- 6 large eggs
- 1/8 teaspoon mustard powder
- 2 tablespoons light mayonnaise

Direction:

1. Sit the eggs in a saucepan, then pour in enough water to cover the egg. Bring to a boil, then boil the eggs for another 8 minutes. Turn off the heat and cover, then let sit for 15 minutes.
2. Transfer the boiled eggs to a pot of cold water and peel under the water.
3. Transfer the eggs to a large plate, then cut in half. Remove the egg yolks and place them in a bowl, then mash with a fork.
4. Add the mustard powder, mayo, salt, and pepper to the bowl of yolks, then stir to mix well.
5. Spoon the yolk mixture in the egg white on the plate. Serve immediately.

Nutrition:
45 calories
1g carbohydrates
0.9g fiber

641. Sautéed Collard Greens and Cabbage

Preparation Time: 10 minutes
Cooking Time: 10 minutes
Serving: 8
Ingredients:

- 2 tablespoons extra-virgin olive oil
- 1 collard greens bunch
- ½ small green cabbage
- 6 garlic cloves
- 1 tablespoon low-sodium soy sauce

Direction:

1. Cook olive oil in a large skillet over medium-high heat.
2. Sauté the collard greens in the oil for about 2 minutes, or until the greens start to wilt.
3. Toss in the cabbage and mix well. Set to medium-low, cover, and cook for 5 to 7 minutes, stirring occasionally, or until the greens are softened.
4. Fold in the garlic and soy sauce and stir to combine. Cook for about 30 seconds more until fragrant.
5. Remove from the heat to a plate and serve.

Nutrition:
73 calories
5.9g carbohydrates
2.9g fiber

642. Roasted Delicata Squash with Thyme

Preparation Time: 10 minutes
Cooking Time: 20 minutes
Serving: 4
Ingredients:

- 1 (1½-pound) Delicata squash
- 1 tablespoon extra-virgin olive oil
- ½ teaspoon dried thyme
- ¼ teaspoon salt
- ¼ teaspoon freshly ground black pepper

Direction:

1. Prep the oven to 400°F (205°C). Ready baking sheet with parchment paper and set aside.
2. Add the squash strips, olive oil, thyme, salt, and pepper in a large bowl, and toss until the squash strips are fully coated.
3. Place the squash strips on the prepared baking sheet in a single layer. Roast for about 20 minutes, flipping the strips halfway through.
4. Remove from the oven and serve on plates.

Nutrition:

78 calories

11.8g carbohydrates

2.1g fiber

643. Roasted Asparagus and Red Peppers

Preparation Time: 5 minutes

Cooking Time: 15 minutes

Serving: 4

Ingredients:

- 1-pound (454 g) asparagus
- 2 red bell peppers, seeded
- 1 small onion
- 2 tablespoons Italian dressing

Direction:

1. Ready oven to (205°C). Wrap baking sheet with parchment paper and set aside.
2. Combine the asparagus with the peppers, onion, dressing in a large bowl, and toss well.
3. Arrange the vegetables on the baking sheet and roast for about 15 minutes. Flip the vegetables with a spatula once during cooking.
4. Transfer to a large platter and serve.

Nutrition:

92 calories

10.7g carbohydrates

4g fiber

644. Tarragon Spring Peas

Preparation Time: 10 minutes

Cooking Time: 12 minutes

Serving: 6

Ingredients:

1 tablespoon unsalted butter

½ Vidalia onion

1 cup low-sodium vegetable broth

3 cups fresh shelled peas

1 tablespoon minced fresh tarragon

Directions:

1. Cook butter in a pan at medium heat.
2. Sauté the onion in the melted butter for about 3 minutes, stirring occasionally.
3. Pour in the vegetable broth and whisk well. Add the peas and tarragon to the skillet and stir to combine.
4. Reduce the heat to low, cover, cook for about 8 minutes more, or until the peas are tender.
5. Let the peas cool for 5 minutes and serve warm.

Nutrition:

82 calories

12g carbohydrates

3.8g fiber

645. Butter-Orange Yams

Preparation Time: 7 minutes

Cooking Time: 45 minutes

Serving: 8

Ingredients:

- 2 medium jewel yams
- 2 tablespoons unsalted butter
- Juice of 1 large orange
- 1½ teaspoons ground cinnamon
- ¼ teaspoon ground ginger
- ¾ teaspoon ground nutmeg
- 1/8 teaspoon ground cloves

Direction:

1. Set oven at 180°C.
2. Arrange the yam dices on a rimmed baking sheet in a single layer. Set aside.
3. Add the butter, orange juice, cinnamon, ginger, nutmeg, and garlic cloves to a medium saucepan over medium-low heat. Cook for 3 to 5 minutes, stirring continuously.
4. Spoon the sauce over the yams and toss to coat well.
5. Bake in the prepared oven for 40 minutes.

6. Let the yams cool for 8 minutes on the baking sheet before removing and serving.

Nutrition:

129 calories

24.7g carbohydrates

5g fiber

646. Roasted Tomato Brussels Sprouts

Preparation Time: 15 minutes

Cooking Time: 20 minutes

Serving: 4

Ingredients:

- 1-pound (454 g) Brussels sprouts
- 1 tablespoon extra-virgin olive oil
- ½ cup sun-dried tomatoes
- 2 tablespoons lemon juice
- 1 teaspoon lemon zest

Directions:

1. Set oven 205°C. Prep large baking sheet with aluminum foil.

2. Toss the Brussels sprouts in the olive oil in a large bowl until well coated. Sprinkle with salt and pepper.

3. Spread out the seasoned Brussels sprouts on the prepared baking sheet in a single layer.

4. Roast for 20 minutes, shake halfway through.

5. Remove from the oven then situate in a bowl. Whisk tomatoes, lemon juice, and lemon zest, to incorporate. Serve immediately.

Nutrition:

111 calories

13.7g carbohydrates

4.9g fiber

647. Simple Sautéed Greens

Preparation Time: 10 minutes

Cooking Time: 10 minutes

Serving: 4

Ingredients:

- 2 tablespoons extra-virgin olive oil
- 1 pound (454 g) Swiss chard
- 1-pound (454 g) kale
- ½ teaspoon ground cardamom
- 1 tablespoon lemon juice

Direction:

1. Heat up olive oil in a big skillet over medium-high heat.

2. Stir in Swiss chard, kale, cardamom, lemon juice to the skillet, and stir to combine. Cook for about 10 minutes, stirring continuously, or until the greens are wilted.

3. Sprinkle with the salt and pepper and stir well.

4. Serve the greens on a plate while warm.

Nutrition:

139 calories

15.8g carbohydrates

3.9g fiber

648. Garlicky Mushrooms

Preparation Time: 10 minutes

Cooking Time: 12 minutes

Serving: 4

Ingredients:

- 1 tablespoon butter
- 2 teaspoons extra-virgin olive oil
- 2 pounds button mushrooms
- 2 teaspoons minced fresh garlic
- 1 teaspoon chopped fresh thyme

Direction:

1. Warm up butter and olive oil in a huge skillet over medium-high heat.

2. Add the mushrooms and sauté for 10 minutes, stirring occasionally.

3. Stir in the garlic and thyme and cook for an additional 2 minutes.

4. Season and serve on a plate.

Nutrition:

96 calories

8.2g carbohydrates

1.7g fiber

649. Green Beans in Oven

Preparation Time: 5 minutes

Cooking Time: 17 minutes

Serving: 3

Ingredients

- 12 oz. green bean pods
- 1 tbsp. olive oil
- 1/2 tsp. onion powder
- 1/8 tsp. pepper
- 1/8 tsp. salt

Directions

1.   Preheat oven to 350°F. Mix green beans with onion powder, pepper, and oil.
2.   Spread the seeds on the baking sheet.
3.   Bake 17 minutes or until you have a delicious aroma in the kitchen.
Nutrition
37 Calories
1.4g Protein
5.5g Carbohydrates

650.   Parmesan Broiled Flounder

Preparation Time: 10 minutes
Cooking Time: 7 minutes
Serving: 2
Ingredients
- 2 (4-oz) flounder
- 1,5 tbsp Parmesan cheese
- 1,5 tbsp mayonnaise
- 1/8 tsp soy sauce
- 1/4 tsp chili sauce
- 1/8 tsp salt-free lemon-pepper seasoning

Directions
1.   Preheat flounder.
2.   Mix cheese, reduced-fat mayonnaise, soy sauce, chili sauce, seasoning.
3.   Put fish on a baking sheet coated with cooking spray, sprinkle with salt and pepper.
4.   Spread Parmesan mixture over flounder.
5.   Broil 6 to 8 minutes or until a crust appears on the fish.
Nutrition
200 Calories
17g Fat
7g Carbohydrate

651.   Fish with Fresh Tomato - Basil Sauce

Preparation Time: 10 minutes
Cooking Time: 15 minutes
Serving: 2
Ingredients
- 2 (4-oz) tilapia fillets
- 1 tbsp fresh basil, chopped
- 1/8 tsp salt
- 1 pinch of crushed red pepper
- 1 cup cherry tomatoes, chopped
- 2 tsp extra virgin olive oil

Directions
1.   Preheat oven to 400°F.
2.   Arrange rinsed and patted dry fish fillets on foil (coat a foil baking sheet with cooking spray).
3.   Sprinkle tilapia fillets with salt and red pepper.
4.   Bake 12 - 15 minutes.
5.   Meanwhile, mix leftover ingredients in a saucepan.
6.   Cook over medium-high heat until tomatoes are tender.
7.   Top fish fillets properly with tomato mixture.
Nutrition
130 Calories
30g Protein
1g Carbohydrates

652.   Baked Chicken

Preparation Time: 15 minutes
Cooking Time: 25 minutes
Serving: 4
Ingredients
- 2 (6-oz) bone-in chicken breasts
- 1/8 tsp salt
- 1/8 tsp pepper
- 3 tsp extra virgin olive oil
- 1/2 tsp dried oregano
- 7 pitted kalamata olives
- 1 cup cherry tomatoes
- 1/2 cup onion
- 1 (9-oz) pkg frozen artichoke hearts
- 1 lemon

Directions
1.   Preheat oven to 400°F.
2.   Sprinkle chicken with pepper, salt, and oregano.
3.   Heat oil, add chicken and cook until it browned.
4.   Place chicken in a baking dish. Arrange tomatoes, coarsely chopped olives, and onion, artichokes and lemon cut into wedges around the chicken.
5.   Bake 20 minutes or until chicken is done and vegetables are tender.
Nutrition:
160 Calories
3g Fat
1g Carbohydrates

653. Seared Chicken with Roasted Vegetables

Preparation Time: 20 minutes
Cooking Time: 30 minutes
Serving: 1
Ingredients

- 1 (8-oz) boneless, skinless chicken breasts
- 3/4 lb. small Brussels sprouts
- 2 large carrots
- 1 large red bell pepper
- 1 small red onion
- 2 cloves garlic halved
- 2 tbsp extra virgin olive oil
- 1/2 tsp dried dill
- 1/4 tsp pepper
- 1/4 tsp salt

Directions
1.   1.Preheat oven to 425°F.
2.   Match Brussels sprouts cut in half, red onion cut into wedges, sliced carrots, bell pepper cut into pieces and halved garlic on a baking sheet.
3.   Sprinkle with 1 tbsp oil and with 1/8 tsp salt and 1/8 tsp pepper. Bake until well-roasted, cool slightly.
4.   In the Meantime, sprinkle chicken with dill, remaining 1/8 tsp salt and 1/8 tsp pepper. Cook until chicken is done. Put roasted vegetables with drippings over chicken.

Nutrition
170 Calories
7g Fat
12g Protein

654. Fish Simmered in Tomato-Pepper Sauce

Preparation Time: 5 minutes
Cooking Time: 10 minutes
Serving: 2
Ingredients

- 2 (4-oz) cod fillets
- 1 big tomato
- 1/3 cup red peppers (roasted)
- 3 tbsp almonds
- 2 cloves garlic
- 2 tbsp fresh basil leaves
- 2 tbsp extra virgin olive oil
- 1/4 tsp salt
- 1/8 tsp pepper

Directions
1.   Toast sliced almonds in a pan until fragrant.
2.   Grind almonds, basil, minced garlic, 1-2 tsp oil in a food processor until finely ground.
3.   Add coarsely-chopped tomato and red peppers; grind until smooth.
4.   Season fish with salt and pepper.
5.   Cook in hot oil in a large pan over medium-high heat until fish is browned. Pour sauce around fish. Cook 6 minutes more.

Nutrition
90 Calories
5g Fat
7g Carbohydrates

655. Cheese Potato and Pea Casserole

Preparation Time: 10 minutes
Cooking Time: 35 minutes
Serving: 3
Ingredients

- 1 tbsp olive oil
- ¾ lb. red potatoes
- ¾ cup green peas
- ½ cup red onion
- ¼ tsp dried rosemary
- ¼ tsp salt
- 1/8 tsp pepper

Direction
1.   Prepare oven to 350°F.
2.   Cook 1 tsp oil in a skillet. Stir in thinly sliced onions and cook. Remove from pan.
3.   Situate half of the thinly sliced potatoes and onions in bottom of skillet; top with peas, crushed dried rosemary, and 1/8 tsp each salt and pepper.
4.   Place remaining potatoes and onions on top. Season with remaining 1/8 tsp salt.
5.   Bake 35 minutes, pour remaining 2 tsp oil and sprinkle with cheese.

Nutrition
80 Calories

2g Protein

18g Carbohydrates

656. Oven-Fried Tilapia

Preparation Time: 7 minutes

Cooking Time: 15 minutes

Serving: 2

Ingredients

- 2 (4-oz) tilapia fillets
- 1/4 cup yellow cornmeal
- 2 tbsp light ranch dressing
- 1 tbsp canola oil
- 1 tsp dill (dried)
- 1/8 tsp salt

Directions

1. Preheat oven to 425°F. Brush both sides of rinsed and patted dry tilapia fish fillets with dressing.
2. Combine cornmeal, oil, dill, and salt.
3. Sprinkle fish fillets with cornmeal mixture.
4. Put fish on a prepared baking sheet.
5. Bake 15 minutes.

Nutrition

96 Calories

21g Protein

2g Fat

657. Chicken with Coconut Sauce

Preparation Time: 15 minutes

Cooking Time: 20 minutes

Serving: 2

Ingredients

- 1/2 lb. chicken breasts
- 1/3 cup red onion
- 1 tbsp paprika (smoked)
- 2 tsp cornstarch
- 1/2 cup light coconut milk
- 1 tsp extra virgin olive oil
- 2 tbsp fresh cilantro
- 1 (10-oz) can tomatoes and green chilis
- 1/4 cup water

Directions

1. Cut chicken into little cubes; sprinkle with 1,5 tsp paprika.
2. Heat oil, add chicken and cook 3 to 5 minutes.

3. Remove from skillet, and fry finely-chopped onion 5 minutes.
4. Return chicken to pan. Add tomatoes,1,5 tsp paprika, and water. Bring to a boil, and then simmer 4 minutes.
5. Mix cornstarch and coconut milk; stir into chicken mixture, and cook until it has done.
6. Sprinkle with chopped cilantro.

Nutrition

200 Calories

13g Protein

10g Fat

658. Fish with Fresh Herb Sauce

Preparation Time: 10 minutes

Cooking Time: 10 minutes

Serving: 2

Ingredients

- 2 (4-oz) cod fillets
- 1/3 cup fresh cilantro
- 1/4 tsp cumin
- 1 tbsp red onion
- 2 tsp extra virgin olive oil
- 1 tsp red wine vinegar
- 1 small clove garlic
- 1/8 tsp salt
- 1/8 black pepper

Directions

1. Combine chopped cilantro, finely chopped onion, oil, red wine vinegar, minced garlic, and salt.
2. Sprinkle both sides of fish fillets with cumin and pepper.
3. Cook fillets 4 minutes per side. Top each fillet with cilantro mixture.

Nutrition

90 Calories

4g Fat

3g Carbohydrates

659. Skillet Turkey Patties

Preparation Time: 7 minutes

Cooking Time: 8 minutes

Serving: 2

Ingredients

- 1/2 lb. lean ground turkey
- 1/2 cup low-sodium chicken broth

- 1/4 cup red onion
- 1/2 tsp Worcestershire sauce
- 1 tsp extra virgin olive oil
- 1/4 tsp oregano (dried)
- 1/8 tsp pepper

Directions

1. Combine turkey, chopped onion, Worcestershire sauce, dried oregano, and pepper; make 2 patties.
2. Warm up oil and cook patties 4 minutes per side; set aside.
3. Add broth to skillet, bring to a boil. Boil 2 minutes, spoon sauce over patties.

Nutrition

180 Calories

11g Fat

9g Carbohydrates

660. Turkey Loaf

Preparation Time: 10 minutes

Cooking Time: 50 minutes

Serving: 2

Ingredients

- 1/2 lb. 93% lean ground turkey
- 1/3 cup panko breadcrumbs
- 1/2 cup green onion
- 1 egg
- 1/2 cup green bell pepper
- 1 tbsp ketchup
- 1/4 cup sauce (Picante)
- 1/2 tsp cumin (ground)

Directions

1. Preheat oven to 350°F. Mix lean ground turkey, 3 tbsp Picante sauce, panko breadcrumbs, egg, chopped green onion, chopped green bell pepper and cumin in a bowl (mix well);
2. Put the mixture into a baking sheet; shape into an oval (about 1,5 inches thick). Bake 45 minutes.
3. Mix remaining Picante sauce and the ketchup; apply over loaf. Bake 5 minutes longer. Let stand 5 minutes.

Nutrition

161 Calories

20g Protein

8g Fat

661. Mushroom Pasta

Preparation Time: 7 minutes

Cooking Time: 10 minutes

Serving: 4

Ingredients

- 4 oz whole-grain linguine
- 1 tsp extra virgin olive oil
- 1/2 cup light sauce
- 2 tbsp green onion
- 1 (8-oz) pkg mushrooms
- 1 clove garlic
- 1/8 tsp salt
- 1/8 tsp pepper

Directions

1. Cook pasta according to package directions, drain.
2. Fry sliced mushrooms 4 minutes.
3. Stir in fettuccine minced garlic, salt and pepper. Cook 2 minutes.
4. Heat light sauce until heated; top pasta mixture properly with sauce and with finely-chopped green onion.

Nutrition

300 Calories

1g Fat

15g Carbohydrates

662. Chicken Tikka Masala

Preparation Time: 5 minutes

Cooking Time: 15 minutes

Serving: 2

Ingredients

- 1/2 lb. chicken breasts
- 1/4 cup onion
- 1.5 tsp extra virgin olive oil
- 1 (14.5-oz) can tomatoes
- 1 tsp ginger
- 1 tsp fresh lemon juice
- 1/3 cup plain Greek yogurt (fat-free)
- 1 tbsp garam masala
- 1/4 tsp salt
- 1/4 tsp pepper

Directions

1. Flavor chicken cut into 1-inch cubes with 1,5 tsp garam masala,1/8 tsp salt and pepper.
2. Cook chicken and diced onion 4 to 5 minutes.
3. Add diced tomatoes, grated ginger, 1.5 tsp garam masala, 1/8 tsp salt. Cook 8 to 10 minutes.

4.   Add lemon juice and yogurt until blended.

Nutrition

200 Calories

26g Protein

10g Fat

663.   Tomato and Roasted Cod

Preparation Time: 10 minutes

Cooking Time: 35 minutes

Serving: 2

Ingredients

- 2 (4-oz) cod fillets
- 1 cup cherry tomatoes
- 2/3 cup onion
- 2 tsp orange rind
- 1 tbsp extra virgin olive oil
- 1 tsp thyme (dried)
- 1/4 tsp salt, divided
- 1/4 tsp pepper, divided

Directions

1.   Preheat oven to 400°F. Mix in half tomatoes, sliced onion, grated orange rind, extra virgin olive oil, dried thyme, and 1/8 salt and pepper. Fry 25 minutes. Remove from oven.

2.   Arrange fish on pan, and flavor with remaining 1/8 tsp each salt and pepper. Put reserved tomato mixture over fish. Bake 10 minutes.

Nutrition

120 Calories

9g Protein

2g Fat

664.   French Broccoli Salad

Preparation Time: 10 minutes,

Cooking Time: 10 minutes;

Servings: 10

Ingredients:

- 8 cups broccoli florets
- 3 strips of bacon, cooked and crumbled
- ¼ cup sunflower kernels
- 1 bunch of green onion, sliced

What you will need from the store cupboard:

- 3 tablespoons seasoned rice vinegar
- 3 tablespoons canola oil
- 1/2 cup dried cranberries

Directions:

1.   Combine the green onion, cranberries, and broccoli in a bowl.

2.   Whisk the vinegar, and oil in another bowl. Blend well.

3.   Now drizzle over the broccoli mix.

4.   Coat well by tossing.

5.   Sprinkle bacon and sunflower kernels before serving.

Nutrition

Calories 121, Carbohydrates 14g, Cholesterol 2mg, Fiber 3g, Sugar 1g, Fat 7g, Protein 3g, Sodium 233mg

665.   Tenderloin Grilled Salad

Preparation Time: 10 minutes, Cooking Time: 20 minutes;

Servings: 5

Ingredients:

- 1 lb. pork tenderloin
- 10 cups mixed salad greens
- 2 oranges, seedless, cut into bite-sized pieces
- 1 tablespoon orange zest, grated

What you will need from the store cupboard:

- 2 tablespoons of cider vinegar
- 2 tablespoons olive oil
- 2 teaspoons Dijon mustard
- 1/2 cup juice of an orange
- 2 teaspoons honey
- 1/2 teaspoon ground pepper

Directions:

1.   Bring together all the dressing ingredients in a bowl.

2.   Grill each side of the pork covered over medium heat for 9 minutes.

3.   Slice after 5 minutes.

4.   Slice the tenderloin thinly.

5.   Keep the greens on your serving plate.

6.   Top with the pork and oranges.

7.   Sprinkle nuts (optional).

Nutrition:

Calories 211, Carbohydrates 13g, Cholesterol 51mg, Fiber 3g, Sugar 0.8g, Fat 9g, Protein 20g, Sodium 113mg

666.   Barley Veggie Salad

Preparation Time: 10 minutes,

Cooking Time: 20 minutes;

Servings: 6

Ingredients:

- 1 tomato, seeded and chopped
- 2 tablespoons parsley, minced
- 1 yellow pepper, chopped
- 1 tablespoon basil, minced
- ¼ cup almonds, toasted

What you will need from the store cupboard:

- 1-1/4 cups vegetable broth
- 1 cup barley
- 1 tablespoon lemon juice
- 2 tablespoons of white wine vinegar
- 3 tablespoons olive oil
- ¼ teaspoon pepper
- 1/2 teaspoon salt
- 1 cup of water

Directions:

1.   Boil the broth, barley, and water in a saucepan.

2.   Reduce heat. Cover and let it simmer for 10 minutes.

3.   Take out from the heat.

4.   In the meantime, bring together the parsley, yellow pepper, and tomato in a bowl.

5.   Stir the barley in.

6.   Whisk the vinegar, oil, basil, lemon juice, water, pepper and salt in a bowl.

7.   Pour this over your barley mix. Toss to coat well.

8.   Stir the almonds in before serving.

Nutrition:

Calories 211, Carbohydrates 27g, Cholesterol 0mg, Fiber 7g, Sugar 0g, Fat 10g, Protein 6g, Sodium 334mg

667.   Spinach Shrimp Salad

Preparation Time: 10 minutes,

Cooking Time: 10 minutes;

Servings: 4

Ingredients:

- 1 lb. uncooked shrimp, peeled and deveined
- 2 tablespoons parsley, minced
- ¾ cup halved cherry tomatoes
- 1 medium lemon

- 4 cups baby spinach

What you will need from the store cupboard:

- 2 tablespoons butter
- 3 minced garlic cloves
- ¼ teaspoon pepper
- ¼ teaspoon salt

Directions:

1. Melt the butter over medium temperature in a nonstick skillet.
2. Add the shrimp.
3. Now cook the shrimp for 3 minutes until your shrimp becomes pink.
4. Add the parsley and garlic.
5. Cook for another minute. Take out from the heat.
6. Keep the spinach in your salad bowl.

7. Top with the shrimp mix and tomatoes.
8. Drizzle lemon juice on the salad.
9. Sprinkle pepper and salt.

Nutrition:

Calories 201, Carbohydrates 6g, Cholesterol 153mg, Fiber 2g, Sugar 0g, Fat 10g, Protein 21g, Sodium 350mg

668. Sweet Potato and Roasted Beet Salad

Preparation Time: 10 minutes,
Cooking Time: 10 minutes;
Servings: 4
Ingredients:

- 2 beets
- 1 sweet potato, peeled and cubed
- 1 garlic clove, minced
- 2 tablespoons walnuts, chopped and toasted
- 1 cup fennel bulb, sliced

What you will need from the store cupboard:

- 3 tablespoons balsamic vinegar
- 1 teaspoon Dijon mustard
- 1 tablespoon honey
- 3 tablespoons olive oil
- ¼ teaspoon pepper
- ¼ teaspoon salt
- 3 tablespoons water

Directions:

1. Scrub the beets. Trim the tops to 1 inch.
2. Wrap in foil and keep on a baking sheet.
3. Bake until tender. Take off the foil.
4. Combine water and sweet potato in a bowl.
5. Cover. Microwave for 5 minutes. Drain off.
6. Now peel the beets. Cut into small wedges.
7. Arrange the fennel, sweet potato and beets on 4 salad plates.
8. Sprinkle nuts.
9. Whisk the honey, mustard, vinegar, water, garlic, pepper and salt.
10. Whisk in oil gradually.
11. Drizzle over the salad.

Nutrition:

Calories 270, Carbohydrates 37g, Cholesterol 0mg, Fiber 6g, Sugar 0.3g, Fat 13g, Protein 5g, Sodium 309mg

669. Potato Calico Salad

Preparation Time: 15 minutes,
Cooking Time: 5 minutes;
Servings: 14
Ingredients:

- 4 red potatoes, peeled and cooked
- 1-1/2 cups kernel corn, cooked
- 1/2 cup green pepper, diced
- 1/2 cup red onion, chopped
- 1 cup carrot, shredded

What you will need from the store cupboard:

- 1/2 cup olive oil

- ¼ cup vinegar
- 1-1/2 teaspoons chili powder
- 1 teaspoon salt
- Dash of hot pepper sauce

Directions:
1. Keep all the ingredients together in a jar.
2. Close it and shake well.
3. Cube the potatoes. Combine with the carrot, onion, and corn in your salad bowl.
4. Pour the dressing over.
5. Now toss lightly.
Nutrition:
Calories 146, Carbohydrates 17g, Cholesterol 0mg, Fiber 0g, Sugar 0g, Fat 9g, Protein 2g, Sodium 212mg

670. Mango and Jicama Salad

Preparation Time: 15 minutes,
Cooking Time: 5 minutes;
Servings: 8
Ingredients:

- 1 jicama, peeled
- 1 mango, peeled
- 1 teaspoon ginger root, minced
- 1/3 cup chives, minced
- 1/2 cup cilantro, chopped

What you will need from the store cupboard:

- ¼ cup canola oil
- 1/2 cup white wine vinegar
- 2 tablespoons of lime juice
- ¼ cup honey
- 1/8 teaspoon pepper
- ¼ teaspoon salt

Directions:
1. Whisk together the vinegar, honey, canola oil, gingerroot, paper, and salt.
2. Cut the mango and jicama into matchsticks.
3. Keep in a bowl.
4. Now toss with the lime juice.
5. Add the dressing and herbs. Combine well by tossing.
Nutrition:
Calories 143, Carbohydrates 20g, Cholesterol 0mg, Fiber 3g, Sugar 1.6g, Fat 7g, Protein 1g, Sodium 78mg

671. Asian Crispy Chicken Salad

Preparation Time: 10 minutes,
Cooking Time: 10 minutes;
Servings: 2
Ingredients:

- 2 chicken breasts halved, skinless
- 1/2 cup panko bread crumbs
- 4 cups spring mix salad greens
- 4 teaspoons of sesame seeds
- 1/2 cup mushrooms, sliced

What you will need from the store cupboard:

- 1 teaspoon sesame oil
- 2 teaspoons of canola oil
- 2 teaspoons hoisin sauce
- ¼ cup sesame ginger salad dressing

Directions:
1. Flatten the chicken breasts to half-inch thickness.
2. Mix the sesame oil and hoisin sauce. Brush over the chicken.
3. Combine the sesame seeds and panko in a bowl.
4. Now dip the chicken mix in it.

5. Cook each side of the chicken for 5 minutes.
6. In the meantime, divide the salad greens between two plates.
7. Top with mushroom.
8. Slice the chicken and keep on top. Drizzle the dressing.

Nutrition:

Calories 386, Carbohydrates 29g, Cholesterol 63mg, Fiber 6g, Sugar 1g, Fat 17g, Protein 30g, Sodium 620mg

672. Kale, Grape and Bulgur Salad

Preparation Time: 10 minutes,
Cooking Time: 15 minutes;
Servings: 6
Ingredients:

- 1 cup bulgur
- 1 cup pecan, toasted and chopped
- ¼ cup scallions, sliced
- 1/2 cup parsley, chopped
- 2 cups California grapes, seedless and halved

What you will need from the store cupboard:

- 2 tablespoons of extra virgin olive oil
- ¼ cup of juice from a lemon
- Pinch of kosher salt
- Pinch of black pepper
- 2 cups of water

Directions:
1. Boil 2 cups of water in a saucepan
2. Stir the bulgur in and 1/2 teaspoon of salt.
3. Take out from the heat.
4. Keep covered. Drain.
5. Stir in the other ingredients.
6. Season with pepper and salt.

Nutrition:

Calories 289, Carbohydrates 33g, Fat 17g, Protein 6g, Sodium 181mg

673. Strawberry Salsa

Preparation Time: 10 minutes,
Cooking Time: 5 minutes;
Servings: 4
Ingredients:

- 4 tomatoes, seeded and chopped
- 1-pint strawberry, chopped
- 1 red onion, chopped
- 2 tablespoons of juice from a lime
- 1 jalapeno pepper, minced

What you will need from the store cupboard:

- 1 tablespoon olive oil
- 2 garlic cloves, minced

Directions:
1. Bring together the strawberries, tomatoes, jalapeno, and onion in the bowl.
2. Stir in the garlic, oil, and lime juice.
3. Refrigerate. Serve with separately cooked pork or poultry.

Nutrition:

Calories 19, Carbohydrates 3g, Fiber 1g, Sugar 0.2g, Cholesterol 0mg, Total Fat 1g, Protein 0g

674. Garden Wraps

Preparation Time: 20 minutes,
Cooking Time: 10 minutes;
Servings: 8
Ingredients:

- 1 cucumber, chopped
- 1 sweet corn
- 1 cabbage, shredded
- 1 tablespoon lettuce, minced
- 1 tomato, chopped

What you will need from the store cupboard:

- 3 tablespoons of rice vinegar
- 2 teaspoons peanut butter
- 1/3 cup onion paste
- 1/3 cup chili sauce
- 2 teaspoons of low-sodium soy sauce

Directions:
1. Cut corn from the cob. Keep in a bowl.
2. Add the tomato, cabbage, cucumber, and onion paste.
3. Now whisk the vinegar, peanut butter, and chili sauce together.
4. Pour this over the vegetable mix. Toss for coating.
5. Let this stand for 10 minutes.
6. Take your slotted spoon and place 1/2 cup salad in every lettuce leaf.
7. Fold the lettuce over your filling.

Nutrition:

Calories 64, Carbohydrates 13g, Fiber 2g, Sugar 1g, Cholesterol 0mg, Total Fat 1g, Protein 2g

675. Party Shrimp

Preparation Time: 15 minutes,

Cooking Time: 10 minutes;

Servings: 30

Ingredients:

- 16 oz. uncooked shrimp, peeled and deveined
- 1-1/2 teaspoons of juice from a lemon
- 1/2 teaspoon basil, chopped
- 1 teaspoon coriander, chopped
- 1/2 cup tomato

What you will need from the store cupboard:

- 1 tablespoon of olive oil
- 1/2 teaspoon Italian seasoning
- 1/2 teaspoon paprika
- 1 sliced garlic clove
- ¼ teaspoon pepper

Directions:

1. Bring together everything except the shrimp in a dish or bowl.
2. Add the shrimp. Coat well by tossing. Set aside.
3. Drain the shrimp. Discard the marinade.
4. Keep them on a baking sheet. It should not be greased.
5. Broil each side for 4 minutes. The shrimp should become pink.

Nutrition:

Calories 14, Carbohydrates 0g, Fiber 0g, Sugar 0g, Cholesterol 18mg, Total Fat 0g, Protein 2g

676. Zucchini Mini Pizzas

Preparation Time: 20 minutes,

Cooking Time: 10 minutes;

Servings: 24

Ingredients:

- 1 zucchini, cut into ¼ inch slices diagonally
- 1/2 cup pepperoni, small slices
- 1 teaspoon basil, minced
- 1/2 cup onion, chopped
- 1 cup tomatoes

What you will need from the store cupboard:

- 1/8 teaspoon pepper
- 1/8 teaspoon salt
- 3/4 cup mozzarella cheese, shredded
- 1/3 cup pizza sauce

Directions:

1. Preheat your broiler. Keep the zucchini in 1 layer on your greased baking sheet.
2. Add the onion and tomatoes. Broil each side for 1 to 2 minutes till they become tender and crisp.
3. Now sprinkle pepper and salt.
4. Top with cheese, pepperoni, and sauce.
5. Broil for a minute. The cheese should melt.
6. Sprinkle basil on top.

Nutrition:

Calories 29, Carbohydrates 1g, Fiber 0g, Sugar 1g, Cholesterol 5mg, Total Fat 2g, Protein 2g

677. Garlic-Sesame Pumpkin Seeds

Preparation Time: 10 minutes

Cooking Time: 20 minutes

Servings: 2

Ingredients:

- 1 egg white
- 1 teaspoon onion, minced
- 1/2 teaspoon caraway seeds
- 2 cups pumpkin seeds
- 1 teaspoon sesame seeds

What you will need from the store cupboard:

- 1 garlic clove, minced

- 1 tablespoon of canola oil
- ¾ teaspoon of kosher salt

Directions:

1. Preheat your oven to 350 °F.
2. Whisk together the oil and egg white in a bowl.
3. Include pumpkin seeds. Coat well by tossing.
4. Now stir in the onion, garlic, sesame seeds, caraway seeds, and salt.
5. Spread in 1 layer in your parchment-lined baking pan.
6. Bake for 15 minutes until it turns golden brown.

Nutrition:

Calories 95, Carbohydrates 9g, Fiber 3g, Sugar 0g, Cholesterol 0mg, Total Fat 5g, Protein 4g

678. Thai Quinoa Salad

Preparation time: 10 minutes
Cooking time: 0 minutes
Servings: 1-2
Ingredients:

Ingredients used for dressing:

- 1 tbsp. Sesame seed
- 1 tsp. Chopped garlic
- 1 tsp. Lemon, fresh juice
- 3 tsp. Apple Cider Vinegar
- 2 tsp. Tamari, gluten-free.
- 1/4 cup of tahini (sesame butter)
- 1 pitted date
- 1/2 tsp. Salt
- 1/2 tsp. toasted Sesame oil

Salad Ingredients:

- 1 cup of quinoa, steamed
- 1 big handful of arugulas
- 1 tomato cut in pieces
- 1/4 of the red onion, diced

Directions:

1. Add the following to a small blender: 1/4 cup + 2 tbsp.
2. Filtered water, the rest of the **Ingredients**. Blend, man. Steam 1 cup of quinoa in a steamer or a rice pan, then set aside.
3. Combine the quinoa, the arugula, the tomatoes sliced, the red onion diced on a serving plate or bowl, add the Thai dressing
4. and serve with a spoon.

Nutrition:

Calories: 100
Carbohydrates: 12 g

679. Green Goddess Bowl and Avocado Cumin Dressing

Preparation time: 10 minutes
Cooking time: 0 minutes
Servings: 1-2
Ingredients:

Ingredients for the dressing of avocado cumin:

- 1 Avocado
- 1 tbsp. Cumin Powder
- 2 limes, freshly squeezed
- 1 cup of filtered water
- 1/4 seconds. sea salt
- 1 tbsp. Olive extra virgin olive oil
- Cayenne pepper dash
- Optional: 1/4 tsp. Smoked pepper

Tahini Lemon Dressing Ingredients:

- 1/4 cup of tahini (sesame butter)
- 1/2 cup of filtered water (more if you want thinner, less thick)
- 1/2 lemon, freshly squeezed
- 1 clove of minced garlic
- 3/4 tsp. Sea salt (Celtic Gray, Himalayan, Redmond Real Salt)
- 1 tbsp. Olive extra virgin olive oil
- black pepper taste

Salad Ingredients:

- 3 cups of kale, chopped
- 1/2 cup of broccoli flowers, chopped
- 1/2 zucchini (make spiral noodles)
- 1/2 cup of kelp noodles, soaked and drained
- 1/3 cup of cherry tomatoes, halved.
- 2 tsp. hemp seeds

Directions:

1. Gently steam the kale and the broccoli (flash the steam for 4 minutes), set aside.
2. Mix the zucchini noodles and kelp noodles and toss with a generous portion of the smoked avocado cumin dressing. Add the cherry tomatoes and stir again.
3. Place the steamed kale and broccoli and drizzle with the lemon tahini dressing. Top the kale and the broccoli with

the noodles and tomatoes and sprinkle the whole dish with the hemp seeds.

Nutrition:

Calories: 89

Carbohydrates: 11g

Fat: 1.2g

Protein: 4g

680. 7 Sweet and Savory Salad

Preparation time: 10 minutes

Cooking time: 0 minutes

Servings: 1-2

Ingredients:

- 1 big head of butter lettuce
- 1/2 of cucumber, sliced
- 1 pomegranate, seed or 1/3 cup of seed
- 1 avocado, 1 cubed
- 1/4 cup of shelled pistachio, chopped

Ingredients for dressing:

- 1/4 cup of apple cider vinegar
- 1/2 cup of olive oil
- 1 clove of garlic, minced

Directions:

1. Put the butter lettuce in a salad bowl.
2. Add the remaining **Ingredients** and toss with the salad dressing.

Nutrition:

Calories: 68

Carbohydrates: 8g

Fat: 1.2g

Protein: 2g

681. Kale Pesto's Pasta

Preparation time: 10 minutes

Cooking time: 0 minutes

Servings: 1-2

Ingredients:

- 1 bunch of kale
- 2 cups of fresh basil
- 1/4 cup of extra virgin olive oil
- 1/2 cup of walnuts
- 2 limes, freshly squeezed
- Sea salt and chili pepper
- 1 zucchini, noodle (spiralizer)

- Optional: garnish with chopped asparagus, spinach leaves, and tomato.

Directions:

1. The night before, soak the walnuts in order to improve absorption.
2. Put all the recipe **Ingredients** in a blender and blend until the consistency of the cream is reached.
3. Add the zucchini noodles and enjoy.

Nutrition:

Calories: 55

Carbohydrates: 9 g

Fat: 1.2g

682. Beet Salad with Basil Dressing

Preparation time: 10 minutes

Cooking time: 0 minutes

Servings: 4

Ingredients:

Ingredients for the dressing

- ¼ cup blackberries
- ¼ cup extra-virgin olive oil
- Juice of 1 lemon
- 2 tablespoons minced fresh basil
- 1 teaspoon poppy seeds
- A pinch of sea salt
- For the salad
- 2 celery stalks, chopped
- 4 cooked beets, peeled and chopped
- 1 cup blackberries
- 4 cups spring mix

Directions:

1. To make the dressing, mash the blackberries in a bowl. Whisk in the oil, lemon juice, basil, poppy seeds, and sea salt.
2. To make the salad: Add the celery, beets, blackberries, and spring mix to the bowl with the dressing.
3. Combine and serve.

Nutrition:

Calories: 192

Fat: 15g

Carbohydrates: 15g

Protein: 2g

683. Basic Salad with Olive Oil Dressing

Preparation time: 10 minutes
Cooking time: 0 minute
Servings: 4
Ingredients:

- 1 cup coarsely chopped iceberg lettuce
- 1 cup coarsely chopped romaine lettuce
- 1 cup fresh baby spinach
- 1 large tomato, hulled and coarsely chopped
- 1 cup diced cucumber
- 2 tablespoons extra-virgin olive oil
- ¼ teaspoon of sea salt

Directions:
1.   In a bowl, combine the spinach and lettuces. Add the tomato and cucumber.
2.   Drizzle with oil and sprinkle with sea salt.
3.   Mix and serve.

Nutrition:
Calories: 77
Fat: 4g
Carbohydrates: 3g
Protein: 1g

684. Spinach & Orange Salad with Oil Drizzle

Preparation time: 10 minutes
Cooking time: 0 minute
Servings: 4
Ingredients:

- 4 cups fresh baby spinach
- 1 blood orange, coarsely chopped
- ½ red onion, thinly sliced
- ½ shallot, finely chopped
- 2 tbsp. minced fennel fronds
- Juice of 1 lemon
- 1 tbsp. extra-virgin olive oil
- Pinch sea salt

Directions:
1.   In a bowl, toss together the spinach, orange, red onion, shallot, and fennel fronds.
2.   Add the lemon juice, oil, and sea salt.
3.   Mix and serve.

Nutrition:
Calories: 79
Fat: 2g
Carbohydrates: 8g
Protein: 1g

685. Fruit Salad with Coconut-Lime Dressing

Preparation time: 5 minutes
Cooking time: 0 minutes
Servings: 4
Ingredients:

Ingredients for the dressing

- ¼ cup full-fat canned coconut milk
- 1 tbsp. raw honey
- Juice of ½ lime
- Pinch sea salt
- For the salad
- 2 bananas, thinly sliced
- 2 mandarin oranges, segmented
- ½ cup strawberries, thinly sliced
- ½ cup raspberries
- ½ cup blueberries

Directions:
1.   To make the dressing: whisk all the dressing **Ingredients** in a bowl.
2.   To make the salad: Add the salad **Ingredients** in a bowl and mix.
3.   Drizzle with the dressing and serve.

Nutrition:
Calories: 141
Fat: 3g
Carbohydrates: 30g
Protein: 2g

686. Cranberry And Brussels Sprouts With Dressing

Preparation time: 10 minutes
Cooking time: 0 minute
Servings: 4
Ingredients:

Ingredients for the dressing

- 1/3 cup extra-virgin olive oil
- 2 tbsp. apple cider vinegar

- 1 tbsp. pure maple syrup
- Juice of 1 orange
- ½ tbsp. dried rosemary
- 1 tbsp. scallion, whites only
- Pinch sea salt

For the salad

- 1 bunch scallions, greens only, finely chopped
- 1 cup Brussels sprouts, stemmed, halved, and thinly sliced
- ½ cup fresh cranberries
- 4 cups fresh baby spinach

Directions:

1. To make the dressing: In a bowl, whisk the dressing **Ingredients**.
2. To make the salad: Add the scallions, Brussels sprouts, cranberries, and spinach to the bowl with the dressing.
3. Combine and serve.

Nutrition:

Calories: 267

Fat: 18g

Carbohydrates: 26g

Protein: 2g

687. Parsnip, Carrot, And Kale Salad with Dressing

Preparation time: 10 minutes

Cooking time: 0 minutes

Servings: 4

Ingredients:

Ingredients for the dressing

- 1/3 cup extra-virgin olive oil
- Juice of 1 lime
- 2 tbsp. minced fresh mint leaves
- 1 tsp. pure maple syrup
- Pinch sea salt

For the salad

- 1 bunch kale, chopped
- ½ parsnip, grated
- ½ carrot, grated
- 2 tbsp. sesame seeds

Directions:

1. To make the dressing, mix all the dressing **Ingredients** in a bowl.

2. To make the salad, add the kale to the dressing and massage the dressing into the kale for 1 minute.
3. Add the parsnip, carrot, and sesame seeds.
4. Combine and serve.

Nutrition:

Calories: 214

Fat: 2g

Carbohydrates: 12g

Protein: 2g

688. Tomato Toasts

Preparation time: 5 minutes

Cooking time: 5 minutes

Servings: 4

Ingredients:

- 4 slices of sprouted bread toasts
- 2 tomatoes, sliced
- 1 avocado, mashed
- 1 teaspoon olive oil
- 1 pinch of salt
- ¾ teaspoon ground black pepper

Directions:

1. Blend together the olive oil, mashed avocado, salt, and ground black pepper.
2. When the mixture is homogenous – spread it over the sprouted bread.
3. Then place the sliced tomatoes over the toasts.
4. Enjoy!

Nutrition:

Calories: 125

Fat: 11.1g

Carbohydrates: 7.0g

Protein: 1.5g

689. Everyday Salad

Preparation time: 10 minutes

Cooking time: 40 minutes

Servings: 6

Ingredients:

- 5 halved mushrooms
- 6 halved Cherry (Plum) Tomatoes
- 6 rinsed Lettuce Leaves
- 10 olives
- ½ chopped cucumber
- Juice from ½ Key Lime

- 1 teaspoon olive oil
- Pure Sea Salt

Directions:

1. Tear rinsed lettuce leaves into medium pieces and put them in a medium salad bowl.

2. Add mushrooms halves, chopped cucumber, olives and cherry tomato halves into the bowl. Mix well. Pour olive and Key Lime juice over salad.

3. Add pure sea salt to taste. Mix it all till it is well combined.

Nutrition:

Calories: 88

Carbohydrates: 11g

Fat: .5g

Protein: .8g

690. Super-Seedy Salad with Tahini Dressing

Preparation time: 10 minutes

Cooking time: 0 minutes

Servings: 1-2

Ingredients:

- 1 slice stale sourdough, torn into chunks
- 50g mixed seeds
- 1 tsp. cumin seeds
- 1 tsp. coriander seeds
- 50g baby kale
- 75g long-stemmed broccoli, blanched for a few minutes then roughly chopped
- ½ red onion, thinly sliced
- 100g cherry tomatoes, halved
- ½ a small bunch flat-leaf parsley, torn

DRESSING

- 100ml natural yogurt
- 1 tbsp. tahini
- 1 lemon, juiced

Directions:

1. Heat the oven to 200°C/fan 180°C/gas 6. Put the bread into a food processor and pulse into very rough breadcrumbs. Put into a bowl with the mixed seeds and spices, season, and spray well with oil. Tip onto a non-stick baking tray and roast for 15-20 minutes, stirring and tossing regularly, until deep golden brown.

2. Whisk together the dressing **Ingredients**, some seasoning and a splash of water in a large bowl. Tip the baby kale, broccoli, red onion, cherry tomatoes and flat-leaf parsley into the dressing, and mix well. Divide between 2 plates and top with the crispy breadcrumbs and seeds.

Nutrition:

Calories: 78

Carbohydrates: 6 g

Fat: 2g

Protein: 1.5g

691. Vegetable Salad

Preparation time: 10 minutes

Cooking time: 0 minutes

Servings: 1-2

Ingredients:

- 4 cups each of raw spinach and romaine lettuce
- 2 cups each of cherry tomatoes, sliced cucumber, chopped baby carrots and chopped red, orange and yellow bell pepper
- 1 cup each of chopped broccoli, sliced yellow squash, zucchini and cauliflower.

Directions:

1. Wash all these vegetables.

2. Mix in a large mixing bowl and top off with a non-fat or low-fat dressing of your choice.

Nutrition:

Calories: 48

Carbohydrates: 11g

Protein: 3g

692. Greek Salad

Preparation time: 10 minutes

Cooking time: 0 minutes

Servings: 1-2

Ingredients:

- 1 Romaine head, torn in bits
- 1 cucumber sliced
- 1 pint cherry tomatoes, halved
- 1 green pepper, thinly sliced
- 1 onion sliced into rings
- 1 cup kalamata olives
- 1 ½ cups feta cheese, crumbled
- For dressing combine:
- 1 cup olive oil

- 1/4 cup lemon juice
- 2 tsp. oregano
- Salt and pepper

Directions:
1.   Lay Ingredients on plate.
2.   Drizzle dressing over salad

Nutrition:
Calories: 107
Carbohydrates: 18g
Fat: 1.2 g
Protein: 1g

693.   Alkaline Spring Salad

Preparation time: 10 minutes
Cooking time: 0 minutes
Servings: 1-2
Eating seasonal fruits and vegetables is a fabulous way of taking care of yourself and the environment at the same time. This alkaline-electric salad is delicious and nutritious.

Ingredients:
- 4 cups seasonal approved greens of your choice
- 1 cup cherry tomatoes
- 1/4 cup walnuts
- 1/4 cup approved herbs of your choice
- For the dressing:
- 3-4 key limes
- 1 tbsp. of homemade raw sesame
- Sea salt and cayenne pepper

Directions:
1.   First, get the juice of the key limes. In a small bowl, whisk together the key lime juice with the homemade raw sesame "tahini" butter. Add sea salt and cayenne pepper, to taste.
2.   Cut the cherry tomatoes in half.
3.   In a large bowl, combine the greens, cherry tomatoes, and herbs. Pour the dressing on top and "massage" with your hands.
4.   Let the greens soak up the dressing. Add more sea salt, cayenne pepper, and herbs on top if you wish. Enjoy!

Nutrition:
Calories: 77
Carbohydrates: 11g

694.   Fresh Tuna Salad

Preparation Time: 10 minutes

Cooking time: none
Servings: 3
Ingredients:
- 1 can tuna (6 oz.)
- 1/3 cup fresh cucumber, chopped
- 1/3 cup fresh tomato, chopped
- 1/3 cup avocado, chopped
- 1/3 cup celery, chopped
- 2 garlic cloves, minced
- 4 tsp. olive oil
- 2 tbsp. lime juice
- Pinch of black pepper

Directions:
1.   Prepare the dressing by combining olive oil, lime juice, minced garlic and black pepper.
2.   Mix the salad ingredients in a salad bowl and drizzle with the dressing.
Nutrition: Carbohydrates: 4.8 g Protein: 14.3 g Total sugars: 1.1 g Calories: 212 g

695.   Roasted Portobello Salad

Preparation Time: 10 minutes
Cooking time: none
Servings: 4
Ingredients:
- 11/2 lb. Portobello mushrooms, stems trimmed
- 3 heads Belgian endive, sliced
- 1 small red onion, sliced
- 4 oz. blue cheese
- 8 oz. mixed salad greens
- Dressing:
- 3 tbsp. red wine vinegar
- 1 tbsp. Dijon mustard
- 2/3 cup olive oil
- Salt and pepper to taste

Directions:
1.   Preheat the oven to 450F.
2.   Prepare the dressing by whisking together vinegar, mustard, salt and pepper. Slowly add olive oil while whisking.
3.   Cut the mushrooms and arrange them on a baking sheet, stem-side up. Coat the mushrooms with some dressing and bake for 15 minutes.
4.   In a salad bowl toss the salad greens with onion, endive and cheese. Sprinkle with the dressing.

5.   Add mushrooms to the salad bowl.
Nutrition: Carbohydrates: 22.3 g Protein: 14.9 g Total sugars: 2.1 g Calories: 501

696. Shredded Chicken Salad

Preparation Time: 5 minutes
Cooking time: 10 minutes
Servings: 6
Ingredients:

- 2 chicken breasts, boneless, skinless
- 1 head iceberg lettuce, cut into strips
- 2 bell peppers, cut into strips
- 1 fresh cucumber, quartered, sliced
- 3 scallions, sliced
- 2 tbsp. chopped peanuts
- 1 tbsp. peanut vinaigrette
- Salt to taste
- 1 cup water

Directions:
1.   In a skillet simmer one cup of salted water.
2.   Add the chicken breasts, cover and cook on low for 5 minutes. Remove the cover. Then remove the chicken from the skillet and shred with a fork.
3.   In a salad bowl mix the vegetables with the cooled chicken, season with salt and sprinkle with peanut vinaigrette and chopped peanuts.
Nutrition: Carbohydrates: 9 g Protein: 11.6 g Total sugars: 4.2 g Calories: 117

697. Broccoli Salad

Preparation Time: 10 minutes
Cooking time: none
Servings: 6
Ingredients:

- 1 medium head broccoli, raw, florets only
- 1/2 cup red onion, chopped
- 12 oz. turkey bacon, chopped, fried until crisp
- 1/2 cup cherry tomatoes, halved
- ¼ cup sunflower kernels
- ¾ cup raisins
- ¾ cup mayonnaise
- 2 tbsp. white vinegar

Directions:
1.   In a salad bowl combine the broccoli, tomatoes and onion.

2.   Mix mayo with vinegar and sprinkle over the broccoli.
3.   Add the sunflower kernels, raisins and bacon and toss well.
Nutrition: Carbohydrates: 17.3 g Protein: 11 g Total sugars: 10 g Calories: 220

698. Cherry Tomato Salad

Preparation Time: 10 minutes
Cooking time: none
Servings: 6
Ingredients:

- 40 cherry tomatoes, halved
- 1 cup mozzarella balls, halved
- 1 cup green olives, sliced
- 1 can (6 oz.) black olives, sliced
- 2 green onions, chopped
- 3 oz. roasted pine nuts
- Dressing:
- 1/2 cup olive oil
- 2 tbsp. red wine vinegar
- 1 tsp. dried oregano
- Salt and pepper to taste

Directions:
1.   In a salad bowl, combine the tomatoes, olives and onions.
2.   Prepare the dressing by combining olive oil with red wine vinegar, dried oregano, salt and pepper.
3.   Sprinkle with the dressing and add the nuts.
4.   Let marinate in the fridge for 1 hour.
Nutrition: Carbohydrates: 10.7 g Protein: 2.4 g Total sugars: 3.6 g

699. Ground Turkey Salad

Preparation Time: 10 minutes
Cooking time: 35 minutes
Servings: 6
Ingredients:

- 1 lb. lean ground turkey
- 1/2-inch ginger, minced
- 2 garlic cloves, minced
- 1 onion, chopped
- 1 tbsp. olive oil
- 1 bag lettuce leaves (for serving)

- ¼ cup fresh cilantro, chopped
- 2 tsp. coriander powder
- 1 tsp. red chili powder
- 1 tsp. turmeric powder
- Salt to taste
- 4 cups water
- Dressing:
- 2 tbsp. fat free yogurt
- 1 tbsp. sour cream, non-fat
- 1 tbsp. low fat mayonnaise
- 1 lemon, juiced
- 1 tsp. red chili flakes
- Salt and pepper to taste

Directions:

1. In a skillet sauté the garlic and ginger in olive oil for 1 minute. Add onion and season with salt. Cook for 10 minutes over medium heat.
2. Add the ground turkey and sauté for 3 more minutes. Add the spices (turmeric, red chili powder and coriander powder).
3. Add 4 cups water and cook for 30 minutes, covered.
4. Prepare the dressing by combining yogurt, sour cream, mayo, lemon juice, chili flakes, salt and pepper.
5. To serve arrange the salad leaves on serving plates and place the cooked ground turkey on them. Top with dressing.

Nutrition: Carbohydrates: 9.1 g Protein: 17.8 g Total sugars: 2.5 g Calories: 176

700. Asian Cucumber Salad

Preparation Time: 10 minutes
Cooking time: none
Servings: 6
Ingredients:

- 1 lb. cucumbers, sliced
- 2 scallions, sliced
- 2 tbsp. sliced pickled ginger, chopped
- ¼ cup cilantro
- 1/2 red jalapeño, chopped
- 3 tbsp. rice wine vinegar
- 1 tbsp. sesame oil
- 1 tbsp. sesame seeds

Directions:

1. In a salad bowl combine all ingredients and toss together.

Nutrition: Carbohydrates: 5.7 g Protein: 1 g Total sugars: 3.1 g Calories: 52

701. Cauliflower Tofu Salad

Preparation time: 10 minutes
Cooking time: 15 minutes
Servings: 4
Ingredients:

- 2 cups cauliflower florets, blended
- 1 fresh cucumber, diced
- 1/2 cup green olives, diced
- 1/3 cup red onion, diced
- 2 tbsp. toasted pine nuts
- 2 tbsp. raisins
- 1/3 cup feta, crumbled
- 1/2 cup pomegranate seeds
- 2 lemons (juiced, zest grated)
- 8 oz. tofu
- 2 tsp. oregano
- 2 garlic cloves, minced
- 1/2 tsp. red chili flakes
- 3 tbsp. olive oil
- Salt and pepper to taste

Directions:

1. Season the processed cauliflower with salt and transfer to a strainer to drain.
2. Prepare the marinade for tofu by combining 2 tbsp. lemon juice, 1.5 tbsp. olive oil, minced garlic, chili flakes, oregano, salt and pepper. Coat tofu in the marinade and set aside.
3. Preheat the oven to 450F.
4. Bake tofu on a baking sheet for 12 minutes.
5. In a salad bowl mix the remaining marinade with onions, cucumber, cauliflower, olives and raisins. Add in the remaining olive oil and grated lemon zest.
6. Top with tofu, pine nuts, and feta and pomegranate seeds.

Nutrition: Carbohydrates: 34.1 g Protein: 11.1 g Total sugars: 11.5 g Calories: 328

702. Scallop Caesar Salad

Preparation Time: 5 minutes
Cooking Time: 2 minutes

Servings: 2

Ingredients:

- 8 sea scallops
- 4 cups romaine lettuce
- 2 tsp. olive oil
- 3 tbsp. Caesar Salad Dressing
- 1 tsp. lemon juice
- Salt and pepper to taste

Directions:

1. In a frying pan heat olive oil and cook the scallops in one layer no longer than 2 minutes per both sides. Season with salt and pepper to taste.
2. Arrange lettuce on plates and place scallops on top.
3. Pour over the Caesar dressing and lemon juice.

Nutrition: Carbohydrates: 14 g Protein: 30.7 g Total sugars: 2.2 g Calories: 340 g

703. Chicken Avocado Salad

Preparation Time: 30 minutes

Cooking time: 15 minutes

Servings: 4

Ingredients:

- 1 lb. chicken breast, cooked, shredded
- 1 avocado, pitted, peeled, sliced
- 2 tomatoes, diced
- 1 cucumber, peeled, sliced
- 1 head lettuce, chopped
- 3 tbsp. olive oil
- 2 tbsp. lime juice
- 1 tbsp. cilantro, chopped
- Salt and pepper to taste

Directions:

1. In a bowl whisk together oil, lime juice, cilantro, salt, and a pinch of pepper.
2. Combine lettuce, tomatoes, cucumber in a salad bowl and toss with half of the dressing.
3. Toss chicken with the remaining dressing and combine with vegetable mixture.
4. Top with avocado.

Nutrition: Carbohydrates: 10 g Protein: 38 g Total sugars: 11.5 g Calories: 380

704. California Wraps

Preparation Time: 5 minutes

Cooking Time: 15 minutes

Servings: 4

Ingredients:

- 4 slices turkey breast, cooked
- 4 slices ham, cooked
- 4 lettuce leaves
- 4 slices tomato
- 4 slices avocado
- 1 tsp. lime juice
- A handful watercress leaves
- 4 tbsp. Ranch dressing, sugar free

Directions:

1. Top a lettuce leaf with turkey slice, ham slice and tomato.
2. In a bowl combine avocado and lime juice and place on top of tomatoes. Top with water cress and dressing.
3. Repeat with the remaining ingredients for 4. Topping each lettuce leaf with a turkey slice, ham slice, tomato and dressing.

Nutrition: Carbohydrates: 4 g Protein: 9 g Total sugars: 0.5 g Calories: 140

705. Chicken Salad in Cucumber Cups

Preparation Time: 5 minutes

Cooking Time: 15 minutes

Servings: 4

Ingredients:

- 1/2 chicken breast, skinless, boiled and shredded
- 2 long cucumbers, cut into 8 thick rounds each, scooped out (won't use in a).
- 1 tsp. ginger, minced
- 1 tsp. lime zest, grated
- 4 tsp. olive oil
- 1 tsp. sesame oil
- 1 tsp. lime juice
- Salt and pepper to taste

Directions:

1. In a bowl combine lime zest, juice, olive and sesame oils, ginger, and season with salt.
2. Toss the chicken with the dressing and fill the cucumber cups with the salad.

Nutrition: Carbohydrates: 4 g Protein: 12 g Total sugars: 0.5 g Calories: 116 g

706. Sunflower Seeds and Arugula Garden Salad

Preparation time: 5 minutes
Cooking time: 10 minutes
Servings: 6
Ingredients:

- ¼ tsp. black pepper
- ¼ tsp. salt
- 1 tsp. fresh thyme, chopped
- 2 tbsp. sunflower seeds, toasted
- 2 cups red grapes, halved
- 7 cups baby arugula, loosely packed
- 1 tbsp. coconut oil
- 2 tsp. honey
- 3 tbsp. red wine vinegar
- 1/2 tsp. stone-ground mustard

Directions:
1. In a small bowl, whisk together mustard, honey and vinegar. Slowly pour oil as you whisk.
2. In a large salad bowl, mix thyme, seeds, grapes and arugula.
3. Drizzle with dressing and serve.

Nutrition: Calories: 86.7g Protein: 1.6g Carbs: 13.1g Fat: 3.1g.

707. Supreme Caesar Salad

Preparation time: 5 minutes
Cooking time: 10 minutes
Servings: 4
Ingredients:

- ¼ cup olive oil
- ¾ cup mayonnaise
- 1 head romaine lettuce, torn into bite sized pieces
- 1 tbsp. lemon juice
- 1 tsp. Dijon mustard
- 1 tsp. Worcestershire sauce
- 3 cloves garlic, peeled and minced
- 3 cloves garlic, peeled and quartered
- 4 cups day old bread, cubed
- 5 anchovy filets, minced
- 6 tbsp. grated parmesan cheese, divided
- Ground black pepper to taste
- Salt to taste

Directions:

1. In a small bowl, whisk well lemon juice, mustard, Worcestershire sauce, 2 tbsp. parmesan cheese, anchovies, mayonnaise, and minced garlic. Season with pepper and salt to taste. Set aside in the ref.
2. On medium fire, place a large nonstick saucepan and heat oil.
3. Sauté quartered garlic until browned around a minute or two. Remove and discard.
4. Add bread cubes in same pan, sauté until lightly browned. Season with pepper and salt. Transfer to a plate.
5. In large bowl, place lettuce and pour in dressing. Toss well to coat. Top with remaining parmesan cheese.
6. Garnish with bread cubes, serve, and enjoy.

Nutrition: Calories: 443.3g Fat: 32.1g Protein: 11.6g Carbs: 27g

708. Tabbouleh- Arabian Salad

Preparation time: 5 minutes
Cooking time: 10 minutes
Servings: 6
Ingredients:

- ¼ cup chopped fresh mint
- 1 2/3 cups boiling water
- 1 cucumber, peeled, seeded and chopped
- 1 cup bulgur
- 1 cup chopped fresh parsley
- 1 cup chopped green onions
- 1 tsp. salt
- 1/3 cup lemon juice
- 1/3 cup olive oil
- 3 tomatoes, chopped
- Ground black pepper to taste

Directions:

1. In a large bowl, mix together boiling water and bulgur. Let soak and set aside for an hour while covered.
2. After one hour, toss in cucumber, tomatoes, mint, parsley, onions, lemon juice and oil. Then season with black pepper and salt to taste. Toss well and refrigerate for another hour while covered before serving.

Nutrition: Calories: 185.5g fat: 13.1g Protein: 4.1g Carbs: 12.8g

709. Aromatic Toasted Pumpkin Seeds

Preparation Time: 5 minutes

Cooking Time: 45 minutes

Serving: 4

Ingredients:

- 1 cup pumpkin seeds
- 1 teaspoon cinnamon
- 2 packets stevia
- 1 tablespoon canola oil
- ¼ teaspoon sea salt

Direction

1. Prep the oven to 300°F (150°C).
2. Combine the pumpkin seeds with cinnamon, stevia, canola oil, and salt in a bowl. Stir to mix well.
3. Pour the seeds in the single layer on a baking sheet, then arrange the sheet in the preheated oven.
4. Bake for 45 minutes or until well toasted and fragrant. Shake the sheet twice to bake the seeds evenly.
5. Serve immediately.

Nutrition:

202 calories

5.1g carbohydrates

2.3g fiber

710. Bacon-Wrapped Shrimps

Preparation Time: 10 minutes

Cooking Time: 6 minutes

Serving: 10

Ingredient:

- 20 shrimps, peeled and deveined
- 7 slices bacon
- 4 leaves romaine lettuce

Direction

1. Set the oven to 205°C.
2. Wrap each shrimp with each bacon strip, then arrange the wrapped shrimps in a single layer on a baking sheet, seam side down.
3. Broil for 6 minutes. Flip the shrimps halfway through the cooking time.
4. Take out from the oven and serve on lettuce leaves.

Nutrition:

70 calories

4.5g fat

7g protein

First Course Recipe

711. Blueberry and Chicken Salad

Preparation Time: 10 minutes
Cooking Time: 0 minute
Serving: 4
Ingredients:

- 2 cups chopped cooked chicken
- 1 cup fresh blueberries
- ¼ cup almonds
- 1 celery stalk
- ¼ cup red onion
- 1 tablespoon fresh basil
- 1 tablespoon fresh cilantro
- ½ cup plain, vegan mayonnaise
- ¼ teaspoon salt
- ¼ teaspoon freshly ground black pepper
- 8 cups salad greens

Direction:
1. Toss chicken, blueberries, almonds, celery, onion, basil, and cilantro.
2. Blend yogurt, salt, and pepper. Stir chicken salad to combine.
3. Situate 2 cups of salad greens on each of 4 plates and divide the chicken salad among the plates to serve.

Nutrition:
207 Calories
11g Carbohydrates
6g Sugars

712. Beef and Red Bean Chili

Preparation Time: 10 minutes
Cooking Time: 6 hours
Serving: 4
Ingredients

- 1 cup dry red beans
- 1 tablespoon olive oil
- 2 pounds boneless beef chuck
- 1 large onion, coarsely chopped
- 1 (14 ounce) can beef broth
- 2 chipotle chili peppers in adobo sauce
- 2 teaspoons dried oregano, crushed
- 1 teaspoon ground cumin
- ½ teaspoon salt
- 1 (14.5 ounce) can tomatoes with mild green chilis
- 1 (15 ounce) can tomato sauce

- ¼ cup snipped fresh cilantro
- 1 medium red sweet pepper

Direction
1. Rinse out the beans and place them into a Dutch oven or big saucepan, then add in water enough to cover them. Allow the beans to boil then drop the heat down. Simmer the beans without a cover for 10 minutes. Take off the heat and keep covered for an hour.
2. In a big frypan, heat up the oil upon medium-high heat, then cook onion and half the beef until they brown a bit over medium-high heat. Move into a 3 1/2- or 4-quart crockery cooker. Do this again with what's left of the beef. Add in tomato sauce, tomatoes (not drained), salt, cumin, oregano, adobo sauce, chipotle peppers, and broth, stirring to blend. Strain out and rinse beans and stir in the cooker.
3. Cook while covered on a low setting for around 10-12 hours or on high setting for 5-6 hours. Spoon the chili into bowls or mugs and top with sweet pepper and cilantro.

Nutrition
288 Calories
24g Carbohydrate
5g Sugar

713. Berry Apple Cider

Preparation Time: 15 minutes
Cooking Time: 3 hours
Serving: 3
Ingredients

- 4 cinnamon sticks, cut into 1-inch pieces
- 1½ teaspoons whole cloves
- 4 cups apple cider
- 4 cups low-calorie cranberry-raspberry juice drink
- 1 medium apple

Direction
1. To make the spice bag, cut out a 6-inch square from double thick, pure cotton cheesecloth. Put in the cloves and cinnamon, then bring the corners up, tie it closed using a clean kitchen string that is pure cotton.
2. In a 3 1/2- 5-quart slow cooker, combine cranberry-raspberry juice, apple cider, and the spice bag.
3. Cook while covered over low heat setting for around 4-6 hours or on a high heat setting for 2-2 1/2 hours.
4. Throw out the spice bag. Serve right away or keep it warm while covered on warm or low-heat setting up to 2 hours, occasionally stirring. Garnish each serving with apples (thinly sliced).

Nutrition
89 Calories

22g Carbohydrate
19g Sugar

714. Brunswick Stew

Preparation Time: 10 minutes
Cooking Time: 45 minutes
Serving: 3
Ingredients

- 4 ounces diced salt pork
- 2 pounds chicken parts
- 8 cups water
- 3 potatoes, cubed
- 3 onions, chopped
- 1 (28 ounce) can whole peeled tomatoes
- 2 cups canned whole kernel corn
- 1 (10 ounce) package frozen lima beans
- 1 tablespoon Worcestershire sauce
- 1/2 teaspoon salt
- 1/4 teaspoon ground black pepper

Direction
1.   Mix and boil water, chicken and salt pork in a big pot on high heat. Lower heat to low. Cover then simmer until chicken is tender for 45 minutes.
2.   Take out chicken. Let cool until easily handled. Take meat out. Throw out bones and skin. Chop meat to bite-sized pieces. Put back in the soup.
3.   Add ground black pepper, salt, Worcestershire sauce, lima beans, corn, tomatoes, onions and potatoes. Mix well. Stir well and simmer for 1 hour, uncovered.

Nutrition
368 Calories
25.9g Carbohydrate
27.9g Protein

715. Buffalo Chicken Salads

Preparation Time: 7 minutes
Cooking Time: 3 hours
Serving: 5
Ingredients

- 1½ pounds chicken breast halves
- ½ cup Wing Time® Buffalo chicken sauce
- 4 teaspoons cider vinegar
- 1 teaspoon Worcestershire sauce
- 1 teaspoon paprika
- 1/3 cup light mayonnaise
- 2 tablespoons fat-free milk
- 2 tablespoons crumbled blue cheese
- 2 romaine hearts, chopped
- 1 cup whole grain croutons
- ½ cup very thinly sliced red onion

Direction
1.   Place chicken in a 2-quarts slow cooker. Mix together Worcestershire sauce, 2 teaspoons of vinegar and Buffalo sauce in a small bowl; pour over chicken. Dust with paprika. Close and cook for 3 hours on low-heat setting.
2.   Mix the leftover 2 teaspoons of vinegar with milk and light mayonnaise together in a small bowl at serving time; mix in blue cheese. While chicken is still in the slow cooker, pull meat into bite-sized pieces using two forks.
3.   Split the romaine among 6 dishes. Spoon sauce and chicken over lettuce. Pour with blue cheese dressing then add red onion slices and croutons on top.

Nutrition
274 Calories
11g Carbohydrate
2g Fiber

716. Cacciatore Style Chicken

Preparation Time: 10 minutes
Cooking Time: 4 hours
Serving: 6
Ingredients

- 2 cups sliced fresh mushrooms
- 1 cup sliced celery
- 1 cup chopped carrot
- 2 medium onions, cut into wedges
- 1 green, yellow, or red sweet peppers
- 4 cloves garlic, minced
- 12 chicken drumsticks
- ½ cup chicken broth
- ¼ cup dry white wine
- 2 tablespoons quick-cooking tapioca
- 2 bay leaves
- 1 teaspoon dried oregano, crushed
- 1 teaspoon sugar
- ½ teaspoon salt

- ¼ teaspoon pepper
- 1 (14.5 ounce) can diced tomatoes
- 1/3 cup tomato paste
- Hot cooked pasta or rice

Direction

1. Mix garlic, sweet pepper, onions, carrot, celery and mushrooms in a 5- or 6-qt. slow cooker. Cover veggies with the chicken. Add pepper, salt, sugar, oregano, bay leaves, tapioca, wine and broth.

2. Cover. Cook for 3–3 1/2 hours on high-heat setting.

3. Take chicken out; keep warm. Discard bay leaves. Turn to high-heat setting if using low-heat setting. Mix tomato paste and undrained tomatoes in. Cover. Cook on high-heat setting for 15 more minutes. Serving: Put veggie mixture on top of pasta and chicken.

Nutrition

324 Calories

7g Sugar:

35g Carbohydrate

717. Carnitas Tacos

Preparation Time: 10 minutes

Cooking Time: 5 hours

Serving: 4

Ingredients

- 3 to 3½-pound bone-in pork shoulder roast
- ½ cup chopped onion
- 1/3 cup orange juice
- 1 tablespoon ground cumin
- 1½ teaspoons kosher salt
- 1 teaspoon dried oregano, crushed
- ¼ teaspoon cayenne pepper
- 1 lime
- 2 (5.3 ounce) containers plain low-fat Greek yogurt
- 1 pinch kosher salt
- 16 (6 inch) soft yellow corn tortillas, such as Mission® brand
- 4 leaves green cabbage, quartered
- 1 cup very thinly sliced red onion
- 1 cup salsa (optional)

Direction

1. Take off meat from the bone; throw away bone. Trim meat fat. Slice meat into 2 to 3-inch pieces; put in a slow cooker of 3 1/2 or 4-quart in size. Mix in cayenne, oregano, salt, cumin, orange juice and onion.

2. Cover and cook for 4 to 5 hours on high. Take out meat from the cooker. Shred meat with two forks. Mix in enough cooking liquid to moisten.

3. Take out 1 teaspoon zest (put aside) for lime crema, then squeeze 2 tablespoons lime juice. Mix dash salt, yogurt, and lime juice in a small bowl.

4. Serve lime crema, salsa (if wished), red onion and cabbage with meat in tortillas. Scatter with lime zest.

Nutrition

301 Calories

28g Carbohydrate

7g Sugar

718. Chicken Chili

Preparation Time: 6 minutes

Cooking Time: 1 hour

Serving: 4

Ingredients

- 3 tablespoons vegetable oil
- 2 cloves garlic, minced
- 1 green bell pepper, chopped
- 1 onion, chopped
- 1 stalk celery, sliced
- 1/4-pound mushrooms, chopped
- 1-pound chicken breast
- 1 tablespoon chili powder
- 1 teaspoon dried oregano
- 1 teaspoon ground cumin
- 1/2 teaspoon paprika
- 1/2 teaspoon cocoa powder
- 1/4 teaspoon salt
- 1 pinch crushed red pepper flakes
- 1 pinch ground black pepper
- 1 (14.5 oz) can tomatoes with juice
- 1 (19 oz) can kidney beans

Direction

1. Fill 2 tablespoons of oil into a big skillet and heat it at moderate heat. Add mushrooms, celery, onion, bell pepper and garlic, sautéing for 5 minutes. Put it to one side.

2. Insert the leftover 1 tablespoon of oil into the skillet. At high heat, cook the chicken until browned and its exterior turns firm. Transfer the vegetable mixture back into skillet.

3. Stir in ground black pepper, hot pepper flakes, salt, cocoa powder, paprika, oregano, cumin and chili powder. Continue stirring for several minutes to avoid burning. Pour

in the beans and tomatoes and lead the entire mixture to boiling point then adjust the setting to low heat. Place a lid on the skillet and leave it simmering for 15 minutes. Uncover the skillet and leave it simmering for another 15 minutes.

Nutrition

308 Calories

25.9g Carbohydrate

29g Protein

719. Chicken Vera Cruz

Preparation Time: 7 minutes

Cooking Time: 10 hours

Serving: 5

Ingredients

- 1 medium onion, cut into wedges
- 1-pound yellow-skin potatoes
- 6 skinless, boneless chicken thighs
- 2 (14.5 oz.) cans no-salt-added diced tomatoes
- 1 fresh jalapeño chili pepper
- 2 tablespoons Worcestershire sauce
- 1 tablespoon chopped garlic
- 1 teaspoon dried oregano, crushed
- ¼ teaspoon ground cinnamon
- 1/8 teaspoon ground cloves
- ½ cup snipped fresh parsley
- ¼ cup chopped pimiento-stuffed green olives

Direction

1. Put onion in a 3 1/2- or 4-quart slow cooker. Place chicken thighs and potatoes on top. Drain and discard juices from a can of tomatoes. Stir undrained and drained tomatoes, cloves, cinnamon, oregano, garlic, Worcestershire sauce and jalapeño pepper together in a bowl. Pour over all in the cooker.

2. Cook with a cover for 10 hours on low-heat setting.

3. To make the topping: Stir chopped pimiento-stuffed green olives and snipped fresh parsley together in a small bowl. Drizzle the topping over each serving of chicken.

Nutrition

228 Calories

9g Sugar

25g Carbohydrate

720. Chicken and Cornmeal Dumplings

Preparation Time: 8 minutes

Cooking Time: 8 hours

Serving: 4

Ingredients

Chicken and Vegetable Filling

- 2 medium carrots, thinly sliced
- 1 stalk celery, thinly sliced
- 1/3 cup corn kernels
- ½ of a medium onion, thinly sliced
- 2 cloves garlic, minced
- 1 teaspoon snipped fresh rosemary
- ¼ teaspoon ground black pepper
- 2 chicken thighs, skinned
- 1 cup reduced sodium chicken broth
- ½ cup fat-free milk
- 1 tablespoon all-purpose flour

Cornmeal Dumplings

- ¼ cup flour
- ¼ cup cornmeal
- ½ teaspoon baking powder
- 1 egg white
- 1 tablespoon fat-free milk
- 1 tablespoon canola oil

Direction

1. Mix 1/4 teaspoon pepper, carrots, garlic, celery, rosemary, corn, and onion in a 1 1/2 or 2-quart slow cooker. Place chicken on top. Pour the broth atop mixture in the cooker.

2. Close and cook on low-heat for 7 to 8 hours.

3. If cooking with the low-heat setting, switch to high-heat setting (or if heat setting is not available, continue to cook). Place the chicken onto a cutting board and let to cool slightly. Once cool enough to handle, chop off chicken from bones and get rid of the bones. Chop the chicken and place back into the mixture in cooker. Mix flour and milk in a small bowl until smooth. Stir into the mixture in cooker.

4. Drop the Cornmeal Dumplings dough into 4 mounds atop hot chicken mixture using two spoons. Cover and cook for 20 to 25 minutes more or until a toothpick come out clean when inserted into a dumpling. (Avoid lifting lid when cooking.) Sprinkle each of the serving with coarse pepper if desired.

5. Mix together 1/2 teaspoon baking powder, 1/4 cup flour, a dash of salt and 1/4 cup cornmeal in a medium bowl. Mix 1 tablespoon canola oil, 1 egg white and 1 tablespoon

fat-free milk in a small bowl. Pour the egg mixture into the flour mixture. Mix just until moistened.

Nutrition

369 Calories

9g Sugar

47g Carbohydrate

721. Chicken and Pepperoni

Preparation Time: 4 minutes

Cooking Time: 4 hours

Serving: 5

Ingredients

- 3½ to 4 pounds meaty chicken pieces
- 1/8 teaspoon salt
- 1/8 teaspoon black pepper
- 2 ounces sliced turkey pepperoni
- ¼ cup sliced pitted ripe olives
- ½ cup reduced-sodium chicken broth
- 1 tablespoon tomato paste
- 1 teaspoon dried Italian seasoning, crushed
- ½ cup shredded part-skim mozzarella cheese (2 ounces)

Direction

1. Put chicken into a 3 1/2 to 5-qt. slow cooker. Sprinkle pepper and salt on the chicken. Slice pepperoni slices in half. Put olives and pepperoni into the slow cooker. In a small bowl, blend Italian seasoning, tomato paste and chicken broth together. Transfer the mixture into the slow cooker.

2. Cook with a cover for 3-3 1/2 hours on high.

3. Transfer the olives, pepperoni and chicken onto a serving platter with a slotted spoon. Discard the cooking liquid. Sprinkle cheese over the chicken. Use foil to loosely cover and allow to sit for 5 minutes to melt the cheese.

Nutrition

243 Calories

1g Carbohydrate

41g Protein

722. Chicken and Sausage Gumbo

Preparation Time: 6 minutes

Cooking Time: 4 hours

Serving: 5

Ingredients

- 1/3 cup all-purpose flour
- 1 (14 ounce) can reduced-sodium chicken broth
- 2 cups chicken breast
- 8 ounces smoked turkey sausage links
- 2 cups sliced fresh okra
- 1 cup water
- 1 cup coarsely chopped onion
- 1 cup sweet pepper
- ½ cup sliced celery
- 4 cloves garlic, minced
- 1 teaspoon dried thyme
- ½ teaspoon ground black pepper
- ¼ teaspoon cayenne pepper
- 3 cups hot cooked brown rice

Direction

1. To make the roux: Cook the flour upon a medium heat in a heavy medium-sized saucepan, stirring periodically, for roughly 6 minutes or until the flour browns. Take off the heat and slightly cool, then slowly stir in the broth. Cook the roux until it bubbles and thickens up.

2. Pour the roux in a 3 1/2- or 4-quart slow cooker, then add in cayenne pepper, black pepper, thyme, garlic, celery, sweet pepper, onion, water, okra, sausage, and chicken.

3. Cook the soup covered on a high setting for 3 - 3 1/2 hours. Take the fat off the top and serve atop hot cooked brown rice.

Nutrition

230 Calories

3g Sugar

19g Protein

723. Chicken, Barley, and Leek Stew

Preparation Time: 10 minutes

Cooking Time: 3 hours

Serving: 2

Ingredients

- 1-pound chicken thighs
- 1 tablespoon olive oil
- 1 (49 ounce) can reduced-sodium chicken broth
- 1 cup regular barley (not quick-cooking)
- 2 medium leeks, halved lengthwise and sliced

- 2 medium carrots, thinly sliced
- 1½ teaspoons dried basil or Italian seasoning, crushed
- ¼ teaspoon cracked black pepper

Direction

1. In the big skillet, cook the chicken in hot oil till becoming brown on all sides. In the 4-5-qt. slow cooker, whisk the pepper, dried basil, carrots, leeks, barley, chicken broth and chicken.

2. Keep covered and cooked over high heat setting for 2 – 2.5 hours or till the barley softens. As you wish, drizzle with the parsley or fresh basil prior to serving.

Nutrition

248 Calories

6g Fiber

27g Carbohydrate

724. Cider Pork Stew

Preparation Time: 9 minutes

Cooking Time: 12 hours

Serving: 3

Ingredients

- 2 pounds pork shoulder roast
- 3 medium cubed potatoes
- 3 medium carrots
- 2 medium onions, sliced
- 1 cup coarsely chopped apple
- ½ cup coarsely chopped celery
- 3 tablespoons quick-cooking tapioca
- 2 cups apple juice
- 1 teaspoon salt
- 1 teaspoon caraway seeds
- ¼ teaspoon black pepper

Direction

1. Chop the meat into 1-in. cubes. In the 3.5- 5.5 qt. slow cooker, mix the tapioca, celery, apple, onions, carrots, potatoes and meat. Whisk in pepper, caraway seeds, salt and apple juice.

2. Keep covered and cook over low heat setting for 10-12 hours. If you want, use the celery leaves to decorate each of the servings.

Nutrition

244 Calories

5g Fiber

33g Carbohydrate

725. Creamy Chicken Noodle Soup

Preparation Time: 7 minutes

Cooking Time: 8 hours

Serving: 4

Ingredients

- 1 (32 fluid ounce) container reduced-sodium chicken broth
- 3 cups water
- 2½ cups chopped cooked chicken
- 3 medium carrots, sliced
- 3 stalks celery
- 1½ cups sliced fresh mushrooms
- ¼ cup chopped onion
- 1½ teaspoons dried thyme, crushed
- ¾ teaspoon garlic-pepper seasoning
- 3 ounces reduced-fat cream cheese (Neufchâtel), cut up
- 2 cups dried egg noodles

Direction

1. Mix together the garlic-pepper seasoning, thyme, onion, mushrooms, celery, carrots, chicken, water and broth in a 5 to 6-quart slow cooker.

2. Put cover and let it cook for 6-8 hours on low-heat setting.

3. Increase to high-heat setting if you are using low-heat setting. Mix in the cream cheese until blended. Mix in uncooked noodles. Put cover and let it cook for an additional 20-30 minutes or just until the noodles become tender.

Nutrition

170 Calories

3g Sugar

2g Fiber

726. Cuban Pulled Pork Sandwich

Preparation Time: 6 minutes

Cooking Time: 5 hours

Serving: 5

Ingredients

- 1 teaspoon dried oregano, crushed
- ¾ teaspoon ground cumin
- ½ teaspoon ground coriander

- ¼ teaspoon salt
- ¼ teaspoon black pepper
- ¼ teaspoon ground allspice
- 1 2 to 2½-pound boneless pork shoulder roast
- 1 tablespoon olive oil
- Nonstick cooking spray
- 2 cups sliced onions
- 2 green sweet peppers, cut into bite-size strips
- ½ to 1 fresh jalapeño pepper
- 4 cloves garlic, minced
- ¼ cup orange juice
- ¼ cup lime juice
- 6 heart-healthy wheat hamburger buns, toasted
- 2 tablespoons jalapeño mustard

Direction

1. Mix allspice, oregano, black pepper, cumin, salt, and coriander together in a small bowl. Press each side of the roast into the spice mixture. On medium-high heat, heat oil in a big non-stick pan; put in roast. Cook for 5mins until both sides of the roast is light brown, turn the roast one time.

2. Using a cooking spray, grease a 3 1/2 or 4qt slow cooker; arrange the garlic, onions, jalapeno, and green peppers in a layer. Pour in lime juice and orange juice. Slice the roast if needed to fit inside the cooker; put on top of the vegetables covered or 4 1/2-5hrs on high heat setting.

3. Move roast to a cutting board using a slotted spoon. Drain the cooking liquid and keep the jalapeno, green peppers, and onions. Shred the roast with 2 forks then place it back in the cooker. Remove fat from the liquid. Mix half cup of cooking liquid and reserved vegetables into the cooker. Pour in more cooking liquid if desired. Discard the remaining cooking liquid.

4. Slather mustard on rolls. Split the meat between the bottom roll halves. Add avocado on top if desired. Place the roll tops to sandwiches.

Nutrition

379 Calories
32g Carbohydrate
4g Fiber

727. Gazpacho

Preparation Time: 15 minutes
Cooking Time: 0 minute
Serving: 4
Ingredients:

- 3 pounds ripe tomatoes
- 1 cup low-sodium tomato juice
- ½ red onion, chopped
- 1 cucumber
- 1 red bell pepper
- 2 celery stalks
- 2 tablespoons parsley
- 2 garlic cloves
- 2 tablespoons extra-virgin olive oil
- 2 tablespoons red wine vinegar
- 1 teaspoon honey
- ½ teaspoon salt
- ¼ teaspoon freshly ground black pepper

Direction

1. In a blender jar, combine the tomatoes, tomato juice, onion, cucumber, bell pepper, celery, parsley, garlic, olive oil, vinegar, honey, salt, and pepper. Pulse until blended but still slightly chunky.

2. Adjust the seasonings as needed and serve.

Nutrition:

170 Calories
24g Carbohydrates
16g Sugars

728. Tomato and Kale Soup

Preparation Time: 10 minutes
Cooking Time: 15 minutes
Servings: 4
Ingredients:

- 1 tablespoon extra-virgin olive oil
- 1 medium onion
- 2 carrots
- 3 garlic cloves
- 4 cups low-sodium vegetable broth
- 1 (28-ounce) can crushed tomatoes
- ½ teaspoon dried oregano
- ¼ teaspoon dried basil
- 4 cups chopped baby kale leaves
- ¼ teaspoon salt

Direction

1. In a huge pot, heat up oil over medium heat. Sauté onion and carrots for 3 to 5 minutes. Add the garlic and sauté for 30 seconds more, until fragrant.

2. Add the vegetable broth, tomatoes, oregano, and basil to the pot and boil. Decrease the heat to low and simmer for 5 minutes.

3. Using an immersion blender, purée the soup.

4. Add the kale and simmer for 3 more minutes. Season with the salt. Serve immediately.

Nutrition:

170 Calories

31g Carbohydrates

13g Sugars

729. Comforting Summer Squash Soup with Crispy Chickpeas

Preparation Time: 10 minutes

Cooking Time: 20 minutes

Serving: 4

Ingredients:

- 1 (15-ounce) can low-sodium chickpeas
- 1 teaspoon extra-virgin olive oil
- ¼ teaspoon smoked paprika
- Pinch salt, plus ½ teaspoon
- 3 medium zucchinis
- 3 cups low-sodium vegetable broth
- ½ onion
- 3 garlic cloves
- 2 tablespoons plain low-fat Greek yogurt
- Freshly ground black pepper

Direction:

1. Preheat the oven to 425°F. Line a baking sheet with parchment paper.

2. In a medium mixing bowl, toss the chickpeas with 1 teaspoon of olive oil, the smoked paprika, and a pinch salt. Transfer to the prepared baking sheet and roast until crispy, about 20 minutes, stirring once. Set aside.

3. Meanwhile, in a medium pot, heat the remaining 1 tablespoon of oil over medium heat.

4. Add the zucchini, broth, onion, and garlic to the pot, and boil. Simmer, and cook for 20 minutes.

5. In a blender jar, purée the soup. Return to the pot.

6. Add the yogurt, remaining ½ teaspoon of salt, and pepper, and stir well. Serve topped with the roasted chickpeas.

Nutrition:

188 Calories

24g Carbohydrates

7g Sugars

730. Curried Carrot Soup

Preparation Time: 10 minutes

Cooking Time: 5 minutes

Serving: 6

Ingredients:

- 1 tablespoon extra-virgin olive oil
- 1 small onion
- 2 celery stalks
- 1½ teaspoons curry powder
- 1 teaspoon ground cumin
- 1 teaspoon minced fresh ginger
- 6 medium carrots
- 4 cups low-sodium vegetable broth
- ¼ teaspoon salt
- 1 cup canned coconut milk
- ¼ teaspoon freshly ground black pepper
- 1 tablespoon chopped fresh cilantro

Direction:

1. Heat an Instant Pot to high and add the olive oil.

2. Sauté the onion and celery for 2 to 3 minutes. Add the curry powder, cumin, and ginger to the pot and cook until fragrant, about 30 seconds.

3. Add the carrots, vegetable broth, and salt to the pot. Close and seal, and set for 5 minutes on high. Allow the pressure to release naturally.

4. In a blender jar, carefully purée the soup in batches and transfer back to the pot.

5. Stir in the coconut milk and pepper, and heat through. Top with the cilantro and serve.

Nutrition:

145 Calories

13g Carbohydrates

4g Sugars

731. Thai Peanut, Carrot, and Shrimp Soup

Preparation Time: 10 minutes

Cooking Time: 10 minutes

Serving: 4

Ingredients:

- 1 tablespoon coconut oil

- 1 tablespoon Thai red curry paste
- ½ onion
- 3 garlic cloves
- 2 cups chopped carrots
- ½ cup whole unsalted peanuts
- 4 cups low-sodium vegetable broth
- ½ cup unsweetened plain almond milk
- ½ pound shrimp,
- Minced fresh cilantro, for garnish

Direction:

1. In a big pan, heat up oil over medium-high heat until shimmering.
2. Cook curry paste, stirring continuously, for 1 minute. Add the onion, garlic, carrots, and peanuts to the pan, and continue to cook for 2 to 3 minutes.
3. Boil broth. Reduce the heat to low and simmer for 5 to 6 minutes.
4. Purée the soup until smooth and return it to the pot. Over low heat, pour almond milk and stir to combine. Cook shrimp in the pot for 2 to 3 minutes.
5. Garnish with cilantro and serve.

Nutrition:

237 Calories

17g Carbohydrates

6g Sugars

732. Chicken Tortilla Soup

Preparation Time: 10 minutes

Cooking Time: 35 minutes

Serving: 4

Ingredients:

- 1 tablespoon extra-virgin olive oil
- 1 onion, thinly sliced
- 1 garlic clove, minced
- 1 jalapeño pepper, diced
- 2 boneless, skinless chicken breasts
- 4 cups low-sodium chicken broth
- 1 roma tomato, diced
- ½ teaspoon salt
- 2 (6-inch) corn tortillas
- Juice of 1 lime
- Minced fresh cilantro, for garnish
- ¼ cup shredded cheddar cheese, for garnish

Direction

1. In a medium pot, cook oil over medium-high heat. Add the onion and cook for 3 to 5 minutes until it begins to soften. Add the garlic and jalapeño, and cook until fragrant, about 1 minute more.
2. Add the chicken, chicken broth, tomato, and salt to the pot and boil. Lower heat to medium and simmer mildly for 20 to 25 minutes. Remove the chicken from the pot and set aside.
3. Preheat a broiler to high.
4. Spray the tortilla strips with nonstick cooking spray and toss to coat. Spread in a single layer on a baking sheet and broil for 3 to 5 minutes, flipping once, until crisp.
5. Once chicken is cooked, shred it with two forks and return to the pot.
6. Season the soup with the lime juice. Serve hot, garnished with cilantro, cheese, and tortilla strips.

Nutrition:

191 Calories

13g Carbohydrates

2g Sugars

733. Beef and Mushroom Barley Soup

Preparation Time: 10 minutes

Cooking Time: 80 minutes

Serving: 6

Ingredients:

- 1-pound beef stew meat, cubed
- ¼ teaspoon salt
- ¼ teaspoon freshly ground black pepper
- 1 tablespoon extra-virgin olive oil
- 8 ounces sliced mushrooms
- 1 onion, chopped
- 2 carrots, chopped
- 3 celery stalks, chopped
- 6 garlic cloves, minced
- ½ teaspoon dried thyme
- 4 cups low-sodium beef broth
- 1 cup water
- ½ cup pearl barley

Direction:

1. Season the meat well.
2. In an Instant Pot, heat the oil over high heat. Cook meat on all sides. Remove from the pot and set aside.

3. Add the mushrooms to the pot and cook for 1 to 2 minutes. Remove the mushrooms and set aside with the meat.

4. Sauté onion, carrots, and celery for 3 to 4 minutes. Add the garlic and continue to cook until fragrant, about 30 seconds longer.

5. Return the meat and mushrooms to the pot, then add the thyme, beef broth, and water. Adjust the pressure on high and cook for 15 minutes. Let the pressure release naturally.

6. Open the Instant Pot and add the barley. Use the slow cooker function on the Instant Pot, affix the lid (vent open), and continue to cook for 1 hour. Serve.

Nutrition:

245 Calories

19g Carbohydrates

3g Sugars

734. Cucumber, Tomato, and Avocado Salad

Preparation Time: 10 minutes

Cooking Time: 0 minute

Serving: 4

Ingredients:

- 1 cup cherry tomatoes
- 1 large cucumber
- 1 small red onion
- 1 avocado
- 2 tablespoons chopped fresh dill
- 2 tablespoons extra-virgin olive oil
- Juice of 1 lemon
- ¼ teaspoon salt
- ¼ teaspoon freshly ground black pepper

Direction:

1. In a big mixing bowl, mix the tomatoes, cucumber, onion, avocado, and dill.

2. In a small bowl, combine the oil, lemon juice, salt, and pepper, and mix well.

3. Drizzle the dressing over the vegetables and toss to combine. Serve.

Nutrition:

151 Calories

11g Carbohydrates

4g Sugars

735. Cabbage Slaw Salad

Preparation Time: 15 minutes

Cooking Time: 0 minute

Serving: 4

Ingredients:

- 2 cups green cabbage
- 2 cups red cabbage
- 2 cups grated carrots
- 3 scallions
- 2 tablespoons extra-virgin olive oil
- 2 tablespoons rice vinegar
- 1 teaspoon honey
- 1 garlic clove
- ¼ teaspoon salt

Direction:

1. Throw together the green and red cabbage, carrots, and scallions.

2. In a small bowl, whisk together the oil, vinegar, honey, garlic, and salt.

3. Pour the dressing over the veggies and mix to combine thoroughly.

4. Serve immediately, or cover and chill for several hours before serving.

Nutrition:

80 Calories

10g Carbohydrates

6g Sugars

736. Green Salad with Blackberries, Goat Cheese, and Sweet Potatoes

Preparation Time: 15 minutes

Cooking Time: 20 minutes

Serving: 4

Ingredients:

For the vinaigrette

- 1-pint blackberries
- 2 tablespoons red wine vinegar
- 1 tablespoon honey
- 3 tablespoons extra-virgin olive oil
- ¼ teaspoon salt
- Freshly ground black pepper

For the salad

- 1 sweet potato, cubed
- 1 teaspoon extra-virgin olive oil
- 8 cups salad greens (baby spinach, spicy greens, romaine)
- ½ red onion, sliced
- ¼ cup crumbled goat cheese

Direction:

For vinaigrette

1. In a blender jar, combine the blackberries, vinegar, honey, oil, salt, and pepper, and process until smooth. Set aside.

For salad

2. Preheat the oven to 425°F. Line a baking sheet with parchment paper.

3. Mix the sweet potato with the olive oil. Transfer to the prepared baking sheet and roast for 20 minutes, stirring once halfway through, until tender. Remove and cool for a few minutes.

4. In a large bowl, toss the greens with the red onion and cooled sweet potato, and drizzle with the vinaigrette. Serve topped with 1 tablespoon of goat cheese per serving.

Nutrition:

196 Calories

21g Carbohydrates

10g Sugars

737. Three Bean and Basil Salad

Preparation Time: 10 minutes

Cooking Time: 0 minute

Serving: 8

Ingredients:

- 1 (15-ounce) can low-sodium chickpeas
- 1 (15-ounce) can low-sodium kidney beans
- 1 (15-ounce) can low-sodium white beans
- 1 red bell pepper
- ¼ cup chopped scallions
- ¼ cup finely chopped fresh basil
- 3 garlic cloves, minced
- 2 tablespoons extra-virgin olive oil
- 1 tablespoon red wine vinegar
- 1 teaspoon Dijon mustard
- ¼ teaspoon freshly ground black pepper

Direction:

1. Toss chickpeas, kidney beans, white beans, bell pepper, scallions, basil, and garlic gently.

2. Blend together olive oil, vinegar, mustard, and pepper. Toss with the salad.

3. Wrap and chill for 1 hour.

Nutrition:

193 Calories

29g Carbohydrates

3g Sugars

738. Rainbow Black Bean Salad

Preparation Time: 15 minutes

Cooking Time: 0 minute

Serving: 5

Ingredients:

- 1 (15-ounce) can low-sodium black beans
- 1 avocado, diced
- 1 cup cherry
- tomatoes, halved
- 1 cup chopped baby spinach
- ½ cup red bell pepper
- ¼ cup jicama
- ½ cup scallions
- ¼ cup fresh cilantro
- 2 tablespoons lime juice
- 1 tablespoon extra-virgin olive oil
- 2 garlic cloves, minced
- 1 teaspoon honey
- ¼ teaspoon salt
- ¼ teaspoon freshly ground black pepper

Direction:

1. Mix black beans, avocado, tomatoes, spinach, bell pepper, jicama, scallions, and cilantro.

2. Blend lime juice, oil, garlic, honey, salt, and pepper. Add to the salad and toss.

3. Chill for 1 hour before serving.

Nutrition:

169 Calories

22g Carbohydrates

3g Sugars

739. Warm Barley and Squash Salad

Preparation Time: 20 minutes

Cooking Time: 40 minutes

Serving: 8

Ingredients:

- 1 small butternut squash
- 3 tablespoons extra-virgin olive oil
- 2 cups broccoli florets
- 1 cup pearl barley
- 1 cup toasted chopped walnuts
- 2 cups baby kale
- ½ red onion, sliced
- 2 tablespoons balsamic vinegar
- 2 garlic cloves, minced
- ½ teaspoon salt
- ¼ teaspoon black pepper

Direction:

1. Preheat the oven to 400°F. Line a baking sheet with parchment paper.

2. Peel off the squash, and slice into dice. In a large bowl, toss the squash with 2 teaspoons of olive oil. Transfer to the prepared baking sheet and roast for 20 minutes.

3. While the squash is roasting, toss the broccoli in the same bowl with 1 teaspoon of olive oil. After 20 minutes, flip the squash and push it to one side of the baking sheet. Add the broccoli to the other side and continue to roast for 20 more minutes until tender.

4. While the veggies are roasting, in a medium pot, cover the barley with several inches of water. Boil, then adjust heat, cover, and simmer for 30 minutes until tender. Drain and rinse.

5. Transfer the barley to a large bowl, and toss with the cooked squash and broccoli, walnuts, kale, and onion.

6. In a small bowl, mix the remaining 2 tablespoons of olive oil, balsamic vinegar, garlic, salt, and pepper. Drizzle dressing over the salad and toss.

Nutrition:

274 Calories

32g Carbohydrates

3g Sugars

740. Winter Chicken and Citrus Salad

Preparation Time: 10 minutes

Cooking Time: 0 minute

Serving: 4

Ingredients:

- 4 cups baby spinach
- 2 tablespoons extra-virgin olive oil
- 1 tablespoon lemon juice
- 1/8 teaspoon salt
- 2 cups chopped cooked chicken
- 2 mandarin oranges
- ½ peeled grapefruit, sectioned
- ¼ cup sliced almonds

Direction:

1. Toss spinach with the olive oil, lemon juice, salt, and pepper.

2. Add the chicken, oranges, grapefruit, and almonds to the bowl. Toss gently.

3. Arrange on 4 plates and serve.

Nutrition:

249 Calories

11g Carbohydrates

7g Sugars

741. Pork Chops with Grape Sauce

Preparation Time: 15 minutes

Cooking Time: 25 minutes

Servings: 4

Ingredients:

- Cooking spray
- 4 pork chops
- ¼ cup onion, sliced
- 1 clove garlic, minced
- 1/2 cup low-sodium chicken broth
- ¾ cup apple juice
- 1 tablespoon cornstarch
- 1 tablespoon balsamic vinegar
- 1 teaspoon honey
- 1 cup seedless red grapes, sliced in half

Directions:

1. Spray oil on your pan.

2. Put it over medium heat.

3. Add the pork chops to the pan.

4. Cook for 5 minutes per side.

5. Remove and set aside.

6. Add onion and garlic.

7. Cook for 2 minutes.

8. Pour in the broth and apple juice.

9. Bring to a boil.

10. Reduce heat to simmer.
11. Put the pork chops back to the skillet.
12. Simmer for 4 minutes.
13. In a bowl, mix the cornstarch, vinegar and honey.
14. Add to the pan.
15. Cook until the sauce has thickened.
16. Add the grapes.
17. Pour sauce over the pork chops before serving.

Nutrition:
Calories 188
Total Fat 4 g
Saturated Fat 1 g
Cholesterol 47 mg
Sodium 117 mg
Total Carbohydrate 18 g
Dietary Fiber 1 g
Total Sugars 13 g
Protein 19 g
Potassium 759 mg

742. Roasted Pork & Apples

Preparation Time: 15 minutes
Cooking Time: 30 minutes
Servings: 4
Ingredients:
- Salt and pepper to taste
- 1/2 teaspoon dried, crushed
- 1 lb. pork tenderloin
- 1 tablespoon canola oil
- 1 onion, sliced into wedges
- 3 cooking apples, sliced into wedges
- 2/3 cup apple cider
- Sprigs fresh sage

Directions:
1. In a bowl, mix salt, pepper and sage.
2. Season both sides of pork with this mixture.
3. Place a pan over medium heat.
4. Brown both sides.
5. Transfer to a roasting pan.
6. Add the onion on top and around the pork.
7. Drizzle oil on top of the pork and apples.
8. Roast in the oven at 425 degrees F for 10 minutes.
9. Add the apples, roast for another 15 minutes.
10. In a pan, boil the apple cider and then simmer for 10 minutes.

11. Pour the apple cider sauce over the pork before serving.

Nutrition:
Calories 239
Total Fat 6 g
Saturated Fat 1 g
Cholesterol 74 mg
Sodium 209 mg
Total Carbohydrate 22 g
Dietary Fiber 3 g
Total Sugars 16 g
Protein 24 g
Potassium 655 mg

743. Pork with Cranberry Relish

Preparation Time: 30 minutes
Cooking Time: 30 minutes
Servings: 4
Ingredients:
- 12 oz. pork tenderloin, fat trimmed and sliced crosswise
- Salt and pepper to taste
- ¼ cup all-purpose flour
- 2 tablespoons olive oil
- 1 onion, sliced thinly
- ¼ cup dried cranberries
- ¼ cup low-sodium chicken broth
- 1 tablespoon balsamic vinegar

Directions:
1. Flatten each slice of pork using a mallet.
2. In a dish, mix the salt, pepper and flour.
3. Dip each pork slice into the flour mixture.
4. Add oil to a pan over medium high heat.
5. Cook pork for 3 minutes per side or until golden crispy.
6. Transfer to a serving plate and cover with foil.
7. Cook the onion in the pan for 4 minutes.
8. Stir in the rest of the ingredients.
9. Simmer until the sauce has thickened.

Nutrition:
Calories 211
Total Fat 9 g
Saturated Fat 2 g
Cholesterol 53 mg
Sodium 116 mg
Total Carbohydrate 15 g

Dietary Fiber 1 g
Total Sugars 6 g
Protein 18 g
Potassium 378 mg

744. Sesame Pork with Mustard Sauce

Preparation Time: 25 minutes
Cooking Time: 25 minutes
Servings: 4
Ingredients:

- 2 tablespoons low-sodium teriyaki sauce
- ¼ cup chili sauce
- 2 cloves garlic, minced
- 2 teaspoons ginger, grated
- 2 pork tenderloins
- 2 teaspoons sesame seeds
- ¼ cup low fat sour cream
- 1 teaspoon Dijon mustard
- Salt to taste
- 1 scallion, chopped

Directions:
1. Preheat your oven to 425 degrees F.
2. Mix the teriyaki sauce, chili sauce, garlic and ginger.
3. Put the pork on a roasting pan.
4. Brush the sauce on both sides of the pork.
5. Bake in the oven for 15 minutes.
6. Brush with more sauce.
7. Top with sesame seeds.
8. Roast for 10 more minutes.
9. Mix the rest of the ingredients.
10. Serve the pork with mustard sauce.

Nutrition:
Calories 135
Total Fat 3 g
Saturated Fat 1 g
Cholesterol 56X mg
Sodium 302 mg
Total Carbohydrate 7 g
Dietary Fiber 1 g
Total Sugars 15 g
Protein 20 g
Potassium 755 mg

745. Steak with Mushroom Sauce

Preparation Time: 20 minutes
Cooking Time: 5 minutes
Servings: 4
Ingredients:

- 12 oz. sirloin steak, sliced and trimmed
- 2 teaspoons grilling seasoning
- 2 teaspoons oil
- 6 oz. broccoli, trimmed
- 2 cups frozen peas
- 3 cups fresh mushrooms, sliced
- 1 cup beef broth (unsalted)
- 1 tablespoon mustard
- 2 teaspoons cornstarch
- Salt to taste

Directions:
1. Preheat your oven to 350 degrees F.
2. Season meat with grilling seasoning.
3. In a pan over medium high heat, cook the meat and broccoli for 4 minutes.
4. Sprinkle the peas around the steak.
5. Put the pan inside the oven and bake for 8 minutes.
6. Remove both meat and vegetables from the pan.
7. Add the mushrooms to the pan.
8. Cook for 3 minutes.
9. Mix the broth, mustard, salt and cornstarch.
10. Add to the mushrooms.
11. Cook for 1 minute.
12. Pour sauce over meat and vegetables before serving.

Nutrition:
Calories 226
Total Fat 6 g
Saturated Fat 2 g
Cholesterol 51 mg
Sodium 356 mg
Total Carbohydrate 16 g
Dietary Fiber 5 g
Total Sugars 6 g
Protein 26 g
Potassium 780 mg

746.   Steak with Tomato & Herbs

Preparation Time: 30 minutes
Cooking Time: 30 minutes
Servings: 2
Ingredients:

- 8 oz. beef loin steak, sliced in half
- Salt and pepper to taste
- Cooking spray
- 1 teaspoon fresh basil, snipped
- ¼ cup green onion, sliced
- 1/2 cup tomato, chopped

Directions:

1. Season the steak with salt and pepper.
2. Spray oil on your pan.
3. Put the pan over medium high heat.
4. Once hot, add the steaks.
5. Reduce heat to medium.
6. Cook for 10 to 13 minutes for medium, turning once.
7. Add the basil and green onion.
8. Cook for 2 minutes.
9. Add the tomato.
10. Cook for 1 minute.
11. Let cool a little before slicing.

Nutrition:
Calories 170
Total Fat 6 g
Saturated Fat 2 g
Cholesterol 66 mg
Sodium 207 mg
Total Carbohydrate 3 g
Dietary Fiber 1 g
Total Sugars 5 g
Protein 25 g
Potassium 477 mg

747.   Barbecue Beef Brisket

Preparation Time: 25 minutes
Cooking Time: 10 hours
Servings: 10
Ingredients:

- 4 lb. beef brisket (boneless), trimmed and sliced
- 1 bay leaf
- 2 onions, sliced into rings
- 1/2 teaspoon dried thyme, crushed
- ¼ cup chili sauce
- 1 clove garlic, minced
- Salt and pepper to taste
- 2 tablespoons light brown sugar
- 2 tablespoons cornstarch
- 2 tablespoons cold water

Directions:

1. Put the meat in a slow cooker.
2. Add the bay leaf and onion.
3. In a bowl, mix the thyme, chili sauce, salt, pepper and sugar.
4. Pour the sauce over the meat.
5. Mix well.
6. Seal the pot and cook on low heat for 10 hours.
7. Discard the bay leaf.
8. Pour cooking liquid in a pan.
9. Add the mixed water and cornstarch.
10. Simmer until the sauce has thickened.
11. Pour the sauce over the meat.

Nutrition:
Calories 182
Total Fat 6 g
Saturated Fat 2 g
Cholesterol 57 mg
Sodium 217 mg
Total Sugars 4 g
Protein 20 g
Potassium 383 mg

748.   Beef & Asparagus

Preparation Time: 15 minutes
Cooking Time: 10 minutes
Servings: 4
Ingredients:

- 2 teaspoons olive oil
- 1 lb. lean beef sirloin, trimmed and sliced
- 1 carrot, shredded
- Salt and pepper to taste
- 12 oz. asparagus, trimmed and sliced
- 1 teaspoon dried herbes de Provence, crushed
- 1/2 cup Marsala
- ¼ teaspoon lemon zest

Directions:
1. Pour oil in a pan over medium heat.
2. Add the beef and carrot.
3. Season with salt and pepper.
4. Cook for 3 minutes.
5. Add the asparagus and herbs.
6. Cook for 2 minutes.
7. Add the Marsala and lemon zest.
8. Cook for 5 minutes, stirring frequently.

Nutrition:
Calories 327
Total Fat 7 g
Saturated Fat 2 g
Cholesterol 69 mg
Sodium 209 mg
Total Carbohydrate 29 g
Dietary Fiber 2 g
Total Sugars 3 g
Protein 28 g
Potassium 576 mg

749. Italian Beef

Preparation Time: 20 minutes
Cooking Time: 1 hour and 20 minutes
Servings: 4
Ingredients:

- Cooking spray
- 1 lb. beef round steak, trimmed and sliced
- 1 cup onion, chopped
- 2 cloves garlic, minced
- 1 cup green bell pepper, chopped
- 1/2 cup celery, chopped
- 2 cups mushrooms, sliced
- 14 1/2 oz. canned diced tomatoes
- 1/2 teaspoon dried basil
- ¼ teaspoon dried oregano
- 1/8 teaspoon crushed red pepper
- 2 tablespoons Parmesan cheese, grated

Directions:
1. Spray oil on the pan over medium heat.
2. Cook the meat until brown on both sides.
3. Transfer meat to a plate.
4. Add the onion, garlic, bell pepper, celery and mushroom to the pan.
5. Cook until tender.

6. Add the tomatoes, herbs, and pepper.
7. Put the meat back to the pan.
8. Simmer while covered for 1 hour and 15 minutes.
9. Stir occasionally.
10. Sprinkle Parmesan cheese on top of the dish before serving.

Nutrition:
Calories 212
Total Fat 4 g
Saturated Fat 1 g
Cholesterol 51 mg
Sodium 296 mg
Total Sugars 6 g
Protein 30 g
Potassium 876 mg

750. Lamb with Broccoli & Carrots

Preparation Time: 20 minutes
Cooking Time: 10 minutes
Servings: 4
Ingredients:

- 2 cloves garlic, minced
- 1 tablespoon fresh ginger, grated
- ¼ teaspoon red pepper, crushed
- 2 tablespoons low-sodium soy sauce
- 1 tablespoon white vinegar
- 1 tablespoon cornstarch
- 12 oz. lamb meat, trimmed and sliced
- 2 teaspoons cooking oil
- 1 lb. broccoli, sliced into florets
- 2 carrots, sliced into strips
- ¾ cup low-sodium beef broth
- 4 green onions, chopped
- 2 cups cooked spaghetti squash pasta

Directions:
1. Combine the garlic, ginger, red pepper, soy sauce, vinegar and cornstarch in a bowl.
2. Add lamb to the marinade.
3. Marinate for 10 minutes.
4. Discard marinade.
5. In a pan over medium heat, add the oil.
6. Add the lamb and cook for 3 minutes.
7. Transfer lamb to a plate.

8. Add the broccoli and carrots.
9. Cook for 1 minute.
10. Pour in the beef broth.
11. Cook for 5 minutes.
12. Put the meat back to the pan.
13. Sprinkle with green onion and serve on top of spaghetti squash.
Nutrition:
Calories 205
Total Fat 6 g
Saturated Fat 1 g
Cholesterol 40 mg
Sodium 659 mg
Total Carbohydrate 17 g

751. Rosemary Lamb

Preparation Time: 15 minutes
Cooking Time: 2 hours
Servings: 14
Ingredients:
- Salt and pepper to taste
- 2 teaspoons fresh rosemary, snipped
- 5 lb. whole leg of lamb, trimmed and cut with slits on all sides
- 3 cloves garlic, slivered
- 1 cup water
Directions:
1. Preheat your oven to 375 degrees F.
2. Mix salt, pepper and rosemary in a bowl.
3. Sprinkle mixture all over the lamb.
4. Insert slivers of garlic into the slits.
5. Put the lamb on a roasting pan.
6. Add water to the pan.
7. Roast for 2 hours.
Nutrition:
Calories 136

Total Fat 4 g
Saturated Fat 1 g
Cholesterol 71 mg
Sodium 218 mg
Protein 23 g
Potassium 248 mg

752. Mediterranean Lamb Meatballs

Preparation Time: 10 minutes
Cooking Time: 20 minutes
Servings: 8
Ingredients:
- 12 oz. roasted red peppers
- 1 1/2 cups whole wheat breadcrumbs
- 2 eggs, beaten
- 1/3 cup tomato sauce
- 1/2 cup fresh basil
- ¼ cup parsley, snipped
- Salt and pepper to taste
- 2 lb. lean ground lamb
Directions:
1. Preheat your oven to 350 degrees F.
2. In a bowl, mix all the ingredients and then form into meatballs.
3. Put the meatballs on a baking pan.
4. Bake in the oven for 20 minutes.
Nutrition:
Calories 94
Total Fat 3 g
Saturated Fat 1 g
Cholesterol 35 mg
Sodium 170 mg
Total Carbohydrate 2 g
Dietary Fiber 1 g
Total Sugars 0 g

Second Course Recipes

753. Cauliflower Rice with

Chicken

Preparation Time: 15 Minutes
Cooking Time: 15 Minutes
Servings: 4
Ingredients

- 1/2 large cauliflower
- 3/4 cup cooked meat
- 1/2 bell pepper
- 1 carrot
- 2 ribs celery
- 1 tbsp. stir fry sauce (low carb)
- 1 tbsp. extra virgin olive oil
- Salt and pepper to taste

Directions
1.   Chop cauliflower in a processor to "rice." Place in a bowl.
2.   Properly chop all vegetables in a food processor into thin slices.
3.   Add cauliflower and other plants to WOK with heated oil. Fry until all veggies are tender.
4.   Add chopped meat and sauce to the wok and fry 10 Minutes.
Serve.
This dish is very mouth-watering!
Nutrition:
Calories 200 / Protein 10 g / Fat 12 g /Carbs 10 g

754. Turkey with Fried Eggs

Preparation Time: 10 Minutes
Cooking Time: 20 Minutes
Servings: 4
Ingredients

- 4 large potatoes
- 1 cooked turkey thigh
- 1 large onion (about 2 cups diced)
- butter
- Chile flakes
- 4 eggs
- salt to taste
- pepper to taste

Directions
1.   Rub the cold boiled potatoes on the coarsest holes of a box grater. Dice the turkey.
2.   Cook the onion in as much unsalted butter as you feel comfortable with until it's just fragrant and translucent.
3.   Add the rubbed potatoes and a cup of diced cooked turkey, salt and pepper to taste, and cook 20 Minutes.
Top each with a fried egg. Yummy!
Nutrition:
Calories 170 / Protein 19 g / Fat 7 g / Carbs 6 g

755. Sweet Potato, Kale, and White Bean Stew

Preparation time: 15 minutes
Cooking time: 25 minutes
Servings: 4
Ingredients:

- 1 (15-ounce) can low-sodium cannellini beans, rinsed and drained, divided
- 1 tablespoon olive oil
- 1 medium onion, chopped
- 2 garlic cloves, minced
- 2 celery stalks, chopped
- 3 medium carrots, chopped
- 2 cups low-sodium vegetable broth
- 1 teaspoon apple cider vinegar
- 2 medium sweet potatoes (about 1¼ pounds)
- 2 cups chopped kale
- 1 cup shelled edamame
- ¼ cup quinoa
- 1 teaspoon dried thyme
- 1/2 teaspoon cayenne pepper

- 1/2 teaspoon salt
- ¼ teaspoon freshly ground black pepper

Directions:

1. Put half the beans into a blender and blend until smooth. Set aside.

2. In a large soup pot over medium heat, heat the oil. When the oil is shining, include the onion and garlic, and cook until the onion softens and the garlic is sweet, about 3 minutes. Add the celery and carrots, and continue cooking until the vegetables soften, about 5 minutes.

3. Add the broth, vinegar, sweet potatoes, unblended beans, kale, edamame, and quinoa, and bring the mixture to a boil. Reduce the heat and simmer until the vegetables soften, about 10 minutes.

4. Add the blended beans, thyme, cayenne, salt, and black pepper, increase the heat to medium-high, and bring the mixture to a boil. Reduce the heat and simmer, uncovered, until the flavors combine, about 5 minutes.

5. Into each of 4 containers, scoop 1¾ cups of stew.

Nutrition: calories: 373; total fat: 7g; saturated fat: 1g; protein: 15g; total carbs: 65g; fiber: 15g; sugar: 13g; sodium: 540mg

756. Slow Cooker Two-Bean Sloppy Joes

Preparation time: 10 minutes
Cooking time: 6 hours
Servings: 4
Ingredients:

- 1 (15-ounce) can low-sodium black beans
- 1 (15-ounce) can low-sodium pinto beans
- 1 (15-ounce) can no-salt-added diced tomatoes
- 1 medium green bell pepper, cored, seeded, and chopped
- 1 medium yellow onion, chopped
- ¼ cup low-sodium vegetable broth
- 2 garlic cloves, minced
- 2 servings (¼ cup) meal prep barbecue sauce or bottled barbecue sauce
- ¼ teaspoon salt
- ¼ teaspoon freshly ground black pepper
- 4 whole-wheat buns

Directions:

1. In a slow cooker, combine the black beans, pinto beans, diced tomatoes, bell pepper, onion, broth, garlic, meal prep barbecue sauce, salt, and black pepper. Stir the ingredients, then cover and cook on low for 6 hours.

2. Into each of 4 containers, spoon 1¼ cups of sloppy joe mix. Serve with 1 whole-wheat bun.

3. Storage: place airtight containers in the refrigerator for up to 1 week. To freeze, place freezer-safe containers in the freezer for up to 2 months. To defrost, refrigerate overnight. To reheat individual portions, microwave uncovered on high for 2 to 21/2 minutes. Alternatively, reheat the entire dish in a saucepan on the stove top. Bring the sloppy joes to a boil, then reduce the heat and simmer until heated through, 10 to 15 minutes. Serve with a whole-wheat bun.

Nutrition: calories: 392; total fat: 3g; saturated fat: 0g; protein: 17g; total carbs: 79g; fiber: 19g; sugar: 15g; sodium: 759mg

757. Lighter Eggplant Parmesan

Preparation time: 15 minutes
Cooking time: 35 minutes
Servings: 4
Ingredients:

- Nonstick cooking spray
- 3 eggs, beaten
- 1 tablespoon dried parsley
- 2 teaspoons ground oregano
- 1/8 teaspoon freshly ground black pepper
- 1 cup panko bread crumbs, preferably whole-wheat
- 1 large eggplant (about 2 pounds)
- 5 servings (21/2 cups) chunky tomato sauce or jarred low-sodium tomato sauce
- 1 cup part-skim mozzarella cheese
- ¼ cup grated parmesan cheese

Directions:

1. Preheat the oven to 450f. Coat a baking sheet with cooking spray.

2. In a medium bowl, whisk together the eggs, parsley, oregano, and pepper.

3. Pour the panko into a separate medium bowl.

4. Slice the eggplant into ¼-inch-thick slices. Dip each slice of eggplant into the egg mixture, shaking off the excess. Then dredge both sides of the eggplant in the panko bread crumbs. Place the coated eggplant on the prepared baking sheet, leaving a 1/2-inch space between each slice.

5. Bake for about 15 minutes until soft and golden brown. Remove from the oven and set aside to slightly cool.

6. Pour 1/2 cup of chunky tomato sauce on the bottom of an 8-by-15-inch baking dish. Using a spatula or the back of a spoon spread the tomato sauce evenly. Place half the slices of cooked eggplant, slightly overlapping, in the dish, and top with 1 cup of chunky tomato sauce, 1/2 cup of mozzarella and 2 tablespoons of grated parmesan. Repeat the layer, ending with the cheese.

7. Bake uncovered for 20 minutes until the cheese is bubbling and slightly browned.

8. Remove from the oven and allow cooling for 15 minutes before dividing the eggplant equally into 4 separate containers.

Nutrition: calories: 333; total fat: 14g; saturated fat: 6g; protein: 20g; total carbs: 35g; fiber: 11g; sugar: 15g; sodium: 994mg

758. Coconut-Lentil Curry

Preparation time: 15 minutes
Cooking time: 35 minutes
Servings: 4
Ingredients:

- 1 tablespoon olive oil
- 1 medium yellow onion, chopped
- 1 garlic clove, minced
- 1 medium red bell pepper, diced
- 1 (15-ounce) can green or brown lentils, rinsed and drained
- 2 medium sweet potatoes, washed, peeled, and cut into bite-size chunks (about 1¼ pounds)
- 1 (15-ounce) can no-salt-added diced tomatoes
- 2 tablespoons tomato paste
- 4 teaspoons curry powder
- 1/8 teaspoon ground cloves
- 1 (15-ounce) can light coconut milk
- ¼ teaspoon salt
- 2 pieces whole-wheat naan bread, halved, or 4 slices crusty bread

Directions:

1. In a large saucepan over medium heat, heat the olive oil. When the oil is shimmering, add both the onion and garlic and cook until the onion softens and the garlic is sweet, for about 3 minutes.

2. Add the bell pepper and continue cooking until it softens, about 5 minutes more. Add the lentils, sweet potatoes, tomatoes, tomato paste, curry powder, and cloves, and bring the mixture to a boil. Reduce the heat to medium-low, cover, and simmer until the potatoes are softened, about 20 minutes.

3. Add the coconut milk and salt, and return to a boil. Reduce the heat and simmer until the flavors combine, about 5 minutes.

4. Into each of 4 containers, spoon 2 cups of curry.

5. Enjoy each serving with half of a piece of naan bread or 1 slice of crusty bread.

Nutrition: calories: 559; total fat: 16g; saturated fat: 7g; protein: 16g; total carbs: 86g; fiber: 16g; sugar: 18g; sodium: 819mg

759. Stuffed Portobello with Cheese

Preparation time: 15 minutes
Cooking time: 25 minutes
Servings: 4
Ingredients:

- 4 Portobello mushroom caps
- 1 tablespoon olive oil
- 1/2 teaspoon salt, divided
- ¼ teaspoon freshly ground black pepper, divided
- 1 cup baby spinach, chopped
- 11/2 cups part-skim ricotta cheese
- 1/2 cup part-skim shredded mozzarella cheese
- ¼ cup grated parmesan cheese
- 1 garlic clove, minced
- 1 tablespoon dried parsley
- 2 teaspoons dried oregano
- 4 teaspoons unseasoned bread crumbs, divided
- 4 servings (4 cups) roasted broccoli with shallots

Directions:

1. Preheat the oven to 375f. Line a baking sheet with aluminum foil.

2. Brush the mushroom caps with the olive oil, and sprinkle with ¼ teaspoon salt and 1/8 teaspoon pepper. Put the mushroom caps on the prepared baking sheet and bake until soft, about 12 minutes.

3. In a medium bowl, mix together the spinach, ricotta, mozzarella, parmesan, garlic, parsley, oregano, and the remaining ¼ teaspoon of salt and 1/8 teaspoon of pepper.

4. Spoon 1/2 cup of cheese mixture into each mushroom cap, and sprinkle each with 1 teaspoon of bread crumbs. Return the mushrooms to the oven for an additional 8 to 10 minutes until warmed through.

5. Remove from the oven and allow the mushrooms to cool for about 10 minutes before placing each in an individual container. Add 1 cup of roasted broccoli with shallots to each container.

Nutrition: calories: 419; total fat: 30g; saturated fat: 10g; protein: 23g; total carbs: 19g; fiber: 2g; sugar: 3g; sodium: 790mg

760. Lighter Shrimp Scampi

Preparation time: 15 minutes
Cooking time: 15 minutes
Servings: 4
Ingredients:

- 11/2 pounds large peeled and deveined shrimp
- ¼ teaspoon salt
- 1/8 teaspoon freshly ground black pepper
- 2 tablespoons olive oil
- 1 shallot, chopped
- 2 garlic cloves, minced
- ¼ cup cooking white wine
- Juice of 1/2 lemon (1 tablespoon)
- 1/2 teaspoon sriracha
- 2 tablespoons unsalted butter, at room temperature
- ¼ cup chopped fresh parsley
- 4 servings (6 cups) zucchini noodles with lemon vinaigrette

Directions:

1. Season the shrimp with the salt and pepper.
2. In a medium saucepan over medium heat, heat the oil. Add the shallot and garlic, and cook until the shallot softens and the garlic is fragrant, about 3 minutes. Add the shrimp, cover, and cook until opaque, 2 to 3 minutes on each side. Using a slotted spoon, transfer the shrimp to a large plate.
3. Add the wine, lemon juice, and sriracha to the saucepan, and stir to combine. Bring the mixture to a boil, then reduce the heat and simmer until the liquid is reduced by about half, 3 minutes. Add the butter and stir until melted, about 3 minutes. Return the shrimp to the saucepan and toss to coat. Add the parsley and stir to combine.

4. Into each of 4 containers, place 11/2 cups of zucchini noodles with lemon vinaigrette, and top with ¾ cup of scampi.

Nutrition: calories: 364; total fat: 21g; saturated fat: 6g; protein: 37g; total carbs: 10g; fiber: 2g; sugar: 6g; sodium: 557mg

761. Maple-Mustard Salmon

Preparation time: 10 minutes, plus 30 minutes marinating time
Cooking time: 20 minutes
Servings: 4
Ingredients:

- Nonstick cooking spray
- 1/2 cup 100% maple syrup
- 2 tablespoons Dijon mustard
- ¼ teaspoon salt
- 4 (5-ounce) salmon fillets
- 4 servings (4 cups) roasted broccoli with shallots
- 4 servings (2 cups) parleyed whole-wheat couscous

Directions:

1. Preheat the oven to 400f. Line a baking sheet with aluminum foil and coat with cooking spray.
2. In a medium bowl, whisk together the maple syrup, mustard, and salt until smooth.
3. Put the salmon fillets into the bowl and toss to coat. Cover and place in the refrigerator to marinate for at least 30 minutes and up to overnight.
4. Shake off excess marinade from the salmon fillets and place them on the prepared baking sheet, leaving a 1-inch space between each fillet. Discard the extra marinade.
5. Bake for about 20 minutes until the salmon is opaque and a thermometer inserted in the thickest part of a fillet reads 145f.
6. Into each of 4 resealable containers, place 1 salmon fillet, 1 cup of roasted broccoli with shallots, and 1/2 cup of parleyed whole-wheat couscous.

Nutrition: calories: 601; total fat: 29g; saturated fat: 4g; protein: 36g; total carbs: 51g; fiber: 3g; sugar: 23g; sodium: 610mg

762. Chicken Salad with Grapes and Pecans

Preparation Time: 15 Minutes
Cooking Time: 5 Minutes
Servings: 4

Ingredients:

- 1/3 cup unsalted pecans, chopped
- 10 ounces cooked skinless, boneless chicken breast or rotisserie chicken, finely chopped
- 1/2 medium yellow onion, finely chopped
- 1 celery stalk, finely chopped
- ¾ cup red or green seedless grapes, halved
- ¼ cup light mayonnaise
- ¼ cup nonfat plain Greek yogurt
- 1 tablespoon Dijon mustard
- 1 tablespoon dried parsley
- ¼ teaspoon salt
- 1/8 teaspoon freshly ground black pepper
- 1 cup shredded romaine lettuce
- 4 (8-inch) whole-wheat pitas

Directions:

1. Heat a small skillet over medium-low heat to toast the pecans. Cook the pecans until fragrant, about 3 minutes. Remove from the heat and set aside to cool.

2. In a medium bowl, mix the chicken, onion, celery, pecans, and grapes.

3. In a small bowl, whisk together the mayonnaise, yogurt, mustard, parsley, salt, and pepper. Spoon the sauce over the chicken mixture and stir until well combined.

4. Into each of 4 containers, place ¼ cup of lettuce and top with 1 cup of chicken salad. Store the pitas separately until ready to serve.

5. When ready to eat, stuff the serving of salad and lettuce into 1 pita.

Nutrition: Calories: 418; Total Fat: 14g; Saturated Fat: 2g; Protein: 31g; Total Carbs: 43g; Fiber: 6g;

763. Roasted Vegetables

Preparation time: 14 minutes
Cooking time: 17 minutes
Servings: 3
Ingredients:

- 4 Tbsp. olive oil, reserve some for greasing
- 2 heads, large garlic, tops sliced off
- 2 large eggplants/aubergine, tops removed, cubed
- 2 large shallots, peeled, quartered
- 1 large carrot, peeled, cubed
- 1 large parsnips, peeled, cubed
- 1 small green bell pepper, deseeded, ribbed, cubed
- 1 small red bell pepper, deseeded, ribbed, cubed
- ½ pound Brussels sprouts, halved, do not remove cores
- 1 sprig, large thyme, leaves picked
- sea salt, coarse-grained

For garnish

- 1 large lemon, halved, ½ squeezed, ½ sliced into smaller wedges
- 1/8 cup fennel bulb, minced

Directions:

1. From 425°F or 220°C preheat oven for at least 5 minutes before using.

2. Line deep roasting pan with aluminum foil; lightly grease with oil. Tumble in bell peppers, Brussels sprouts, carrots, eggplants, garlic, parsnips, rosemary leaves, shallots, and thyme. Add a pinch of sea salt; drizzle in remaining oil and lemon juice. Toss well to combine.

3. Cover roasting pan with a sheet of aluminum foil. Place this on middle rack of oven. Bake for 20 to 30 minutes. Remove aluminum foil. Roast, for another 5 to 10 minutes, or until some vegetables brown at the edges. Remove roasting pan from oven. Cool slightly before ladling equal portions into plates.

4. Garnish with fennel and a wedge of lemon. Squeeze lemon juice on top of dish before eating.

Nutrition:
Calories 163
Total Fat 4.2 g
Saturated Fat 0.8 g
Cholesterol 0 mg
Sodium 861 mg
Total Carbs 22.5 g
Fiber 6.3 g
Sugar 2.3 g
Protein 9.2 g

764. Millet Pilaf

Preparation time: 10 minutes
Cooking time: 15 minutes
Servings: 4
Ingredients:

- 1 cup millet
- 2 tomatoes, rinsed, seeded, and chopped
- 1¾ cups filtered water
- 2 tablespoons extra-virgin olive oil

- ¼ cup chopped dried apricot
- Zest of 1 lemon
- Juice of 1 lemon
- ½ cup fresh parsley, rinsed and chopped
- Himalayan pink salt
- Freshly ground black pepper

Directions:

1. In an electric pressure cooker, combine the millet, tomatoes, and water. Lock the lid into place, select Manual and High Pressure, and cook for 7 minutes.

2. When the beep sounds, quick release the pressure by pressing Cancel and twisting the steam valve to the Venting position. Carefully remove the lid.

3. Stir in the olive oil, apricot, lemon zest, lemon juice, and parsley. Taste, season with salt and pepper, and serve.

Nutrition:

Calories: 270

Total fat: 8g

Total carbohydrates: 42g

Fiber: 5g

Sugar: 3g

Protein: 6g

765. Sweet and Sour Onions

Preparation time: 10 minutes

Cooking time: 11 minutes

Servings: 4

Ingredients:

- 4 large onions, halved
- 2 garlic cloves, crushed
- 3 cups vegetable stock
- 1 ½ tablespoon balsamic vinegar
- ½ teaspoon Dijon mustard
- 1 tablespoon sugar

Directions:

1. Combine onions and garlic in a pan. Fry for 3 minutes, or till softened.

2. Pour stock, vinegar, Dijon mustard, and sugar. Bring to a boil.

3. Reduce heat. Cover and let the combination simmer for 10 minutes.

4. Get rid of from heat. Continue stirring until the liquid is reduced and the onions are brown. Serve.

Nutrition:

Calories 203

Total Fat 41.2 g

Saturated Fat 0.8 g

Cholesterol 0 mg

Sodium 861 mg

Total Carbs 29.5 g

Fiber 16.3 g

Sugar 29.3 g

Protein 19.2 g

766. Sautéed Apples and Onions

Preparation time: 14 minutes

Cooking time: 16 minutes

Servings: 3

Ingredients:

- 2 cups dry cider
- 1 large onion, halved
- 2 cups vegetable stock
- 4 apples, sliced into wedges
- Pinch of salt
- Pinch of pepper

Directions:

1. Combine cider and onion in a saucepan. Bring to a boil until the onions are cooked and liquid almost gone.

2. Pour the stock and the apples. Season with salt and pepper. Stir occasionally. Cook for about 10 minutes or until the apples are tender but not mushy. Serve.

Nutrition:

Calories 343

Total Fat 51.2 g

Saturated Fat 0.8 g

Cholesterol 0 mg

Sodium 861 mg

Total Carbs 22.5 g

Fiber 6.3 g

Sugar 2.3 g

Protein 9.2 g

767. Zucchini Noodles with Portabella Mushrooms

Preparation time: 14 minutes

Cooking time: 16 minutes

Servings: 3

Ingredients:

- 1 zucchini, processed into spaghetti-like noodles
- 3 garlic cloves, minced

- 2 white onions, thinly sliced
- 1 thumb-sized ginger, julienned
- 1 lb. chicken thighs
- 1 lb. portabella mushrooms, sliced into thick slivers
- 2 cups chicken stock
- 3 cups water
- Pinch of sea salt, add more if needed
- Pinch of black pepper, add more if needed
- 2 tsp. sesame oil
- 4 Tbsp. coconut oil, divided
- ¼ cup fresh chives, minced, for garnish

Directions:

1.   Pour 2 tablespoons of coconut oil into a large saucepan. Fry mushroom slivers in batches for 5 minutes or until seared brown. Set aside. Transfer these to a plate.

2.   Sauté the onion, garlic, and ginger for 3 minutes or until tender. Add in chicken thighs, cooked mushrooms, chicken stock, water, salt, and pepper stir mixture well. Bring to a boil.

3.   Decrease gradually the heat and allow simmering for 20 minutes or until the chicken is forking tender. Tip in sesame oil.

4.   Serve by placing an equal amount of zucchini noodles into bowls. Ladle soup and garnish with chives.

Nutrition:

Calories 163
Total Fat 4.2 g
Saturated Fat 0.8 g
Cholesterol 0 mg
Sodium 861 mg
Total Carbs 22.5 g
Fiber 6.3 g
Sugar 2.3 g
Protein 9.2 g

768.   Grilled Tempeh with Pineapple

Preparation time: 12 minutes
Cooking time: 16 minutes
Servings: 3
Ingredients:

- 10 oz. tempeh, sliced
- 1 red bell pepper, quartered
- 1/4 pineapple, sliced into rings

- 6 oz. green beans
- 1 tbsp. coconut aminos
- 2 1/2 tbsp. orange juice, freshly squeeze
- 1 1/2 tbsp. lemon juice, freshly squeezed
- 1 tbsp. extra virgin olive oil
- 1/4 cup hoisin sauce

Directions:

1.   Blend together the olive oil, orange and lemon juices, coconut aminos or soy sauce, and hoisin sauce in a bowl. Add the diced tempeh and set aside.

2.   Heat up the grill or place a grill pan over medium high flame. Once hot, lift the marinated tempeh from the bowl with a pair of tongs and transfer them to the grill or pan.

3.   Grille for 2 to 3 minutes, or until browned all over.

4.   Grill the sliced pineapples alongside the tempeh, then transfer them directly onto the serving platter.

5.   Place the grilled tempeh beside the grilled pineapple and cover with aluminum foil to keep warm.

6.   Meanwhile, place the green beans and bell peppers in a bowl and add just enough of the marinade to coat.

7.   Prepare the grill pan and add the vegetables. Grill until fork tender and slightly charred.

8.   Transfer the grilled vegetables to the serving platter and arrange artfully with the tempeh and pineapple. Serve at once.

Nutrition:

Calories 163
Total Fat 4.2 g
Saturated Fat 0.8 g
Cholesterol 0 mg
Sodium 861 mg
Total Carbs 22.5 g
Fiber 6.3 g
Sugar 2.3 g
Protein 9.2 g

769.   Courgettes In Cider Sauce

Preparation time: 13 minutes
Cooking time: 17 minutes
Servings: 3
Ingredients:

- 2 cups baby courgettes
- 3 tablespoons vegetable stock
- 2 tablespoons apple cider vinegar

- 1 tablespoon light brown sugar
- 4 spring onions, finely sliced
- 1-piece fresh gingerroot, grated
- 1 teaspoon corn flour
- 2 teaspoons water

Directions:

1. Bring a pan with salted water to a boil. Add courgettes. Bring to a boil for 5 minutes.

2. Meanwhile, in a pan, combine vegetable stock, apple cider vinegar, brown sugar, onions, gingerroot, lemon juice and rind, and orange juice and rind. Take to a boil. Lower the heat and allow simmering for 3 minutes.

3. Mix the corn flour with water. Stir well. Pour into the sauce. Continue stirring until the sauce thickens.

4. Drain courgettes. Transfer to the serving dish. Spoon over the sauce. Toss to coat courgettes. Serve.

Nutrition:
Calories 173
Total Fat 9.2 g
Saturated Fat 0.8 g
Cholesterol 0 mg
Sodium 861 mg
Total Carbs 22.5 g
Fiber 6.3 g
Sugar 2.3 g
Protein 9.2 g

770. Baked Mixed Mushrooms

Preparation time: 8 minutes
Cooking time: 20 minutes
Servings: 3
Ingredients:

- 2 cups mixed wild mushrooms
- 1 cup chestnut mushrooms
- 2 cups dried porcini
- 2 shallots
- 4 garlic cloves
- 3 cups raw pecans
- ½ bunch fresh thyme
- 1 bunch flat-leaf parsley
- 2 tablespoons olive oil
- 2 fresh bay leaves
- 1 ½ cups stale bread

Directions:

1. Remove skin and finely chop garlic and shallots. Roughly chop the wild mushrooms and chestnut mushrooms. Pick the leaves of the thyme and tear the bread into small pieces. Put inside the pressure cooker.

2. Place the pecans and roughly chop the nuts. Pick the parsley leaves and roughly chop.

3. Place the porcini in a bowl then add 300ml of boiling water. Set aside until needed.

4. Heat oil in the pressure cooker. Add the garlic and shallots. Cook for 3 minutes while stirring occasionally.

5. Drain porcini and reserve the liquid. Add the porcini into the pressure cooker together with the wild mushrooms and chestnut mushrooms. Add the bay leaves and thyme.

6. Position the lid and lock in place. Put to high heat and bring to high pressure. Adjust heat to stabilize. Cook for 10 minutes. Adjust taste if necessary.

7. Transfer the mushroom mixture into a bowl and set aside to cool completely.

8. Once the mushrooms are completely cool, add the bread, pecans, a pinch of black pepper and sea salt, and half of the reserved liquid into the bowl. Mix well. Add more reserved liquid if the mixture seems dry.

9. Add more than half of the parsley into the bowl and stir. Transfer the mixture into a 20cm x 25cm lightly greased baking dish and cover with tin foil.

10. Bake in the oven for 35 minutes. Then, get rid of the foil and cook for another 10 minutes. Once done, sprinkle the remaining parsley on top and serve with bread or crackers. Serve.

Nutrition:
Calories 343
Total Fat 4.2 g
Saturated Fat 0.8 g
Cholesterol 0 mg
Sodium 861 mg
Total Carbs 22.5 g

Fiber 6.3 g

Sugar 2.3 g

Protein 9.2 g

771. Spiced Okra

Preparation time: 14 minutes

Cooking time: 16 minutes

Servings: 3

Ingredients:

- 2 cups okra
- ¼ teaspoon stevia
- 1 teaspoon chilli powder
- ½ teaspoon ground turmeric
- 1 tablespoon ground coriander
- 2 tablespoons fresh coriander, chopped
- 1 tablespoon ground cumin
- ¼ teaspoon salt
- 1 tablespoon desiccated coconut
- 3 tablespoons vegetable oil
- ½ teaspoon black mustard seeds
- ½ teaspoon cumin seeds
- Fresh tomatoes, to garnish

Directions:

1. Trim okra. Wash and dry.

2. Combine stevia, chilli powder, turmeric, ground coriander, fresh coriander, cumin, salt, and desiccated coconut in a bowl.

3. Heat the oil in a pan. Cook mustard and cumin seeds for 3 minutes. Stir continuously. Add okra. Tip in the spice mixture. Cook on low heat for 8 minutes.

4. Transfer to a serving dish. Garnish with fresh tomatoes.

Nutrition:

Calories 163

Total Fat 4.2 g

Saturated Fat 0.8 g

Cholesterol 0 mg

Sodium 861 mg

Total Carbs 22.5 g

Fiber 6.3 g

Sugar 2.3 g

Protein 9.2 g

772. Lemony Salmon Burgers

Preparation Time: 10 Minutes

Cooking Time: 10 Minutes

Servings: 4

Ingredients

- 2 (3-oz) cans boneless, skinless pink salmon
- 1/4 cup panko breadcrumbs
- 4 tsp. lemon juice
- 1/4 cup red bell pepper

- 1/4 cup sugar-free yogurt
- 1 egg
- 2 (1.5-oz) whole wheat hamburger toasted buns

Directions

1. Mix drained and flaked salmon, finely-chopped bell pepper, panko breadcrumbs.

2. Combine 2 tbsp. cup sugar-free yogurt, 3 tsp. fresh lemon juice, and egg in a bowl. Shape mixture into 2 (3-inch) patties, bake on the skillet over medium heat 4 to 5 Minutes per side.

3. Stir together 2 tbsp. sugar-free yogurt and 1 tsp. lemon juice; spread over bottom halves of buns.

4. Top each with 1 patty, and cover with bun tops. This dish is very mouth-watering!

Nutrition:

Calories 131 / Protein 12 / Fat 1 g / Carbs 19 g

773. Caprese Turkey Burgers

Preparation Time 10 Minutes

Cooking Time: 10 Minutes

Servings: 4

Ingredients

- 1/2 lb. 93% lean ground turkey
- 2 (1,5-oz) whole wheat hamburger buns (toasted)
- 1/4 cup shredded mozzarella cheese (part-skim)
- 1 egg
- 1 big tomato
- 1 small clove garlic
- 4 large basil leaves

- 1/8 tsp. salt
- 1/8 tsp. pepper

Directions

1. Combine turkey, white egg, Minced garlic, salt, and pepper (mix until combined);

2. Shape into 2 cutlets. Put cutlets into a skillet; cook 5 to 7 Minutes per side.

3. Top cutlets properly with cheese and sliced tomato at the end of cooking.

4. Put 1 cutlet on the bottom of each bun.

5. Top each patty with 2 basil leaves. Cover with bun tops.

My guests enjoy this dish every time they visit my home.

Nutrition:

Calories 180 / Protein 7 g / Fat 4 g / Carbs 20 g

774. Pasta Salad

Preparation Time: 15 Minutes

Cooking Time: 15 Minutes

Servings: 4

Ingredients

- 8 oz. whole-wheat pasta
- 2 tomatoes
- 1 (5-oz) pkg spring mix
- 9 slices bacon
- 1/3 cup mayonnaise (reduced-fat)
- 1 tbsp. Dijon mustard
- 3 tbsp. apple cider vinegar
- 1/4 tsp. salt
- 1/2 tsp. pepper

Directions

1. Cook pasta.

2. Chilled pasta, chopped tomatoes and spring mix in a bowl.

3. Crumble cooked bacon over pasta.

4. Combine mayonnaise, mustard, vinegar, salt and pepper in a small bowl.

5. Pour dressing over pasta, stirring to coat.

Understanding diabetes is the first step in curing.

Nutrition:

Calories 200 / Protein 15 g / Fat 3 g / Carbs 6 g

775. Chicken, Strawberry, And Avocado Salad

Preparation Time: 10 Minutes

Cooking Time: 5 Minutes

Ingredients

- 1,5 cups chicken (skin removed)
- 1/4 cup almonds
- 2 (5-oz) pkg salad greens
- 1 (16-oz) pkg strawberries
- 1 avocado
- 1/4 cup green onion
- 1/4 cup lime juice
- 3 tbsp. extra virgin olive oil
- 2 tbsp. honey
- 1/4 tsp. salt
- 1/4 tsp. pepper

Directions

1. Toast almonds until golden and fragrant.

2. Mix lime juice, oil, honey, salt, and pepper.

3. Mix greens, sliced strawberries, chicken, diced avocado, and sliced green onion and sliced almonds; drizzle with dressing. Toss to coat.

Yummy!

Nutrition:

Calories 150 / Protein 15 g / Fat 10 g / Carbs 5 g

776. Lemon-Thyme Eggs

Preparation Time: 10 Minutes

Cooking Time: 5 Minutes

Servings: 4

Ingredients

- 7 large eggs
- 1/4 cup mayonnaise (reduced-fat)
- 2 tsp. lemon juice
- 1 tsp. Dijon mustard
- 1 tsp. chopped fresh thyme
- 1/8 tsp. cayenne pepper

Directions

1. Bring eggs to a boil.
2. Peel and cut each egg in half lengthwise.
3. Remove yolks to a bowl. Add mayonnaise, lemon juice, mustard, thyme, and cayenne to egg yolks; mash to blend. Fill egg white halves with yolk mixture.
4. Chill until ready to serve.

Please your family with a delicious meal.

Nutrition:

Calories 40 / Protein 10 g / Fat 6 g / Carbs 2 g

777. Spinach Salad with Bacon

Preparation Time: 15 Minutes

Cooking Time: 0 Minutes

Servings: 4

Ingredients

- 8 slices center-cut bacon
- 3 tbsp. extra virgin olive oil
- 1 (5-oz) pkg baby spinach
- 1 tbsp. apple cider vinegar
- 1 tsp. Dijon mustard
- 1/2 tsp. honey
- 1/4 tsp. salt
- 1/2 tsp. pepper

Directions

1. Mix vinegar, mustard, honey, salt and pepper in a bowl.
2. Whisk in oil. Place spinach in a serving bowl; drizzle with dressing, and toss to coat.
3. Sprinkle with cooked and crumbled bacon.

Nutrition:

Calories 110 / Protein 6 g / Fat 2 g / Carbs 1 g

778. Pea and Collards Soup

Preparation Time: 10 Minutes

Cooking Time: 50 Minutes

Servings: 4

Ingredients

- 1/2 (16-oz) pkg black-eyed peas
- 1 onion
- 2 carrots
- 1,5 cups ham (low-sodium)
- 1 (1-lb) bunch collard greens (trimmed)
- 1 tbsp. extra virgin olive oil
- 2 cloves garlic
- 1/2 tsp. black pepper
- Hot sauce

Directions

1. Cook chopped onion and carrots 10 Minutes.
2. Add peas, diced ham, collards, and Minced garlic. Cook 5 Minutes.

3.   Add broth, 3 cups water, and pepper. Bring to a boil; simmer 35 Minutes, adding water if needed.
Serve with favorite sauce.
Nutrition:
Calories 86 / Protein 15 g / Fat 2 g / Carbs 9 g

779. Spanish Stew

Preparation Time: 10 Minutes
Cooking Time: 25 Minutes
Servings: 4
Ingredients
- 1.1/2 (12-oz) pkg smoked chicken sausage links
- 1 (5-oz) pkg baby spinach
- 1 (15-oz) can chickpeas
- 1 (14.5-oz) can tomatoes with basil, garlic, and oregano
- 1/2 tsp. smoked paprika
- 1/2 tsp. cumin
- 3/4 cup onions
- 1 tbsp. extra virgin olive oil

Directions
1.   Cook sliced the sausage in hot oil until browned. Remove from pot.
2.   Add chopped onions; cook until tender.
3.   Add sausage, drained and rinsed chickpeas, diced tomatoes, paprika, and ground cumin. Cook 15 Minutes.
4.   Add in spinach; cook 1 to 2 Minutes.
This dish is ideal for every day and for a festive table.
Nutrition:
Calories 200 / Protein 10 g / Fat 20 g / Carbs 1 g

780. Creamy Taco Soup

Preparation Time: 10 Minutes
Cooking Time: 20 Minutes
Servings: 4
Ingredients
- 3/4 lb. ground sirloin
- 1/2 (8-oz) cream cheese
- 1/2 onion
- 1 clove garlic
- 1 (10-oz) can tomatoes and green chiles

- 1 (14.5-oz) can beef broth
- 1/4 cup heavy cream
- 1,5 tsp. cumin
- 1/2 tsp. chili powder

Directions
1.   Cook beef, chopped onion, and Minced garlic until meat is browned and crumbly; drain and return to pot.
2.   Add ground cumin, chili powder, and cream cheese cut into small pieces and softened, stirring until cheese is melted.
3.   Add diced tomatoes, broth, and cream; bring to a boil, and simmer 10 Minutes. Season with pepper and salt to taste.
You've got to give someone the recipe for this soup dish!
Nutrition:
Calories 60 / Protein 3 g / Fat 1 g / Carbs 8 g

781. Chicken with Caprese Salsa

Preparation Time: 15 Minutes
Cooking Time: 5 Minutes
Servings: 4
Ingredients
- 3/4 lb. boneless, skinless chicken breasts
- 2 big tomatoes
- 1/2 (8-oz) ball fresh mozzarella cheese
- 1/4 cup red onion
- 2 tbsp. fresh basil

- 1 tbsp. balsamic vinegar
- 2 tbsp. extra virgin olive oil (divided)
- 1/2 tsp. salt (divided)
- 1/4 tsp. pepper (divided)

Directions
1. Sprinkle cut in half lengthwise chicken with 1/4 tsp. salt and 1/8 tsp. pepper.
2. Heat 1 tbsp. olive oil, cook chicken 5 Minutes.
3. Meanwhile, mix chopped tomatoes, diced cheese, finely chopped onion, chopped basil, vinegar, 1 tbsp. oil, and 1/4 tsp. salt and 1/8 tsp. pepper.
4. Spoon salsa over chicken.
Chicken with Caprese Salsa is a nutritious, simple and very tasty dish that can be prepared in a few Minutes.
Nutrition:
Calories 210 / Protein 28 g / Fat 17 g / Carbs 0, 1 g

782. Balsamic-Roasted Broccoli

Preparation Time: 10 Minutes
Cooking Time: 15 Minutes
Servings: 4
Ingredients
- 1 lb. broccoli
- 1 tbsp. extra virgin olive oil
- 1 tbsp. balsamic vinegar
- 1 clove garlic
- 1/8 tsp. salt

- Pepper to taste

Directions
1. Preheat oven to 450F.
2. Combine broccoli, olive oil, vinegar, Minced garlic, salt, and pepper; toss.
3. Spread broccoli on a baking sheet.
4. Bake 12 to 15 Minutes.
Really good!
Nutrition:
Calories 27 / Protein 3 g / Fat 0, 3 g / Carbs 4 g

783. Hearty Beef and Vegetable Soup

Preparation Time: 10 Minutes
Cooking Time: 30 Minutes
Servings: 4
Ingredients
- 1/2 lb. lean ground beef
- 2 cups beef broth
- 1,5 tbsp. vegetable oil (divided)
- 1 cup green bell pepper
- 1/2 cup red onion
- 1 cup green cabbage
- 1 cup frozen mixed vegetables
- 1/2 can tomatoes
- 1,5 tsp. Worcestershire sauce
- 1 small bay leaf
- 1,8 tsp. pepper
- 2 tbsp. ketchup

Directions
1. Cook beef in 1/2 tbsp. hot oil 2 Minutes.
2. Stir in chopped bell pepper and chopped onion; cook 4 Minutes.
3. Add chopped cabbage, mixed vegetables, stewed tomatoes, broth, Worcestershire sauce, bay leaf, and pepper; bring to a boil.
4. Reduce heat to medium; cover, and cook 15 Minutes.
5. Stir in ketchup and 1 tbsp. oil, and remove from heat. Let stand 10 Minutes.
The right diet is excellent diabetes remedy.
Nutrition:
Calories 170 / Protein 17 g / Fat 8 g / Carbs 3 g

784. Cauliflower Muffin

Preparation Time: 15 Minutes
Cooking Time: 30 Minutes
Servings: 4
Ingredients

- 2,5 cup cauliflower
- 2/3 cup ham
- 2,5 cups of cheese
- 2/3 cup champignon
- 1,5 tbsp. flaxseed
- 3 eggs
- 1/4 tsp. salt
- 1/8 tsp. pepper

Directions
1. 1. Preheat oven to 375 F.
2. Put muffin liners in a 12-muffin tin.
3. Combine diced cauliflower, ground flaxseed, beaten eggs, cup diced ham, grated cheese, and diced mushrooms, salt, pepper.
4. Divide mixture rightly between muffin liners.
5. Bake 30 Minutes.
This is a great lunch for the whole family.
Nutrition:
Calories 116 / Protein 10 g / Fat 7 g / Carbs 3 g

785. Ham and Egg Cups

Preparation Time: 10 Minutes
Cooking Time: 15 Minutes
Servings: 4
Ingredients

- 5 slices ham

- 4 tbsp. cheese

- 1,5 tbsp. cream
- 3 egg whites
- 1,5 tbsp. pepper (green)
- 1 tsp. salt
- pepper to taste

Directions
1. Preheat oven to 350 F.
2. Arrange each slice of thinly sliced ham into 4 muffin tin.
3. Put 1/4 of grated cheese into ham cup.
4. Mix eggs, cream, salt and pepper and divide it into 2 tins.
5. Bake in oven 15 Minutes; after baking, sprinkle with green onions.
If you want to keep your current shape, also pay attention to this dish.
Nutrition:
Calories 180 / Protein 13 g / Fat 13 g / Carbs 2 g

786. Lemony Salmon

Preparation Time: 10 minutes
Cooking Time: 3 Minutes
Servings: 3
Ingredients:

- 1 pound salmon fillet, cut into 3 pieces
- 3 teaspoons fresh dill, chopped
- 5 tablespoons fresh lemon juice, divided
- Salt and ground black pepper, as required

Directions:
1. Arrange a steamer trivet in Instant Pot and pour ¼ cup of lemon juice.
2. Season the salmon with salt and black pepper evenly.
3. Place the salmon pieces on top of trivet, skin side down and drizzle with remaining lemon juice.
4. Now, sprinkle the salmon pieces with dill evenly.

5. Close the lid and place the pressure valve to "Seal" position.

6. Press "Steam" and use the default time of 3 minutes.

7. Press "Cancel" and allow a "Natural" release.

8. Open the lid and serve hot.

Nutrition: Calories: 20 Fats: 9.6g, Carbs: 1.1g, Sugar: 0.5g, Proteins: 29.7g, Sodium: 74mg

787. Shrimp with Green Beans

Preparation Time: 10 minutes

Cooking Time: 2 Minutes

Servings: 4

Ingredients:

- ¾ pound fresh green beans, trimmed
- 1-pound medium frozen shrimp, peeled and deveined
- 2 tablespoons fresh lemon juice
- 2 tablespoons olive oil
- Salt and ground black pepper, as required

Directions:

1. Arrange a steamer trivet in the Instant Pot and pour cup of water.

2. Arrange the green beans on top of trivet in a single layer and top with shrimp.

3. Drizzle with oil and lemon juice.

4. Sprinkle with salt and black pepper.

5. Close the lid and place the pressure valve to "Seal" position.

6. Press "Steam" and just use the default time of 2 minutes.

7. Press "Cancel" and allow a "Natural" release.

8. Open the lid and serve.

9. Nutrition: Calories: 223, Fats: 1g, Carbs: 7.9g, Sugar: 1.4g, Proteins: 27.4g, Sodium: 322mg

788. Crab Curry

Preparation Time: 10 minutes

Cooking Time: 20 Minutes

Servings: 2

Ingredients:

- 0.5lb chopped crab
- 1 thinly sliced red onion
- 0.5 cup chopped tomato
- 3tbsp curry paste
- 1tbsp oil or ghee

Directions:

1. Set the Instant Pot to sauté and add the onion, oil, and curry paste.

2. When the onion is soft, add the remaining ingredients and seal.

3. Cook on Stew for 20 minutes.

4. Release the pressure naturally.

Nutrition: Calories: 2; Carbs: 11; Sugar: 4; Fat: 10; Protein: 24; GL: 9

789. Mixed Chowder

Preparation Time: 10 minutes

Cooking Time: 35 Minutes

Servings: 2

Ingredients:

- 1lb fish stew mix
- 2 cups white sauce
- 3tbsp old bay seasoning

Directions:

1. Mix all the ingredients in your Instant Pot.

2. Cook on Stew for 35 minutes.

3. Release the pressure naturally.

Nutrition: Calories: 320; Carbs: 9; Sugar: 2; Fat: 16; Protein: GL: 4

790. Mussels in Tomato Sauce

Preparation Time: 10 minutes

Cooking Time: 3 Minutes

Servings: 4

Ingredients:

- 2 tomatoes, seeded and chopped finely
- 2 pounds mussels, scrubbed and de-bearded
- 1 cup low-sodium chicken broth
- 1 tablespoon fresh lemon juice
- 2 garlic cloves, minced

Directions:

1. In the pot of Instant Pot, place tomatoes, garlic, wine and bay leaf and stir to combine.

2. Arrange the mussels on top.

3. Close the lid and place the pressure valve to "Seal" position.

4. Press "Manual" and cook under "High Pressure" for about 3 minutes.

5. Press "Cancel" and carefully allow a "Quick" release.

6. Open the lid and serve hot.

Nutrition: Calories: 213, Fats: 25.2g, Carbs: 11g, Sugar: 1. Proteins: 28.2g, Sodium: 670mg

791. Citrus Salmon

Preparation Time: 10 minutes
Cooking Time: 7 Minutes
Servings: 4
Ingredients:

- 4 (4-ounce) salmon fillets
- 1 cup low-sodium chicken broth
- 1 teaspoon fresh ginger, minced
- 2 teaspoons fresh orange zest, grated finely
- 3 tablespoons fresh orange juice
- 1 tablespoon olive oil
- Ground black pepper, as required

Directions:
1. In Instant Pot, add all ingredients and mix.
2. Close the lid and place the pressure valve to "Seal" position.
3. Press "Manual" and cook under "High Pressure" for about 7 minutes.
4. Press "Cancel" and allow a "Natural" release.
5. Open the lid and serve the salmon fillets with the topping of cooking sauce.

Nutrition: Calories: 190, Fats: 10.5g, Carbs: 1.8g, Sugar: 1g, Proteins: 22. Sodium: 68mg

792. Herbed Salmon

Preparation Time: 10 minutes
Cooking Time: 3 Minutes
Servings: 4
Ingredients:

- 4 (4-ounce) salmon fillets
- ¼ cup olive oil
- 2 tablespoons fresh lemon juice
- 1 garlic clove, minced
- ¼ teaspoon dried oregano
- Salt and ground black pepper, as required
- 4 fresh rosemary sprigs
- 4 lemon slices

Directions:
1. For dressing: in a large bowl, add oil, lemon juice, garlic, oregano, salt and black pepper and beat until well co combined.
2. Arrange a steamer trivet in the Instant Pot and pour 11/2 cups of water in Instant Pot.
3. Place the salmon fillets on top of trivet in a single layer and top with dressing.
4. Arrange 1 rosemary sprig and 1 lemon slice over each fillet.
5. Close the lid and place the pressure valve to "Seal" position.
6. Press "Steam" and just use the default time of 3 minutes.
7. Press "Cancel" and carefully allow a "Quick" release.
8. Open the lid and serve hot.

Nutrition: Calories: 262, Fats: 17g, Carbs: 0.7g, Sugar: 0.2g, Proteins: 22.1g, Sodium: 91mg

793. Salmon in Green Sauce

Preparation Time: 10 minutes
Cooking Time: 12 Minutes
Servings: 4
Ingredients:

- 4 (6-ounce) salmon fillets
- 1 avocado, peeled, pitted and chopped
- 1/2 cup fresh basil, chopped
- 3 garlic cloves, chopped
- 1 tablespoon fresh lemon zest, grated finely

Directions:
1. Grease a large piece of foil.
2. In a large bowl, add all ingredients except salmon and water and with a fork, mash completely.
3. Place fillets in the center of foil and top with avocado mixture evenly.
4. Fold the foil around fillets to seal them.
5. Arrange a steamer trivet in the Instant Pot and pour 1/2 cup of water.
6. Place the foil packet on top of trivet.
7. Close the lid and place the pressure valve to "Seal" position.
8. Press "Manual" and cook under "High Pressure" for about minutes.
9. Meanwhile, preheat the oven to broiler.
10. Press "Cancel" and allow a "Natural" release.
11. Open the lid and transfer the salmon fillets onto a broiler pan.
12. Broil for about 3-4 minutes.
13. Serve warm.

Nutrition: Calories: 333, Fats: 20.3g, Carbs: 5.5g, Sugar: 0.4g, Proteins: 34.2g, Sodium: 79mg

794.   Braised Shrimp

Preparation Time: 10 minutes
Cooking Time: 4 Minutes
Servings: 4
Ingredients:

- 1-pound frozen large shrimp, peeled and deveined
- 2 shallots, chopped
- ¾ cup low-sodium chicken broth
- 2 tablespoons fresh lemon juice
- 2 tablespoons olive oil
- 1 tablespoon garlic, crushed
- Ground black pepper, as required

Directions:
1.   In the Instant Pot, place oil and press "Sauté". Now add the shallots and cook for about 2 minutes.
2.   Add the garlic and cook for about 1 minute.
3.   Press "Cancel" and stir in the shrimp, broth, lemon juice and black pepper.
4.   Close the lid and place the pressure valve to "Seal" position.
5.   Press "Manual" and cook under "High Pressure" for about 1 minute.
6.   Press "Cancel" and carefully allow a "Quick" release.
7.   Open the lid and serve hot.
Nutrition: Calories: 209, Fats: 9g, Carbs: 4.3g, Sugar: 0.2g, Proteins: 26.6g, Sodium: 293mg

795.   Shrimp Coconut Curry

Preparation Time: 10 minutes
Cooking Time: 20 Minutes
Servings: 2
Ingredients:

- 0.5lb cooked shrimp
- 1 thinly sliced onion
- 1 cup coconut yogurt
- 3tbsp curry paste
- 1tbsp oil or ghee

Directions:
1.   Set the Instant Pot to sauté and add the onion, oil, and curry paste.
2.   When the onion is soft, add the remaining ingredients and seal.
3.   Cook on Stew for 20 minutes.
4.   Release the pressure naturally.

Nutrition: Calories: 380; Carbs: 13; Sugar: 4; Fat: 22; Protein: 40; GL: 14

796.   Trout Bake

Preparation Time: 10 minutes
Cooking Time: 35 Minutes
Servings: 2
Ingredients:

- 1lb trout fillets, boneless
- 1lb chopped winter vegetables
- 1 cup low sodium fish broth
- 1tbsp mixed herbs
- sea salt as desired

Directions:
1.   Mix all the ingredients except the broth in a foil pouch.
2.   Place the pouch in the steamer basket your Instant Pot.
3.   Pour the broth into the Instant Pot.
4.   Cook on Steam for 35 minutes.
5.   Release the pressure naturally.
Nutrition: Calories: 310; Carbs: 14; Sugar: 2; Fat: 12; Protein: 40; GL: 5

797.   Sardine Curry

Preparation Time: 10 minutes
Cooking Time: 35 Minutes
Servings: 2
Ingredients:

- 5 tins of sardines in tomato
- 1lb chopped vegetables
- 1 cup low sodium fish broth
- 3tbsp curry paste

Directions:
1.   Mix all the ingredients in your Instant Pot.
2.   Cook on Stew for 35 minutes.
3.   Release the pressure naturally.
Nutrition: Calories: 320; Carbs: 8; Sugar: 2; Fat: 16; Protein: GL: 3

798.   Swordfish Steak

Preparation Time: 10 minutes
Cooking Time: 35 Minutes
Servings: 2
Ingredients:

- 1lb swordfish steak, whole

- 1lb chopped Mediterranean vegetables
- 1 cup low sodium fish broth
- 2tbsp soy sauce

Directions:

1. Mix all the ingredients except the broth in a foil pouch.
2. Place the pouch in the steamer basket for your Instant Pot.
3. Pour the broth into the Instant Pot. Lower the steamer basket into the Instant Pot.
4. Cook on Steam for 35 minutes.
5. Release the pressure naturally.

Nutrition: Calories: 270; Carbs: 5; Sugar: 1; Fat: 10; Protein: 48; GL: 1

799. Lemon Sole

Preparation Time: 10 minutes
Cooking Time: 5 Minutes
Servings: 2
Ingredients:

- 1lb sole fillets, boned and skinned
- 1 cup low sodium fish broth
- 2 shredded sweet onions
- juice of half a lemon
- 2tbsp dried cilantro

Directions:

1. Mix all the ingredients in your Instant Pot.
2. Cook on Stew for 5 minutes.
3. Release the pressure naturally.

Nutrition: Calories: 230; Carbs: Sugar: 1; Fat: 6; Protein: 46; GL: 1

800. Tuna Sweet corn Casserole

Preparation Time: 10 minutes
Cooking Time: 35 Minutes
Servings: 2
Ingredients:

- 3 small tins of tuna
- 0.5lb sweet corn kernels
- 1lb chopped vegetables
- 1 cup low sodium vegetable broth
- 2tbsp spicy seasoning

Directions:

1. Mix all the ingredients in your Instant Pot.
2. Cook on Stew for 35 minutes.

3. Release the pressure naturally.

Nutrition: Calories: 300; Carbs: 6; Sugar: 1; Fat: 9; Protein: GL: 2

801. Lemon Pepper Salmon

Preparation Time: 10 minutes
Cooking Time: 10 Minutes
Servings: 4
Ingredients:

- 3 tbsps. ghee or avocado oil
- 1 lb. skin-on salmon filet
- 1 julienned red bell pepper
- 1 julienned green zucchini
- 1 julienned carrot
- ¾ cup water
- A few sprigs of parsley, tarragon, dill, basil or a combination
- 1/2 sliced lemon
- 1/2 tsp. black pepper
- ¼ tsp. sea salt

Directions:

1. Add the water and the herbs into the bottom of the Instant Pot and put in a wire steamer rack making sure the handles extend upwards.
2. Place the salmon filet onto the wire rack, with the skin side facing down.
3. Drizzle the salmon with ghee, season with black pepper and salt, and top with the lemon slices.
4. Close and seal the Instant Pot, making sure the vent is turned to "Sealing".
5. Select the "Steam" setting and cook for 3 minutes.
6. While the salmon cooks, julienne the vegetables, and set aside.
7. Once done, quick release the pressure, and then press the "Keep Warm/Cancel" button.
8. Uncover and wearing oven mitts, carefully remove the steamer rack with the salmon.
9. Remove the herbs and discard them.
10. Add the vegetables to the pot and put the lid back on.
11. Select the "Sauté" function and cook for 1-2 minutes.
12. Serve the vegetables with salmon and add the remaining fat to the pot.

13.   Pour a little of the sauce over the fish and vegetables if desired.

Nutrition: Calories 296, Carbs 8g, Fat 15 g, Protein 31 g, Potassium (K) 1084 mg, Sodium (Na) 284 mg

802.   Baked Salmon with Garlic Parmesan Topping

Preparation time: 5 minutes,
Cooking time: 20 minutes,
Servings: 4
Ingredients:

- 1 lb. wild caught salmon filets
- 2 tbsp. margarine
- What you'll need from store cupboard:
- ¼ cup reduced fat parmesan cheese, grated
- ¼ cup light mayonnaise
- 2-3 cloves garlic, diced
- 2 tbsp. parsley
- Salt and pepper

Directions:

1.   Heat oven to 350 and line a baking pan with parchment paper.

2.   Place salmon on pan and season with salt and pepper.

3.   In a medium skillet, over medium heat, melt butter. Add garlic and cook, stirring 1 minute.

4.   Reduce heat to low and add remaining Ingredients. Stir until everything is melted and combined.

5.   Spread evenly over salmon and bake 15 minutes for thawed fish or 20 for frozen. Salmon is done when it flakes easily with a fork. Serve.

Nutrition: Calories 408 Total Carbs 4g Protein 41g Fat 24g Sugar 1g Fiber 0g

803.   Blackened Shrimp

Preparation time: 5 minutes
Cooking time: 5 minutes
Servings: 4
Ingredients:

- 1 1/2 lbs. shrimp, peel & devein
- 4 lime wedges
- 4 tbsp. cilantro, chopped
- What you'll need from store cupboard:
- 4 cloves garlic, diced
- 1 tbsp. chili powder
- 1 tbsp. paprika
- 1 tbsp. olive oil
- 2 tsp. Splenda brown sugar
- 1 tsp. cumin
- 1 tsp. oregano
- 1 tsp. garlic powder
- 1 tsp. salt
- 1/2 tsp. pepper

Directions:

1.   In a small bowl combine seasonings and Splenda brown sugar.

2.   Heat oil in a skillet over med-high heat. Add shrimp, in a single layer, and cook 1-2 minutes per side.

3.   Add seasonings, and cook, stirring, 30 seconds. Serve garnished with cilantro and a lime wedge.

Nutrition: Calories 252 Total Carbs 7g Net Carbs 6g Protein 39g Fat 7g Sugar 2g Fiber 1g

804.   Cajun Catfish

Preparation time: 5 minutes
Cooking time: 15 minutes
Servings: 4
Ingredients:

- 4 (8 oz.) catfish fillets
- What you'll need from store cupboard:
- 2 tbsp. olive oil
- 2 tsp. garlic salt
- 2 tsp. thyme
- 2 tsp. paprika
- 1/2 tsp. cayenne pepper
- 1/2 tsp. red hot sauce
- ¼ tsp. black pepper
- Nonstick cooking spray

Directions:

1.   Heat oven to 450 degrees. Spray a 9x13-inch baking dish with cooking spray.

2.   In a small bowl whisk together everything but catfish. Brush both sides of fillets, using all the spice mix.

3.   Bake 10-13 minutes or until fish flakes easily with a fork. Serve.

Nutrition: Calories 366 Total Carbs 0g Protein 35g Fat 24g Sugar 0g Fiber 0g

805. Cajun Flounder & Tomatoes

Preparation time: 10 minutes
Cooking time: 15 minutes
Servings: 4
Ingredients:

- 4 flounder fillets
- 2 1/2 cups tomatoes, diced
- ¾ cup onion, diced
- ¾ cup green bell pepper, diced
- What you'll need from store cupboard:
- 2 cloves garlic, diced fine
- 1 tbsp. Cajun seasoning
- 1 tsp. olive oil

Directions:

1. Heat oil in a large skillet over med-high heat. Add onion and garlic and cook 2 minutes, or until soft. Add tomatoes, peppers and spices, and cook 2-3 minutes until tomatoes soften.
2. Lay fish over top. Cover, reduce heat to medium and cook, 5-8 minutes, or until fish flakes easily with a fork. Transfer fish to serving plates and top with sauce.

Nutrition: Calories 194 Total Carbs 8g Net Carbs 6g Protein 32g Fat 3g Sugar 5g Fiber 2g

806. Cajun Shrimp & Roasted Vegetables

Preparation time: 5 minutes
Cooking time: 15 minutes
Servings: 4
Ingredients:

- 1 lb. large shrimp, peeled and deveined
- 2 zucchinis, sliced
- 2 yellow squash, sliced
- 1/2 bunch asparagus, cut into thirds
- 2 red bell pepper, cut into chunks
- What you'll need from store cupboard:
- 2 tbsp. olive oil
- 2 tbsp. Cajun Seasoning
- Salt & pepper, to taste

Directions:

1. Heat oven to 400 degrees.

2. Combine shrimp and vegetables in a large bowl. Add oil and seasoning and toss to coat.
3. Spread evenly in a large baking sheet and bake 15-20 minutes, or until vegetables are tender. Serve.

Nutrition: Calories 251 Total Carbs 13g Net Carbs 9g Protein 30g Fat 9g Sugar 6g Fiber 4g

807. Cilantro Lime Grilled Shrimp

Preparation time: 5 minutes,
Cooking time: 5 minutes,
Servings: 6
Ingredients:

- 1 1/2 lbs. large shrimp raw, peeled, deveined with tails on
- Juice and zest of 1 lime
- 2 tbsp. fresh cilantro chopped
- What you'll need from store cupboard:
- ¼ cup olive oil
- 2 cloves garlic, diced fine
- 1 tsp. smoked paprika
- ¼ tsp. cumin
- 1/2 teaspoon salt
- ¼ tsp. cayenne pepper

Directions:

1. Place the shrimp in a large Ziploc bag.
2. Mix remaining Ingredients in a small bowl and pour over shrimp. Let marinate 20-30 minutes.
3. Heat up the grill. Skewer the shrimp and cook 2-3 minutes, per side, just until they turn pick. Be careful not to overcook them. Serve garnished with cilantro.

Nutrition: Calories 317 Total Carbs 4g Protein 39g Fat 15g Sugar 0g Fiber 0g

808. Crab Frittata

Preparation time: 10 minutes
Cooking time: 50 minutes
Servings: 4
Ingredients:

- 4 eggs
- 2 cups lump crabmeat
- 1 cup half-n-half
- 1 cup green onions, diced
- What you'll need from store cupboard:
- 1 cup reduced fat parmesan cheese, grated

- 1 tsp. salt
- 1 tsp. pepper
- 1 tsp. smoked paprika
- 1 tsp. Italian seasoning
- Nonstick cooking spray

Directions:

1.	Heat oven to 350 degrees. Spray an 8-inch springform pan, or pie plate with cooking spray.

2.	In a large bowl, whisk together the eggs and half-n-half. Add seasonings and parmesan cheese, stir to mix.

3.	Stir in the onions and crab meat. Pour into prepared pan and bake 35-40 minutes, or eggs are set and top is lightly browned.

4.	Let cool 10 minutes, then slice and serve warm or at room temperature.

Nutrition: Calories 276 Total Carbs 5g Net Carbs 4g Protein 25g Fat 17g Sugar 1g Fiber 1g

## 809.	Crunchy Lemon Shrimp

Preparation time: 5 minutes
Cooking time: 10 minutes,
Servings: 4
Ingredients:

- 1 lb. raw shrimp, peeled and deveined
- 2 tbsp. Italian parsley, roughly chopped
- 2 tbsp. lemon juice, divided
- What you'll need from store cupboard:
- 2/3 cup panko bread crumbs
- 2 1/2 tbsp. olive oil, divided
- Salt and pepper, to taste

Directions:

1.	Heat oven to 400 degrees.

2.	Place the shrimp evenly in a baking dish and sprinkle with salt and pepper. Drizzle on 1 tablespoon lemon juice and 1 tablespoon of olive oil. Set aside.

3.	In a medium bowl, combine parsley, remaining lemon juice, bread crumbs, remaining olive oil, and ¼ tsp. each of salt and pepper. Layer the panko mixture evenly on top of the shrimp.

4.	Bake 8-10 minutes or until shrimp are cooked through and the panko is golden brown.

Nutrition: Calories 283 Total Carbs 15g Net Carbs 14g Protein 28g Fat 12g Sugar 1g Fiber 1g

## 810.	Grilled Tuna Steaks

Preparation time: 5 minutes

Cooking time: 10 minutes,
Servings: 6
Ingredients:

- 6 6 oz. tuna steaks
- 3 tbsp. fresh basil, diced
- What you'll need from store cupboard:
- 4 1/2 tsp. olive oil
- ¾ tsp. salt
- ¼ tsp. pepper
- Nonstick cooking spray

Directions:

1.	Heat grill to medium heat. Spray rack with cooking spray.

2.	Drizzle both sides of the tuna with oil. Sprinkle with basil, salt and pepper.

3.	Place on grill and cook 5 minutes per side, tuna should be slightly pink in the center. Serve.

Nutrition: Calories 343 Total Carbs 0g Protein 51g Fat 14g Sugar 0g Fiber 0g

## 811.	Red Clam Sauce & Pasta

Preparation time: 10 minutes,
Cooking time: 3 hours,
Servings: 4
Ingredients:

- 1 onion, diced
- ¼ cup fresh parsley, diced
- What you'll need from store cupboard:
- 2 6 1/2 oz. cans clams, chopped, undrained
- 14 1/2 oz. tomatoes, diced, undrained
- 6 oz. tomato paste
- 2 cloves garlic, diced
- 1 bay leaf
- 1 tbsp. sunflower oil
- 1 tsp. Splenda
- 1 tsp. basil
- 1/2 tsp. thyme
- 1/2 Homemade Pasta, cook & drain

Directions:

1.	Heat oil in a small skillet over med-high heat. Add onion and cook until tender, add garlic and cook 1 minute more. Transfer to crock pot.

2.	Add remaining Ingredients, except pasta, cover and cook on low 3-4 hours.

3.   Discard bay leaf and serve over cooked pasta.

Nutrition: Calories 223 Total Carbs 32g Net Carbs 27g Protein 12g Fat 6g Sugar 15g Fiber 5g

812. Salmon Milano

Preparation time: 10 minutes,

Cooking time: 20 minutes,

Servings: 6

Ingredients:

- 2 1/2 lb. salmon filet
- 2 tomatoes, sliced
- 1/2 cup margarine
- What you'll need from store cupboard:
- 1/2 cup basil pesto

Directions:

1.   Heat the oven to 400 degrees. Line a 9x15-inch baking sheet with foil, making sure it covers the sides. Place another large piece of foil onto the baking sheet and place the salmon filet on top of it.

2.   Place the pesto and margarine in blender or food processor and pulse until smooth. Spread evenly over salmon. Place tomato slices on top.

3.   Wrap the foil around the salmon, tenting around the top to prevent foil from touching the salmon as much as possible. Bake 15-25 minutes, or salmon flakes easily with a fork. Serve.

Nutrition: Calories 444 Total Carbs 2g Protein 55g Fat 24g Sugar 1g Fiber 0g

813. Shrimp & Artichoke Skillet

Preparation time: 5 minutes

Cooking time: 10 minutes

Servings: 4

Ingredients:

- 1 1/2 cups shrimp, peel & devein
- 2 shallots, diced
- 1 tbsp. margarine
- What you'll need from store cupboard
- 2 12 oz. jars artichoke hearts, drain & rinse
- 2 cups white wine
- 2 cloves garlic, diced fine

Directions:

1.   Melt margarine in a large skillet over med-high heat. Add shallot and garlic and cook until they start to brown, stirring frequently.

2.   Add artichokes and cook 5 minutes. Reduce heat and add wine. Cook 3 minutes, stirring occasionally.

3.   Add the shrimp and cook just until they turn pink. Serve.

Nutrition: Calories 487 Total Carbs 26g Net Carbs 17g Protein 64g Fat 5g Sugar 3g Fiber 9g

814. Tuna Carbonara

Preparation time: 5 minutes

Cooking time: 25 minutes

Servings: 4

Ingredients:

- 1/2 lb. tuna fillet, cut in pieces
- 2 eggs
- 4 tbsp. fresh parsley, diced
- What you'll need from store cupboard:
- 1/2 Homemade Pasta, cook & drain,
- 1/2 cup reduced fat parmesan cheese
- 2 cloves garlic, peeled
- 2 tbsp. extra virgin olive oil
- Salt & pepper, to taste

Directions:

1.   In a small bowl, beat the eggs, parmesan and a dash of pepper.

2.   Heat the oil in a large skillet over med-high heat. Add garlic and cook until browned. Add the tuna and cook 2-3 minutes, or until tuna is almost cooked through. Discard the garlic.

3.   Add the pasta and reduce heat. Stir in egg mixture and cook, stirring constantly, 2 minutes. If the sauce is too thick, thin with water, a little bit at a time, until it has a creamy texture.

4.   Salt and pepper to taste and serve garnished with parsley.

Nutrition: Calories 409 Total Carbs 7g Net Carbs 6g Protein 25g Fat 30g Sugar 3g Fiber 1g

815. Mediterranean Fish Fillets

Preparation Time: 10 minutes

Cooking Time: 3 minutes

Servings: 4

Ingredients:

- 4 cod fillets
- 1 lb. grape tomatoes, halved
- 1 cup olives, pitted and sliced

- 2 tbsp. capers
- 1 tsp. dried thyme
- 2 tbsp. olive oil
- 1 tsp. garlic, minced
- Pepper
- Salt

Directions:

1. Pour 1 cup water into the instant pot then place steamer rack in the pot.
2. Spray heat-safe baking dish with cooking spray.
3. Add half grape tomatoes into the dish and season with pepper and salt.
4. Arrange fish fillets on top of cherry tomatoes. Drizzle with oil and season with garlic, thyme, capers, pepper, and salt.
5. Spread olives and remaining grape tomatoes on top of fish fillets.
6. Place dish on top of steamer rack in the pot.
7. Seal pot with a lid and select manual and cook on high for 3 minutes.
8. Once done, release pressure using quick release. Remove lid.
9. Serve and enjoy.

Nutrition: Calories 212 Fat 11.9 g Carbohydrates 7.1 g Sugar 3 g Protein 21.4 g Cholesterol 55 mg

Side Dish Recipes

816. Brussels Sprouts

Preparation Time: 5 minutes
Cooking Time: 3 minutes
Servings: 5
Ingredients:

- 1 tsp. extra-virgin olive oil
- 1 lb. halved Brussels sprouts
- 3 tbsps. apple cider vinegar
- 3 tbsps. gluten-free tamari soy sauce
- 3 tbsps. chopped sun-dried tomatoes

Direction:

1. Select the "Sauté" function on your Instant Pot, add oil and allow the pot to get hot.
2. Cancel the "Sauté" function and add the Brussels sprouts.
3. Stir well and allow the sprouts to cook in the residual heat for 2-3 minutes.
4. Add the tamari soy sauce and vinegar, and then stir.
5. Cover the Instant Pot, sealing the pressure valve by pointing it to "Sealing."
6. Select the "Manual, High Pressure" setting and cook for 3 minutes.
7. Once the cook cycle is done, do a quick pressure release, and then stir in the chopped sun-dried tomatoes.
8. Serve immediately.

Nutrition:
62 Calories
10g Carbohydrates
1g Fat

817. Garlic and Herb Carrots

Preparation Time: 2 minutes
Cooking Time: 18 minutes
Servings: 3
Ingredients:

- 2 tbsps. butter
- 1 lb. baby carrots
- 1 cup water
- 1 tsp. fresh thyme or oregano
- 1 tsp. minced garlic
- Black pepper
- Coarse sea salt

Direction:

1. Fill water to the inner pot of the Instant Pot, and then put in a steamer basket.
2. Layer the carrots into the steamer basket.
3. Close and seal the lid, with the pressure vent in the "Sealing" position.
4. Select the "Steam" setting and cook for 2 minutes on high pressure.
5. Quick release the pressure and then carefully remove the steamer basket with the steamed carrots, discarding the water.
6. Add butter to the inner pot of the Instant Pot and allow it to melt on the "Sauté" function.
7. Add garlic and sauté for 30 seconds, and then add the carrots. Mix well.
8. Stir in the fresh herbs, and cook for 2-3 minutes.
9. Season with salt and black pepper, and the transfer to a serving bowl.
10. Serve warm and enjoy!

Nutrition:
122 Calories
12g Carbohydrates
7g Fat

818. Cilantro Lime Drumsticks

Preparation Time: 5 minutes
Cooking Time: 15 minutes
Servings: 6
Ingredients:

- 1 tbsp. olive oil
- 6 chicken drumsticks
- 4 minced garlic cloves
- ½ cup low-sodium chicken broth
- 1 tsp. cayenne pepper
- 1 tsp. crushed red peppers
- 1 tsp. fine sea salt
- Juice of 1 lime

To Serve:

- 2 tbsp. chopped cilantro
- Extra lime zest

Direction:

1. Pour olive oil to the Instant Pot and set it on the "Sauté" function.

2. Once the oil is hot adding the chicken drumsticks, and season them well.

3. Using tongs, stir the drumsticks and brown the drumsticks for 2 minutes per side.

4. Add the lime juice, fresh cilantro, and chicken broth to the pot.

5. Lock and seal the lid, turning the pressure valve to "Sealing."

6. Cook the drumsticks on the "Manual, High Pressure" setting for 9 minutes.

7. Once done let the pressure release naturally.

8. Carefully transfer the drumsticks to an aluminum-foiled baking sheet and broil them in the oven for 3-5 minutes until golden brown.

9. Serve warm, garnished with more cilantro and lime zest.

Nutrition:

480 Calories

3.3g Carbohydrates

29g Fat

819. Eggplant Spread

Preparation Time: 5 minutes

Cooking Time: 18 minutes

Servings: 5

Ingredients:

- 4 tbsps. extra-virgin olive oil
- 2 lbs. eggplant
- 4 skin-on garlic cloves
- ½ cup water
- ¼ cup pitted black olives
- 3 sprigs fresh thyme
- Juice of 1 lemon
- 1 tbsp. tahini
- 1 tsp. sea salt
- Fresh extra-virgin olive oil

Direction:

1. Peel the eggplant in alternating stripes, leaving some areas with skin and some with no skin.

2. Slice into big chunks and layer at the bottom of your Instant Pot.

3. Add olive oil to the pot, and on the "Sauté" function, fry and caramelize the eggplant on one side, about 5 minutes.

4. Add in the garlic cloves with the skin on.

5. Flip over the eggplant and then add in the remaining uncooked eggplant chunks, salt, and water.

6. Close the lid, ensure the pressure release valve is set to "Sealing."

7. Cook for 5 minutes on the "Manual, High Pressure" setting.

8. Once done, carefully open the pot by quick releasing the pressure through the steam valve.

9. Discard most of the brown cooking liquid.

10. Remove the garlic cloves and peel them.

11. Add the lemon juice, tahini, cooked and fresh garlic cloves and pitted black olives to the pot.

12. Using a hand-held immersion blender, process all the ingredients until smooth.

13. Pour out the spread into a serving dish and season with fresh thyme, whole black olives and some extra-virgin olive oil, prior to serving.

Nutrition:

155 Calories

16.8g Carbohydrates

11.7g Fat

820. Carrot Hummus

Preparation Time: 15 minutes

Cooking Time: 10 minutes

Servings: 2

Ingredients:

- 1 chopped carrot
- 2 oz. cooked chickpeas
- 1 tsp. lemon juice
- 1 tsp. tahini
- 1 tsp. fresh parsley

Direction:

1. Place the carrot and chickpeas in your Instant Pot.

2. Add a cup of water, seal, cook for 10 minutes on Stew.

3. Depressurize naturally. Blend with the remaining ingredients.

Nutrition:

58 Calories

8g Carbohydrates

2g Fat

821. Vegetable Rice Pilaf

Preparation Time: 5 minutes

Cooking Time: 25 minutes

Servings: 6

Ingredients:

- 1 tablespoon olive oil
- ½ medium yellow onion, diced
- 1 cup uncooked long-grain brown rice
- 2 cloves minced garlic
- ½ teaspoon dried basil
- Salt and pepper
- 2 cups fat-free chicken broth
- 1 cup frozen mixed veggies

Direction:

1. Cook oil in a large skillet over medium heat.
2. Add the onion and sauté for 3 minutes until translucent.
3. Stir in the rice and cook until lightly toasted.
4. Add the garlic, basil, salt, and pepper then stir to combined.
5. Stir in the chicken broth then bring to a boil.
6. Decrease heat and simmer, covered, for 10 minutes.
7. Stir in the frozen veggies then cover and cook for another 10 minutes until heated through. Serve hot.

Nutrition:

90 Calories

12.6g Carbohydrates

2.2g Fiber

822. Curry Roasted Cauliflower Florets

Preparation Time: 5 minutes

Cooking Time: 25 minutes

Servings: 6

Ingredients:

- 8 cups cauliflower florets
- 2 tablespoons olive oil
- 1 teaspoon curry powder
- ½ teaspoon garlic powder
- Salt and pepper

Direction:

1. Prep the oven to 425°F and line a baking sheet with foil.
2. Toss the cauliflower with the olive oil and spread on the baking sheet.
3. Sprinkle with curry powder, garlic powder, salt, and pepper.
4. Roast for 25 minutes or until just tender. Serve hot.

Nutrition:

75 Calories

7.4g Carbohydrates

3.5g Fiber

823. Mushroom Barley Risotto

Preparation Time: 5 minutes

Cooking Time: 25 minutes

Servings: 8

Ingredients:

- 4 cups fat-free beef broth
- 2 tablespoons olive oil
- 1 small onion, diced well
- 2 cloves minced garlic
- 8 ounces thinly sliced mushrooms
- ¼ tsp dried thyme
- Salt and pepper
- 1 cup pearled barley
- ½ cup dry white wine

Direction:

1. Heat the beef broth in a medium saucepan and keep it warm.
2. Heat the oil in a large, deep skillet over medium heat.
3. Add the onions and garlic and sauté for 2 minutes then stir in the mushrooms and thyme.
4. Season with salt and pepper and sauté for 2 minutes more.
5. Add the barley and sauté for 1 minute then pour in the wine.
6. Ladle about ½ cup of beef broth into the skillet and stir well to combine.
7. Cook until most of the broth has been absorbed then add another ladle.
8. Repeat until you have used all of the broth and the barley is cooked to al dente.
9. Season and serve hot.

Nutrition:

155 Calories

21.9g Carbohydrates

4.4g Fiber

824. Braised Summer Squash

Preparation Time: 10 minutes

Cooking Time: 20 minutes

Servings: 6

Ingredients:

- 3 tablespoons olive oil
- 3 cloves minced garlic
- ¼ teaspoon crushed red pepper flakes
- 1-pound summer squash, sliced
- 1-pound zucchini, sliced
- 1 teaspoon dried oregano

- Salt and pepper

Direction:

1.Cook oil in a large skillet over medium heat.

2.Add the garlic and crushed red pepper and cook for 2 minutes.

3.Add the summer squash and zucchini and cook for 15 minutes, stirring often, until just tender.

4.Stir in the oregano then season with salt and pepper to taste. serve hot.

Nutrition:

90 Calories

6.2g Carbohydrates

1.8g Fiber

825. Lemon Garlic Green Beans

Preparation time: 5 minutes

Cooking Time: 10 minutes

Servings: 6

Ingredients:

- 1 1/2 pounds green beans, trimmed
- 2 tablespoons olive oil
- 1 tablespoon fresh lemon juice
- 2 cloves minced garlic
- Salt and pepper

Directions:

1. Fill a large bowl with ice water and set aside.

2. Bring a pot of salted water to boil then add the green beans.

3. Cook for 3 minutes then drain and immediately place in the ice water.

4. Cool the beans completely then drain them well.

5. Heat the oil in a large skillet over medium-high heat.

6. Add the green beans, tossing to coat, then add the lemon juice, garlic, salt, and pepper.

7. Sauté for 3 minutes until the beans are tender-crisp then serve hot.

Nutrition:

Calories 75, Total Fat 4.8g, Saturated Fat 0.7g, Total Carbs 8.5g, Net Carbs 4.6g, Protein 2.1g, Sugar 1.7g, Fiber 3.9g, Sodium 7mg

826. Brown Rice & Lentil Salad

Preparation time: 10 minutes

Cooking Time: 10 minutes

Servings: 4

Ingredients:

- 1 cup water
- 1/2 cup instant brown rice
- 2 tablespoons olive oil
- 2 tablespoons red wine vinegar
- 1 tablespoon Dijon mustard
- 1 tablespoon minced onion
- 1/2 teaspoon paprika
- Salt and pepper
- 1 (15-ounce) can brown lentils, rinsed and drained
- 1 medium carrot, shredded
- 2 tablespoons fresh chopped parsley

Directions:

1. Stir together the water and instant brown rice in a medium saucepan.

2. Bring to a boil then simmer for 10 minutes, covered.

3. Remove from heat and set aside while you prepare the salad.

4. Whisk together the olive oil, vinegar, Dijon mustard, onion, paprika, salt, and pepper in a medium bowl.

5. Toss in the cooked rice, lentils, carrots, and parsley.

6. Adjust seasoning to taste then stir well and serve warm.

Nutrition:

Calories 145, Total Fat 7.7g, Saturated Fat 1g, Total Carbs 13.1g, Net Carbs 10.9g, Protein 6g, Sugar 1g, Fiber 2.2g, Sodium 57mg

827. Mashed Butternut Squash

Preparation time: 5 minutes

Cooking Time: 25 minutes

Servings: 6

Ingredients:

- 3 pounds whole butternut squash (about 2 medium)
- 2 tablespoons olive oil
- Salt and pepper

Directions:

1. Preheat the oven to 400F and line a baking sheet with parchment.

2. Cut the squash in half and remove the seeds.

3. Cut the squash into cubes and toss with oil then spread on the baking sheet.

4. Roast for 25 minutes until tender then place in a food processor.

5. Blend smooth then season with salt and pepper to taste.

Nutrition:
Calories 90, Total Fat 4.8g, Saturated Fat 0.7g, Total Carbs 12.3g, Net Carbs 10.2g, Protein 1.1g, Sugar 2.3g, Fiber 2.1g, Sodium 4mg

828. Cilantro Lime Quinoa

Preparation time: 5 minutes
Cooking Time: 25 minutes
Servings: 6
Ingredients:

- 1 cup uncooked quinoa
- 1 tablespoon olive oil
- 1 medium yellow onion, diced
- 2 cloves minced garlic
- 1 (4-ounce) can diced green chiles, drained
- 1 1/2 cups fat-free chicken broth
- ¾ cup fresh chopped cilantro
- 1/2 cup sliced green onion
- 2 tablespoons lime juice
- Salt and pepper

Directions:
1.   Rinse the quinoa thoroughly in cool water using a fine mesh sieve.
2.   Heat the oil in a large saucepan over medium heat.
3.   Add the onion and sauté for 2 minutes then stir in the chile and garlic.
4.   Cook for 1 minute then stir in the quinoa and chicken broth.
5.   Bring to a boil then reduce heat and simmer, covered, until the quinoa absorbs the liquid – about 20 to 25 minutes.
6.   Remove from heat then stir in the cilantro, green onions, and lime juice.
7.   Season with salt and pepper to taste and serve hot.
Nutrition:
Calories 150, Total Fat 4.1g, Saturated Fat 0.5g, Total Carbs 22.5g, Net Carbs 19.8g, Protein 6g, Sugar 1.7g, Fiber 2.7g, Sodium 179mg

829. Oven-Roasted Veggies

Preparation time: 5 minutes
Cooking Time: 25 minutes
Servings: 6
Ingredients:

- 1 pound cauliflower florets
- 1/2-pound broccoli florets
- 1 large yellow onion, cut into chunks
- 1 large red pepper, cored and chopped
- 2 medium carrots, peeled and sliced
- 2 tablespoons olive oil
- 2 tablespoons apple cider vinegar
- Salt and pepper

Directions:
1.   Preheat the oven to 425F and line a large rimmed baking sheet with parchment.
2.   Spread the veggies on the baking sheet and drizzle with oil and vinegar.
3.   Toss well and season with salt and pepper.
4.   Spread the veggies in a single layer then roast for 20 to 25 minutes, stirring every 10 minutes, until tender.
5.   Adjust seasoning to taste and serve hot.
Nutrition:
Calories 100, Total Fat 5g, Saturated Fat 0.7g, Total Carbs 12.4g, Net Carbs 8.2g, Protein 3.2g, Sugar 5.5g, Fiber 4.2g, Sodium 51mg

830. Parsley Tabbouleh

Preparation time: 5 minutes
Cooking Time: 25 minutes
Servings: 6
Ingredients:

- 1 cup water
- 1/2 cup bulgur
- ¼ cup fresh lemon juice
- 2 tablespoons olive oil
- 2 cloves minced garlic
- Salt and pepper
- 2 cups fresh chopped parsley
- 2 medium tomatoes, died
- 1 small cucumber, diced
- ¼ cup fresh chopped mint

Directions:
1.   Bring the water and bulgur to a boil in a small saucepan then remove from heat.
2.   Cover and let stand until the water are fully absorbed, about 25 minutes.
3.   Meanwhile, whisk together the lemon juice, olive oil, garlic, salt, and pepper in a medium bowl.
4.   Toss in the cooked bulgur along with the parsley, tomatoes, cucumber, and mint.
5.   Season with salt and pepper to taste and serve.

Nutrition:
Calories 110, Total Fat 5.3g, Saturated Fat 0.9g, Total Carbs 14.4g, Net Carbs 10.5g, Protein 3g, Sugar 2.4g, Fiber 3.9g, Sodium 21mg

831. Garlic Sautéed Spinach

Preparation time: 5 minutes
Cooking Time: 10 minutes
Servings: 4
Ingredients:

- 1 1/2 tablespoons olive oil
- 4 cloves minced garlic
- 6 cups fresh baby spinach
- Salt and pepper

Directions:
1. Heat the oil in a large skillet over medium-high heat.
2. Add the garlic and cook for 1 minute.
3. Stir in the spinach and season with salt and pepper.
4. Sauté for 1 to 2 minutes until just wilted. Serve hot.

Nutrition:
Calories 60, Total Fat 5.5g, Saturated Fat 0.8g, Total Carbs 2.6g, Net Carbs 1.5g, Protein 1.5g, Sugar 0.2g, Fiber 1.1g, Sodium 36mg

832. French Lentils

Preparation time: 5 minutes
Cooking Time: 25 minutes
Servings: 10
Ingredients:

- 2 tablespoons olive oil
- 1 medium onion, diced
- 1 medium carrot, peeled and diced
- 2 cloves minced garlic
- 5 1/2 cups water
- 2 ¼ cups French lentils, rinsed and drained
- 1 teaspoon dried thyme
- 2 small bay leaves
- Salt and pepper

Directions:
1. Heat the oil in a large saucepan over medium heat.
2. Add the onions, carrot, and garlic and sauté for 3 minutes.
3. Stir in the water, lentils, thyme, and bay leaves – season with salt.

4. Bring to a boil then reduce to a simmer and cook until tender, about 20 minutes.
5. Drain any excess water and adjust seasoning to taste. Serve hot.

Nutrition:
Calories 185, Total Fat 3.3g, Saturated Fat 0.5g, Total Carbs 27.9g, Net Carbs 14.2g, Protein 11.4g, Sugar 1.7g, Fiber 13.7g, Sodium 11mg

833. Grain-Free Berry Cobbler

Preparation time: 5 minutes
Cooking Time: 25 minutes
Servings: 10
Ingredients:

- 4 cups fresh mixed berries
- 1/2 cup ground flaxseed
- ¼ cup almond meal
- ¼ cup unsweetened shredded coconut
- 1/2 tablespoon baking powder
- 1 teaspoon ground cinnamon
- ¼ teaspoon salt
- Powdered stevia, to taste
- 6 tablespoons coconut oil

Directions:
1. Preheat the oven to 375F and lightly grease a 10-inch cast-iron skillet.
2. Spread the berries on the bottom of the skillet.
3. Whisk together the dry ingredients in a mixing bowl.
4. Cut in the coconut oil using a fork to create a crumbled mixture.
5. Spread the crumble over the berries and bake for 25 minutes until hot and bubbling.
6. Cool the cobbler for 5 to 10 minutes before serving.

Nutrition:
Calories 215 Total Fat 16.8g, Saturated Fat 10.4g, Total Carbs 13.1g, Net Carbs 6.7g, Protein 3.7g, Sugar 5.3g, Fiber 6.4g, Sodium 61mg

834. Coffee-Steamed Carrots

Preparation Time: 10 minutes
Cooking Time: 3 minutes
Servings: 4
Ingredients:

- 1 cup brewed coffee
- 1 teaspoon light brown sugar
- ½ teaspoon kosher salt

- Freshly ground black pepper
- 1-pound baby carrots
- Chopped fresh parsley
- 1 teaspoon grated lemon zest

Directions:

1. Pour the coffee into the electric pressure cooker. Stir in the brown sugar, salt, and pepper. Add the carrots.
2. Close the pressure cooker. Set to sealing.
3. Cook on high pressure for minutes.
4. Once complete, click Cancel and quick release the pressure.
5. Once the pin drops, open and remove the lid.
6. Using a slotted spoon, portion carrots to a serving bowl. Topped with the parsley and lemon zest, and serve.

Nutrition:

51 Calories

12g Carbohydrates

4g Fiber

835. Rosemary Potatoes

Preparation Time: 5 minutes

Cooking Time: 25 minutes

Servings: 2

Ingredients:

- 1lb red potatoes
- 1 cup vegetable stock
- 2tbsp olive oil
- 2tbsp rosemary sprigs

Directions:

1. Situate potatoes in the steamer basket and add the stock into the Instant Pot.
2. Steam the potatoes in your Instant Pot for 15 minutes.
3. Depressurize and pour away the remaining stock.
4. Set to sauté and add the oil, rosemary, and potatoes.
5. Cook until brown.

Nutrition: Per serving:

195 Calories

31g Carbohydrates

1g Fat

836. Corn on the Cob

Preparation Time: 10 minutes

Cooking Time: 5 minutes

Servings: 12

Ingredients:

- 6 ears corn

Directions:

1. Take off husks and silk from the corn. Cut or break each ear in half.
2. Pour 1 cup of water into the bottom of the electric pressure cooker. Insert a wire rack or trivet.
3. Place the corn upright on the rack, cut-side down. Seal lid of the pressure cooker.
4. Cook on high pressure for 5 minutes.
5. When its complete, select Cancel and quick release the pressure.
6. When pin drops, unlock and take off lid.
7. Pull out the corn from the pot. Season as desired and serve immediately.

Nutrition

62 Calories

14g Carbohydrates

1g Fiber

837. Chili Lime Salmon

Preparation Time: 6 minutes

Cooking Time: 10 minutes

Servings: 2

Ingredients:

For Sauce:

- 1 jalapeno pepper
- 1 tablespoon chopped parsley
- 1 teaspoon minced garlic
- 1/2 teaspoon cumin
- 1/2 teaspoon paprika
- 1/2 teaspoon lime zest
- 1 tablespoon honey
- 1 tablespoon lime juice
- 1 tablespoon olive oil
- 1 tablespoon water

For Fish:

- 2 salmon fillets, each about 5 ounces
- 1 cup water
- 1/2 teaspoon salt
- 1/8 teaspoon ground black pepper

Directions:

1. Prepare salmon and for this, season salmon with salt and black pepper until evenly coated.
2. Plugin instant pot, insert the inner pot, pour in water, then place steamer basket and place seasoned salmon on it.

3.Seal instant pot with its lid, press the 'steam' button, then press the 'timer' to set the cooking time to 5 minutes and cook on high pressure, for 5 minutes.

4.Transfer all the ingredients for the sauce in a bowl, whisk until combined and set aside until required.

5.When the timer beeps, press 'cancel' button and do quick pressure release until pressure nob drops down.

6.Open the instant pot, then transfer salmon to a serving plate and drizzle generously with prepared sauce.

7.Serve straight away.

Nutrition:

305 Calories

29g Carbohydrates

6g Fiber

838. Collard Greens

Preparation Time: 5 minutes

Cooking Time: 6 hours

Servings: 12

Ingredients:

- 2 pounds chopped collard greens
- ¾ cup chopped white onion
- 1 teaspoon onion powder
- 1 teaspoon garlic powder
- 1 teaspoon salt
- 2 teaspoons brown sugar
- ½ teaspoon ground black pepper
- ½ teaspoon red chili powder
- ¼ teaspoon crushed red pepper flakes
- 3 tablespoons apple cider vinegar
- 2 tablespoons olive oil
- 14.5-ounce vegetable broth
- 1/2 cup water

Directions:

1.Plugin instant pot, insert the inner pot, add onion and collard and then pour in vegetable broth and water.

2.Close instant pot with its lid, seal, press the 'slow cook' button, then press the 'timer' to set the cooking time to 6 hours at high heat setting.

3.When the timer beeps, press 'cancel' button and do natural pressure release until pressure nob drops down.

4.Open the instant pot, add remaining ingredients and stir until mixed.

5.Then press the 'sauté/simmer' button and cook for 3 to minutes or more until collards reach to desired texture.

6.Serve straight away.

Nutrition:

49 Calories

2.3g Carbohydrates

0.5g Fiber

839. Mashed Pumpkin

Preparation Time: 9 minutes

Cooking Time: 15 minutes

Servings: 2

Ingredients:

- 2 cups chopped pumpkin
- 0.5 cup water
- 2tbsp powdered sugar-free sweetener of choice
- 1tbsp cinnamon

Directions:

1.Place the pumpkin and water in your Instant Pot.

2.Seal and cook on Stew 15 minutes.

3.Remove and mash with the sweetener and cinnamon.

Nutrition:

12 Calories

3g Carbohydrates

1g Sugar

840. Parmesan-Topped Acorn Squash

Preparation Time: 8 minutes

Cooking Time: 20 minutes

Servings: 4

Ingredients:

- 1 acorn squash (about 1 pound)
- 1 tablespoon extra-virgin olive oil
- 1 teaspoon dried sage leaves, crumbled
- ¼ teaspoon freshly grated nutmeg
- 1/8 teaspoon kosher salt
- 1/8 teaspoon freshly ground black pepper
- 2 tablespoons freshly grated Parmesan cheese

Directions:

1.Chop acorn squash in half lengthwise and remove the seeds. Cut each half in half for a total of 4 wedges. Snap off the stem if it's easy to do.

2.In a small bowl, combine the olive oil, sage, nutmeg, salt, and pepper. Brush the cut sides of the squash with the olive oil mixture.

3. Fill 1 cup of water into the electric pressure cooker and insert a wire rack or trivet.

4. Place the squash on the trivet in a single layer, skin-side down.

5. Set the lid of the pressure cooker on sealing.

6. Cook on high pressure for 20 minutes.

7. Once done, press Cancel and quick release the pressure.

8. Once the pin drops, open it.

9. Carefully remove the squash from the pot, sprinkle with the Parmesan, and serve.

Nutrition:

85 Calories

12g Carbohydrates

2g Fiber

841. Quinoa Tabbouleh

Preparation Time: 8 minutes

Cooking Time: 16 minutes

Servings: 6

Ingredients:

- 1 cup quinoa, rinsed
- 1 large English cucumber
- 2 scallions, sliced
- 2 cups cherry tomatoes, halved
- 2/3 cup chopped parsley
- 1/2 cup chopped mint
- ½ teaspoon minced garlic
- 1/2 teaspoon salt
- ½ teaspoon ground black pepper
- 2 tablespoon lemon juice
- 1/2 cup olive oil

Directions:

1. Plugin instant pot, insert the inner pot, add quinoa, then pour in water and stir until mixed.

2. Close instant pot with its lid and turn the pressure knob to seal the pot.

3. Select 'manual' button, then set the 'timer' to 1 minute and cook in high pressure, it may take 7 minutes.

4. Once the timer stops, select 'cancel' button and do natural pressure release for 10 minutes and then do quick pressure release until pressure nob drops down.

5. Open the instant pot, fluff quinoa with a fork, then spoon it on a rimmed baking sheet, spread quinoa evenly and let cool.

6. Meanwhile, place lime juice in a small bowl, add garlic and stir until just mixed.

7. Then add salt, black pepper, and olive oil and whisk until combined.

8. Transfer cooled quinoa to a large bowl, add remaining ingredients, then drizzle generously with the prepared lime juice mixture and toss until evenly coated.

9. Taste quinoa to adjust seasoning and then serve.

Nutrition:

283 Calories

30.6g Carbohydrates

3.4g Fiber

842. Wild Rice Salad with Cranberries and Almonds

Preparation Time: 6 minutes

Cooking Time: 25 minutes

Servings: 18

Ingredients:

For the rice

- 2 cups wild rice blend, rinsed
- 1 teaspoon kosher salt
- 2½ cups Vegetable Broth

For the dressing

- ¼ cup extra-virgin olive oil
- ¼ cup white wine vinegar
- 1½ teaspoons grated orange zest
- Juice of 1 medium orange (about ¼ cup)
- 1 teaspoon honey or pure maple syrup

For the salad

- ¾ cup unsweetened dried cranberries
- ½ cup sliced almonds, toasted
- Freshly ground black pepper

Directions:

1. To make the rice

2. In the electric pressure cooker, combine the rice, salt, and broth.

3. Close and lock the lid. Set the valve to sealing.

4. Cook on high pressure for 25 minutes.

5. When the cooking is complete, hit Cancel and allow the pressure to release naturally for 1minutes, then quick release any remaining pressure.

6. Once the pin drops, unlock and remove the lid.

7. Let the rice cool briefly, then fluff it with a fork.

8. To make the dressing

9. While the rice cooks, make the dressing: In a small jar with a screw-top lid, combine the olive oil, vinegar, zest, juice, and honey. (If you don't have a jar, whisk the ingredients together in a small bowl.) Shake to combine.

10. To make the salad

11. Mix rice, cranberries, and almonds.

12. Add the dressing and season with pepper.

13. Serve warm or refrigerate.

Nutrition

126 Calories

18g Carbohydrates

2g Fiber

843. Low Fat Roasties

Preparation Time: 8 minutes

Cooking Time: 25 minutes

Servings: 2

Ingredients:

- 1lb roasting potatoes
- 1 garlic clove
- 1 cup vegetable stock
- 2tbsp olive oil

Directions:

1. Position potatoes in the steamer basket and add the stock into the Instant Pot.

2. Steam the potatoes in your Instant Pot for 15 minutes.

3. Depressurize and pour away the remaining stock.

4. Set to sauté and add the oil, garlic, and potatoes. Cook until brown.

Nutrition:

201 Calories

3g Carbohydrates

6g Fat

844. Roasted Parsnips

Preparation Time: 9 minutes

Cooking Time: 25 minutes

Servings: 2

Ingredients:

- 1lb parsnips
- 1 cup vegetable stock
- 2tbsp herbs
- 2tbsp olive oil

Directions:

1. Put the parsnips in the steamer basket and add the stock into the Instant Pot.

2. Steam the parsnips in your Instant Pot for 15 minutes.

3. Depressurize and pour away the remaining stock.

4. Set to sauté and add the oil, herbs and parsnips.

5. Cook until golden and crisp.

Nutrition:

130 Calories

14g Carbohydrates

4g Protein

845. Lower Carb Hummus

Preparation Time: 9 minutes

Cooking Time: 60 minutes

Servings: 2

Ingredients:

- 0.5 cup dry chickpeas
- 1 cup vegetable stock
- 1 cup pumpkin puree
- 2tbsp smoked paprika
- salt and pepper to taste

Directions:

1. Soak the chickpeas overnight.

2. Place the chickpeas and stock in the Instant Pot.

3. Cook on Beans 60 minutes.

4. Depressurize naturally.

5. Blend the chickpeas with the remaining ingredients.

Nutrition:

135 Calories

18g Carbohydrates

3g Fat

846. Sweet and Sour Red Cabbage

Preparation Time: 7 minutes

Cooking Time: 10 minutes

Servings: 8

Ingredients:

- 2 cups Spiced Pear Applesauce
- 1 small onion, chopped
- ½ cup apple cider vinegar
- ½ teaspoon kosher salt
- 1 head red cabbage

Directions:

1. In the electric pressure cooker, combine the applesauce, onion, vinegar, salt, and cup of water. Stir in the cabbage.

2. Seal lid of the pressure cooker.

3.Cook on high pressure for 10 minutes.

4.When the cooking is complete, hit Cancel and quick release the pressure.

5.Once the pin drops, unlock and remove the lid.

6.Spoon into a bowl or platter and serve.

Nutrition:

91 Calories

18g Carbohydrates

4g Fiber

847. Pinto Beans

Preparation Time: 6 minutes

Cooking Time: 55 minutes

Servings: 10

Ingredients:

- 2 cups pinto beans, dried
- 1 medium white onion
- 1 ½ teaspoon minced garlic
- ¾ teaspoon salt
- 1/4 teaspoon ground black pepper
- 1 teaspoon red chili powder
- 1/4 teaspoon cumin
- 1 tablespoon olive oil
- 1 teaspoon chopped cilantro
- 5 ½ cup vegetable stock

Directions:

1.Plugin instant pot, insert the inner pot, press sauté/simmer button, add oil and when hot, add onion and garlic and cook for 3 minutes or until onions begin to soften.

2.Add remaining ingredients, stir well, then press the cancel button, shut the instant pot with its lid and seal the pot.

3.Click 'manual' button, then press the 'timer' to set the cooking time to 45 minutes and cook at high pressure.

4.Once done, click 'cancel' button and do natural pressure release for 10 minutes until pressure nob drops down.

5.Open the instant pot, spoon beans into plates and serve.

Nutrition:

107 Calories

11.7g Carbohydrates

4g Fiber

848. Parmesan Cauliflower Mash

Preparation Time: 19 minutes

Cooking Time: 5 minutes

Servings: 4

Ingredients:

- 1 head cauliflower
- ½ teaspoon kosher salt
- ½ teaspoon garlic pepper
- 2 tablespoons plain Greek yogurt
- ¾ cup freshly grated Parmesan cheese
- 1 tablespoon unsalted butter or ghee (optional)
- Chopped fresh chives

Directions:

1.Pour cup of water into the electric pressure cooker and insert a steamer basket or wire rack.

2.Place the cauliflower in the basket.

3.Cover lid of the pressure cooker to seal.

4.Cook on high pressure for 5 minutes.

5.Once complete, hit Cancel and quick release the pressure.

6.When the pin drops, remove the lid.

7.Remove the cauliflower from the pot and pour out the water. Return the cauliflower to the pot and add the salt, garlic pepper, yogurt, and cheese. Use an immersion blender to purée or mash the cauliflower in the pot.

8.Spoon into a serving bowl, and garnish with butter (if using) and chives.

Nutrition:

141 Calories

12g Carbohydrates

4g Fiber

849. Steamed Asparagus

Preparation Time: 3 minutes

Cooking Time: 2 minutes

Servings: 4

Ingredients:

- 1 lb. fresh asparagus, rinsed and tough ends trimmed
- 1 cup water

Direction:

1.Place the asparagus into a wire steamer rack, and set it inside your Instant Pot.

2.Add water to the pot. Close and seal the lid, turning the steam release valve to the "Sealing" position.

3.Select the "Steam" function to cook on high pressure for 2 minutes.

4.Once done, do a quick pressure release of the steam.

5. Lift the wire steamer basket out of the pot and place the asparagus onto a serving plate.

6. Season as desired and serve.

Nutrition:

22 Calories

4g Carbohydrates

2g Protein

850. Squash Medley

Preparation Time: 10 minutes

Cooking Time: 20 minutes.

Servings: 2

Ingredients:

- 2 lbs. mixed squash
- ½ cup mixed veg
- 1 cup vegetable stock
- 2 tbsps. olive oil
- 2 tbsps. mixed herbs

Direction:

1. Put the squash in the steamer basket and add the stock into the Instant Pot.

2. Steam the squash in your Instant Pot for 10 minutes.

3. Depressurize and pour away the remaining stock.

4. Set to sauté and add the oil and remaining ingredients.

5. Cook until a light crust form.

Nutrition:

100 Calories

10g Carbohydrates

6g Fat

851. Eggplant Curry

Preparation Time: 15 minutes

Cooking Time: 20 minutes

Servings: 2

Ingredients:

- 3 cups chopped eggplant
- 1 thinly sliced onion
- 1 cup coconut milk
- 3 tbsps. curry paste
- 1 tbsp. oil or ghee

Direction:

1. Select Instant Pot to sauté and put the onion, oil, and curry paste.

2. Once the onion is soft, stir in remaining ingredients and seal.

3. Cook on Stew for 20 minutes. Release the pressure naturally.

Nutrition:

350 Calories

15g Carbohydrates

25g Fat

852. Lentil and Eggplant Stew

Preparation Time: 15 minutes

Cooking Time: 35 minutes

Servings: 2

Ingredients:

- 1 lb. eggplant
- 1 lb. dry lentils
- 1 cup chopped vegetables
- 1 cup low sodium vegetable broth

Direction:

1. Incorporate all the ingredients in your Instant Pot, cook on Stew for 35 minutes.

2. Release the pressure naturally and serve.

Nutrition:

310 Calories

22g Carbohydrates

10g Fat

853. Tofu Curry

Preparation Time: 15 minutes

Cooking Time: 20 minutes

Servings: 2

Ingredients:

- 2 cups cubed extra firm tofu
- 2 cups mixed stir fry vegetables
- ½ cup soy yogurt
- 3 tbsps. curry paste
- 1 tbsp. oil or ghee

Direction:

1. Set the Instant Pot to sauté and add the oil and curry paste.

2. Once soft, place the remaining ingredients except for the yogurt and seal.

3. Cook on Stew for 20 minutes.

4. Release the pressure naturally and serve with a scoop of soy yogurt.

Nutrition:

300 Calories

9g Carbohydrates

14g Fat

854. Lentil and Chickpea Curry

Preparation Time: 15 minutes
Cooking Time: 20 minutes
Servings: 2
Ingredients:

- 2 cups dry lentils and chickpeas
- 1 thinly sliced onion
- 1 cup chopped tomato
- 3 tbsps. curry paste
- 1 tbsp. oil or ghee

Direction:

1. Press Instant Pot to sauté and mix onion, oil, and curry paste.
2. Once the onion is cooked, stir the remaining ingredients and seal.
3. Cook on Stew for 20 minutes.
4. Release the pressure naturally and serve.

Nutrition:
360 Calories
26g Carbohydrates
19g Fat

855. Split Pea Stew

Preparation Time: 5 minutes
Cooking Time: 35 minutes
Servings: 2
Ingredients:

- 1 cup dry split peas
- 1 lb. chopped vegetables
- 1 cup mushroom soup
- 2 tbsps. old bay seasoning

Direction:

1. Incorporate all the ingredients in Instant Pot, cook for 33 minutes.
2. Release the pressure naturally.

Nutrition:
300 Calories
7g Carbohydrates
2g Fat

856. Fried Tofu Hotpot

Preparation Time: 15 minutes
Cooking Time: 15 minutes
Servings: 2

Ingredients:

- ½ lb. fried tofu
- 1 lb. chopped Chinese vegetable mix
- 1 cup low sodium vegetable broth
- 2 tbsps. 5 spice seasoning
- 1 tbsp. smoked paprika

Direction:

1. Combine all the ingredients in your Instant Pot, set on Stew for 15 minutes.
2. Release the pressure naturally and serve.

Nutrition:
320 Calories
11g Carbohydrates
23g Fat

857. Chili Sin Carne

Preparation Time: 15 minutes
Cooking Time: 35 minutes
Servings: 2
Ingredients:

- 3 cups mixed cooked beans
- 2 cups chopped tomatoes
- 1 tbsp. yeast extract
- 2 squares very dark chocolate
- 1 tbsp. red chili flakes

Direction:

1. Combine all the ingredients in your Instant Pot, cook for 35 minutes.
2. Release the pressure naturally and serve.

Nutrition:
240 Calories
20g Carbohydrates
3g Fat

858. Chick Pea and Kale Dish

Preparation time: 10 minutes
Cooking time: 25-30 minutes
Servings:4
Ingredients:

- 2 cups chickpea flour
- 1/2 cup green bell pepper, diced
- 1/2 cup onions, minced
- 1 tablespoon oregano
- 1 tablespoon salt
- 1 teaspoon cayenne

- 4 cups spring water
- 2 tablespoons Grape Seed Oil

Directions:

1. Boil spring water in a large pot
2. Lower heat into medium and whisk in chickpea flour
3. Add some minced onions, diced green bell pepper, seasoning to the pot and cook for 10 minutes
4. Cover dish using a baking sheet, grease with oil
5. Pour batter into the sheet and spread with a spatula
6. Cover with another sheet
7. Transfer to a fridge and chill, for 20 minutes
8. Remove from freezer and cut batter into fry shapes
9. Preheat the Air Fryer, to 385 degrees F
10. Transfer fries into the cooking basket, lightly greased and cover with parchment
11. Bake for about 15 minutes, flip and bake for 10 minutes more until golden brown
12. Serve and enjoy!

Nutrition:

Calories: 271 kcal

Carbohydrates: 28 g

Fat: 15 g

Protein: 9 g

859. Zucchini Chips

Preparation time: 10 minutes

Cooking time: 12-15 minutes

Servings:4

Ingredients:

- Salt as needed
- Grape seed oil as needed
- 6 zucchinis

Directions:

1. Into 330 F, pre heat the Air Fryer
2. Wash zucchini, slice zucchini into thin strips
3. Put slices in a bowl and add oil, salt, and toss
4. Spread over the cooking basket, fry for 12-15 minutes
5. Serve and enjoy!

Nutrition:

Calories: 92 kcal

Carbohydrates: 6 g

Fat: 7 g

Protein: 2 g

860. Classic Blueberry Spelt Muffins

Preparation time: 10 minutes

Cooking time: 12-15 minutes

Servings:4

Ingredients:

- 1/4 sea salt
- 1/3 cup maple syrup
- 1 teaspoon baking powder
- 1/2 cup sea moss
- 3/4 cup spelt flour
- 3/4 cup Kamut flour
- 1 cup hemp milk
- 1 cup blueberries

Directions:

1. Into 380 degrees F pre heat Air Fryer
2. Take your muffin tins and gently grease them
3. Take a bowl and add flour, syrup, salt, baking powder, seamless and mix well
4. Add milk and mix well
5. Fold in blueberries
6. Pour into muffin tins
7. Transfer to the cooking basket, bake for 20-25 minutes until nicely baked
8. Serve and enjoy!

Nutrition:

Calories: 217 kcal,

Carbohydrates: 32 g

Fat: 9 g

Protein: 4 g

861. Genuine Healthy Crackers

Preparation time: 10 minutes

Cooking time: 12-15 minutes

Servings:4

Ingredients:

- 1/2 cup Rye flour
- 1 cup spelt flour
- 2 teaspoons sesame seed
- 1 teaspoon agave syrup
- 1 teaspoon salt
- 2 tablespoons grapeseed oil
- 3/4 cup spring water

Directions:

1. Into 330 degrees F, Preheat the Air Fryer
2. Take a medium bowl and add all **Ingredients**, mix well
3. Make dough ball
4. Prepare a place for rolling out the dough, cover with a piece of parchment
5. Lightly grease paper with grape seed oil, place dough
6. Roll out, dough with a rolling pin, add more flour if needed
7. Take a shape cutter and cut dough into squares
8. Place squares in Air Fryer cooking basket
9. Brush with more oil
10. Sprinkle salt
11. Bake for 10-15 minutes until golden
12. Let it cool, serve, and enjoy!

Nutrition:
Calories: 226 kcal
Carbohydrates: 41 g
Fat: 3 g
Protein: 11 g

862. Tortilla Chips

Preparation time: 10 minutes
Cooking time: 8-12 minutes
Servings: 4
Ingredients:

- 2 cups of spelt flour
- 1 teaspoon of salt
- 1/2 cup of spring water
- 1/3 cup of grapeseed oil

Directions:
1. Preheat your Air Fryer into 320 degrees F
2. Take the food processor then add salt, flour, and process well for 15 seconds
3. Gradually add grapeseed oil until mixed
4. Keep mixing until you have a nice dough
5. Formulate work surface and cover in a piece of parchment, sprinkle flour
6. Knead the dough for 1-2 minutes
7. Grease cooking basket with oil
8. Transfer dough on the cooking basket, brush oil and sprinkle salt
9. Cut dough into 8 triangles
10. Bake for about 8-12 minutes until golden brown
11. Serve and enjoy once done!

Nutrition:
Calories: 288 kcal
Carbohydrates: 18 g
Fat: 17 g
Protein: 16 g

863. Pumpkin Spice Crackers

Preparation time: 10 minutes
Cooking time: 60 minutes
Servings: 06
Ingredients:

- 1/3 cup coconut flour
- 2 tablespoons pumpkin pie spice
- ¾ cup sunflower seeds
- ¾ cup flaxseed
- 1/3 cup sesame seeds
- 1 tablespoon ground psyllium husk powder
- 1 teaspoon sea salt
- 3 tablespoons coconut oil, melted
- 11/3 cups alkaline water

Directions:
1. Set your oven to 300 degrees F.
2. Combine all dry **Ingredients** in a bowl.
3. Add water and oil to the mixture and mix well.
4. Let the dough stay for 2 to 3 minutes.
5. Spread the dough evenly on a cookie sheet lined with parchment paper.
6. Bake for 30 minutes.
7. Reduce the oven heat to low and bake for another 30 minutes.
8. Crack the bread into bite-size pieces.
9. Serve

Nutrition:
Calories 248
Total Fat 15.7 g
Saturated Fat 2.7 g
Cholesterol 75 mg
Sodium 94 mg
Total Carbs 0.4 g
Fiber 0g
Sugar 0 g
Protein 24.9 g

864. Spicy Roasted Nuts

Preparation time: 10 minutes
Cooking time: 15 minutes

Servings: 4

Ingredients:

- 8 oz. pecans or almonds or walnuts
- 1 teaspoon sea salt
- 1 tablespoon olive oil or coconut oil
- 1 teaspoon ground cumin
- 1 teaspoon paprika powder or chili powder

Directions:

1. Add all the **Ingredients** to a skillet.
2. Roast the nuts until golden brown.
3. Serve and enjoy.

Nutrition:

Calories 287

Total Fat 29.5 g

Saturated Fat 3 g

Cholesterol 0 mg

Total Carbs 5.9 g

Sugar 1.4g

Fiber 4.3 g

Sodium 388 mg

Protein 4.2 g

865. Wheat Crackers

Preparation time: 10 minutes

Cooking time: 20 minutes

Servings: 4

Ingredients:

- 1 3/4 cups almond flour
- 1 1/2 cups coconut flour
- 3/4 teaspoon sea salt
- 1/3 cup vegetable oil
- 1 cup alkaline water
- Sea salt for sprinkling

Directions:

1. Set your oven to 350 degrees F.
2. Mix coconut flour, almond flour and salt in a bowl.
3. Stir in vegetable oil and water. Mix well until smooth.
4. Spread this dough on a floured surface into a thin sheet.
5. Cut small squares out of this sheet.
6. Arrange the dough squares on a baking sheet lined with parchment paper.
7. For about 20 minutes, bake until light golden in color.

8. Serve.

Nutrition:

Calories 64

Total Fat 9.2 g

Saturated Fat 2.4 g

Cholesterol 110 mg

Sodium 276 mg

Total Carbs 9.2 g

Fiber 0.9 g

Sugar 1.4 g

Protein 1.5 g

866. Potato Chips

Preparation time: 10 minutes

Cooking time: 20 minutes

Servings: 4

Ingredients:

- 1 tablespoon vegetable oil
- 1 potato, sliced paper thin
- Sea salt, to taste

Directions:

1. Toss potato with oil and sea salt.
2. Spread the slices in a baking dish in a single layer.
3. Cook in a microwave for 5 minutes until golden brown.
4. Serve.

Nutrition:

Calories 80

Total Fat 3.5 g

Saturated Fat 0.1 g

Cholesterol 320 mg

Sodium 350 mg

Total Carbs 11.6 g

Fiber 0.7 g

Sugar 0.7 g

Protein 1.2 g

867. Zucchini Pepper Chips

Preparation time: 10 minutes

Cooking time: 15 minutes

Servings: 04

Ingredients:

- 1 2/3 cups vegetable oil
- 1 teaspoon garlic powder
- 1 teaspoon onion powder
- 1/2 teaspoon black pepper

- 3 tablespoons crushed red pepper flakes
- 2 zucchinis, thinly sliced

Directions:

1. Mix oil with all the spices in a bowl.
2. Add zucchini slices and mix well.
3. Transfer the mixture to a Ziplock bag and seal it.
4. Refrigerate for 10 minutes.
5. Spread the zucchini slices on a greased baking sheet.
6. Bake for 15 minutes
7. Serve.

Nutrition:

Calories 172
Total Fat 11.1 g
Saturated Fat 5.8 g
Cholesterol 610 mg
Sodium 749 mg
Total Carbs 19.9 g
Fiber 0.2 g
Sugar 0.2 g
Protein 13.5 g

868. Apple Chips

Preparation time: 5 minutes
Cooking time: 45 minutes
Servings:4
Ingredients:

- 2 Golden Delicious apples, cored and thinly sliced
- 1 1/2 teaspoons white sugar
- 1/2 teaspoon ground cinnamon

Directions:

1. Set your oven to 225 degrees F.
2. Place apple slices on a baking sheet.
3. Sprinkle sugar an
4. d cinnamon over apple slices.
5. Bake for 45 minutes.
6. Serve

Nutrition:

Calories 127
Total Fat 3.5 g
Saturated Fat 0.5 g
Cholesterol 162 mg
Sodium 142 mg
Total Carbs 33.6g
Fiber 0.4 g
Sugar 0.5 g
Protein 4.5 g

869. Kale Crisps

Preparation time: 10 minutes
Cooking time: 10 minutes
Servings: 04
Ingredients:

- 1 bunch kale, remove the stems, leaves torn into even pieces
- 1 tablespoon olive oil
- 1 teaspoon sea salt

Directions:

1. Set your oven to 350 degrees F. Layer a baking sheet with parchment paper.
2. Spread the kale leaves on a paper towel to absorb all the moisture.
3. Toss the leaves with sea salt, and olive oil.
4. Kindly spread them, on the baking sheet and bake for 10 minutes.
5. Serve.

Nutrition:

Calories 113
Total Fat 7.5 g
Saturated Fat 1.1 g
Cholesterol 20 mg
Sodium 97 mg
Total Carbs 1.4 g
Fiber 0 g
Sugar 0 g
Protein 1.1g

870. Carrot Chips

Preparation time: 5 minutes
Cooking time: 12 minutes
Servings: 4
Ingredients:

- 4 carrots, washed, peeled and sliced
- 2 teaspoons extra-virgin olive oil
- 1/4 teaspoon sea salt

Directions:

1. Set your oven to 350 degrees F.
2. Toss carrots with salt and olive oil.

3. Spread the slices into two baking sheets in a single layer.

4. Bake for 6 minutes on upper and lower rack of the oven.

5. Switch the baking racks and bake for another 6 minutes.

6. Serve.

Nutrition:

Calories 153

Total Fat 7.5 g

Saturated Fat 1.1 g

Cholesterol 20 mg

Sodium 97 mg

Total Carbs 20.4 g

Fiber 0 g

Sugar 0 g

Protein 3.1g

871. Pita Chips

Preparation time: 5 minutes

Cooking time: 12 minutes

Servings: 4

Ingredients:

- 12 pita bread pockets, sliced into triangles
- 1/2 cup olive oil
- 1/2 teaspoon ground black pepper
- 1 teaspoon garlic salt
- 1/2 teaspoon dried basil
- 1 teaspoon dried chervil

Directions:

1. Set your oven to 400 degrees F.

2. Toss pita with all the remaining **Ingredients** in a bowl.

3. Spread the seasoned triangles on a baking sheet.

4. Bake for 7 minutes until golden brown.

5. Serve with your favorite hummus.

Nutrition:

Calories 201

Total Fat 5.5 g

Saturated Fat 2.1 g

Cholesterol 10 mg

Sodium 597 mg

Total Carbs 2.4 g

Fiber 0 g

Sugar 0 g

Protein 3.1g

872. Sweet Potato Chips

Preparation time: 5 minutes

Cooking time: 5 minutes

Servings: 4

Ingredients:

- 1 sweet potato, thinly sliced
- 2 teaspoons olive oil, or as needed
- Coarse sea salt, to taste

Directions:

1. Toss sweet potato with oil and salt.

2. Spread the slices in a baking dish in a single layer.

3. Cook in a microwave for 5 minutes until golden brown.

4. Serve.

Nutrition:

Calories 213

Total Fat 8.5 g

Saturated Fat 3.1 g

Cholesterol 120 mg

Sodium 497 mg

Total Carbs 21.4 g

Fiber 0 g

Sugar 0 g

Protein 0.1g

873. Spinach and Sesame Crackers

Preparation time: 5 minutes

Cooking time: 15 minutes

Servings: 4

Ingredients:

- 2 tablespoons white sesame seeds
- 1 cup fresh spinach, washed
- 1 2/3 cups all-purpose flour
- 1/2 cup water
- 1/2 teaspoon baking powder
- 1 teaspoon olive oil
- 1 teaspoon salt

Directions:

1. Transfer the spinach to a blender with a half cup water and blend until smooth.

2. Add 2 tablespoons white sesame seeds, ½ teaspoon baking powder, 1 2/3 cups all-purpose flour, and 1 teaspoon salt to a bowl and stir well until combined. Add in 1

teaspoon olive oil and spinach water. Mix again and knead by using your hands until you obtain a smooth dough.

3.   If the made dough is too gluey, then add more flour.

4.   Using your parchment paper lightly roll out the dough as thin as possible. Cut into squares with a pizza cutter.

5.   Bake into a preheated oven at 400°, for about 15to 20 minutes. Once done, let cool and then serve.

Nutrition:

223 calories

3g fat

41g total carbohydrates

6g protein

874.   Mini Nacho Pizzas

Preparation time: 5 minutes

Cooking time: 10 minutes

Servings: 4

Ingredients:

- 1/4 cup refried beans, vegan
- 2 tablespoons tomato, diced
- 2 English muffins, split in half
- 1/4 cup onion, sliced
- 1/3 cup vegan cheese, shredded
- 1 small jalapeno, sliced
- 1/3 cup roasted tomato salsa
- 1/2 avocado, diced and tossed in lemon juice

Directions:

1.   Add the refried beans/salsa onto the muffin bread. Sprinkle with shredded vegan cheese followed by the veggie toppings.

2.   Transfer to a baking sheet and place in a preheated oven at 350 to 400 F on a top rack.

3.   Put into the oven for 10 minutes and then broil for 2minutes, so that the top becomes bubbly.

4.   Take out from the oven and let them cool at room temperature.

5.   Top with avocado. Enjoy!

Nutrition:

133 calories

4.2g fat

719g total carbohydrates

6g protein

875.   Pizza Sticks

Preparation time: 10 minutes

Cooking time: 30 minutes

Servings: 16 sticks

Ingredients:

- 5 tablespoons tomato sauce
- Few pinches of dried basil
- 1 block extra firm tofu
- 2 tablespoon + 2 teaspoon **Nutrition**al yeast

Directions:

1.   Cape the tofu in a paper tissue and put a cutting board on top, place something heavy on top and drain for about 10 to 15 minutes.

2.   In the meantime, line your baking sheet with parchment paper. Cut the tofu into 16 equal pieces and place them on a baking sheet.

3.   Spread each pizza stick with a teaspoon of marinara sauce.

4.   Sprinkle each stick with half teaspoon of yeast, followed by basil on top.

5.   Bake into a preheated oven at 425 F for about 28 to 30 minutes. Serve and enjoy!

Nutrition:

33 calories

1.7g fat

2g total carbs

3g protein

876.   Raw Broccoli Poppers

Preparation time: 2 minutes

Cooking time: 8 minutes

Servings: 4

Ingredients:

- 1/8 cup water
- 1/8 teaspoon fine sea salt
- 4 cups broccoli florets, washed and cut into 1-inch pieces
- 1/4 teaspoon turmeric powder
- 1 cup unsalted cashews, soaked overnight or at least 3-4 hours and drained
- 1/4 teaspoon onion powder
- 1 red bell pepper, seeded and
- 2 heaping tablespoons **Nutrition**al
- 2 tablespoons lemon juice

Directions:

1. Transfer the drained cashews to a high-speed blender and pulse for about 30 seconds. Add in the chopped pepper and pulse again for 30seconds.

2. Add some 2 tablespoons lemon juice, 1/8 cup water, 2heaping tablespoons **Nutrition**al yeast, ¼ teaspoon onion powder, 1/8 teaspoon fine sea salt, and 1/4 teaspoon turmeric powder. Pulse for about 45 seconds until smooth.

3. Handover the broccoli into a bowl and add in chopped cheesy cashew mixture. Toss well until coated.

4. Transfer the pieces of broccoli to the trays of a yeast dehydrator.

5. Follow the dehydrator's instructions and dehydrate for about 8 minutes at 125 F or until crunchy.

Nutrition:
408 calories
32g fat
22g total carbohydrates
15g protein

877. Blueberry Cauliflower

Preparation time: 2 minutes
Cooking time: 5 minutes
Servings: 1
Ingredients:

- ¼ cup frozen strawberries
- 2 teaspoons maple syrup
- ¾ cup unsweetened cashew milk
- 1 teaspoon vanilla extract
- ½ cup plain cashew yogurt
- 5 tablespoons powdered peanut butter
- ¾ cup frozen wild blueberries
- ½ cup cauliflower florets, coarsely chopped

Directions:

1. Add all the smoothie **Ingredients** to a high-speed blender.

2. Blitz to combine until smooth.

3. Pour into a chilled glass and serve.

Nutrition:
340 calories
11g fat
48g total carbohydrates
16g protein

878. Candied Ginger

Preparation time: 10 minutes
Cooking time: 40 minutes

Servings: 3 to 5
Ingredients:

- 2 1/2 cups salted pistachios, shelled
- 1 1/4 teaspoons powdered ginger
- 3 tablespoons pure maple syrup

Directions:

1. Add 1 1/4 teaspoons powdered ginger to a bowl with pistachios. Stir well until combined. There

2. should be no lumps.

3. Drizzle with 3 tablespoons of maple syrup and stir well.

4. Transfer to a baking sheet lined with parchment paper and spread evenly.

5. Cook into a preheated oven at 275 F for about 20 minutes.

6. Take out from oven, stir, and cook for further 10 to 15 minutes.

7. Let it cool for about few minutes until crispy. Enjoy!

Nutrition:
378 calories
27.6g fat
26g total carbohydrates
13g protein

879. Chia Crackers

Preparation time: 20 minutes
Cooking time: 1 hour
Servings: 24-26 crackers
Ingredients:

- 1/2 cup pecans, chopped
- 1/2 cup chia seeds
- 1/2 teaspoon cayenne pepper
- 1 cup water
- 1/4 cup **Nutrition**al yeast
- 1/2 cup pumpkin seeds
- 1/4 cup ground flax
- Salt and pepper, to taste

Directions:

1. Mix around 1/2 cup chia seeds and 1 cup water. Keep it aside.

2. Take another bowl and combine all the remaining **Ingredients**. Combine well and stir in the chia water mixture until you obtained dough.

3. Transfer the dough onto a baking sheet and rollout (¼" thick).

4. Transfer into a preheated oven at 325°F and bake for about half an hour.

5. Take out from the oven, flip over the dough, and cut it into desired cracker shape/squares.

6. Spread and back again for further half an hour, or until crispy and browned.

7. Once done, take out from oven and let them cool at room temperature. Enjoy!

Nutrition:

41 calories

3.1g fat

2g total carbohydrates

2g protein

880. Orange- Spiced Pumpkin Hummus

Preparation time: 2 minutes

Cooking time: 5 minutes

Servings: 4 cups

Ingredients:

- 1 tablespoon maple syrup
- 1/2 teaspoon salt
- 1 can (16oz.) garbanzo beans,
- 1/8 teaspoon ginger or nutmeg
- 1 cup canned pumpkin Blend,
- 1/8 teaspoon cinnamon
- 1/4 cup tahini
- 1 tablespoon fresh orange juice
- Pinch of orange zest, for garnish
- 1 tablespoon apple cider vinegar

Directions:

1. Mix all the **Ingredients** to a food processor blender and blend until slightly chunky.

2. Serve right away and enjoy!

Nutrition:

291 calories

22.9g fat

15g total carbohydrates

12g protein

881. Cinnamon Maple Sweet Potato Bites

Preparation time: 5 minutes

Cooking time: 25 minutes

Servings: 3 to 4

Ingredients:

- ½ teaspoon corn-starch
- 1 teaspoon cinnamon
- 4 medium sweet potatoes, then peeled, and cut into bite-size cubes
- 2 to 3 tablespoons maple syrup
- 3 tablespoons butter, melted

Directions:

1. Transfer the potato cubes to a Ziploc bag and add in 3 tablespoons of melted butter. Seal and shake well until the potato cubes are coated with butter.

2. Add in the remaining **Ingredients** and shake again.

3. Transfer the potato cubes to a parchment-lined baking sheet. Cubes shouldn't be stacked on one another.

4. Sprinkle with cinnamon, if needed, and bake in a preheated oven at 425°F for about 25 to 30 minutes, stirring once during cooking.

5. Once done, take them out and stand at room temperature. Enjoy!

Nutrition:

436 calories

17.4g fat

71.8g total carbohydrates

4.1g protein

882. Cheesy Kale Chips

Preparation time: 3 minutes

Cooking time: 12 minutes

Servings: 4

Ingredients:

- 3 tablespoons **Nutrition**al yeast
- 1 head curly kale, washed, ribs
- 3/4 teaspoon garlic powder
- 1 tablespoon olive oil
- 1 teaspoon onion powder
- Salt, to taste

Directions:

1. Line cookie sheets with parchment paper.

2. Drain the kale leaves and spread on a paper removed and leaves torn into chip-

3. towel. Then, kindly transfer the leaves to a bowl and sized pieces

4. add in 1 teaspoon onion powder, 3 tablespoons **Nutrition**al yeast, 1 tablespoon olive oil, and 3/4

5. teaspoon garlic powder. Mix with your hands.

6. Spread the kale onto prepared cookie sheets. They shouldn't touch each other.

7. Bake into a preheated oven for about 350 F for about 10to 12 minutes.

8. Once crisp, take out from the oven, and sprinkle with a bit of salt. Serve and enjoy!

Nutrition:

71 calories

4g fat

5g total carbohydrates

4g protein

883. Lemon Roasted Bell Pepper

Preparation time: 10 minutes

Cooking time: 5 minutes

Servings: 4

Ingredients:

- 4 bell peppers
- 1 teaspoon olive oil
- 1 tablespoon mango juice
- 1/4 teaspoon garlic, minced
- 1 teaspoons oregano
- 1 pinch salt
- 1 pinch pepper

Directions:

1. Start heating the Air Fryer to 390 degrees F

2. Place some bell pepper in the Air fryer

3. Drizzle it with the olive oil and air fry for 5 minutes

4. Take a serving plate and transfer it

5. Take a small bowl and add garlic, oregano, mango juice, salt, and pepper

6. Mix them well and drizzle the mixture over the peppers

7. Serve and enjoy!

Nutrition:

Calories: 59 kcal

Carbohydrates: 6 g

Fat: 5 g

Protein: 4 g

884. Subtle Roasted Mushrooms

Preparation time: 10 minutes

Cooking time: 5 minutes

Servings: 4

Ingredients:

- 2 teaspoons mixed Sebi Friendly herbs
- 1 tablespoon olive oil
- 1/2 teaspoon garlic powder
- 2 pounds mushrooms
- 2 tablespoons date sugar

Directions:

1. Wash mushrooms and turn dry in a plate of mixed greens spinner

2. Quarter them and put in a safe spot

3. Put garlic, oil, and spices in the dish of your oar type air fryer

4. Warmth for 2 minutes

5. Stir it.

6. Add some mushrooms and cook 25 minutes

7. Then include vermouth and cook for 5 minutes more

8. Serve and enjoy!

Nutrition:

Calories: 94 kcal

Carbohydrates: 3 g

Fat: 8 g

Protein: 2 g.

885. Fancy Spelt Bread

Preparation time: 10 minutes

Cooking time: 5 minutes

Servings: 4

Ingredients:

- 1 cup spring water
- 1/2 cup of coconut milk
- 3 tablespoons avocado oil
- 1 teaspoon baking soda
- 1 tablespoon agave nectar
- 4 and 1/2 cups spelt flour
- 1 and 1/2 teaspoon salt

Directions:

1. Pre-heat your Air Fryer to 355 degrees F

2. Take a big bowl and add baking soda, salt, flour whisk well

3. Add 3/4 cup of water, plus coconut milk, oil and mix well

4. Sprinkle your working surface with flour, add dough to the flour

5. Roll well

6. Knead for about three minutes, adding small amounts of flour until dough is a nice ball
7. Place parchment paper in your cooking basket
8. Lightly grease your pan and put the dough inside
9. Transfer into Air Fryer and bake for 30-45 minutes until done
10. Remove then insert a stick to check for doneness
11. If done already serve and enjoy, if not, let it cook for a few minutes more

Nutrition:

Calories: 203 kcal

Carbohydrates: 37 g

Fat: 4g

Protein: 7 g

Carbohydrates: 5 g

Fat: 5 g

Protein: 5 g

886. Crispy Crunchy Hummus

Preparation time: 10 minutes

Cooking time: 10-15 minutes

Servings:4

Ingredients:

- 1/2 a red onion
- 2 tablespoons fresh coriander
- 1/4 cup cherry tomatoes
- 1/2 a red bell pepper
- 1 tablespoon dulse flakes
- Juice of lime
- Salt to taste
- 3 tablespoons olive oil
- 2 tablespoons tahini
- 1 cup warm chickpeas

Directions:

1. Prepare your Air Fryer cooking basket
2. Add chickpeas to your cooking container and cook for 10-15 minutes, making a point to continue blending them every once in a while, until they are altogether warmed
3. Add warmed chickpeas to a bowl and include tahini, salt, lime
4. Utilize a fork to pound chickpeas and fixings in a glue until smooth
5. Include hacked onion, cherry tomatoes, ringer pepper, dulse drops, and olive oil
6. Blend well until consolidated
7. Serve hummus with a couple of cuts of spelt bread

Nutrition:

Calories: 95 kcal

Soups & Stews

887. Dill Celery Soup

Preparation time: 10 minutes
Cooking time: 30 minutes
Servings: 4
Ingredients:

- 6 cups celery stalk, chopped
- 2 cups filtered alkaline water
- 1 medium onion, chopped
- 1/2 tsp. dill
- 1 cup of coconut milk
- 1/4 tsp. sea salt

Directions:

1.   Combine all elements into the direct pot and mix fine.
2.   Cover pot with lid and select soup mode it takes 30 minutes.
3.   Release pressure using the quick release **Directions:** than open lid carefully.
4.   Blend the soup utilizing a submersion blender until smooth.
5.   Stir well and serve.

Nutrition:

Calories 193
Fat 15.3 g
Carbohydrates 10.9 g
Protein 5.2 g
Sugar 5.6 g
Cholesterol 0 mg

888. Creamy Avocado-Broccoli Soup

Preparation time: 10 minutes
Cooking time: 15 minutes
Servings: 1-2
Ingredients:

-
-3 flowers broccoli

- 1 small avocado
- 1 yellow onion
- 1 green or red pepper
- 1 celery stalk
- 2 cups vegetable broth (yeast-free)
- Celtic Sea Salt to taste

Directions:

1.   Warmth vegetable stock (don't bubble). Include hacked onion and broccoli, and warm for a few minutes. At that point put in blender, include the avocado, pepper and celery and Blend until the soup is smooth (include some more water whenever wanted). Flavor and serve warm. Delicious!!

Nutrition:

Calories: 60g
Carbohydrates: 11g
Fat: 2 g
Protein: 2g

889. Fresh Garden Vegetable Soup

Preparation time: 7 minutes
Cooking time: 20 minutes
Servings: 1-2
Ingredients:

- 2 huge carrots
- 1 little zucchini
- 1 celery stem
- 1 cup of broccoli
- 3 stalks of asparagus
- 1 yellow onion
- 1 quart of (antacid) water
- 4-5 tsps. Of sans yeast vegetable stock
- 1 tsp. new basil
- 2 tsps. Ocean salt to taste

Directions:

1.   Put water in pot, include the vegetable stock just as the onion and bring to bubble.
2.   In the meantime, cleave the zucchini, the broccoli and the asparagus, and shred the carrots and the celery stem in a food processor.
3.   When the water is bubbling, it would be ideal if you turn off the oven as we would prefer not to heat up the

vegetables. Simply put them all in the high temp water and hold up until the vegetables arrive at wanted delicacy.

4.   Permit to cool somewhat, at that point put all fixings into blender and blend until you get a thick, smooth consistency.

Nutrition:

Calories: 43

Carbohydrates: 7g

Fat: 1 g

890.   Raw Some Gazpacho Soup

Preparation time: 7 minutes

Cooking time: 3 hours

Servings: 3-4

Ingredients:

- 500g tomatoes
- 1 small cucumber
- 1 red pepper
- 1 onion
- 2 cloves of garlic
- 1 small chili
- 1 quart of water (preferably alkaline water)
- 4 tbsp. cold-pressed olive oil
- Juice of one fresh lemon
- 1 dash of cayenne pepper
- Sea salt to taste

Directions:

1.   Remove the skin of the cucumber and cut all vegetables in large pieces.

2.   Put all **Ingredients** except the olive oil in a blender and mix until smooth.

3.   Add the olive oil and mix again until oil is emulsified.

4.   Put the soup in the fridge and chill for at least 2 hours (soup should be served ice cold).

5.   Add some salt and pepper to taste, mix, place the soup in bowls, garnish with chopped scallions, cucumbers, tomatoes and peppers and enjoy!

Nutrition:

Calories: 39

Carbohydrates: 8g

Fat: 0.5 g

Protein: 0.2g

891.   Alkaline Carrot Soup with Fresh Mushrooms

Preparation time: 10 minutes

Cooking time: 20 minutes

Servings: 1-2

Ingredients:

- 4 mid-sized carrots
- 4 mid-sized potatoes
- 10 enormous new mushrooms (champignons or chanterelles)
- 1/2 white onion
- 2 tbsp. olive oil (cold squeezed, additional virgin)
- 3 cups vegetable stock
- 2 tbsp. parsley, new and cleaved
- Salt and new white pepper

Directions:

1.   Wash and strip carrots and potatoes and dice them.

2.   Warm up vegetable stock in a pot on medium heat. Cook carrots and potatoes for around 15 minutes. Meanwhile finely shape onion and braise them in a container with olive oil for around 3 minutes.

3.   Wash mushrooms, slice them to wanted size and add to the container, cooking approx. an additional 5 minutes, blending at times. Blend carrots, vegetable stock and potatoes, and put substance of the skillet into pot.

4.   When nearly done, season with parsley, salt and pepper and serve hot. Appreciate this alkalizing soup!

Nutrition:

Calories: 75

Carbohydrates: 13g

Fat: 1.8g

Protein: 1 g

892.   Swiss Cauliflower-Omental-Soup

Preparation time: 10 minutes

Cooking time: 15 minutes

Servings: 3-4

Ingredients:

- 2 cups cauliflower pieces
- 1 cup potatoes, cubed
- 2 cups vegetables stock (without yeast)
- 3 tbsp. Swiss Omental cheddar, cubed
- 2 tbsp. new chives

- 1 tbsp. pumpkin seeds
- 1 touch of nutmeg and cayenne pepper

Directions:

1. Cook cauliflower and potato in vegetable stock until delicate and Blend with a blender.

2. Season the soup with nutmeg and cayenne, and possibly somewhat salt and pepper.

3. Include Emmenthal cheddar and chives and mix a couple of moments until the soup is smooth and prepared to serve. Enhance it with pumpkin seeds.

Nutrition:

Calories: 65

Carbohydrates: 13g

Fat: 2g

Protein: 1g

893. Chilled Parsley-Gazpacho with Lime & Cucumber

Preparation time: 10 minutes

Cooking time: 2 hours

Servings: 1

Ingredients:

- 4-5 middle sized tomatoes
- 2 tbsp. olive oil, extra virgin and cold pressed
- 2 large cups fresh parsley
- 2 ripe avocados
- 2 cloves garlic, diced
- 2 limes, juiced
- 4 cups vegetable broth
- 1 middle sized cucumber
- 2 small red onions, diced
- 1 tsp. dried oregano
- 1½ tsp. paprika powder
- ½ tsp. cayenne pepper
- Sea salt and freshly ground pepper to taste

Directions:

1. In a pan, heat up olive oil and sauté onions and garlic until translucent. Set aside to cool down.

2. Use a large blender and blend parsley, avocado, tomatoes, cucumber, vegetable broth, lime juice and onion-garlic mix until smooth. Add some water if desired, and season with cayenne pepper, paprika powder, oregano, salt and pepper. Blend again and put in the fridge for at least 1, 5 hours.

3. Tip: Add chives or dill to the gazpacho. Enjoy this great alkaline (cold) soup!

Nutrition:

Calories: 48

Carbohydrates: 12 g

Fat: 0.8g

894. Chilled Avocado Tomato Soup

Preparation time: 7 minutes

Cooking time: 20 minutes

Servings: 1-2

Ingredients:

- 2 small avocados
- 2 large tomatoes
- 1 stalk of celery
- 1 small onion
- 1 clove of garlic
- Juice of 1 fresh lemon
- 1 cup of water (best: alkaline water)
- A handful of fresh lavages
- Parsley and sea salt to taste

Directions:

1. Scoop the avocados and cut all veggies in little pieces.

2. Spot all fixings in a blender and blend until smooth.

3. Serve chilled and appreciate this nutritious and sound soluble soup formula!

Nutrition:

Calories: 68

Carbohydrates: 15g

Fat: 2g

Protein: .8g

895. Pumpkin and White Bean Soup with Sage

Preparation time: 10 minutes

Cooking time: 40 minutes

Servings: 3-4

Ingredients:

- 1 ½ pound pumpkin
- ½ pound yams
- ½ pound white beans
- 1 onion

- 2 cloves of garlic
- 1 tbsp. of cold squeezed additional virgin olive oil
- 1 tbsp. of spices (your top picks)
- 1 tbsp. of sage
- 1 ½ quart water (best: antacid water)
- A spot of ocean salt and pepper

Directions:

1. Cut the pumpkin and potatoes in shapes, cut the onion and cut the garlic, the spices and the sage in fine pieces.
2. Sauté the onion and also the garlic in olive oil for around two or three minutes.
3. Include the potatoes, pumpkin, spices and sage and fry for an additional 5 minutes.
4. At that point include the water and cook for around 30 minutes (spread the pot with a top) until vegetables are delicate.
5. At long last include the beans and some salt and pepper. Cook for an additional 5 minutes and serve right away. Prepared!! Appreciate this antacid soup. Alkalizing tasty!

Nutrition:

Calories: 78

Carbohydrates: 12g

896. Alkaline Carrot Soup with Millet

Preparation time: 7 minutes

Cooking time: 40 minutes

Servings: 3-4

Ingredients:

- 2 cups cauliflower pieces
- 1 cup potatoes, cubed
- 2 cups vegetables stock (without yeast)
- 3 tbsp. Swiss Emmenthal cheddar, cubed
- 2 tbsp. new chives
- 1 tbsp. pumpkin seeds

1 touch of nutmeg and cayenne pepper

Directions:

1. Cook cauliflower and potato in vegetable stock until delicate and Blend with a blender.
2. Season the soup with nutmeg and cayenne, and possibly somewhat salt and pepper.

3. Include Emmenthal cheddar and chives and mix a couple of moments until the soup is smooth and prepared to serve. Can enhance with pumpkin seeds.

Nutrition:

Calories: 65

Carbohydrates: 15g

Fat: 1g

Protein: 2g

897. Alkaline Pumpkin Tomato Soup

Preparation time: 15 minutes

Cooking time: 30 minutes

Servings: 3-4

Ingredients:

- 1 quart of water (if accessible: soluble water)
- 400g new tomatoes, stripped and diced
- 1 medium-sized sweet pumpkin
- 5 yellow onions
- 1 tbsp. Cold squeezed additional virgin olive oil
- 2 tsp. ocean salt or natural salt
- Touch of Cayenne pepper
- Your preferred spices (discretionary)
- Bunch of new parsley

Directions:

1. Cut onions in little pieces and sauté with some oil in a significant pot.
2. Cut the pumpkin down the middle, at that point remove the stem and scoop out the seeds.
3. At long last scoop out the fragile living creature and put it in the pot.
4. Include likewise the tomatoes and the water and cook for around 20 minutes.
5. At that point empty the soup into a food processor and blend well for a couple of moments. Sprinkle with salt pepper and other spices.
6. Fill bowls and trimming with new parsley. Make the most of your alkalizing soup!

Nutrition:

Calories: 78

Carbohydrates: 20

Fat: 0.5g

Protein: 1.5g

898. Alkaline Pumpkin Coconut Soup

Preparation time: 10 minutes
Cooking time: 15 minutes
Servings: 3-4
Ingredients:

- 2lb pumpkin
- 6 cups water (best: soluble water delivered with a water ionizer)
- 1 cup low fat coconut milk
- 5 ounces potatoes
- 2 major onions
- 3 ounces leek
- 1 bunch of new parsley
- 1 touch of nutmeg
- 1 touch of cayenne pepper
- 1 tsp. ocean salt or natural salt
- 4 tbsp. cold squeezed additional virgin olive oil

Directions:

1. As a matter of first significance: cut the onions, the pumpkin, and the potatoes just as the hole into little pieces.
2. At that point, heat the olive oil in a significant pot and sauté the onions for a couple of moments.
3. At that point include the water and heat up the pumpkin, potatoes and the leek until delicate.
4. Include the coconut milk.
5. Presently utilize a hand blender and puree for around 1 moment. The soup should turn out to be extremely velvety.
6. Season with salt, pepper and nutmeg lastly include the parsley. 7. Appreciate this alkalizing pumpkin soup hot or cold!

Nutrition:
Calories: 88
Carbohydrates: 23g
Fat: 2.5 g
Protein: 1.8g

899. Cold Cauliflower-Coconut Soup

Preparation time: 7 minutes
Cooking time: 20 minutes
Servings: 3-4
Ingredients:

- 1 pound (450g) new cauliflower
- 1 ¼ cup (300ml) unsweetened coconut milk
- 1 cup water (best: antacid water)
- 2 tbsp. new lime juice
- 1/3 cup cold squeezed additional virgin olive oil
- 1 cup new coriander leaves, slashed
- Spot of salt and cayenne pepper
- 1 bunch of unsweetened coconut chips

Directions:

1. Steam cauliflower for around 10 minutes.
2. At that point, set up the cauliflower with coconut milk and water in a food processor and procedure until extremely smooth.
3. Include new lime squeeze, salt and pepper, a large portion of the cleaved coriander and the oil and blend for an additional couple of moments.
4. Pour in soup bowls and embellishment with coriander and coconut chips. Appreciate!

Nutrition:
Calories: 65
Carbohydrates: 11g
Fat: 0.3g
Protein: 1.5g

900. Raw Avocado-Broccoli Soup with Cashew Nuts

Preparation time: 10 minutes
Cooking time: 30 minutes
Servings: 1-2
Ingredients:

- ½ cup water (if available: alkaline water)
- ½ avocado
- 1 cup chopped broccoli
- ½ cup cashew nuts
- ½ cup alfalfa sprouts
- 1 clove of garlic
- 1 tbsp. cold pressed extra virgin olive oil
- 1 pinch of sea salt and pepper
- Some parsley to garnish

Directions:

1. Put the cashew nuts in a blender or food processor, include some water and puree for a couple of moments.

2. Include the various fixings (with the exception of the avocado) individually and puree each an ideal opportunity for a couple of moments.

3. Dispense the soup in a container and warm it up to the normal room temperature. Enhance with salt and pepper. In the interim dice the avocado and slash the parsley.

4. Dispense the soup in a container or plate; include the avocado dices and embellishment with parsley.

5. That's it! Enjoy this excellent healthy soup!

Nutrition:
Calories: 48
Carbohydrates: 18g
Fat: 3g
Protein: 1.4g

901. White Bean Soup

Preparation time: 10 minutes
Cooking time: 40 minutes
Servings: 6
Ingredients:

- 2 cups white beans, rinsed
- ¼ tsp. cayenne pepper
- 1 tsp. dried oregano
- ½ tsp. fresh rosemary, chopped
- 3 cups filtered alkaline water
- 3 cups unsweetened almond milk
- 3 garlic cloves, minced
- 2 celery stalks, diced
- 1 onion, chopped
- 1 tbsp. olive oil
- ½ tsp. sea salt

Directions:
1. Add oil into the instant pot and set the pot on sauté mode.

2. Add carrots, celery, and onion in oil and sauté until softened, about 5 minutes.

3. Add garlic and sauté for a minute.

4. Add beans, seasonings, water, and almond milk and stir to combine.

5. Cover pot with lid and cook on high pressure for 35 minutes.

6. When finished, allow to release pressure naturally then open the lid.

7. Stir well and serve.

Nutrition:

Calories 276
Fat 4.8 g
Carbohydrates 44.2 g
Sugar 2.3 g
Protein 16.6 g
Cholesterol 0 mg

902. Kale Cauliflower Soup

Preparation time: 10 minutes
Cooking time: 25 minutes
Servings: 4
Ingredients:

- 2 cups baby kale
- ½ cup unsweetened coconut milk
- 4 cups of water
- 1 large cauliflower head, chopped
- 3 garlic cloves, peeled
- 2 carrots, peeled and chopped
- 2 onion, chopped
- 3 tbsp. olive oil
- Pepper
- Salt

Directions:
1. Add oil into the instant pot and set the pot on sauté mode.

2. Add carrot, garlic, and onion to the pot and sauté for 5-7 minutes.

3. Add water and cauliflower and stir well.

4. Cover pot with lid and cook on high pressure for 20 minutes.

5. When finished, release pressure using the quick release **Directions:** than open the lid.

6. Add kale and coconut milk and stir well.

7. Blend the soup utilizing a submersion blender until smooth.

8. Season with pepper and salt.

Nutrition:
Calories 261
Fat 18.1 g
Carbohydrates 23.9 g
Sugar 9.9 g
Protein 6.6 g
Cholesterol 0 mg

903. Healthy Broccoli Asparagus Soup

Preparation time: 10 minutes
Cooking time: 20 minutes
Servings: 6
Ingredients:

- 2 cups broccoli florets, chopped
- 15 asparagus spear, ends trimmed and chopped
- 1 tsp. dried oregano
- 1 tbsp. fresh thyme leaves
- ½ cup unsweetened almond milk
- 3 ½ cups filtered alkaline water
- 2 cups cauliflower florets, chopped
- 2 tsp. garlic, chopped
- 1 cup onion, chopped
- 2 tbsp. olive oil
- Pepper
- Salt

Directions:

1. Add oil in the instant pot and set the pot on sauté mode.
2. Add onion to the olive oil and sauté until onion is softened.
3. Add garlic and sauté for 30 seconds.
4. Add all vegetables and water and stir well.
5. Cover pot with lid and cook on manual mode for 3 minutes.
6. When finished, allow to release pressure naturally then open the lid.
7. Blend the soup utilizing a submersion blender until smooth.
8. Stir in almond milk, herbs, pepper, and salt.
9. Serve and enjoy.

Nutrition:
Calories 85
Fat 5.2 g
Carbohydrates 8.8 g
Sugar 3.3 g
Protein 3.3 g
Cholesterol 0 mg

904. Creamy Asparagus Soup

Preparation time: 10 minutes

Cooking time: 30 minutes
Servings: 6
Ingredients:

- 2 lbs. fresh asparagus cut off woody stems
- ¼ tsp. lime zest
- 2 tbsp. lime juice
- 14 oz. coconut milk
- 1 tsp. dried thyme
- ½ tsp. oregano
- ½ tsp. sage
- 1 ½ cups filtered alkaline water
- 1 cauliflower head, cut into florets
- 1 tbsp. garlic, minced
- 1 leek, sliced
- 3 tbsp. coconut oil
- Pinch of Himalayan salt

Directions:

- Preheat the oven to 400 F/ 200 C.
- Line baking tray with parchment paper and set aside.
- Arrange asparagus spears on a baking tray. Drizzle with 2 tablespoons of coconut oil and sprinkle with salt, thyme, oregano, and sage.
- Bake in preheated oven for 20-25 minutes.
- Add remaining oil in the instant pot and set the pot on sauté mode.
- Put some garlic and leek to the pot and sauté for 2-3 minutes.
- Add cauliflower florets and water in the pot and stir well.
- Cover pot with lid and select steam mode and set timer for 4 minutes.
- When finished, release pressure using the quick release **Directions**.
- Add roasted asparagus, lime zest, lime juice, and coconut milk and stir well.
- Blend the soup utilizing a submersion blender until smooth.
- Serve and enjoy.

Nutrition:
Calories 265
Fat 22.9 g
Carbohydrates 14.7 g
Sugar 6.7 g

Protein 6.1 g
Cholesterol 0 mg

905. Quick Broccoli Soup

Preparation time: 5 minutes
Cooking time: 10 minutes
Servings: 6
Ingredients:

- 1 lb. broccoli, chopped
- 6 cups filtered alkaline water
- 1 onion, diced
- 2 tbsp. olive oil
- Pepper
- Salt

Directions:

1. Add oil into the instant pot and set the pot on sauté mode.
2. Add onion in olive oil and sauté until softened.
3. Add broccoli and water and stir well.
4. Cover pot with top and cook on manual high pressure for 3 minutes.
5. When finished, release pressure using the quick release **Directions:** than open the lid.
6. Blend the soup utilizing a submersion blender until smooth.
7. Season soup with pepper and salt.
8. Serve and enjoy.

Nutrition:
Calories 73
Fat 4.9 g
Carbohydrates 6.7 g
Protein 2.3 g
Sugar 2.1 g
Cholesterol 0 mg

906. Green Lentil Soup

Preparation time: 10 minutes
Cooking time: 30 minutes
Servings: 4
Ingredients:

- 1 ½ cups green lentils, rinsed
- 4 cups baby spinach
- 4 cups filtered alkaline water
- 1 tsp. Italian seasoning
- 2 tsp. fresh thyme
- 14 oz. tomatoes, diced

- 3 garlic cloves, minced
- 2 celery stalks, chopped
- 1 carrot, chopped
- 1 onion, chopped
- Pepper
- Sea salt

Directions:

1. Add all Ingredients except spinach into the direct pot and mix fine.
2. Cover pot with top and cook on manual high pressure for 18 minutes.
3. When finished, release pressure using the quick release **Directions:** than open the lid.
4. Add spinach and stir well.
5. Serve and enjoy.

Nutrition:
Calories 306
Fat 1.5 g
Carbohydrates 53.7 g
Sugar 6.4 g
Protein 21 g
Cholesterol 1 mg

907. Squash Soup

Preparation time: 10 minutes
Cooking time: 40 minutes
Servings: 4
Ingredients:

- 3 lbs. butternut squash, peeled and cubed
- 1 tbsp. curry powder
- 1/2 cup unsweetened coconut milk
- 3 cups filtered alkaline water
- 2 garlic cloves, minced
- 1 large onion, minced
- 1 tsp. olive oil

Directions:

1. Add olive oil in the instant pot and set the pot on sauté mode.
2. Add onion and cook until tender, about 8 minutes.
3. Add curry powder and garlic and sauté for a minute.
4. Add butternut squash, water, and salt and stir well.
5. Cover pot with lid and cook on soup mode for 30 minutes.

6. When finished, allow to release pressure naturally for 10 minutes then release using quick release Directions: than open the lid.

7. Blend the soup utilizing a submersion blender until smooth.

8. Add coconut milk and stir well.

9. Serve warm and enjoy.

Nutrition:

Calories 254

Fat 8.9 g

Carbohydrates 46.4 g

Sugar 10.1 g

Protein 4.8 g

Cholesterol 0 mg

908. Tomato Soup

Preparation time: 5 minutes

Cooking time: 20 minutes

Servings: 4

Ingredients:

- 6 tomatoes, chopped
- 1 onion, diced
- 14 oz. coconut milk
- 1 tsp. turmeric
- 1 tsp. garlic, minced
- 1/4 cup cilantro, chopped
- 1/2 tsp. cayenne pepper
- 1 tsp. ginger, minced
- 1/2 tsp. sea salt

Directions:

1. Add all **Ingredients** to the direct pot and mix fine.

2. Cover instant pot with lid and cook on manual high pressure for 5 minutes.

3. When finished, allow to release pressure naturally for 10 minutes then release using the quick release **Directions:**

4. Blend the soup utilizing a submersion blender until smooth.

5. Stir well and serve.

Nutrition:

Calories 81

Fat 3.5 g

Carbohydrates 11.6 g

Sugar 6.1 g

Protein 2.5 g

Cholesterol 0 mg

909. Basil Zucchini Soup

Preparation time: 10 minutes

Cooking time: 20 minutes

Servings: 4

Ingredients:

- 3 medium zucchinis, peeled and chopped
- 1/4 cup basil, chopped
- 1 large leek, chopped
- 3 cups filtered alkaline water
- 1 tbsp. lemon juice
- 3 tbsp. olive oil
- 2 tsp. sea salt

Directions:

1. Add 2 tbsp. oil into the pot and set the pot on sauté mode.

2. Add zucchini and sauté for 5 minutes.

3. Add basil and leeks and sauté for 2-3 minutes.

4. Add lemon juice, water, and salt. Stir well.

5. Cover pot with lid and cook on high pressure for 8 minutes.

6. When finished, allow to release pressure naturally then open the lid.

7. Blend the soup utilizing a submersion blender until smooth.

8. Top with remaining olive oil and serve.

Nutrition:

Calories 157

Fat 11.9 g

Carbohydrates 8.9 g

Protein 5.8 g

Sugar 4 g

Cholesterol 0 mg

910. Summer Vegetable Soup

Preparation time: 5 minutes

Cooking time: 20 minutes

Servings: 10

Ingredients:

- 1/2 cup basil, chopped
- 2 bell peppers, seeded and sliced
- 1/ cup green beans, trimmed and cut into pieces
- 8 cups filtered alkaline water

- 1 medium summer squash, sliced
- 1 medium zucchini, sliced
- 2 large tomatoes, sliced
- 1 small eggplant, sliced
- 6 garlic cloves, smashed
- 1 medium onion, diced
- Pepper
- Salt

Directions:

1. Combine all elements into the direct pot and mix fine.

2. Cover pot with lid and cook on soup mode for 10 minutes.

3. Release pressure using quick release **Directions:** than open the lid.

4. Blend the soup utilizing a submersion blender until smooth.

5. Serve and enjoy.

Nutrition:

Calories 84

Fat 1.6 g

Carbohydrates 12.8 g

Protein 6.1 g

Sugar 6.1 g

Cholesterol 0 mg

911. Almond-Red Bell Pepper Dip

Preparation time: 14 minutes
Cooking time: 16 minutes
Servings: 3
Ingredients:

- Garlic, 2-3 cloves
- Sea salt, one (1) pinch
- Cayenne pepper, one (1) pinch
- Extra virgin olive oil (cold pressed), one (1) tablespoon
- Almonds, 60g
- Red bell pepper, 280g

Directions:

1. First of all, cook garlic and pepper until they are soft.

2. Add all **Ingredients** in a mixer and blend until the mix becomes smooth and creamy.

3. Finally, add pepper and salt to taste.

4. Serve.

Nutrition:

Calories: 51

Carbohydrates: 10g

Fat: 1g

Protein: 2g

912. Spicy Carrot Soup

Preparation time: 10 minutes
Cooking time: 20 minutes
Servings: 6
Ingredients:

- 8 large carrots, peeled and chopped
- 1 1/2 cups filtered alkaline water
- 14 oz. coconut milk
- 3 garlic cloves, peeled
- 1 tbsp. red curry paste
- 1/4 cup olive oil
- 1 onion, chopped
- Salt

Directions:

1. Combine all elements into the direct pot and mix fine.

2. Cover pot with lid and select manual and set timer for 15 minutes.

3. Allow to release pressure naturally then open the lid.

4. Blend the soup utilizing a submersion blender until smooth.

5. Serve and enjoy.

Nutrition:

Calories 267

Fat 22 g

Carbohydrates 13 g

Protein 4 g

Sugar 5 g

Cholesterol 20 mg

913. Zucchini Soup

Preparation time: 10 minutes
Cooking time: 30 minutes
Servings: 10
Ingredients:

- 10 cups zucchini, chopped
- 32 oz. filtered alkaline water
- 13.5 oz. coconut milk

- 1 tbsp. Thai curry paste

Directions:

1. Combine all elements into the direct pot and mix fine.
2. Cover pot with lid and cook on manual high pressure for 10 minutes.
3. Release pressure using quick release **Directions:** than open the lid.
4. Using blender Blend the soup until smooth.
5. Serve and enjoy.

Nutrition:

Calories 122

Fat 9.8 g

Carbohydrates 6.6 g

Protein 4.1 g

Sugar 3.6 g

Cholesterol 0 mg

914. Kidney Bean Stew

Preparation time: 15 minutes

Cooking time: 15 minutes

Servings: 2

Ingredients:

- 1lb cooked kidney beans
- 1 cup tomato passata
- 1 cup low sodium beef broth
- 3tbsp Italian herbs

Recipe:

1. Mix all the ingredients in your Instant Pot.
2. Cook on Stew for 15 minutes.
3. Release the pressure naturally.

Nutrition:

Calories: 270

Carbs: 16

Sugar: 3

Fat: 10

Protein: 23

GL: 8

915. Cabbage Soup

Preparation time: 15 minutes

Cooking time: 35 minutes

Servings: 2

Ingredients:

- 1lb shredded cabbage
- 1 cup low sodium vegetable broth

- 1 shredded onion
- 2tbsp mixed herbs
- 1tbsp black pepper

Recipe:

1. Mix all the ingredients in your Instant Pot.
2. Cook on Stew for 35 minutes.
3. Release the pressure naturally.

Nutrition:

Calories: 60

Carbs: 2

Sugar: 0

Fat: 2

Protein: 4

GL: 1

916. Pumpkin Spice Soup

Preparation time: 10 minutes

Cooking time: 35 minutes

Servings: 2

Ingredients:

- 1lb cubed pumpkin
- 1 cup low sodium vegetable broth
- 2tbsp mixed spice

Recipe:

1. Mix all the ingredients in your Instant Pot.
2. Cook on Stew for 35 minutes.
3. Release the pressure naturally.
4. Blend the soup.

Nutrition:

Calories: 100

Carbs: 7

Sugar: 1

Fat: 2

Protein: 3

GL: 1

917. Cream of Tomato Soup

Preparation time: 15 minutes

Cooking time: 15 minutes

Servings: 2

Ingredients:

- 1lb fresh tomatoes, chopped
- 1.5 cups low sodium tomato puree
- 1tbsp black pepper

Recipe:

1. Mix all the ingredients in your Instant Pot.

2.   Cook on Stew for 15 minutes.
3.   Release the pressure naturally.
4.   Blend.

Nutrition:

Calories: 20

Carbs: 2

Sugar: 1

Fat: 0

Protein: 3

GL: 1

918. Shiitake Soup

Preparation time: 15 minutes

Cooking time: 35 minutes

Servings: 2

Ingredients:

- 1 cup shiitake mushrooms
- 1 cup diced vegetables
- 1 cup low sodium vegetable broth
- 2tbsp 5 spice seasoning

Recipe:

1.   Mix all the ingredients in your Instant Pot.
2.   Cook on Stew for 35 minutes.
3.   Release the pressure naturally.

Nutrition:

Calories: 70

Carbs: 5

Sugar: 1

Fat: 2

Protein: 2

GL: 1

919. Spicy Pepper Soup

Preparation time: 15 minutes

Cooking time: 15 minutes

Servings: 2

Ingredients:

- 1lb chopped mixed sweet peppers
- 1 cup low sodium vegetable broth
- 3tbsp chopped chili peppers
- 1tbsp black pepper

Recipe:

1.   Mix all the ingredients in your Instant Pot.
2.   Cook on Stew for 15 minutes.
3.   Release the pressure naturally. Blend.

Nutrition:

Calories: 100

Carbs: 11

Sugar: 4

Fat: 2

Protein: 3

GL: 6

920. Zoodle Won-Ton Soup

Preparation time: 15 minutes

Cooking time: 5 minutes

Servings: 2

Ingredients:

- 1lb spiralized zucchini
- 1 pack unfried won-tons
- 1 cup low sodium beef broth
- 2tbsp soy sauce

Recipe:

1.   Mix all the ingredients in your Instant Pot.
2.   Cook on Stew for 5 minutes.
3.   Release the pressure naturally.

Nutrition:

Calories: 300

Carbs: 6

Sugar: 1

Fat: 9

Protein: 43

GL: 2

921. Broccoli Stilton Soup

Preparation time: 15 minutes

Cooking time: 35 minutes

Servings: 2

Ingredients:

- 1lb chopped broccoli
- 0.5lb chopped vegetables
- 1 cup low sodium vegetable broth
- 1 cup Stilton

Recipe:

1.   Mix all the ingredients in your Instant Pot.
2.   Cook on Stew for 35 minutes.
3.   Release the pressure naturally.
4.   Blend the soup.

Nutrition:

Calories: 280

Carbs: 9

Sugar: 2
Fat: 22
Protein: 13
GL: 4

922. Lamb Stew

Preparation time: 15 minutes
Cooking time: 35 minutes
Servings: 2
Ingredients:
- 1lb diced lamb shoulder
- 1lb chopped winter vegetables
- 1 cup low sodium vegetable broth
- 1tbsp yeast extract
- 1tbsp star anise spice mix

Recipe:
1. Mix all the ingredients in your Instant Pot.
2. Cook on Stew for 35 minutes.
3. Release the pressure naturally.

Nutrition:
Calories: 320
Carbs: 10
Sugar: 2
Fat: 8
Protein: 42
GL: 3

923. Irish Stew

Preparation time: 15 minutes
Cooking time: 35 minutes
Servings: 2
Ingredients:
- 1.5lb diced lamb shoulder
- 1lb chopped vegetables
- 1 cup low sodium beef broth
- 3 minced onions
- 1tbsp ghee

Recipe:
1. Mix all the ingredients in your Instant Pot.
2. Cook on Stew for 35 minutes.
3. Release the pressure naturally.

Nutrition:
Calories: 330
Carbs: 9
Sugar: 2
Fat: 12

Protein: 49
GL: 3

924. Sweet and Sour Soup

Preparation time: 15 minutes
Cooking time: 35 minutes
Servings: 2
Ingredients:
- 1lb cubed chicken breast
- 1lb chopped vegetables
- 1 cup low carb sweet and sour sauce
- 0.5 cup diabetic marmalade

Recipe:
1. Mix all the ingredients in your Instant Pot.
2. Cook on Stew for 35 minutes.
3. Release the pressure naturally.

925. Meatball Stew

Preparation time: 15 minutes
Cooking time: 25 minutes
Servings: 2
Ingredients:
- 1lb sausage meat
- 2 cups chopped tomato
- 1 cup chopped vegetables
- 2tbsp Italian seasonings
- 1tbsp vegetable oil

Recipe:
1. Roll the sausage into meatballs.
2. Put the Instant Pot on Sauté and fry the meatballs in the oil until brown.
3. Mix all the ingredients in your Instant Pot.
4. Cook on Stew for 25 minutes.
5. Release the pressure naturally.

Nutrition:
Calories: 300
Carbs: 4
Sugar: 1
Fat: 12
Protein: 40
GL: 2

926. Kebab Stew

Preparation time: 15 minutes

Cooking time: 35 minutes

Servings: 2

Ingredients:

- 1lb cubed, seasoned kebab meat
- 1lb cooked chickpeas
- 1 cup low sodium vegetable broth
- 1tbsp black pepper

Recipe:

1. Mix all the ingredients in your Instant Pot.
2. Cook on Stew for 35 minutes.
3. Release the pressure naturally.

Nutrition:

Calories: 290

Carbs: 22

Sugar: 4

Fat: 10

Protein: 34

GL: 6

927. French Onion Soup

Preparation time: 35 minutes

Cooking time: 35 minutes

Servings: 2

Ingredients:

- 6 onions, chopped finely
- 2 cups vegetable broth
- 2tbsp oil
- 2tbsp Gruyere

Recipe:

1. Place the oil in your Instant Pot and cook the onions on Sauté until soft and brown.
2. Mix all the ingredients in your Instant Pot.
3. Cook on Stew for 35 minutes.
4. Release the pressure naturally.

Nutrition:

Calories: 110

Carbs: 8

Sugar: 3

Fat: 10

Protein: 3

GL: 4

928. Meatless Ball Soup

Preparation time: 15 minutes

Cooking time: 15 minutes

Servings: 2

Ingredients:

- 1lb minced tofu
- 0.5lb chopped vegetables
- 2 cups low sodium vegetable broth
- 1tbsp almond flour
- salt and pepper

Recipe:

1. Mix the tofu, flour, salt and pepper.
2. Form the meatballs.
3. Place all the ingredients in your Instant Pot.
4. Cook on Stew for 15 minutes.
5. Release the pressure naturally.

Nutrition:

Calories: 240

Carbs: 9

Sugar: 3

Fat: 10

Protein: 35

GL: 5

929. Fake-On Stew

Preparation time: 15 minutes

Cooking time: 25 minutes

Servings: 2

Ingredients:

- 0.5lb soy bacon
- 1lb chopped vegetables
- 1 cup low sodium vegetable broth
- 1tbsp nutritional yeast

Recipe:

1. Mix all the ingredients in your Instant Pot.
2. Cook on Stew for 25 minutes.
3. Release the pressure naturally.

Nutrition:

Calories: 200

Carbs: 12

Sugar: 3

Fat: 7

Protein: 41

GL: 5

930. Chickpea Soup

Preparation time: 15 minutes
Cooking time: 35 minutes
Servings: 2
Ingredients:

- 1lb cooked chickpeas
- 1lb chopped vegetables
- 1 cup low sodium vegetable broth
- 2tbsp mixed herbs

Recipe:
1. Mix all the ingredients in your Instant Pot.
2. Cook on Stew for 35 minutes.
3. Release the pressure naturally.

Nutrition:
Calories: 310
Carbs: 20
Sugar: 3
Fat: 5
Protein: 27
GL: 5

931. Chicken Zoodle Soup

Preparation time: 15 minutes
Cooking time: 35 minutes
Servings: 2
Ingredients:

- 1lb chopped cooked chicken
- 1lb spiralized zucchini
- 1 cup low sodium chicken soup
- 1 cup diced vegetables

Recipe:
1. Mix all the ingredients except the zucchini in your Instant Pot.
2. Cook on Stew for 35 minutes.
3. Release the pressure naturally.
4. Stir in the zucchini and allow to heat thoroughly.

Nutrition:
Calories: 250
Carbs: 5
Sugar: 0
Fat: 10
Protein: 40
GL: 1

932. Lemon-Tarragon Soup

Preparation time: 10 minutes
Cooking time: 10 minutes
Servings: 1-2

Cashews and coconut milk replace heavy cream in this healthy version of lemon-tarragon soup, balanced by tart freshly squeezed lemon juice and fragrant tarragon. It's a light, airy soup that you won't want to miss.

Ingredients:

- 1 tablespoon avocado oil
- ½ cup diced onion
- 3 garlic cloves, crushed
- ¼ plus 1/8 teaspoon sea salt
- ¼ plus 1/8 teaspoon freshly ground black pepper
- 1 (13.5-ounce) can full-fat coconut milk
- 1 tablespoon freshly squeezed lemon juice
- ½ cup raw cashews
- 1 celery stalk
- 2 tablespoons chopped fresh tarragon

Directions:
1. In a medium skillet over medium-high warmth, heat the avocado oil. Add the onion, garlic, salt, and pepper, and sauté for 3 to 5 minutes or until the onion is soft.
2. In a high-speed blender, blend together the coconut milk, lemon juice, cashews, celery, and tarragon with the onion mixture until smooth. Adjust seasonings, if necessary.
3. Fill 1 huge or 2 little dishes and enjoy immediately, or transfer to a medium saucepan and warm on low heat for 3 to 5 minutes before serving.

Nutrition:
Calories: 60
Carbohydrates: 13 g
Protein: 0.8 g

933. Chilled Cucumber and Lime Soup

Preparation time: 5 minutes
Cooking time: 20 minutes
Servings: 1-2
Ingredients:

- 1 cucumber, peeled
- ½ zucchini, peeled
- 1 tablespoon freshly squeezed lime juice
- 1 tablespoon fresh cilantro leaves
- 1 garlic clove, crushed

- ¼ teaspoon sea salt

Directions:

1. In a blender, blend together the cucumber, zucchini, lime juice, cilantro, garlic, and salt until well combined. Add more salt, if necessary.

2. Fill 1 huge or 2 little dishes and enjoy immediately, or refrigerate for 15 to 20 minutes to chill before serving.

Nutrition:

Calories: 48

Carbohydrates: 8 g

Fat: 1g

Protein: .5g

934. Coconut, Cilantro, And Jalapeño Soup

Preparation time: 5 minutes

Cooking time: 5 minutes

Servings: 1-2

This soup is a nutrient dream. Cilantro is a natural anti-inflammatory and is also excellent for detoxification. And one single jalapeño has an entire day's worth of vitamin C!

Ingredients:

- 2 tablespoons avocado oil
- ½ cup diced onions
- 3 garlic cloves, crushed
- ¼ teaspoon sea salt
- 1 (13.5-ounce) can full-fat coconut milk
- 1 tablespoon freshly squeezed lime juice
- ½ to 1 jalapeño
- 2 tablespoons fresh cilantro leaves

Directions:

1. In a medium skillet over medium-high warmth, heat the avocado oil. Include the garlic, onion salt, and pepper, and sauté for 3 to 5 minutes, or until the onions are soft.

2. In a blender, blend together the coconut milk, lime juice, jalapeño, and cilantro with the onion mixture until creamy.

3. Fill 1 huge or 2 little dishes and enjoy.

Nutrition:

Calories: 75

Carbohydrates: 13 g

Fat: 2 g

Protein: 4 g

935. Spicy Watermelon Gazpacho

Preparation time: 5 minutes

Cooking time: 5 minutes

Servings: 1-2

At first taste, this soup may have you wondering if you're lunching on a hot and spicy salsa. It has the heat and seasonings of a traditional tomato-based salsa, but it also has a faint sweetness from the cool watermelon. The soup is really hot with a whole jalapeño, so if you don't like food too hot, just use half a jalapeño.

Ingredients:

- 2 cups cubed watermelon
- ¼ cup diced onion
- ¼ cup packed cilantro leaves
- ½ to 1 jalapeño
- 2 tablespoons freshly squeezed lime juice

Directions:

1. In a blender or food processor, pulse to combine the watermelon, onion, cilantro, jalapeño, and lime juice only long enough to break down the **Ingredients**, leaving them very finely diced and taking care to not over process.

2. Pour into 1 large or 2 small bowls and enjoy.

Nutrition:

Calories: 35

Carbohydrates: 12

Fat: .4 g

936. Roasted Carrot and Leek Soup

Preparation time: 4 minutes

Cooking time: 30 minutes

Servings: 3-4

The carrot, a root vegetable, is an excellent source of antioxidants (1 cup has 113 percent of your daily value of vitamin A) and fiber (1 cup has 14 percent of your daily value). This bright and colorful soup freezes well to enjoy later when you're short on time.

Ingredients:

- 6 carrots
- 1 cup chopped onion
- 1 fennel bulb, cubed
- 2 garlic cloves, crushed
- 2 tablespoons avocado oil

- 1 teaspoon sea salt
- 1 teaspoon freshly ground black pepper
- 2 cups almond milk, plus more if desired

Directions:

1. Preheat the oven to 400°F. Line a baking sheet with parchment paper.
2. Cut the carrots into thirds, and then cut each third in half. Transfer to a medium bowl.
3. Add the onion, fennel, garlic, and avocado oil, and toss to coat. Season with the salt and pepper, and toss again.
4. Transfer the vegetables to the prepared baking sheet, and roast for 30 minutes.
5. Remove from the oven and allow the vegetables to cool.
6. In a high-speed blender, blend together the almond milk and roasted vegetables until creamy and smooth. Adjust the seasonings, if necessary, and add additional milk if you prefer a thinner consistency.
7. Pour into 2 large or 4 small bowls and enjoy.

Nutrition:

Calories: 55
Carbohydrates: 12g
Fat: 1.5 g
Protein: 1.8 g

937. Creamy Lentil and Potato Stew

Preparation time: 10 minutes
Cooking time: 30 minutes
Servings: 4

This is a hearty stew that is sure to be a favorite. It's a one-pot meal that is the perfect comfort food. With fresh vegetables and herbs along with protein-rich lentils, it's both healthy and filling. Any lentil variety would work, even a mixed, sprouted lentil blend. Another bonus of this recipe: It's freezer-friendly.

Ingredients:

- 2 tablespoons avocado oil
- ½ cup diced onion
- 2 garlic cloves, crushed
- 1 to 1½ teaspoons sea salt
- 1 teaspoon freshly ground black pepper
- 1 cup dry lentils
- 2 carrots, sliced
- 1 cup peeled and cubed potato

- 1 celery stalk, diced
- 2 fresh oregano sprigs, chopped
- 2 fresh tarragon sprigs, chopped
- 5 cups vegetable broth, divided
- 1 (13.5-ounce) can full-fat coconut milk

Directions:

1. In a great soup pot over average-high hotness, heat the avocado oil. Include the garlic, onion, salt, and pepper, and sauté for 3 to 5 minutes, or until the onion is soft.
2. Add the lentils, carrots, potato, celery, oregano, tarragon, and 2½ cups of vegetable broth, and stir.
3. Get to a boil, decrease the heat to medium-low, and cook, stirring frequently and adding additional vegetable broth a half cup at a time to make sure there is enough liquid for the lentils and potatoes to cook, for 20 to 25 minutes, or until the potatoes and lentils are soft.
4. Take away from the heat, and stirring in the coconut milk. Pour into 4 soup bowls and enjoy.

Nutrition:

Calories: 85
Carbohydrates: 20g
Fat: 3g
Protein: 3g

938. Roasted Garlic and Cauliflower Soup

Preparation time: 10 minutes
Cooking time: 35 minutes
Servings: 1-2

Roasted garlic is always a treat, and paired with cauliflower in this wonderful soup, what you get is a deeply satisfy soup with savory, rustic flavors. Blended, the result is a smooth, thick, and creamy soup, but if you prefer a thinner consistency, just adds a little more vegetable broth to thin it out. Cauliflower is anti-inflammatory, high in antioxidants, and a good source of vitamin C (1 cup has 86 percent of your daily value).

Ingredients:

- 4 cups bite-size cauliflower florets
- 5 garlic cloves
- 1½ tablespoons avocado oil
- ¾ teaspoon sea salt
- ½ teaspoon freshly ground black pepper
- 1 cup almond milk
- 1 cup vegetable broth, plus more if desired

Directions:

1. Preheat the oven to 450°F. Line a baking sheet with parchment paper.

2. In a medium bowl, toss the cauliflower and garlic with the avocado oil to coat. Season with the salt and pepper, and toss again.

3. Transfer to the prepared baking sheet and roast for 30 minutes. Cool before adding to the blender.

4. In a high-speed blender, blend together the cooled vegetables, almond milk, and vegetable broth until creamy and smooth. Adjust the salt and pepper, if necessary, and add additional vegetable broth if you prefer a thinner consistency.

5. Transfer to a medium saucepan, and lightly warm on medium-low heat for 3 to 5 minutes.

6. Ladle into 1 large or 2 small bowls and enjoy.

Nutrition:

Calories: 48

Carbohydrates: 11g

Protein: 1.5g

939. Beefless "Beef" Stew

Preparation time: 10 minutes

Cooking time: 0 minutes

Servings: 4

The potatoes, carrots, aromatics, and herbs in this soup meld so well together, you'll forget there's typically beef in this stew. Hearty and flavorful, this one-pot comfort food is perfect for a fall or winter dinner.

Ingredients:

- 1 tablespoon avocado oil
- 1 cup onion, diced
- 2 garlic cloves, crushed
- 1 teaspoon sea salt
- 1 teaspoon freshly ground black pepper
- 3 cups vegetable broth, plus more if desired
- 2 cups water, plus more if desired
- 3 cups sliced carrot
- 1 large potato, cubed
- 2 celery stalks, diced
- 1 teaspoon dried oregano
- 1 dried bay leaf

Directions:

1. In a medium soup pot over medium heat, heat the avocado oil. Include the onion, garlic, salt, and pepper, and sauté for 2 to 3 minutes, or until the onion is soft.

2. Add the vegetable broth, water, carrot, potato, celery, oregano, and bay leaf, and stir. Get to a boil, decrease the heat to medium-low, and cook for 30 to 45 minutes, or until the potatoes and carrots be soft.

3. Adjust the seasonings, if necessary, and add additional water or vegetable broth, if a soupier consistency is preferred, in half-cup increments.

4. Ladle into 4 soup bowls and enjoy.

Nutrition:

Calories: 59

Carbohydrates: 12g

940. Creamy Mushroom Soup

Preparation time: 5 minutes

Cooking time: 20 minutes

Servings: 4

This savory, earthy soup is a must try if you love mushrooms. Shiitake and baby Portobello (cremini) mushrooms are used here, but you can substitute them with your favorite mushroom varieties. Full-fat coconut milk gives it that close-your-eyes-and-savor-it creaminess that pushes the soup into the comfort food realm—perfect for those cold evenings when you need a warm soup to heat up your insides.

Ingredients:

- 1 tablespoon avocado oil
- 1 cup sliced shiitake mushrooms
- 1 cup sliced cremini mushrooms
- 1 cup diced onion
- 1 garlic clove, crushed
- ¾ teaspoon sea salt
- ½ teaspoon freshly ground black pepper
- 1 cup vegetable broth
- 1 (13.5-ounce) can full-fat coconut milk
- ½ teaspoon dried thyme
- 1 tablespoon coconut aminos

Directions:

1. In a great soup pot over average-high hotness, heat the avocado oil. Add the mushrooms, onion, garlic, salt, and pepper, and sauté for 2 to 3 minutes, or until the onion is soft.

2. Add the vegetable broth, coconut milk, thyme, and coconut aminos. Reduce the heat to medium-low, and simmer for about 15 minutes, stirring occasionally.

3.   Adjust seasonings, if necessary, ladle into 2 large or 4 small bowls, and enjoy.

Nutrition:

Calories: 65

Carbohydrates: 12g

Fat: 2g

Protein: 2g

941.   Chilled Berry and Mint Soup

Preparation time: 5 minutes

Cooking time: 20 minutes

Servings: 1-2

There's no better way to cool down when it's hot outside than with this chilled, sweet mixed berry soup. It's light and showcases summer's berry bounty: raspberries, blackberries, and blueberries. The fresh mint brightens the soup and keeps the sweetness in check. This soup isn't just for lunch or dinner either—tries it for a quick breakfast, too! If you like a thinner consistency for this, just add a little extra water.

Ingredients:

FOR THE SWEETENER

- ¼ cup unrefined whole cane sugar, such as Sucanat
- ¼ cup water, plus more if desired
- FOR THE SOUP
- 1 cup mixed berries (raspberries, blackberries, blueberries)
- ½ cup water
- 1 teaspoon freshly squeezed lemon juice
- 8 fresh mint leaves

Directions:

1.   To prepare the sweetener

2.   In a small saucepan over medium-low, heat the sugar and water, stirring continuously for 1 to 2 minutes, until the sugar is dissolved. Cool.

3.   To prepare the soup

4.   In a blender, blend together the cooled sugar water with the berries, water, lemon juice, and mint leaves until well combined.

5.   Transfer the mixture to the refrigerator and allow chilling completely, about 20 minutes.

6.   Ladle into 1 large or 2 small bowls and enjoy.

Nutrition:

Calories: 89

Carbohydrates: 12g

Fat: 6g

Protein: 2.2 g

942.   Vegetable Soup

Preparation Time: 10 Minutes

Cooking Time: 30 Minutes

Servings: 5

Ingredients:

- 8 cups Vegetable Broth
- 2 tbsp. Olive Oil
- 1 tbsp. Italian Seasoning
- 1 Onion, large & diced
- 2 Bay Leaves, dried
- 2 Bell Pepper, large & diced
- Sea Salt & Black Pepper, as needed
- 4 cloves of Garlic, minced
- 28 oz. Tomatoes, diced
- 1 Cauliflower head, medium & torn into florets
- 2 cups Green Beans, trimmed & chopped

Directions:

1.   Heat oil in a Dutch oven over medium heat.

2.   Once the oil becomes hot, stir in the onions and pepper.

3.   Cook for 10 minutes or until the onion is softened and browned.

4.   Spoon in the garlic and sauté for a minute or until fragrant.

5.   Add all the remaining ingredients to it. Mix until everything comes together.

6.   Bring the mixture to a boil. Lower the heat and cook for further 20 minutes or until the vegetables have softened.

7.   Serve hot.

Nutrition:

Calories – 79kL

Fat – 2g

Carbohydrates – 8g

Protein – 2g

Sodium – 187mg

Desserts

943. Peanut Butter Cups

Preparation Time: 5 minutes
Cooking Time: 10 minutes
Servings: 4
Ingredients:

* 1 packet plain gelatin
* ¼ cup sugar substitute
* 2 cups nonfat cream
* ½ teaspoon vanilla
* ¼ cup low-fat peanut butter
* 2 tablespoons unsalted peanuts, chopped

Directions:
1. Mix gelatin, sugar substitute and cream in a pan.
2. Let sit for 5 minutes.
3. Place over medium heat and cook until gelatin has been dissolved.
4. Stir in vanilla and peanut butter.
5. Pour into custard cups. Chill for 3 hours.
6. Top with the peanuts and serve.
Nutrition:
171 Calories
21g Carbohydrate
6.8g Protein

944. Fruit Pizza

Preparation Time: 5 minutes
Cooking Time: 10 minutes
Servings: 4
Ingredients:

* 1 teaspoon maple syrup
* ¼ teaspoon vanilla extract
* ½ cup coconut milk yogurt
* 2 round slices watermelon
* ½ cup blackberries, sliced
* ½ cup strawberries, sliced
* 2 tablespoons coconut flakes (unsweetened)

Directions:
1. Mix maple syrup, vanilla and yogurt in a bowl.
2. Spread the mixture on top of the watermelon slice.
3. Top with the berries and coconut flakes.
Nutrition:

70 Calories
14.6g Carbohydrate
1.2g Protein

945. Choco Peppermint Cake

Preparation Time: 5 minutes
Cooking Time: 10 minutes
Servings: 4
Ingredients:

* Cooking spray
* 1/3 cup oil
* 15 oz. package chocolate cake mix
* 3 eggs, beaten
* 1 cup water
* ¼ teaspoon peppermint extract

Directions:
1. Spray slow cooker with oil.
2. Mix all the ingredients in a bowl.
3. Use an electric mixer on medium speed setting to mix ingredients for 2 minutes.
4. Pour mixture into the slow cooker.
5. Cover the pot and cook on low for 3 hours.
6. Let cool before slicing and serving.
Nutrition:
185 Calories
27g Carbohydrate
3.8g Protein

946. Roasted Mango

Preparation Time: 5 minutes
Cooking Time: 10 minutes
Servings: 4
Ingredients:

* 2 mangoes, sliced
* 2 teaspoons crystallized ginger, chopped
* 2 teaspoons orange zest
* 2 tablespoons coconut flakes (unsweetened)

Directions:
1. Preheat your oven to 350 degrees F.
2. Add mango slices in custard cups.
3. Top with the ginger, orange zest and coconut flakes.
4. Bake in the oven for 10 minutes.

Nutrition:

89 Calories

20g Carbohydrate

0.8g Protein

947. Roasted Plums

Preparation Time: 5 minutes

Cooking Time: 10 minutes

Servings: 4

Ingredients:

- Cooking spray
- 6 plums, sliced
- ½ cup pineapple juice (unsweetened)
- 1 tablespoon brown sugar
- 2 tablespoons brown sugar
- ¼ teaspoon ground cardamom
- ½ teaspoon ground cinnamon
- 1/8 teaspoon ground cumin

Directions:

1. Combine all the ingredients in a baking pan.
2. Roast in the oven at 450 degrees F for 20 minutes.

Nutrition:

102 Calories

18.7g Carbohydrate

2g Protein

948. Figs with Honey & Yogurt

Preparation Time: 5 minutes

Cooking Time: 10 minutes

Servings: 4

Ingredients:

- ½ teaspoon vanilla
- 8 oz. nonfat yogurt
- 2 figs, sliced
- 1 tablespoon walnuts, chopped and toasted
- 2 teaspoons honey

Directions:

1. Stir vanilla into yogurt.
2. Mix well.
3. Top with the figs and sprinkle with walnuts.
4. Drizzle with honey and serve.

Nutrition:

157 Calories

24g Carbohydrate

7g Protein

949. Flourless Chocolate Cake

Preparation Time: 10 minutes

Cooking Time: 45 minutes

Servings: 6

Ingredients:

- ½ Cup of stevia
- 12 Ounces of unsweetened baking chocolate
- 2/3 Cup of ghee
- 1/3 Cup of warm water
- ¼ Teaspoon of salt
- 4 Large pastured eggs
- 2 Cups of boiling water

Directions:

1. Line the bottom of a 9-inch pan of a spring form with a parchment paper.
2. Heat the water in a small pot; then add the salt and the stevia over the water until wait until the mixture becomes completely dissolved.
3. Melt the baking chocolate into a double boiler or simply microwave it for about 30 seconds.
4. Mix the melted chocolate and the butter in a large bowl with an electric mixer.
5. Beat in your hot mixture; then crack in the egg and whisk after adding each of the eggs.
6. Pour the obtained mixture into your prepared spring form tray.
7. Wrap the spring form tray with a foil paper.
8. Place the spring form tray in a large cake tray and add boiling water right to the outside; make sure the depth doesn't exceed 1 inch.
9. Bake the cake into the water bath for about 45 minutes at a temperature of about 350 F.
10. Remove the tray from the boiling water and transfer to a wire to cool.
11. Let the cake chill for an overnight in the refrigerator.

Nutrition

295 Calories

6g Carbohydrates

4g Fiber

950. Lava Cake

Preparation Time: 10 minutes

Cooking Time: 10 minutes

Servings: 2

Ingredients:

- 2 Oz of dark chocolate; you should at least use chocolate of 85% cocoa solids
- 1 Tablespoon of super-fine almond flour
- 2 Oz of unsalted almond butter
- 2 Large eggs

Directions:

1. Heat your oven to a temperature of about 350 Fahrenheit.
2. Grease 2 heat proof ramekins with almond butter.
3. Now, melt the chocolate and the almond butter and stir very well.
4. Beat the eggs very well with a mixer.
5. Add the eggs to the chocolate and the butter mixture and mix very well with almond flour and the swerve; then stir.
6. Pour the dough into 2 ramekins.
7. Bake for about 9 to 10 minutes.
8. Turn the cakes over plates and serve with pomegranate seeds!

Nutrition

459 Calories

3.5g Carbohydrates

0.8g Fiber

951. Cheese Cake

Preparation Time: 15 minutes
Cooking Time: 50 minutes
Servings: 6
Ingredients:

For Almond Flour Cheesecake Crust:

- 2 Cups of Blanched almond flour
- 1/3 Cup of almond Butter
- 3 Tablespoons of Erythritol (powdered or granular)
- 1 Teaspoon of Vanilla extract

For Keto Cheesecake Filling:

- 32 Oz of softened Cream cheese
- 1 and ¼ cups of powdered erythritol
- 3 Large Eggs
- 1 Tablespoon of Lemon juice
- 1 Teaspoon of Vanilla extract

Directions:

1. Preheat your oven to a temperature of about 350 degrees F.
2. Grease a spring form pan of 9" with cooking spray or just line its bottom with a parchment paper.
3. In order to make the cheesecake rust, stir in the melted butter, the almond flour, the vanilla extract and the erythritol in a large bowl.

4. The dough will get will be a bit crumbly; so, press it into the bottom of your prepared tray.
5. Bake for about 12 minutes; then let cool for about 10 minutes.
6. In the meantime, beat the softened cream cheese and the powdered sweetener at a low speed until it becomes smooth.
7. Crack in the eggs and beat them in at a low to medium speed until it becomes fluffy. Make sure to add one a time.
8. Add in the lemon juice and the vanilla extract and mix at a low to medium speed with a mixer.
9. Pour your filling into your pan right on top of the crust. You can use a spatula to smooth the top of the cake.
10. Bake for about 45 to 50 minutes.
11. Remove the baked cheesecake from your oven and run a knife around its edge.
12. Let the cake cool for about 4 hours in the refrigerator.
13. Serve and enjoy your delicious cheese cake!

Nutrition

325 Calories

6g Carbohydrates

1g Fiber

952. Orange Cake

Preparation Time: 10 minutes
Cooking Time: 50minutes
Servings: 8
Ingredients:

- 2 and ½ cups of almond flour
- 2 Unwaxed washed oranges
- 5 Large separated eggs
- 1 Teaspoon of baking powder
- 2 Teaspoons of orange extract
- 1 Teaspoon of vanilla bean powder
- 6 Seeds of cardamom pods crushed
- 16 drops of liquid stevia; about 3 teaspoons
- 1 Handful of flaked almonds to decorate

Directions:

1. Preheat your oven to a temperature of about 350 Fahrenheit.
2. Line a rectangular bread baking tray with a parchment paper.
3. Place the oranges into a pan filled with cold water and cover it with a lid.
4. Bring the saucepan to a boil, then let simmer for about 1 hour and make sure the oranges are totally submerged.

5. Make sure the oranges are always submerged to remove any taste of bitterness.

6. Cut the oranges into halves; then remove any seeds; and drain the water and set the oranges aside to cool down.

7. Cut the oranges in half and remove any seeds, then puree it with a blender or a food processor.

8. Separate the eggs; then whisk the egg whites until you see stiff peaks forming.

9. Add all your ingredients except for the egg whites to the orange mixture and add in the egg whites; then mix.

10. Pour the batter into the cake tin and sprinkle with the flaked almonds right on top.

11. Bake your cake for about 50 minutes.

12. Remove the cake from the oven and set aside to cool for 5 minutes.

Nutrition

164 Calories

7.1g Carbohydrates

2.7g Fiber

953. Madeleine

Preparation Time: 10 minutes

Cooking Time: 15 minutes

Servings: 12

Ingredients

- 2 Large pastured eggs
- ¾ Cup of almond flour
- 1 and ½ Tablespoons of Swerve
- ¼ Cup of cooled, melted coconut oil
- 1 Teaspoon of vanilla extract
- 1 Teaspoon of almond extract
- 1 Teaspoon of lemon zest
- ¼ Teaspoon of salt

Directions

1. Preheat your oven to a temperature of about 350 F.

2. Combine the eggs with the salt and whisk on a high speed for about 5 minutes.

3. Slowly add in the Swerve and keep mixing on high for 2 additional minutes.

4. Stir in the almond flour until it is very well-incorporated; then add in the vanilla and the almond extracts.

5. Add in the melted coconut oil and stir all your ingredients together.

6. Pour the obtained batter into equal parts in a greased Madeleine tray.

7. Bake your Ketogenic Madeleine for about 13 minutes or until the edges start to have a brown color.

8. Flip the Madeleines out of the baking tray.

Nutrition

87 Calories

3g Carbohydrates

3g Fiber

954. Waffles

Preparation Time: 20 minutes

Cooking Time: 30 minutes

Servings: 3

Ingredients:

For Ketogenic waffles:

- 8 Oz of cream cheese
- 5 Large pastured eggs
- 1/3 Cup of coconut flour
- ½ Teaspoon of Xanthan gum
- 1 Pinch of salt
- ½ Teaspoon of vanilla extract
- 2 Tablespoons of Swerve
- ¼ Teaspoon of baking soda
- 1/3 Cup of almond milk

Optional ingredients:

- ½ Teaspoon of cinnamon pie spice
- ¼ Teaspoon of almond extract

For low-carb Maple Syrup:

- 1 Cup of water
- 1 Tablespoon of Maple flavor
- ¾ Cup of powdered Swerve
- 1 Tablespoon of almond butter
- ½ Teaspoon of Xanthan gum

Directions

For the waffles:

1. Make sure all your ingredients are exactly at room temperature.

2. Place all your ingredients for the waffles from cream cheese to pastured eggs, coconut flour, Xanthan gum, salt, vanilla extract, the Swerve, the baking soda and the almond milk except for the almond milk with the help of a processor.

3. Blend your ingredients until it becomes smooth and creamy; then transfer the batter to a bowl.

4. Add the almond milk and mix your ingredients with a spatula.

5. Heat a waffle maker to a temperature of high.

6.Spray your waffle maker with coconut oil and add about ¼ of the batter in it evenly with a spatula into your waffle iron.

7.Close your waffle and cook until you get the color you want.

8.Carefully remove the waffles to a platter.

For the Ketogenic Maple Syrup:

9.Place 1 and ¼ cups of water, the swerve and the maple in a small pan and bring to a boil over a low heat; then let simmer for about 10 minutes.

10.Add the coconut oil.

11.Sprinkle the Xanthan gum over the top of the waffle and use an immersion blender to blend smoothly.

12.Serve and enjoy your delicious waffles!

Nutrition

316 Calories

7g Carbohydrates

3g Fiber

955. Pretzels

Preparation Time: 10 minutes

Cooking Time: 20 minutes

Servings: 8

Ingredients:

- 1 and ½ cups of pre-shredded mozzarella
- 2 Tablespoons of full fat cream cheese
- 1 Large egg
- ¾ Cup of almond flour+ 2 tablespoons of ground almonds or almond meal
- ½ Teaspoon of baking powder
- 1 Pinch of coarse sea salt

Directions:

1.Heat your oven to a temperature of about 180 C/356 F.

2.Melt the cream cheese and the mozzarella cheese and stir over a low heat until the cheeses are perfectly melted.

3.If you choose to microwave the cheese, just do that for about 1 minute no more and if you want to do it on the stove, turn off the heat as soon as the cheese is completely melted.

4.Add the large egg to the prepared warm dough; then stir until your ingredients are very well combined. If the egg is cold; you will need to heat it gently.

5.Add in the ground almonds or the almond flour and the baking powder and stir until your ingredients are very well combined.

6.Take one pinch of the dough of cheese and toll it or stretch it in your hands until it is about 18 to 20 cm of length; if your dough is sticky, you can oil your hands to avoid that.

7.Now, form pretzels from the cheese dough and nicely shape it; then place it over a baking sheet.

8.Sprinkle with a little bit of salt and bake for about 17 minutes.

Nutrition

113 Calories

2.5g Carbohydrates

0.8g Fiber

956. Cheesy Taco Bites

Preparation Time: 5 minutes

Cooking Time: 10minutes

Serving: 12

Ingredients

- 2 Cups of Packaged Shredded Cheddar Cheese
- 2 Tablespoon of Chili Powder
- 2 Tablespoons of Cumin
- 1 Teaspoon of Salt
- 8 Teaspoons of coconut cream for garnishing
- Use Pico de Gallo for garnishing as well

Directions:

1.Preheat your oven to a temperature of about 350 F.

2.Over a baking sheet lined with a parchment paper, place 1 tablespoon piles of cheese and make sure to a space of 2 inches between each.

3.Place the baking sheet in your oven and bake for about 5 minutes.

4.Remove from the oven and let the cheese cool down for about 1 minute; then carefully lift up and press each into the cups of a mini muffin tin.

5.Make sure to press the edges of the cheese to form the shape of muffins mini.

6.Let the cheese cool completely; then remove it.

7.While you continue to bake the cheese and create your cups.

8.Fill the cheese cups with the coconut cream, then top with the Pico de Gallo.

Nutrition

73 Calories

3g Carbohydrates

4g Protein

957. Nut Squares

Preparation Time: 30 minutes
Cooking Time: 10 minutes
Serving: 10
Ingredients:

- 2 Cups of almonds, pumpkin seeds, sunflower seeds and walnuts
- ½ Cup of desiccated coconut
- 1 Tablespoon of chia seeds
- ¼ Teaspoon of salt
- 2 Tablespoons of coconut oil
- 1 Teaspoon of vanilla extract
- 3 Tablespoons of almond or peanut butter
- 1/3 Cup of Sukrin Gold Fiber Syrup

Directions:

1. Line a square baking tin with a baking paper; then lightly grease it with cooking spray
2. Chop all the nuts roughly; then slightly grease it too, you can also leave them as whole
3. Mix the nuts in a large bowl; then combine them in a large bowl with the coconut, the chia seeds and the salt
4. In a microwave-proof bowl; add the coconut oil; then add the vanilla, the coconut butter or oil, the almond butter and the fiber syrup and microwave the mixture for about 30 seconds
5. Stir your ingredients together very well; then pour the melted mixture right on top of the nuts
6. Press the mixture into your prepared baking tin with the help of the back of a measuring cup and push very well
7. Freeze your treat for about 1 hour before cutting it
8. Cut your frozen nut batter into small cubes or squares of the same size

Nutrition
268 Calories
14g Carbohydrates
1g Fiber

958. Pumpkin & Banana Ice Cream

Preparation Time: 5 minutes
Cooking Time: 10 minutes
Servings: 4
Ingredients:

- 15 oz. pumpkin puree
- 4 bananas, sliced and frozen
- 1 teaspoon pumpkin pie spice
- Chopped pecans

Directions:

1. Add pumpkin puree, bananas and pumpkin pie spice in a food processor.
2. Pulse until smooth.
3. Chill in the refrigerator.
4. Garnish with pecans.

Nutrition:
71 Calories
18g Carbohydrate
1.2g Protein

959. Brulee Oranges

Preparation Time: 5 minutes
Cooking Time: 10 minutes
Servings: 4
Ingredients:

- 4 oranges, sliced into segments
- 1 teaspoon ground cardamom
- 6 teaspoons brown sugar
- 1 cup nonfat Greek yogurt

Directions:

1. Preheat your broiler.
2. Arrange orange slices in a baking pan.
3. In a bowl, mix the cardamom and sugar.
4. Sprinkle mixture on top of the oranges. Broil for 5 minutes.
5. Serve oranges with yogurt.

Nutrition:
168 Calories
26.9g Carbohydrate
6.8g Protein

960. Frozen Lemon & Blueberry

Preparation Time: 5 minutes
Cooking Time: 10 minutes
Servings: 4
Ingredients:

- 6 cup fresh blueberries
- 8 sprigs fresh thyme
- ¾ cup light brown sugar
- 1 teaspoon lemon zest
- ¼ cup lemon juice
- 2 cups water

Directions:

1.Add blueberries, thyme and sugar in a pan over medium heat.
2.Cook for 6 to 8 minutes.
3.Transfer mixture to a blender.
4.Remove thyme sprigs.
5.Stir in the remaining ingredients.
6.Pulse until smooth.
7.Strain mixture and freeze for 1 hour.
Nutrition:
78 Calories
20g Carbohydrate
3g Protein

961. Peanut Butter Choco Chip Cookies

Preparation Time: 5 minutes
Cooking Time: 10 minutes
Servings: 4
Ingredients:

- 1 egg
- ½ cup light brown sugar
- 1 cup natural unsweetened peanut butter
- Pinch salt
- ¼ cup dark chocolate chips

Directions:
1.Preheat your oven to 375 degrees F.
2.Mix egg, sugar, peanut butter, salt and chocolate chips in a bowl.
3.Form into cookies and place in a baking pan.
4.Bake the cookie for 10 minutes.
5.Let cool before serving.
Nutrition:
159 Calories
12g Carbohydrate
4.3g Protein

962. Watermelon Sherbet

Preparation Time: 5 minutes
Cooking Time: 3 minutes
Servings: 4
Ingredients:

- 6 cups watermelon, sliced into cubes
- 14 oz. almond milk
- 1 tablespoon honey
- ¼ cup lime juice

- Salt to taste

Directions:
1.Freeze watermelon for 4 hours.
2.Add frozen watermelon and other ingredients in a blender.
3.Blend until smooth.
4.Transfer to a container with seal.
5.Seal and freeze for 4 hours.
Nutrition:
132 Calories
24.5g Carbohydrate
3.1g Protein

963. Strawberry & Mango Ice Cream

Preparation Time: 5 minutes
Cooking Time: 10 minutes
Servings: 4
Ingredients:

- 8 oz. strawberries, sliced
- 12 oz. mango, sliced into cubes
- 1 tablespoon lime juice

Directions:
1.Add all ingredients in a food processor.
2.Pulse for 2 minutes.
3.Chill before serving.
Nutrition:
70 Calories
17.4g Carbohydrate
1.1g Protein

964. Sparkling Fruit Drink

Preparation Time: 5 minutes
Cooking Time: 10 minutes
Servings: 4
Ingredients:

- 8 oz. unsweetened grape juice
- 8 oz. unsweetened apple juice
- 8 oz. unsweetened orange juice
- 1 qt. homemade ginger ale
- Ice

Directions:
1.Makes 7 servings. Mix first 4 ingredients together in a pitcher. Stir in ice cubes and 9 ounces of the beverage to each glass. Serve immediately.

Nutrition:
60 Calories
1.1g Protein

965. Tiramisu Shots

Preparation Time: 5 minutes
Cooking Time: 10 minutes
Servings: 4
Ingredients:

- 1 pack silken tofu
- 1 oz. dark chocolate, finely chopped
- ¼ cup sugar substitute
- 1 teaspoon lemon juice
- ¼ cup brewed espresso
- Pinch salt
- 24 slices angel food cake
- Cocoa powder (unsweetened)

Directions:
1. Add tofu, chocolate, sugar substitute, lemon juice, espresso and salt in a food processor.
2. Pulse until smooth.
3. Add angel food cake pieces into shot glasses.
4. Drizzle with the cocoa powder.
5. Pour the tofu mixture on top.
6. Top with the remaining angel food cake pieces.
7. Chill for 30 minutes and serve.
Nutrition:
75 Calories
12g Carbohydrate
2.9g Protein

966. Ice Cream Brownie Cake

Preparation Time: 5 minutes
Cooking Time: 10 minutes
Servings: 4
Ingredients:

- Cooking spray
- 12 oz. no-sugar brownie mix
- ¼ cup oil
- 2 egg whites
- 3 tablespoons water
- 2 cups sugar-free ice cream

Directions:
1. Preheat your oven to 325 degrees F.
2. Spray your baking pan with oil.
3. Mix brownie mix, oil, egg whites and water in a bowl.
4. Pour into the baking pan.
5. Bake for 25 minutes.
6. Let cool.
7. Freeze brownie for 2 hours.
8. Spread ice cream over the brownie.
9. Freeze for 8 hours.
Nutrition:
198 Calories
33g Carbohydrate
3g Protein

967. Berry Sorbet

Preparation time: 10 minutes
Cooking time: 20 minutes
Servings: 6
Ingredients:

- Water, 2 c
- Blend strawberries, 2 c
- Spelt Flour, 1.5 tsp.
- Date sugar, .5 c

Directions:
1. Add the water into a large pot and let the water begin to warm. Add the flour and date sugar and stir until dissolved. Allow this mixture to start boiling and continue to cook for around ten minutes. It should have started to thicken. Take off the heat and set to the side to cool.
2. Once the syrup has cooled off, add in the strawberries, and stir well to combine.
3. Pour into a container that is freezer safe and put it into the freezer until frozen.
4. Take sorbet out of the freezer, cut into chunks, and put it either into a blender or a food processor. Hit the pulse button until the mixture is creamy.
5. Pour this into the same freezer-safe container and put it back into the freezer for four hours.
Nutrition:
Calories: 99
Carbohydrates: 8 g

968. Quinoa Porridge

Preparation time: 5 minutes
Cooking time: 15 minutes
Servings: 04
Ingredients:

- Zest of one lime

- Coconut milk, .5 c
- Cloves, .5 tsp.
- Ground ginger, 1.5 tsp.
- Spring water, 2 c
- Quinoa, 1 c
- Grated apple, 1

Directions:

1.   Cook the quinoa. Follow the instructions on the package. When the quinoa has been cooked, drain well. Place it back into the pot and stir in spices.

2.   Add coconut milk and stir well to combine.

3.   Grate the apple now and stir well.

4.   Divide equally into bowls and add the lime zest on top. Sprinkle with nuts and seeds of choice.

Nutrition:

Calories: 180

Fat: 3 g

Carbohydrates: 40 g

Protein: 10 g

969. Apple Quinoa

Preparation time: 15 minutes

Cooking time: 30 minutes

Servings: 04

Ingredients:

- Coconut oil, 1 tbsp.
- Ginger
- Key lime .5
- Apple, 1
- Quinoa, .5 c
- Optional toppings
- Seeds
- Nuts
- Berries

Directions:

1.   Fix the quinoa according to the instructions on the package. When you are getting close to the end of the **Cooking time**, grate in the apple and cook for 30 seconds.

2.   Zest the lime into the quinoa and squeeze the juice in. Stir in the coconut oil.

3.   Divide evenly into bowls and sprinkle with some ginger.

4.   You can add in some berries, nuts, and seeds right before you eat.

Nutrition:

Calories: 146

Fiber: 2.3 g

Fat: 8.3 g

970. Kamut Porridge

Preparation time: 10 minutes

Cooking time: 25 minutes

Servings: 04

Ingredients:

- Agave syrup, 4 tbsp.
- Coconut oil, 1 tbsp.
- Sea salt, .5 tsp.
- Coconut milk, 3.75 c
- Kamut berries, 1 c
- Optional toppings
- Berries
- Coconut chips
- Ground nutmeg
- Ground cloves

Directions:

1.   You need to "crack" the Kamut berries. You can try this by placing the berries into a food processor and pulsing until you have 1.25 cups of Kamut.

2.   Place the cracked Kamut in a pot with salt and coconut milk. Give it a good stir in order to combine everything. Allow this mixture to come to a full rolling boil and then turn the heat down until the mixture is simmering. Stir every now and then until the Kamut has thickened to your likeness. This normally takes about ten minutes.

3.   Take off heat, stir in agave syrup and coconut oil.

4.   Garnish with toppings of choice and enjoy.

Nutrition:

Calories: 114

Protein: 5 g

Carbohydrates: 24g

Fiber: 4 g

971. Hot Kamut With Peaches, Walnuts, And Coconut

Preparation time: 10 minutes

Cooking time: 35 minutes

Servings: 04

Ingredients:

- Toasted coconut, 4 tbsp.
- Toasted and chopped walnuts, .5 c

- Chopped dried peaches, 8
- Coconut milk, 3 c
- Kamut cereal, 1 c

Directions:

1. Mix the coconut milk into a saucepan and allow it to warm up. When it begins simmering, add in the Kamut. Let this cook about 15 minutes, while stirring every now and then.

2. When done, divide evenly into bowls and top with the toasted coconut, walnuts, and peaches.

3. You could even go one more and add some fresh berries.

Nutrition:

Calories: 156
Protein: 5.8 g
Carbohydrates: 25 g
Fiber: 6 g

972. Overnight "Oats"

Preparation time: 5 minutes
Cooking time: 0 minutes
Servings: 04
Ingredients:

- Berry of choice, .5 c
- Walnut butter, .5 tbsp.
- Burro banana, .5
- Ginger, .5 tsp.
- Coconut milk, .5 c
- Hemp seeds, .5 c

Directions:

1. Put the hemp seeds, salt, and coconut milk into a glass jar. Mix well.

2. Place the lid on the jar then put in the refrigerator to sit overnight.

3. The next morning, add the ginger, berries, and banana. Stir well and enjoy.

Nutrition:

Calories: 139
Fat: 4.1 g
Protein: 9 g
Sugar: 7 g

973. Blueberry Cupcakes

Preparation time: 15 minutes
Cooking time: 40 minutes

Servings: 04
Ingredients:

- Grapeseed oil
- Sea salt, .5 tsp.
- Sea moss gel, .25 c
- Agave, .3 c
- Blueberries, .5 c
- Teff flour, .75 c
- Spelt flour, .75 c
- Coconut milk, 1 c

Directions:

1. Warm your oven to 365. Place paper liners into a muffin tin.

2. Place sea moss gel, sea salt, agave, flour, and milk in large bowl. Mix well to combine. Gently fold in blueberries.

3. Gently pour batter into paper liners. Place in oven and bake 30 minutes.

4. They are done if they have turned a nice golden color, and they spring back when you touch them.

Nutrition:

Calories: 85
Fat: 0.7 g
Carbohydrates: 12 g
Protein: 1.4 g
Fiber: 5 g

974. Brazil Nut Cheese

Preparation time: 2 hours
Cooking time: 0 minutes
Servings: 04
Ingredients:

- Grapeseed oil, 2 tsp.
- Water, 1.5 c
- Hemp milk, 1.5 c
- Cayenne, .5 tsp.
- Onion powder, 1 tsp.
- Juice of .5 lime
- Sea salt, 2 tsp.
- Brazil nuts, 1 lb.
- Onion powder, 1 tsp.

Directions:

1. You will need to start process by soaking the Brazil nuts in some water. You just put the nuts into a bowl and make sure the water covers them. Soak no less than two hours or overnight. Overnight would be best.

2. Now you need to put everything except water into a food processor or blender.

3. Add just .5 cups water and blend for two minutes

4. Continue adding .5 cup water and blending until you have the consistency you want.

5. Scrape into an airtight container and enjoy.

Nutrition:

Calories: 187.

Protein: 4.1 g

Fat: 19 g

Carbs: 3.3 g

Fiber: 2.1 g

975. Slow Cooker Peaches

Preparation Time: 10 minutes

Cooking time: 4 hours 20 minutes

Servings: 4-6

Ingredients

- 4 cups peaches, sliced
- 2/3 cup rolled oats
- 1/3 cup Bisques
- 1/4 teaspoon cinnamon
- 1/2 cup brown sugar
- 1/2 cup granulated sugar

Directions:

1. Spray the slow cooker pot with a cooking spray.

2. Mix oats, Bisques, cinnamon and all the sugars in the pot.

3. Add peaches and stir well to combine. Cook on low for 4-6 hours.

Nutrition: 617 calories; 3.6 g fat; 13 g total carbs; 9 g protein

976. Pumpkin Custard

Preparation Time: 10 minutes

Cooking time: 2 hours 30 minutes

Servings: 6

Ingredients

- 1/2 cup almond flour
- 4 eggs
- 1 cup pumpkin puree
- 1/2 cup stevia/erythritol blend, granulated
- 1/8 teaspoon sea salt
- 1 teaspoon vanilla extract or maple flavoring
- 4 tablespoons butter, ghee, or coconut oil melted
- 1 teaspoon pumpkin pie spice

Directions:

1. Grease or spray a slow cooker with butter or coconut oil spray.

2. In a medium mixing bowl, beat the eggs until smooth. Then add in the sweetener.

3. To the egg mixture, add in the pumpkin puree along with vanilla or maple extract.

4. Then add almond flour to the mixture along with the pumpkin pie spice and salt. Add melted butter, coconut oil or ghee.

5. Transfer the mixture into a slow cooker. Close the lid. Cook for 2-2 ¾ hours on low.

6. When through, serve with whipped cream, and then sprinkle with little nutmeg if need be. Enjoy!

7. Set slow-cooker to the low setting. Cook for 2-2.45 hours, and begin checking at the two-hour mark. Serve warm with stevia sweetened whipped cream and a sprinkle of nutmeg.

Nutrition: 147 calories; 12 g fat; 4 g total carbs; 5 g protein

977. Blueberry Lemon Custard Cake

Preparation Time: 10 minutes

Cooking time: 3 hours

Servings: 12

Ingredients

- 6 eggs, separated
- 2 cups light cream
- 1/2 cup coconut flour
- 1/2 teaspoon salt
- 2 teaspoon lemon zest
- 1/2 cup granulated sugar substitute
- 1/3 cup lemon juice
- 1/2 cup blueberries fresh
- 1 teaspoon lemon liquid stevia

Directions:

1. Into a stand mixer, add the egg whites and whip them well until stiff peaks have formed; set aside.

2. Whisk the yolks together with the remaining ingredients except blueberries, to form batter.

3. When done, fold egg whites into the formed batter a little at a time until slightly combined.

4. Grease the crock pot and then pour in the mixture. Then sprinkle batter with the blueberries.

5. Close the lid then cook for 3 hours on low. When the cooking time is over, open the lid and let cool for an hour, and then let chill in the refrigerator for at least 2 hours or overnight.

6. Serve cold with little sugar free whipped cream and enjoy!

Nutrition: 165 calories; 10 g fat; 14 g total carbs; 4 g protein

978. Sugar Free Carrot Cake

Cooking time: 4 hours

Servings: 8

Ingredients

For Carrot cake:

- 2 eggs
- 1 1/2 almond flour
- 1/2 cup butter, melted
- ¼ cup heavy cream
- 1 teaspoon baking powder
- 1 teaspoon vanilla extract or almond extract, optional
- 1 cup sugar substitute
- 1 cup carrots, finely shredded
- 1 teaspoon cinnamon
- ¼ teaspoon nutmeg
- 1/8 teaspoon allspice
- 1 teaspoon ginger
- 1/2 teaspoon baking soda

For cream cheese frosting:

- 1 cup confectioner's sugar substitute
- ¼ cup butter, softened
- 1 teaspoon almond extract
- 4 oz. cream cheese, softened

Directions:

1. Grease a loaf pan well and then set it aside.

2. Using a mixer, combine butter together with eggs, vanilla, sugar substitute and heavy cream in a mixing bowl, until well blended.

3. Combine almond flour together with baking powder, spices and the baking soda in another bowl until well blended.

4. When done, combine the wet ingredients together with the dry ingredients until well blended, and then stir in carrots.

5. Pour the mixer into the prepared loaf pan, and then place the pan into a slow cooker on a trivet. Add 1 cup water inside.

6. Cook for about 4-5 hours on low. Be aware that the cake will be very moist.

7. When the cooking time is over, let the cake cool completely.

8. To prepare the cream cheese frosting: blend the cream cheese together with extract, butter and powdered sugar substitute until frosting is formed.

9. Top the cake with the frosting.

Nutrition: 299 calories; 25.4 g fat; 15 g total carbs; 4 g protein

979. Sugar Free Chocolate Molten Lava Cake

Preparation Time: 10 minutes

Cooking time: 3 hours

Servings: 12

Ingredients

- 3 egg yolks
- 1 1/2 cups Swerve sweetener, divided
- 1 teaspoon baking powder
- 1/2 cup flour, gluten free
- 3 whole eggs
- 5 tablespoons cocoa powder, unsweetened, divided
- 4 oz. chocolate chips, sugar free
- 1/2 teaspoon salt
- 1/2 teaspoon vanilla liquid stevia
- 1/2 cup butter, melted, cooled
- 2 cups hot water
- 1 teaspoon vanilla extract

Directions:

1. Grease the crockpot well with cooking spray.

2. Whisk 1 ¼ cups of swerve together with flour, salt, baking powder and 3 tablespoons cocoa powder in a bowl.

3. Stir the cooled melted butter together with eggs, yolks, liquid stevia and the vanilla extract in a separate bowl.

4. When done, add the wet ingredients to the dry ingredient until nicely combined, and then pour the mixture into the prepared crock pot.

5. Then top the mixture in the crockpot with chocolate chips.

6. Whisk the rest of the swerve sweetener and the remaining cocoa powder with the hot water, and then pour this mixture over the chocolate chips top.

7. Close the lid and cook for 3 hours on low. When the cooking time is over, let cool a bit and then serve. Enjoy!

Nutrition: 157 calories; 13 g fat; 10.5 g total carbs; 3.9 g protein

980. Chocolate Quinoa Brownies

Preparation Time: 10 minutes
Cooking time: 2 hours
Servings: 16
Ingredients

- 2 eggs
- 3 cups quinoa, cooked
- 1 teaspoon vanilla liquid stevia
- 1 ¼ chocolate chips, sugar free
- 1 teaspoon vanilla extract
- 1/3 cup flaxseed ground
- ¼ teaspoon salt
- 1/3 cup cocoa powder, unsweetened
- 1/2 teaspoon baking powder
- 1 teaspoon pure stevia extract
- 1/2 cup applesauce, unsweetened

Sugar- frees frosting:

- ¼ cup heavy cream
- 1 teaspoon chocolate liquid stevia
- ¼ cup cocoa powder, unsweetened
- 1/2 teaspoon vanilla extract

DIRECTIONS:

1. Add all the ingredients to a food processor. Then process until well incorporated.

2. Line a crock pot with a parchment paper, and then spread the batter into the lined pot.

3. Close the lid and cook for 4 hours on LOW or 2 hours on HIGH. Let cool.

4. Prepare the frosting. Whisk all the ingredients together and then microwave for 20 seconds. Taste and adjust on sweetener if desired.

5. When the frosting is ready, stir it well again and then pour it over the sliced brownies.

6. Serve and enjoy!

Nutrition: 133 calories; 7.9 g fat; 18.4 g total carbs; 4.3 g protein

981. Blueberry Crisp

Preparation Time: 10 minutes
Cooking time: 3-4 hours
Servings: 10
Ingredients

- 1/4 cup butter, melted
- 24 oz. blueberries, frozen
- 3/4 teaspoon salt
- 1 1/2 cups rolled oats, coarsely ground
- 3/4 cup almond flour, blanched
- 1/4 cup coconut oil, melted
- 6 tablespoons sweetener
- 1 cup pecans or walnuts, coarsely chopped

Directions:

1. Using a non-stick cooking spray, spray the slow cooker pot well.

2. Into a bowl, add ground oats and chopped nuts along with salt, blanched almond flour, brown sugar, stevia granulated sweetener, and then stir in the coconut/butter mixture. Stir well to combine.

3. When done, spread crisp topping over blueberries. Cook for 3-4 hours, until the mixture has become bubbling hot and you can smell the blueberries.

4. Serve while still hot with the whipped cream or the ice cream if desired. Enjoy!

Nutrition: 261 calories; 16.6 g fat; 32 g total carbs; 4 g protein

982. Maple Custard

Preparation Time: 10 minutes
Cooking time: 2 hours
Servings: 6
Ingredients

- 1 teaspoon maple extract
- 2 egg yolks
- 1 cup heavy cream
- 2 eggs
- 1/2 cup whole milk
- 1/4 teaspoon salt
- 1/4 cup Sukrin Gold or any sugar-free brown sugar substitute
- 1/2 teaspoon cinnamon

Directions:

1.   Combine all ingredients together in a blender, process well.

2.   Grease 6 ramekins and then pour the batter evenly into each ramekin.

3.   To the bottom of the slow cooker, add 4 ramekins and then arrange the remaining 2 against the side of a slow cooker, and not at the top of bottom ramekins.

4.   Close the lid and cook on high for 2 hours, until the center is cooked through but the middle is still jiggly.

5.   Let cool at a room temperature for an hour after removing from the slow cooker, and then chill in the fridge for at least 2 hours.

6.   Serve and enjoy with a sprinkle of cinnamon and little sugar free whipped cream.

Nutrition: 190 calories; 18 g fat; 2 g total carbs; 4 g protein

983. Raspberry Cream Cheese Coffee Cake

Preparation Time: 10 minutes
Cooking time: 4 hours
Servings: 12
Ingredients

- 1 1/4 almond flour
- 2/3 cup water
- 1/2 cup Swerve
- 3 eggs
- 1/4 cup coconut flour
- 1/4 cup protein powder
- 1/4 teaspoon salt
- 1/2 teaspoon vanilla extract
- 1 1/2 teaspoon baking powder
- 6 tablespoons butter, melted

For the Filling:

- 1 1/2 cup fresh raspberries
- 8 oz. cream cheese
- 1 large egg
- 1/3 cup powdered Swerve
- 2 tablespoon whipping cream

DIRECTIONS:

1.   Grease the slow cooker pot. Prepare the cake batter. In a bowl, combine almond flour together with coconut flour, sweetener, baking powder, protein powder and salt, and then stir in the melted butter along with eggs and water until well combined. Set aside.

2.   Prepare the filling. Beat cream cheese thoroughly with the sweetener until have smoothened, and then beat in whipping cream along with the egg and vanilla extract until well combined.

3.   Assemble the cake. Spread around 2/3 of batter in the slow cooker as you smoothen the top using a spatula or knife.

4.   Pour cream cheese mixture over the batter in the pan, evenly spread it, and then sprinkle with raspberries. Add the rest of batter over filling.

5.   Cook for 3-4 hours on low. Let cool completely.

6.   Serve and enjoy!

Nutrition: 239 calories; 19.18 g fat; 6.9 g total carbs; 7.5 g protein

984. Pumpkin Pie Bars

Preparation Time: 10 minutes
Cooking time: 3 hours
Servings: 16
Ingredients
For the Crust:

- 3/4 cup coconut, shredded
- 4 tablespoons butter, unsalted, softened
- 1/4 cup cocoa powder, unsweetened
- 1/4 teaspoon salt
- 1/2 cup raw sunflower seeds or sunflower seed flour
- 1/4 cup confectioners Swerve

Filling:

- 2 teaspoons cinnamon liquid stevia
- 1 cup heavy cream
- 1 can pumpkin puree
- 6 eggs
- 1 tablespoon pumpkin pie spice
- 1/2 teaspoon salt
- 1 tablespoon vanilla extract
- 1/2 cup sugar-free chocolate chips, optional

Directions:

1.   Add all the crust ingredients to a food processor. Then process until fine crumbs are formed.

2.   Grease the slow cooker pan well. When done, press crust mixture onto the greased bottom.

3.   In a stand mixer, combine all the ingredients for the filling, and then blend well until combined.

4.   Top the filling with chocolate chips if using, and then pour the mixture onto the prepared crust.

5. Close the lid and cook for 3 hours on low. Open the lid and let cool for at least 30 minutes, and then place the slow cooker into the refrigerator for at least 3 hours.

6. Slice the pumpkin pie bar and serve it with sugar free whipped cream. Enjoy!

Nutrition: 169 calories; 15 g fat; 6 g total carbs; 4 g protein

985. Dark Chocolate Cake

Preparation Time: 10 minutes
Cooking time: 3 hours
Servings: 10
Ingredients

- 1 cup almond flour
- 3 eggs
- 2 tablespoons almond flour
- 1/4 teaspoon salt
- 1/2 cup Swerve Granular
- 3/4 teaspoon vanilla extract
- 2/3 cup almond milk, unsweetened
- 1/2 cup cocoa powder
- 6 tablespoons butter, melted
- 1 1/2 teaspoon baking powder
- 3 tablespoons unflavored whey protein powder or egg white protein powder
- 1/3 cup sugar-free chocolate chips, optional

Directions:

1. Grease the slow cooker well.

2. Whisk the almond flour together with cocoa powder, sweetener, whey protein powder, salt and baking powder in a bowl. Then stir in butter along with almond milk, eggs and the vanilla extract until well combined, and then stir in the chocolate chips if desired.

3. When done, pour into the slow cooker. Allow to cook for 2-2 1/2 hours on low.

4. When through, turn off the slow cooker and let the cake cool for about 20-30 minutes.

5. When cooled, cut the cake into pieces and serve warm with lightly sweetened whipped cream. Enjoy!

Nutrition: 205 calories; 17 g fat; 8.4 g total carbs; 12 g protein

986. Lemon Custard

Preparation Time: 10 minutes
Cooking time: 3 hours
Servings: 4
Ingredients:

- 2 cups whipping cream or coconut cream
- 5 egg yolks
- 1 tablespoon lemon zest
- 1 teaspoon vanilla extract
- 1/4 cup fresh lemon juice, squeezed
- 1/2 teaspoon liquid stevia
- Lightly sweetened whipped cream

Directions:

1. Whisk egg yolks together with lemon zest, liquid stevia, lemon zest and vanilla in a bowl, and then whisk in heavy cream.

2. Divide the mixture among 4 small jars or ramekins.

3. To the bottom of a slow cooker add a rack, and then add ramekins on top of the rack and add enough water to cover half of ramekins.

4. Close the lid and cook for 3 hours on low. Remove ramekins.

5. Let cool to room temperature, and then place into the refrigerator to cool completely for about 3 hours.

6. When through, top with the whipped cream and serve. Enjoy!

Nutrition: 319 calories; 30 g fat; 3 g total carbs; 7 g protein

987. Baked Stuffed Pears

Preparation time: 15 minutes
Cooking time: 35 minutes
Servings: 04
Ingredients:

- Agave syrup, 4 tbsp.
- Cloves, .25 tsp.
- Chopped walnuts, 4 tbsp.
- Currants, 1 c
- Pears, 4

Directions:

1. Make sure your oven has been warmed to 375.

2. Slice the pears in two lengthwise and remove the core. To get the pear to lay flat, you can slice a small piece off the back side.

3. Place the agave syrup, currants, walnuts, and cloves in a small bowl and mix well. Set this to the side to be used later.

4. Put the pears on a cookie sheet that has parchment paper on it. Make sure the cored sides are facing up. Sprinkle each pear half with about .5 tablespoon of the chopped walnut mixture.

5.	Place into the oven and cook for 25 to 30 minutes. Pears should be tender.

Nutrition:

Calories: 103.9

Fiber: 3.1 g

Carbohydrates: 22 g

## 988.	Butternut Squash Pie

Preparation time: 25 minutes

Cooking time: 35 minutes

Servings: 04

Ingredients:

- For the Crust
- Cold water
- Agave, splash
- Sea salt, pinch
- Grapeseed oil, .5 c
- Coconut flour, .5 c
- Spelt Flour, 1 c
- For the Filling
- Butternut squash, peeled, chopped
- Water
- Allspice, to taste
- Agave syrup, to taste
- Hemp milk, 1 c
- Sea moss, 4 tbsp.

Directions:

1.	You will need to warm your oven to 350.

2.	For the Crust

3.	Place the grapeseed oil and water into the refrigerator to get it cold. This will take about one hour.

4.	Place all **Ingredients** into a large bowl. Now you need to add in the cold water a little bit in small amounts until a dough form. Place this onto a surface that has been sprinkled with some coconut flour. Knead for a few minutes and roll the dough as thin as you can get it. Carefully, pick it up and place it inside a pie plate.

5.	Place the butternut squash into a Dutch oven and pour in enough water to cover. Bring this to a full rolling boil. Let this cook until the squash has become soft.

6.	Completely drain and place into bowl. Using a potato masher, mash the squash. Add in some allspice and agave to taste. Add in the sea moss and hemp milk. Using a hand mixer, blend well. Pour into the pie crust.

7.	Place into an oven and bake for about one hour.

Nutrition:

Calories: 245

Carbohydrates: 50 g

Fat: 10 g

## 989.	Coconut Chia Cream Pot

Preparation time: 5 minutes

Cooking time: 5 minutes

Servings: 04

Ingredients:

- Date, one (1)
- Coconut milk (organic), one (1) cup
- Coconut yogurt, one (1) cup
- Vanilla extract, ½ teaspoon
- Chia seeds, ¼ cup
- Sesame seeds, one (1) teaspoon
- Flaxseed (ground), one (1) tablespoon or flax meal, one (1) tablespoon
- Toppings:
- Fig, one (1)
- Blueberries, one (1) handful
- Mixed nuts (brazil nuts, almonds, pistachios, macadamia, etc.)
- Cinnamon (ground), one teaspoon

Directions:

1.	First, blend the date with coconut milk (the idea is to sweeten the coconut milk).

2.	Get a mixing bowl and add the coconut milk with the vanilla, sesame seeds, chia seeds, and flax meal.

3.	Refrigerate for between twenty to thirty minutes or wait till the chia expands.

4.	To serve, pour a layer of coconut yogurt in a small glass, then add the chia mix, followed by pouring another layer of the coconut yogurt.

5.	It's alkaline, creamy and delicious.

Nutrition:

Calories: 310

Carbohydrates: 39 g

Protein: 4 g

Fiber: 8.1 g

## 990.	Chocolate Avocado Mousse

Preparation time: 10 minutes

Cooking time: 5 minutes

Servings: 04

Ingredients:

- Coconut water, 2/3 cup
- Avocado, ½ hass
- Raw cacao, 2 teaspoons
- Vanilla, 1 teaspoon
- Dates, three (3)
- Sea salt, 0ne (1) teaspoon
- Dark chocolate shavings

Directions:
1. Blend all **Ingredients**.
2. Blast until it becomes thick and smooth, as you wish.
3. Put in a fridge and allow it to get firm.

Nutrition:
Calories: 181.8
Fat: 151. g
Protein: 12 g

991. Chia Vanilla Coconut Pudding

Preparation time: 5 minutes
Cooking time: 5 minutes
Servings: 2
Ingredients:

- Coconut oil, 2 tablespoons
- Raw cashew, ½ cup
- Coconut water, ½ cup
- Cinnamon, 1 teaspoon
- Dates (pitted), 3
- Vanilla, 2 teaspoons
- Coconut flakes (unsweetened), 1 teaspoon
- Salt (Himalayan or Celtic Grey)
- Chia seeds, 6 tablespoons
- Cinnamon or pomegranate seeds for garnish (optional)

Directions:
1. Get a blender, add all the **Ingredients** (minus the pomegranate and chia seeds), and blend for about forty to sixty seconds.
2. Reduce the blender speed to the lowest and add the chia seeds.
3. Pour the content into an airtight container and put in a refrigerator for five to six hours.
4. To serve, you can garnish with the cinnamon powder of pomegranate seeds.

Nutrition:

Calories: 201
Fat: 10 g
Sodium: 32.8 mg

992. Sweet Tahini Dip with Ginger Cinnamon Fruit

Preparation time: 10 minutes
Cooking time: 5 minutes
Servings: 2
Ingredients:

- Cinnamon, one (1) teaspoon
- Green apple, one (1)
- Pear, one (1)
- Fresh ginger, two (2) – three (3)
- Celtic sea salt, one (1) teaspoon
- Ingredient for sweet Tahini
- Almond butter (raw), three (3) teaspoons
- Tahini (one big scoop), three (3) teaspoons
- Coconut oil, two (2) teaspoons
- Cayenne (optional), ¼ teaspoons
- Wheat-free tamari, two (2) teaspoons
- Liquid coconut nectar, one (1) teaspoon

Directions:
1. Get a clean mixing bowl.
2. Grate the ginger, add cinnamon, sea salt and mix together in the bowl.
3. Dice apple and pear into little cubes, turn into the bowl and mix.
4. Get a mixing bowl and mix all the **Ingredients**.
5. Then add the Sprinkle the Sweet Tahini Dip all over the Ginger Cinnamon Fruit.
6. Serve.

Nutrition:
Calories: 109
Fat: 10.8 g
Sodium: 258 mg

993. Coconut Butter and Chopped Berries with Mint

Preparation time: 5 minutes
Cooking time: 5 minutes
Servings: 04
Ingredients:

- Chopped mint, one (1) tablespoon

- Coconut butter (melted), two (2) tablespoons
- Mixed berries (strawberries, blueberries, and raspberries)

Directions:

1. Get a small bowl and add the berries.
2. Drizzle the melted coconut butter and sprinkle the mint.
3. Serve.

Nutrition:

Calories: 159

Fat: 12 g

Carbohydrates: 18 g

994. Alkaline Raw Pumpkin Pie

Preparation time: 5 minutes

Cooking time: 5 minutes

Servings: 04

Ingredients:

Ingredients for Pie Crust

- Cinnamon, one (1) teaspoon
- Dates/Turkish apricots, one (1) cup
- Raw almonds, one (1) cup
- Coconut flakes (unsweetened), one (1) cup

Ingredients for Pie Filling

- Dates, six (6)
- Cinnamon, ½ teaspoon
- Nutmeg, ½ teaspoon
- Pecans (soaked overnight), one (1) cup
- Organic pumpkin Blends (12 oz.), 1 ¼ cup
- Nutmeg, ½ teaspoon
- Sea salt (Himalayan or Celtic Sea Salt), ¼ teaspoon
- Vanilla, 1 teaspoon
- Gluten-free tamari

Directions:

Directions for pie crust

1. Get a food processor and blend all the pie crust **Ingredients** at the same time.
2. Make sure the mixture turns oily and sticky before you stop mixing.
3. Put the mixture in a pie pan and mold against the sides and floor, to make it stick properly.

Directions for the pie filling

1. Mix Ingredients together in a blender.
2. Add the mixture to fill in the pie crust.
3. Pour some cinnamon on top.

4. Then refrigerate till it's cold.
5. Then mold.

Nutrition:

Calories 135

Calories from Fat 41.4.

Total Fat 4.6 g

Cholesterol 11.3 mg

995. Strawberry Sorbet

Preparation time: 5 minutes

Cooking time: 4 Hours

Servings: 4

Ingredients:

- 2 cups of Strawberries*
- 1 1/2 teaspoons of Spelt Flour
- 1/2 cup of Date Sugar
- 2 cups of Spring Water

Directions:

- Add Date Sugar, Spring Water, and Spelt Flour to a medium pot and boil on low heat for about ten minutes. Mixture should thicken, like syrup.
- Remove the pot from the heat and allow it to cool.
- After cooling, add Blend Strawberry and mix gently.
- Put mixture in a container and freeze.
- Cut it into pieces, put the sorbet into a processor and blend until smooth.
- Put everything back in the container and leave in the refrigerator for at least four hours.
- Serve and enjoy your Strawberry Sorbet!

Nutrition:

Calories: 198

Carbohydrates: 28 g

996. Blueberry Muffins

Preparation time: 5 minutes

Cooking time: 1 Hour

Servings: 3

Ingredients:

- 1/2 cup of Blueberries
- 3/4 cup of Teff Flour
- 3/4 cup of Spelt Flour
- 1/3 cup of Agave Syrup
- 1/2 teaspoon of Pure Sea Salt
- 1 cup of Coconut Milk

- 1/4 cup of Sea Moss Gel (optional, check information)
- Grape Seed Oil

Directions:
1. Preheat your oven to 365 degrees Fahrenheit.
2. Grease or line 6 standard muffin cups.
3. Add Teff, Spelt flour, Pure Sea Salt, Coconut Milk, Sea Moss Gel, and Agave Syrup to a large bowl. Mix them together.
4. Add Blueberries to the mixture and mix well.
5. Divide muffin batter among the 6 muffin cups.
6. Bake for 30 minutes until golden brown.
7. Serve and enjoy your Blueberry Muffins!

Nutrition:
Calories: 65
Fat: 0.7 g
Carbohydrates: 12 g
Protein: 1.4 g
Fiber: 5 g

997. Banana Strawberry Ice Cream

Preparation time: 5 minutes
Cooking time: 4 Hours
Servings: 5
Ingredients:
- 1 cup of Strawberry*
- 5 quartered Baby Bananas*
- 1/2 Avocado, chopped
- 1 tablespoon of Agave Syrup
- 1/4 cup of Homemade Walnut Milk

Directions:
1. Mix Ingredients into the blender and blend them well.
2. Taste. If it is too thick, add extra Milk or Agave Syrup if you want it sweeter.
3. Put in a container with a lid and allow to freeze for at least 5 to 6 hours.
4. Serve it and enjoy your Banana Strawberry Ice Cream!

Nutrition:
Calories: 200
Fat: 0.5 g
Carbohydrates: 44 g

998. Homemade Whipped Cream

Preparation time: 5 minutes
Cooking time: 10 Minutes
Servings: 1 Cup
Ingredients:
- 1 cup of Aquafaba
- 1/4 cup of Agave Syrup

Directions:
1. Add Agave Syrup and Aquafaba into a bowl.
2. Mix at high speed around 5 minutes with a stand mixer or 10 to 15 minutes with a hand mixer.
3. Serve and enjoy your Homemade Whipped Cream!

Nutrition:
Calories: 21
Fat: 0g
Sodium: 0.3g
Carbohydrates: 5.3g
Fiber: 0g
Sugars: 4.7g
Protein: 0g

999. Chocolate Crunch Bars

Preparation time: 5 minutes
Cooking time: 5 minutes
Servings: 4
Ingredients:
- 1 1/2 cups sugar-free chocolate chips
- 1 cup almond butter
- Stevia to taste
- 1/4 cup coconut oil
- 3 cups pecans, chopped

Directions:
1. Layer an 8-inch baking pan with parchment paper.
2. Mix chocolate chips with butter, coconut oil, and sweetener in a bowl.
3. Melt it by heating in a microwave for 2 to 3 minutes until well mixed.
4. Stir in nuts and seeds. Mix gently.
5. Pour this batter carefully into the baking pan and spread evenly.
6. Refrigerate for 2 to 3 hours.
7. Slice and serve.

Nutrition:
Calories 316

Total Fat 30.9 g

Saturated Fat 8.1 g

Cholesterol 0 mg

Total Carbs 8.3 g

Sugar 1.8 g

Fiber 3.8 g

Sodium 8 mg

Protein 6.4 g

1000. Homemade Protein Bar

Preparation time: 5 minutes

Cooking time: 10 minutes

Servings: 4

Ingredients:

- 1 cup nut butter
- 4 tablespoons coconut oil
- 2 scoops vanilla protein
- Stevia, to taste
- ½ teaspoon sea salt
- Optional **Ingredients:**
- 1 teaspoon cinnamon

1. **Directions:**
2. Mix coconut oil with butter, protein, stevia, and salt in a dish.
3. Stir in cinnamon and chocolate chip.
4. Press the mixture firmly and freeze until firm.
5. Cut the crust into small bars.
6. Serve and enjoy.

Nutrition:

Calories 179

Total Fat 15.7 g

Saturated Fat 8 g

Cholesterol 0 mg

Total Carbs 4.8 g

Sugar 3.6 g

Fiber 0.8 g

Sodium 43 mg

Protein 5.6 g

1001. Shortbread Cookies

Preparation time: 10 minutes

Cooking time: 70 minutes

Servings: 6

Ingredients:

- 2 1/2 cups almond flour
- 6 tablespoons nut butter

- 1/2 cup erythritol
- 1 teaspoon vanilla essence

Directions:

1. Preheat your oven to 350 degrees F.
2. Layer a cookie sheet with parchment paper.
3. Beat butter with erythritol until fluffy.
4. Stir in vanilla essence and almond flour. Mix well until becomes crumbly.
5. Spoon out a tablespoon of cookie dough onto the cookie sheet.
6. Add more dough to make as many cookies.
7. Bake for 15 minutes until brown.
8. Serve.

Nutrition:

Calories 288

Total Fat 25.3 g

Saturated Fat 6.7 g

Cholesterol 23 mg

Total Carbs 9.6 g

Sugar 0.1 g

Fiber 3.8 g

Sodium 74 mg

Potassium 3 mg

Protein 7.6 g

1002. Coconut Chip Cookies

Preparation time: 10 minutes

Cooking time: 15 minutes

Servings: 4

Ingredients:

- 1 cup almond flour
- ½ cup cacao nibs
- ½ cup coconut flakes, unsweetened
- 1/3 cup erythritol
- ½ cup almond butter
- ¼ cup nut butter, melted
- ¼ cup almond milk
- Stevia, to taste
- ¼ teaspoon sea salt

Directions:

1. Preheat your oven to 350 degrees F.
2. Layer a cookie sheet with parchment paper.
3. Add and then combine all the dry **Ingredients** in a glass bowl.

4.	Whisk in butter, almond milk, vanilla essence, stevia, Protein 6.5 g and almond butter.

5.	Beat well then stir in dry mixture. Mix well.

6.	Spoon out a tablespoon of cookie dough on the cookie sheet.

7.	Add more dough to make as many as 16 cookies.

8.	Flatten each cookie using your fingers.

9.	Bake for 25 minutes until golden brown.

10.	Let them sit for 15 minutes.

11.	Serve.

Nutrition:

Calories 192

Total Fat 17.44 g

Saturated Fat 11.5 g

Cholesterol 125 mg

Total Carbs 2.2 g

Sugar 1.4 g

Fiber 2.1 g

Sodium 135 mg

Protein 4.7 g

1003. Peanut Butter Bars

Preparation time: 10 minutes

Cooking time: 10 minutes

Servings: 6

Ingredients:

- 3/4 cup almond flour
- 2 oz. almond butter
- 1/4 cup Swerve
- 1/2 cup peanut butter
- 1/2 teaspoon vanilla

Directions:

1.	Combine all the **Ingredients** for bars.

2.	Transfer this mixture to 6-inch small pan. Press it firmly.

3.	Refrigerate for 30 minutes.

4.	Slice and serve.

Nutrition:

Calories 214

Total Fat 19 g

Saturated Fat 5.8 g

Cholesterol 15 mg

Total Carbs 6.5 g

Sugar 1.9 g

Fiber 2.1 g

Sodium 123 mg

1004. Zucchini Bread Pancakes

Preparation time: 15 minutes

Cooking time: 35 minutes

Servings: 3

Ingredients:

- Grapeseed oil, 1 tbsp.
- Chopped walnuts, .5 c
- Walnut milk, 2 c
- Shredded zucchini, 1 c
- Mashed burro banana, .25 c
- Date sugar, 2 tbsp.
- Kamut flour or spelt, 2 c

Directions:

1.	Place the date sugar and flour into a bowl. Whisk together.

2.	Add in the mashed banana and walnut milk. Stir until combined. Remember to scrape the bowl to get all the dry mixture. Add in walnuts and zucchini. Stir well until combined.

3.	Place the grapeseed oil onto a griddle and warm.

4.	Pour .25 cup batter on the hot griddle. Leave it along until bubbles begin forming on to surface. Carefully turn over the pancake and cook another four minutes until cooked through.

5.	Place the pancakes onto a serving plate and enjoy with some agave syrup.

Nutrition:

Calories: 246

Carbohydrates: 49.2 g

Fiber: 4.6 g

Protein: 7.8

1005. Flourless Chocolate Cake

Preparation time: 10 minutes

Cooking time: 45 minutes

Servings: 6

Ingredients:

- 1/2 Cup of stevia
- 12 Ounces of unsweetened baking chocolate
- 2/3 Cup of ghee
- 1/3 Cup of warm water
- ¼ Teaspoon of salt
- 4 Large pastured eggs
- 2 Cups of boiling water

Directions:

1. Line the bottom of a 9-inch pan of a spring form with a parchment paper.
2. Heat the water in a small pot; then add the salt and the stevia over the water until wait until the mixture becomes completely dissolved.
3. Melt the baking chocolate into a double boiler or simply microwave it for about 30 seconds.
4. Mix the melted chocolate and the butter in a large bowl with an electric mixer.
5. Beat in your hot mixture; then crack in the egg and whisk after adding each of the eggs.
6. Pour the obtained mixture into your prepared spring form tray.
7. Wrap the spring form tray with a foil paper.
8. Place the spring form tray in a large cake tray and add boiling water right to the outside; make sure the depth doesn't exceed 1 inch.
9. Bake the cake into the water bath for about 45 minutes at a temperature of about 350 F.
10. Remove the tray from the boiling water and transfer to a wire to cool.
11. Let the cake chill for an overnight in the refrigerator.
12. Serve and enjoy your delicious cake!

Nutrition:

Calories: 295 | Fat: 26g | Carbohydrates: 6g | Fiber: 4g | Protein: 8g

1006. Raspberry Cake With White Chocolate Sauce

Preparation time: 15 minutes

Cooking time: 60 minutes

Servings: 6

Ingredients:

- 5 Ounces of melted cacao butter
- 2 Ounces of grass-fed ghee
- 1/2 Cup of coconut cream
- 1 Cup of green banana flour

- 3 Teaspoons of pure vanilla
- 4 Large eggs
- 1/2 Cup of as Lakanto Monk Fruit
- 1 Teaspoon of baking powder
- 2 Teaspoons of apple cider vinegar
- 2 Cup of raspberries

For the white chocolate sauce:

- 3 and 1/2 ounces of cacao butter
- 1/2 Cup of coconut cream
- 2 Teaspoons of pure vanilla extract
- 1 Pinch of salt

Directions:

1. Preheat your oven to a temperature of about 280 degrees Fahrenheit.
2. Combine the green banana flour with the pure vanilla extract, the baking powder, the coconut cream, the eggs, the cider vinegar and the monk fruit and mix very well.
3. Leave the raspberries aside and line a cake loaf tin with a baking paper.
4. Pour in the batter into the baking tray and scatter the raspberries over the top of the cake.
5. Place the tray in your oven and bake it for about 60 minutes; in the meantime, prepare the sauce by

Directions for sauce:

6. Combine the cacao cream, the vanilla extract, the cacao butter and the salt in a saucepan over a low heat.
7. Mix all your ingredients with a fork to make sure the cacao butter mixes very well with the cream.
8. Remove from the heat and set aside to cool a little bit; but don't let it harden.
9. Drizzle with the chocolate sauce.
10. Scatter the cake with more raspberries.

11.   Slice your cake; then serve and enjoy it!

Nutrition:

Calories: 323| Fat: 31.5g | Carbohydrates: 9.9g | Fiber: 4g |Protein: 5g

1007. Ketogenic Lava Cake

Preparation time: 10 minutes

Cooking time: 10 minutes

Servings: 2

Ingredients:

• 2 Oz of dark chocolate; you should at least use chocolate of 85% cocoa solids

• 1 Tablespoon of super-fine almond flour

• 2 Oz of unsalted almond butter

• 2 Large eggs

Directions:

1.   Heat your oven to a temperature of about 350 Fahrenheit.

2.   Grease 2 heat proof ramekins with almond butter.

3.   Now, melt the chocolate and the almond butter and stir very well.

4.   Beat the eggs very well with a mixer.

5.   Add the eggs to the chocolate and the butter mixture and mix very well with almond flour and the swerve; then stir.

6.   Pour the dough into 2 ramekins.

7.   Bake for about 9 to 10 minutes.

8.   Turn the cakes over plates and serve with pomegranate seeds!

Nutrition:

Calories: 459| Fat: 39g | Carbohydrates: 3.5g | Fiber: 0.8g |Protein: 11.7g

1008. Ketogenic Cheese Cake

Preparation time: 15 minutes

Cooking time: 50 minutes

Servings: 6

Ingredients:

For the Almond Flour Cheesecake Crust:

• 2 Cups of Blanched almond flour

• 1/3 Cup of almond Butter

• 3 Tablespoons of Erythritol (powdered or granular)

• 1 Teaspoon of Vanilla extract

For the Keto Cheesecake Filling:

• 32 Oz of softened Cream cheese

• 1 and ¼ cups of powdered erythritol

• 3 Large Eggs

• 1 Tablespoon of Lemon juice

• 1 Teaspoon of Vanilla extract

Directions:

1.   Preheat your oven to a temperature of about 350 degrees F.

2.   Grease a spring form pan of 9" with cooking spray or just line its bottom with a parchment paper.

3.   In order to make the cheesecake rust, stir in the melted butter, the almond flour, the vanilla extract and the erythritol in a large bowl.

4.   The dough will get will be a bit crumbly; so, press it into the bottom of your prepared tray.

5.   Bake for about 12 minutes; then let cool for about 10 minutes.

6.   In the meantime, beat the softened cream cheese and the powdered sweetener at a low speed until it becomes smooth.

7.   Crack in the eggs and beat them in at a low to medium speed until it becomes fluffy. Make sure to add one a time.

8.   Add in the lemon juice and the vanilla extract and mix at a low to medium speed with a mixer.

9.   Pour your filling into your pan right on top of the crust. You can use a spatula to smooth the top of the cake.

10.   Bake for about 45 to 50 minutes.

11.   Remove the baked cheesecake from your oven and run a knife around its edge.

12.   Let the cake cool for about 4 hours in the refrigerator.

13.   Serve and enjoy your delicious cheese cake!

Nutrition:

Calories: 325 | Fat: 29g | Carbohydrates: 6g | Fiber: 1g | Protein: 7g

1009. Cake with Whipped Cream Icing

Preparation time: 20 minutes

Cooking time: 25 minutes

Servings: 7

Ingredients:

- ¾ Cup Coconut flour
- ¾ Cup of Swerve Sweetener
- 1/2 Cup of Cocoa powder
- 2 Teaspoons of Baking powder
- 6 Large Eggs
- 2/3 Cup of Heavy Whipping Cream
- 1/2 Cup of Melted almond Butter

For the whipped Cream Icing:

- 1 Cup of Heavy Whipping Cream
- ¼ Cup of Swerve Sweetener
- 1 Teaspoon of Vanilla extract
- 1/3 Cup of Sifted Cocoa Powder

Directions:

1.   Pre-heat your oven to a temperature of about 350 F.

2.   Grease an 8x8 cake tray with cooking spray.

3.   Add the coconut flour, the Swerve sweetener; the cocoa powder, the baking powder, the eggs, the melted butter; and combine very well with an electric or a hand mixer.

4.   Pour your batter into the cake tray and bake for about 25 minutes.

5.   Remove the cake tray from the oven and let cool for about 5 minutes.

For the Icing

6.   Whip the cream until it becomes fluffy; then add in the Swerve, the vanilla and the cocoa powder.

7.   Add the Swerve, the vanilla and the cocoa powder; then continue mixing until your ingredients are very well combined.

8.   Frost your baked cake with the icing; then slice it; serve and enjoy your delicious cake!

Nutrition:

Calories: 357 | Fat: 33g | Carbohydrates: 11g | Fiber: 2g | Protein: 8g

1010. Walnut-Fruit Cake

Preparation time: 15 minutes

Cooking time: 20 minutes

Servings: 6

Ingredients:

- 1/2 Cup of almond butter (softened)
- ¼ Cup of so Nourished granulated erythritol
- 1 Tablespoon of ground cinnamon
- 1/2 Teaspoon of ground nutmeg
- ¼ Teaspoon of ground cloves
- 4 Large pastured eggs
- 1 Teaspoon of vanilla extract
- 1/2 Teaspoon of almond extract
- 2 Cups of almond flour
- 1/2 Cup of chopped walnuts
- ¼ Cup of dried of unsweetened cranberries
- ¼ Cup of seedless raisins

Directions:

1.   Preheat your oven to a temperature of about 350 F and grease an 8-inch baking tin of round shape with coconut oil.

2.   Beat the granulated erythritol on a high speed until it becomes fluffy.

3.   Add the cinnamon, the nutmeg, and the cloves; then blend your ingredients until they become smooth.

4.   Crack in the eggs and beat very well by adding one at a time, plus the almond extract and the vanilla.

5.   Whisk in the almond flour until it forms a smooth batter then fold in the nuts and the fruit.

6.   Spread your mixture into your prepared baking pan and bake it for about 20 minutes.

7.   Remove the cake from the oven and let cool for about 5 minutes.

8.   Dust the cake with the powdered erythritol.

9.   Serve and enjoy your cake!

Nutrition:

Calories: 250| Fat: 11g | Carbohydrates: 12g | Fiber: 2g | Protein: 7g

1011. Ginger Cake

Preparation time: 15 minutes
Cooking time: 20 minutes
Servings: 9
Ingredients:

•   1/2 Tablespoon of unsalted almond butter to grease the pan

•   4 Large eggs

•   ¼ Cup coconut milk

•   2 Tablespoons of unsalted almond butter

•   1 and 1/2 teaspoons of stevia

•   1 Tablespoon of ground cinnamon

•   1 Tablespoon of natural unweeded cocoa powder

•   1 Tablespoon of fresh ground ginger

•   1/2 Teaspoon of kosher salt

•   1 and 1/2 cups of blanched almond flour

•   1/2 Teaspoon of baking soda

Directions:

1.   Preheat your oven to a temperature of 325 F.

2.   Grease a glass baking tray of about 8X8 inches generously with almond butter.

3.   In a large bowl, whisk all together the coconut milk, the eggs, the melted almond butter, the stevia, the cinnamon, the cocoa powder, the ginger and the kosher salt.

4.   Whisk in the almond flour, then the baking soda and mix very well.

5.   Pour the batter into the prepared pan and bake for about 20 to 25 minutes.

6.   Let the cake cool for about 5 minutes; then slice; serve and enjoy your delicious cake.

Nutrition:

Calories: 175| Fat: 15g | Carbohydrates: 5g | Fiber: 1.9g | Protein: 5g

1012. Ketogenic Orange Cake

Preparation time: 10 minutes

Cooking time: 50minutes
Servings: 8
Ingredients:

•   2 and 1/2 cups of almond flour

•   2 Unwaxed washed oranges

•   5 Large separated eggs

•   1 Teaspoon of baking powder

•   2 Teaspoons of orange extract

•   1 Teaspoon of vanilla bean powder

•   6 Seeds of cardamom pods crushed

•   16 drops of liquid stevia; about 3 teaspoons

•   1 Handful of flaked almonds to decorate

Directions:

1.   Preheat your oven to a temperature of about 350 Fahrenheit.

2.   Line a rectangular bread baking tray with a parchment paper.

3.   Place the oranges into a pan filled with cold water and cover it with a lid.

4.   Bring the saucepan to a boil, then let simmer for about 1 hour and make sure the oranges are totally submerged.

5. Make sure the oranges are always submerged to remove any taste of bitterness.

6. Cut the oranges into halves; then remove any seeds; and drain the water and set the oranges aside to cool down.

7. Cut the oranges in half and remove any seeds, then puree it with a blender or a food processor.

8. Separate the eggs; then whisk the egg whites until you see stiff peaks forming.

9. Add all your ingredients except for the egg whites to the orange mixture and add in the egg whites; then mix.

10. Pour the batter into the cake tin and sprinkle with the flaked almonds right on top.

11. Bake your cake for about 50 minutes.

12. Remove the cake from the oven and set aside to cool for 5 minutes.

13. Slice your cake; then serve and enjoy its incredible taste!

Nutrition:

Calories: 164| Fat: 12g | Carbohydrates: 7.1 | Fiber: 2.7g |Protein: 10.9g

1013. Lemon Cake

Preparation time: 20 minutes
Cooking time: 20minutes
Servings: 6
Ingredients:
- 2 Medium lemons
- 4 Large eggs
- 2 Tablespoons of almond butter
- 2 Tablespoons of avocado oil
- 1/3 cup of coconut flour
- 4-5 tablespoons of honey (or another sweetener of your choice)
- 1/2 tablespoon of baking soda

Directions:
1. Preheat your oven to a temperature of about 350 F.

2. Crack the eggs in a large bowl and set two egg whites aside.

3. Whisk the 2 whites of eggs with the egg yolks, the honey, the oil, the almond butter, the lemon zest and the juice and whisk very well together.

4. Combine the baking soda with the coconut flour and gradually add this dry mixture to the wet ingredients and keep whisking for a couple of minutes.

5. Beat the two eggs with a hand mixer and beat the egg into foam.

6. Add the white egg foam gradually to the mixture with a silicone spatula.

7. Transfer your obtained batter to tray covered with a baking paper.

8. Bake your cake for about 20 to 22 minutes.

9. Let the cake cool for 5 minutes; then slice your cake.

10. Serve and enjoy your delicious cake!

Nutrition:

Calories: 164| Fat: 12g | Carbohydrates: 7.1 | Fiber: 2.7g |Protein: 10.9g

1014. Cinnamon Cake

Preparation time: 15 minutes
Cooking time: 35minutes
Servings: 6
Ingredients
For the Cinnamon Filling:
- 3 Tablespoons of Swerve Sweetener
- 2 Teaspoons of ground cinnamon
For the Cake:
- 3 Cups of almond flour
- ¾ Cup of Swerve Sweetener
- ¼ Cup of unflavored whey protein powder
- 2 Teaspoon of baking powder
- 1/2 Teaspoon of salt
- 3 large pastured eggs
- 1/2 Cup of melted coconut oil

- 1/2 Teaspoon of vanilla extract
- 1/2 Cup of almond milk
- 1 Tablespoon of melted coconut oil

For the cream cheese Frosting:
- 3 Tablespoons of softened cream cheese
- 2 Tablespoons of powdered Swerve Sweetener
- 1 Tablespoon of coconut heavy whipping cream
- 1/2 Teaspoon of vanilla extract

Directions:

1. Preheat your oven to a temperature of about 325 F and grease a baking tray of 8x8 inch.
2. For the filling, mix the Swerve and the cinnamon in a mixing bowl and mix very well; then set it aside.
3. For the preparation of the cake; whisk all together the almond flour, the sweetener, the protein powder, the baking powder, and the salt in a mixing bowl.
4. Add in the eggs, the melted coconut oil and the vanilla extract and mix very well.
5. Add in the almond milk and keep stirring until your ingredients are very well combined.
6. Spread about half of the batter in the prepared pan; then sprinkle with about two thirds of the filling mixture.
7. Spread the remaining mixture of the batter over the filling and smooth it with a spatula.
8. Bake for about 35 minutes in the oven.
9. Brush with the melted coconut oil and sprinkle with the remaining cinnamon filling.
10. Prepare the frosting by beating the cream cheese, the powdered erythritol, the cream and the vanilla extract in a mixing bowl until it becomes smooth.
11. Drizzle frost over the cooled cake.
12. Slice the cake; then serve and enjoy your cake!

Nutrition:
Calories: 222| Fat: 19.2g | Carbohydrates: 5.4g | Fiber: 1.5g |Protein: 7.3g

1015. Banana Nut Muffins

Preparation time: 5 minutes
Cooking time: 1 Hour
Servings: 6
Ingredients
Dry **Ingredients**:
- 1 1/2 cups of Spell or Teff Flour
- 1/2 teaspoon of Pure Sea Salt
- 3/4 cup of Date Syrup

Wet **Ingredients**:
- 2 medium Blend Burro Bananas
- ¼ cup of Grape Seed Oil
- ¾ cup of Homemade Walnut Milk (see recipe)*
- 1 tablespoon of Key Lime Juice

Filling **Ingredients**:
- ½ cup of chopped Walnuts (plus extra for decorating)
- 1 chopped Burro Banana

Directions:

1. Preheat your oven to 400 degrees Fahrenheit.
2. Take a muffin tray and grease 12 cups or line with cupcake liners.
3. Put all dry **Ingredients** in a large bowl and mix them thoroughly.
4. Add all wet **Ingredients** to a separate, smaller bowl and mix well with Blend Bananas.
5. Mix **Ingredients** from the two bowls in one large container. Be careful not to over mix.
6. Add the filling **Ingredients** and fold in gently.
7. Pour muffin batter into the 12 prepared muffin cups and garnish with a couple Walnuts.
8. Bake it for 22 to 26 minutes until golden brown.
9. Allow to cool for 10 minutes.
10. Serve and enjoy your Banana Nut Muffins!

Nutrition:
Calories: 150
Fat: 10 g
Carbohydrates: 30 g
Protein: 2.4 g
Fiber: 2 g

1016. Mango Nut Cheesecake

Cooking time: 4 Hour 30 Minutes
Servings: 8 **Servings**
Ingredients
Filling:
- 2 cups of Brazil Nuts
- 5 to 6 Dates
- 1 tablespoon of Sea Moss Gel (check information)
- 1/4 cup of Agave Syrup
- 1/4 teaspoon of Pure Sea Salt
- 2 tablespoons of Lime Juice
- 1 1/2 cups of Homemade Walnut Milk (see recipe)*

Crust:

- 1 1/2 cups of quartered Dates
- 1/4 cup of Agave Syrup
- 1 1/2 cups of Coconut Flakes
- 1/4 teaspoon of Pure Sea Salt

Toppings:

- Sliced Mango
- Sliced Strawberries

Directions:

1. Put all crust Ingredients, in a food processor and blend for 30 seconds.
2. With parchment paper, cover a baking form and spread out the blended crust Ingredients.
3. Put sliced Mango across the crust and freeze for 10 minutes.
4. Mix all filling Ingredients, using a blender until it becomes smooth
5. Pour the filling above the crust, cover with foil or parchment paper and let it stand for about 3 to 4 hours in the refrigerator.
6. Take out from the baking form and garnish with toppings.
7. Serve and enjoy your Mango Nut Cheesecake!

1017. Blackberry Jam

Preparation time: 5 minutes
Cooking time: 4 Hour 30 Minutes
Servings: 1 Cup
Ingredients:

- 3/4 cup of Blackberries
- 1 tablespoon of Key Lime Juice
- 3 tablespoons of Agave Syrup
- ¼ cup of Sea Moss Gel + extra 2 tablespoons (check information)

Directions:

1. Put rinsed Blackberries into a medium pot and cook on medium heat.
2. Stir Blackberries until liquid appears.
3. Once berries soften, use your immersion blender to chop up any large pieces. If you don't have a blender, put the mixture in a food processor, mix it well, then return to the pot.
4. Add Sea Moss Gel, Key Lime Juice and Agave Syrup to the blended mixture. Boil on medium heat and stir well until it becomes thick.

5. Remove from the heat and leave it to cool for 10 minutes.
6. Serve it with bread pieces or the Flatbread (see recipe).
7. Enjoy your Blackberry Jam!

Nutrition:

Calories: 43

Fat: 0.5 g

Carbohydrates: 13 g

1018. Blackberry Bars

Preparation time: 5 minutes
Cooking time: 1 Hour 20 Minutes
Servings: 4
Ingredients:

- 3 Burro Bananas or 4 Baby Bananas
- 1 cup of Spelt Flour
- 2 cups of Quinoa Flakes
- 1/4 cup of Agave Syrup
- 1/4 teaspoon of Pure Sea Salt
- 1/2 cup of Grape Seed Oil
- 1 cup of prepared Blackberry Jam

Directions:

1. Preheat your oven to 350 degrees Fahrenheit.
2. Remove skin of Bananas and mash with a fork in a large bowl.
3. Combine Agave Syrup and Grape Seed Oil with the Blend and mix well.
4. Add Spelt Flour and Quinoa Flakes. Knead the dough until it becomes sticky to your fingers.
5. Cover a 9x9-inch baking pan with parchment paper.
6. Take 2/3 of the dough and smooth it out over the parchment pan with your fingers.
7. Spread Blackberry Jam over the dough.
8. Crumble the remainder dough and sprinkle on the top.
9. Bake for 20 minutes.
10. Remove from the oven and let it cool for at 10 to 15 minutes.
11. Cut into small pieces.
12. Serve and enjoy your Blackberry Bars!

Nutrition:

Calories: 43

Fat: 0.5 g

Carbohydrates: 10 g

Protein: 1.4 g

Fiber: 5 g

1019. Detox Berry Smoothie

Preparation time: 15 minutes

Cooking time: 0

Servings: 1

Ingredients:

- Spring water
- 1/4 avocado, pitted
- One medium burro banana
- One Seville orange
- Two cups of fresh lettuce
- One tablespoon of hemp seeds
- One cup of berries (blueberries or an aggregate of blueberries, strawberries, and raspberries)

Directions:

1. Add the spring water to your blender.
2. Put the fruits and vegies right inside the blender.
3. Blend all **Ingredients** till smooth.

Nutrition:

Calories: 202.4

Fat: 4.5g

Carbohydrates: 32.9g

Protein: 13.3g

Juice and Smoothie Recipes

1020. Dandelion Avocado Smoothie

Preparation time: 15 minutes
Cooking time: 0
Servings: 1
Ingredients:

- One cup of Dandelion
- One Orange (juiced)
- Coconut water
- One Avocado
- One key lime (juice)

Directions:

1. In a high-speed blender until smooth, blend Ingredients.

Nutrition:

Calories: 160
Fat: 15 grams
Carbohydrates: 9 grams
Protein: 2 grams

1021. Amaranth Greens and Avocado Smoothie

Preparation time: 15 minutes
Cooking time: 0
Servings: 1
Ingredients:

- One key lime (juice).
- Two sliced apples (seeded).
- Half avocado.
- Two cupsful of amaranth greens.
- Two cupsful of watercress.
- One cupful of water.

Directions:

1. Add the whole recipes together and transfer them into the blender. Blend thoroughly until smooth.

Nutrition:

Calories: 160
Fat: 15 grams
Carbohydrates: 9 grams
Protein: 2 grams

1022. Lettuce, Orange and Banana Smoothie

Preparation time: 15 minutes
Cooking time: 0
Servings: 1
Ingredients:

- One and a half cupsful of fresh lettuce.
- One large banana.
- One cup of mixed berries of your choice.
- One juiced orange.

Directions:

1. First, add the orange juice to your blender.
2. Add the remaining recipes and blend thoroughly.
3. Enjoy the rest of your day.

Nutrition:

Calories: 252.1
Protein: 4.1 g

1023. Delicious Elderberry Smoothie

Preparation time: 15 minutes
Cooking time: 0
Servings: 1
Ingredients:

- One cupful of Elderberry
- One cupful of Cucumber
- One large apple
- A quarter cupful of water

Directions:

1. Add the whole recipes together into a blender. Grind very well until they are uniformly smooth and enjoy.

Nutrition:

Calories: 106
Carbohydrates: 26.68

1024. Peaches Zucchini Smoothie

Preparation time: 15 minutes

Cooking time: 0

Servings: 1

Ingredients:

- A half cupful of squash.
- A half cupful of peaches.
- A quarter cupful of coconut water.
- A half cupful of Zucchini.

Directions:

1. Add the whole recipes together into a blender and blend until smooth and serve.

Nutrition:

55 Calories

0g Fat

2g Of Protein

10mg Sodium

14 G Carbohydrate

2g Of Fiber

1025. Ginger Orange and Strawberry Smoothie

Preparation time: 15 minutes

Cooking time: 0

Servings: 1

Ingredients:

- One cup of strawberry.
- One large orange (juice)
- One large banana.
- Quarter small sized ginger (peeled and sliced).

Directions:

2. Transfer the orange juice to a clean blender.

3. Add the remaining recipes and blend thoroughly until smooth.

4. Enjoy. Wow! You have ended the 9th day of your weight loss and detox journey.

Nutrition:

32 Calories

0.3g Fat

2g Of Protein

10mg Sodium

14g Carbohydrate

Water

2g Of Fiber.

1026. Kale Parsley and Chia Seeds Detox Smoothie

Preparation time: 15 minutes

Cooking time: 0

Servings: 1

Ingredients:

- Three tbsp. chia seeds (grounded).
- One cupful of water.
- One sliced banana.
- One pear (chopped).
- One cupful of organic kale.
- One cupful of parsley.
- Two tbsp. of lemon juice.
- A dash of cinnamon.

Directions:

1. Add the whole recipes together into a blender and pour the water before blending. Blend at high speed until smooth and enjoy. You may or may not place it in the refrigerator depending on how hot or cold the weather appears.

Nutrition:

75 calories

1g fat

5g protein

10g fiber

1027. Watermelon Limenade

Preparation time: 5 Minutes

Cooking time: 0 minutes

Servings: 6

When it comes to refreshing summertime drinks, lemonade is always near the top of the list. This Watermelon "Limenade" is perfect for using up leftover watermelon or for those early fall days when stores and farmers are almost giving them away. You can also substitute 4 cups of ice for the cold water to create a delicious summertime slushy.

Ingredients

- 4 cups diced watermelon
- 4 cups cold water
- 2 tablespoons freshly squeezed lemon juice
- 1 tablespoon freshly squeezed lime juice

Directions

1. In a blender, combine the watermelon, water, lemon juice, and lime juice, and blend for 1 minute.

2. Strain the contents through a fine-mesh sieve or nut-milk bag. Serve chilled. Store in the refrigerator for up to 3 days.

SERVING TIP: Slice up a few lemon or lime wedges to serve with your Watermelon Limenade, or top it with a few fresh mint leaves to give it an extra-crisp, minty flavor.

Nutrition

Calories: 60

1028. Bubbly Orange Soda

Preparation time: 5 Minutes
Cooking time: 0 minutes
Servings: 4

Soda can be one of the toughest things to give up when you first adopt a WFPB diet. That's partially because refined sugars and caffeine are addictive, but it can also be because carbonated beverages are fun to drink! With sweetness from the orange juice and bubbliness from the carbonated water, this orange "soda" is perfect for assisting in the transition from SAD to WFPB.

Ingredients

- 4 cups carbonated water
- 2 cups pulp-free orange juice (4 oranges, freshly squeezed and strained)

Directions

1. For each serving, pour 2 parts carbonated water and 1-part orange juice over ice right before serving.
2. Stir and enjoy.

SERVING TIP: This recipe is best made right before drinking. The amount of fizz in the carbonated water will decrease the longer it's open, so if you're going to make it ahead of time, make sure it's stored in an airtight, refrigerator-safe container.

Nutrition

Calories: 56

1029. Creamy Cashew Milk

Preparation time: 5 Minutes
Cooking time: 0 minutes
Servings: 8

Learning how to make your own plant-based milks can be one of the best ways to save money and ditch dairy for good. This is one of the easiest milk recipes to master, and if you have a high-speed blender, you can skip the straining step and go straight to a refrigerator-safe container. Large mason jars work great for storing plant-based milk, as they allow you to give a quick shake before each use.

Ingredients

- 4 cups water

- ¼ cup raw cashews, soaked overnight

Directions

1. In a blender, blend the water and cashews on high speed for 2 minutes.
2. Strain with a nut-milk bag or cheesecloth, then store in the refrigerator for up to 5 days.

VARIATION TIP: This recipe makes unsweetened cashew milk that can be used in savory and sweet dishes. For a creamier version to put in your coffee, cut the amount of water in half. For a sweeter version, add 1 to 2 tablespoons maple syrup and 1 teaspoon vanilla extract before blending.

Nutrition

Calories: 18

1030. Homemade Oat Milk

Preparation time: 5 Minutes
Cooking time: 0 minutes
Servings: 8

Oat milk is a fantastic option if you need a nut-free milk or just want an extremely inexpensive plant-based milk. Making a half-gallon jar at home costs a fraction of the price of other plant-based or dairy milks. Oat milk can be used in both savory and sweet dishes.

Ingredients

- 1 cup rolled oats
- 4 cups water

Directions

1. Put the oats in a medium bowl, and cover with cold water. Soak for 15 minutes, then drain and rinse the oats.
2. Pour the cold water and the soaked oats into a blender. Blend for 60 to 90 seconds, or just until the mixture is a creamy white color throughout. (Blending any further may over blend the oats, resulting in a gummy milk.)
3. Strain through a nut-milk bag or colander, then store in the refrigerator for up to 5 days.

Nutrition

Calories: 39

1031. Lucky Mint Smoothie

Preparation time: 5 Minutes
Cooking time: 0 minutes
Servings: 2

As spring approaches and mint begins to take over the garden once again, "Irish"-themed green shakes begin to pop up as well. In contrast to the traditionally high-fat, sugary shakes, this smoothie is a wonderful option for sunny spring days. So next time you want to sip on something cool and minty, do so with a health-promoting Lucky Mint Smoothie.

Ingredients

- 2 cups plant-based milk (here or here)
- 2 frozen bananas, halved
- 1 tablespoon fresh mint leaves or ¼ teaspoon peppermint extract
- 1 teaspoon vanilla extract

Directions

1. In a blender, combine the milk, bananas, mint, and vanilla. Blend on high for 1 to 2 minutes, or until the contents reach a smooth and creamy consistency, and serve.

VARIATION TIP: If you like to sneak greens into smoothies, add a cup or two of spinach to boost the health benefits of this smoothie and give it an even greener appearance.

Nutrition

Calories: 152

1032. Paradise Island Smoothie

Preparation time: 5 Minutes
Cooking time: 0 minutes
Servings: 2
Ingredients:

- 2 cups plant-based milk (here or here)
- 1 frozen banana
- ½ cup frozen mango chunks
- ½ cup frozen pineapple chunks
- 1 teaspoon vanilla extract

Directions:

1. In a blender, combine the milk, banana, mango, pineapple, and vanilla. Blend on high for 1 to 2 minutes, or until the contents reach a smooth and creamy consistency, and serve.

LEFTOVER TIP: If you have any leftover smoothie, you can put it in a jar with some rolled oats and allow the mixture to soak in the refrigerator overnight to create a tropical version of overnight oats.

Nutrition

Calories: 176

1033. Apple Pie Smoothie

Preparation time: 5 Minutes
Cooking time: 0 minutes
Servings: 2

This smoothie is great for a quick breakfast or a cool dessert. Its combination of sweet apples and warming cinnamon is sure to win over children and adults alike. If the holidays find you in a warm area, this smoothie may just be the cool treat you've been looking for to take the place of pie at dessert time.

Ingredients

- 2 sweet crisp apples, cut into 1-inch cubes
- 2 cups plant-based milk (here or here)
- 1 cup ice
- 1 tablespoon maple syrup
- 1 teaspoon ground cinnamon
- 1 teaspoon vanilla extract

Direction

1. In a blender, combine the apples, milk, ice, maple syrup, cinnamon, and vanilla. Blend on high for 1 to 2 minutes, or until the contents reach a smooth and creamy consistency, and serve.

VARIATION TIP: You can also use this recipe for making overnight oatmeal. Blend your smoothie, mix it with 2 cups rolled oats, and refrigerate overnight for a premade breakfast for two.

Nutrition

Calories: 198

1034. Choco-Nut Milkshake

Preparation Time: 10 minutes
Cooking Time: 0 minute
Serving: 2
Ingredients

- 2 cups unsweetened coconut, almond
- 1 banana, sliced and frozen
- ¼ cup unsweetened coconut flakes
- 1 cup ice cubes
- ¼ cup macadamia nuts, chopped
- 3 tablespoons sugar-free sweetener
- 2 tablespoons raw unsweetened cocoa powder
- Whipped coconut cream

Directions

1.Place all ingredients into a blender and blend on high until smooth and creamy.

2.Divide evenly between 4 "mocktail" glasses and top with whipped coconut cream, if desired.

3.Add a cocktail umbrella and toasted coconut for added flair.

4.Enjoy your delicious Choco-nut smoothie!
Nutrition
12g Carbohydrates
3g Protein
199 Calories

1035. Pineapple & Strawberry Smoothie

Preparation Time: 7 minutes
Cooking Time: 0 minute
Serving: 2
Ingredients:

- 1 cup strawberries
- 1 cup pineapple, chopped
- ¾ cup almond milk
- 1 tablespoon almond butter

Directions:
1.Add all ingredients to a blender.
2.Blend until smooth.
3.Add more almond milk until it reaches your desired consistency.
4.Chill before serving.
Nutrition:
255 Calories
39g Carbohydrate
5.6g Protein

1036. Cantaloupe Smoothie

Preparation Time: 11 minutes
Cooking Time: 0 minute
Serving: 2
Ingredients:

- ¾ cup carrot juice
- 4 cups cantaloupe, sliced into cubes
- Pinch of salt
- Frozen melon balls
- Fresh basil

Directions:
1.Add the carrot juice and cantaloupe cubes to a blender. Sprinkle with salt.
2.Process until smooth.
3.Transfer to a bowl.
4.Chill in the refrigerator for at least 30 minutes.
5.Top with the frozen melon balls and basil before serving.
Nutrition:

135 Calories
31g Carbohydrate
3.4g Protein

1037. Berry Smoothie with Mint

Preparation Time: 7 minutes
Cooking Time: 0 minute
Serving: 2
Ingredients:

- ¼ cup orange juice
- ½ cup blueberries
- ½ cup blackberries
- 1 cup reduced-fat plain kefir
- 1 tablespoon honey
- 2 tablespoons fresh mint leaves

Directions:
1.Add all the ingredients to a blender.
2.Blend until smooth.
Nutrition:
137 Calories
27g Carbohydrate
6g Protein

1038. Green Smoothie

Preparation Time: 12 minutes
Cooking Time: 0 minute
Serving: 2
Ingredients:

- 1 cup vanilla almond milk (unsweetened)
- ¼ ripe avocado, chopped
- 1 cup kale, chopped
- 1 banana
- 2 teaspoons honey
- 1 tablespoon chia seeds
- 1 cup ice cubes

Directions:
1.Combine all the ingredients in a blender.
2.Process until creamy.
Nutrition:
343 Calories
14.7g Carbohydrate
5.9g Protein

1039. Banana, Cauliflower & Berry Smoothie

Preparation Time: 9 minutes
Cooking Time: 0 minute
Serving: 2
Ingredients:
- 2 cups almond milk (unsweetened)
- 1 cup banana, sliced
- ½ cup blueberries
- ½ cup blackberries
- 1 cup cauliflower rice
- 2 teaspoons maple syrup

Directions:
1. Pour almond milk into a blender.
2. Stir in the rest of the ingredients.
3. Process until smooth.
4. Chill before serving.

Nutrition:
149 Calories
29g Carbohydrate
3g Protein

1040. Berry & Spinach Smoothie

Preparation Time: 11 minutes
Cooking Time: 0 minute
Serving: 2
Ingredients:
- 2 cups strawberries
- 1 cup raspberries
- 1 cup blueberries
- 1 cup fresh baby spinach leaves
- 1 cup pomegranate juice
- 3 tablespoons milk powder (unsweetened)

Directions:
1. Mix all the ingredients in a blender.
2. Blend until smooth.
3. Chill before serving.

Nutrition:
118 Calories
25.7g Carbohydrate
4.6g Protein

1041. Peanut Butter Smoothie with Blueberries

Preparation Time: 12 minutes
Cooking Time: 0 minute
Serving: 2

Ingredients:
- 2 tablespoons creamy peanut butter
- 1 cup vanilla almond milk (unsweetened)
- 6 oz. soft silken tofu
- ½ cup grape juice
- 1 cup blueberries
- Crushed ice

Directions:
1. Mix all the ingredients in a blender.
2. Process until smooth.

Nutrition:
247 Calories
30g Carbohydrate
10.7g Protein

1042. Peach & Apricot Smoothie

Preparation Time: 11 minutes
Cooking Time: 0 minute
Serving: 2
Ingredients:
- 1 cup almond milk (unsweetened)
- 1 teaspoon honey
- ½ cup apricots, sliced
- ½ cup peaches, sliced
- ½ cup carrot, chopped
- 1 teaspoon vanilla extract

Directions:
1. Mix milk and honey.
2. Pour into a blender.
3. Add the apricots, peaches and carrots.
4. Stir in the vanilla.
5. Blend until smooth.

Nutrition:
153 Calories
30g Carbohydrate
32.6g Protein

1043. Tropical Smoothie

Preparation Time: 8 minutes
Cooking Time: 0 minute
Serving: 2
Ingredients:
- 1 banana, sliced
- 1 cup mango, sliced
- 1 cup pineapple, sliced

- 1 cup peaches, sliced
- 6 oz. nonfat coconut yogurt
- Pineapple wedges

Directions:

1.Freeze the fruit slices for 1 hour.

2.Transfer to a blender.

3.Stir in the rest of the ingredients except pineapple wedges.

4.Process until smooth.

5.Garnish with pineapple wedges.

Nutrition:

102 Calories

22.6g Carbohydrate

2.5g Protein

1044. Banana & Strawberry Smoothie

Preparation Time: 7 minutes

Cooking Time: 0 minute

Serving: 2

Ingredients:

- 1 banana, sliced
- 4 cups fresh strawberries, sliced
- 1 cup ice cubes
- 6 oz. yogurt
- 1 kiwi fruit, sliced

Directions:

1.Add banana, strawberries, ice cubes and yogurt in a blender.

2.Blend until smooth.

3.Garnish with kiwi fruit slices and serve.

Nutrition:

54 Calories

11.8g Carbohydrate

1.7g Protein

1045. Cantaloupe & Papaya Smoothie

Preparation Time: 9 minutes

Cooking Time: 0 minute

Serving: 2

Ingredients:

- ¾ cup low-fat milk
- ½ cup papaya, chopped

- ½ cup cantaloupe, chopped
- ½ cup mango, cubed
- 4 ice cubes
- Lime zest

Directions:

1.Pour milk into a blender.

2.Add the chopped fruits and ice cubes.

3.Blend until smooth.

4.Garnish with lime zest and serve.

Nutrition:

207 Calories

18.4g Carbohydrate

7.7g Protein

1046. Watermelon & Cantaloupe Smoothie

Preparation Time: 10 minutes

Cooking Time: 0 minute

Serving: 2

Ingredients:

- 2 cups watermelon, sliced
- 1 cup cantaloupe, sliced
- ½ cup nonfat yogurt
- ¼ cup orange juice

Directions:

1.   Add all the ingredients to a blender.

2.   Blend until creamy and smooth.

3.   Chill before serving.

Nutrition:

114 Calories

13g Carbohydrate

4.8g Protein

1047. Raspberry and Peanut Butter Smoothie

Preparation Time: 10 minutes

Cooking Time: 0 minute

Serving: 2

Ingredients:

- Peanut butter, smooth and natural [2 tbsp]
- Skim milk [2 tbsp]
- Raspberries, fresh [1 or 1 ½ cups]
- Ice cubes [1 cup]
- Stevia [2 tsp]

Directions:

1.   Situate all the ingredients in your blender. Set the mixer to puree. Serve.

Nutrition:

170 Calories

8.6g Fat

20g Carbohydrate

1048. Strawberry, Kale and Ginger Smoothie

Preparation Time: 13 minutes

Cooking Time: 0 minute

Serving: 2

Ingredients:

*   Curly kale leaves, fresh and large with stems removed [6 pcs]

*   Grated ginger, raw and peeled [2 tsp]

*   Water, cold [½ cup]

*   Lime juice [3 tbsp]

*   Honey [2 tsp]

*   Strawberries, fresh and trimmed [1 or 1 ½ cups]

*   Ice cubes [1 cup]

Directions:

1.   Position all the ingredients in your blender. Set to puree. Serve.

Nutrition:

205 Calories

2.9g Fat

42.4g Carbohydrates

1049. Berry Mint Smoothie

Preparation Time: 5 Minutes

Cooking Time: 5 Minutes

Servings: 2

Ingredients:

*   1 tbsp. Low-carb Sweetener of your choice

*   1 cup Kefir or Low Fat-Yoghurt

*   2 tbsp. Mint

*   ¼ cup Orange

*   1 cup Mixed Berries

Directions:

1.   Place all of the ingredients in a high-speed blender and then blend it until smooth.

2.   Transfer the smoothie to a serving glass and enjoy it.

Nutrition:

Calories: 137Kcal

Carbohydrates: 11g

Proteins: 6g

Fat: 1g

Sodium: 64mg

1050. Greenie Smoothie

Preparation Time: 5 Minutes
Cooking Time: 5 Minutes
Servings: 2
Ingredients:

- 1 1/2 cup Water
- 1 tsp. Stevia
- 1 Green Apple, ripe
- 1 tsp. Stevia
- 1 Green Pear, chopped into chunks
- 1 Lime
- 2 cups Kale, fresh
- ¾ tsp. Cinnamon
- 12 Ice Cubes
- 20 Green Grapes
- 1/2 cup Mint, fresh

Directions:
1.   Pour water, kale, and pear in a high-speed blender and blend them for 2 to 3 minutes until mixed.
2.   Stir in all the remaining ingredients into it and blend until it becomes smooth.
3.   Transfer the smoothie to serving glass.
Nutrition:
Calories: 123Kcal
Carbohydrates: 27g
Proteins: 2g
Fat: 2g
Sodium: 30mg

1051. Coconut Spinach Smoothie

Preparation Time: 5 Minutes
Cooking Time: 5 Minutes
Servings: 2
Ingredients:

- 1 ¼ cup Coconut Milk
- 2 Ice Cubes
- 2 tbsp. Chia Seeds
- 1 scoop of Protein Powder, preferably vanilla
- 1 cup Spin

Directions:
1.   Pour coconut milk along with spinach, chia seeds, protein powder, and ice cubes in a high-speed blender.
2.   Blend for 2 minutes to get a smooth and luscious smoothie.
3.   Serve in a glass and enjoy it.
Nutrition:
Calories: 251Kcal
Carbohydrates: 10.9g
Proteins: 20.3g
Fat: 15.1g
Sodium: 102mg

1052. Oats Coffee Smoothie

Preparation Time: 5 Minutes

Cooking Time: 5 Minutes

Servings: 2

Ingredients:

- 1 cup Oats, uncooked & grounded
- 2 tbsp. Instant Coffee
- 3 cup Milk, skimmed
- 2 Banana, frozen & sliced into chunks
- 2 tbsp. Flax Seeds, grounded

Directions:

1. Place all of the ingredients in a high-speed blender and blend for 2 minutes or until smooth and luscious.
2. Serve and enjoy.

Nutrition:

Calories: 251Kcal

Carbohydrates: 10.9g

Proteins: 20.3g

Fat: 15.1g

Sodium: 102mg

1053. Veggie Smoothie

Preparation Time: 5 Minutes

Cooking Time: 5 Minutes

Servings: 1

Ingredients:

- ¼ of 1 Red Bell Pepper, sliced
- 1/2 tbsp. Coconut Oil
- 1 cup Almond Milk, unsweetened
- ¼ tsp. Turmeric
- 4 Strawberries, chopped
- Pinch of Cinnamon
- 1/2 of 1 Banana, preferably frozen

Directions:

1. Combine all the ingredients required to make the smoothie in a high-speed blender.
2. Blend for 3 minutes to get a smooth and silky mixture.
3. Serve and enjoy.

Nutrition:

Calories: 169cal

Carbohydrates: 17g

Proteins: 2.3g

Fat: 9.8g

Sodium: 162mg

1054. Avocado Smoothie

Preparation Time: 10 Minutes

Cooking Time: 0 Minutes

Servings: 2

Ingredients:

- 1 Avocado, ripe & pit removed
- 2 cups Baby Spinach
- 2 cups Water
- 1 cup Baby Kale
- 1 tbsp. Lemon Juice
- 2 sprigs of Mint
- 1/2 cup Ice Cubes

Directions:

1. Place all the ingredients needed to make the smoothie in a high-speed blender then blend until smooth.
2. Transfer to a serving glass and enjoy it.

Nutrition:

Calories: 214cal

Carbohydrates: 15g

Proteins: 2g

Fat: 17g

Sodium: 25mg

1055. Orange Carrot Smoothie

Preparation Time: 5 Minutes

Cooking Time: 0 Minutes

Servings: 1

Ingredients:

- 1 1/2 cups Almond Milk
- ¼ cup Cauliflower, blanched & frozen
- 1 Orange
- 1 tbsp. Flax Seed
- 1/3 cup Carrot, grated
- 1 tsp. Vanilla Extract

Directions:

1. Mix all the ingredients in a high-speed blender and blend for 2 minutes or until you get the desired consistency.
2. Transfer to a serving glass and enjoy it.

Nutrition:

Calories: 216cal

Carbohydrates: 10g

Proteins: 15g

Fat: 7g

Sodium: 25mg

1056. Blackberry Smoothie

Preparation Time: 5 Minutes

Cooking Time: 0 Minutes

Servings: 1

Ingredients:

- 1 1/2 cups Almond Milk

- ¼ cup Cauliflower, blanched & frozen
- 1 Orange
- 1 tbsp. Flax Seed
- 1/3 cup Carrot, grated
- 1 tsp. Vanilla Extract

Directions:

1.   Place all the ingredients needed to make the blackberry smoothie in a high-speed blender and blend for 2 minutes until you get a smooth mixture.

2.   Transfer to a serving glass and enjoy it.

Nutrition:
Calories: 275cal
Carbohydrates: 9g
Proteins: 11g
Fat: 17g
Sodium: 73mg

1057. Key Lime Pie Smoothie

Preparation Time: 5 Minutes
Cooking Time: 0 Minutes
Servings: 1
Ingredients:

- 1/2 cup Cottage Cheese
- 1 tbsp. Sweetener of your choice
- 1/2 cup Water
- 1/2 cup Spinach
- 1 tbsp. Lime Juice
- 1 cup Ice Cubes

Directions:

1.   Spoon in the ingredients to a high-speed blender and blend until silky smooth.

2.   Transfer to a serving glass and enjoy it.

Nutrition:
Calories: 180cal
Carbohydrates: 7g
Proteins: 36g
Fat: 1g
Sodium: 35mg

1058. Cinnamon Roll Smoothie

Preparation Time: 5 Minutes
Cooking Time: 0 Minutes
Servings: 1
Ingredients:

- 1 tsp. Flax Meal or oats, if preferred
- 1 cup Almond Milk
- 1/2 tsp. Cinnamon
- 2 tbsp. Protein Powder

- 1 cup Ice
- ¼ tsp. Vanilla Extract
- 4 tsp. Sweetener of your choice

Directions:

1.   Pour the milk into the blender, followed by the protein powder, sweetener, flax meal, cinnamon, vanilla extract, and ice.

2.   Blend for 40 seconds or until smooth.

3.   Serve and enjoy.

Nutrition:

Calories: 145cal

Carbohydrates: 1.6g

Proteins: 26.5g

Fat: 3.25g

Sodium: 30mg

1059. Strawberry Cheesecake Smoothie

Preparation Time: 5 Minutes

Cooking Time: 0 Minutes

Servings: 1

Ingredients:

- ¼ cup Soy Milk, unsweetened
- 1/2 cup Cottage Cheese, low-fat
- 1/2 tsp. Vanilla Extract
- 2 oz. Cream Cheese
- 1 cup Ice Cubes
- 1/2 cup Strawberries
- 4 tbsp. Low-carb Sweetener of your choice

Directions:

1.   Add all the ingredients for making the strawberry cheesecake smoothie to a high-speed blender until you get the desired smooth consistency.

2.   Serve and enjoy.

Nutrition:

Calories: 347cal

Carbohydrates: 10.05g

Proteins: 17.5g

Fat: 24g

Sodium: 45mg

1060. Peanut Butter Banana Smoothie

Preparation Time: 5 Minutes

Cooking Time: 2 Minutes

Servings: 1

Ingredients:

- ¼ cup Greek Yoghurt, plain
- 1/2 tbsp. Chia Seeds
- 1/2 cup Ice Cubes
- 1/2 of 1 Banana
- 1/2 cup Water
- 1 tbsp. Peanut Butter

Directions:

1.   Place all the ingredients needed to make the smoothie in a high-speed blender and blend to get a smooth and luscious mixture.

2.   Transfer the smoothie to a serving glass and enjoy it.

Nutrition:

Calories: 202cal

Carbohydrates: 14g

Proteins: 10g

Fat: 9g

Sodium: 30mg

1061. Avocado Turmeric

Smoothie

Preparation Time:
5 Minutes
Cooking Time: 2 Minutes
Servings: 1
Ingredients:

- 1/2 of 1 Avocado
- 1 cup Ice, crushed
- ¾ cup Coconut Milk, full-fat
- 1 tsp. Lemon Juice
- ¼ cup Almond Milk
- 1/2 tsp. Turmeric
- 1 tsp. Ginger, freshly grated

Directions:
1.   Place all the ingredients excluding the crushed ice in a high-speed blender and blend for 2 to 3 minutes or until smooth.
2.   Transfer to a serving glass and enjoy it.
Nutrition:
Calories: 232cal
Carbohydrates: 4.1g
Proteins: 1.7g
Fat: 22.4g
Sodium: 25mg

1062. Lemon Blueberry Smoothie

Preparation Time: 5 Minutes

Cooking Time: 2 Minutes
Servings: 2
Ingredients:

- 1 tbsp. Lemon Juice
- 1 ¾ cup Coconut Milk, full-fat
- 1/2 tsp. Vanilla Extract
- 3 oz. Blueberries, frozen

Directions:
1.   Combine coconut milk, blueberries, lemon juice, and vanilla extract in a high-speed blender.
2.   Blend for 2 minutes for a smooth and luscious smoothie.
3.   Serve and enjoy.
Nutrition:
Calories: 417cal
Carbohydrates: 9g
Proteins: 4g
Fat: 43g
Sodium: 35mg

1063. Matcha Green Smoothie

Preparation Time: 5 Minutes
Cooking Time: 2 Minutes
Servings: 2
Ingredients:

- ¼ cup Heavy Whipping Cream
- 1/2 tsp. Vanilla Extract
- 1 tsp. Matcha Green Tea Powder
- 2 tbsp. Protein Powder
- 1 tbsp. Hot Water
- 1 ¼ cup Almond Milk, unsweetened
- 1/2 of 1 Avocado, medium

Directions:
1.   Place all the ingredients in the high-blender for one to two minutes.
2.   Serve and enjoy.
Nutrition:
Calories: 229cal
Carbohydrates: 1.5g
Proteins: 14.1g
Fat: 43g
Sodium: 35mg

1064. Blueberry Smoothie

Preparation Time: 10 minutes

Cooking Time: 0 minutes

Servings: 2

Ingredients:

- 2 cups frozen blueberries
- 1 small banana
- 1½ cups unsweetened almond milk
- ¼ cup ice cubes

Directions:

1. Place all the ingredients in a high-speed blender and pulse until creamy.
2. Pour the smoothie into two glasses and serve immediately.

Nutrition: Calories 158 Total Fat 3.3 g Saturated Fat 0.3 g Cholesterol 0 mg Sodium 137 mg Total Carbs 34 g Fiber 5.6 g Sugar 20.6 g Protein 2.4 g

1065. Beet & Strawberry Smoothie

Preparation Time: 10 minutes

Cooking Time: 0 minutes

Servings: 2

Ingredients:

- 2 cups frozen strawberries, pitted and chopped
- 2/3 cup roasted and frozen beet, chopped
- 1 teaspoon fresh ginger, peeled and grated
- 1 teaspoon fresh turmeric, peeled and grated
- ½ cup fresh orange juice
- 1 cup unsweetened almond milk

Directions:

1. Place all the ingredients in a high-speed blender and pulse until creamy.
2. Pour the smoothie into two glasses and serve immediately.

Nutrition: Calories 258 Total Fat 1.5 g Saturated Fat 0.1 g Cholesterol 0 mg Sodium 134 mg Total Carbs 26.7g Fiber 4.9 g Sugar 18.7 g Protein 2.9 g

1066. Kiwi Smoothie

Preparation Time: 10 minutes

Cooking Time: 0 minutes

Servings: 2

Ingredients:

- 4 kiwis
- 2 small bananas, peeled

- 1½ cups unsweetened almond milk
- 1-2 drops liquid stevia
- ¼ cup ice cubes

Directions:

1. Place all the ingredients in a high-speed blender and pulse until creamy.
2. Pour the smoothie into two glasses and serve immediately.

Nutrition: Calories 228 Total Fat 3.8 g Saturated Fat 0.4 g Cholesterol 0 mg Sodium 141 mg Total Carbs 50.7 g Fiber 8.4 g Sugar 28.1 g Protein 3.8 g

1067. Pineapple & Carrot Smoothie

Preparation Time: 10 minutes

Cooking Time: 0 minutes

Servings: 2

Ingredients:

- 1 cup frozen pineapple
- 1 large ripe banana, peeled and sliced
- ½ tablespoon fresh ginger, peeled and chopped
- ¼ teaspoon ground turmeric
- 1 cup unsweetened almond milk
- ½ cup fresh carrot juice
- 1 tablespoon fresh lemon juice

Directions:

1. Place all the ingredients in a high-speed blender and pulse until creamy.
2. Pour the smoothie into two glasses and serve immediately.

Nutrition: Calories 132 Total Fat 2.2 g Saturated Fat 0.3 g Cholesterol 0 mg Sodium 113 mg Total Carbs 629.3 g Fiber 4.1 g Sugar 16.9 g Protein 2 g

1068. Oats & Orange Smoothie

Preparation Time: 10 minutes

Cooking Time: 0 minutes

Servings: 4

Ingredients:

- 2/3 cup rolled oats
- 2 oranges, peeled, seeded, and sectioned
- 2 large bananas, peeled and sliced
- 2 cups unsweetened almond milk
- 1 cup ice cubes, crushed

Directions:

1. Place all the ingredients in a high-speed blender and pulse until creamy.
2. Pour the smoothie into four glasses and serve immediately.

Nutrition: Calories 175
Total Fat 3 g Saturated Fat 0.4 g Cholesterol 0 mg Sodium 93 mg Total Carbs 36.6 g Fiber 5.9 g Sugar 17.1 g Protein 3.9 g

1069. Pumpkin Smoothie

Preparation Time: 10 minutes
Cooking Time: 0 minutes
Servings: 2
Ingredients:

- 1 cup homemade pumpkin puree
- 1 medium banana, peeled and sliced
- 1 tablespoon maple syrup
- 1 teaspoon ground flaxseeds
- ½ teaspoon ground cinnamon
- ¼ teaspoon ground ginger
- 1½ cups unsweetened almond milk
- ¼ cup ice cubes

Directions:
1. Place all the ingredients in a high-speed blender and pulse until creamy.
2. Pour the smoothie into two glasses and serve immediately.

Nutrition: Calories 159 Total Fat 3.6 g Saturated Fat 0.5 g Cholesterol 0 mg Sodium 143 mg Total Carbs 32.6 g Fiber 6.5 g Sugar 17.3 g Protein 3 g

1070. Grape & Swiss Chard Smoothie

Preparation Time: 10 minutes
Cooking Time: 0 minutes
Servings: 2
Ingredients:

- 2 cups seedless green grapes
- 2 cups fresh Swiss chard, trimmed and chopped
- 2 tablespoons maple syrup
- 1 teaspoon fresh lemon juice
- 1½ cups water
- 4 ice cubes

Directions:
1. Place all the ingredients in a high-speed blender and pulse until creamy.

2. Pour the smoothie into two glasses and serve immediately.

Nutrition: Calories 176 Total Fat 0.2 g Saturated Fat 0 g Cholesterol 0 mg Sodium 83 mg Total Carbs 44.9 g Fiber 1.7 g Sugar 37.9 g Protein 0.7 g

1071. Mango Smoothie

Preparation Time: 10 minutes
Cooking Time: 0 minutes
Servings: 2
Ingredients:

- 2 cups frozen mango, peeled, pitted and chopped
- ¼ cup almond butter
- Pinch of ground turmeric
- 2 tablespoons fresh lemon juice
- 1¼ cups unsweetened almond milk
- ¼ cup ice cubes

Directions:
1. Add all the ingredients in a high-speed blender and pulse until smooth.
2. Pour the smoothie into two glasses and serve immediately.

Nutrition: Calories 140 Total Fat 4.1 g Saturated Fat 0.6 g Cholesterol 0 mg Sodium 118 mg Total Carbs 26.8 g Fiber 3.6 g Sugar 23 g Protein 2.5 g

1072. Pineapple Smoothie

Preparation Time: 10 minutes
Cooking Time: 0 minutes
Servings: 2
Ingredients:

- 2 cups pineapple, chopped
- ½ teaspoon fresh ginger, peeled and chopped
- ½ teaspoon ground turmeric
- 1 teaspoon natural immune support supplement *
- 1 teaspoon chia seeds
- 1½ cups cold green tea
- ½ cup ice, crushed

Directions:
1. Add all the ingredients in a high-speed blender and pulse until smooth.
2. Pour the smoothie into two glasses and serve immediately.

Nutrition: Calories 152 Total Fat 1 g Saturated Fat 0 g Cholesterol 0 mg Sodium 9 mg Total Carbs 30 g Fiber 3.5 g Sugar 29.8 g Protein 1.5 g

1073. Kale & Pineapple Smoothie

Preparation Time: 15 minutes
Cooking Time: 0 minutes
Servings: 2
Ingredients:

- 1½ cups fresh kale, trimmed and chopped
- 1 frozen banana, peeled and chopped
- ½ cup fresh pineapple chunks
- 1 cup unsweetened coconut milk
- ½ cup fresh orange juice
- ½ cup ice

Directions:

1. Add all the ingredients in a high-speed blender and pulse until smooth.
2. Pour the smoothie into two glasses and serve immediately.

Nutrition: Calories 148 Total Fat 2.4 g Saturated Fat 2.1 g Cholesterol 0 mg Sodium 23 mg Total Carbs 31.6 g Fiber 3.5 g Sugar 16.5 g Protein 2.8 g

1074. Raisins – Plume Smoothie (RPS)

Preparation time: 10 minutes
Cooking time: 0 minutes
Servings: 1
Ingredients:

- 1 Teaspoon Raisins
- 2 Sweet Cherry
- 1 Skinned Black Plume
- 1 Cup Dr. Sebi's Stomach Calming Herbal Tea/ Cuachalate back powder,
- ¼ Coconut Water

Directions:

1. Flash 1 teaspoon of Raisin in warm water for 5 seconds and drain the water completely.
2. Rinse, cube Sweet Cherry and skinned black Plum
3. Get 1 cup of water boiled; put ¾ Dr. Sebi's Stomach Calming Herbal Tea for 10 – 15minutes.
4. If you are unable to get Dr. Sebi's Stomach Calming Herbal tea, you can alternatively, cook 1 teaspoon of powdered Cuachalate with 1 cup of water for 5 – 10 minutes, remove the extract and allow it to cool.
5. Pour all the ARPS items inside a blender and blend till you achieve a homogenous smoothie.
6. It is now okay, for you to enjoy the inevitable detox smoothie.

Nutrition:
Calories: 150
Fat: 1.2 g
Carbohydrates: 79 g
Protein: 3.1 g

1075. Nori Clove Smoothies (NCS)

Preparation time: 10 minutes
Cooking time: 0 minutes
Servings: 1
Ingredients:

- ¼ Cup Fresh Nori
- 1 Cup Cubed Banana
- 1 Teaspoon Diced Onion or ¼ Teaspoon Powdered Onion
- ½ Teaspoon Clove
- 1 Cup Dr. Sebi Energy Booster
- 1 Tablespoon Agave Syrup

Directions:

1. Rinse ANCS Items with clean water.
2. Finely chop the onion to take one teaspoon and cut fresh Nori
3. Boil 1½ teaspoon with 2 cups of water, remove the particle, allow to cool, measure 1 cup of the tea extract
4. Pour all the items inside a blender with the tea extract and blend to achieve homogenous smoothies.
5. Transfer into a clean cup and have a nice time with a lovely body detox and energizer.

Nutrition:
Calories: 78
Fat: 2.3 g
Carbohydrates: 5 g
Protein: 6 g

1076. Brazil Lettuce Smoothies (BLS)

Preparation time: 10 minutes
Cooking time: 0 minutes

Servings: 1

Ingredients:

- 1 Cup Raspberries
- ½ Handful Romaine Lettuce
- ½ Cup Homemade Walnut Milk
- 2 Brazil Nuts
- ½ Large Grape with Seed
- 1 Cup Soft jelly Coconut Water
- Date Sugar to Taste

Directions:

1. In a clean bowl rinse, the vegetable with clean water.
2. Chop the Romaine Lettuce and cubed Raspberries and add other items into the blender and blend to achieve homogenous smoothies.
3. Serve your delicious medicinal detox.

Nutrition:

Calories: 168

Fat: 4.5 g

Carbohydrates: 31.3 g

Sugar: 19.2 g

Protein: 3.6 g

1077. Apple – Banana Smoothie (Abs)

Preparation time: 10 minutes

Cooking time: 0 minutes

Servings: 1

Ingredients:

- I Cup Cubed Apple
- ½ Burro Banana
- ½ Cup Cubed Mango
- ½ Cup Cubed Watermelon
- ½ Teaspoon Powdered Onion
- 3 Tablespoon Key Lime Juice
- Date Sugar to Taste (If you like)

Directions:

1. In a clean bowl rinse, the vegetable with clean water.
2. Cubed Banana, Apple, Mango, Watermelon and add other items into the blender and blend to achieve homogenous smoothies.
3. Serve your delicious medicinal detox.
4. Alternatively, you can add one tablespoon of finely dices raw red Onion if powdered Onion is not available.

Nutrition:

Calories: 99

Fat: 0.3g

Carbohydrates: 23 grams

Protein: 1.1 g

1078. Ginger – Pear Smoothie (GPS)

Preparation time: 10 minutes

Cooking time: 0 minutes

Servings: 1

Ingredients:

- 1 Big Pear with Seed and Cured
- ½ Avocado
- ¼ Handful Watercress
- ½ Sour Orange
- ½ Cup Ginger Tea
- ½ Cup Coconut Water
- ¼ Cup Spring Water
- 2 Tablespoon Agave Syrup
- Date Sugar to satisfaction

Directions:

1. Firstly boil 1 cup of Ginger Tea, cover the cup and allow it cool to room temperature.
2. Pour all the AGPS Items into your clean blender and homogenize them to smooth fluid.
3. You have just prepared yourself a wonderful Detox Romaine Smoothie.

Nutrition:

Calories: 101.

Protein: 1 g

Carbs: 27 g

Fiber: 6 g

1079. Cantaloupe – Amaranth Smoothie (CAS)

Preparation time: 10 minutes

Cooking time: 0 minutes

Servings: 1

Ingredients:

- ½ Cup Cubed Cantaloupe
- ¼ Handful Green Amaranth
- ½ Cup Homemade Hemp Milk
- ¼ Teaspoon Dr. Sebi's Bromide Plus Powder
- 1 Cup Coconut Water

- 1 Teaspoon Agave Syrup

Directions:

1. You will have to rinse all the ACAS items with clean water.

2. Chop green Amaranth, cubed Cantaloupe, transfer all into a blender and blend to achieve homogenous smoothie.

3. Pour into a clean cup; add Agave syrup and homemade Hemp Milk.

4. Stir them together and drink.

Nutrition:

Calories: 55

Fiber: 1.5 g

Carbohydrates: 8 mg

1080. Garbanzo Squash Smoothie (GSS)

Preparation time: 10 minutes

Cooking time: 0 minutes

Servings: 1

Ingredients:

- 1 Large Cubed Apple
- 1 Fresh Tomatoes
- 1 Tablespoon Finely Chopped Fresh Onion or ¼ Teaspoon Powdered Onion
- ¼ Cup Boiled Garbanzo Bean
- ½ Cup Coconut Milk
- ¼ Cubed Mexican Squash Chayote
- 1 Cup Energy Booster Tea

Directions:

1. You will need to rinse the AGSS items with clean water.

2. Boil 1½ Dr. Sebi's Energy Booster Tea with 2 cups of clean water. Filter the extract, measure 1 cup and allow it to cool.

3. Cook Garbanzo Bean, drain the water and allow it to cool.

4. Pour all the AGSS items into a high-speed blender and blend to achieve homogenous smoothie.

5. You may add Date Sugar.

6. Serve your amazing smoothie and drink.

Nutrition:

Calories: 82.

Carbs: 22 g

Protein: 2 g

Fiber: 7 g

1081. Strawberry – Orange Smoothies (SOS)

Preparation time: 10 minutes

Cooking time: 0 minutes

Servings: 1

Ingredients:

- 1 Cup Diced Strawberries
- 1 Removed Back of Seville Orange
- ¼ Cup Cubed Cucumber
- ¼ Cup Romaine Lettuce
- ½ Kelp
- ½ Burro Banana
- 1 Cup Soft Jelly Coconut Water
- ½ Cup Water
- Date Sugar.

Directions:

1. Use clean water to rinse all the vegetable items of ASOS into a clean bowl.

2. Chop Romaine Lettuce; dice Strawberry, Cucumber, and Banana; remove the back of Seville Orange and divide into four.

3. Transfer all the ASOS items inside a clean blender and blend to achieve a homogenous smoothie.

4. Pour into a clean big cup and fortify your body with a palatable detox.

Nutrition:

Calories 298

Calories from Fat 9.

Fat 1g

Cholesterol 2mg

Sodium 73mg

Potassium 998mg

Carbohydrates 68g

Fiber 7g

Sugar 50g

1082. Tamarind – Pear Smoothie (TPS)

Preparation time: 10 minutes

Cooking time: 0 minutes

Servings: 1

Ingredients:

- ½ Burro Banana

- ½ Cup Watermelon
- 1 Raspberries
- 1 Prickly Pear
- 1 Grape with Seed
- 3 Tamarind
- ½ Medium Cucumber
- 1 Cup Coconut Water
- ½ Cup Distilled Water

Directions:

1. Use clean water to rinse all the ATPS items.
2. Remove the pod of Tamarind and collect the edible part around the seed into a container.
3. If you must use the seeds then you have to boil the seed for 15mins and add to the Tamarind edible part in the container.
4. Cubed all other vegetable fruits and transfer all the items into a high-speed blender and blend to achieve homogenous smoothie.

Nutrition:

Calories: 199
Carbohydrates: 47 g
Fat: 1g
Protein: 6g

1083. Currant Elderberry Smoothie (CES)

Preparation time: 10 minutes
Cooking time: 0 minutes
Servings: 1
Ingredients:

- ¼ Cup Cubed Elderberry
- 1 Sour Cherry
- 2 Currant
- 1 Cubed Burro Banana
- 1 Fig
- 1Cup 4 Bay Leaves Tea
- 1 Cup Energy Booster Tea
- Date Sugar to your satisfaction

Directions:

1. Use clean water to rinse all the ACES items
2. Initially boil ¾ Teaspoon of Energy Booster Tea with 2 cups of water on a heat source and allow boiling for 10 minutes.

3. Add 4 Bay leaves and boil together for another 4minutes.
4. Drain the Tea extract into a clean big cup and allow it to cool.
5. Transfer all the items into a high-speed blender and blend till you achieve a homogenous smoothie.
6. Pour the palatable medicinal smoothie into a clean cup and drink.

Nutrition:

Calories: 63
Fat: 0.22g
Sodium: 1.1mg
Carbohydrates: 15.5g
Fiber: 4.8g
Sugars: 8.25g
Protein: 1.6g

1084. Sweet Dream Strawberry Smoothie

Preparation time:1 5 minutes
Cooking time: 0
Servings: 1
Ingredients:

- 5 Strawberries
- 3 Dates – Pits eliminated
- 2 Burro Bananas or small bananas
- Spring Water for 32 fluid ounces of smoothie

Directions:

1. Strip off skin of the bananas.
2. Wash the dates and strawberries.
3. Include bananas, dates, and strawberries to a blender container.
4. Include a couple of water and blend.
5. Keep on including adequate water to persuade up to be 32 oz. of smoothie.

Nutrition:

Calories: 282
Fat: 11g
Carbohydrates: 4g
Protein: 7g

1085. Alkaline Green Ginger and Banana Cleansing Smoothie

Preparation time: 15 minutes
Cooking time: 0
Servings: 1

Ingredients:

- One handful of kale
- one banana, frozen
- Two cups of hemp seed milk
- One inch of ginger, finely minced
- Half cup of chopped strawberries, frozen
- 1 tablespoon of agave or your preferred sweetener

Directions:

1. Mix all the **Ingredients** in a blender and mix on high speed.
2. Allow it to blend evenly.
3. Pour into a pitcher with a few decorative straws and voila you are one happy camper.
4. Enjoy!

Nutrition:

Calories: 350

Fat: 4g

Carbohydrates: 52g

Protein: 16g

1086. Orange Mixed Detox Smoothie

Preparation time: 15 minutes

Cooking time: 0

Servings: 1

Ingredients:

- One cup of vegies (Amaranth, Dandelion, Lettuce or Watercress)
- Half avocado
- One cup of tender-jelly coconut water
- One seville orange
- Juice of one key lime
- One tablespoon of bromide plus powder

Directions:

1. Peel and cut the Seville orange in chunks.
2. Mix all the **Ingredients** collectively in a high-speed blender until done.

Nutrition:

Calories: 71

Fat: 1g

Carbohydrates: 12g

Protein: 2g

1087. Cucumber Toxin Flush Smoothie

Preparation time: 15 minutes

Cooking time: 0

Servings: 1

Ingredients:

- 1 Cucumber
- 1 Key Lime
- 1 cup of watermelon (seeded), cubed

Directions:

1. Mix all the above **Ingredients** in a high-speed blender.
2. Considering that watermelon and cucumbers are largely water, you may not want to add any extra, however you can so if you want.
3. Juice the key lime and add into your smoothie.
4. Enjoy!

Nutrition:

Calories: 219

Fat: 4g

Carbohydrates: 48g

Protein: 5g

1088. Apple Blueberry Smoothie

Preparation time: 15 minutes

Cooking time: 0

Servings: 1

Ingredients:

- Half apple
- One Date
- Half cup of blueberries
- Half cup of sparkling callaloo
- One tablespoon of hemp seeds
- One tablespoon of sesame seeds
- Two cups of sparkling soft-jelly coconut water
- Half of tablespoon of bromide plus powder

Directions:

1. Mix all of the **Ingredients** in a high-speed blender and enjoy!

Nutrition:

Calories: 167.4

Fat: 6.4g

Carbohydrates: 22.5g

Protein: 6.7g

Low Sugar Recipes

1089. Red Veggie & Fruit Smoothie

Preparation Time: 10 minutes
Cooking Time: 0 minutes
Servings: 2
Ingredients:

- ½ cup fresh raspberries
- ½ cup fresh strawberries
- ½ red bell pepper, seeded and chopped
- ½ cup red cabbage, chopped
- 1 small tomato
- 1 cup water
- ½ cup ice cubes

Directions:
1. Place all the ingredients in a high-speed blender and pulse until creamy.
2. Pour the smoothie into two glasses and serve immediately.
Nutrition: Calories 39 Cholesterol 0 mg Saturated Fat 0 g Sodium 10 mg Total Carbs 8.9 g Fiber 3.5 g Sugar 4.8 g Protein 1.3 g Total Fat 0.4 g

1090. Kale Smoothie

Preparation Time: 10 minutes
Cooking Time: 0 minutes
Servings: 2
Ingredients:

- 3 stalks fresh kale, trimmed and chopped
- 1-2 celery stalks, chopped
- ½ avocado, peeled, pitted, and chopped
- ½-inch piece ginger root, chopped
- ½-inch piece turmeric root, chopped
- 2 cups coconut milk

Directions:
1. Place all the ingredients in a high-speed blender and pulse until creamy.
2. Pour the smoothie into two glasses and serve immediately.

Nutrition: Calories 248 Total Fat 21.8 g Saturated Fat 12 g Cholesterol 0 mg Sodium 59 mg Total Carbs 11.3 g Fiber 4.2 g Sugar 0.5 g Protein 3.5 g

1091. Green Tofu Smoothie

Preparation Time: 10 minutes
Cooking Time: 0 minutes
Servings: 2
Ingredients:

- 1½ cups cucumber, peeled and chopped roughly
- 3 cups fresh baby spinach
- 2 cups frozen broccoli
- ½ cup silken tofu, drained and pressed
- 1 tablespoon fresh lime juice
- 4-5 drops liquid stevia
- 1 cup unsweetened almond milk
- ½ cup ice, crushed

Directions:
1. Place all the ingredients in a high-speed blender and pulse until creamy.
2. Pour the smoothie into two glasses and serve immediately.
Nutrition: Calories 118 Total Fat 15 g Saturated Fat 0.8 g Cholesterol 0 mg Sodium 165 mg Total Carbs 12.6 g Fiber 4.8 g Sugar 3.4 g Protein 10 g

1092. Green Veggies Smoothie

Preparation Time: 15 minutes
Cooking Time: 0 minutes
Servings: 2
Ingredients:

- 1 medium avocado, peeled, pitted, and chopped
- 1 large cucumber, peeled and chopped
- 2 fresh tomatoes, chopped
- 1 small green bell pepper, seeded and chopped
- 1 cup fresh spinach, torn
- 2 tablespoons fresh lime juice
- 2 tablespoons homemade vegetable broth
- 1 cup alkaline water

Directions:

1. Add all the ingredients in a high-speed blender and pulse until smooth.
2. Pour the smoothie into glasses and serve immediately.

Nutrition: Calories 275 Total Fat 20.3 g Saturated Fat 4.2 g Cholesterol 0 mg Sodium 76 mg Total Carbs 24.1 g Fiber 10.1 g Sugar 9.3 g Protein 5.3 g

1093. Avocado & Spinach Smoothie

Preparation Time: 10 minutes
Cooking Time: 0 minutes
Servings: 2
Ingredients:

- 2 cups fresh baby spinach
- ½ avocado, peeled, pitted, and chopped
- 4-6 drops liquid stevia
- ½ teaspoon ground cinnamon
- 1 tablespoon hemp seeds
- 2 cups chilled alkaline water

Directions:
1. Add all the ingredients in a high-speed blender and pulse until smooth.
2. Pour the smoothie into two glasses and serve immediately.

Nutrition: Calories 132 Total Fat 11.7 g Saturated Fat 2.2 g Cholesterol 0 mg Sodium 27 mg Total Carbs 6.1 g Fiber 4.5 g Sugar 0.4 g Protein 3.1 g

1094. Sarsaparilla Syrup

Preparation time: 15 minutes
Cooking time: 4 hours
Servings: 4
Ingredients:
Date sugar, 1 c
Sassafras root, 1 tbsp.
Sarsaparilla root, 1 c
Water, 2 c
Directions:
1. Firstly, add all of the **Ingredients** to a mason jar. Screw on the lid, tightly, and shake everything together. Heat a water bath up to 160. Sit the mason jar into the water bath and allow it to infuse for about two to four hours.
2. When the infusion time is almost up, set up an ice bath. Add half and half water and ice to a bowl. Carefully take the mason jar out of the water bath and place it into the ice bath. Allow it to sit in the ice bath for 15 to 20 minutes.
3. Strain the infusion out and into another clean jar.
Nutrition:
Calories 37
Sugar 2g
Protein 0.4g
Fat 0.3

1095. Misto Quente

Preparation time: 5 minutes
Cooking time: 10 minutes
Servings: 4
Ingredients:

- 4 slices of bread without shell
- 4 slices of turkey breast
- 4 slices of cheese
- 2 tbsp. cream cheese
- 2 spoons of butter

Directions:
1. Preheat the air fryer. Set the timer of 5 minutes and the temperature to 200C.
2. Pass the butter on one side of the slice of bread, and on the other side of the slice, the cream cheese.
3. Mount the sandwiches placing two slices of turkey breast and two slices cheese between the breads, with the cream cheese inside and the side with butter.
4. Place the sandwiches in the basket of the air fryer. Set the timer of the air fryer for 5 minutes and press the power button.
Nutrition: Calories: 340 Fat: 15g Carbohydrates: 32g Protein: 15g Sugar: 0g Cholesterol: 0mg

1096. Garlic Bread

Preparation time: 10 minutes
Cooking time: 15 minutes
Servings: 4-5
Ingredients:

- 2 stale French rolls
- 4 tbsp. crushed or crumpled garlic
- 1 cup of mayonnaise
- Powdered grated Parmesan
- 1 tbsp. olive oil

Directions:

1. Preheat the air fryer. Set the time of 5 minutes and the temperature to 2000C.
2. Mix mayonnaise with garlic and set aside.
3. Cut the baguettes into slices, but without separating them completely.
4. Fill the cavities of equals. Brush with olive oil and sprinkle with grated cheese.
5. Place in the basket of the air fryer. Set the timer to 10 minutes, adjust the temperature to 1800C and press the power button.

Nutrition: Calories: 340 Fat: 15g Carbohydrates: 32g Protein: 15g Sugar: 0g Cholesterol: 0mg

1097. Bruschetta

Preparation time: 5 minutes
Cooking time: 10 minutes
Servings: 2
Ingredients:

- 4 slices of Italian bread
- 1 cup chopped tomato tea
- 1 cup grated mozzarella tea
- Olive oil
- Oregano, salt, and pepper
- 4 fresh basil leaves

Directions:
1. Preheat the air fryer. Set the timer of 5 minutes and the temperature to 2000C.
2. Sprinkle the slices of Italian bread with olive oil. Divide the chopped tomatoes and mozzarella between the slices. Season with salt, pepper, and oregano.
3. Put oil in the filling. Place a basil leaf on top of each slice.
4. Put the bruschetta in the basket of the air fryer being careful not to spill the filling. Set the timer of 5 minutes, set the temperature to 180C, and press the power button.
5. Transfer the bruschetta to a plate and serve.

Nutrition: Calories: 434 Fat: 14g Carbohydrates: 63g Protein: 11g Sugar: 8g Cholesterol: 0mg

1098. Cream Buns with Strawberries

Preparation time: 10 minutes
Cooking time: 12 minutes
Servings: 6
Ingredients:

- 240g all-purpose flour
- 50g granulated sugar
- 8g baking powder
- 1g of salt
- 85g chopped cold butter
- 84g chopped fresh strawberries
- 120 ml whipping cream
- 2 large eggs
- 10 ml vanilla extract
- 5 ml of water

Directions:
1. Sift flour, sugar, baking powder and salt in a large bowl. Put the butter with the flour with the use of a blender or your hands until the mixture resembles thick crumbs.
2. Mix the strawberries in the flour mixture. Set aside for the mixture to stand. Beat the whipping cream, 1 egg and the vanilla extract in a separate bowl.
3. Put the cream mixture in the flour mixture until they are homogeneous, and then spread the mixture to a thickness of 38 mm.
4. Use a round cookie cutter to cut the buns. Spread the buns with a combination of egg and water. Set aside
5. Preheat the air fryer, set it to 180C.
6. Place baking paper in the preheated inner basket.
7. Place the buns on top of the baking paper and cook for 12 minutes at 180C, until golden brown.

Nutrition: Calories: 150 Fat: 14g Carbohydrates: 3g Protein: 11g Sugar: 8g Cholesterol: 0mg

1099. Blueberry Buns

Preparation time: 10 minutes
Cooking time: 12 minutes
Servings: 6
Ingredients:

- 240g all-purpose flour
- 50g granulated sugar
- 8g baking powder
- 2g of salt
- 85g chopped cold butter
- 85g of fresh blueberries
- 3g grated fresh ginger
- 113 ml whipping cream
- 2 large eggs
- 4 ml vanilla extract
- 5 ml of water

Directions:
1. Put sugar, flour, baking powder and salt in a large bowl.
2. Put the butter with the flour using a blender or your hands until the mixture resembles thick crumbs.
3. Mix the blueberries and ginger in the flour mixture and set aside
4. Mix the whipping cream, 1 egg and the vanilla extract in a different container.
5. Put the cream mixture with the flour mixture until combined.
6. Shape the dough until it reaches a thickness of approximately 38 mm and cut it into eighths.
7. Spread the buns with a combination of egg and water. Set aside Preheat the air fryer set it to 180C.
8. Place baking paper in the preheated inner basket and place the buns on top of the paper. Cook for 12 minutes at 180C, until golden brown
Nutrition: Calories: 105 Fat: 1.64g Carbohydrates: 20.09gProtein: 2.43g Sugar: 2.1g Cholesterol: 0mg

1100. Cauliflower Potato Mash

Preparation Time: 30 minutes Servings: 4
Cooking Time: 5 minutes
Ingredients:
- 2 cups potatoes, peeled and cubed
- 2 tbsp. butter
- ¼ cup milk
- 10 oz. cauliflower florets
- ¾ tsp. salt

Directions:
1. Add water to the saucepan and bring to boil.
2. Reduce heat and simmer for 10 minutes.
3. Drain vegetables well. Transfer vegetables, butter, milk, and salt in a blender and blend until smooth.
4. Serve and enjoy.
Nutrition: Calories 128 Fat 6.2 g, Sugar 3.3 g, Protein 3.2 g, Cholesterol 17 mg

1101. French toast in Sticks

Preparation time: 5 minutes
Cooking time: 10 minutes
Servings: 4
Ingredients:
- 4 slices of white bread, 38 mm thick, preferably hard
- 2 eggs
- 60 ml of milk
- 15 ml maple sauce
- 2 ml vanilla extract
- Nonstick Spray Oil
- 38g of sugar
- 3ground cinnamon
- Maple syrup, to serve
- Sugar to sprinkle

Directions:
1. Cut each slice of bread into thirds making 12 pieces. Place sideways
2. Beat the eggs, milk, maple syrup and vanilla.
3. Preheat the air fryer, set it to 175C.
4. Dip the sliced bread in the egg mixture and place it in the preheated air fryer. Sprinkle French toast generously with oil spray.
5. Cook French toast for 10 minutes at 175C. Turn the toast halfway through cooking.
6. Mix the sugar and cinnamon in a bowl.
7. Cover the French toast with the sugar and cinnamon mixture when you have finished cooking.
8. Serve with Maple syrup and sprinkle with powdered sugar
Nutrition: Calories 128 Fat 6.2 g, Carbohydrates 16.3 g, Sugar 3.3 g, Protein 3.2 g, Cholesterol 17 mg

1102. Stuffed French toast

Preparation time: 4 minutes
Cooking time: 10 minutes
Servings: 1
Ingredients:
- 1 slice of brioche bread,
- 64 mm thick, preferably rancid
- 113g cream cheese
- 2 eggs
- 15 ml of milk
- 30 ml whipping cream
- 38g of sugar
- 3g cinnamon
- 2 ml vanilla extract
- Nonstick Spray Oil
- Pistachios chopped to cover
- Maple syrup, to serve

Directions:

1. Preheat the air fryer, set it to 175C.

2. Cut a slit in the middle of the muffin.

3. Fill the inside of the slit with cream cheese. Leave aside.

4. Mix the eggs, milk, whipping cream, sugar, cinnamon, and vanilla extract.

5. Moisten the stuffed French toast in the egg mixture for 10 seconds on each side.

6. Sprinkle each side of French toast with oil spray.

7. Place the French toast in the preheated air fryer and cook for 10 minutes at 175C

8. Stir the French toast carefully with a spatula when you finish cooking.

9. Serve topped with chopped pistachios and acrid syrup.

Nutrition: Calories: 159Fat: 7.5g Carbohydrates: 25.2g Protein: 14g Sugar: 0g Cholesterol: 90mg

1103. Chili Chicken Wings

Preparation Time: 10 minutes
Cooking Time: 1 hour 10 minutes
Servings: 4
Ingredients:

- 2 lbs. chicken wings
- 1/8 tsp. paprika
- 1/2 cup coconut flour
- 1/4 tsp. garlic powder
- 1/4 tsp. chili powder

Directions:

1. Preheat the oven to 400 F/ 200 C.

2. In a mixing bowl, add all ingredients except chicken wings and mix well.

3. Add chicken wings to the bowl mixture and coat well and place on a baking tray.

4. Bake in preheated oven for 55-60 minutes.

5. Serve and enjoy.

Nutrition:
Calories 440 Fat 17.1 g, Carbohydrates 1.3 g, Sugar 0.2 g, Protein 65.9 g, Cholesterol 202 mg

1104. Garlic Chicken Wings

Preparation Time: 10 minutes
Cooking Time: 55 minutes
Servings: 6
Ingredients:

- 12 chicken wings

- 2 garlic cloves, minced
- 3 tbsp. ghee
- 1/2 tsp. turmeric
- 2 tsp. cumin seeds

Directions:

1. Preheat the oven to 425 F/ 215 C.

2. In a large bowl, mix together 1 teaspoon cumin, 1 tbsp. ghee, turmeric, pepper, and salt.

3. Add chicken wings to the bowl and toss well.

4. Spread chicken wings on a baking tray and bake in preheated oven for 30 minutes.

5. Turn chicken wings to another side and bake for 8 minutes more.

6. Meanwhile, heat remaining ghee in a pan over medium heat.

7. Add garlic and cumin to the pan and cook for a minute.

8. Remove pan from heat and set aside.

9. Remove chicken wings from oven and drizzle with ghee mixture/

10. Bake chicken wings 5 minutes more.

11. Serve and enjoy.

Nutrition:
Calories 378 Fat 27.9 g, Carbohydrates 11.4 g, Sugar 0 g, Protein 19.7 g, Cholesterol 94 mg

1105. Spinach Cheese Pie

Preparation Time: 10 minutes
Cooking Time: 40 minutes
Servings: 8
Ingredients:

- 6 eggs, lightly beaten
- 2 boxes frozen spinach, chopped
- 2 cup cheddar cheese, shredded
- 15 oz. cottage cheese
- 1 tsp. salt

Directions:

1. Preheat the oven to 375 F/ 190 C.

2. Spray an 8*8-inch baking dish with cooking spray and set aside.

3. In a mixing bowl, combine together spinach, eggs, cheddar cheese, cottage cheese, pepper, and salt.

4. Pour spinach mixture into the prepared baking dish and bake in preheated oven for 10 minutes.

5. Serve and enjoy.

Nutrition:

Calories 229 Fat 14 g, Carbohydrates 5.4 g, Sugar 0.9 g, Protein 21 g, Cholesterol 157 mg

1106. Tasty Harissa Chicken

Preparation Time: 10 minutes

Cooking Time: 4 hours 10 minutes

Servings: 4

Ingredients:

- 1 lb. chicken breasts, skinless and boneless
- 1/2 tsp. ground cumin
- 1 cup harissa sauce
- 1/4 tsp. garlic powder
- 1/2 tsp. kosher salt

Directions:

1. Season chicken with garlic powder, cumin, and salt.
2. Place chicken to the slow cooker.
3. Pour harissa sauce over the chicken.
4. Cover slow cooker with lid and cook on low for 4 hours.
5. Remove chicken from slow cooker and shred using a fork.
6. Return shredded chicken to the slow cooker and stir well.
7. Serve and enjoy.

Nutrition:

Calories 232 Fat 9.7 g, Carbohydrates 1.3 g, Sugar 0.1 g, Protein 32.9 g, Cholesterol 101 mg

1107. Roasted Balsamic Mushrooms

Preparation Time: 10 minutes

Cooking Time: 50 minutes

Servings: 4

Ingredients:

- 8 oz. mushrooms, sliced
- 1/2 tsp. thyme
- 2 tbsp. balsamic vinegar
- 2 tbsp. extra virgin olive oil
- 2 onions, sliced

Directions:

1. Preheat the oven to 375 F/ 190 C.
2. Line baking tray with aluminum foil and spray with cooking spray and set aside.
3. In a mixing bowl, add all ingredients and mix well.

4. Spread mushroom mixture onto a prepared baking tray.
5. Roast in preheated oven for 45 minutes.
6. Season with pepper and salt.
7. Serve and enjoy.

Nutrition:

Calories 96 Fat 7.2 g, Carbohydrates 7.2 g, Sugar 3.3 g, Protein 2.4 g, Cholesterol 0 mg

1108. Roasted Cumin Carrots

Preparation Time: 10 minutes

Cooking Time: 45 minutes

Servings: 4

Ingredients:

- 8 carrots, peeled and cut into 1/2-inch-thick slices
- 1 tsp. cumin seeds
- 1 tbsp. olive oil
- 1/2 tsp. kosher salt

Directions:

1. Preheat the oven to 400 F/ 200 C.
2. Line baking tray with parchment paper.
3. Add carrots, cumin seeds, olive oil, and salt in a large bowl and toss well to coat.
4. Spread carrots on a prepared baking tray and roast in preheated oven for 20 minutes.
5. Turn carrots to another side and roast for 20 minutes more.
6. Serve and enjoy.

Nutrition:

Calories 82 Fat 3.6 g, Carbohydrates 12.2 g, Sugar 6 g, Protein 1.1 g, Cholesterol 0 mg

1109. Tasty & Tender Brussels Sprouts

Preparation Time: 10 minutes

Cooking Time: 35 minutes

Servings: 4

Ingredients:

- 1 lb. Brussels sprouts, trimmed cut in half
- ¼ cup balsamic vinegar
- 1 onion, sliced
- 1 tbsp. olive oil

Directions:

1. Add water in a saucepan and bring to boil.

2.   Add Brussels sprouts and cook over medium heat for 20 minutes. Drain well.
3.   Heat oil in a pan over medium heat.
4.   Add onion and cook until softened. Add sprouts and vinegar and stir well and cook for 1-2 minutes.
5.   Serve and enjoy.
Nutrition:
Calories 93 Fat 3.9 g, Carbohydrates 13 g, Sugar 3.7 g, Protein 4.2 g, Cholesterol 0 mg

1110. Sautéed Veggies

Preparation Time: 10 minutes
Cooking Time: 15 minutes
Servings: 4
Ingredients:

- 1/2 cup mushrooms, sliced
- 1 zucchini, diced
- 1 squash, diced
- 2 1/2 tsp. southwest seasoning
- 3 tbsp. olive oil

Directions:
1.   In a medium bowl, whisk together southwest seasoning, pepper, olive oil, and salt.
2.   Add vegetables to a bowl and mix well to coat.
3.   Heat pan over medium-high heat.
4.   Add vegetables in the pan and sauté for 5-7 minutes.
5.   Serve and enjoy.
Nutrition:
Calories 107 Fat 10.7 g, Carbohydrates 3.6 g, Sugar 1.5 g, Protein 1.2 g, Cholesterol 0 mg

1111. Mustard Green Beans

Preparation Time: 10 minutes
Cooking Time: 20 minutes
Servings: 4
Ingredients:

- 1 lb. green beans, washed and trimmed
- 1 tsp. whole grain mustard
- 1 tbsp. olive oil
- 2 tbsp. apple cider vinegar
- 1/4 cup onion, chopped

Directions:
1.   Steam green beans in the microwave until tender.
2.   Meanwhile, in a pan heat olive oil over medium heat.
3.   Add the onion in a pan sauté until softened.

4.   Add water, apple cider vinegar, and mustard in the pan and stir well.
5.   Add green beans and stir to coat and heat through.
6.   Season green beans with pepper and salt.
7.   Serve and enjoy.
Nutrition:
Calories 71 Fat 3.7 g, Carbohydrates 8.9 g, Sugar 1.9 g, Protein 2.1 g, Cholesterol 0 mg

1112. Zucchini Fries

Preparation Time: 10 minutes
Cooking Time: 40 minutes
Servings: 4
Ingredients:

- 1 egg
- 2 medium zucchinis, cut into fry's shape
- 1 tsp. Italian herbs
- 1 tsp. garlic powder
- 1 cup parmesan cheese, grated

Directions:
1.   Preheat the oven to 425 F/ 218 C.
2.   Spray a baking tray with cooking spray and set aside.
3.   In a small bowl, add egg and lightly whisk it.
4.   In a separate bowl, mix together spices and parmesan cheese.
5.   Dip zucchini fries in egg then coat with parmesan cheese mixture and place on a baking tray.
6.   Bake in preheated oven for 25-30 minutes. Turn halfway through.
7.   Serve and enjoy.
Nutrition:
Calories 184 Fat 10.3 g, Carbohydrates 3.9 g, Sugar 2 g, Protein 14.7 g, Cholesterol 71 mg

1113. Broccoli Nuggets

Preparation Time: 10 minutes
Cooking Time: 25 minutes
Servings: 4
Ingredients:

- 2 cups broccoli florets
- 1/4 cup almond flour
- 2 egg whites
- 1 cup cheddar cheese, shredded
- 1/8 tsp. salt

Directions:

1. Preheat the oven to 350 F/ 180 C.
2. Spray a baking tray with cooking spray and set aside.
3. Using potato masher breaks the broccoli florets into small pieces.
4. Add remaining ingredients to the broccoli and mix well.
5. Drop 20 scoops onto baking tray and press lightly into a nugget shape.
6. Bake in preheated oven for 20 minutes.
7. Serve and enjoy.

Nutrition:

Calories 148 Fat 10.4 g, Carbohydrates 3.9 g, Sugar 1.1 g, Protein 10.5 g, Cholesterol 30 mg

1114. Zucchini Cauliflower Fritters

Preparation Time: 10 minutes
Cooking Time: 15 minutes
Servings: 4
Ingredients:

- 2 medium zucchinis, grated and squeezed
- 3 cups cauliflower florets
- 1 tbsp. coconut oil
- 1/4 cup coconut flour
- 1/2 tsp. sea salt

Directions:

1. Steam cauliflower florets for 5 minutes.
2. Add cauliflower into the food processor and process until it looks like rice.
3. Add all ingredients except coconut oil to the large bowl and mix until well combined.
4. Make small round patties from the mixture and set aside.
5. Heat coconut oil in a pan over medium heat.
6. Place patties in a pan and cook for 3-4 minutes on each side.
7. Serve and enjoy.

Nutrition:

Calories 68 Fat 3.8 g, Carbohydrates 7.8 g, Sugar 3.6 g, Protein 2.8 g, Cholesterol 0 mg

1115. Roasted Chickpeas

Preparation Time: 10 minutes
Cooking Time: 30 minutes
Servings: 4

Ingredients:

- 15 oz. can chickpeas, drained, rinsed and pat dry
- 1/2 tsp. paprika
- 1 tbsp. olive oil
- 1/2 tsp. pepper
- 1/2 tsp. salt

Directions:

1. Preheat the oven to 450 F/ 232 C.
2. Spray a baking tray with cooking spray and set aside.
3. In a large bowl, toss chickpeas with olive oil, paprika, pepper, and salt.
4. Spread chickpeas on a prepared baking tray and roast in preheated oven for 25 minutes. Stir every 10 minutes.
5. Serve and enjoy.

Nutrition:

Calories 158 Fat 4.8 g, Carbohydrates 24.4 g, Sugar 0 g, Protein 5.3 g, Cholesterol 0 mg

1116. Peanut Butter Mousse

Preparation Time: 10 minutes
Cooking Time: 10 minutes
Servings: 2
Ingredients:

- 1 tbsp. peanut butter
- 1 tsp. vanilla extract
- 1 tsp. stevia
- 1/2 cup heavy cream

Directions:

1. Add all ingredients into the bowl and whisk until soft peak forms.
2. Spoon into the serving bowls and enjoy.

Nutrition:

Calories 157 Fat 15.1 g, Carbohydrates 5.2 g, Sugar 3.6 g, Protein 2.6 g, Cholesterol 41 mg

1117. Coffee Mousse

Preparation Time: 10 minutes
Cooking Time: 20 minutes
Servings: 8
Ingredients:

- 4 tbsp. brewed coffee
- 16 oz. cream cheese, softened
- 1/2 cup unsweetened almond milk
- 1 cup whipping cream

- 2 tsp. liquid stevia

Directions:

1. Add coffee and cream cheese in a blender and blend until smooth.
2. Add stevia, and milk and blend again until smooth.
3. Add cream and blend until thickened.
4. Pour into the serving glasses and place in the refrigerator.
5. Serve chilled and enjoy.

Nutrition:

Calories 244 Fat 24.6 g, Carbohydrates 2.1 g, Sugar 0.1 g, Protein 4.7 g, Cholesterol 79 mg

Low Carb Recipes

1118. Chicken Thigh and Kale Stew

Preparation time: 20 minutes
Cooking time: 6 hours
Servings: 6
Ingredients:

- 3 tablespoons extra-virgin olive oil, divided
- 1 pound (454 g) boneless chicken thighs, diced into 1½-inch pieces
- ½ sweet onion, chopped
- 2 teaspoons minced garlic
- 2 cups chicken broth
- 2 celery stalks, diced
- 1 carrot, diced
- 1 teaspoon dried thyme
- 1 cup shredded kale
- 1 cup coconut cream
- Salt, for seasoning
- Freshly ground black pepper, for seasoning

Directions:
1. Lightly grease the insert of the slow cooker with 1 tablespoon of the olive oil.
2. In a large skillet over medium-high heat, heat the remaining 2 tablespoons of the olive oil. Add the chicken and sauté until it is just cooked through, about 7 minutes.
3. Add the onion and garlic and sauté for an additional 3 minutes.
4. Transfer the chicken mixture to the insert, and stir in the broth, celery, carrot, and thyme.
5. Cover and cook on low for 6 hours.
6. Stir in the kale and coconut cream.
7. Season with salt and pepper, and serve warm.

Nutrition:
Calories: 277 | fat: 22.0g | protein: 17.0g | carbs: 6.0g | net carbs: 4.0g | fiber: 2.0g

1119. Bell Pepper Turkey Casserole

Preparation time: 10 minutes
Cooking time: 25 minutes
Servings: 5
Ingredients:

- 3 teaspoons olive oil
- 1 cup bell peppers, sliced
- 1 yellow onion, thinly sliced
- 1½ pounds (680 g) turkey breast
- Se salt and ground black pepper, to taste
- 1 cup chicken bone broth
- 1 cup double cream
- ½ cup Swiss cheese, shredded

Directions:
1. Heat 2 teaspoons of the olive oil in a sauté pan over a moderate flame. Sauté the peppers and onion until they have softened; reserve.
2. In the same sauté pan, heat the remaining teaspoon of olive oil and sear the turkey breasts until no longer pink.
3. Layer the peppers and onions in a lightly greased baking pan. Add the turkey breast; sprinkle with salt and pepper.
4. Mix the chicken bone broth with the double cream; pour the mixture over the turkey breasts. Bake in the preheated oven at 350°F (180°C) for 20 minutes; top with the Swiss cheese.
5. Bake an additional 5 minutes or until golden brown on top. Bon appétit!

Nutrition:
Calories: 465 | fat: 28.5g | protein: 45.4g | carbs: 4.5g | net carbs: 4.2g | fiber: 0.3g

1120. Asian Turkey and Bird's Eye Soup

Preparation time: 10 minutes
Cooking time: 15 minutes
Servings: 5
Ingredients:

- 2 tablespoons canola oil
- 2 Oriental sweets peppers, deseeded and chopped
- 1 Bird's eye chili, deseeded and chopped
- 2 green onions, chopped

- 5 cups vegetable broth
- 1 pound (454 g) turkey thighs, deboned and cut into halves
- ½ teaspoon five-spice powder
- 1 teaspoon oyster sauce
- Kosher salt, to taste

Directions:

1.   Heat the olive oil in a stockpot over a moderate flame. Then, sauté the peppers and onions until they have softened or about 4 minutes

2.   Add in the other ingredients and bring to a boil. Turn the heat to simmer, cover, and continue to cook an additional 12 minutes.

3.   Ladle into individual bowls and serve warm. Enjoy!

Nutrition:

Calories: 180 | fat: 7.5g | protein: 21.4g | carbs: 6.7g | net carbs: 5.5g | fiber: 1.2g

1121. Chicken and Bell Pepper Kabobs

Preparation time: 10 minutes
Cooking time: 10 minutes
Servings: 6
Ingredients:

- 2 tablespoons olive oil
- 4 tablespoons dry sherry
- 1 tablespoon stone-ground mustard
- 1½ pounds (680 g) chicken, skinless, boneless and cubed
- 2 red onions, cut into wedges
- 1 green bell pepper, cut into 1-inch pieces
- 1 red bell pepper, cut into 1-inch pieces
- 1 yellow bell pepper, cut into 1-inch pieces
- ½ teaspoon sea salt
- ¼ teaspoon ground black pepper, or more to taste

Directions:

1.   In a mixing bowl, combine the olive oil, dry sherry, mustard and chicken until well coated.

2.   Alternate skewering the chicken and vegetables until you run out of ingredients. Season with salt and black pepper.

3.   Preheat your grill to medium-high heat.

4.   Place the kabobs on the grill, flipping every 2 minutes and cook to desired doneness. Serve warm.

Nutrition:

Calories: 201 | fat: 8.2g | protein: 24.3g | carbs:7.0 g | net carbs: 5.7g | fiber: 1.3g

1122. Chicken Drumsticks in Capocollo

Preparation time: 10 minutes
Cooking time: 35 minutes
Servings: 5
Ingredients:

- 2 pounds (907 g) chicken drumsticks, skinless and boneless
- 1 garlic clove, peeled and halved
- ½ teaspoon smoked paprika
- Coarse sea salt and ground black pepper, to taste
- 10 thin slices of capocollo

Directions:

1.   Using a sharp kitchen knife, butterfly cut the chicken drumsticks in half.

2.   Lay each chicken drumstick flat on a cutting board and rub garlic halves over the surface of chicken drumsticks. Season with paprika, salt, and black pepper.

3.   Lay a slice of capocollo on each piece, pressing lightly. Roll them up and secure with toothpicks.

4.   Bake in the preheated oven at 420ºF (216ºC) for about 15 minutes until the edges of the chicken begin to brown.

5.   Turnover and bake for a further 15 to 20 minutes. Bon appétit!

Nutrition:

Calories: 486 | fat: 33.7g | protein: 39.1g | carbs: 3.6g | net carbs: 2.6g | fiber: 1.0g

1123. Olla Tapada

Preparation time: 15 minutes
Cooking time: 25 minutes
Servings: 3
Ingredients:

- 2 teaspoons canola oil
- 1 red bell pepper, deveined and chopped
- 1 shallot, chopped
- ½ cup celery rib, chopped

- ½ cup chayote, peeled and cubed
- 1 pound (454 g) duck breasts, boneless, skinless, and chopped into small chunks
- 1½ cups vegetable broth
- ½ stick Mexican cinnamon
- 1 thyme sprig
- 1 rosemary sprig
- Sea salt and freshly ground black pepper, to taste

Directions:

1. Heat the canola oil in a soup pot (or clay pot) over a medium-high flame. Now, sauté the bell pepper, shallot and celery until they have softened about 5 minutes.

2. Add the remaining ingredients and stir to combine. Once it starts boiling, turn the heat to simmer and partially cover the pot.

3. Let it simmer for 17 to 20 minutes or until thoroughly cooked. Enjoy!

Nutrition:

Calories: 230 | fat: 9.6g | protein: 30.5g | carbs: 3.3g | net carbs: 2.3g | fiber: 1.0g

1124. Cheddar Bacon Stuffed Chicken Fillets

Preparation time: 10 minutes
Cooking time: 25 minutes
Servings: 2
Ingredients:

- 2 chicken fillets, skinless and boneless
- ½ teaspoon oregano
- ½ teaspoon tarragon
- ½ teaspoon paprika
- ¼ teaspoon ground black pepper
- Sea salt, to taste
- 2 (1-ounce / 28-g) slices bacon
- 2 (1-ounce / 28-g) slices Cheddar cheese
- 1 tomato, sliced

Directions:

1. Sprinkle the chicken fillets with oregano, tarragon, paprika, black pepper, and salt.

2. Place the bacon slices and cheese on each chicken fillet. Roll up the fillets and secure with toothpicks. Place the stuffed chicken fillets on a lightly greased baking pan. Scatter the sliced tomato around the fillets.

3. Bake in the preheated oven at 390°F (199°C) for 15 minutes; turn on the other side and bake an additional 5 to 10 minutes or until the meat is no longer pink.

4. Discard the toothpicks and serve immediately. Bon appétit!

Nutrition:

Calories: 400 | fat: 23.8g | protein: 41.3g | carbs: 3.6g | net carbs: 2.4g | fiber: 1.2g

1125. Herbed Balsamic Turkey

Preparation time: 15 minutes
Cooking time: 15 minutes
Servings: 2
Ingredients:

- 1 turkey drumstick, skinless and boneless
- 1 tablespoon balsamic vinegar
- 1 tablespoon whiskey
- 3 tablespoons olive oil
- 1 tablespoon stone ground mustard
- ½ teaspoon tarragon
- 1 teaspoon rosemary
- 1 teaspoon sage
- 1 garlic clove, pressed
- Kosher salt and ground black pepper, to season
- 1 brown onion, peeled and chopped

Directions:

1. Place the turkey drumsticks in a ceramic dish. Toss them with the balsamic vinegar, whiskey, olive oil, mustard, tarragon, rosemary, sage, and garlic.

2. Cover with plastic wrap and refrigerate for 3 hours. Heat your grill to the hottest setting.

3. Grill the turkey drumsticks for about 13 minutes per side. Season with salt and pepper to taste and serve with brown onion. Bon appétit!

Nutrition:

Calories: 389 | fat: 19.6g | protein: 42.0g | carbs: 6.0g | net carbs: 4.6g | fiber: 1.4g

1126. Turkish Chicken Thigh Kebabs

Preparation time: 15 minutes
Cooking time: 9 to 12 minutes
Servings: 2

Ingredients:
- 1 pound (454 g) chicken thighs, boneless, skinless and halved
- ½ cup Greek yogurt
- Sea salt, to taste
- 1 tablespoon Aleppo red pepper flakes
- ½ teaspoon ground black pepper
- ¼ teaspoon dried oregano
- ½ teaspoon mustard seeds
- 1/8 teaspoon ground cinnamon
- ½ teaspoon sumac
- 2 Roma tomatoes, chopped
- 2 tablespoons olive oil
- 1½ ounces (43 g) Swiss cheese, sliced

Directions:
1. Place the chicken thighs, yogurt, salt, red pepper flakes, black pepper, oregano, mustard seeds, cinnamon, sumac, tomatoes, and olive oil in a ceramic dish. Cover and let it marinate in your refrigerator for 4 hours.
2. Preheat your grill for medium-high heat and lightly oil the grate. Thread the chicken thighs onto skewers, making a thick log shape.
3. Cook your kebabs for 3 or 4 minutes; turn over and continue cooking for 3 to 4 minutes more. An instant-read thermometer should read about 165°F (74°C).
4. Add the cheese and let it cook for a further 3 to 4 minutes or until completely melted. Bon appétit!

Nutrition:
Calories: 500 | fat: 23.3g | protein: 61.0g | carbs: 6.2g | net carbs: 4.5g | fiber: 1.7g

1127. Spiced Duck Goulash

Preparation time: 15 minutes
Cooking time: 5 minutes
Servings: 2
Ingredients:
- 2 (1-ounce / 28-g) slices bacon, chopped
- ½ pound (227 g) duck legs, skinless and boneless
- 2 cups chicken broth, preferably homemade
- ½ cup celery ribs, chopped
- 2 green garlic stalks, chopped
- 2 green onion stalks, chopped
- 1 ripe tomato, puréed

- Kosher salt, to season
- ¼ teaspoon red pepper flakes
- ½ teaspoon Hungarian paprika
- ½ teaspoon ground black pepper
- ½ teaspoon mustard seeds
- ½ teaspoon sage
- 1 bay laurel

Directions:
1. Heat a stockpot over medium-high heat; once hot, fry the bacon until it is crisp or about 3 minutes. Add in the duck legs and cook until they are no longer pink.
2. Chop the meat, discarding any remaining skin and bones. Then, reserve the bacon and meat.
3. Pour in a splash of chicken broth to deglaze the pan.
4. Now, sauté the celery, green garlic and onions for 2 to 3 minutes, stirring periodically. Add the remaining ingredients to the pot, including the reserved bacon and meat.
5. Stir to combine and reduce the heat to medium-low. Let it cook, covered, until everything is thoroughly heated or about 1 hour. Serve in individual bowls and enjoy!

Nutrition:
Calories: 364 | fat: 22.4g | protein: 33.2g | carbs: 5.1g | net carbs: 3.7g | fiber: 1.4g

1128. Chicken Mélange

Preparation time: 15 minutes
Cooking time: 35 minutes
Servings: 3
Ingredients:
- 2 ounces (57 g) bacon, diced
- ¾ pound (340 g) whole chicken, boneless and chopped
- ½ medium-sized leek, chopped
- 1 teaspoon ginger garlic paste
- 1 teaspoon poultry seasoning mix
- Sea salt, to taste
- 1 bay leaf
- 1 thyme sprig
- 1 rosemary sprig
- 1 cup chicken broth
- ½ cup cauliflower, chopped into small florets
- 2 vine-ripe tomatoes, puréed

Directions:

1.   Heat a medium-sized pan over medium-high heat; once hot, fry the bacon until it is crisp or about 3 minutes. Add in the chicken and cook until it is no longer pink; reserve.

2.   Then, sauté the leek until tender and fragrant. Stir in the ginger garlic paste, poultry seasoning mix, salt, bay leaf, thyme, and rosemary.

3.   Pour in the chicken broth and reduce the heat to medium; let it cook for 15 minutes, stirring periodically.

4.   Add in the cauliflower and tomatoes along with the reserved bacon and chicken. Decrease the temperature to simmer and let it cook for a further 15 minutes or until warmed through. Bon appétit!

Nutrition:

Calories: 353 | fat: 14.4g | protein: 44.1g | carbs: 5.9g | net carbs: 3.5g | fiber: 2.4g

1129. Teriyaki Turkey with Peppers

Preparation time: 15 minutes

Cooking time: 10 minutes

Servings: 3

Ingredients:

- ¾ pound (340 g) lean ground turkey
- 1 brown onion, chopped
- 1 red bell pepper, deveined and chopped
- 1 serrano pepper, deveined and chopped
- 1 tablespoon rice vinegar
- 1 garlic clove, pressed
- 1 tablespoon sesame oil
- ½ teaspoon ground cumin
- ½ teaspoon hot sauce
- 2 tablespoons peanut butter
- Sea salt and cayenne pepper, to season
- ½ teaspoon celery seeds
- ½ teaspoon mustard seeds
- 1 rosemary sprig, leaves chopped
- 2 tablespoons fresh Thai basil, snipped

Directions:

1.   Heat a medium-sized pan over medium-high heat; once hot, brown the ground turkey for 4 to 6 minutes; reserve.

2.   Then cook the onion and peppers in the pan drippings for a further 2 to 3 minutes.

3.   Add ¼ cup of cold water to another saucepan and heat over medium heat. Now, stir in vinegar, garlic, sesame oil, cumin, hot sauce, peanut butter, salt, cayenne pepper, celery seeds, and mustard seeds.

4.   Let it simmer, stirring occasionally, until the mixture begins to bubble slightly. Bring the mixture to a boil; then, immediately remove from the heat and add the cooked ground turkey and sautéed onion/pepper mixture.

5.   Ladle into serving bowls and garnish with the rosemary and Thai basil. Enjoy!

Nutrition:

Calories: 411 | fat: 27.2g | protein: 36.6g | carbs: 6.5g | net carbs: 5.5g | fiber: 1.0g

1130. Chicken, Pepper, and Tomato Bake

Preparation time: 10 minutes

Cooking time: 25 minutes

Servings: 3

Ingredients:

- 1 tablespoon olive oil
- ¾ pound (340 g) chicken breast fillets, chopped into bite-sized chunks
- 2 garlic cloves, sliced
- ¼ teaspoon Korean chili pepper flakes
- ¼ teaspoon Himalayan salt
- ½ teaspoon poultry seasoning mix
- 1 bell pepper, deveined and chopped
- 2 ripe tomatoes, chopped
- ¼ cup heavy whipping cream
- ¼ cup sour cream

Directions:

1.   Brush a casserole dish with olive oil. Add the chicken, garlic, Korean chili pepper flakes, salt, and poultry seasoning mix to the casserole dish.

2.   Next, layer the pepper and tomatoes. Whisk the heavy whipping cream and sour cream in a mixing bowl.

3.   Top everything with the cream mixture. Bake in the preheated oven at 390°F (199°C) for about 25 minutes or until thoroughly heated. Bon appétit!

Nutrition:

Calories: 411 | fat: 20.6g | protein: 50.0g | carbs: 6.2g | net carbs: 4.7g | fiber: 1.5g

1131. Mediterranean Roasted Chicken Drumettes

Preparation time: 15 minutes
Cooking time: 20 minutes
Servings: 5
Ingredients:

- 2 tablespoons olive oil
- 1½ pounds (680 g) chicken drumettes
- 2 cloves garlic, minced
- 1 thyme sprig
- 1 rosemary sprig
- ½ teaspoon dried oregano
- Sea salt and freshly ground black pepper, to taste
- 2 tablespoons Greek cooking wine
- ½ cup chicken bone broth
- 1 red onion, cut into wedges
- 2 bell peppers, sliced

Directions:
1.   Start by preheating your oven to 420°F (216°C). Brush the sides and bottom a baking dish with 1 tablespoon of olive oil.
2.   Heat the remaining tablespoon of olive oil in a saucepan over a moderate flame. Brown the chicken drumettes for 5 to 6 minutes per side.
3.   Transfer the warm chicken drumettes to a baking dish. Add the garlic, spices, wine and broth. Scatter red onion and peppers around chicken drumettes.
4.   Roast in the preheated oven for about 13 minutes. Serve immediately and enjoy!
Nutrition:
Calories: 219 | fat: 9.2g | protein: 28.5g | carbs: 4.2g | net carbs: 3.5g | fiber: 0.7g

1132. Italian Asiago and Pepper Stuffed Turkey

Preparation time: 15 minutes
Cooking time: 50 minutes
Servings: 6
Ingredients:

- 2 tablespoons extra-virgin olive oil
- 1 tablespoon Italian seasoning mix
- Sea salt and freshly ground black pepper, to season
- 2 garlic cloves, sliced
- 6 ounces (170 g) Asiago cheese, sliced
- 2 bell peppers, thinly sliced
- 1½ pounds (680 g) turkey breasts
- 2 tablespoons Italian parsley, roughly chopped

Directions:
1.   Brush the sides and bottom of a casserole dish with 1 tablespoon of extra-virgin olive oil. Preheat an oven to 360°F (182°C).
2.   Sprinkle the turkey breast with the Italian seasoning mix, salt, and black pepper on all sides.
3.   Make slits in each turkey breast and stuff with garlic, cheese, and bell peppers. Drizzle the turkey breasts with the remaining tablespoon of olive oil.
4.   Bake in the preheated oven for 50 minutes or until an instant-read thermometer registers 165°F (74°C).
5.   Garnish with Italian parsley and serve warm. Bon appétit!
Nutrition:
Calories: 350 | fat: 22.3g | protein: 32.1g | carbs: 3.0g | net carbs: 2.4g | fiber: 0.6g

1133. Simple White Wine Drumettes

Preparation time: 10 minutes
Cooking time: 35 minutes
Servings: 4
Ingredients:

- 1 pound (454 g) chicken drumettes
- 1 tablespoon olive oil
- 2 tablespoons butter, melted
- 1 garlic cloves, sliced
- Fresh juice of ½ lemon
- 2 tablespoons white wine
- Salt and ground black pepper, to taste
- 1 tablespoon fresh scallions, chopped

Directions:
1.   Start by preheating your oven to 450°F (235°C). Place the chicken in a parchment-lined baking pan. Drizzle with olive oil and melted butter.

2. Add the garlic, lemon, wine, salt, and black pepper.
3. Bake in the preheated oven for about 35 minutes. Serve garnished with fresh scallions. Enjoy!

Nutrition:
Calories: 210 | fat: 12.3g | protein: 23.3g | carbs: 0.5g | net carbs: 0.4g | fiber: 0.1g

1134. Turkey Wing Curry

Preparation time: 15 minutes
Cooking time: 55 minutes
Servings: 4
Ingredients:
- 3 teaspoons sesame oil
- 1 pound (454 g)turkey wings, boneless and chopped
- 2 cloves garlic, finely chopped
- 1 small-sized red chili pepper, minced
- ½ teaspoon turmeric powder
- ½ teaspoon ginger powder
- 1 teaspoon red curry paste
- 1 cup unsweetened coconut milk, preferably homemade
- ½ cup water
- ½ cup turkey consommé
- Kosher salt and ground black pepper, to taste

Directions:
1. Heat sesame oil in a sauté pan. Add the turkey and cook until it is light brown about 7 minutes.
2. Add garlic, chili pepper, turmeric powder, ginger powder, and curry paste and cook for 3 minutes longer.
3. Add the milk, water, and consommé. Season with salt and black pepper. Cook for 45 minutes over medium heat. Bon appétit!

Nutrition:
Calories: 296 | fat: 19.6g | protein: 25.6g | carbs: 3.0g | net carbs: 3.0g | fiber: 0g

1135. Double-Cheese Ranch Chicken

Preparation time: 15 minutes
Cooking time: 20 minutes
Servings: 4
Ingredients:
- 2 chicken breasts

- 2 tablespoons butter, melted
- 1 teaspoon salt
- ½ teaspoon garlic powder
- ½ teaspoon cayenne pepper
- ½ teaspoon black peppercorns, crushed
- ½ tablespoon ranch seasoning mix
- 4 ounces (113 g) Ricotta cheese, room temperature
- ½ cup Monterey-Jack cheese, grated
- 4 slices bacon, chopped
- ¼ cup scallions, chopped

Directions:
1. Start by preheating your oven to 370°F (188°C).
2. Drizzle the chicken with melted butter. Rub the chicken with salt, garlic powder, cayenne pepper, black pepper, and ranch seasoning mix.
3. Heat a cast iron skillet over medium heat. Cook the chicken for 3 to 5 minutes per side. Transfer the chicken to a lightly greased baking dish.
4. Add cheese and bacon. Bake about 12 minutes. Top with scallions just before serving. Bon appétit!

Nutrition:
Calories: 290 | fat: 19.3g | protein: 25.1g | carbs: 2.5g | net carbs: 2.5g | fiber: 0g

1136. Asiago Drumsticks with Spinach

Preparation time: 10 minutes
Cooking time: 12 minutes
Servings: 2
Ingredients:
- 1 tablespoon peanut oil
- 2 chicken drumsticks
- ½ cup vegetable broth
- ½ cup cream cheese
- 2 cups baby spinach
- Sea salt and ground black pepper, to taste
- ½ teaspoon parsley flakes
- ½ teaspoon shallot powder
- ½ teaspoon garlic powder
- ½ cup Asiago cheese, grated

Directions:
1. Heat the oil in a pan over medium-high heat. Then cook the chicken for 7 minutes, turning occasionally; reserve.

2. Pour in broth; add cream cheese and spinach; cook until spinach has wilted. Add the chicken back to the pan.

3. Add seasonings and Asiago cheese; cook until everything is thoroughly heated, an additional 4 minutes. Serve immediately and enjoy!

Nutrition:

Calories: 588 | fat: 46.0g | protein: 37.6g | carbs: 5.7g | net carbs: 4.7g | fiber: 1.0g

1137. Turkey and Canadian Bacon Pizza

Preparation time: 10 minutes
Cooking time: 32 minutes
Servings: 4
Ingredients:

- ½ pound (227 g) ground turkey
- ½ cup Parmesan cheese, freshly grated ½ cup Mozzarella cheese, grated
- Salt and ground black pepper, to taste
- 1 bell pepper, sliced
- 2 slices Canadian bacon, chopped
- 1 tomato, chopped
- 1 teaspoon oregano
- ½ teaspoon basil

Directions:

1. In mixing bowl, thoroughly combine the ground turkey, cheese, salt, and black pepper.

2. Then, press the cheese-chicken mixture into a parchment-lined baking pan. Bake in the preheated oven, at 390°F (199°C) for 22 minutes.

3. Add bell pepper, bacon, tomato, oregano, and basil. Bake an additional 10 minutes and serve warm. Bon appétit!

Nutrition:

Calories: 361 | fat: 22.6g | protein: 32.5g | carbs: 5.8g | net carbs: 5.2g | fiber: 0.6g

Infusion And Herbal Tea Recipes

1138. Lemon Rooibos Iced Tea

Preparation Time: 10 minutes
Cooking Time: 0 minute
Serving: 4
Ingredient:

- 4 bags natural, unflavored rooibos tea
- 4 cups boiling water
- 3 tablespoons freshly squeezed lemon juice
- 30–40 drops liquid stevia

Directions

1.Situate tea bags into tea pot and pour the boiling water over the bags.
2.Set aside to room temperature, then refrigerate the tea until it is ice-cold.
3.Remove the tea bags. Squeeze them gently.
4.Add the lemon juice and liquid stevia to taste and stir until well mixed.
5.Serve immediately, preferably with ice cubes and some nice garnishes, like lemon wedges.
Nutrition:
70 Calories
16g Carbohydrates
1g Protein

1139. Lemon Lavender Iced Tea

Preparation Time: 15minutes
Cooking Time: 0 minute
Serving: 4
Ingredients:

- 2 bags natural, unflavored rooibos tea
- 2 oz lemon chunks without peel and pith, seeds removed
- 1 teaspoon dried lavender blossoms placed in a tea ball
- 4 cups water, at room temperature
- 20–40 drops liquid stevia

Directions

1.Place the tea bags, lemon chunks and the tightly-closed tea ball with the lavender blossoms in a 1.5 qt (1.5 l) pitcher.
2.Pour in the water.
3.Refrigerate overnight.
4.Remove the tea bags, lemon chunks and the tea ball with the lavender on the next day. Squeeze the tea bags gently to save as much liquid as possible.
5.Add liquid stevia to taste and stir until well mixed.
6.Serve immediately with ice cubes and lemon wedges.
Nutrition:
81 Calories
12g Carbohydrates
3g Protein

1140. Cherry Vanilla Iced Tea

Preparation Time: 12 minutes
Cooking Time: 0 minute
Serving: 4
Ingredients:

- 4 bags natural, unflavored rooibos tea
- 4 cups boiling water
- 2 tablespoons freshly squeezed lime juice
- 1–2 tablespoons cherry flavoring
- 30–40 drops (or to taste) liquid vanilla stevia

Directions

1.Place tea bags into tea pot and pour the boiling water over the bags.
2.Put aside the tea cool down first, then refrigerate the tea until it is ice-cold.
3.Remove the tea bags. Squeeze them lightly.
4.Add the lime juice, cherry flavoring and the vanilla stevia and stir until well mixed.
5.Serve immediately, preferably with ice cubes and some nice garnishes like lime wedges and fresh cherries.
Nutrition:
89 Calories
14g Carbohydrates
2g Protein

1141. Elegant Blueberry Rose Water Iced Tea

Preparation Time: 12 minutes

Cooking Time: 0 minute

Serving: 4

Ingredient:

- 2 bags herbal blueberry tea
- 4 cups boiling water
- 20 drops liquid stevia
- 1 tablespoon rose water

Directions

1.Position tea bags into tea pot and pour the boiling water over the bags.

2.Allow tea cool down first, then refrigerate the tea until it is ice-cold.

3.Remove the tea bags. Press them gently.

4.Add the liquid stevia and the rose water and stir until well mixed.

5.Serve immediately, preferably with ice cubes and some nice garnishes, like fresh blueberries or natural rose petals

Nutrition:

75 Calories

10g Carbohydrates

2g Protein

1142. Melba Iced Tea

Preparation Time: 10 minutes

Cooking Time: 0 minute

Serving: 4

Ingredients:

- 1 bag herbal raspberry tea
- 1 bag herbal peach tea
- 4 cups boiling water
- 10 drops liquid peach stevia
- 20–40 drops (or to taste) liquid vanilla stevia

Directions

1.Pour the boiling water over the tea bags.

2.Leave tea cool down on room temperature, then refrigerate the tea until it is ice-cold.

3.Remove the tea bags. Press lightly.

4.Add the peach stevia and stir until well mixed.

5.Add vanilla stevia to taste and stir until well mixed.

6.Serve immediately, preferably with ice cubes and some nice garnishes, like vanilla bean, fresh raspberries or peach slices.

Nutrition:

81 Calories

14g Carbohydrates

4g Protein

1143. Merry Raspberry Cherry Iced Tea

Preparation Time: 11 minutes

Cooking Time: 0 minute

Serving: 4

Ingredients:

- 2 bags herbal raspberry tea
- 4 cups boiling water
- 1 teaspoon stevia-sweetened cherry-flavored drink mix
- 1 teaspoon freshly squeezed lime juice
- 10–20 drops (or to taste) liquid stevia

Directions

1.Put the tea bags into tea pot and fill in boiling water over the bags.

2.Let the tea cool down first to room temperature, then chill until it is ice-cold.

3.Discard tea bags. Squeeze them.

4.Add the cherry-flavored drink mix and the lime juice and stir until the drink mix is dissolved.

5.Add liquid stevia to taste and stir until well mixed.

6.Serve immediately, preferably with ice cubes or crushed ice and some nice garnishes, like fresh raspberries and cherries.

Nutrition:

82 Calories

11g Carbohydrates

4g Protein

1144. Vanilla Kissed Peach Iced Tea

Preparation Time: 13 minutes

Cooking Time: 0 minute

Serving: 4

Ingredients:

- 2 bags herbal peach tea
- 4 cups boiling water
- 1 teaspoon vanilla extract
- 1 teaspoon freshly squeezed lemon juice
- 30–40 drops (or to taste) liquid stevia

Directions

1.Soak tea bags over boiling water.

2.Allow to cool down on room temperature, then refrigerate the tea until it is ice-cold.

3.Remove and press tea bags.

4.Add the vanilla extract and the lemon juice and stir until well mixed.

5.Add liquid stevia to taste and stir until well mixed.

6.Serve immediately, preferably with ice cubes and some nice garnishes, like peach slices.

Nutrition:

88 Calories

14g Carbohydrates

3g Protein

1145. Xtreme Berried Iced Tea

Preparation Time: 10 minutes

Cooking Time: 0 minute

Serving: 4

Ingredients:

- 2 bags herbal Wild Berry Tea
- 4 cups = 950 ml boiling water
- 2 teaspoons freshly squeezed lime juice
- 40 drops berry-flavored liquid stevia
- 10 drops (or to taste) liquid stevia

Directions

1.Submerge tea bags into boiling water.

2.Set aside to cool down, then refrigerate the tea until it is ice-cold.

3.Pull out tea bags. Squeeze.

4.Add the lime juice and the berry stevia and stir until well mixed.

5.Add liquid stevia to taste and stir until well mixed.

6.Serve immediately.

Nutrition:

76 Calories

14g Carbohydrates

4g Protein

1146. Refreshingly Peppermint Iced Tea

Preparation Time: 15 minutes

Cooking Time: 0 minute

Serving: 5

Ingredients:

- 4 bags peppermint tea
- 4 cups = 950 ml boiling water
- 2 teaspoons stevia-sweetened lime-flavored drink mix
- 1 cup = 240 ml ice-cold sparkling water

Directions

1.Immerse tea bags on boiling water.

2.Set aside before cooling until it is ice-cold.

3.Take out tea bags then press.

4.Add the lime-flavored drink mix and stir until it is properly dissolved.

5.Add the sparkling water and stir very gently.

6.Serve immediately, preferably with ice cubes, mint leaves and lime wedges.

Nutrition:

78 Calories

17g Carbohydrates

4g Protein

1147. Lemongrass Mint Iced Tea

Preparation Time: 12 minutes

Cooking Time: 0 minute

Serving: 4

Ingredients:

- 1 stalk lemongrass, chopped in 1-inch
- 1/2 cup chopped, loosely packed mint sprigs
- 4 cups boiling water

Directions

1.Put the lemongrass and the mint into tea pot and pour the boiling water over them.

2.Let cool down first to room temperature, then refrigerate until the tea is ice-cold.

3.Filter out the lemongrass and the mint.

4.Add liquid vanilla stevia to taste if you prefer some sweetness and stir until well mixed.

5.Serve immediately, preferably with ice cubes and some nice garnishes, like mint sprigs and lemongrass stalks.

Nutrition:

89 Calories

17g Carbohydrates

5g Protein

1148. Spiced Tea

Preparation Time: 8 minutes

Cooking Time: 0 minute

Serving: 4

Ingredients:

- 2 bags Bengal Spice tea
- 2 teaspoons freshly squeezed lemon juice
- 1 packet zero-carb vanilla stevia
- 1 packet zero-carb stevia

- 4 cups boiling water

Directions

1. Put the tea bags, lemon juice and the both stevia into tea pot.
2. Pour in the boiling water.
3. Put aside to cool over room temperature, then refrigerate.
4. Pull away tea bags then squeeze it.
5. Stir gently.
6. Serve immediately, preferably with ice cubes or crushed ice and some lemon wedges or slices.

Nutrition:

91 Calories

16g Carbohydrates

1g Protein

1149. Infused Pumpkin Spice Latte

Preparation Time: 11 minutes

Cooking Time: 0 minute

Serving: 2

Ingredients:

- 2 cups almond milk
- ¼ cup coconut cream
- 2 teaspoons cannabis coconut oil
- ¼ cup pure pumpkin, canned
- ½ teaspoon vanilla extract
- 1 ½ teaspoon pumpkin spice
- ½ cup coconut whipped cream
- 1 pinch of salt

Direction:

1. Place all ingredients except the coconut whipped cream, in pan over a medium low heat stove.
2. Whisk well and allow to simmer but don't boil!
3. Simmer for about 5 minutes.
4. Pour into mugs and serve.

Nutrition:

94 Calories

17g Carbohydrates

3g Protein

1150. Infused Turmeric-Ginger Tea

Preparation Time: 9 minutes

Cooking Time: 0 minute

Serving: 1

Ingredients:

- 1 cup water
- ½ cup coconut milk
- 1 teaspoon cannabis oil
- ½ teaspoon ground turmeric
- ¼ cup fresh ginger root, sliced
- 1 pinch Stevia or maple syrup, to taste

Direction:

1. Combine all ingredients in a small saucepan over medium heat.
2. Heat until simmer and turn heat low.
3. Take pan off the heat after 2 minutes
4. Let it cool, strain mixture into cup or mug.

Nutrition:

98 Calories

14g Carbohydrates

2g Protein

1151. Infused London Fog

Preparation Time: 17 minutes

Cooking Time: 0 minute

Serving: 2

Ingredients:

- 1 cup hot water
- 1 Earl Grey teabag
- 1 teaspoon cannabis coconut oil
- ¼ cup almond milk
- ¼ teaspoon vanilla extract
- 1 pinch Stevia or sugar, to taste

Direction:

1. Fill up half a mug with boiling water.
2. Add teabag; if you prefer your tea strong, add two.
3. Add cannabis oil and stir well.
4. Add almond milk to fill your mug and stir through with the vanilla extract
5. Use Stevia or sugar to sweeten your Earl Grey to taste.

Nutrition:

76 Calories

14g Carbohydrates

2g Protein

1152. Infused Cranberry-Apple Snug

Preparation Time: 10 minutes

Cooking Time: 0 minute

Serving: 1

Ingredients:

- ½ cup fresh cranberry juice
- ½ cup fresh apple juice, cloudy
- ½ stick cinnamon
- 2 whole cloves
- ¼ lemon, sliced
- 1 pinch of Stevia or sugar, to taste
- cranberries for garnish (optional)

Direction:

1. Combine all ingredients in a small saucepan over medium heat.
2. Heat until simmer and turn heat low.
3. Let it cool, strain the mixture into a mug.
4. Serve with cinnamon stick and cranberries in a mug.

Nutrition:

88 Calories

15g Carbohydrates

3g Protein

1153. Stomach Soother

Preparation time: 5 minutes

Cooking time: 3 minutes

Servings: 1

Ingredients:

- Agave syrup, 1 tbsp.
- Ginger tea, .5 c
- Dr. Sebi's Stomach Relief Herbal Tea
- Burro banana, 1

Directions:

1. Fix the herbal tea according to the **Directions** on the package. Set it aside to cool.
2. Once the tea is cool, place it along with all the other **Ingredients** into a blender. Switch on the blender and let it run until it is creamy.

Nutrition:

Calories 25

Sugar 3g

Protein 0.3g

Fat 0.5

1154. Dandelion "Coffee"

Preparation time: 15 minutes

Cooking time: 10 minutes

Servings: 4

Ingredients:

- Nettle leaf, a pinch
- Roasted dandelion root, 1 tbsp.
- Water, 24 oz.

Directions:

1. To start, we will roast the dandelion root to help bring out its flavors. Feel free to use raw dandelion root if you want to, but roasted root brings out an earthy and complex flavor, which is perfect for cool mornings.
2. Simply add the dandelion root to a pre-warmed cast iron skillet. Allow the pieces to roast on medium heat until they start to darken in color, and you start to smell their rich aroma. Make sure that you don't let them burn because this will ruin your teas taste.
3. As the root is roasting, have the water in a pot and allow it to come up to a full, rapid boil. Once your dandelion is roasted, add it to the boiling water with the nettle leaf. Steep this for ten minutes.
4. Strain. You can flavor your tea with some agave if you want to. Enjoy.

Nutrition:

Calories 43

Sugar 1g

Protein 0.2g

Fat 0.3

1155. Chamomile Delight

Preparation time: 5 minutes

Cooking time: 10 minutes

Servings: 3

Ingredients:

- Date sugar, 1 tbsp.
- Walnut milk, .5 c
- Dr. Sebi's Nerve/Stress Relief Herbal Tea, .25 c
- Burro banana, 1

Directions:

1. Prepare the tea according to the package **Directions**. Set to the side and allow to cool.
2. Once the tea is cooled, add it along with the above **Ingredients** to a blender and process until creamy and smooth.

Nutrition:

Calories 21

Sugar 0.8g

Protein 1.0g

Fat 0.2g

1156. Mucus Cleanse Tea

Preparation time: 10 minutes
Cooking time: 5 minutes
Servings: 2
Ingredients:

- Blue Vervain
- Bladder wrack
- Irish Sea Moss

Directions:

1. Add the sea moss to your blender. This would be best as a gel. Just make sure that it is totally dry.
2. Place equal parts of the bladder wrack to the blender. Again, this would be best as a gel. Just make sure that it is totally dry. To get the best results you need to chop these by hand.
3. Add equal parts of the blue vervain to the blender. You can use the roots to increase your iron intake and **Nutrition**al healing values.
4. Process the herbs until they form a powder. This can take up to three minutes.
5. Place the powder into a non-metal pot and put it on the stove. Fill the pot half full of water. Make sure the herbs are totally immersed in water. Turn on the heat and let the liquid boil. Don't let it boil more than five minutes.
6. Carefully strain out the herbs. You can save these for later use in other recipes.
7. You can add in some agave nectar, date sugar, or key lime juice for added flavor.

Nutrition:
Calories 36
Sugar 6g
Protein 0.7g
Fat 0.3g

1157. Immune Tea

Preparation time: 10 minutes
Cooking time: 20 minutes
Servings: 1
Ingredients:

- Echinacea, 1 part
- Astragalus, 1 part
- Rosehip, 1 part
- Chamomile, 1 part
- Elderflowers, 1 part
- Elderberries, 1 part

Directions:

1. Mix the herbs together and place them inside an airtight container.
2. When you are ready to make a cup of tea, place one teaspoon into a tea ball or bag, and put it in eight ounces of boiling water. Let this sit for 20 minutes.

Nutrition:
Calories 39
Sugar 1g
Protein 2g
Fat 0.6g

1158. Ginger Turmeric Tea

Preparation time: 5 minutes
Cooking time: 15 minutes
Servings: 2
Ingredients:

- Juice of one key lime
- Turmeric finger, couple of slices
- Ginger root, couple of slices
- Water, 3 c

Directions:

1. Pour the water into a pot and let it boil. Remove from heat and put the turmeric and ginger in. Stir well. Place lid on pot and let it sit 15 minutes.
2. While you are waiting on your tea to finish steeping, juice one key lime, and divide between two mugs.
3. Once the tea is ready, remove the turmeric and ginger and pour the tea into mugs and enjoy. If you want your tea a bit sweet, add some agave syrup or date sugar.

Nutrition:
Calories 27
Sugar 5g
Protein 3g
Fat 1.0g

1159. Tranquil Tea

Preparation time: 5 minutes
Cooking time: 10 minutes
Servings: 2
Ingredients:

- Rose petals, 2 parts
- Lemongrass, 2 parts
- Chamomile, 4 parts

Directions:

1. Pour all the herbs into a glass jar and shake well to mix.

2. When you are ready to make a cup of tea, add one teaspoon of the mixture for every serving to a tea strainer, ball, or bag. Cover with water that has boiled and let it sit for ten minutes.

3. If you like a little sweetness in your tea, you can add some agave syrup or date sugar.

Nutrition:

Calories 35

Sugar 3.4g

Protein 2.3g

Fat 1.5g

1160. Energizing Lemon Tea

Preparation time: 5 minutes

Cooking time: 15 minutes

Servings: 3

Ingredients:

- Lemongrass, .5 tsp. dried herb
- Lemon thyme, .5 tsp. dried herb
- Lemon verbena, 1 tsp. dried herb

Directions:

1. Place the dried herbs into a tea strainer, bag, or ball and place it in one cup of water that has boiled. Let this sit 15 minutes. Carefully strain out the tea. You can add agave syrup or date sugar if needed.

Nutrition:

Calories 40

Sugar 6g

Protein 2.2g

Fat 0.3

1161. Respiratory Support Tea

Preparation time: 5 minutes

Cooking time: 18 minutes

Servings: 4

Ingredients:

- Rosehip, 2 parts
- Lemon balm, 1 part
- Coltsfoot leaves, 1 part
- Mullein, 1 part
- Osha root, 1 part
- Marshmallow root, 1 part

Directions:

1. Place three cups of water into a pot. Place the Osha root and marshmallow root into the pot. Allow to boil. Let this simmer for ten minutes

2. Now put the remaining **Ingredients** into the pot and let this steep another eight minutes. Strain.

3. Drink four cups of this tea each day.

4. It's almost that time of year again when everyone is suffering from the dreaded cold. Then that cold turns into a nasty lingering cough. Having these **Ingredients** on hand will help you be able to get ahead of this year's cold season. When you buy your ingredient, they need to be stored in glass jars. The roots and leaves need to be put into separate jars. You can drink this tea at any time, but it is great for when you need some extra respiratory support.

Nutrition:

Calories 35

Sugar 3.4g

Protein 2.3g

Fat 1.5g

1162. Thyme and Lemon Tea

Preparation time: 5 minutes

Cooking time: 10 minutes

Servings: 2

Ingredients:

- Key lime juice, 2 tsp.
- Fresh thyme sprigs, 2

Directions:

1. Place the thyme into a canning jar. Boil enough water to cover the thyme sprigs. Cover the jar with a lid and leave it alone for ten minutes. Add the key lime juice. Carefully strain into a mug and add some agave nectar if desired.

Nutrition:

Calories 22

Sugar 1.4g

Protein 5.3g

Fat 0.6g

1163. Sore Throat Tea

Preparation time: 8 minutes

Cooking time: 15 minutes

Servings: 4

Ingredients:

- Sage leaves, 8 to 10 leaves

Directions:

1.   Place the sage leaves into a quart canning jar and add water that has boiled until it covers the leaves. Pour the lid on the jar and let sit for 15 minutes.

2.   You can use this tea as a gargle to help ease a sore or scratchy throat. Usually, the pain will ease up before you even finish your first cup. This can also be used for inflammations of the throat, tonsils, and mouth since the mucous membranes get soothed by the sage oil. A normal dose would be between three to four cups each day. Every time you take a sip, roll it around in your mouth before swallowing it.

Nutrition:

Calories 26

Sugar 2.0g

Protein 7.6g

Fat 3.2g

1164. Autumn Tonic Tea

Preparation time: 10 minutes

Cooking time: 15 minutes

Servings: 2

Ingredients:

- Dried ginger root, 1 part
- Rosehip, 1 part
- Red clover, 2 parts
- Dandelion root and leaf, 2 parts
- Mullein leaf, 2 parts
- Lemon balm, 3 parts
- Nettle leaf, 4 parts

Directions:

1.   Place all of these **Ingredients** above into a bowl. Stir everything together to mix well. Put into a glass jar with a lid and keep it in a dry place that stays cool.

2.   When you want a cup of tea, place four cups of water into a pot. Let this come to a full rolling boil. Place the desired amount of tea blend into a tea strainer, ball, or bag and cover with boiling water. Let sit for 15 minutes. Strain out the herbs and drink it either cold or hot. If you like your tea sweet, add some agave syrup or date sugar.

Nutrition:

Calories 43

Sugar 3.8g

Protein 6.5g

Fat 3.9g

1165. Adrenal and Stress Health

Preparation time: 12 minutes

Cooking time: 20 minutes

Servings: 2

Ingredients:

Bladder wrack, .5 c

Tulsi holy basil, 1 c

Shatavari root, 1 c

Ashwagandha root, 1 c

Directions:

1.   Place these **Ingredients** into a bowl. Stir well to combine.

2.   Place mixture in a glass jar with a lid and store in a dry place that stays cool.

3.   When you want a cup of tea, place two tablespoons of the tea mixture into a medium pot. Pour in two cups of water. Let this come to a full rolling boil. Turn down heat. Let this simmer 20 minutes. Strain well. If you prefer your tea sweet, you can add some agave syrup or date sugar.

Nutrition:

Calories 43

Sugar 2.2g

Protein 4.1g

Fat 2.3g

1166. Lavender Tea

Preparation time: 5 minutes

Cooking time: 15 minutes

Servings: 2

Ingredients:

- Agave syrup, to taste
- Dried lavender flowers, 2 tbsp.
- Fresh lemon balm, handful
- Water, 3 c

Directions:

1.   Pour the water in a pot and allow to boil.

2.   Pour over the lavender and lemon balm. Cover and let sit for five minutes.

3.   Strain well. If you prefer your tea sweet, add some agave syrup.

Nutrition:

Calories 59

Sugar 6.8g

Protein 3.3g

Fat 1.6g

Other Diabetic Recipes

1167. Scallion Sandwich

Preparation Time: 10 minutes
Cooking Time: 10 minutes
Servings: 1
Ingredients:

- 2 slices wheat bread
- 2 teaspoons butter, low fat
- 2 scallions, sliced thinly
- 1 tablespoon of parmesan cheese, grated
- 3/4 cup of cheddar cheese, reduced fat, grated

Directions:

1. Preheat the Air fryer to 356 degrees.
2. Spread butter on a slice of bread. Place inside the cooking basket with the butter side facing down.
3. Place cheese and scallions on top. Spread the rest of the butter on the other slice of bread Put it on top of the sandwich and sprinkle with parmesan cheese.
4. Cook for 10 minutes.

Nutrition: Calorie: 154Carbohydrate: 9g Fat: 2.5g Protein: 8.6g Fiber: 2.4g

1168. Lean Lamb and Turkey Meatballs with Yogurt

Preparation Time: 10 minutes
Servings: 4
Cooking Time: 8 minutes
Ingredients:

- 1 egg white
- 4 ounces ground lean turkey
- 1 pound of ground lean lamb
- 1 teaspoon each of cayenne pepper, ground coriander, red chili pastes, salt, and ground cumin
- 2 garlic cloves, minced
- 1 1/2 tablespoons parsley, chopped
- 1 tablespoon mint, chopped
- 1/4 cup of olive oil

For the yogurt

- 2 tablespoons of buttermilk
- 1 garlic clove, minced
- 1/4 cup mint, chopped

- 1/2 cup of Greek yogurt, non-fat
- Salt to taste

Directions:

1. Set the Air Fryer to 390 degrees.
2. Mix all the ingredients for the meatballs in a bowl. Roll and mold them into golf-size round pieces. Arrange in the cooking basket. Cook for 8 minutes.
3. While waiting, combine all the ingredients for the mint yogurt in a bowl. Mix well.
4. Serve the meatballs with the mint yogurt. Top with olives and fresh mint.
5. Nutrition: Calorie: 154 Carbohydrate: 9g Fat: 2.5g Protein: 8.6g Fiber: 2.4g

1169. Air Fried Section and Tomato

Preparation Time: 10 minutes
Cooking Time: 5 minutes
Servings: 2
Ingredients:

- 1 aubergine, sliced thickly into 4 disks
- 1 tomato, sliced into 2 thick disks
- 2 tsp. feta cheese, reduced fat
- 2 fresh basil leaves, minced
- 2 balls, small buffalo mozzarella, reduced fat, roughly torn
- Pinch of salt
- Pinch of black pepper

Directions:

1. Preheat Air Fryer to 330 degrees F.
2. Spray small amount of oil into the Air fryer basket. Fry aubergine slices for 5 minutes or until golden brown on both sides. Transfer to a plate.
3. Fry tomato slices in batches for 5 minutes or until seared on both sides.
4. To serve, stack salad starting with an aborigine base, buffalo mozzarella, basil leaves, tomato slice, and 1/2-teaspoon feta cheese.
5. Top of with another slice of aborigine and 1/2 tsp. feta cheese. Serve.

Nutrition: Calorie: 140.3Carbohydrate: 26.6Fat: 3.4g Protein: 4.2g Fiber: 7.3g

1170. Cheesy Salmon Fillets

Preparation Time: 15 minutes
Cooking Time: 20 minutes
Servings: 2-3
Ingredients: For the salmon fillets

- 2 pieces, 4 oz. each salmon fillets, choose even cuts
- 1/2 cup sour cream, reduced fat
- ¼ cup cottage cheese, reduced fat
- ¼ cup Parmigiano-Reggiano cheese, freshly grated

Garnish:

- Spanish paprika
- 1/2-piece lemon, cut into wedges

Directions:
1.   Preheat Air Fryer to 330 degrees F.
2.   To make the salmon fillets, mix sour cream, cottage cheese, and Parmigiano-Reggiano cheese in a bowl.
3.   Layer salmon fillets in the Air fryer basket. Fry for 20 minutes or until cheese turns golden brown.
4.   To assemble, place a salmon fillet and sprinkle paprika. Garnish with lemon wedges and squeeze lemon juice on top. Serve.
Nutrition: Calorie: 274Carbohydrate: 1g Fat: 19g Protein: 24g Fiber: 0.5g

1171. Salmon with Asparagus

Preparation Time: 5 Minutes
Cooking Time: 10 Minutes
Servings: 3
Ingredients:

- 1 lb. Salmon, sliced into fillets
- 1 tbsp. Olive Oil
- Salt & Pepper, as needed

- 1 bunch of Asparagus, trimmed
- 2 cloves of Garlic, minced
- Zest & Juice of 1/2 Lemon
- 1 tbsp. Butter, salted

Directions:
1.   Spoon in the butter and olive oil into a large pan and heat it over medium-high heat.
2.   Once it becomes hot, place the salmon and season it with salt and pepper.
3.   Cook for 4 minutes per side and then cook the other side.
4.   Stir in the garlic and lemon zest to it.
5.   Cook for further 2 minutes or until slightly browned.
6.   Off the heat and squeeze the lemon juice over it.
7.   Serve it hot.
Nutrition:
Calories: 409Kcal
Carbohydrates: 2.7g
Proteins: 32.8g
Fat: 28.8g
Sodium: 497mg

1172. Shrimp in Garlic Butter

Preparation Time: 5 Minutes
Cooking Time: 20 Minutes
Servings: 4
Ingredients:

- 1 lb. Shrimp, peeled & deveined
- ¼ tsp. Red Pepper Flakes
- 6 tbsp. Butter, divided
- 1/2 cup Chicken Stock
- Salt & Pepper, as needed
- 2 tbsp. Parsley, minced
- 5 cloves of Garlic, minced
- 2 tbsp. Lemon Juice

Directions:
1.   Heat a large bottomed skillet over medium-high heat.
2.   Spoon in two tablespoons of the butter and melt it. Add the shrimp.
3.   Season it with salt and pepper. Sear for 4 minutes or until shrimp gets cooked.
4.   Transfer the shrimp to a plate and stir in the garlic.
5.   Sauté for 30 seconds or until aromatic.

6. Pour the chicken stock and whisk it well. Allow it to simmer for 5 to 10 minutes or until it has reduced to half.

7. Spoon the remaining butter, red pepper, and lemon juice to the sauce. Mix.

8. Continue cooking for another 2 minutes.

9. Take off the pan from the heat and add the cooked shrimp to it.

10. Garnish with parsley and transfer to the serving bowl.

11. Enjoy.

Nutrition:

Calories: 307Kcal

Carbohydrates: 3g

Proteins: 27g

Fat: 20g

Sodium: 522mg

1173. Cobb Salad

Keto & Under 30 Minutes

Preparation Time: 5 Minutes

Cooking Time: 5 Minutes

Servings: 1

Ingredients:

- 4 Cherry Tomatoes, chopped
- ¼ cup Bacon, cooked & crumbled
- 1/2 of 1 Avocado, chopped
- 2 oz. Chicken Breast, shredded
- 1 Egg, hardboiled
- 2 cups Mixed Green salad
- 1 oz. Feta Cheese, crumbled

Directions:

1. Toss all the ingredients for the Cobb salad in a large mixing bowl and toss well.

2. Serve and enjoy it.

Nutrition:

Calories: 307Kcal

Carbohydrates: 3g

Proteins: 27g

Fat: 20g

Sodium: 522mg

1174. Seared Tuna Steak

Preparation Time: 10 Minutes

Cooking Time: 10 Minutes

Serving Size: 2

Ingredients:

- 1 tsp. Sesame Seeds

- 1 tbsp. Sesame Oil
- 2 tbsp. Soya Sauce
- Salt & Pepper, to taste
- 2 × 6 oz. Ahi Tuna Steaks

Directions:

1. Seasoning the tuna steaks with salt and pepper. Keep it aside on a shallow bowl.

2. In another bowl, mix soya sauce and sesame oil.

3. pour the sauce over the salmon and coat them generously with the sauce.

4. Keep it aside for 10 to 15 minutes and then heat a large skillet over medium heat.

5. Once hot, keep the tuna steaks and cook them for 3 minutes or until seared underneath.

6. Flip the fillets and cook them for a further 3 minutes.

7. Transfer the seared tuna steaks to the serving plate and slice them into 1/2-inch slices. Top with sesame seeds.

Nutrition:

Calories: 255Kcal

Fat: 9g

Carbohydrates: 1g

Proteins: 40.5g

Sodium: 293mg

1175. Beef Chili

Preparation Time: 10 Minutes

Cooking Time: 20 Minutes

Serving Size: 4

Ingredients:

- 1/2 tsp. Garlic Powder
- 1 tsp. Coriander, grounded
- 1 lb. Beef, grounded
- 1/2 tsp. Sea Salt
- 1/2 tsp. Cayenne Pepper
- 1 tsp. Cumin, grounded
- 1/2 tsp. Pepper, grounded
- 1/2 cup Salsa, low-carb & no-sugar

Directions:

1. Heat a large-sized pan over medium-high heat and cook the beef in it until browned.

2. Stir in all the spices and cook them for 7 minutes or until everything is combined.

3. When the beef gets cooked, spoon in the salsa.

4. Bring the mixture to a simmer and cook for another 8 minutes or until everything comes together.

5. Take it from heat and transfer to a serving bowl.

Nutrition:

Calories: 229Kcal

Fat: 10g

Carbohydrates: 2g

Proteins: 33g

Sodium: 675mg

1176. Greek Broccoli Salad

Preparation Time: 10 Minutes

Cooking Time: 15 Minutes

Servings: 4

Ingredients:

- 1 ¼ lb. Broccoli, sliced into small bites
- ¼ cup Almonds, sliced
- 1/3 cup Sun-dried Tomatoes
- ¼ cup Feta Cheese, crumbled
- ¼ cup Red Onion, sliced

For the dressing:

- 1/4 cup Olive Oil
- Dash of Red Pepper Flakes
- 1 Garlic clove, minced
- ¼ tsp. Salt
- 2 tbsp. Lemon Juice
- 1/2 tsp. Dijon Mustard
- 1 tsp. Low Carb Sweetener Syrup
- 1/2 tsp. Oregano, dried

Directions:

1. Mix broccoli, onion, almonds and sun-dried tomatoes in a large mixing bowl.

2. In another small-sized bowl, combine all the dressing ingredients until emulsified.

3. Spoon the dressing over the broccoli salad.

4. Allow the salad to rest for half an hour before serving.

Nutrition:

Calories: 272Kcal

Carbohydrates: 11.9g

Proteins: 8g

Fat: 21.6g

Sodium: 321mg

1177. Cheesy Cauliflower Gratin

Preparation Time: 5 Minutes

Cooking Time: 25 Minutes

Servings: 6

Ingredients:

- 6 deli slices Pepper Jack Cheese
- 4 cups Cauliflower florets
- Salt and Pepper, as needed
- 4 tbsp. Butter
- 1/3 cup Heavy Whipping Cream

Directions:

1. Mix the cauliflower, cream, butter, salt, and pepper in a safe microwave bowl and combine well.

2. Microwave the cauliflower mixture for 25 minutes on high until it becomes soft and tender.

3. Remove the ingredients from the bowl and mash with the help of a fork.

4. Taste for seasonings and spoon in salt and pepper as required.

5. Arrange the slices of pepper jack cheese on top of the cauliflower mixture and microwave for 3 minutes until the cheese starts melting.

6. Serve warm.

Nutrition:

Calories: 421Kcal

Carbohydrates: 3g

Proteins: 19g

Fat: 37g

Sodium: 111mg

1178. Strawberry Spinach Salad

Preparation Time: 5 Minutes

Cooking Time: 10 Minutes

Servings: 4

Ingredients:

- 4 oz. Feta Cheese, crumbled
- 8 Strawberries, sliced
- 2 oz. Almonds
- 6 Slices Bacon, thick-cut, crispy and crumbled
- 10 oz. Spinach leaves, fresh
- 2 Roma Tomatoes, diced
- 2 oz. Red Onion, sliced thinly

Directions:

1. For making this healthy salad, mix all the ingredients needed to make the salad in a large-sized bowl and toss them well.

Nutrition:

Calories – 255kcal

Fat – 16g

Carbohydrates – 8g

Proteins – 14g

Sodium: 27mg

1179. Muffins Sandwich

Preparation time: 2 minutes

Cooking time: 10 minutes

Servings: 1

Ingredients:

- Nonstick Spray Oil
- 1 slice of white cheddar cheese
- 1 slice of Canadian bacon
- 1 English muffin, divided
- 15 ml hot water
- 1 large egg
- Salt and pepper to taste

Directions:

1. Spray the inside of an 85g mold with oil spray and place it in the air fryer.

2. Preheat the air fryer, set it to 160C.

3. Add the Canadian cheese and bacon in the preheated air fryer.

4. Pour the hot water and the egg into the hot pan and season with salt and pepper.

5. Select Bread, set to 10 minutes.

6. Take out the English muffins after 7 minutes, leaving the egg for the full time.

7. Build your sandwich by placing the cooked egg on top of the English muffing and serve

Nutrition: Calories 400 Fat 26g, Carbohydrates 26g, Sugar 15 g, Protein 3 g, Cholesterol 155 mg

1180. Bacon BBQ

Preparation time: 2 minutes

Cooking time: 8 minutes

Servings: 2

Ingredients:

- 13g dark brown sugar
- 5g chili powder
- 1g ground cumin
- 1g cayenne pepper
- 4 slices of bacon, cut in half

Directions:

1. Mix seasonings until well combined.

2. Dip the bacon in the dressing until it is completely covered. Leave aside.

3. Preheat the air fryer, set it to 160C.

4. Place the bacon in the preheated air fryer

5. Select Bacon and press Start/Pause.

Nutrition: Calories: 1124 Fat: 72g Carbohydrates: 59g Protein: 49g Sugar: 11g Cholesterol: 77mg

1181. Wild Rice and Black Lentils Bowl

Preparation time: 10 minutes

Cooking time: 50 minutes

Servings: 4

Ingredients:

- Wild rice
- 2 cups wild rice, uncooked
- 4 cups spring water
- ½ teaspoon salt
- 2 bay leaves
- Black lentils
- 2 cups black lentils, cooked
- 1 ¾ cups coconut milk, unsweetened
- 2 cups vegetable stock
- 1 teaspoon dried thyme
- 1 teaspoon dried paprika
- ½ of medium purple onion; peeled, sliced
- 1 tablespoon minced garlic
- 2 teaspoons creole seasoning
- 1 tablespoon coconut oil
- Plantains
- 3 large plantains, chopped into ¼-inch-thick pieces
- 3 tablespoons coconut oil
- Brussels sprouts
- 10 large brussels sprouts, quartered
- 2 tablespoons spring water
- 1 teaspoon sea salt
- ½ teaspoon ground black pepper

Directions:

1. Prepare the rice: take a medium pot, place it over medium-high heat, pour in water, and add bay leaves and salt.

2.   Bring the water to a boil, then switch heat to medium, add rice, and then cook for 30–45 minutes or more until tender.

3.   When done, discard the bay leaves from rice, drain if any water remains in the pot, remove it from heat, and fluff by using a fork. Set aside until needed.

4.   While the rice boils, prepare lentils: take a large pot, place it over medium-high heat and when hot, add onion and cook for 5 minutes or until translucent.

5.   Stir garlic into the onion, cook for 2 minutes until fragrant and golden, then add remaining **Ingredients** for the lentils and stir until mixed.

6.   Bring the lentils to a boil, then switch heat to medium and simmer the lentils for 20 minutes until tender, covering the pot with a lid.

7.   When done, remove the pot from heat and set aside until needed.

8.   While rice and lentils simmer, prepare the plantains: chop them into ¼-inch-thick pieces.

9.   Take a large skillet pan, place it over medium heat, add coconut oil and when it melts, add half of the plantain pieces and cook for 7–10 minutes per side or more until golden-brown.

10.   When done, transfer browned plantains to a plate lined with paper towels and repeat with the remaining plantain pieces; set aside until needed.

11.   Prepare the sprouts: return the skillet pan over medium heat, add more oil if needed, and then add brussels sprouts.

12.   Toss the sprouts until coated with oil, and then let them cook for 3–4 minutes per side until brown.

13.   Drizzle water over sprouts, cover the pan with the lid, and then cook for 3–5 minutes until steamed.

14.   Season the sprouts with salt and black pepper, toss until mixed, and transfer sprouts to a plate.

15.   Assemble the bowl: divide rice evenly among four bowls and then top with lentils, plantain pieces, and sprouts.

16.   Serve immediately.

Nutrition:
Calories: 333
Carbohydrates: 49.2 grams
Fat: 10.7 grams
Protein: 6.2 grams

1182. Alkaline Spaghetti Squash Recipe

Preparation time: 10 minutes
Cooking time: 30 minutes
Servings: 4
Ingredients:

- 1 spaghetti squash
- Grapeseed oil
- Sea salt
- Cayenne powder (optional)
- Onion powder (optional)

Directions:
1.   Preheat your oven to 375°f
2.   Carefully chop off the ends of the squash and cut it in half.
3.   Scoop out the seeds into a bowl.
4.   Coat the squash with oil.
5.   Season the squash and flip it over for the other side to get baked. When properly baked, the outside of the squash will be tender.
6.   Allow the squash to cool off, then, use a fork to scrape the inside into a bowl.
7.   Add seasoning to taste.
8.   Dish your alkaline spaghetti squash!

Nutrition:
Calories: 672
Carbohydrates: 65 grams
Fat: 47 grams
Protein: 12 grams

1183. Dairy-Free Fruit Tarts

Preparation time: 15 minutes
Cooking time: 15 minutes
Servings: 2
Ingredients:
1 cup Coconut Whipped Cream
½ Easy Shortbread Crust (dairy-free option)
Fresh mint Sprigs
½ cup mixed fresh Berries

Directions:
Grease two 4" pans with detachable bottoms. Pour the shortbread mixture into pans and firmly press into the edges and bottom of each pan. Refrigerate for 15 minutes.
Loosen the crust carefully to remove from the pan.
Distribute the whipped cream between the tarts and evenly spread to the sides. Refrigerate for 1-2 hours to make it firm.
Use the berries and sprig of mint to garnish each of the tarts
Nutrition:

Fat: 28.9g
Carbs: 8.3g
Protein: 5.8g
Calories: 306

1184. Spaghetti Squash with Peanut Sauce

Preparation time: 15 minutes
Cooking time: 15 minutes
Servings: 4

Ingredients:

- 1 cup cooked shelled edamame; frozen, thawed
- 3-pound spaghetti squash
- ½ cup red bell pepper, sliced
- ¼ cup scallions, sliced
- 1 medium carrot, shredded
- 1 teaspoon minced garlic
- ½ teaspoon crushed red pepper
- 1 tablespoon rice vinegar
- ¼ cup coconut aminos
- 1 tablespoon maple syrup
- ½ cup peanut butter
- ¼ cup unsalted roasted peanuts, chopped
- ¼ cup and 2 tablespoons spring water, divided
- ¼ cup fresh cilantro, chopped
- 4 lime wedges

Directions:

1. Prepare the squash: cut each squash in half lengthwise and then remove seeds.
2. Take a microwave-proof dish, place squash halves in it cut-side-up, drizzle with 2 tablespoons water, and then microwave at high heat setting for 10–15 minutes until tender.
3. Let squash cool for 15 minutes until able to handle. Use a fork to scrape its flesh lengthwise to make noodles, and then let noodles cool for 10 minutes.
4. While squash microwaves, prepare the sauce: take a medium bowl, add butter in it along with red pepper and garlic, pour in vinegar, coconut aminos, maple syrup, and water, and then whisk until smooth.
5. When the squash noodles have cooled, distribute them evenly among four bowls, top with scallions, carrots,

bell pepper, and edamame beans, and then drizzle with prepared sauce.
6. Sprinkle cilantro and peanuts and serve each bowl with a lime wedge.

Nutrition:
Calories: 419
Carbohydrates: 32.8 grams
Fat: 24 grams
Protein: 17.6 grams

1185. Cauliflower Alfredo Pasta

Preparation time: 10 minutes
Cooking time: 30 minutes
Servings: 4

Ingredients:

- Alfredo sauce
- 4 cups cauliflower florets, fresh
- 1 tablespoon minced garlic
- ¼ cup **Nutrition**al yeast
- ½ teaspoon garlic powder
- ¾ teaspoon sea salt
- ½ teaspoon onion powder
- ½ teaspoon ground black pepper
- ½ tablespoon olive oil
- 1 tablespoon lemon juice, and more as needed for serving
- ½ cup almond milk, unsweetened
- Pasta
- 1 tablespoon minced parsley
- 1 lemon, juiced
- ½ teaspoon sea salt
- ¼ teaspoon ground black pepper
- 12 ounces spelt pasta; cooked, warmed

Directions:

1. Take a large pot half full with water, place it over medium-high heat, and then bring it to a boil.
2. Add cauliflower florets, cook for 10–15 minutes until tender, drain them well, and then return florets to the pot.
3. Take a medium skillet pan, place it over low heat, add oil and when hot, add garlic and cook for 4–5 minutes until fragrant and golden-brown.
4. Spoon garlic into a food processor, add remaining **Ingredients** for the sauce in it, along with cauliflower florets, and then pulse for 2–3 minutes until smooth.

5. Tip the sauce into the pot, stir it well, place it over medium-low heat, and then cook for 5 minutes until hot.

6. Add pasta into the pot, toss well until coated, taste to adjust seasoning, and then cook for 2 minutes until pasta gets hot.

7. Divide pasta and sauce among four plates, season with salt and black pepper, drizzle with lemon juice, and then top with minced parsley.

8. Serve straight away.

Nutrition:

Calories: 360

Carbohydrates: 59 grams

Fat: 9 grams

Protein: 13 grams

1186. Sloppy Joe

Preparation time: 8 minutes

Cooking time: 12 minutes

Servings: 4

Ingredients:

- 2 cups kamut or spelt wheat, cooked
- ½ cup white onion, diced
- 1 roma tomato, diced
- 1 cup chickpeas, cooked
- ½ cup green bell peppers, diced
- 1 teaspoon sea salt
- 1/8 teaspoon cayenne pepper
- 1 teaspoon onion powder
- 1 tablespoon grapeseed oil
- 1 ½ cups barbecue sauce, alkaline

Directions:

1. Plug in a high-power food processor, add chickpeas and spelt, cover with the lid, and then pulse for 15 seconds.

2. Take a large skillet pan, place it over medium-high heat, add oil and when hot, add onion and bell pepper, season with salt, cayenne pepper, and onion powder, and then stir until well combined.

3. Cook the vegetables for 3–5 minutes until tender. Add tomatoes, add the pulsed mixture, pour in barbecue sauce, and then stir until well mixed.

4. Simmer for 5 minutes, then remove the pan from heat and serve sloppy joe with alkaline flatbread.

Nutrition:

Calories: 333

Carbohydrates: 65 grams

Fat: 5 grams

Protein: 14 grams

1187. Amaretti

Preparation time: 15 minutes

Cooking time: 22 minutes

Servings: 2

Ingredients:

- ½ cup of granulated Erythritol-based Sweetener
- 165g (2 cups) sliced Almonds
- ¼ cup of powdered of Erythritol-based sweetener
- 4 large egg whites
- Pinch of salt
- ½ tsp. almond extract

Directions:

Heat the oven to 300° F and use parchment paper to line 2 baking sheets. Grease the parchment slightly.

Process the powdered sweetener, granulated sweetener, and sliced almonds in a food processor until it appears like coarse crumbs.

Beat the egg whites plus the salt and almond extracts using an electric mixer in a large bowl until they hold soft peaks. Fold in the almond mixture so that it becomes well combined.

Drop spoonful of the dough onto the prepared baking sheet and allow for a space of 1 inch between them. Press a sliced almond into the top of each cookie.

Bake in the oven for 22 minutes until the sides becomes brown. They will appear jellylike when they are taken out from the oven but will begin to be firms as it cools down.

Nutrition: Fat: 8.8g

Carbs: 4.1g

Protein: 5.3g

Calories: 117

1188. Green Fruit Juice

Preparation time: 10 minutes

Cooking time: 0 minutes

Servings: 2

Ingredients:

- 3 large kiwis, peeled and chopped
- 3 large green apples, cored and sliced
- 2 cups seedless green grapes
- 2 teaspoons fresh lime juice

Directions:

Add all ingredients into a juicer and extract the juice according to the manufacturer's method.

Pour into 2 glasses and serve immediately.

Nutrition:

Calories 304

Total Fat 2.2 g

Saturated Fat 0 g

Protein 6.2 g

1189. Kale Chickpea Mash

Preparation time: 15 minutes

Cooking time: 12 minutes

Servings: 1

Ingredients:

- 1 shallot
- 3 tbsp garlic
- A bunch of kale
- 1/2 cup boiled chickpea
- 2 tbsp coconut oil
- Sea salt

Directions:

1.   Add some garlic in olive oil
2.   Chop shallot and fry it with oil in a nonstick skillet.
3.   Cook until the shallot turns golden brown.
4.   Add kale and garlic in the skillet and stir well.
5.   Add chickpeas and cook for 6 minutes. Add the rest of the **Ingredients** and give a good stir.
6.   Serve and enjoy

Nutrition:

Calories: 149

Total fat: 8 grams

Saturated fat: 1 gram

Net carbohydrates: 13 grams

Protein: 4 grams

Sugars 6g

Fiber 3g

Sodium 226mg

Potassium 205mg

1190. Quinoa and Apple

The combination of quinoa and apple yields a delicious and filling lunch dish that can be carried to work in your lunch box.

Preparation time: 15 minutes

Cooking time: 12 minutes

Servings: 1

Ingredients:

- 1/2 cup quinoa
- 1 apple
- 1/2 lemon
- Cinnamon to taste

Directions:

1.   Cook quinoa according to the packet **Directions**.
2.   Grate the apple and add to the cooked quinoa. Cook for 30 seconds.
3.   Serve in a bowl then sprinkle lime and cinnamon. Enjoy.

Nutrition:

Calories 229

Total fat: 3.2 grams

Net carbs: 32.3 grams

Protein: 6.1 grams

Sugars: 4.2 grams

Fiber: 3.3 grams

Sodium: 35.5 milligrams

Potassium: 211.8 milligrams

1191. Warm Avo And Quinoa Salad

This is an amazing alkaline quinoa dish that will blow your mind away. It's an easy dish that will be ready in less than 20 minutes.

Preparation time: 5 minutes

Cooking time: 12 minutes

Servings: 4

Ingredients:

- 4 ripe avocados, quartered
- 1 cup quinoa
- 0.9 lb. Chickpeas, drained
- 1 oz flat leaf parsley

Directions:

1.   Add quinoa in a pot with 2 cups of water. Bring to boil then simmer for 12 minutes or until all the water has evaporated. The grains should be glassy and swollen.
2.   Toss the quinoa with all other **Ingredients** and season with salt and pepper to taste.
3.   Serve with olive oil and lemon wedges. Enjoy.

Nutrition:

Calories: 354

Total fat: 16 grams

Saturated fat: 2 grams

Net carbs: 31 grams
Protein: 15 grams
Sugars: 6 grams
Fiber: 15 grams
Sodium: 226 milligrams
Potassium: 205 milligrams

1192. Tuna Salad

Preparation Time: 15 minutes
Cooking time: 30 minutes
Servings: 2
Ingredients:

- 2 (5-ounce) cans water packed tuna, drained
- 2 tablespoons fat-free plain Greek yogurt
- Salt and ground black pepper, as required
- 2 medium carrots, peeled and shredded
- 2 apples, cored and chopped
- 2 cups fresh spinach, torn

Directions:
1. In a large bowl, add the tuna, yogurt, salt and black pepper and gently, stir to combine.
2. Add the carrots and apples and stir to combine.
3. Serve immediately.

Nutrition:
Calories 306
Total Fat 1.8g
Saturated Fat 0 g
Cholesterol 63 mg
Total Carbs 38 g
Sugar 26 g
Fiber 7.6 g
Sodium 324 mg
Potassium 602 mg
Protein 35.8 g

1193. Herring & Veggies Soup

Preparation Time: 15 minutes
Cooking Time: 25 minutes
Servings: 5
Ingredients:

- 2 tablespoons olive oil
- 1 shallot, chopped
- 2 small garlic cloves, minced
- 1 jalapeño pepper, chopped
- 1 head cabbage, chopped
- 1 small red bell pepper, seeded and chopped finely

- 1 small yellow bell pepper, seeded and chopped finely
- 5 cups low-sodium chicken broth
- 2 (4-ounce) boneless herring fillets, cubed
- ¼ cup fresh cilantro, minced
- 2 tablespoons fresh lemon juice
- Ground black pepper, as required
- 2 scallions, chopped

Directions:
1. In a large soup pan, heat the oil over medium heat and sauté shallot and garlic for 2-3 minutes.
2. Add the cabbage and bell peppers and sauté for about 3-4 minutes.
3. Add the broth and bring to a boil over high heat.
4. Now, reduce the heat to medium-low and simmer for about 10 minutes.
5. Add the herring cubes and cook for about 5-6 minutes.
6. Stir in the cilantro, lemon juice, salt and black pepper and cook for about 1-2 minutes.
7. Serve hot with the topping of scallion.

Nutrition:
Calories 215
Total Fat 11.2g
Saturated Fat 2.1 g
Cholesterol 35 mg
Total Carbs 14.7 g
Sugar 7 g
Fiber 4.5 g
Sodium 152 mg
Potassium 574 mg
Protein 15.1 g

1194. Salmon Soup

Preparation Time: 15 minutes
Cooking Time: 20 minutes
Servings: 4
Ingredients:

- 1 tablespoon olive oil
- 1 yellow onion, chopped
- 1 garlic clove, minced
- 4 cups low-sodium chicken broth
- 1-pound boneless salmon, cubed
- 2 tablespoon fresh cilantro, chopped
- Ground black pepper, as required

- 1 tablespoon fresh lime juice

Directions:

1. In a large pan heat the oil over medium heat and sauté the onion for about 5 minutes.
2. Add the garlic and sauté for about 1 minute.
3. Stir in the broth and bring to a boil over high heat.
4. Now, reduce the heat to low and simmer for about 10 minutes.
5. Add the salmon and soy sauce and cook for about 3-4 minutes.
6. Stir in black pepper, lime juice, and cilantro and serve hot.

Nutrition:

Calories 208
Total Fat 10.5 g
Saturated Fat 1.5 g
Cholesterol 50 mg
Total Carbs 3.9 g
Sugar 1.2 g
Fiber 0.6 g
Sodium 121 mg
Potassium 331 mg
Protein 24.4 g

1195. Salmon & Shrimp Stew

Preparation Time: 20 minutes
Cooking Time: 21 minutes
Servings: 6

Ingredients:

- 2 tablespoons olive oil
- 1/2 cup onion, chopped finely
- 2 garlic cloves, minced
- 1 Serrano pepper, chopped
- 1 teaspoon smoked paprika
- 4 cups fresh tomatoes, chopped
- 4 cups low-sodium chicken broth
- 1 pound salmon fillets, cubed
- 1 pound shrimp, peeled and deveined
- 2 tablespoons fresh lime juice
- ¼ cup fresh basil, chopped
- ¼ cup fresh parsley, chopped
- Ground black pepper, as required
- 2 scallions, chopped

Directions:

1. In a large soup pan, melt coconut oil over medium-high heat and sauté the onion for about 5-6 minutes.
2. Add the garlic, Serrano pepper and smoked paprika and sauté for about 1 minute.
3. Add the tomatoes and broth and bring to a gentle simmer over medium heat.
4. Simmer for about 5 minutes.
5. Add the salmon and simmer for about 3-4 minutes.
6. Stir in the remaining seafood and cook for about 4-5 minutes.
7. Stir in the lemon juice, basil, parsley, sea salt and black pepper and remove from heat.
8. Serve hot with the garnishing of scallion.

Nutrition:

Calories 271
Total Fat 11 g
Saturated Fat 1.8 g
Cholesterol 193 mg
Total Carbs 8.6 g
Sugar 3.8 g
Fiber 2.1 g
Sodium 273 mg
Potassium 763 mg
Protein 34.7 g

1196. Salmon Curry

Preparation Time: 15 minutes
Cooking Time: 30 minutes
Servings: 6

Ingredients:

- 6 (4-ounce) salmon fillets
- 1 teaspoon ground turmeric, divided
- Salt, as required
- 3 tablespoon olive oil, divided
- 1 yellow onion, chopped finely
- 1 teaspoon garlic paste
- 1 teaspoon fresh ginger paste
- 3-4 green chilies, halved
- 1 teaspoon red chili powder
- 1/2 teaspoon ground cumin
- 1/2 teaspoon ground cinnamon
- ¾ cup fat-free plain Greek yogurt, whipped
- ¾ cup filtered water
- 3 tablespoon fresh cilantro, chopped

Directions:

1. Season each salmon fillet with 1/2 teaspoon of the turmeric and salt.
2. In a large skillet, melt 1 tablespoon of the butter over medium heat and cook the salmon fillets for about 2 minutes per side.
3. Transfer the salmon onto a plate.
4. In the same skillet, melt the remaining butter over medium heat and sauté the onion for about 4-5 minutes.
5. Add the garlic paste, ginger paste, green chilies, remaining turmeric and spices and sauté for about 1 minute.
6. Now, reduce the heat to medium-low.
7. Slowly, add the yogurt and water, stirring continuously until smooth.
8. Cover the skillet and simmer for about 10-15 minutes or until desired doneness of the sauce.
9. Carefully, add the salmon fillets and simmer for about 5 minutes.
10. Serve hot with the garnishing of cilantro.

Nutrition:
Calories 242
Total Fat 14.3 g
Saturated Fat 2 g
Cholesterol 51 mg
Total Carbs 4.1 g
Sugar 2 g
Fiber 0.8 g
Sodium 98 mg
Potassium 493 mg
Protein 25.4 g

1197. Salmon with Bell Peppers

Preparation Time: 15 minutes
Cooking Time: 20 minutes
Servings: 6
Ingredients:

- 6 (3-ounce) salmon fillets
- Pinch of salt
- Ground black pepper, as required
- 1 yellow bell pepper, seeded and cubed
- 1 red bell pepper, seeded and cubed
- 4 plum tomatoes, cubed
- 1 small onion, sliced thinly
- 1/2 cup fresh parsley, chopped
- ¼ cup olive oil
- 2 tablespoons fresh lemon juice

Directions:
1. Preheat the oven to 400 degrees F.
2. Season each salmon fillet with salt and black pepper lightly.
3. In a bowl, mix together the bell peppers, tomato and onion.
4. Arrange 6 foil pieces onto a smooth surface.
5. Place 1 salmon fillet over each foil paper and sprinkle with salt and black pepper.
6. Place veggie mixture over each fillet evenly and top with parsley and capers evenly.
7. Drizzle with oil and lemon juice.
8. Fold each foil around salmon mixture to seal it.
9. Arrange the foil packets onto a large baking sheet in a single layer.
10. Bake for about 20 minutes.
11. Serve hot.

Nutrition:
Calories 220
Total Fat 14 g
Saturated Fat 2 g
Cholesterol 38 mg
Total Carbs 7.7 g
Sugar 4.8 g
Fiber 2 g
Sodium 74 mg
Potassium 647 mg
Protein 17.9 g

1198. Shrimp Salad

Preparation Time: 20 minutes
Cooking Time: 4 minutes
Servings: 6
Ingredients:
For Salad:

- 1 pound shrimp, peeled and deveined
- Salt and ground black pepper, as required
- 1 teaspoon olive oil
- 1 1/2 cups carrots, peeled and julienned
- 1 1/2 cups red cabbage, shredded
- 1 1/2 cup cucumber, julienned
- 5 cups fresh baby arugula
- ¼ cup fresh basil, chopped
- ¼ cup fresh cilantro, chopped
- 4 cups lettuce, torn

- ¼ cup almonds, chopped

For Dressing:
- 2 tablespoons natural almond butter
- 1 garlic clove, crushed
- 1 tablespoon fresh cilantro, chopped
- 1 tablespoon fresh lime juice
- 1 tablespoon unsweetened applesauce
- 2 teaspoons balsamic vinegar
- 1/2 teaspoon cayenne pepper
- Salt, as required
- 1 tablespoon water
- 1/3 cup olive oil

Directions:
1. Slowly, add the oil, beating continuously until smooth.
2. For salad: in a bowl, add shrimp, salt, black pepper and oil and toss to coat well.
3. Heat a skillet over medium-high heat and cook the shrimp for about 2 minutes per side.
4. Remove from the heat and set aside to cool.
5. In a large bowl, add the shrimp, vegetables and mix well.
6. For dressing: in a bowl, add all ingredients except oil and beat until well combined.
7. Place the dressing over shrimp mixture and gently, toss to coat well.
8. Serve immediately.

Nutrition:
Calories 274
Total Fat 17.7 g
Saturated Fat 2.4 g
Cholesterol 159 mg
Total Carbs 10 g
Sugar 3.8 g
Fiber 2.9 g
Sodium 242 mg
Potassium 481 mg
Protein 20.5 g

1199. Shrimp & Veggies Curry

Preparation Time: 20 minutes
Cooking Time: 20 minutes
Servings: 6
Ingredients:
- 2 teaspoons olive oil

- 11/2 medium white onions, sliced
- 2 medium green bell peppers, seeded and sliced
- 3 medium carrots, peeled and sliced thinly
- 3 garlic cloves, chopped finely
- 1 tablespoon fresh ginger, chopped finely
- 21/2 teaspoons curry powder
- 11/2 pounds shrimp, peeled and deveined
- 1 cup filtered water
- 2 tablespoons fresh lime juice
- Salt and ground black pepper, as required
- 2 tablespoons fresh cilantro, chopped

Directions:
1. In a large skillet, heat oil over medium-high heat and sauté the onion for about 4-5 minutes.
2. Add the bell peppers and carrot and sauté for about 3-4 minutes.
3. Add the garlic, ginger and curry powder and sauté for about 1 minute.
4. Add the shrimp and sauté for about 1 minute.
5. Stir in the water and cook for about 4-6 minutes, stirring occasionally.
6. Stir in lime juice and remove from heat.
7. Serve hot with the garnishing of cilantro.

Nutrition:
Calories 193
Total Fat 3.8 g
Saturated Fat 0.9 g
Cholesterol 239 mg
Total Carbs 12 g
Sugar 4.7 g
Fiber 2.3 g
Sodium 328 mg
Potassium 437 mg
Protein 27.1 g

1200. Shrimp with Zucchini

Preparation Time: 20 minutes
Cooking Time: 8 minutes
Servings: 4
Ingredients:
- 3 tablespoons olive oil
- 1-pound medium shrimp, peeled and deveined
- 1 shallot, minced
- 4 garlic cloves, minced
- ¼ teaspoon red pepper flakes, crushed

- Salt and ground black pepper, as required
- ¼ cup low-sodium chicken broth
- 2 tablespoons fresh lemon juice
- 1 teaspoon fresh lemon zest, grated finely
- 1/2-pound zucchini, spiralized with Blade C

Directions:

1. In a large skillet, heat the oil and butter over medium-high heat and cook the shrimp, shallot, garlic, red pepper flakes, salt and black pepper for about 2 minutes, stirring occasionally.
2. Stir in the broth, lemon juice and lemon zest and bring to a gentle boil.
3. Stir in zucchini noodles and cook for about 1-2 minutes.
4. Serve hot.

Nutrition:
Calories 245
Total Fat 12.6 g
Saturated Fat 2.2 g
Cholesterol 239 mg
Total Carbs 5.8 g
Sugar 1.2 g
Fiber 08 g
Sodium 289 mg
Potassium 381 mg
Protein 27 g

1201. Shrimp with Broccoli

Preparation Time: 15 minutes
Cooking Time: 12 minutes
Servings: 6
Ingredients:

- 2 tablespoons olive oil, divided
- 4 cups broccoli, chopped
- 2-3 tablespoons filtered water
- 11/2 pounds large shrimp, peeled and deveined
- 2 garlic cloves, minced
- 1 (1-inch) piece fresh ginger, minced
- Salt and ground black pepper, as required

Directions:

1. In a large skillet, heat 1 tablespoon of oil over medium-high heat and cook the broccoli for about 1-2 minutes stirring continuously.
2. Stir in the water and cook, covered for about 3-4 minutes, stirring occasionally.

3. With a spoon, push the broccoli to side of the pan.
4. Add the remaining oil and let it heat.
5. Add the shrimp and cook for about 1-2 minutes, tossing occasionally.
6. Add the remaining ingredients and sauté for about 2-3 minutes.
7. Serve hot.

Nutrition:
Calories 197
Total Fat 6.8 g
Saturated Fat 1.3 g
Cholesterol 239 mg
Total Carbs 6.1 g
Sugar 1.1 g
Fiber 1.6 g
Sodium 324 mg
Potassium 389 mg
Protein 27.6 g

1202. Pork Chop Diane

Preparation Time: 10 minutes
Cooking Time: 20 minutes
Serving: 4
Ingredients:

- ¼ cup low-sodium chicken broth
- 1 tablespoon freshly squeezed lemon juice
- 2 teaspoons Worcestershire sauce
- 2 teaspoons Dijon mustard
- 4 (5-ounce) boneless pork top loin chops
- 1 teaspoon extra-virgin olive oil
- 1 teaspoon lemon zest
- 1 teaspoon butter
- 2 teaspoons chopped fresh chives

Direction:

1. Blend together the chicken broth, lemon juice, Worcestershire sauce, and Dijon mustard and set it aside.
2. Season the pork chops lightly.
3. Situate large skillet over medium-high heat and add the olive oil.
4. Cook the pork chops, turning once, until they are no longer pink, about 8 minutes per side.
5. Put aside the chops.
6. Pour the broth mixture into the skillet and cook until warmed through and thickened, about 2 minutes.
7. Blend lemon zest, butter, and chives.

8.　　Garnish with a generous spoonful of sauce.

Nutrition:

200 Calories

8g Fat

1g Carbohydrates

1203. Autumn Pork Chops with Red Cabbage and Apples

Preparation Time: 15 minutes

Cooking Time: 30 minutes

Serving: 4

Ingredients:

- ¼ cup apple cider vinegar
- 2 tablespoons granulated sweetener
- 4 (4-ounce) pork chops, about 1 inch thick
- 1 tablespoon extra-virgin olive oil
- ½ red cabbage, finely shredded
- 1 sweet onion, thinly sliced
- 1 apple, peeled, cored, and sliced
- 1 teaspoon chopped fresh thyme

Direction:

1. Scourge together the vinegar and sweetener. Set it aside.

2. Season the pork with salt and pepper.

3. Position huge skillet over medium-high heat and add the olive oil.

4. Cook the pork chops until no longer pink, turning once, about 8 minutes per side.

5. Put chops aside.

6. Add the cabbage and onion to the skillet and sauté until the vegetables have softened, about 5 minutes.

7. Add the vinegar mixture and the apple slices to the skillet and bring the mixture to a boil.

8. Adjust heat to low and simmer, covered, for 5 additional minutes.

9. Return the pork chops to the skillet, along with any accumulated juices and thyme, cover, and cook for 5 more minutes.

Nutrition:

223 Calories

12g Carbohydrates

3g Fiber

1204. Chipotle Chili Pork Chops

Preparation Time: 4 hours

Cooking Time: 20 minutes

Serving: 4

Ingredients:

- Juice and zest of 1 lime
- 1 tablespoon extra-virgin olive oil
- 1 tablespoon chipotle chili powder
- 2 teaspoons minced garlic
- 1 teaspoon ground cinnamon
- Pinch sea salt
- 4 (5-ounce) pork chops

Direction:

1. Combine the lime juice and zest, oil, chipotle chili powder, garlic, cinnamon, and salt in a resealable plastic bag. Add the pork chops. Remove as much air as possible and seal the bag.

2. Marinate the chops in the refrigerator for at least 4 hours, and up to 24 hours, turning them several times.

3. Ready the oven to 400°F and set a rack on a baking sheet. Let the chops rest at room temperature for 15 minutes, then arrange them on the rack and discard the remaining marinade.

4. Roast the chops until cooked through, turning once, about 10 minutes per side.

5. Serve with lime wedges.

Nutrition:

204 Calories

1g Carbohydrates

1g Sugar

1205. Orange-Marinated Pork Tenderloin

Preparation Time: 2 hours

Cooking Time: 30 minutes

Serving: 4

Ingredients:

- ¼ cup freshly squeezed orange juice
- 2 teaspoons orange zest
- 2 teaspoons minced garlic
- 1 teaspoon low-sodium soy sauce
- 1 teaspoon grated fresh ginger
- 1 teaspoon honey
- 1½ pounds pork tenderloin roast
- 1 tablespoon extra-virgin olive oil

Direction:

1. Blend together the orange juice, zest, garlic, soy sauce, ginger, and honey.

2. Pour the marinade into a resealable plastic bag and add the pork tenderloin.

3. Remove as much air as possible and seal the bag. Marinate the pork in the refrigerator, turning the bag a few times, for 2 hours.

4. Preheat the oven to 400°F.

5. Pull out tenderloin from the marinade and discard the marinade.

6. Position big ovenproof skillet over medium-high heat and add the oil.

7. Sear the pork tenderloin on all sides, about 5 minutes in total.

8. Position skillet to the oven and roast for 25 minutes.

9. Put aside for 10 minutes before serving.

Nutrition:

228 Calories

4g Carbohydrates

3g Sugar

1206. Homestyle Herb Meatballs

Preparation Time: 10 minutes

Cooking Time: 15 minutes

Serving: 4

Ingredients:

- ½ pound lean ground pork
- ½ pound lean ground beef
- 1 sweet onion, finely chopped
- ¼ cup bread crumbs
- 2 tablespoons chopped fresh basil
- 2 teaspoons minced garlic
- 1 egg

Direction:

1. Preheat the oven to 350°F.

2. Ready baking tray with parchment paper and set it aside.

3. In a large bowl, mix together the pork, beef, onion, bread crumbs, basil, garlic, egg, salt, and pepper until very well mixed.

4. Roll the meat mixture into 2-inch meatballs.

5. Transfer the meatballs to the baking sheet and bake until they are browned and cooked through, about 15 minutes.

6. Serve the meatballs with your favorite marinara sauce and some steamed green beans.

Nutrition:

332 Calories

13g Carbohydrates

3g Sugar

1207. Lime-Parsley Lamb Cutlets

Preparation Time: 4 hours

Cooking Time: 10 minutes

Serving: 4

Ingredients:

- ¼ cup extra-virgin olive oil
- ¼ cup freshly squeezed lime juice
- 2 tablespoons lime zest
- 2 tablespoons chopped fresh parsley
- 12 lamb cutlets (about 1½ pounds total)

Direction:

1. Scourge the oil, lime juice, zest, parsley, salt, and pepper.

2. Pour marinade to a resealable plastic bag.

3. Add the cutlets to the bag and remove as much air as possible before sealing.

4. Marinate the lamb in the refrigerator for about 4 hours, turning the bag several times.

5. Preheat the oven to broil.

6. Remove the chops from the bag and arrange them on an aluminum foil–lined baking sheet. Discard the marinade.

7. Broil the chops for 4 minutes per side for medium doneness.

8. Let the chops rest for 5 minutes before serving.

Nutrition:

413 Calories

1g Carbohydrates

31g Protein

1208. Mediterranean Steak Sandwiches

Preparation Time: 1 hour

Cooking Time: 10 minutes

Serving: 4

Ingredients:

- 2 tablespoons extra-virgin olive oil
- 2 tablespoons balsamic vinegar
- 2 teaspoons garlic
- 2 teaspoons lemon juice
- 2 teaspoons fresh oregano
- 1 teaspoon fresh parsley
- 1-pound flank steak
- 4 whole-wheat pitas
- 2 cups shredded lettuce
- 1 red onion, thinly sliced

- 1 tomato, chopped
- 1 ounce low-sodium feta cheese

Direction:

1. Scourge olive oil, balsamic vinegar, garlic, lemon juice, oregano, and parsley.
2. Add the steak to the bowl, turning to coat it completely.
3. Marinate the steak for 1 hour in the refrigerator, turning it over several times.
4. Preheat the broiler. Line a baking sheet with aluminum foil.
5. Put steak out of the bowl and discard the marinade.
6. Situate steak on the baking sheet and broil for 5 minutes per side for medium.
7. Set aside for 10 minutes before slicing.
8. Stuff the pitas with the sliced steak, lettuce, onion, tomato, and feta.

Nutrition:

344 Calories

22g Carbohydrates

3g Fiber

1209. Roasted Beef with Peppercorn Sauce

Preparation Time: 10 minutes

Cooking Time: 90 minutes

Serving: 4

Ingredients:

- 1½ pounds top rump beef roast
- 3 teaspoons extra-virgin olive oil
- 3 shallots, minced
- 2 teaspoons minced garlic
- 1 tablespoon green peppercorns
- 2 tablespoons dry sherry
- 2 tablespoons all-purpose flour
- 1 cup sodium-free beef broth

Direction:

1. Heat the oven to 300°F.
2. Season the roast with salt and pepper.
3. Position huge skillet over medium-high heat and add 2 teaspoons of olive oil.
4. Brown the beef on all sides, about 10 minutes in total, and transfer the roast to a baking dish.
5. Roast until desired doneness, about 1½ hours for medium. When the roast has been in the oven for 1 hour, start the sauce.
6. In a medium saucepan over medium-high heat, sauté the shallots in the remaining 1 teaspoon of olive oil until translucent, about 4 minutes.
7. Stir in the garlic and peppercorns, and cook for another minute. Whisk in the sherry to deglaze the pan.
8. Whisk in the flour to form a thick paste, cooking for 1 minute and stirring constantly.
9. Fill in the beef broth and whisk for 4 minutes. Season the sauce.
10. Serve the beef with a generous spoonful of sauce.

Nutrition:

330 Calories

4g Carbohydrates

36g Protein

21-Day Meal Plan

Day	Breakfast	First Course	Second Course	Dessert
1	Blueberry Breakfast Cake	Blueberry and Chicken Salad	Cauliflower Rice with Chicken	Peanut Butter Cups
2	Whole-Grain Pancakes	Beef and Red Bean Chili	Turkey with Fried Eggs	Fruit Pizza
3	Buckwheat Grouts Breakfast Bowl	Berry Apple Cider	Sweet Potato, Kale, And White Bean Stew	Choco Peppermint Cake
4	Peach Muesli Bake	Brunswick Stew	Slow Cooker Two-Bean Sloppy Joes	Roasted Mango
5	Steel-Cut Oatmeal Bowl with Fruit and Nuts	Buffalo Chicken Salads	Lighter Eggplant Parmesan	Roasted Plums
6	Whole-Grain Dutch Baby Pancake	Cacciatore Style Chicken	Coconut-Lentil Curry	Figs with Honey & Yogurt
7	Mushroom, Zucchini, And Onion Frittata	Carnitas Tacos	Stuffed Portobello With Cheese	Flourless Chocolate Cake
8	Spinach and Cheese Quiche	Chicken Chili	Lighter Shrimp Scampi	Lava Cake
9	Spicy Jalapeno Popper Deviled Eggs	Chicken Vera Cruz	Maple-Mustard Salmon	Cheese Cake
10	Lovely Porridge	Chicken and Cornmeal Dumplings	Chicken Salad with Grapes and Pecans	Orange Cake
11	Salty Macadamia Chocolate Smoothie	Chicken and Pepperoni	Roasted Vegetables	Madeleine
12	Basil and Tomato Baked Eggs	Chicken and Sausage Gumbo	Millet Pilaf	Waffles
13	Cinnamon and Coconut Porridge	Chicken, Barley, And Leek Stew	Sweet and Sour Onions	Pretzels
14	An Omelet of Swiss Chard	Cider Pork Stew	Sautéed Apples and Onions	Cheesy Taco Bites
15	Cheesy Low-Carb Omelet	Creamy Chicken Noodle Soup	Zucchini Noodles with Portabella Mushrooms	Nut Squares
16	Yogurt and Kale Smoothie	Cuban Pulled Pork Sandwich	Grilled Tempeh with Pineapple	Pumpkin & Banana Ice Cream
17	Bacon and Chicken Garlic Wrap	Gazpacho	Courgettes in Cider Sauce	Brulee Oranges
18	Grilled Chicken Platter	Tomato and Kale Soup	Baked Mixed Mushrooms	Frozen Lemon & Blueberry
19	Parsley Chicken Breast	Comforting Summer Squash Soup with Crispy Chickpeas	Spiced Okra	Peanut Butter Choco Chip Cookies
20	Mustard Chicken	Curried Carrot Soup	Lemony Salmon Burgers	Watermelon Sherbet

| 21 | Balsamic Chicken | Thai Peanut, Carrot, And Shrimp Soup | Caprese Turkey Burgers | Strawberry & Mango Ice Cream |

100 day Food Plan

Day	Breakfast	First Course	Second Course	Dessert
1	Apple Topped French Toast	Asparagus with Scallops	Wholesome Broccoli Pork Chops	Ketogenic Lava Cake
2	Café Mocha Smoothies	Butter Cod with Asparagus	Italian Pork Chops	Keto Donuts
3	Cheese Spinach Waffles	Cilantro Lime Shrimp	Tomato Steak Kebabs	Coconut Milk Pear Shake
4	Cottage Cheese Pancake	Asparagus and Scallop Skillet with Lemony	Garlic Chicken Balls	Fruit Pizza
5	Ham & Jicama Hash	Tomato Tuna Melts	Lemony Dijon Meat Loaf	Roasted Mango
6	Hot Maple Porridge	Peppercorn-Crusted Baked Salmon	Mu Shu Lunch Pork	Waffles
7	Jicama Hash Brown	Roasted Salmon with Honey-Mustard Sauce	Creole Braised Sirloin	Pumpkin and Banana Ice Cream
8	Whole-Grain Pancakes	Roasted Salmon with Honey-Mustard Sauce	Crispy Chicken Wings	Roasted Plum
9	Blueberry Breakfast Cake	Whole Veggie-Stuffed Trout	Rosemary Lemon Lamb Chops	Brulee Oranges
10	Peach Muesli Bake	Ginger-Garlic Cod Cooked in Paper	Delicious Lamb Chops	Frozen Lemon and Blueberry
11	Whole-Grain Dutch Baby Pancake	Roasted Halibut with Red Peppers, Green Beans	Pork Tenderloin with Bell Peppers	Easy Air Fry Brownies
12	Café Mocha Smoothies	Blackened Tilapia with Mango Salsa	Pork Rolls	Tiramisu Shots
13	Buckwheat Grouts Breakfast Bowl	Scallops and Asparagus Skillet	Pork Sausage Casserole	Peanut Butter Choco Chip Cookies
14	Cheese Spinach Waffles	Baked Oysters	Tuna Burgers	Watermelon Sherbet
15	Steel-Cut Oatmeal Bowl with Fruit and Nuts	Tropical Shrimp Cocktail	Lemon Chili Salmon	Keto Vanilla Mug Cake
16	Whole-Grain Dutch Baby Pancake	Pork Chop Diane	Spicy Catfish	Chia Pudding
17	Mushroom, Zucchini and Onion Frittata	Chopotle Chili Pork Chops	Salmon Patties	Lemon Custard
18	Spinach and Cheese Quiche	Orange-Marinated Pork Tenderloin	Vinegar Halibut	Ice Cream Brownie Cake
19	Spicy Jalapeno Popper Deviled Eggs	Lime-Parsley Lamb Cutlets	Honey-Glazed Salmon	Chocolate Mousse
20	Lovely Porridge	Roasted Beef with Peppercorn Sauce	Basil-Parmesan Crusted Salmon	Air Fried Sugar-Free Chocolate Souffle
21	Cinnamon Apple Granola	Pork Chops with Grape Sauce	Ginger Cod Chard Bake	Chocolate Ice Cream
22	Blueberry Breakfast Cake	Blueberry and Chicken Salad	Cauliflower Rice with Chicken	Peanut Butter Cups

23	Whole-Grain Pancakes	Beef and Red Bean Chili	Turkey with Fried Eggs	Fruit Pizza
24	Buckwheat Grouts Breakfast Bowl	Berry Apple Cider	Sweet Potato, Kale, And White Bean Stew	Choco Peppermint Cake
25	Peach Muesli Bake	Brunswick Stew	Slow Cooker Two-Bean Sloppy Joes	Roasted Mango
26	Steel-Cut Oatmeal Bowl with Fruit and Nuts	Buffalo Chicken Salads	Lighter Eggplant Parmesan	Roasted Plums
27	Whole-Grain Dutch Baby Pancake	Cacciatore Style Chicken	Coconut-Lentil Curry	Figs with Honey & Yogurt
28	Mushroom, Zucchini, And Onion Frittata	Carnitas Tacos	Stuffed Portobello With Cheese	Flourless Chocolate Cake
29	Spinach and Cheese Quiche	Chicken Chili	Lighter Shrimp Scampi	Lava Cake
30	Spicy Jalapeno Popper Deviled Eggs	Chicken Vera Cruz	Maple-Mustard Salmon	Cheese Cake
31	Lovely Porridge	Chicken and Cornmeal Dumplings	Chicken Salad with Grapes and Pecans	Orange Cake
32	Salty Macadamia Chocolate Smoothie	Chicken and Pepperoni	Roasted Vegetables	Madeleine
33	Basil and Tomato Baked Eggs	Chicken and Sausage Gumbo	Millet Pilaf	Waffles
34	Cinnamon and Coconut Porridge	Chicken, Barley, And Leek Stew	Sweet and Sour Onions	Pretzels
35	An Omelet of Swiss Chard	Cider Pork Stew	Sautéed Apples and Onions	Cheesy Taco Bites
36	Cheesy Low-Carb Omelet	Creamy Chicken Noodle Soup	Zucchini Noodles with Portabella Mushrooms	Nut Squares
37	Yogurt and Kale Smoothie	Cuban Pulled Pork Sandwich	Grilled Tempeh with Pineapple	Pumpkin & Banana Ice Cream
38	Bacon and Chicken Garlic Wrap	Gazpacho	Courgettes in Cider Sauce	Brulee Oranges
39	Grilled Chicken Platter	Tomato and Kale Soup	Baked Mixed Mushrooms	Frozen Lemon & Blueberry
40	Parsley Chicken Breast	Comforting Summer Squash Soup with Crispy Chickpeas	Spiced Okra	Peanut Butter Choco Chip Cookies
41	Mustard Chicken	Curried Carrot Soup	Lemony Salmon Burgers	Watermelon Sherbet
42	Balsamic Chicken	Thai Peanut, Carrot, And Shrimp Soup	Caprese Turkey Burgers	Strawberry & Mango Ice Cream
43	Turkey Sausage Breakfast Muffins	Pork Chop Diane	Dumplings	Apple Crisp
44	Tortilla Breakfast Scramble	Autumn Pork Chops with Red Cabbage and Apples	Spaghetti Bolognese	Apple Pear and Pecan Dessert Squares
45	Mushroom and Asparagus Frittata	Chipotle Chili Pork Chops	Cauliflower Pizza	Apricot Soufflé
46	Vegetable Breakfast Skillet	Orange-Marinated Pork Tenderloin	Tuscan Kale	Autumn Skillet Cake

DASH DIET COOKBOOK FOR BEGINNERS
Dr. Lindsay Burton

Page 450

450

47	Cinnamon Apple Oatmeal	Home-style Herb Meatballs	Broccoli And Almonds	Baked Maple Custard
48	Egg White Zucchini Frittata	Lime-Parsley Lamb Cutlets	Strawberry-Arugula Salad	Blackberry Crostata
49	Mushroom and Spinach Scrambled Eggs	Mediterranean Steak Sandwiches	Chicken Salad	Blackberry Soufflés
50	Onion and Herb Frittata	Roasted Beef with Peppercorn Sauce	Roasted Vegetable Medley	Blueberry Lemon "Cup" Cakes
51	Apple French Toast	Coffee-and-Herb-Marinated Steak	Vegetable Egg Bake	Blueberry No-Bake Cheesecake
52	Salsa Breakfast Casserole	Traditional Beef Stroganoff	Italian Seafood Stew	Broiled Stone Fruit
53	Fruit Crepes	Chicken and Roasted Vegetable Wraps	Lemon Cauliflower and Pine Nuts	Café Mocha Torte
54	Asparagus Frittata	Spicy Chicken Cacciatore	Beef Tenderloin and Avocado Cream	Cappuccino Mousse
55	Oatmeal Yogurt Breakfast	Ginger Citrus Chicken Thighs	Salmon and Citrus Sauce	Caramel Pecan Pie
56	Apple Muffins	Chicken with Creamy Thyme Sauce	Orange-Avocado Salad	Carrot Cupcakes
57	Cinnamon Pumpkin Waffles	One-Pot Roast Chicken Dinner	Avocados with Walnut-Herb	Chocolate Cherry Cake Roll
58	Banana Pancakes	Almond-Crusted Salmon	Barbecue Brisket	Chocolate Orange Bread Pudding
59	Pumpkin Walnut Oatmeal	Chicken and Veggie Bowl with Brown Rice	Broccoli and Hot Sauce	Chocolate Torte
60	Blueberry Nut Muffins	Beef Fajitas	Chicken Thighs	Cinnamon Bread Pudding
61	Raisin French Toast	Italian Pork Chops	Creamy Bell Pepper-Corn Salad and Seared Zucchini	Coconut Cream Pie
62	Whole Wheat Blueberry Pancakes	Chicken Mushroom Stroganoff	Corn Tortillas and Spinach Salad	Coconut Milk Shakes
63	Broccoli Quiche	Grilled Tuna Kebabs	Smoky Carrot and Black Bean Stew	Coconutty Pudding Clouds
64	Turkey and Fried Eggs	Tilapia with Coconut Rice	Oven-Baked Potatoes and Green Beans	Cream Cheese Pound Cake
65	Ham and Egg Cups	Spicy Turkey Tacos	Hummus and Salad Pita Flats	Dark Chocolate Coffee Cupcakes
66	Cauliflower Muffin	Quick and Easy Shrimp Stir-Fry	Lettuce Salad with Lemon	German Chocolate Cake Bars
67	Zucchini Noodles with Creamy Avocado Pesto	Chicken Burrito Bowl with Quinoa	Pork Chops and Butternut Squash Salad	Gingerbread Soufflés
68	Avocado Chicken Salad	Baked Salmon Cakes	Low Carb Stuffed Peppers	Lemon Meringue Ice Cream
69	Pancakes With Berries	Rice and Meatball Stuffed Bell Peppers	Chicken Cordon Bleu	Mini Bread Puddings

70	Omelette à la Margherita	Stir-Fried Steak and Cabbage	Beef Goulash	Mini Key Lime Tarts
71	Reduced Carb Berry Parfaits	Gazpacho	Pork Chop Diane	Pumpkin & Banana Ice Cream
72	Healthy Avocado Toast	Tomato and Kale Soup	Autumn Pork Chops with Red Cabbage	Brulee Oranges
73	Whole Egg Baked Sweet Potatoes	Curried Carrot Soup	Chipotle Chili Pork Chops	Frozen Lemon & Blueberry
74	Berry Avocado Smoothie	Thai, Peanut, Carrot and Shrimp Soup	Orange-Marinated Pork Tenderloin	Peanut Butter Choco Chip Cookies
75	Bagel Hummus Toast	Chicken Tortilla Soup	Homestyle Herb Meatballs	Watermelon Sorbet
76	Black Bean Tacos Breakfast	Beef and Mushroom Barley Soup	Lime-Parsley Lamb Cutlets	Strawberry & Mango Ice Cream
77	Strawberry Coconut Bake	Cucumber, Tomato and Avocado Salad	Mediterranean Steak Sandwiches	Tiramisu Shots
78	Reduced Carb Berry Parfaits	Gazpacho	Pork Chop Diane	Pumpkin & Banana Ice Cream
79	Healthy Avocado Toast	Tomato and Kale Soup	Autumn Pork Chops with Red Cabbage	Brulee Oranges
80	Whole Egg Baked Sweet Potatoes	Curried Carrot Soup	Chipotle Chili Pork Chops	Frozen Lemon & Blueberry
81	Berry Avocado Smoothie	Thai, Peanut, Carrot and Shrimp Soup	Orange-Marinated Pork Tenderloin	Peanut Butter Choco Chip Cookies
82	Bagel Hummus Toast	Chicken Tortilla Soup	Homestyle Herb Meatballs	Watermelon Sorbet
83	Black Bean Tacos Breakfast	Beef and Mushroom Barley Soup	Lime-Parsley Lamb Cutlets	Strawberry & Mango Ice Cream
84	Strawberry Coconut Bake	Cucumber, Tomato and Avocado Salad	Mediterranean Steak Sandwiches	Tiramisu Shots
85	Reduced Carb Berry Parfaits	Gazpacho	Pork Chop Diane	Pumpkin & Banana Ice Cream
86	Healthy Avocado Toast	Tomato and Kale Soup	Autumn Pork Chops with Red Cabbage	Brulee Oranges
87	Whole Egg Baked Sweet Potatoes	Curried Carrot Soup	Chipotle Chili Pork Chops	Frozen Lemon & Blueberry
88	Berry Avocado Smoothie	Thai, Peanut, Carrot and Shrimp Soup	Orange-Marinated Pork Tenderloin	Peanut Butter Choco Chip Cookies
89	Bagel Hummus Toast	Chicken Tortilla Soup	Homestyle Herb Meatballs	Watermelon Sorbet
90	Black Bean Tacos Breakfast	Beef and Mushroom Barley Soup	Lime-Parsley Lamb Cutlets	Strawberry & Mango Ice Cream
91	Strawberry Coconut Bake	Cucumber, Tomato and Avocado Salad	Mediterranean Steak Sandwiches	Tiramisu Shots
92	Reduced Carb Berry Parfaits	Gazpacho	Pork Chop Diane	Pumpkin & Banana Ice Cream
93	Healthy Avocado Toast	Tomato and Kale Soup	Autumn Pork Chops with Red Cabbage	Brulee Oranges

94	Whole Egg Baked Sweet Potatoes	Curried Carrot Soup	Chipotle Chili Pork Chops	Frozen Lemon & Blueberry
95	Berry Avocado Smoothie	Thai, Peanut, Carrot and Shrimp Soup	Orange-Marinated Pork Tenderloin	Peanut Butter Choco Chip Cookies
96	Bagel Hummus Toast	Chicken Tortilla Soup	Homestyle Herb Meatballs	Watermelon Sorbet
97	Black Bean Tacos Breakfast	Beef and Mushroom Barley Soup	Lime-Parsley Lamb Cutlets	Strawberry & Mango Ice Cream
98	Strawberry Coconut Bake	Cucumber, Tomato and Avocado Salad	Mediterranean Steak Sandwiches	Tiramisu Shots
99	Lovely Porridge	Chicken, Strawberry, And Avocado Salad	Creamed Spinach	Tabbouleh- Arabian Salad
100	Salty Macadamia Chocolate Smoothie	Lemon-Thyme Eggs	Stuffed Mushrooms	Arugula Garden Salad

Conclusion

Being diagnosed with diabetes will bring some major changes in your lifestyle. From the time you are diagnosed with it, it would always be a constant battle with food. You need to become a lot more careful with your food choices and the quantity that you ate. Every meal will feel like a major effort. You will be planning every day for the whole week, well in advance. Depending upon the type of food you ate, you have to keep checking your blood sugar levels. You may get used to taking long breaks between meals and staying away from snacks between dinner and breakfast.

Managing diabetes can be a very, very stressful ordeal. There will be many times that you will mark your glucose levels down on a piece of paper like you are plotting graph lines or something. You will mix your insulin shots up and then stress about whether or not you are giving yourself the right dosage. You will always be over-cautious because it involves a LOT of math and a really fine margin of error. But now, those days are gone!

The warning symptoms of diabetes type 1 are the same as type 2; however, in type 1, these signs and symptoms tend to occur slowly over a period of months or years, making them harder to spot and recognize. Some of these symptoms can even occur after the disease has progressed.

Diabetes can occur at any age. However, being too young or too old means your body is not in its best form, and therefore, this increases the risk of developing diabetes.

That sounds scary. However, diabetes only occurs with the presence of a combination of these risk factors. Most of the risk factors can be minimized by taking action. For example, developing a more active lifestyle, taking care of your habits, and attempting to lower your blood glucose sugar by restricting your sugar intake. If you start to notice you are prediabetic or getting overweight, etc., there is always something you can do to modify the situation. Recent studies show that developing healthy eating habits and following diets that are low in carbs, losing excess weight, and leading an active lifestyle can help to protect you from developing diabetes, especially diabetes type 2, by minimizing the risk factors of developing the disorder.

You can also have an oral glucose tolerance test in which you will have a fasting glucose test first, and then you will be given a sugary drink and then having your blood glucose tested 2 hours after that to see how your body responds to glucose meals. In healthy individuals, the blood glucose should drop 2 hours post sugary meals again due to the action of insulin.

Another indicative test is the HbA1C. This test reflects the average of your blood glucose level over the last 2 to 3 months. It is also a test to see how well you manage your diabetes.

All the above goes in the direction that you need to avoid a starchy diet because of its tendency to raise blood glucose levels. Too many carbohydrates can lead to insulin sensitivity and pancreatic fatigue, as well as weight gain with all its associated risk factors for cardiovascular disease and hypertension.

When your body is low on sugars, it will be forced to use a subsequent molecule to burn for energy; in that case, this will be fat. The burning of fat will lead you to lose weight.

Made in the USA
Coppell, TX
07 February 2022